MATERIALITY AND SOCIAL PRACTICE

Transformative Capacities of Intercultural Encounters

Edited by

Joseph Maran and Philipp W. Stockhammer

Oxbow Books
Oxford & Philadelphia

Published in the United Kingdom in 2012 by
OXBOW BOOKS
10 Hythe Bridge Street, Oxford OX1 2EW

and in the United States by
OXBOW BOOKS
908 Darby Road, Havertown, PA 19083

Reprinted in paperback 2013

Paperback Edition: ISBN 978-1-78297-541-0
Digtial Edition: ISBN 978-1-84217-909-3

A CIP record for this book is available from the British Library

Library of Congress Cataloging-in-Publication Data

Materiality and social practice : transformative capacities of intercultural encounters / edited by Joseph Maran and Philipp W. Stockhammer. -- 1st ed.
p. cm.
Includes bibliographical references.
ISBN 978-1-84217-458-6
1. Bronze age--Mediterraean Region. 2. Commerce, Prehistoric--Mediterraean Region. 3. Material culture--Mediterraean Region. 4. Ceremonial objects--Mediterraean Region. 5. Social archaeology--Mediterraean Region. 6. Mediterranean Region--Relations. 7. Mediterranean Region--Antiquities. I. Maran, Joseph. II. Stockhammer, Philipp.
GN778.25M386 2012
937--dc23
2011040894

For a complete list of Oxbow titles, please contact:

UNITED KINGDOM
Oxbow Books
Telephone (01865) 241249, Fax (01865) 794449
Email: oxbow@oxbowbooks.com
www.oxbowbooks.com

UNITED STATES OF AMERICA
Oxbow Books
Telephone (800) 791-9354, Fax (610) 853-9146
Email: queries@casemateacademic.com
www.casemateacademic.com/oxbow

Oxbow Books is part of the Casemate Group

Front cover: Megiddo Ivories, Pl. 32, 160. © Permission from the Oriental Institute Chicago

Contents

1.

Introduction

Joseph Maran and Philipp W. Stockhammer

The contributions in this volume are based on papers delivered at the conference *Materiality and Practice: Transformative Capacities of Intercultural Encounters*, that took place in the Internationales Wissenschaftsforum Heidelberg on March 25 to 27, 2010. The conference was part of our research project 'Materiality and Practice: Cultural Entanglements of 2nd millennium BC East Mediterranean Societies'. Our research and the publication of this volume were generously funded by the Deutsche Forschungsgemeinschaft (German Research Foundation) within the Cluster of Excellence 270/1 'Asia and Europe in a Global Context' at Heidelberg University. We are grateful to the directorate of the Cluster of Excellence for enabling us to undertake the interdisciplinary project from which the idea of this symposium took its start. The conference and its publication were facilitated by the support of specific people and institutions, to whom the organisers are very thankful. In particular, we would like to thank the director of the Internationales Wissenschaftsforum Heidelberg, Professor Jan Christian Gertz, and the manager, Dr Ellen Peerenboom, for allowing us to convene at the wonderful venue of the Wissenschaftsforum. Moreover, we would like to thank our student assistants Nadine Becker, Maribel Dorka Moreno, Martina Riedl and Kristina Sauer, whose highly contagious enthusiasm in the organisation of the symposium was much appreciated. Special thanks are due to Kristina Sauer for the layout of this publication, and to Éilís Monahan for her careful language editing of the texts. Finally, we would like to express our gratitude to two peer reviewers whose insightful comments helped us to optimise the quality of the contributions and our publisher Oxbow, especially Julie Gardiner, whose support made the publication of this volume an easy task.

The contributions in this volume aim to investigate the transformative potential arising from the interplay between material forms, social practices and intercultural relations. Such a focus necessitates first, an approach that takes a transcultural perspective as a fundamental methodology and second, a broader understanding of the inter-relationship between humans and objects.

Adopting a transcultural approach forces us to change archaeology's stance towards items coming from the outside. By using them mostly for reconstructing systems of exchange or for chronology, archaeology has for a long time reduced them to their properties as objects and as being foreign. In contrast, our research is based on the notion that the significance of such items does not derive from the transfer from one place to another as such but, rather, from the ways in which they were used and contextualised. The main question is how, through their integration into discourses and practices, new frameworks of meaning were created conforming neither with what had existed in the receiving society nor in the area of origin of the objects.

As is well known, in the 1980s cultural studies and the social sciences increasingly turned to subjects of interculturality and materiality as research topics. This development superseded a long period of neglect of such issues, in which social and cultural anthropology focused on local societies that were approached as if they could be studied as self-contained entities. At that time, the investigation of material forms was regarded as the realm of an outdated, antiquarian approach with no relevance for the analysis of the social world, which was imagined as mostly abstract and detached from materiality. Hans-Peter Hahn (2008) and Bernhard Streck (2000) have recently pointed out that the renunciation of this 'atomistic approach' in cultural studies, and the turning of attention to questions of cultural globalisation, in some cases has led to the re-appearance of a vocabulary, and of ways of representation, that are strangely reminiscent of the 'culture-historical school' which dominated German ethnography in the early 20th century. One of the shortcomings of this diffusionist school of thought of the early 20th century was that the appearance of the same form was taken to represent the same origin and the same meaning, or as Jonathan Friedman (1997) has put it 'culture was contained in its embodiment rather than its generativity'. On the other hand, as Hans-Peter Hahn has reminded us, it should not be forgotten that the culture-historical school was founded on the almost revolutionary insight that the mobility of cultural forms does not necessarily require a complex political organization, thus conceding a high degree of agency to people of non-modern societies who, at the turn of the 20th century, were usually thought to be incapable of achievements like long-distance travel and the creation of wide-ranging exchange networks.

For archaeology, the post-structuralist re-discovery of the significance of materiality and interculturality has opened up new perspectives for dealing with such issues, although this requires careful reflection on the flaws of the culture-historical approach to avoid the risks of repeating earlier mistakes and inadvertently creating a sort of Neo-Diffusionist paradigm. One especially has to be aware of this danger in Germany where, in contrast to the United Kingdom and the USA, the ideas of diffusionism and culture history continued to exert an influence on archaeology long after the 2nd World War (when they had long been abandoned in ethnography). The flaws of culture-history and its diffusionist approach consisted, above all, in the object-like approach towards culture, the lack of concepts of agency and of practice, as well as the obsession with origins, and finally the concentration on abstract 'influences' and 'flows' of cultural traits and the disinterest in the actual contextualisation of cultural forms and possible shifts of meaning (Maran 2012).

In order to avoid the pitfalls of culture-history, the focus must thus be on the generative, rather than the representative character of culture, and the highly localised approach of post-diffusionist social and cultural anthropology needs to be merged with an outlook that transcends the local level and is open to the manifold repercussions of interculturality. In other words, the effects of intercultural relations must be investigated locally, which means concentrating on phenomena of appropriation and studying how foreign cultural forms were re-contextualised through their integration in social practices and discourses. This publication sets out to take a step in this direction by tackling the overarching topic of the transformative capacities of intercultural encounters from various points of view. While the main thrust of many of the contributions lies on aspects related to the Mediterranean interaction spheres of the 2nd and early 1st millennia BCE, others enrich our issue by approaching it from different thematic angles. In our view, it is necessary to analyse the relation between agency and materiality in the constitution of what is perceived as social realities. Until quite recently, it seemed self-evident that social relations are tantamount to human relations, and that such relations, as already mentioned, could be studied on a largely abstract level, ignoring the world of social goods. Recently, this position has been challenged by discussions within the social sciences and cultural studies deriving from the insight that the realms of the social and the material are closely interwoven and that social practices and discourses constitute the interface between them. This raises the important issue of whether the concept of agency should be stripped of its exclusively anthropocentric meaning and extended to include non-human agents (*cf.* Latour 1986; 2007; Law 1992)?

In our opinion, this broader concept of agency is necessary to understand better the relationship between humans and objects. Following the first modernists of the late 18th and 19th centuries, modernity had always aimed at understanding and explaining the world on the basis of a single worldview. Since the 1970s, post-structuralism has tried to move past this approach by emphasising the multiplicity of the discourses and codes that are supposed to explain the world. While acknowledging plurality, however, in one important respect post-structuralism did not overcome modernity, since its focus was still on worldviews and texts rather than on the analysis of the engagement of individual agents with the world. In contrast to this, we try to merge lines of thought introduced by Pierre Bourdieu (1982), Bruno Latour (1986; 2007) and John Law (1992) to emphasise the decisive role of the habitus, individual agency and the material world. Thus, we argue the necessity of shifting the focus from discourses and codes towards practices and the intimate entanglement between humans and their surroundings on the basis of those practices. We assume that the relationship between humans and objects comprises at least three dimensions: firstly, the creation of objects as functional tools to adapt to our surroundings, as proclaimed by Leslie White (1959, 8; *cf.* Binford 1962, 218 – *i.e.* the basic notion of modernity and the connected ideas of processual archaeology); secondly, the creation of objects as symbols in non-verbal discourses (as one of the basic notions of post-processual archaeology; *cf.* Hodder 1982); and thirdly, a silent discourse between humans and objects that is neither functional in its modern sense nor symbolic in its post-structuralist sense. In the course of our interaction with objects, a dialogue develops in which the objects become agents that are able to trigger or influence our action. This dialogue is non-verbal and non-symbolic and is completely dependent on each specific individual context. However, the way humans and objects communicate during social practices is very powerful: it makes us naturalise our man-made surroundings, it persuades us to change either the surroundings or ourselves and it forces us to believe that objects have a will of their own.

Following this line of thought, landscapes created by many generations of humans influence our idea of what constitutes a natural landscape, the smell of burning food tells us to change our cooking habits, and puppets tell the puppet master how they want to act. Although the objects do not speak, they address our senses (smelling, seeing, tasting, feeling) in such a powerful way that our worldviews cannot be understood without including materiality and social practices in our analysis.

References

Binford, L. R. (1962) Archaeology as Anthropology. *American Antiquity* 28/2, 217–225.

Bourdieu, P. (1982) *Die feinen Unterschiede*. Frankfurt a. Main, Suhrkamp.

Friedman, J. (1997) Global Crises, the Struggle for Cultural Identity and Intellectual Porkbarelling: Cosmopolitans versus Locals, Ethnics and Nationals in an Era of De-hegemonisation. In P. Werbner and T. Modood (eds), *Debating Cultural Hybridity: Multi-Cultural Identities and the Politics of Anti-Racism*, 70–89. London and New Jersey, Zed Books.

Hahn, H. P. (2008) Diffusionism, Appropriation, and Globalization. Some Remarks on Current Debates in Anthropology. *Anthropos* 103, 191–202.

Hodder, I. (1982) *Symbols in Action: Ethnoarchaeological Studies in Material Culture*. New Studies in Archaeology. Cambridge, University Press.

Latour, B. (1986) The Powers of Association. In J. Law (ed.), *Power, Action and Belief: A New Sociology of Knowledge?* Sociological Review Monograph 32, 264–280. London, Boston and Henley, Routledge and Kegan

Latour, B. (2007) *Reassembling the Social: An Introduction to Actor-Network-Theory*. Oxford, University Press.

Law, J. (1992) Notes on the Theory of the Actor-Network: Ordering, Strategy and Heterogeneity. *Systems Practice* 5, 379–393.

Maran, J. (2012) One World is not Enough: The Transformative Potential of Intercultural Exchange in Prehistoric Societies. In P. W. Stockhammer (ed.), *Conceptualizing Cultural Hybridization: A Transdisciplinary Approach. Papers of the Conference, Heidelberg, 21st–22nd September 2009*. Transcultural Research. Heidelberg Studies on Asia and Europe in a Global Context, 59–66. Berlin and Heidelberg, Springer.

Streck, B. (2000) Diffusion und Rekontextualisierung – Einführung. In U. Engel, A. Jones and R. Kappel (eds), *Afrika 2000*. 17. Tagung der Vereinigung von Afrikanisten (VAD) in Deutschland, Leipzig, 30. März bis 1. April 2000. Selbstverlag der VAD, published without place.

White, L. A. (1959) *The Evolution of Culture*. New York, McGraw-Hill Book Company.

2.

Words and things: reflections on people's interaction with the material world

Hans P. Hahn

> 'In order to "dissolve" the problems of the nature of material objects and our knowledge of them, it is necessary not merely to describe in full our use of material-objects expressions, but also to present, in succession, the various opposed old, non-linguistic theories'
>
> (Ernest Gellner (1959) *Words and Things*, 115)

Introduction

The 20th century was the era of materialism and material culture. It has been suggested that in the history of mankind there has never before been such a huge quantity of material possessions per individual as during the last one or two generations (Linde 1972). People own a plethora of things. For most men and women in the so-called 'consumer societies', it seems possible to become the owner of thousands of objects without any particular effort (Galbraith 1958).

Not only is the number of items rapidly increasing, but also the share of the artificially produced objects is enlarging, while the relative number of the natural objects diminishes. Industrial modes of production and engineering knowledge are the basis for more and more objects in everyday life. This is valid even with regard to food and meals. Hardly any of the foodstuffs in current use are natural products or come directly from a farmstead. In most cases, modern food is an industrial product, and therefore requires considerable awareness with regard to the ingredients.

Complementary to these developments are significant changes at the level of the materials in use. For a considerable time, the constant expansion of the number of available materials has made it more or less impossible for individual users to know which material one actually is dealing with, when using any kind of typical everyday object (Küchler 2009). The constantly accelerating speed of invention of new materials grows in step with new technical requirements. Many of the new materials that get into the users' and owners' hands often remain completely unknown to them. Some specific properties of new materials reveal themselves in their daily usage, but most of their complex, and often harmful, entanglements with the environment become clear only at the end of their lifespan, when it comes to the question which of these objects may pass into the garbage bin and which may not (Hahn and Soentgen 2010).

To some degree, it is justified to describe this 'getting out of control' as the 'revenge of the things' (Rötzer 1991). Among all societies worldwide, it is the heirs of Greek philosophy, those civilizations that had once established the principles of the superiority of the intellectual and the orientation to ideas (or ideologies), that are now losing control over the material world (Mauss [1939] 1969). The material world slips away from the control of mankind and possibly threatens the biological balance of our planet (Scherhorn 1997).

Perhaps the tradition of Greek philosophy explains why in the humanities this phenomenon was recognized as an important issue only very recently. Early discussions about the relevance of ordinary things are biased by the complaints about their negative influence. Georg Simmel is prominent in this context. He deplored the 'atrophy of the individual' in modern times, which he assumed to be simultaneous with the appearance of ever more sophisticated objects ([1907] 1989, 620). Simmel can be regarded as one of the early representatives of an important research tradition that is still vital and defended by many scholars (Schechter 2002; Levine 2007). This line of thought addresses consumption in a critical manner. It revolves around the idea that mankind would possibly be happier with less consumption and less material possessions. Another prominent representative of this approach, who condemns consumption without even considering its relevance to everyday life, is Theodor Adorno, and quite similar positions can be found among other exponents of 'critical theory' (Schor, Slater, Zukin and Zelizer 2010).

When speaking about the culture industry, Adorno designates consumption as 'betrayal' of the citizen, who becomes a passive consumer (Horkheimer and Adorno 1944, 166). Another, quite recent example of the tradition of critical reflections on consumption is Juliet Schor's book, published in 2008 with the title 'The Consuming Child'. She warns of a possible risk of development disturbances, which may occur when children are excessively handling material things. Nobody knows whether this is true. Nevertheless, in nursery schools it has become an accepted practice to organize 'no toy'-days as an educational measure.

This rejection of the material world, motivated by its assumed threatening, disturbing or at least irrelevant character, is not as isolated and radical as it might appear. On the contrary, it is just the outcome of a continuing tradition that refuses to acknowledge the relevance of the material in general and of consumption in particular. Strangely, this tradition is also reflected in so-called 'object theory'. In 1904 in his 'Theory of things', Alexius Meinong (1988) repudiates any difference between an actual object and the 'idea' as an object. He sketched a new phenomenology in which both phenomena (the thing and the idea) are treated without difference. The American philosopher Mark Baldwin (1895) made some quite similar statements. In an essay published in 1895, he insinuates that – at the beginning of any kind of reflection – thinking about an object must start with an abstract concept that completely separates the thing from its substance and materiality as relevant features.

These remarks just underline the widely acknowledged assumption that Western thinking is based on a thorough divide between the sphere of the mind and the sphere of things, whereas the realm of the non-material – the mind, thoughts, and words – is given priority. This article will show how this problematic dichotomy is perpetuated even in some major theories of current material culture studies. The article will point at the shortcomings of this division and give some suggestions how to overcome it and thereby contribute to a better understanding of materiality and people's interaction with material objects.

Scientific traditions of dealing with the material world

Of course this does not mean that there is no scientific interest in the material world. After all, the age of capitalism is also the epoch of materialism, and there is an ongoing debate whether it is possible to identify some kind of 'material turn' in history. This term was designed by historians of consumption (Rappaport 2008; Trentmann 2009) in order to designate a particular moment when consumption became the most important form of the acquisition and incorporation of material goods. The 'material turn' refers to the idea that – from this moment onwards – the majority of society acknowledges the possibility of the articulation of identity through consumption and the possession of things acquired as commodities. If it is possible to identify a 'material turn,' then there is the question when this might have occurred. The early colonial period would be a good candidate for this event, because it corresponds with the arrival of sugar and other colonial goods, which – within a short span of time – turned from luxury goods into popular necessities in British society (Mintz 1985).

This contribution will not engage in the discussion about whether and when a 'material turn' could have taken place. Instead, some of the more recent and widely acknowledged theories, tackling the realm of the material and the cultural relevance of objects, will be outlined here. The aim of this short overview is to show the achievements, but also the shortcomings of these approaches. The best starting point is Karl Marx and his concept of 'commodity fetishism'. As a matter of fact, Marx has succeeded in expressing something important by using that term: as soon as a product becomes a commodity, its value has little to do with its production costs and, in particular, it is totally disconnected from its use value. Ironically, Marx speaks about the 'silly ideas' in the 'blockhead of the wooden table' which begins to dance, when it becomes a commodity.[1] As such, the table – taken here as the model for any commodity – acquires wondrous qualities, which have nothing to do with its materiality, but definitely creates its particular appeal through the social mechanisms of ascribing properties and transmitting 'prestige' to its owner. This is one of the most astonishing effects of consumerism – what kinds of things can be commodities and thereby 'things with silly properties' (Kockelman 2006).

Pointing to the disconnection of an object and its culturally defined meanings and valuations, Marx can be considered as one of the founders of a field of research focusing on the meanings of things. This field, which is commonly labelled the 'semiotic approach to things', enjoys an increasing relevance up to the present (Ritzer, Goodman and Wiedenhoft 2001). Material properties of things, their substances, are of no real import in this line of thought. What is much more relevant is the quality (prestige, stigma, association with a given lifestyle) of the owner articulated through the possession of the object. Owning and using an object is a prerogative. It may be an expression of reputation, namely a mark of distinction from all the others who do not possess this special table, expensive car or exclusive clothes.

The list of prominent scholars who have dealt with the semiotics of objects is quite long. Roland Barthes (1957) has written a widely acknowledged essay on the Citroën DS, a fashionable car model of the 1950s. Barthes explains how dreams of luxury and extravagance are associated with this object, thereby rendering many of the material properties irrelevant. The Citroën connects the person and these dreams, if only the person is able to acquire such a car. However, Barthes (1967) went on in one of his subsequent publications to assume the equal status of objects, texts and images as carriers of such dreams of meanings. The later publications concerning his concept reveal a serious shortcoming of the semiotic approach in general: Although the meanings give reasons why some objects are highly relevant and receive an outstanding appreciation, the semiotic approach does not address the question of ordinary objects, the wide range of things everybody uses in everyday life. These objects exist without dreaming about them and even without having an idea whether the object is in fashion or not.

Thorstein Veblen (1899), another theorist of the semiotic approach, describes the extravagances of the rich as providing a disastrous example for the rest of the society. In his model, the other members, down to the worker, have no choice but to imitate the quirks of the super rich. Meanwhile Marx's notion of 'fetishism' resonates a considerable astonishment about the insignificance of material qualities of the thing, Veblen's model of the evaluation of things assumes a close relation between social hierarchies and material meanings: Whatever the 'upper class' defines as desirable and adopts as a form of 'conspicuous consumption', the rest of society accepts as a meaningful object. Obviously, Veblen's model implies a dangerous simplification of what might constitute culture and society (Horkheimer and Adorno 1944). To the quest for the relevance of the material, it contributes very little.

Finally Mary Douglas (with Baron Isherwood, 1979) and Daniel Miller (1995) stand at the forefront of the recent boom of *material culture studies*. These two scholars boosted the study of material things in the field of semiotics. Starting with the questions of consumption and commoditisation, already tackled by Marx, they focus on the capacity of appreciated objects to articulate social milieus, class consciousness, lifestyle, and identity. People acquire things in order to create meaningful signs. They seem to believe that these objects are read and understood as material signs, and that their meaningful messages are successfully conveyed to other members of society. Things constitute society; they are a mirror of society, at least insofar as the idea of society as a social structure is concerned. More than others, Jean Baudrillard (1968) is quite explicit concerning the power of unlimited 'semiosis', the chain of signs referring to each other.

However, Baudrillard (1972) himself is also critical of the claims of the semiotic approach. He points to the irritating mode of current usage of the term 'commodity fetishism,' which – in contrast to Marx' initial usage – has become devoid of irony. Baudrillard makes clear that semiotic theory perfectly fits into the fetishism approach, although it contributes little explaining the relevance of most material properties of everyday objects (Böhme 2008). Things are reduced to signs; and semiotics are instrumental in realising this reduction.

With this, the limitations of the meaning oriented concept becomes clear; it has only a limited potential to explain the materiality of things. However, there is another framework, which is of almost equal prominence, and does not have the drawback of reducing objects to signs and meanings. This second approach focuses on the issue of needs and uses, which are also present in the works of Karl Marx (Knight 1963). The category of 'need' is contained in Marx's notion of 'use value'. This line of thought has been elaborated more explicitly by Abraham Maslow (1943; 1954), who has coined the term, 'the pyramid of needs'. Maslow's metaphorical approach locates basic needs at the bottom of the pyramid. Basic needs are indispensable for all people. The next level is constituted by secondary needs, which comprise less necessary features, such as fashion, religion and leisure. At the top of the pyramid are the least useful objects, which are pure symbols and objects that have just cultural value, but no everyday use. The lure for those things that are not necessities requires a learning process. Only by training do people become eager to appropriate the 'top of the pyramid'-things (Witt 2001).

In a critical re-evaluation of this approach, Colin Campbell (1987) describes convincingly how it has become a condition of the modern individual to adopt permanently new desires that appear on the horizon. The desperate desire – or is it a 'need'? – can be sated only temporarily by the acquisition of new goods. Campbell calls this condition 'the spirit of consumerism'. This is an articulation of the romantic ethic, which is characterized by the infinite search for a better existence. Zygmunt Bauman (2001) has polemically addressed the slippery notion of what a need is and what a desire is with the figure of the hunter. Consumers are hunters. They are in pursuit of ever-newer things, which become meaningless as soon as they manage to acquire them. As this metaphor makes clear, the actual properties of things are of no great relevance any more in the 'spirit of consumerism' model. Once again the material properties have dropped out from the scope of observation, as the theory directs the awareness to a domain of thinking about things and not the actual dealing with things.

This short *tour d'horizon*, dealing with two recent and widely acknowledged theories on things in society is far from being comprehensive. However it reveals two major trends. On the one hand, there is an unquestioned acceptance of the infinitely expandable world of meanings, signifiers, and tools of social differentiation. On the other hand, there is an infinitely expandable universe of needs, motives and desires. The isolation of the individual and the individual's need to find a distinctive place in society are basic drivers in both concepts.

The best way to synthesise the two approaches is by considering them as complementary. Both are completely convincing in explaining the rapid increase of the individuals' material possession. The unproblematic quantitative multiplication of the material world is, in effect, a 'built-in feature', and one might wonder how people living before the era of the 'material turn' were able to survive with so few things. These astonishing implications call for more thorough reflection on further implications of these widely acknowledged theories.

Critique of the existing approaches

Having introduced the main approaches to the study of material culture, it is time now to elaborate further how these approaches by and large fall short of uncovering the meaning of materiality in our lives. The critique is mainly directed toward some of the implicit assumptions of these approaches. The critique will also shed some light on the grounds of their popularity and their limitations. The first critical aspect is the affirmative relation toward capitalism. The idea that any material object (and most other stuff) can become a commodity is – in contrast to Marx's position – no surprise, but part of the inherent logic in these approaches.

The second criticism is more important with regard to the conceptualisation of the interaction of people with the material. Both theories insinuate that people only deal with the things they possess. Acquisition, owning, and showing achieve the status of social norms or instructions. This could be labelled as 'signalling behaviour', and it seems to be accepted without any resistance as the standard procedure of dealing with things by all members of society. Both traditions assume without further ado that people not only deal with the very many objects they possess, but also do so in complete accordance with social norms. Dealing with things becomes the most important social behaviour. People react to what an individual does with the material object in his or her reach. Anything else is irrelevant. According to these theories, some important aspects of everyday dealing with things are pushed into the background and tend to be neglected. Yet, people also use things they are not aware of, *i.e.* unconsciously; people own things without being conscious about their possession; and – last but not least – some of the most important things are just imagined (and were never acquired as a commodity). As Olsen (2006, 97) has pointed out, with reference to Heidegger, the 'inconspicuous familiarity' is left out in these theories.

Colin Campbell uses an everyday observation in order to make his criticism more evident. His example concerns the moments when people stand in front of the wardrobe, choosing their clothing, and – eventually – taking into consideration its relevance for social distinctions. The choice of clothes, the communication of meaning through fashion, is one of the evident fields of semiotic theory, as many of the theorists, including Veblen and Barthes, have dealt with clothes and the social status of their wearers of fashion. Imagining the moment in front of the wardrobe and the need to select suitable clothing makes clear that such a decision is more complex than the link between the particular clothing and the sign, the social meaning, and the communication of status might suggest (Campbell 1996a).

A close observation reveals further complications: Very often the choice of a garment depends not only on the appearance, but also on questions of whether the owner remembers that it was pleasant to wear it or how appropriate the particular material (cotton, linen or synthetic fibres) is for the particular weather of the respective day. Campbell's (1996b) critical comments on the reduction to 'socially significant meanings' allow him to discuss the 'myth of social action'. As the choice in front of the wardrobe depends on a wide range of possible factors – reaching far beyond the scope of socially relevant meanings – this applies for the everyday dealings with material objects in general. The example of clothing illustrates that any object contains more relevant perceptions and references than what is observable in public. The consideration of social meaning is just the surface, and more precisely, in the case of clothes, it is only one side that everybody can see. Whether the garment feels unpleasant on the skin, or whether it is unpleasant to carry because it fits badly, because the waist size of the owner has changed, all these qualities are left out of the observation.

As the last example shows, the perception of materiality is not adequately addressed by the semiotic approach (Olsen 2003). Therefore it is possible to say that the outcome of these theories is a stunted look on the material world, mated with hectic activity and reduced to the appearance of things. Looking through the lens of the two dominant theories, dealing with things seems to have only one goal: to achieve something that is considered to be relevant on the social level. The things themselves are forced in the straightjacket of a functional context, and, by doing so, they are already numb. Most of our sensual abilities have become irrelevant; much of the inherent complexity of the perceptions of the material is left out (Baudrillard 1986).

The third criticism of the two dominant theories requires a look back into the history of archaeology and anthropology. Both disciplines claim 'material culture' as one of their founding research fields. The history of the anthropological study of material culture in the 19th century can be read as a history of obsession with forms. Eminent anthropologists of that time were convinced that a careful examination of forms is the key for the reconstruction of the history of civilizations. Examples of this are Adolf Bastian (Fiedermutz-Laun 1986) and Henry Balfour (Larson 2007). These and other scholars considered the finest details of the formal design of any object to be the best circumstantial evidence for the historical legacy of a culture. The craftsman was the person who – without having any consciousness about that – condensed 'culture' into the material by association with a particular 'form'.[2]

Although it was only some decades later, in the 1920s, that Cologne Museum's anthropologist Fritz Graebner (1923), defined the rules of the so called 'Formkritierium', this concept was already in common use 30 years prior to its publication. For example Leo Frobenius (1897) uses this method in an essay on the history of West Africa. In a later publication (1909, 780f.) he reproduces drawings of two gongs, one in bronze and from ancient 'Faraka', the other made of iron and documented by himself from Northern Togo. He tells the reader that the transition from bronze to iron – like any other change from one material to another – is irrelevant, as long as it is possible for the culture to produce the very specific traditional and meaningful form. Following Frobenius, these forms are linked to the (mythical) 'Culture of Atlantis' that had been brought to West Africa by Phoenician traders. He assumes that the similarity of forms are sufficient evidence for the import into and survival of ancient cultures in the West African Savannah.

At that time, material culture was regarded as the medium by which culturally and traditionally meaningful forms became visible, transportable and scientifically representable. During the last decades of the 19th century, when masses of objects arrived from the new colonies, the ethnographic museums filled up very quickly (Penny 2003). All these objects were collected as witnesses for millennium-old cultural-historical connections. The materiality and the actual dealing with these things in everyday contexts were of little relevance.

With this, some parallels emerge between the obsession with the form of things in the 19th century and the focus on the social meanings of things at the end of 20th century. In both lines of thought an 'excess of perceptions' is removed. Both approaches are reductionist, insofar as they select a specific range of contexts and a particular kind of perception at the expense of other dimensions. Many highly relevant aspects of everyday life were declared to be insignificant and excluded from consideration. In return, two selected domains, namely form and meaning, were declared as the central criteria.

Until now, science historians have not been able to find a valid criterion for the distinction between the museum and the department store. Both are outcomes of astonishingly similar concepts (Fliedl 1997; Kleindorfer-Marx and Löffler 2000). The ways in which objects are collected and classified in the museum, stripped of most contextual connections, are similar to the mode of display in a department store, where they are laid on a counter in order to be bought. The surprising simultaneity in the emergence of the department store and the museum is another indication for the fact that similar principles are at work (König 2009). In both cases the implicit objective and undeclared motive of these arrangements is to attain control over the perception of things. Museums and department stores both define what sensual qualities befit the item stored, and which properties are excluded. Obviously some specific properties, like smell, are hardly ever accepted in any of these contexts.

The same problematic limitation of relevant properties is perpetuated in the actual *material culture studies*. Furthermore, it is almost impossible to find any critical argument against consumption in the relevant publications of this research field. Unquestionably, consumption is one of the organising principles of present societies. But is there really no life outside the unlimited availability of things and the social control of their meanings? Can a theory be convincing that has such a bias towards a particular mode of dealing with things?

Perception as an approach to people's interaction with the material world

So far, the argument of this contribution has been a critique directed towards the dominant traditions in material culture studies; the question that has been raised is whether they are able to deal with everyday encounters with the material world. There are very few positive indications for alternative approaches. Eventually the tightness of clothes and the unacceptable smell of a museum object might be two examples of the obvious qualities of material practices, which came up in the context of the criticism above. These phenomena have been used here as pure illustrations, however they might give an indication in which direction a broadened approach to material culture should be developed.

There are good reasons to expect that such unforeseen but not uncommon perceptions of the material are a step on the way to a more integrated approach to material culture, thereby avoiding the fallacies of the reductionist theories. The challenge of developing such approach to material culture is not the question of how to apply a framework (the sign-quality, the need or desire, or the museum-object), but merely the fact that any broader framework should find a way to represent the properties of objects beyond their 'control' or 'functionality'. It is the 'Trickiness of the Object' that refers to the excess of (sometimes unexpected) perceptions (Ferus and Rübel 2009) and that should receive more awareness in the approach to the realm of the material. The material world is a challenge because perceptions are broader and richer as one might expect. Material culture is one of the fundamental topics in the humanities, precisely because the things in everyday life are a permanent challenge to man's capacity to control his environment. Scientific approaches should therefore try to integrate this aspect of immediate perception, of the regular presence of things, including those objects that are below the 'threshold' of consciousness (Nöth 1988, 178).

This is not a simple task because, like all theories, concepts of material culture have a tendency not to allow too many entanglements with contradictory or unexpected encounters. One strategy to overcome this difficulty is related to findings in the field of the development of the human mind. In fact, in the development of sensory abilities, 'unknown' objects and 'unconscious' encounters play a crucial role. This is the case in particular for the earliest phases of a child's development. Anyone who has watched a small child exploring a new object will confirm this. Jean Piaget (1974 [1950]) has suggested a differentiated model that distinguishes between different layers of assimilation and accommodation during the developmental phases before language acquisition. Initially in mental development, there is no such thing as 'formal thinking'. This stage is achieved only later, together with the learning of language skills. Only then, object properties like material and form are associated with a name for the thing in order to become the 'cultural concept' of an object, integrating its name *etc* . In this model, the association of a word with a thing is not an enlargement of the perception of the thing. Having words for things constitutes a complex restructuring, including a reduction. After the adoption of a 'cultural concept', concrete perceptions are considered to be just examples for abstract categories. What someone sees, touches or smells is only the actual experience; it has to be contextualized with culturally defined expectations towards the object. The cultural power of 'classifying' any object then dominates all other modes. It forces the individual to describe a thing by referring to abstract categories. This 'retrieval function' categorizes knowledge with regard to the proper name of the object, social contexts, status, *etc* .

Within psychoanalysis, it took all the years from Sigmund Freud to Jacques Lacan to understand that 'object relations' are not only neurotic disturbances, but fundamental abilities of transferring sensibility and binding energy from one domain to another. Lacan has rehabilitated 'things', in the sense of material perceptible objects, by showing how the ego is permanently challenged by his attempt to control relations with things (Johnson 2008). This kind of promotion of things might appear as a co-directional dynamic compared to *material culture studies*, as both are contributing to the promotion of objects in the humanities. However, there is an important difference, insofar as the assumed stability of a material object in the Freudian concept is undermined by the more recent approaches. In contrast to such assumptions, Lacan refers to the unsafe ground of material things (Zupancic 2001). The constancy of subjective perception is a condition of identity, and, at the same time, it is a challenge.

These remarks about cognitive development in early childhood and about recent developments in psychoanalysis might appear to be far-fetched concepts regarding the question of an appropriate way of dealing with material culture. However, there is a third fragment that should be mentioned here in support of the argument about the 'excess of perception', which has so far been underutilised in the humanities.

This aspect concerns the *workplace studies* established currently in sociology (Knoblauch and Heath 1999). Within this new conceptual framework, micro-ethnographic studies have stressed to what extent high-frequency and seemingly routine activities require constant and exact perception by the actors. In these activities, things are not simply 'objects' in the Latin sense of 'objectus', but they constitute an active partner in an interaction with no predetermined result. It is only due to a highly reactive strategy that the human protagonists keep the situation under control. Language has only minor relevance, while social conventions and 'social acting' do not play a major role. A case study might elucidate the relevance of such studies in order to understand 'interaction with things'. The case study was realised by John Gatewood on the basis of his ethnographic research on a fish trawler. In the related publication, entitled 'Actions speak louder than words', Gatewood (1985) describes in detail, how these fishermen work hard, and struggle in order to master the material properties of the equipment with which they work. The coordination of the work in a group is achieved not by speaking, but through corresponding actions. When a rope is too tight, the person in charge feels it through the muscular tension in his arms and will untighten it as quickly as possible. When the fishing net is too heavy, it must be immediately loosened to prevent the loss of fish due to a break due to its own weight.

A second example from *workplace studies* further highlights the relevance of immediate interaction between man and material. This case study had been carried out by Peter Richardson (2009) and documents the working context in a sawmill. It is the task of the workers at the entry control to sort out the bad planks immediately after the trunk has been cut. Of course there are considerable margins, depending on whether there is a preference to take as much wood as possible to the processing or rather the priority is given to the highest quality of timber. Based on immediate and routinised perceptions of colour, weight and hardness of the material, the workers must make a quick choice. Sometimes they recognize by the noise of the saw, that the wooden plank that will come out next must have a flaw.

There is a complex set of formal guidelines, known to all workers, regulating the strategic conflict between larger quantity and higher quality. However, as Richardson found out, it is not these regulations, but the immediate perception of the workers that directs their actions. In the presence of the heavy wooden planks, which – in effect – tell the worker merely by their colour, hardness and noise what to do next, the idea of formulating the rules through language proves to be ineffective. Interaction and knowledge of the material are based on direct perceptions. Linguistic representations may be available, but they are only of secondary relevance as they cannot keep up with the requirements of the situation. Both these examples from *workplace studies* are based on the detailed study of perceptions. Investigations dealing with the interplay of different kinds of perception appear therefore to be the key to understanding the material world. Language can only cover a portion of man's interaction with things.

Within the recent ethnoarchaeological debate, a similar observation had been documented in the framework of the *chaîne opératoire*, which describes the subsequent steps in the skilful production of handcrafted objects (Desrosiers 1991; Dobres 2010). The *chaîne opératoire* can probably be considered as a special approach within *workplace studies*. Both concepts refer to a hidden knowledge when dealing with material objects. Both regard the nonverbal interaction between man and the material world as a key to understanding the role of things in everyday life. This does not apply to professional contexts alone (*i.e.* fishermen, workers in the sawmill, craftspeople *etc* .), but also to the infinite number of everyday encounters with the material, where non-language interaction is relevant.

Conclusion

Recently Martin Scharfe (2009) published a paper on 'cultural materiality,' in which he recalled the '*Signaturenlehre*' (= 'doctrine of the signatures') of Jacob Böhme from the 17th century. Böhme has a precise model of what perception of things can achieve. As Böhme said, 'everything has his mouth' (he means 'speech'); and every object informs the careful observer about many of its particular properties, if only the observation techniques are sufficiently refined. Probably and without exaggeration, Sherlock Holmes can be considered as someone who has perfected this '*Signaturenlehre*', as he could read completely all traces and signs in any object. He observed objects like others would read a text in a book. Very often archaeologists believe themselves to be investigators in a quite similar sense: they intend to give things a voice.

But it is not this kind of 'speaking' of objects that is the focus of the *workplace studies*, which served in this contribution as examples for an elaborate study of perception and action. Böhme's '*Signaturenlehre*', as well as Sherlock Holmes investigative approach, miss a crucial level for understanding the interaction between people and things which remains very often below the level of what is perceived as noteworthy or even below the level of consciousness. Lacan has stressed this in his notion of the 'notorious instability' of perceptions, which constitute the particular role of the material. Perceptions of the material are not constant and controllable. They should rather be viewed as a challenge and as something reconfigured by practice. Interaction always means to recognise, understand and act appropriately simultaneously. This form of the interaction justifies speaking about the 'power of the material'.

It has become obvious that the concern of this contribution is not to plead for a 'language of the material'. This would have been a standard assumption of *material culture studies*. The intention is rather to draw awareness to frequently overlooked moments of direct interaction between man and the material. In the context of these direct interactions, an astonishing density of perceptions can be found and – related – the option for informed actions. This can be troubling, and was referred to here as the 'excess of perceptions'. This very fundamental level of perceptions is often neglected in theories of material culture, because it lacks a linguistic representation and does not appear to be relevant for 'social meanings'. Examples of these perceptions have been the discomfort of clothes that were too tight, the unpleasant smell of museum objects, the pulling of the tightened rope or the noise of the saw when cutting wood.

Sensitivity to the immediate perception of the material world in the context of these very diverse practices, however ephemeral and brief such sensual events might be, opens a sustainable access to the true relevance of material culture. Inevitably this approach will be in conflict with philosophical models that declare 'language' to be the key to understanding the world.

Notes

1. "Nichtsdestoweniger bleibt der Tisch Holz, ein ordinäres sinnliches Ding. Aber sobald er als Ware auftritt, verwandelt er

sich in ein sinnlich übersinnliches Ding. Er steht nicht nur mit seinen Füßen auf dem Boden, sondern er stellt sich allen andren Waren gegenüber auf den Kopf und entwickelt aus seinem Holzkopf Grillen, viel wunderlicher, als wenn er aus freien Stücken zu tanzen begänne." Marx 1876[1968], 85.

2. Arjun Appadurai (2006) recently pointed to this tradition in a critical manner. In his view, the apparent permanence of a form is incompatible with its materiality, because most materials change their consistency and surface with time. Objects are always rendered into an abstract entity, when form is given priority over substance.

References

Appadurai, A. (2006) The Thing Itself. *Public Culture* 18/1, 15–22.

Baldwin, J. M. (1895) The Origin of a 'Thing' and its Nature. *Psychological Review*, 2/6, 551–573.

Barthes, R. (1957) *Mythologies.* Paris: Édition du Seuil.

Barthes, R. (1967) *Système de la mode.* Paris.

Baudrillard, J. (1968) *Le système des objets*. Paris, Gallimard.

Baudrillard, J. (1972) Fétichisme et idéologie: La réduction sémiologique. In J. Baudrillard (ed.), *Pour une critique de l'économie politique du signe*, 94–113. Paris, Gallimard.

Bauman, Z. (2001) Consuming Life. *Journal of Consumer Culture*, 1/1, 9–29.

Baudrillard, J. (1986) *Amerique.* Paris, Grasset.

Böhme, G. (2008) Zur Kritik der Ästhetischen Ökonomie. In K. Maase (ed.), *Die Schönheiten des Populären. Ästhetische Erfahrung der Gegenwart*, 28–41. Frankfurt, Campus.

Campbell, C. (1987) *The Romantic Ethic and the Spirit of Modern Consumerism.* Oxford, Blackwell.

Campbell, C. (1996a) The Meaning of Objects and the Meaning of Actions. A Critical Note on the Sociology of Consumption. *Journal of Material Culture* 1/1, 93–105.

Campbell, C. (1996b) *The Myth of Social Action.* Cambridge, Cambridge University.

Desrosiers, S. (1991) Sur le concept de la chaîne opératoire. In H. Balfet (ed.), *Observer l'action technique: des chaînes opératoires, pour quoi faire?*, 21–25. Paris, CNRS.

Dobres, M.-A. (2010) Archaeologies of Technology. *Cambridge Journal of Economics* 34, 103–114.

Douglas, M. and Isherwood, B. (1979) *The World of Goods. Towards an Anthropology of Consumption.* London, Routledge.

Ferus, K. and Rübel, D. (2009) *Die Tücke des Objekts - Vom Umgang mit Dingen.* Berlin, Reimer.

Fiedermutz-Laun, A. (1986) Adolf Bastian und die Begründung der deutschen Ethnologie im 19. Jahrhundert. *Berichte zur Wissenschaftsgeschichte* 9/3, 167–181.

Fliedl, G. (1997) *Wa(h)re Kunst. Der Museumshop als Wunderkammer; theoretische Objekte, Fakes und Souvenirs.* Schriftenreihe Offenes Kulturhaus, Werkbund-Archiv 24.

Frobenius, L. (1897) Der westafrikanische Kulturkreis. *Petermanns Mitteilungen* 43, 225–271.

Frobenius, L. (1909) Ethnologische Ergebnisse der zweiten Reiseperiode der Deutschen Innerafrikanischen Forschungsexpedition (DIAFE). *Zeitschrift für Ethnologie* 6, 759–783.

Galbraith, J. K. (1958) How Much Should a Country Consume? In H. Jarrett (ed.), *Perspectives on Conservation*, 89–99. Baltimore, John Hopkins University.

Gatewood, J. B. (1985) Actions Speak Louder than Words. In J. Dougherty (ed.), *Directions in Cognitive Anthropology*, 199–219. Urbana, University of Illinois.

Gellner, E. (1959) *Words and Things. A Critical Account of Linguistic Philosophy and a Study in Ideology.* London, Gollanz.

Graebner, F. (1923): Ethnologie. In G. Schwalbe, G. and E. Fischer (ed.), *Anthropologie. Kultur der Gegenwart*, 435–587. Leipzig, B. G. Teubner.

Hahn, H. P. and Soentgen, J. (2010) Acknowledging Substances. Looking at the Hidden Side of the Material. *Philosophy and Technology* 24/1, 19–33.

Horkheimer, M. and Adorno, T. W. (1944) *Dialektik der Aufklärung.* New York/Los Angeles, Institute of Social Research.

Johnson, B. (2008) *Persons and Things*. Boston, Harvard.

Kleindorfer-Marx, B. and Löffler, K. (2000) *Museum und Kaufhaus. Warenwelten im Vergleich*. Regensburg, Regensburger Verein für Volkskunde.

Knight, F. H. (1963) Value and Price. In D. L. Sills (ed.), *International Encyclopedia of the Social Sciences*, 218–225. New York, Macmillan.

Knoblauch, H. and Heath, C. (1999) Technologie, Interaktion und Organisation: Die Workplace Studies. *Schweizerische Zeitschrift für Soziologie* 25/2, 163–181.

Kockelman, P. (2006) A Semiotic Ontology of the Commodity. *Journal of Linguistic Anthropology* 16, 76–102.

Küchler, S. (2009) Was Dinge tun: eine anthropologische Kritik medialer Dingtheorie. In K. Ferus and D. Rübel (eds), *Die Tücke des Objekts - Vom Umgang mit Dingen*, 231–247. Berlin, Reimer.

König, G. M. (2009) *Konsumkultur. Inszenierte Warenwelt um 1900*. Wien, Böhlau.

Larson, F. (2007) Anthropology as Comparative Anatomy? Reflecting on the Study of Material Culture During the Late 1800s and the Late 1900s. *Journal of Material Culture* 12/1, 89–112.

Levine, J. (2007) *No Buying! My Year Without Shopping.* New York, Free Press.

Linde, H. (1972) *Sachdominanzen in Sozialstrukturen.* Tübingen, J.C.B. Mohr.

Marx, K. 1876 [1968] *Das Kapital. Kritik der politischen Ökonomie*. Band I. Berlin, Dietz.

Maslow, A. H. (1943) A Theory of Human Motivation. *Psychological Review* 50/4, 370–396.

Maslow, A. H. (1954) *Motivation and Personality.* New York.

Mauss, M. (1969 [1939]) Conceptions qui ont précédé la notion de matière. In M. Mauss (ed.), *Oeuvres Band: 2. Représentations collectives et diversité des civilisations*, 161–168. Paris, Minuit.

Meinong, A. (1988 [1904]) *Untersuchungen zur Gegenstandstheorie und Psychologie*. Hamburg, Meiner.

Miller, D. (1995) Consumption as the Vanguard of History. In D. Miller (ed.), *Acknowledging Consumption*, 1–57. London, Routledge.

Mintz, S. W. (1985) *Sweetness and Power. The Place of Sugar in Modern History*. New York, Viking/Penguin.

Nöth, W. (1988) The Language of Commodities. Groundwork for a Semiotics of Consumer Goods. *International Journal of Research in Marketing* 4/3, 173–186.

Olsen, B. (2003) Material Culture after Text. Re-Membering Things. *Norwegian Archaeological Review* 36/2, 87–104.

Olsen, B. (2006) Scenes from a Troubled Engagement: Poststructuralism and Material Culture Studies. In C. Tilley (ed.), *Handbook of Material Culture*, 85–105. London, Sage.

Penny, H. G. (2003) *Objects of Culture. Ethnology and Ethnographic Museums in Imperial Germany*. Chapel Hill, University of North Carolina.

Piaget, J. (1974 [1950]) *Der Aufbau der Wirklichkeit beim Kinde.* Stuttgart, Klett. (originally: La construction du réel chez l'enfant, Neuchâtel 1950).

Rappaport, E. (2008) Imperial Possessions, Cultural Histories, and the Material Turn: Response. *Victorian Studies* 50/2, 289–296.

Richardson, P. (2009) Doing Things with Wood. Builders, Managers and Wittgenstein in an Idaho Sawmill. *Critique of Anthropology* 29/2, 160–182.

Ritzer, G., Goodman, D. J. and Wiedenhoft, W. (2001) Theories of Consumption. In G. Ritzer and B. Smart (eds), *Handbook of Social Theory*, 410–427. London, Sage.

Rötzer, F. (1991) Die Rache der Dinge (= postface to the German translation). In J. Baudrillard (ed.), *Das System der Dinge. Über unser Verhältnis zu den alltäglichen Gegenständen*, 250–261. Frankfurt, Campus.

Scharfe, M. (2009) Kulturelle Materialität. In K. C. Berger (ed.), *Erb.gut? Kulturelles Erbe in Wissenschaft und Gesellschaft.* Referate der 25. Österreichischen Volkskundetagung vom 14.–17.11.2007 in Innsbruck, 15–33. Wien, Verein für Volkskunde.

Schechter, H. (2002) *Entrümpeln Sie Ihr Leben! So befreien Sie sich von Andenken, Altlasten und anderem Ballast.* München, mvg. (originally: 'Let Go of Clutter', New York, 2001).

Scherhorn, G. (1997) Das Ganze der Güter. In K. M. Meyer-Abich (ed.), *Vom Baum der Erkenntnis zum Baum des Lebens*, 162–251. München, Beck.

Schor, J. B., Slater, D., Zukin, S. and Zelizer, V. A. (2010) Critical and Moral Stances in Consumer Studies. *Journal of Consumer Culture* 10, 274–291.

Simmel, G. (1989 [1900, 1907]) *Philosophie des Geldes*. Frankfurt, Suhrkamp.

Trentmann, F. (2009) Consumption and Globalization in History. *Journal of Consumer Culture* 9/2, 187–220.

Veblen, T. (1899) The Theory of the Leisure Class. An Economic Study of Institutions, New York: Macmillan 1899).

Witt, U. (2001) Learning to Consume. *Journal of Evolutionary Economics* 11, 23–36.

Zupancic, A. (2001) *Das Reale einer Illusion – Kant und Lacan*. Frankfurt, Suhrkamp.

3.

Magic, materials and matter: understanding different ontologies

Chris Gosden

In the western world of the 21st century we have a particular set of relationships to the material world: we live in a state of mass consumption, with global flows and people, materials and money, as well as holding a generally scientific attitude towards materials. It might be thought that all these characteristics differentiate us from the world of the eastern Mediterranean in the second and first millennia. However, I shall argue that it is the last of the characteristics, a scientific ethos, which most differentiates us from those worlds of the past. Admittedly, levels of consumption today are huge compared with any period of the past and consumption *en masse* reaches further down the social scale. The mining of iron ore in Western Australia to be exported to China for the manufacture of finished products, which are then sold in Europe or Africa, links parts of the world which were until relatively recently ignorant of each other's existence. But it might be argued that the most striking contrast between past and present is one of scale and degree, rather than in the simple existence of mass consumption or the flow of materials across borders of various kinds. As other papers in this volume amply demonstrate, mass consumption, for at least some in ancient societies, was key to many aspects of power and identity. We are also coming to see the Bronze and Iron Age worlds as melting pots in which people, ideas, raw materials, and finished products moved constantly and consequentially. Elsewhere, I have used the image of a circulation system in which things and people move, changing their values and significances and causing changes in the cultural formations through which they move (Gosden 2004). If large-scale consumption and the regular and long distant movement of materials do not differentiate the ancient and modern worlds, what of an acceptance of science? Such a question is, of course, anachronistic, in that a rigorous, experimental, and objective science has only come into existence in the last few hundred years. Key, then, to many differences between past and present, when considering people's entanglements with materials, may be the existence (or otherwise) of a set of scientific practices. I use the word 'practices' deliberately to indicate that science is as much an attitude of the body as the mind, a set of physical engagements with materials and peoples, which aim to produce results of a particular kind. Science as practice is consonant with the contemporary field of Science and Technology Studies (Latour and Woolgar 1986; Barad 2007) and fits in with the broader idea that people and things are entangled; interwoven through repeated patterns of action to which each contributes. If the ancient world lacked the set of practices we now call science, how then to characterize people's forms of engagement with materials in the second and first millennia BCE and what consequences might these have for our understanding of archaeological evidence? I shall develop first a notion of ontology, before focusing on the changing role of metals and their role both in ontologies and notions of reproduction.

Social ontologies

Over the last few hundred years we have separated the terms religion, magic and science. This seems a natural separation to us, but is in fact historically and culturally unusual. In thinking about periods of the past like the Iron Age, our task is not so much to imagine what it would be like to recombine these terms, but to think what it would be like if we had never separated them in the first place. In our ontology, science denotes eternal, unchanging, and empirically verifiable forms of cause and effect contained today within the laws of biology, physics, and chemistry; religion attributes power to single or multiple sets of divine powers; and magic is a tricky and often denigrated term, so that dictionary definitions encompass meanings which include the ability to produce illusions or tricks, the use of incantations and spells to procure desired outcomes, and the human control of supernatural agencies. Magic is also linked to enchantment.

Nineteenth century thinkers, including the sociologist Weber and the anthropologist Tylor, thought the human history of engagement with the world moved from magic to religion to science, each more institutionally based and objectively correct than the previous. As part of this progressive movement of history, people moved from a belief in spirits and magical powers, to a belief in many gods and then just one, to finally emancipate themselves through the application of reason, which found its purest expression in science. The separation between science and religion is now being questioned (Gaukroger 2006), whereby religion is seen to provide the context for science over the last few centuries when vicars have been naturalists, chemists or geologists. Only in the last century has real antagonism grown up and then only on the part of a few. Science and magic have also been closely related: Maynard Keynes described Newton not as the first of the age of reason, but as the last of the magicians, struggling to understand the riddles of the universe in the same manner as the ancient Magi. The progressive move from magic to science provides too partial an account and in all our minds there are aspects of religion (even if we are atheists), magic (despite our rationalism), as well as a broader scientific idiom. The history of the three terms is not one of replacement, but of co-existence in cultural worlds emphasizing each in different measure.

There are grounds for thinking that in many periods of the prehistoric past the mix of these three terms was different from at present and indeed seamless, so that separate concepts for each may not have existed at all. In order to look at varying conceptions of powers in the world and human relations with plants, animals and things the term 'ontology' is becoming central. Ontology is conventionally used as a singular noun to refer either to the study of being, or being in general. In this latter usage, which is the one I shall develop, ontology refers to the things of which the universe is composed and the relationships between them. In a western approach to ontology, it is the specification of energy, mass, chemical composition or biochemical operations that are important. In such an objective view of the world there can be only one reality, so that our use of ontologies in the plural is controversial. I am not so much arguing that matter, or cause and effect, take multiple forms, but rather that people engage with the multiplicity of the universe in different ways. Each cultural engagement highlights and renders differing aspects of the world, each with their own concepts of cause and effect. The world and its workings become apparent to people not through passive contemplation, but through practice and practical knowledge. Skilled action represents a series of little experiments in what it is possible to do with materials in concert or competition with other people. Each cultural form has a different skills base and consequently understands the world differently. The Bronze and Iron Age periods of the eastern Mediterranean are different from our own and may well have had notions of transformation that linked people and things in ways that seem unusual to us.

In an older usage of the word, ontology came to designate the really real, the nature and structure of reality which humans attempted to apprehend and work with or against (Gosden 2008). Brute, inanimate reality stood opposed to the lively and active intentions or desires of human beings. As Viveros de Castro has written (1998, 469) a series of opposed terms connect to reality on the one hand and human society on the other, so that nature opposes culture, as a universal against the particular, the objective to the subjective, the physical to the social, fact to value, the given to the initiated, body to mind, necessity to spontaneity and so on. This series of oppositions has grown up in a western, scientific mindset and not all cultural forms take these divisions for granted. Descola (1994) lays out three different ways of conceiving of the world – animism, totemism and naturalism. The last of these is the Western view, dividing nature (to be investigated by the physical or biological sciences) from culture (probed by social sciences and humanities), which is historically particular, having grown up in the last few hundred years.

Both animism and totemism blur the difference between culture and nature. The former term does this by allowing aspects of personhood to animals, plants, rocks, rivers and so on, which may have desires and intentions in some ways cognate with human motivations. Totemism mixes things up in the opposite direction as it were – if a wallaby or cockatoo can be emblematic of a clan or other human group then people may share characteristics of behaviour or inclination with those species, which are not truly separate from the human group. A particularly influential account of such blurring between our categories of people and the broader world is contained in the work of Viveiros de Castro, who coins the term 'perspectivism' to understand the manner in which Amazonian plants and animals are seen as subjects who apprehend reality from their own points of view, but in manners which echo human perceptions and relations. Animals and spirits see themselves as humans of slightly different kinds and outward differences of the body conceal a human goal within a jaguar or tapir. He says that where Westerners see a world of multiculturalism in which there is both difference and equivalence between human cultures, Amerindian people see multinaturalism in which various species have their differences underpinned by basic similarities of spirit (Viveiros de Castro 1998, 470). The echoes between varying types of being require particular kinds of respect, so that these schemes of reality have a moral element to them, telling people what they need to do to live well.

Both Descola and Viveiros de Castro draw their ideas from work with Amerindian hunter-gatherers and horticulturalists. Similar ideas are developed by Ingold (2000) stemming from understandings of circum-polar hunter-gatherers. These insights are drawn from the American continent and from amongst mobile peoples, providing an interesting but rather particular empirical basis to the ethnography. Recently there has been a growing discussion of ontology (or animism) within archaeology (see the special section in the *Cambridge Archaeological Journal* volume 19, 2009 and that in *Archaeological Method and Theory* volume 15, 2008). Within archaeology the term ontology has useful overlaps with other discussions, principally those concerning ritual and functional action (Brück 1999; Bradley 2005) and that around the agency of objects or their ability to affect people. As with the broader discussions from which they derive archaeological thoughts on ontology oppose two sets of dualisms: that between mind and body and the difference made between culture and nature. Things, plants and animals can be mindful, purposive and able to influence people, so that they might be seen as persons, having many of the key characteristics of personhood. If things can be persons then it makes less sense to see them as nature and outside of culture, blurring or dissolving this distinction. In a western ontology, nature is governed by laws that are outside history and are invariant over time and space. If nature is done away with, then the possibility arises that things can act differently at varying times, depending on the relationships they are enmeshed in. Human beings may relate to things, such as metal artefacts, as animate objects with whom they have to cultivate relationships both with the objects themselves and the powers that lie behind them. The idea of reciprocity is not limited to the human world in which gifts must be acknowledged and repaid, but to many other things. Or rather, the human world is extended to include persons of many different kinds, some of which might look to us like objects or biological species. Such beliefs are not random, irrational or optional, but part of how the structure of the world is seen to be. They can be debated, challenged and rethought, just as our own beliefs can, but it would be dangerous in the extreme to ignore or refuse to engage with the most potent powers in the world. The task of the archaeologist is to layout the key relationships and the human/material practices associated with them.

Bronze and iron

Metalwork is a quick medium, taking on changes of form and decoration readily through the mutability of metal. Changes in metalwork may consequently provide a useful diagnostic for broader changes elsewhere in cultural forms and forces. I shall look briefly at the addition of iron to the metalworking traditions of Europe and use this to think about some of the broader shifts in the nature of transformations this might have brought about. Ironwork often had an everydayness about it, as compared to more deliberately spectacular products in bronze, gold, glass or lapis lazuli. Iron becomes much more ubiquitous from the very end of the second millennium onwards, working its way deep into the cultural process and transforming cycles of change and reproduction. An older view sees a process of invention and spread of iron whereby people were the active element, as inventors and technicians. In tune with broader explorations of what materials can do to people, I would like to develop a more interactive view – it was not just technical barriers that prevented people from making iron, and once these were overcome the functional properties of iron were so obvious as to lead to its rapid spread. Instead, we should see a more complicated and interactive process, in which iron was active too. A key contrast between bronze, gold, silver and glass on the one hand and iron on the other is that the former substances could be taken from a solid to a liquid state before resolidifying. Cast iron does not appear to have been present in Europe before the early modern period, so that iron in the period in question was always worked in a solid state (the process known as smithing), although made malleable by the effects of heat. In some ways this makes it more like stone, which was often heated before being reduced. Furthermore, bronze, gold and silver do not change dramatically once buried, whereas iron rusts fairly rapidly, thereby turning into a substance similar to the surrounding earth when buried. The life cycle of pre-modern iron linked it to the earth, often occurring in nodules or iron pans in its raw state and rapidly returning to the earth once finished products were buried. As we shall see, iron was a reluctant technology, being worked for hundreds or even thousands of years before becoming widespread. The barriers to mass iron working were less technical than conceptual – bronze fit into well-known sets of cycles, being an obviously magical technology, going from solid to liquid and back to solid. Iron had to make room for itself in the practices of humans, perhaps helping to develop a greater emphasis on land and agricultural production that underlay the population rises and re-urbanisation of the first millennium BCE. If this view has some truth to it, iron, through its own properties, helped make a space for itself, sending echoes through the ontologies of the day, changing notions of transformations, as well as the human and supernatural powers that lay behind these transformations. New notions of fertility and fecundity came about as iron became common, partly as a result of this fact. Furthermore iron did not replace bronze, but repositioned it, affirming some old magical values linking bronze to fine products, which were cast or made in sheet. These are complicated issues played out across Europe as the second millennium gives way to the first and the manner in which the addition of iron occurs has its own regional peculiarities and tropes, as I shall try to briefly indicate.

The transition from the Bronze to Iron Ages has been given both positive and negative values. A central idea, inherent in the progressive structure of the Three Age System, is that an iron technology was superior to a bronze one – iron is particularly suited to implements for cutting and piercing, given iron's qualities of hardness and sharpness. Iron implements, it was thought, quickly became widespread and accessible to more (all?) levels of society and so brought about a democratization of arts and crafts generally (a classic statement of this view is put forward by Snodgrass: 1971, Chapter 5; 1980; 1982; for the Aegean building on Childe 1942, 183). What can be seen as technical gains in the Iron Age, however, resulted in a loss of magic from the world as characterised by the Bronze Age, which was open and international in large part because of the trade in copper and tin ores or in finished bronze artefacts. John Evans (1881) was one of the first to laud the open and aristocratic nature of the Bronze Age world, sentiments echoed most recently by Kristiansen (1998) and Kristiansen and Larsson (2005). The Iron Age was a more pragmatic, technically effective and to some degree more democratic world, but lacked the openness, innovation and heroism of warfare and travel seen in the Bronze Age.

This is a popular and widespread narrative contrasting the second and first millennia BCE, but when looked at from the point of view of metal, it does not stand up to close scrutiny. Indeed it may well help to obscure a more interesting take on the relationship not only between bronze and iron, but also with other metals, notably gold and silver.

A first point to make is that iron objects are almost as old as those of bronze, going back in very small numbers to the third millennium BCE, in many cases predating the movement to a full-scale bronze technology (see Pare 2000, fig. 14.1). In some places, notably Anatolia in the Old Assyrian period (2000–1600 BCE), iron was being regularly produced, albeit in small amounts so that its value was ten times that of gold and many times more expensive than copper (Haarer 2001, 264). From this period the value of iron gradually but continually declined against that of other metals, whereas it appears that the value of bronze stayed constant (Haarer 2001, 264). By the 9th century BCE Assyria had a well-developed iron industry capable of producing iron in huge amounts.

It is now recognized that different regions moved to producing bronze in greater amounts at different times, the British Isles being relatively precocious with bronze production pre-dating 2000 BCE, while Crete may not have produced its own bronze until at least 500 years later. Iron follows a similar, but more exaggerated version of this pattern of delayed and regionally differentiated uptake. Second millennium ironworking was largely restricted to Anatolia and Georgia as far as we know, with occasional iron objects, such as the dagger from Ganovce in Slovakia dating back well into this millennium (Harding 2000, 240). Precocious working of iron is also in evidence, notably at Hartshill Copse near Reading in southern Britain around 1000 BCE, where it was carried out in conjunction with bronze working (Collard *et al.* 2006). We can conclude that iron was a known, if minor, element of people's material culture throughout Europe and throughout much of the second millennium BCE, although iron working was a reluctant and restricted technology.

Bronze and iron had a long-term relationship, well predating the formal Iron Age. How does the recognition of this longevity fit with the idea of a rapid transition from bronze to iron? As mentioned above, one of the classic statements of the shift from bronze to iron is provided by Snodgrass. His scheme for change had three stages. In Stage 1, which predates 1150 BCE in the Aegean, his personal period of interest, iron was known, but used in small quantities, and had a semi-precious value. In Stage 2 (1150–1050 BCE in Greece) a shortage of bronze causes experimentation with iron working which becomes more proficient and efficient. In Stage 3 iron is widely available and largely replaces bronze for making practical artefacts (Snodgrass 1971, Chapter 5). Snodgrass's scheme is reprised, although often in less explicit form, across Europe (1971, Chapter 5). Haarer (2001) uses historical records ranging between the Old Assyrian period (2000–1600 BCE) and fourth century Greece to show that between the start of the second millennium BCE and the middle of the first, iron experienced a continuous decline in value, whereas bronze kept a more constant worth. This has two implications – first, there was no sudden drop in the value of iron to make it much more accessible (indeed it was still relatively valuable at the beginning of the first millennium BCE, being found in rich graves along with gold); second, there was no sudden spike in the value of bronze indicating a crisis in supply. Even after iron started to become common this did not happen everywhere, with the result that iron only became common in Mesopotamia after 750 BCE (Haarer 2001, 265), several centuries after this happened in Cyprus, Crete or Greece (Sherratt 1994). The advantages of iron were not immediately self-evident, but were enmeshed in a complex system of values.

The Aegean arguments, both those of Snodgrass, for a crisis in bronze supply, and those of Haarer and Sherratt against, are now repeated elsewhere in Europe, where, it must be said, the ideas of a bronze crisis and rapid shift to iron still predominate. There are slight differences as to whether the shift happened due to a crisis in the bronze supply or whether a sudden increase in iron caused a hiatus in bronze.

This latter idea is often prevalent in northwestern Europe, because it helps explain the otherwise strange occurrence of the large-scale deposition of bronze in the eighth and seventh centuries BCE. Further features of these late Bronze Age depositions are the large numbers of identical axes, some of which have very high levels of lead, making them functionally useless as chopping tools (O'Connor, 1980 Huth 2000, 184–188). Given the scale of this deposition at the end of the Bronze Age, many are now concluding that bronze was not in short supply. The opposite might even be true – 'over-production probably killed bronze's symbolic value and attraction' (Verlaecht 2000, 203). Rather than supply and demand as straightforward economic drives, it is preferable to see complicated shifts in value systems as the cause of change.

If a collapse in bronze supply is less likely to have brought the Bronze Age way of life to a shuddering halt, what about the rise of iron production? Following the argument for transformation we have developed above, bronze may have fit into sets of ideas about the transformations of the world and indeed held a central place within them. Bronze could transmute from solid ore to liquid metal and back into a solid artefact. It could repeat this transformation any number of times, perhaps linking it to both the elements of earth and water (as well as fire). Iron could not be cast until the early modern period, lacking the association with water through a liquid phase. It is notable that iron is much less often deposited in water than bronze, and items such as iron swords, which were thrown into water, were often part of complex composite items that also had major bronze components. Hingley (1997) argues that the capacity of iron to rust, returning it to a state like that of soil, gave it a series of links to notions of fertility which influenced its deposition in ditches and pits. If this argument is correct, iron became common in the middle Iron Age not just (or mainly) because methods for working iron became more sophisticated, but rather because it achieved a new and interesting position within the notions of transformation that were developing from around 400 BCE onwards. Iron did not replace bronze but repositioned it, as can be seen by looking at the evidence from the later Bronze Age onwards for the two metals.

After around 800 BCE, the deposition of bronze declines markedly and this is true of hoards, river finds, and settlement evidence (O'Connor 1980; Needham 2007), there being few burials at this time, as we have seen. The deposition of iron does not become common until about 400 BCE. Looking at the Danebury sequence, the number and weight of iron objects only increases in ceramic phase 6, which is currently dated as starting in 400 BCE (Salter and Ehrenreich 1984, figs 10.4 and 10.5). It might be that there is little iron in evidence before this date because it was scarce and being recycled. However, the data on production that we have, which are albeit fairly slim, indicate specialist smelting and smithing sites become more common after 400 BCE (Salter and Ehrenreich 1984, 151). Rachel Pope (pers. comm.) has found the same pattern when looking at evidence of production in individual houses. Looking again at deposition, Hingley (2006) has found a considerably larger number of iron objects being deposited after the 5th century BCE.

Technologies, magics and sciences

Questions concerning technologies have been at the heart of archaeological thought for the last 200 years. Technologies were once seen as the cutting edge of history: greater sophistication of technological means more energy may be harvested from the environment for each unit of effort expended, in turn allowing greater population densities, sedentism, and social complexity. More recent views would see technologies as the means to bring about desired effects, but those effects might include our relationship with the gods or with each other, as well as a greater yield of calories for a given expenditure of productive effort. Books like Gell's (1998) *Art and Agency* follow this trend, focusing not on what spectacular objects (which we might call art) mean, but what they do. The sorts of things they might do include enchanting and overwhelming one's exchange partners through especially powerful products. In this view, technologies shape people and their relations, rather than being shaped by them, setting up a reciprocal relationship between people and things, and not relatioships in which cause runs from the active intentions of people to the passive objects of interest. New materials, with their own special properties, like iron, do new and different things. The cycles of production and disposal of iron might have been too new for a long time, not fitting into existing cycles of reproduction. Innovation can be resisted if it has no initial role in shaping the world. Eventually (but not inevitably) iron developed a place in which its peculiar capacities became valued and important. Iron also seems to have been linked in part to the sphere of agricultural production. In the twenty-third book of the *Iliad* Achilles holds funeral games for his dead companion, Patroclus, at which very expensive items are offered as prizes, including a large lump of iron –

> He stood up straight and spoke out thus:
> 'Rise up, you who would endeavour to win this prize also.

> For although the rich demesnes of him who Wins it lie far off
> indeed, yet for the succession of five years he will have it
> to use; for his shepherd for want of iron will not have to go in
> to the city for it, nor his ploughman either. This will supply them.'
>
> *Iliad* 23.826–35 (Lattimore trans.)

There is pragmatism and magic mixed here: the ploughing of fields will be facilitated by a lump of iron which appears hard to exhaust, even within a five year period. The working of iron may have been seen as less magical than that of bronze, leading to the common Greek trope that the Age of Iron saw some loss of magic from the world. This does not mean, however, that the ironsmith was a proto-scientist concerned only with temperature, with how much carbon to include, or when and how to quench. She (or he) was able to do all these things, or else iron products would not have become common. But we know that smithing had its own gods and the production of *obeloi* (iron spits) were partly for deposit in sanctuaries, partly as currency, and partly as raw materials which could be made into finished products. Kostoglou (2003) has argued that in 6th century BCE Thrace there was a difference between the iron spits found in settlement sites and those of steel in sanctuaries. If this result can be generalized at all, it may mean that there were fine discriminations being made as to which types of *obelai* were most appropriate for specific contexts. We might need to pay as much attention to the nature of ancient materials as did the ancients themselves.

The period after the collapse of key eastern Mediterranean powers after 1200 BCE brought about a realignment of values and politics. Much attention has been paid to the causes of these collapses, but slightly less to their effects. The increase in iron production and the repositioning of other materials was one element of a complex set of cultural realignments that occurred at this time. However, in order to understand such realignments we also have to take materials seriously as causes as well as effects. Iron was a technology, but one designed to please the gods, set up human relations with new value, as well as helping to plough the fields. Those making iron were technologists, in that they had a fine appreciation of heat and substance and the force needed to work iron. But their technology went beyond what we might see as pragmatics, into questions of the appropriate nature of materials for a sanctuary or for a plough. Such considerations bring into play factors that we would label as religious or magical. It is part of the excitement of the past that such terms do not help us straightforwardly and this is in large part because magic, religion and science cannot be distinguished in the ways we have come to use. Instead, we would be better off considering the materials themselves – looking at the characteristics of iron, for instance, which varied a great deal along a spectrum from iron to hardened steel. But we then also need to locate these forms of iron within a broader universe of materials and entanglements, allowing them to be active rather than passive, to shape people as well as being shaped by them.

References

Barad, K. (2007) *Meeting the Universe Halfway. Quantum Physics and the Entanglement of Matter and Meaning.* Durham and London, Duke University Press.

Bradley, R. (2005) *Ritual and Domestic Life in Prehistoric Europe*. London, Routledge.

Brück, J. (1999) Houses, Lifecycles and Deposition in Middle Bronze Age Settlements in Southern England. *Proceedings of the Prehistoric Society* 65, 1–22.

Childe, G. (1942) *What Happened in History*. Harmondsworth/Middlesex, Penguin Books.

Collard, M., Darvill, T. and Watts, M. (2006) Ironworking in the Bronze Age? Evidence from a 10th Century BC Settlement at Hartshill Copse, Upper Bucklebury, West Berkshire, *Proceedings of the Prehistoric Society* 72, 367–421.

Descola, P. (1994) *In the Society of Nature: a Native Ecology in Amazonia*. Cambridge, Cambridge University Press.

Evans, J. (1881) *The Ancient Bronze Implements, Weapons and Ornaments of Great Britain and Ireland*. London, Longmans, Green and Co.

Gaukroger, S. (2006) *The Emergence of a Scientific Culture: Science and the Shaping of Modernity 1210–1685*. Oxford, Clarendon Press.

Gell, A. (1998) *Art and Agency: an Anthropological Theory*. Oxford, Clarendon Press.

Gosden, C. (2004) *Archaeology and Colonialism. Cultural Contact from 5000 BC to the Present*. Cambridge, Cambridge University Press.

Gosden, C. (2008) Social Ontologies. *Philosophical Transactions of the Royal Society B* 363, 2003–2010.

Haarer, P. (2001) Problematising the Transition from Bronze to Iron. In A. Shortland (ed.), *The Social Context of Technological Change, Egypt and the Near East 1650–1550 BC* 255–273. Oxford, Oxbow Books.

Harding, A. (2000) *European Societies in the Bronze Age*. Cambridge, Cambridge University Press.

Hingley, R. (1997) Iron, Iron Working and Regeneration: a Study of the Symbolic Meaning of Metalworking in Iron Age Britain. In A. Gwilt and C. Haselgrove (eds), *Reconstructing Iron Age Societies* 9–18. Oxford, Oxbow Monographs 71.

Hingley, R. (2006) The Deposition of Iron Objects in Britain During the Later Prehistoric and Roman Periods: Contextual

Analysis and the Significance of Iron. *Britannia* 37, 213–57.

Huth, C. (2000) Metal Circulation, Communication and Traditions of Craftmanship in Late Bronze Age and Early Iron Age Europe. In C. Pare (ed.), *Metals Make the World Go Round: the supply and Circulation of Metals in Bronze Age Europe*, 176–193. Oxford, Oxbow Books.

Ingold, T. (2000) *The Perception of the Environment: Essays on Livelihood, Dwelling and Skills*. London, Routledge.

Kostoglou, M. (2003) Iron and Steel Currency Bars in Ancient Greece. *Mediterranean Archaeology and Archaeometry* 3, 63–68.

Kristiansen, K. (1998) *Europe Before History*. Cambridge, Cambridge University Press.

Kristiansen, K. and Larsson, T. (2005) *The Rise of Bronze Age Society. Travels, Transmissions and Transformations*. Cambridge, Cambridge University Press.

Latour, B. and Woolgar, S. (1986) *Laboratory Life. The Construction of Scientific Facts*. Princeton, Princeton University Press.

Needham, S. (2007) 800 BC, The Great Divide. In C. Haselgrove and R. Pope (eds), *The Earlier Iron Age in Britain and the Near Continent* 39–63. Oxford, Oxbow Books.

O'Connor, B. (1980) *Cross-Channel Relations in the Later Bronze Age*. Two Parts. Oxford, British Archaeological Reports, International Series 91 (i and ii).

Pare, C. (2000) Bronze and the Bronze Age. In C. Pare (ed.), *Metals Make the World Go Round: the supply and Circulation of Metals in Bronze Age Europe* 1–38. Oxford, Oxbow Books.

Salter, C. and Ehrenreich, M. (1984) Iron Age Iron Metallurgy in Central Southern Britain. In B. Cunliffe and D. Miles (eds), *Aspects of the Iron Age in Central Southern Britain*, 146–161. Oxford, Oxford University Committee for Archaeology.

Sherratt, S. (1994) Commerce, Iron and Ideology: Metallurgical Innovation in 12th–11th Century Cyprus. In V. Karageorghis (ed.), *Cyprus in the 11th Century BC*, 59–106. Nicosia, A. G. Leventis Foundation.

Snodgrass, A. (1971) *The Dark Age of Greece: an Archaeological Survey of the Eleventh to the Eighth Centuries BC*. Edinburgh, Edinburgh University Press.

Snodgrass, A. M. (1980) *Archaic Greece: The Age of Experiment*. London, Dent Press.

Snodgrass, A. M. (1982) Cyprus and the Beginnings of Iron Technology in the Eastern Mediterranean. In J. D. Muhly, R. Maddin and V. Karageorghis (eds), *Early Metallurgy in Cyprus*, 285–296. Nicosia, Pierides Foundation.

Verlaecht, K. (2000) Hoarding and the Circulation of Metalwrok in Late Bronze Age Denmark: Quantification and Beyond. In C. Pare (ed.), *Metals Make the World Go Round: the supply and Circulation of Metals in Bronze Age Europe*, 194–208. Oxford, Oxbow Books.

Viveiros de Castro, E. (1998) Cosmological Deixis and Amerindian Perspectivism. *Journal of the Royal Anthropological Institute* 4, 469–488.

4.

Material concerns and colonial encounters

Peter van Dommelen and Michael Rowlands

Material culture lies at the heart of social interaction, because people exchange 'things' as they interact with each other, peacefully or otherwise. It is therefore certainly no exaggeration to claim that '[c]olonialism exists where material culture moves people … [out of] a desire for material culture' (Gosden 2004, 153). It also implies that material culture is intrinsically important to colonialism and to cultural interaction in the broadest sense of the term. This holds in particular for archaeology, if only because material culture is usually all that remains from the past, and archaeological agendas have accordingly been dominated by 'trade' and 'colonisation'. In the Mediterranean, as elsewhere, archaeologists have long focused on tracing movements of both objects and materials by tracking their 'original' places of extraction and manufacture. Using ever more sophisticated scientific analyses, huge efforts have been made to detect connections between items across regions large and small and to create ever more refined distribution maps of artefact types and classes. The Mediterranean of the Bronze and Iron Ages is perhaps a particularly acute case in point, because it is not only practically defined by numerous instances of long-distance contacts ranging from top-level elite 'diplomatic' exchanges to the establishment of full-scale settlers' colonies (*e.g.* Feldman 2006; Hodos 2006), but it has also seen numerous inventories and distribution maps of key materials (*e.g.* Cline 1994; see Manning and Hulin 2005, 270–274).

In the archaeology of the Bronze and Iron Age Mediterranean, as well as elsewhere, material culture has typically been treated as an unproblematic category that can straightforwardly be used to identify connections between regions and to track people and cultures across space and time. As long as the archaeological basics, in particular find contexts, were taken into consideration, it has long been, and continues to be, widely assumed that the resulting find distributions provide a solid basis for charting people's movements and cultural interactions (Cline 1994; van Wijngaarden 2002). This perspective has contributed much to maintain the one-sided 'Hellenocentric' perspective that has pervaded Classical and Mediterranean archaeology since its inception, as these distribution maps underpin the use of sweeping terms like 'the Mycenaean world' to cover much of the Mediterranean, even if only a few handfuls of sherds are involved in many of these regions (Blake 2008). While the one-sided and colonialist nature of conventional approaches to Iron Age and Archaic-Classical Greek and Phoenician 'colonisation' have increasingly come under fire from so-called postcolonial perspectives and have extensively been discussed in recent years, these critiques have only begun to be extended to the earlier contacts and cultural encounters of the Bronze Age Mediterranean (Knapp 2008, 264–280; Voskos and Knapp 2008).

It is from these two topics and approaches – material culture and postcolonial theory – that we take our lead in this paper to discuss cultural encounters in conceptual terms. It is our aim in particular to explore how material culture articulates these contact situations and how our assumptions about the role(s) played by objects impacts on our perception of cultural encounters.

Postcolonial matters

Postcolonial studies have rapidly emerged as a major influence on the social sciences and humanities in the past two decades or so and they have certainly not passed unnoticed in archaeology (*e.g.* Webster and Cooper 1996; Liebmann

Fig. 4.1: View and plan of the Sardinian Bronze Age site of nuraghe Antigori (Sarroch), where imported Mycenaean pottery is usually interpreted as evidence of interaction between indigenous Sardinians and foreign sailors (cf. Russell 2010, fig. 4).

and Rizvi 2008; Lydon and Rizvi 2010). This is all the more remarkable because of their consistent disregard for material culture in general and of archaeology in particular. The tendency of postcolonial studies to focus on the textual, if not literary, dimension of colonialism has repeatedly been criticised as a one-sided turning away from the colonised realities on the ground, as 'discussions of text and image mask this reality of empire: the numbers who died in the colonial wars and labour gangs, or as a result of disease, starvation and transportation' (Boehmer 1995, 20). This shortcoming was long ago already explicitly diagnosed as 'the exorbitation of discourse and a related incuriosity about the enabling socio-economic and political institutions and other forms of social praxis' (Parry 1987, 43).

More generally referred to as a lack of contextualisation (Turner 1995), these critiques have been found to lack the context of the encompassing economic and political structures. This point has been made most forcibly by Arif Dirlik, who has labelled the disregard of the capitalist background of Europe's colonial enterprises in the Third World as amounting to 'a culturalism … that blurs the power relationships that dynamized it and endowed it with hegemonic pervasiveness' (Dirlik 1994, 307; *cf.* Hall 1996, 243–244). It is in fact this kind of context that is most readily related to common associations of colonialism with occupation, domination and exploitation and to images of colonisers and colonised whose 'first encounter was marked by violence and their existence together – that is to say the exploitation of the native by the settler' (Fanon 1967, 28). While the significance of cultural domination in itself may be beyond doubt, these early criticisms clearly voice a concern about the apparent failure of text-based studies to address the immediate contexts of colonialism and to bridge the gap between discourse analysis and (Marxist-inspired) studies of colonial domination and exploitation.

The relevance of 'local context' was nevertheless already emphasised by Edward Said, following Foucault's insistence that discourse is reproduced through practice and in institutions. Although his own study largely remained a textual analysis, Said did recognise the significance of the 'extra-textual reality' as he called it, which was made up of 'cultural traditions, worldly circumstance and stabilizing influences like schools, libraries and government' and which together 'regularised' Orientalist writing (Said 1978, 201). By considering an unusually wide range of documents related to those institutions such as academic studies and colonial policy papers, he successfully widened his analytical scope beyond literary texts (Said 1978, 201–206). The critical difference of *Orientalism* is that Said emphasised his analysis as one of *Western* representation and not of the colonial Middle East: Orientalism, he noted significantly, 'has less to do with the Orient than it has to do with "our" world' (Said 1978, 12).

Contexts of practice

Because 'context' is also an eminently archaeological concept and one that is particularly associated with postprocessual archaeology (Hodder 1986, 118–146), we see this notion as critically important for an archaeological understanding of cultural, including colonial, encounters, because local contexts represent the actual places where it all happened, where people met and where meanings were forged (Fig. 4.1). Precisely because the local context of a colonial situation is where the contacts were acted out, observed, (mis)understood and reacted upon, 'context' is a useful shorthand for referring to the myriad factors that surrounded and influenced those encounters.

Local contexts, we argue, are important because they 'set the stage' for the daily practices of the inhabitants of the colonial situation concerned in both a metaphorical and a literal way. Metaphorically, 'local context' refers to the specific social and economic situation as experienced by the social actors. It therefore distinguishes between the various gender, age, class and ethnicity-based groups that make up the 'colonised' and the 'colonisers' and recognises those groups who straddle the alleged colonial divide. Even if subconscious, the *habitus* of these groups is part and parcel of these local contexts. It is also the place of interplay between people's actions and the wider structural conditions of a colonial situation, which is the kind of broader historical context advocated for discourse analysis. In a literal sense, the 'stage' of the local context is made up of the material culture present in the colonial situation. This not only forms the backdrop against which people live their lives but it also contributes actively to the recreation of their *habitus* by directing their actions and influencing their perceptions.

A double rationale thus exists for the study of material culture in colonial situations: first of all, because colonial encounters consist of material and 'tactile' relationships between people and their material worlds and secondly, because of the impact of the material surroundings on people's daily life in terms of both actions and perceptions.

That is not to say of course that material culture has never been considered in colonial situations. Material culture has long attracted attention from researchers as diverse as archaeologists, ethnographers and geographers, but their interest has always been very much artefact-oriented and has more than anything else been associated with collecting objects (Thomas 1997; 1991, 125–184). The kinds of objects that were studied and collected – which usually went together – were consequently mainly spectacular artefacts such as statuettes, elaborate clothing and weapons, architecture, and of course, jewellery (Fig. 4.2). Famous examples include the shields and spears from Polynesia, the Minangkabau longhouses from Sumatra and Moroccan jewellery. Even these studies, however, have more often than not been carried out without explicit reference to colonialism, despite the colonial contexts in which they were realised (Gosden 1999, 15–32; Gosden and Knowles 2001).

The significance of material culture for social and cultural life has been strongly and explicitly underscored in recent years by both anthropologists and archaeologists, as is most evident in two recently published handbooks (Tilley *et al.* 2006; Hicks and Beaudry 2010). These material culture studies emphasise in particular the significance of more mundane material culture as opposed to the spectacular objects previously collected. Daniel Miller refers for instance to what he calls the 'humility of objects', which enables material culture to play such a profound role: artefacts are such a common appearance that people take their presence for granted and end up hardly noting their presence at all (Miller 1987, 98–108). From his ethnographic work in Trinidad (1994), he has concluded that items such as furnishings and wallpaper are only noted when something is 'wrong' with them, when they are for instance damaged or of an 'inappropriate' design. The implication is that 'good' furnishings and wallpaper then objectify the culturally preferred choices. In his extensive study of four neighbouring communities of a small town in central Trinidad, Miller indeed found that people used 'the arrays of objects as found in the living-room as the media by which their ideals are formulated and their problems argued through' (Miller 1994, 315).

All kinds of portable and fixed types of material culture that make up people's material life worlds are thus meaningful in people's activities and houses, and specific household items are therefore no less significant than field systems, artisanal workshops, or even industrial activity areas. In theoretical terms, the connection between objects and social structures is based on Bourdieu's concept of *habitus*, because material culture is an important guiding principle of people's 'practical knowledge' which in turn generates their classificatory schemes and perceptions of the surrounding world – in short their *habitus* (Bourdieu 1977, 96–158).

For all these reasons, we argue that material culture is indeed a truly 'critical matter' in colonial situations (Pels 1993, 5), as it marks the different value and belief systems of the various participants in the colonial situation. Through the juxtaposition of various sets and traditions of material culture in one and the same contact situation, material culture is also the medium through which people can communicate with each other, even if they do so only subconsciously. The key to this capability is their co-presence, which 'is not merely a condition for communication, it *is* communication; it also points out the possibility that communication is actually achieved without recourse to discourse' (Pels 1999, 27).

A case-study which makes this point well in a colonial context is Nicholas Thomas's study of the introduction of cloth and Western-style clothing in Polynesia (Thomas 1999). His argument is that the substitution of 'traditional' *tapa* (barkcloth) garments by Western clothes is dependent on the subtly different meanings that were attributed to these

Fig. 4.2: Collection of indigenous material culture (cf. Ratzel 1888, pl. Amerikanische Altertümer).

items by different groups, as is demonstrated by the Samoan *tiputa* which appears to have represented both Christian values of chastity and a Samoan understanding of power. Both pre-existing indigenous and newly imported colonial values and objects were thus at the same time involved in this instance of (material) culture change. It is therefore these unassuming and familiar objects that make up the 'critical matters' of colonial contexts because of the role they play in the everyday interactions between colonising and colonised communities and in the Foucauldian 'microphysics of power' that shape interactions and relationships in colonial situations (Pels 1999, 1–43).

Modes of contact

Our emphasis on the significance of local contexts requires us to consider the wide range of variation covered by terms like 'contact situations', 'cultural entanglement' or 'colonial encounter.' While no one could seriously call into question the sheer variety of what we generically call 'contact situations', attempts to capture them in a limited number of clear-cut categories has proven to be fraught with difficulties. The tripartite scheme proposed by Chris Gosden (2004, 24–40) has many merits, not least because it is based on a much longer chronological scale and because it considers a far greater variety of colonial situations than most historical studies. A typical recent example of the latter is Burbanks and Cooper's (2010) otherwise wide-ranging study of empire that is restricted to just this category of 'imperial polities'. The relevance of Gosden's approach is nevertheless diminished by his reliance on a rough and ready classification of states and societies, within which contacts took place. More specifically, his 'typology of forms' (2004, 26) categorises the wider colonial societies in which contacts occurred rather than the colonial situations as such.

In order to steer clear from problematic categorisations like these and at the same time to maintain our focus on local contexts rather than overarching social formations, we propose to adopt a rather minimalist but also more flexible approach that is squarely centred on the contact situations themselves. Taking our lead from these contexts not only enables us to acknowledge the huge variability of contact situations but also makes it also much easier to draw cross-cultural and diachronic comparisons, as our criteria ensure a basic compatibility between contexts. This is particularly useful given the frequent concerns of archaeologists and historians about what they perceive as anachronistic and thus inappropriate comparisons (*e.g.* Owen 2005, 9–18).

What is relatively clear from all these studies is that the axis of variation extends along what we may term the 'degree of intensity' of interaction (*cf.* Burke 2009, 66–67; Stein 2005). It roughly ranges from situations with occasional and temporary visitors to outright military conquest, economic exploitation and enslavement. Power and inequality may thus be put forward as the first key criteria for classifying contact situations (Burke 2009, 67–70; *cf.* van Dommelen 1997, 306). This distinction corresponds with the definition of colonialism in which the existence or absence of unequal relationships are critical, as we have previously proposed (Rowlands 1998, 30–32; van Dommelen 2002, 122–129).

A second key criterion follows from our earlier discussion of 'contexts of practice' and material culture, where we concluded that physical co-presence and immediate juxtaposition of both people and objects represent truly 'critical matters' of contact situations.

While we would not wish to claim that these criteria are exhaustive, we do submit that they allow us to make critical distinctions between different contact situations. Take, for example, the very different contexts in which 16th–17th century Catholic missionaries in China and Latin America found themselves: in the former case, they had little choice but to adapt to local cultural traditions, to the point that it was said that the missionaries had been converted rather than the other way around, while in the latter situations Catholic forms of Christianity represented the norm, as conversion strategies were backed up by the force of Spanish and Portuguese colonial authorities (Burke 2009, 67–70). Despite the roughly comparable forms of social organisation, missionaries from the same background faced very different contact situations on the ground.

More pertinent still is that the two criteria can also be used quite straightforwardly in relation to archaeological contexts. If we look at the late prehistoric Mediterranean, they may help our understanding of for instance the many sites where Mycenaean pottery has been found in the southern central Mediterranean. Because the quantities of imported pottery found are very low in most cases (Manning and Hulin 2005, 282–286; Blake 2008, 9–12), and because most sites concerned do not substantially differ from local indigenous Bronze Age sites in any way, these contexts rank relatively low on the scale of intensity of contact. In other words, in the absence of other indications, it is improbable that direct co-presence between people from the Aegean and Eastern Mediterranean was a major factor in the interaction at these sites (Blake 2008, 22–24; Russell 2010, 118–122).

Ontologies of contact

> 'The development of an archaeology of European expansion … celebrates the successes of European nations in taking control of large portions of the planet over a short segment of time … Not surprisingly,

> the negative connotations of the Africans' side of the equation have to be attenuated with metaphors. Some prefer terms like "cultural encounter", "cultural entanglement", or "embracing of modernity". Others focus on "resistance" or "governance innovation", *etc.*'
>
> (Schmidt 2009, 3)

A term increasingly used in discussions of contact situations is 'appropriation', because it focuses attention on the act of possessing the 'other' as something positive rather than a 'negative connotation attenuated with metaphors' (Schmidt 2009, 3; *cf.* Stockhammer 2012). The suggestion is that the active connotations of the term that imply people's agency overcome the criticism that contact has usually been regarded as a one-sided relationship. Following Latour (1993), it has been argued that the symmetrical relation between 'us' and 'them', or between colonised and coloniser, can be seen as a consequence of the analogous separation of Nature and Culture or, for that matter, of person and thing. Highlighting translation as an essential act of mediation between purified categories, Latour has drawn attention to the 'fuzzy' nature of social life in order to refer to the presence of hybrids as mediations of a strict divide between humans and non-humans (Latour 1993). The implication is that European colonisers in the 19th century would have operated with such a naturalising logic but it is nevertheless quite improbable that the 'natives' they came in contact with would at the same time have constituted themselves in a likewise reactive mode.

Appropriation, as a concept, therefore has to be considered in terms of a wider debate that contrasts its use to the binary oppositions of nature:culture, person:thing, human:non-human or coloniser:colonised. There is no reason to assume that appropriation should necessarily imply the 'foreign' as universal in the exclusive sense of the absolutely unlike. We may instead think of more complex issues of shared attributes and their re-appropriation or recognition based on long-term 'fuzzy' relations that are by no means best understood in terms of discrete encounters of the coloniser *versus* colonised kind (*cf.* Stoler 1989; Rowlands 1998; van Dommelen 2002). Notions of the body and materials are the most prominent examples of how the familiar (Western) concepts of the unity of nature and plurality of cultures may be faced with alternative perspectives that pose the existence of cosmologies based on 'spiritual unity and corporeal diversity' (*cf.* Viveiros de Castro 1998, 470). Viveiros de Castro argues that his case of 'Amazonian Amerindian thought' is based on a representational unity that allows one to think that a unified spirit substance may be objectified in different corporeal forms (human, jaguar, *etc.*) depending on context and perspective. Crucially such points of view are not projected onto objects, but it is the things and objects themselves that are points of view. Hybridity may therefore not be understood as the mixing of unlike things but as an example how a common sense of spirit substance may be objectified in different locally specific embodiments and object forms, depending on perceptions of their differing efficacies. The display of ontological entanglements or cross specific ambiguities are what we might expect in shamanistic and totemic worlds where cosmological origins figure prominently as the mythological basis for an original undifferentiated existence. But these are also features of origin myths of wider cosmological form that explain the existence of discrete beings as images that materialise/make visible in particular localities and circumstances what they must hold in common for existence to be possible. Appropriation is therefore the active process of creating images that will capture the efficacy of something perceived to be shared by creating a zone of indistinction, of indiscernability or ambiguity in which synthesis can be explored.

Research in material culture studies has demonstrated that novel things can be assimilated to create new 'fuzzy' categories (Thomas 1991). In the Samoan case-study already cited above (Thomas 1999), Nicholas Thomas has shown how things can be re-contextualised within existing indigenous categories. In the case of the Pacific, he argues, clothes introduced by Europeans in the 19th century acted as a technology of conversion to Christianity but how this worked for the Polynesians involved was clearly quite different from what the missionaries thought was going on (Thomas 1999, 18). To understand appropriation from the Polynesian perspective requires a focus on the materiality of the objects involved rather than immediately assuming that there must be a more general contextual argument to explain the objects. In Polynesia, barkcloth (*tapa*) was widely produced and used to cover the skin in ways analogous to tattoos and other ways of body decoration. Barkcloth in particular marked the dangerous sacredness of a person and it served to represent ancestral deities and to protect the body at moments of peculiar ritual intensity. Given this background, conversion to Christianity alone cannot sufficiently answer the question asked by European observers to native Tahitians and Samoans concerning what the cloth and guns they wanted meant to them or how they found them effective.

In other words, we need to go beyond defining these items simply as 'local appropriations of a pervasive European derived form' (Thomas 1999, 16). Considering this process as an instance of localisation of a global form assumes a motivation of emulation or copying that sees the power of the European as an absolute. Thomas's study makes it very clear that the Tahitians and Samoans remade themselves in a process that went further than simply copying or emulating European missionaries. That still leaves open the question of what conversion meant to Pacific islanders, but we can safely surmise that there was some connection with the power of wearing *tapa* (barkcloth) and the protective binding of wearing cloth in rituals. At the same time, however, wearing European clothes did instil new ideas of modesty and respectability, and certainly in the case of Samoa this meant that a pre-existing form of bodily display was transformed in a novel way. Perhaps the most important point to note is that Samoan bodies were not necessarily seen as discrete physical entities but that cloth, skin and the interior of the body and body substances rather constituted extensions of each other. With their belief that the coming of clothing would introduce a new moral economy to the Pacific, missionaries were obviously right that clothing was of critical importance but they failed to recognise why it was so important for islanders, who attributed life-giving qualities to fabric, which they viewed as vehicles of spiritual power (Küchler and Were 2005, 84).

Appropriating the foreign

It is of course a simple argument that misattributions like that shown in the case of the Samoan *tiputa* are just due to failures of communication and understanding. The more interesting and pertinent point is its cosmopolitanism. Pacific islanders actively sought after the life-giving powers of European cloth and Europeans responded accordingly. The whiteness of the cloth, the fact that it folded in ways that fibres and bark-cloth could not, and the use of recycled clothing that could be picked apart to make the threads for embroidery and needlework patterns, all played a profound if, from the European point of view, unintended role. In Tonga, for example, techniques of mat-weaving continued after missionaries introduced sumptuary laws that prohibited the making of painted barkcloth, because what they regarded as a positive 'work of patience' was for Tongans a means to define status and health of the body (Küchler and Were 2005, 90).

We can replicate many such examples of what is now increasingly termed 'appropriation' in material forms that emphasise how the materiality of things and the making of things allow transformed identities including both coloniser and colonised. The impact of West African sculpture on European art is reciprocated by the role of the photographic image in mediating the relationship between coloniser and colonised in Africa (Landau and Kaspin 2002). Christraud Geary (1988) has shown how Njoya, king of Bamum in Cameroon during the German colonial period, very quickly saw the advantages of photography and displayed himself in staged poses and dressed in selected clothing of different types. With some he emphasised his Muslim Adamawa connections and with others he played up his European alliances. Such negotiations between Africans and Europeans over what constituted an appropriate photographic image gave each what they wanted to see: Europeans gained illusions of mastery and control through a process of separation involving human/non-human quasi distinctions and Africans obtained images of the appropriation of European power through a perception of increasing shared spiritual substances, but both were tendentiously related to the realities of politics and labour in which their relationships were forged.

By shifting from object to image and back we can recognise another feature of appropriation. Clothing in the Pacific draws our attention to materials such as leaves, fibres, fruits, and bark of trees, as well as to the flexibility of European cloth and the capacity for being recycled into threads and fibres. In the Pacific, these materials were already embedded in contexts of magical efficacy and ideas of reproductive success, which were in turn embedded in ideas of the body. As a result, notions of what is human and non-human overlapped with perceptions of embodied shared substances and ideas of pattern based on techniques of binding, knotting, plaiting, stamping, and rubbing (Küchler and Were 2005, 7). Appropriation is therefore more complex in the Pacific than ideas of status-copying and emulation might lead a Eurocentric view of mimicry to imagine. The focus on the latter explains why carved wooden objects, incised shell ornaments and weapons figure prominently in collections of Pacific 'art' in European museums, while the more fragile forms of mats and barkcloth are relatively underrepresented. Yet the relation between materials and innovative designs in the Pacific has been richly documented, and we now know much more about the flow of designs from fibre products back to Europe in the 18th and 19th century; we now also have a better understanding of their reciprocal return as dyed patterns on cotton cloth.

An additional factor in this regard is the influence of designs on 19th century evolutionism, as ideas developed that geometric patterns were less complex than, and thus inferior to, the ornamental elaboration of European styles, even though it was Pacific patterns that were introduced into European ornamentation at this time. Large quantities of basketry, fans, feather artefacts and mats were brought to Europe but were never mentioned in academic literature or museum catalogues of the period, which means we only have indirect means of understanding their impact. Contrast this with the impact of photography and how images of men posing with ritual objects, often with attendant Europeans, created many of the stereotypes of the Pacific islander that are still with us today.

What a focus on materials and patterns also demonstrates is a very archaeological theme of typology. Patterns are mobile and move from mats and cloth to architecture and decorating the human body. They traverse cultural boundaries and translate from artefact to performance and back to artefact again (Küchler and Were 2005, 197), and end up occupying different positions in terms of repetition and assertions of continuity in conditions of change. In West Africa, for example, a study of a single divinity called *mami wata* ('mother of water') demonstrates how a German poster of an exotic snake charmer in India is incorporated into coastal and riverine cults, the shrine rooms of which are devoted to the reception of exotic alien things. Substantial evidence suggests that the image of *mami wata* can be traced to early encounters between Africans and Europeans in the 15th century and that the cult spread along the west-central African coast with the slave trade. The foreignness of *mami wata* is shown in her stress on her own 'otherness', which gives access to wealth outside social norms and constraints and which usually involves dreams or visions of journeys to her fabulous underwater realm (Drewal 2002). The argument that the image is originally derived from figures, presumably mermaids, on the prows of European ships is quite credible, as is the better known transformation of her imagery with the diffusion of the snake charmer lithograph at the beginning of the 20th century. But 'fuzziness' dictates that none of these origins are emphasised and instead 'Europeans' become part of a watery invisible world of 'whiteness', ghosts, ancestors and sources of unexplainable wealth. Appropriating the 'foreign' by West Africans (*e.g.* Lipps 1966) is therefore not their attempt to emulate or to become 'European' but rather to grasp the cosmological truths shared, as they see them, both by Africans and Europeans. This contrasts markedly with the general European lack of curiosity to understand the 'other' and their preference to simply identify with the potency of the 'foreignness' of objects. This West African case-study offers yet another example, as it implies that, unlike as in the Pacific, West African shrines are about locating and fixing the potency of materials and things and about inhibiting or limiting their flow and access to their potency.

We cannot investigate these changing modes of 'contact' and appropriation without moving to a more substantial understanding of notions of body/personhood and identity in these different historical and social circumstances (*cf.* Knapp and van Dommelen 2008). In his discussion of the appearance of the culture concept in Europe from the 17th century, Descola contrasts naturalism with animism. In the former, it is the acceptance of the separation of mind from body that makes humans separate themselves from non-humans (Descola 2010). European appropriation of the 'other' in this period of expansion was therefore not only rooted in the primacy of conversion as the way to make the him or her human, but it also recognised that this was always an incomplete act. Moreover, culture was a way of talking about the collective spirit or consciousness of group so that they could distinguish themselves from each other by shared language and material practices. Appropriating the 'foreign' as alien, as far as European contact is concerned, was and still is a matter of conversion and of absorbing the non-human into the humanised world. But this exclusionist ontology did not match African perceptions of Europeans. Throughout west-central Africa, a person at death moves from human to ancestor and from the latter state to a fusion with the spirit world, from where (s)he returns to the living in a composite human/spirit form. In the Pacific, by contrast, a strict dichotomy exists between, on the one hand, the human-ancestor-deity continuum in the wider Pacific and, on the other hand, the human-ancestor fusions in Melanesia. In other words, neither do they see the human body as affixed in form, nor do they set it apart from all others, but instead conceive of it more as composite or capable of transforming into analogous images.

It is thus the European image of the 'foreign' that is 'other' in the more naturalising sense of the 'primitive'. In the European perception, the foreign is to be rejected as a totality, but aspects of it may be appropriated through acts of conversion and translation. In fact, this is a much earlier feature found in early Christianity, so 'naturalism' has much deeper roots than its later reformulation in European modernism. Africans or Pacific islanders differ both from each other and from Europeans in their capacity to absorb the latter into their object and image worlds. Once we accept these ontological differences, we are released from the idea of a universal human disposition to mimic or to share that is graded only by relations of dominance and dependence. It is only when we accept these differences, that we can consider more complex notions of hybridity.

Material contacts and hybrid practices

Hybridity is a concept that has come to dominate postcolonial theories, presumably because of its constructivist conception of identity and meaning and its potential to contribute to alternative histories of colonial and other contact situations (Young 1995; Papastergiadis 2000, 168–195; Burke 2009, 1–12). It has also made its way into archaeological debates, in particular in the Mediterranean, where it is increasingly prominent in discussions of cultural contacts and exchanges (van Dommelen 1997; 2002; Feldman 2006, 30–61; Knapp 2008, 57–62; Voskos and Knapp 2008; Vives-Ferrándiz Sánchez 2008; Stiglitz 2010; Jiménez 2011).

Theoretically, it is underpinned by the notion of ambivalence as theorised by Bhabha (1984), who situates it between the divergent ambitions to 'civilise the natives' and to keep them distinct from the European colonisers (Comaroff and Comaroff 1991; Pels 1997, 171–172). As argued by Bhabha (1992), ambiguity goes hand in hand with stereotypes, because reality is always 'messier' than expected and inevitably falls short of binary classifications. This point is underscored by the fact that the widespread stereotype of 'the lazy native' has not discouraged early modern European colonisers from employing or enslaving large numbers of indigenous people as a workforce. While the particular content of stereotypes is surely historically specific and may thus vary widely across colonial contexts, ambivalence and stereotypes as such can be regarded as common and recurrent characteristics of colonial encounters (van Dommelen 2002, 126–129; 2006, 136–138).

Cultural hybridity is closely related to ambivalence and ambiguity, because it is about in-betweenness, about being both coloniser and colonised and yet being neither in full. It roots in the ambivalent spaces of colonial situations that Bhabha refers to as the 'third space' and where, in his words, hybridity 'displaces the histories that constitute it, and sets up new structures of authority' (1990, 211). Cultural hybridity is thus rooted in local contexts and has to be examined in local terms in relation to the groups and communities that make up the colonial situation concerned. The implication is that processual terms like 'hybridisation' or 'creolisation' are less than helpful, because they imply or presuppose all-embracing processes, in which cultural elements are somehow 'mixed' into new combinations. Such a perspective not only draws on a well-outdated conception of culture but also ignores the local context and the involvement of local people on the ground (van Dommelen 2006, 139–140; Jiménez 2011).

This emphasis on the local context of colonial situations takes us back to our earlier discussion of 'contexts of practice' and suggests a way forward through the related notion of 'hybrid practices'. With this term we refer to everyday activities undertaken by people in a colonial situation, where a sustained co-presence of different groups and communities enabled interaction in the broadest sense of the term and of sufficient intensity to encourage, or indeed force, some people to share and to recombine some of their practices. In our view, hybridity is not a catch-all, new notion of postcolonial theory to avoid colonialist biases but rather a specific concept to describe a peculiar type of colonial context. As we have argued above, material culture is part and parcel of both the context and the interaction as it is the 'critical matter' of colonial contexts, and to separate it from practices would not only be artificial but also, and more importantly, entirely beside the point. Together, we contend, hybrid practices and material culture enable us to gauge the intensity of contact and to begin to grasp how colonial situations developed on the ground.

Subtle as it may seem, the archaeological relevance of this distinction is notable, as it allows us to move away from, and indeed beyond, the increasingly frequent references to 'hybrid objects' in archaeological discussions that focus exclusively on the formal characteristics of objects (*e.g.* Antonaccio 2003). A 'practical perspective', as we advocate here, that takes material culture seriously, redirects attention to the activities that involved material culture, and does not distinguish between practices and objects.

Returning to the alleged Mycenaean, or more generically Aegean, presence in the Late Bronze Age Mediterranean, the locally produced 'Aegean-style' pottery in South Italy is a much-debated case in point that is usually considered as a hybrid product of colonial intervention (van Wijngaarden 2008, 135; *cf.* Russell 2010, 113–118). An even more explicit instance can be found in discussions of Mycenaean influence in Cyprus, in which there is consistent reference to 'stylistic hybrids' and 'hybrid products' (Knapp 2008, 264–265, with references). The pottery and other objects concerned are time and again described as 'mixing,' or a 'fusion of,' elements from two distinct cultures, namely the indigenous Cypriot one and that of the Aegean foreigners.

A typical example, albeit from a later date, is the discussion of a so-called 'Corinthianising krater' of late 7th century date from the indigenous Iron Age settlement of Morgantina in central Sicily that is defined as a 'hybrid object … that must be local', as it is 'certainly not a colonial product'. The object is labelled as hybrid, because it 'combines elements from the indigenous and colonial repertoires to create something that … partakes of two different cultures' (Antonaccio 2005, 104–105). In both Iron Age Sicily and Bronze Age Cyprus, the mixed or hybrid appearance of individual objects is taken directly to reflect a local culture that was equally mixed and hybrid.

The problem with descriptions like these is not only that they reify the objects – note how the krater is said to 'combine elements' and to 'partake of different cultures' – and ignore the people who used them, but also that they provide little or no information about the contexts, in which the objects concerned were found. As a consequence, we are left to guess after the activities they played a role in and the people who used them. It is difficult to find out, for instance, whether the Corinthianising krater was used as a substitute for local vessels in practices that otherwise remained unchanged or whether the innovative shape was part of a wider transformation. It is highly significant, however, that an analysis of 'real' imported Greek pottery in Sicilian Iron Age settlements (8th–7th centuries BCE) found that those imports represented a very specific selection of available Greek pottery, produced in either Greece or Greek colonial settlements in Sicily, as it matched existing indigenous pottery types very closely (Hodos 2000; 2006, 129–142). The implication of that analysis is that local indigenous practices, in particular those associated with drinking and feasting, did not change structurally despite contacts with and imports from nearby Greek colonial settlements (Hodos 2006, 154–155, 202). It is worth noting that large vessels for mixing wine like the Corinthianising krater, which had no indigenous equivalent in Iron Age Sicily, are represented by only very few specimens in indigenous contexts before the 6th century BCE, which suggests that mixing wine with other substances was not an element of Sicilian drinking and feasting practices (Hodos 2010, 85–88). That does not preclude that Sicilians diluted their wine, but it suggests that doing so was not an occasion for display as in Greece. If drinking and feasting practices underwent relatively few changes during the 8th and 7th centuries BCE, the imported drinking and pouring vessels cannot be used to argue that these Sicilian communities 'were hybridised.' The evidence suggests rather that the level of interaction between the indigenous Sicilian settlements inland and the Greek colonial foundations on the coast was not remarkably intensive.

In contrast, a very different situation has been described for the Spanish 18th–19th century missionary settlements in Alta California, where indigenous converts of diverse descent lived together in strict accordance with the rules of the Franciscan order and under close supervision of the Spanish (Mexican) priests. They had adopted a fully Spanish way of life and only had access to colonial material culture. Archaeological evidence has nevertheless demonstrated that many of the meals prepared and eaten in the neophyte compounds were more in accordance with indigenous taste and traditions than with Spanish colonial cuisine, even if they were prepared using the available Spanish material culture (Lightfoot 2005, 49–113). Another case takes us to the Mediterranean of the Classical period (4th–3rd centuries BCE), where the cult of the originally Greek goddess Demeter was transported from Greek Sicily to the Punic world of the western Mediterranean. On the islands of Sardinia and Ibiza, the cult was locally transformed in accordance with existing local fertility rituals, and imported or locally manufactured objects of new types suggest that new practices were created that added to and in part replaced existing ritual traditions (van Dommelen 2006, 140–144; van Dommelen and López Bertran forthcoming).

In the latter two instances, practices underwent a range of changes or were wholly and newly invented by local people drawing on locally available materials and activities, some or most of which had been brought to the area from elsewhere. The common element in these contexts is the sustained co-presence of the people involved, Spanish-Mexican missionaries and indigenous neophytes in the Californian case and Punic settlers from Sicily and North Africa and indigenous inhabitants on the Mediterranean islands of Sardinia and Ibiza.

Conclusions: colonialism in practice

To conclude, in this paper our arguments have focused on the materiality of cultural contacts in general and colonial encounters in particular. In our discussion, we have concentrated on two aspects, the first one of which is the intimate entanglement of people's practices and the associated material culture, for which we offered a double rationale. To us, this means that an exclusive focus on the latter, *i.e.* on objects as such, is superficial and overlooks the underlying social and cultural richness of material culture. Because we see people's activities and the material culture involved as intimately entangled aspects, we call for what we may term a 'practical' and 'material' approach to contact and colonial situations.

The other aspect is the conceptual background of 'colonial encounters' in the widest sense of the term. To us, this concerns firstly how we perceive what it means to adopt or to imitate objects. Because imitation and emulation are not neutral concepts, we have surveyed a range of contact and colonial situations across space and time to argue for a complex and nuanced as well as contextualised understanding of the ways in which people adopt, adapt, or reject specific objects. Equally significant is a better appreciation of the often subtle differences of the range of variations from contact to colonial situations: we have drawn attention in particular to the significance of sustained co-presence, which generally comes with the foundation of colonial settlements and arrival of settlers.

Acknowledgements

This joint paper draws on numerous discussions about material culture, Mediterranean archaeology and West African ethnography over many years but it has particularly benefitted from meetings held in the context of the 'Material Connections' project that we co-directed with Bernard Knapp in 2008–09 with support of the AHRC (AH/G00109X/1) and that resulted in the edited volume *Material Connections in the Ancient Mediterranean* (edited by P. van Dommelen and A. B. Knapp; London, Routledge 2010).

References

Antonaccio, C. (2003) Hybridity and the Cultures within Greek Culture. In C. Dougherty and L. Kurke (eds), *The Cultures within Ancient Greek Culture. Contact, Conflict, Collaboration*, 57–74. Cambridge, Cambridge University Press.

Antonaccio, C. (2005) Excavating Colonization. In Hurst and Owen 2005, 97–113.

Bhabha, H. K. (1984) Of Mimicry and Men: The Ambivalence of Colonial Discourse. In H. Bhabha (ed.), *The Location of Culture*, 85–92. London, Routledge.

Bhabha, H. K. (1990) The Third Space. Interview with Homi Bhabha. In J. Rutherford (ed.), *Identity: Community, Culture and Difference*, 207–221. London, Lawrence and Wishart.

Bhabha, H. K. (1992) The Other Question. Stereotype, Discrimination and the Discourse of Colonialism. In H. Bhabha (ed.), *The Location of Culture*, 66–84. London, Routledge.

Blake, E. (2008) The Mycenaeans in Italy: A Minimalist Position. *Papers of the British School at Rome* 76, 1–34.

Boehmer, E. (1995) *Colonial and Postcolonial Literature*. Oxford, Oxford University Press.

Bourdieu, P. (1977) *Outline of a Theory of Practice*. Cambridge, Cambridge University Press.

Burbank, J. and Cooper, F. (2010) *Empires in World History, Power and the Politics of Difference*. Princeton, Princeton University Press.

Burke, P. (2009) *Cultural Hybridity*. Cambridge, Polity Press.

Cline, E. H. (1994) *Sailing the Wine-Dark Sea. International Trade and the Late Bronze Age Aegean.* British Archaeological Reports, International Series 591. Oxford, British Archaeological Reports.

Comaroff, J. and Comaroff, J. (1991) *Of Revelation and Revolution 1: Christianity, Colonialism and Consciousness in South Africa*. Chicago/London, University of Chicago Press.

Descola, P. (2010) *La Fabrique des Images.* Paris, Musee de Qui Branley.

Dirlik, A. (1994) The Postcolonial Aura: Third World Criticism in the Age of Global Capitalism. In P. Mongia (ed.), *Contemporary Postcolonial Theory. A Reader*, 294–320. London, Arnold.

Drewal, H. J. (2002) Mami Wata and Santa Marta: Imag(in)ing Self and Others in Africa. In Landau and Kaspin 2002, 193–212.

Fanon, F. (1967) *The Wretched of the Earth*. Harmondsworth, Penguin books.

Feldman, M. (2006) *Diplomacy by Design: Luxury Arts and an 'International Style' in the Ancient Near East, 1400–1200 BCE*. Chicago, University of Chicago Press.

Geary, C. (1988) *Images from Bamum: German Colonial Photography at the Court of King Njoya.* Washington, Smithsonian Institue.

Gosden, C. (1999) *Anthropology and Archaeology. A Changing Relationship*. London/New York, Routledge.

Gosden, C. (2004) *Archaeology and Colonialism. Cultural Contact from 5000 BC to the Present*. Cambridge, Cambridge University Press.

Gosden, C. and Knowles, C. (2001) *Collecting Colonialism: Material Culture and Colonial Change*. Oxford, Berg.

Hall, C. (1996) Histories, Empires and the Post-colonial Moment. In I. Chambers and L. Curti (eds), *The Post-Colonial Question. Common Sies, Divided Horizons*, 65–77. London/New York, Routledge.

Hicks, D. and Beaudry, M. (2010) *The Oxford Handbook of Material Culture Studies.* Oxford, Oxford University Press.

Hodder, I. (1986) *Reading the Past. Current Approaches to Interpretation in Archaeology*. Cambridge, Cambridge University Press.

Hodos, T. (2000) Wine Wares in Protohistoric Eastern Sicily. In C. Smith and J. Serrati (eds), *Sicily from Aeneas to Augustus. New approaches in archaeology and history*, 41–54. Edinburgh, Edinburgh University Press.

Hodos, T. (2006) *Local Responses to Colonisation in the Iron Age Mediterranean*. London, Routledge.

Hodos, T. (2010) Globalization and Colonization: A View from Iron Age Sicily. *Journal of Mediterranean Archaeology* 23/1, 81–106.

Hurst, H. and Owen, S. (2005) *Ancient Colonisations: Analogy, Similarity and Difference.* London, Duckworth.

Jiménez, A. (2011) Pure Hybridism. Late Iron Age Sculpture in Southern Iberia. *World Archaeology* 43/1, 102–123.

Knapp, A. B. (2008) *Prehistoric and Protohistoric Cyprus. Identity, Insularity, and Connectivity*. Oxford, Oxford University Press.

Knapp, A. B. and van Dommelen, P. (2008) Past Practices: Rethinking Individuals and Agents in Archaeology. *Cambridge Archaeological Journal* 18/1, 15–34.

Küchler, S. and Were, G. (2005) *Pacific Pattern.* London, Thames and Hudson.

Landau, P. S. and Kaspin, D. (2002) *Images and Empires Visuality in Colonial and Postcolonial Africa.* Los Angeles, University of California Press.

Latour, B. (1993) *We Have Never Been Modern.* Cambridge, Harvard University Press.

Liebmann, M. and Rizvi, U. (2008) *Archaeology and the Postcolonial Critique* (Archaeology in Society). Lanham, AltaMira Press.

Lightfoot, K. (2005) *Indians, Missionaries, and Merchants: the Legacy of Colonial Encounters on the California Frontiers*. Berkeley, University of California Press.

Lipps, J. (1966) *The Savage Hits Back.* New York, University Books.

Lydon, J. and Rizvi, U. (2010) *Handbook of Postcolonial Archaeology* (World Archaeological Congress Research. Handbooks in Archaeology). Walnut Creek, Left Coast Press.

Manning, S. and Hulin, L. (2005) Maritime Commerce and Geographies of Mobility in the Late Bronze Age of the East Mediterranean: Problematizations. In E. Blake and A. B. Knapp (eds), *The Archaeology of Mediterranean Prehistory*. Blackwell Studies in Global Archaeology 6, 270–302. Malden, MA/Oxford, Blackwell.

Miller, D. (1987) *Material Culture and Mass Consumption*. Oxford, Blackwell.

Miller, D. (1994) *Modernity. An Ethnographic Approach. Dualism and Mass Consumption in Trinidad*. Oxford/Providence, Berg.

Owen, S. (2005) Analogy, Archaeology and Archaic Colonization. In Hurst and Owen 2005, 5–22.

Papastergiadis, N. (2000) *The Turbulence of Migration. Globalization, Deterritorialization and Hybridity*. Cambridge, Polity Press.

Parry, B. (1987) Problems in Current Theories of Colonial Discourse. *Oxford Literary Review* 9/1–2, 27–58.

Pels, P. (1993) *Critical Matters. Interactions between Missionaries and Waluguru in Colonial Tanganyika, 1930–1961*. Amsterdam, Amsterdam School of Social Research.

Pels, P. (1997) The Anthropology of Colonialism: Culture, History, and the Emergence of Western Governmentality. *Annual Review of Anthropology* 26, 163–183.

Pels, P. (1999) *A Politics of Presence: Contacts between Missionaries and Waluguru in Late Colonial Tanganyika.* History and Anthropology 22. Amsterdam, Harwood Academic publishers.

Rowlands, M. (1998) The Archaeology of Colonialism. In K. Kristiansen and M. Rowlands (eds), *Social Transformations in Archaeology. Global and Local Perspectives.* Material Cultures. Interdisciplinary Studies in the Material Construction of Social Worlds, 327–333. London, Routledge.

Russell, A. (2010) Foreign Materials, Island Mobility and Elite Identity in Late Bronze Age Sardinia. In P. van Dommelen and A. B. Knapp (eds), *Material Connections in the Ancient Mediterranean: Mobility, Materiality and Mediterranean Identities*, 106–126. London, Routledge.

Said, E. (1978) *Orientalism*. New York, Vintage books.

Schmidt, P. R. (2009) What is Postcolonial about Archaeologies in Africa? In P. R. Schmidt (ed.), *Postcolonial Archaeologies in Africa*. School of American Research Advanced Seminars, 1–20. Santa Fe: School of American Research.

Stiglitz, A. (2010) Un'isola meticcia: le molte identità della Sardegna antica. Geografia di una frontiera, *Bollettino di Archeologia Online* 0. 'La Sardegna dai Fenici ai Romani: incontri e relazioni tra culture', ed. C. Tronchetti: http://151.12.58.75/archeologia/index.php?option=com_content&view=article&id=13&Itemid=13.

Stockhammer, P. (2012) Conceptualizing Cultural Hybridization in Archaeology. In P. Stockhammer (ed.), *Conceptualizing Cultural Hybridization: A Transdisciplinary Approach. Papers of the Conference in Heidelberg, 21–22 September 2009*. Transcultural Research. Heidelberg Studies on Asia and Europe in a Global Context, 43–58. Berlin and Heidelberg, Springer.

Stoler, A. (1989) Rethinking Colonial Categories European Communities and the Boundaries of Rule. *Comparative Studies in Society and History* 31, 134–161.

Thomas, N. (1991) *Entangled Objects: Exchange, Colonialism and Material Culture in the Pacific*. Cambridge, Mass., Harvard University Press.

Thomas, N. (1997) *In Oceania. Vision, Artifacts, Histories*. Durham, Duke University Press.

Thomas, N. (1999) The Case of the Misplaced Ponchos. Speculations Concerning the History of Cloth in Polynesia. *Journal of Material Culture* 4/1, 5–20.

Tilley, C., Keane, W., Küchler, S., Rowlands, M. and Spyer, P. (2006) *Handbook of Material Culture*. London, Sage.

Turner, L. (1995) Consuming Colonialism. *Critique of Anthropology* 15, 203–212.

van Dommelen, P. (1997) Colonial Constructs: Colonialism and Archaeology in the Mediterranean. *World Archaeology* 28/3, 305–323.

van Dommelen, P. (2002) Ambiguous Matters: Colonialism and Local Identities in Punic Sardinia. In C. Lyons and J. Papadopoulos (eds), *The Archaeology of Colonialism* (Issues & Debates), 121–147. Los Angeles, Getty Research Institute.

van Dommelen, P. (2006) The Orientalizing Phenomenon: Hybridity and Material Culture in the Western Mediterranean. In C. Riva and N. Vella (eds), *Debating Orientalization. Multidisciplinary Approaches to Processes of Change in the Ancient Mediterranean* Monographs in Mediterranean Archaeology 10, 135–152. London, Equinox.

van Dommelen, P. and López Bertran, M. (forthcoming) Hellenism as Subaltern Culture: Rural Cults in the Punic World. In J. Prag and J. Quinn (eds), *The Hellenistic West*. Cambridge, Cambridge University Press.

van Wijngaarden, G. J. (2002) *Use and Appreciation of Mycenaean Pottery in the Levant, Cyprus and Italy (1600–1200 BC). The Significance of Context,* Amsterdam Archaeological Studies 8. Amsterdam, University of Amsterdam Press.

van Wijngaarden, G. J. (2008) The Relevance of Authenticity. Mycenaean-type Pottery in the Mediterranean. In P. Biehl and Y. Rassamakin (eds), *Import and Imitation in Archaeology*. Schriften des Zentrums für Archäologie und Kulturgeschichte des Schwarzmeerraumes 11, 125–146. Langweissbach, Beier & Beran.

Viveiros de Castro, E. (1998) Cosmological Deixis and Amerindian Perspectivism. *Journal of the Royal Anthropological Institute* 4/3, 469–488.

Vives-Ferrándiz Sánchez, J. (2008) Negotiating Colonial Encounters: Hybrid Practices and Consumption in Eastern Iberia (8th–6th centuries BC). *Journal of Mediterranean Archaeology* 21/2, 241–272.

Voskos, Y. and Knapp, A. B. (2008) Cyprus at the End of the Late Bronze Age: Crisis and Colonization or Continuity and Hybridization. *American Journal of Archaeology* 112, 659–684.

Webster, J. and Cooper N. (1996) *Roman Imperialism: Post-Colonial Perspectives,* Leicester Archaeology Monographs 3. Leicester, Leicester University Press.

Young, R. (1995) *Colonial Desire. Hybridity in Theory, Culture and Race*. London and New York, Routledge.

5.

Matter of fact: transcultural contacts in the Late Bronze Age Eastern Mediterranean

A. Bernard Knapp

In a recent study, Voskos and Knapp (2008) reconsidered traditional interpretations of cultural contacts between Cyprus and the Aegean world between about 1200–1000 BCE. Examining a wide range of material evidence, we questioned the long-standing colonisation model and argued that the material culture and new mortuary traditions of 12th–11th century BCE Cyprus reflect an amalgamation of Cypriot, Aegean and Levantine materialities. These transcultural encounters involved hybridisation practices associated with the formation of a new élite identity. In this study, I investigate in further detail the contexts of several of these items, the fluidity of meaning that may have been assigned to them, and the ways they were appropriated and used on Cyprus. It is argued that the entanglements reflected in the material connections between Cyprus, the Aegean and the Levant formed a basic, constituting feature of new social identities emerging on Cyprus at this time. Finally, I consider how materiality and connectivity, rather than conquering Mycenaeans, impacted on new political regimes that formed during the Early Iron Age.

Introduction

Voskos and Knapp (2008) recently reconsidered traditional interpretations of cultural contacts between Cyprus and the Aegean world between about 1200–1000 BCE. Examining a wide range of material evidence – pottery, metalwork, ivory, architecture and coroplastic art – we suggested that during the late 13th–11th centuries BCE, some people with an Aegean cultural background were involved in transcultural encounters with the indigenous people of Cyprus. Over an extended period of time, those Aegean people who came to Cyprus underwent intensive social transformations. In developing these arguments, we questioned long-standing views about the end of the Bronze Age in the eastern Mediterranean and argued that the so-called 'Mycenaean colonisation' of Cyprus was neither Mycenaean, nor a colonisation. Instead, we suggested that the material culture and new mortuary traditions of this era reflect an amalgamation of Cypriot, Aegean and Levantine materialities.

In this paper, I investigate in more detail the find contexts of several objects treated in the earlier study, the fluidity of meaning that may have been assigned to them and the ways that they were appropriated and used on Cyprus. I argue that the transcultural entanglements reflected in the material connections between Cyprus, the Aegean and the Levant formed a basic, constituting feature of new social identities emerging on Cyprus at this time. Finally, I discuss briefly how materiality and connectivity – not conquering Mycenaeans – impacted on new political regimes that formed during the Early Iron Age.

Hybridisation practices, connectivity and materiality

Peoples and cultures are perennially engaged in conversation with other cultures and peoples, and all cultural products – material and social – form parts of such a conversation. If you accept this statement of the obvious, the concept of hybridisation may seem to offer little that will help archaeologists engage more meaningfully with the transformative capacities of intercultural encounters, or to show how we might link the realms of the material and immaterial. The outcome of hybridisation practices, however, is often imprinted in a wide range of material culture (van Dommelen 2005, 118), and so archaeology has important insights to offer here.

Some archaeologists have argued recently that 'hybridity' as a concept has little analytical force (*e.g.* Jung 2009, 82; Stockhammer, in press). If, however, we understand hybridisation as the process underlying cultural mixtures that result from the practice of mixed origins (Friedman 1997, 88; van Dommelen 2006a, 119), then it provides a conceptual tool that allows Bhabha's (1994, 53–55) points about ambivalence and 'third space' to be related actively to material culture and social practices (Nederveen Pieterse 1995; van Dommelen 2006b, 138–140). I have discussed the concept of hybridisation and my use of it elsewhere (Knapp 2008, 57–61), and provided archaeological and ethnographic examples of hybridisation practices in 19th century South Africa, Polynesia and California, as well as in Punic-era Sardinia; I see no reason to repeat any of these discussions here. Others may term such meetings and mixings 'entanglement' (*e.g.* Thomas 1991; Stockhammer 2012), acculturation (*cf.* Cusick 1998b), enculturation or even 'hybridity' in a passive and descriptive manner; all such terms are problematic for different reasons, but above all because they tend to view social and cultural in a one-sided manner: from the top down.

Hybridisation practices occur in many instances of intercultural contact. Postcolonial theory is based on the notion that a colonial situation involves an interactive process stemming from the cultural entanglements that occur between indigenous and intrusive groups (van Dommelen 2005, 117). This reciprocal process involves interchangeable features that result in equal alterations of various material and social aspects of both groups (Dietler 2005, 54). According to Bhabha (1994), hybridisation practices involve the creation of new transcultural forms – whether political, economic, linguistic or cultural – that emerge during colonial encounters. For archaeologists, it is the material aspect of culture that matters. Differences in culture or material culture are never static but rather always changing, open to multiple interpretations (Bhabha 1994, 36). This is the space of hybridisation, of ambivalence and ambiguity, where the different actors involved in transcultural encounters negotiate strategies directed toward the construction of identity (Vives-Ferrándiz Sánchez 2007, 538). Ambiguity and ambivalence are inherent features of colonialism, and social archaeologists increasingly have turned to postcolonial studies in reaction to one-sided interpretative models such as 'Hellenisation' or 'Romanisation' (*e.g.* Dietler 2005, 55–61; Mattingly 2002).

The concept of hybridisation, then, refers in part to the social meetings, mixings and negotiations that take place between colonists and the colonised. Subaltern, or subordinated groups play a key role here; focusing on local peoples and contexts ensures that adequate attention is given to all the social dynamics involved in these encounters. Dietler (1998, 289) has emphasized that indigenous groups already had '... complex and dynamic histories that were very much in motion' when they came into contact with a colonising group. Any interpretation that perceives such encounters or social exchanges in terms of one-sided power relations misconstrues them (Thomas 1991, 83–84). Through interaction and negotiation, any group engaged in transcultural entanglements contributes to the shaping of a hybridised culture. Such encounters typically result in new social and material realities – the emergence of 'third-space' phenomena – forged by different customs, objects, values and traditions. In turn, and as a result of multiple interacting behaviours, differences, choices and exclusions involving self-representation within and amongst these groups, a new social identity emerges (van Dommelen 2005, 117–118, 136).

When it comes to the entangled objects of archaeology, we need to focus on the ways that innovations were adopted by different groups of people, and adapted to prevailing material and social practices. And we need to consider more fully the contexts in which the intersections of persons and things in motion led to entirely new forms and meanings of the objects involved. A contextual analysis, of course, is widely agreed to be vital for understanding socio-cultural changes and symbolic meanings. For example, if Mycenaean pottery is found primarily in domestic contexts within the Aegean and often in mortuary or ceremonial contexts in Cyprus or the Levant, we can assume that the domestic item was used by the living for everyday purposes, and held no specific social status. The item found in mortuary or other special contexts, however, suggests a different meaning and likely a different social status. In order to assess further the meanings of such exotica, one can look at particular types of foreign objects in local assemblages as a whole, and see if they are associated with other exotica, or with any specific types of local material, or if they seem to replace other object types previously used (Russell 2011). In other words, we need to examine the 'contexts of consumption' of imported goods (Dietler 2005, 66), their patterns of association and their relative quantitative presence, as well as their spatial distribution.

The concepts of materiality and connectivity are crucial if we wish to treat objects as an integral dimension of culture (van Dommelen and Knapp, 2010). Materiality lies at the heart of attempts to engage with objects as an integral dimension of human culture; human behaviour cannot be contemplated without taking into account the role of objects, of things in motion (DeMarrais *et al.* 2005; Meskell 2005). Connectivity – mobility, trade, exchange – by sea has formed a key feature of island life in the Mediterranean from prehistoric times to the present day (Horden and Purcell 2000, 123–172, 225–228); from the very earliest movement of people in the Mediterranean, some level of external communication and exchange – social or material – must have existed.

In this study, I focus on the materiality of cultural encounters during the Late Bronze Age in the eastern Mediterranean, and its role in restructuring existing identities and formulating new, hybridised identities. Although many archaeologists now focus on internal processes in attempting to understand the situation on Cyprus at the transition between the Bronze and Iron Ages, that is, during the 12th–11th centuries BCE, there lingers still a tendency to regard this island as a bridge between superior cultures and to see the material culture of Cyprus as an inevitable, pragmatic reflection of those in surrounding regions. Whether one embraces a 'Hellenising' or an 'Orientalising' perspective, the outcome is the same: high culture, like water, is seen to flow downhill (Dietler 1998, 295–296; 2005, 56–57). By contrast, in this paper I examine the material contexts of several exotic things, ostensibly imports – pottery, metalwork, ivory, faience vessels, cylinder seals – from this transitional era on Cyprus. These objects I regard as active transmitters of social exchange; in order to understand better how they may have been appropriated and used in a transcultural situation, I treat them in the context of their local consumption (similarly, Antoniadou 2005; 2007).

Material matters

During the 16th to mid-13th centuries BCE (Late Cypriot (LC) I–LC IIC early), *i.e.* the centuries that led up to the period of focus here, the Cypriot archaeological record reveals a range of objects that exemplify hybridisation practices (Voskos and Knapp 2008, 663–664). In two separate studies that adopt a more contextual approach, Antoniadou (2005; 2007) examined various imported objects (*i.e.* finished products) and what she terms 'hybrid products' (objects made of imported raw materials, or produced in a foreign technology and style, *e.g.* ivory and gold objects, seals, locally made Mycenaean style pottery), all found widely distributed in diverse contexts at seven different Late Cypriot sites. Amongst several tantalising conclusions, she notes that prior to the 13th century BCE, most imports at Enkomi came from mortuary deposits and would have been perceived as rare and exotic. In contrast, during the 13th and early 12th centuries BCE, most exotic objects, materials, and traits had become well integrated into local practices and systems of meaning – appearing in both settlement and mortuary contexts (gold jewellery and precious metal vessels appear only in tombs) – and thus began to impact on local social identities.

All these objects thus reflect local practices, which became much more intense during the 12th–11th centuries BCE. Nonetheless most archaeologists still see these hybridised objects as the products of intrusive peoples and external influences. I forego further discussion of them here, but it must be remembered that they form the crucial background to any consideration of a wide range of material culture used between the 13th–11th centuries BCE (LC IIC–LC IIIB; further discussion in Voskos and Knapp 2008, 663–664).

Despite the limitations that affect any data set stemming from excavations carried out over a period of some 100 years, with differing methodologies, interests and levels of detail, and with inadequate attention given to stratigraphic analysis or depositional processes, Antoniadou's work (2004; 2005; 2007) has demonstrated the potential of a contextual approach with Cypriot Bronze Age material. This does not mean such an attempt is by any means straightforward. Although, for example, archaeological site reports from Cyprus ostensibly provide a 'full' account of finds and architectural remains, the actual context of many objects is not always clear, and determining the function of such contexts is itself a bit of a guessing game. Finally, it is obviously impossible to treat in a study of this scope every single class of material that exists, or even the majority of objects in any given class. Given all these limitations, my aim here is to *explore* the possibility of using a contextual analysis to consider the fluidity of meaning that may have been assigned to certain objects in motion, objects that I regard as indicative of hybridisation practices. I reiterate that I am focusing primarily on objects and materials discussed in two previous studies without the benefit of a contextual analysis (Knapp 2008; Voskos and Knapp 2008).

Pottery

A coarsely made pottery known as Handmade Burnished Ware (HBW), previously known in the Aegean, first appeared in late 13th century BCE (LC IIIA) contexts alongside locally-manufactured Late Helladic-type wares (*i.e.*, Late Helladic IIIC: 1b) at Maa *Palaeokastro*, Kition, Enkomi, Sinda and Hala Sultan Tekke (Pilides 1991; 1994, 49–67). Although an extremely wide range of origins has been proposed for this ware, its appearance on Cyprus has been attributed to displaced Aegean settlers (Karageorghis 1986, who summarises many of the proposed origins). Like all foreign pottery found on Cyprus, the HBW accounts for only a tiny percentage of the total pottery repertoire of the Late Cypriot period (Steel 2004a, 74). It occurs at Kition (22 examples), Enkomi (4), Hala Sultan Tekke (3), Maa *Palaeokastro* (1),

Item no./type	Site	Area/Room	Context	Date BCE
654/body frag	Kition	I/39	industrial/domestic	13th–12th century
693d/rim frag	Kition	I/40	industrial/domestic	13th–12th century
353–1/cup base frag	Kition	I/26	industrial/domestic	12th–11th century
334/cup rim/body frag	Kition	I/24	industrial/domestic	12th–11th century
334/cup base/body frag	Kition	I/24	industrial/domestic	12th–11th century
674/shallow dish rim/body frag	Kition	I/6+22	domestic (well)	12th–11th century
646–647/body frags	Kition	I/8	industrial/domestic	11th century
Body frag	Kition	I/8	industrial/domestic	11th century
Jar rim and body frags	Kition	I/8	industrial/domestic	11th century
647/body frags	Kition	I/8	industrial/domestic	11th century
1/handle and body frags	Kition	II/16	Ceremonial	12th–11th century
1/jar rim frag	Kition	II/Courtyard A	?	12th–11th century
4/jar body frag	Kition	II/Tower C	?	12th–11th century
299B/rim and body frags	Kition	II/city wall	?	12th–11th century
299B/large body frag	Kition	II/city wall	?	12th–11th century
299B/bowl rim+body frag	Kition	II/city wall	?	12th–11th century
372/cup base+body frags	Kition	II/city wall	?	unstratified
318/bowl base+body frags	Kition	II/city wall	?	unstratified
33/two body frags	Kition	II/Temenos A	Ceremonial	11th century
313/rim frag	Kition	II/city wall	?	unstratified
313/rim frag	Kition	II/city wall	?	unstratified
3409/neck+body frag	Enkomi	Room 72E	destruction level	13th–12th century
6028/body frag	Enkomi	I/47 Ashlar Bldg	ceremonial?	12th century
2531–4/rim frag	Enkomi	III/2	Domestic	12th–11th century
6236A/rim+body frag	Enkomi	III/13/Well 7	ceremonial?	12th–11th century
N1604/rim+body+base frags	HST	?	Domestic	13th–12th century
F7010/jar collar+body frags	HST	Well	Domestic	13th–12th century
F3008/	HST	?	Domestic	13th–12th century
255/jar complete	Maa *Pal*	III/70	Domestic	12th century
RP1.2/deep bowl rim+body frag	Sinda	?	domestic?	13th–12th century

Table 5.1: Context, date and find-spot of handmade burnished wares (based on Pilides 1994, 85–89).

and Sinda (1) (Pilides 1991, 141–143, figs. 14.1–14.4; 1994, 85–89) (see Table 5.1). The earliest finds (from Kition Area I) belong to the late 13th or early 12th century BCE (*i.e.*, the transitional LC IIC–LC III A period), whilst the latest finds – from the same area – belong to 11th–early 10th century BCE (*i.e.* LC IIIB or Cypro-Geometric). Area I is regarded as an 'industrial-residential' compound, whilst Area II is interpreted as a 'sacred area' (Karageorghis and Demas 1985, 434).

HBW, in other words, has been found in what have been defined as domestic, industrial, ceremonial/ritual and destruction-level contexts at five Late Cypriot sites – all but one of them coastal – dated mainly to the 12th–11th centuries BCE. Many of the assumed ceremonial contexts are problematic, and we cannot even guess the meaning of sherds found on or in between floors associated with the city wall. As is the case with its occurrences everywhere from the central Mediterranean through the Aegean and southeast Europe, and now at Tell Kazel in Syria (Boileau *et al.* 2010; Jung, this volume), HBW is an enigmatic type of pottery that occurs in minute quantities in diverse contexts at what is presented as a crucial 'historical' conjuncture. Its peculiar qualities, *i.e.* handmade and burnished, and vanishingly small numbers may make it stand out from thousands of local wares, but we have no idea who made this type of pottery; at least some of the HBW material analysed by Jones (in Karageorghis 1986, 259–264) is not inconsistent with local production, nor is that from Tel Kazel in Syria (Boileau *et al.* 2010, 1685–1686). Nonetheless, an enigmatic phenomenon such as HBW should never be used to argue for an Aegean colonisation of Cyprus and nor, despite the intricate analyses carried out on the HBW found at Tel Kazel in Syria, can it support the notion of a 'Sea Peoples' presence there, following routes of Italo-Greek contact and exchange (Boileau *et al.* 2010, 1686–1688; Jung, this volume).

When it comes to the much more prominent Mycenaean (*i.e.* Late Helladic) pottery, I can do no better than quote Louise Steel (2001, 161) on the subject: '… the equation of Mycenaean pottery with a Mycenaean colonisation of the island became central to twentieth century discourse on the Late Cypriot period, in an archaeological commentary on both the Greek foundation legends of the classical period and the island's linguistic inheritance' (see also Knapp

2008, 250–255). Indeed, Mycenaean pottery has always formed the crux of arguments for a 12th century BCE Aegean colonisation of Cyprus, despite the transition to its production locally during the mid-late 13th century BCE. Whether imported or locally made, Late Helladic pottery has been found all over Cyprus, but again predominantly in large sites along or near the southern and eastern coasts: *e.g.* Enkomi, Kition, Hala Sultan Tekke, Maroni, Kalavasos and Kourion/Episkopi (Steel 2004a, 71–72). The quantities of Late Helladic pottery found in these sites must be set against the overall Late Cypriot ceramic repertoire; at best it never amounts to more than about 1–2% of the total pottery corpus (Steel 1998, 286 and n. 5; 2004a, 74–75). Moreover, as Manning and Hulin (2005, 282–286) have argued, the amount of Late Helladic pottery found throughout the eastern Mediterranean has little bearing on the scope or extent of Mycenaean trade or the presence of Mycenaean merchants, much less Aegean colonists.

Having examined the occurrences of hundreds of examples of Late Helladic ('Mycenaean') pottery from the sites of Enkomi, Kition, Maa *Palaekastro*, Episkopi *Bamboula*, Pyla *Kokkinokremos*, Athienou *Bamboulari tis Koukouninnas* and Myrtou *Pigadhes*, Antoniadou (2004, 161–163 (summary); 2007, 495) found it to be widely distributed in diverse contexts at all sites; it is thus unlikely to have served as exotic item of restricted circulation. Nonetheless, large centres such as Enkomi, Kition or Episkopi had a greater variety of Late Helladic pottery shapes than did smaller coastal sites such as Maa and Pyla, or inland 'sanctuary' sites such as Athienou or Myrtou *Pigadhes* (see also Steel 1998, 286; 2004a, 74–78). This may indicate only that sites directly involved in trade had access to a wider range of imports. More importantly, the association of Late Helladic pottery with domestic, industrial, craft-working and ceremonial contexts indicates that it had become integrated into the everyday practices of people living in the towns of Cyprus during the 13th–early 12th centuries BCE.

Small quantities of Late Helladic pottery occur at almost every excavated 13th century BCE (LC IIC) site in both tombs and settlement deposits (Sherratt 1999, 170; van Wijngaarden 2002, 187–191). At sites such as Kalavasos *Ayios Dhimitrios*, Alassa and Maroni *Vournes*, Late Helladic wares and other imports were found mainly in mortuary contexts (Antoniadou 2004, 176–179). At Enkomi specifically, there are no indications that imported Late Helladic pottery was associated with an elite group or even a special activity (Wijngaarden 2002, 149; 2007, 468). By the mid-late 13th century BCE (LC IIC), moreover, imported Mycenaean wares are found in the same contexts with local imitations and indigenous Cypriot wares, indicating that there was little differentiation in the purposes for which they were used. The only apparent distinction between the imported and locally made Mycenaean wares in the seven sites analysed by Antoniadou is the absence of highly specialised vessels – the *kernos* and the *rhyton* – from the local repertoire and from ritual contexts. Otherwise, vessels typically associated with domestic contexts are also found in ritual contexts, indicating a wide usage and acceptance of locally made Mycenaean wares.

At the same time that Mycenaean imports decreased towards the end of the 13th century BCE, local production of various Mycenaean-type wares was on the rise, as it was elsewhere in the eastern Mediterranean. Previously termed Rude or Pastoral Style, Levanto-Helladic ware, Late Helladic (LH) IIIB: 2 and LH IIIC: 1b, and Decorated Late Cypriot III wares, all of these matt-painted wheelmade wares are now (or should be) called, collectively, White Painted Wheelmade III (WPWM) ware (Åström 1972, 276; Kling 1991, 183; 2000, 281–282). This is the dominant type of pottery found in most 12th century BCE (LC IIIA) contexts but it made its first appearance somewhat earlier (and, crucially, before any Cypriot towns were destroyed at the end of 13th century BCE). The classification of these Aegean-style wares produced on Cyprus was based on their assumed chronological and historical significance rather than on clearly defined typological distinctions (Kling 1987; 1989a). Thus Aegean-style pottery found in 13th century BCE (LC IIC) levels was defined as LH IIIB, whereas in 12th century BCE (LC IIIA) levels it was identified as Late Helladic IIIC or Decorated LC III. Sherratt (1991, 187) also observed that the typological boundaries set up to define the various categories into which LC IIC and LC IIIA have been divided are in fact 'extremely fluid'. Some of these different types, it now seems clear, were in fact identical, and in Aegean terms could be either LH IIIB or IIIC. Nonetheless, it was often the case that when pottery defined as locally made LH IIIC:1b ware was recovered from late 13th–early 12th century BCE (*i.e.* post-LC IIC) destruction deposits at several sites across the island, these deposits were seen as marking a large-scale migration of Aegean colonists.

In several publications over the years, Kling (1987; 1989a; 2000) argued against the use of this pottery-driven methodology to establish an historical scenario. She emphasized the continuity in various features, even in shapes (*e.g.* shallow conical bowls), between the 13th and 12th centuries BCE (*i.e.* between LC IIC and IIIA), and she also noted '... the existence in the painted pottery of LC IIIA of stylistic hybrids that combine local, Aegean and Near Eastern elements' (Kling 1991, 182; similarly Sherratt 1992, 319–320; Mountjoy 2005, 209–210).

Let us now consider a few specific examples of these hybridised pottery wares, which show various foreign stylistic features on vessels of traditional Cypriot shape, or on Aegean vessel types already integrated into the local

Type/item no.	Site	Area/Room	Context	Date BCE
Low hemispherical bowl	Kourion	Tomb 89	Mortuary	11th century
Bell kraters/277–288	Enkomi	Area III buildings	industrial, domestic	12th–11th century
Amphoroid krater/3806	Kition	Room 58, Area II	Ceremonial	12th century
Strainer jug/33	Kouklia	Tomb KA T1	Mortuary	12th century
Strainer jug/87	Alassa *PM*	Tomb 3	Mortuary	12th century
Semi-globular bowl	Kouklia	*Mantissa* tomb	Mortuary	13th–12th century

Table 5.2: Context, date and find-spot of hybridised pottery wares.

repertoire. Furumark (1944, 235, fig. 10.9; 239) illustrated and discussed a low hemispherical bowl (a cup according to him) with raised wishbone handle and decorated with various geometric designs of specifically Aegean character. This type of bowl had a long tradition on Cyprus. Along with many others of similar type (Kling 1989b, 139), this vessel was found in Tomb 89 at Kourion (Episkopi) *Bamboula* and may be dated to the 11th century BCE, *i.e.* LC IIIB (Murray *et al.* 1900, 74–75, fig. 129, bottom centre). Within this same category are some of the numerous LH IIIC: 1b bell kraters and krater fragments found at 12th–11th century BCE Enkomi and decorated with bird and/or fish motifs inspired by Aegean, Levantine and Cypriot traditions (Dikaios 1969–1971, 286–287, 852, nos. 277–288, pl. 81.26–36). The bell krater is an Aegean shape that had been integrated into the Cypriot pottery-making tradition before the end of 13th century BCE, and produced in the Rude (or 'Pastoral') Style (Kling 1989b, 122–124). The vessels in question all derive from the destruction of Level IIIB buildings (Area III) at Enkomi, and are variously defined as being industrial (copper-working) or domestic in nature (Dikiaios 1969–1971, 136–147, 876–877, pl. 256).

An amphoroid krater from Kition, decorated in pictorial and abstract motifs, is not only similar to Levantine examples, but also has forerunners, vessels of very similar shape and size that appeared in the Levant already in the Middle Bronze Age (Yannai 2006, 98–102). Kraters of this type are known on Cyprus by the 16th–15th centuries BCE (LC I–II periods), in White Painted Wheelmade I–II and Proto-White Wheelmade I wares (*e.g.* Sjöqvist 1940, 56, fig. 14.63, 17). Some individual motifs in the top panel of the Kition krater reveal influences from both the Levant (butterfly ornament, fish in vertical row) and the Aegean (the bird and a specific type of fish) (Karageorghis *et al.* 1981, 8, no. 23, pls. VI.23, XIII). Despite this array of influences, the end product seems purely Cypriot. This vessel, dated to 12th century BCE (LC IIIA), was recovered from Room 58, on Floor IIIA in Area II of 'Temple' 5 (Karageorghis 1985, Pt. 1, 74–76; Pt. 2, 104, no. 3806). Rooms 58 and 58A are defined as the main hall within this structure, whose function is purportedly ceremonial.

In other cases, older decorative elements were combined in creative new ways, for example on a strainer jug from Tomb KA T1 (no. 33) at Kouklia (probably the *Marcello* location but none of several publications that describe the object in exhausting detail are clear about its provenance – *e.g.* Catling 1979, 274; Kling 1988, 271–272). Strainer jugs are usually thought to be of Aegean origin, yet they are rare in Mycenaean pottery outside of the Dodecanese and combine features of the Levantine wine set (strainer and jug) in one vessel (Franken 1992, 79, 82, figs. 5–7). With its Aegean- or Levantine-style birds and Cypriot 'Pastoral' Style bulls, this vessel's decoration blends earlier Aegean traditions (*e.g.*, birds found on examples from Rhodes and the Greek mainland) with the predominant ware of 12th century BCE Cyprus (Kling 1988, 272). The feature we wish to emphasize here, however, is its mortuary context. Other strainer jugs from Alassa *Pano Mandilares* (Hadjisavvas 1991, 173–177, figs. 17.1–2, 17.4–5) were found in both mortuary and settlement contexts. Most are decorated with a range of Aegean-style motifs (spirals, net patterns, geometric designs), but one – a tall, ovoid strainer jug (Tomb 3/87) with running spirals on its shoulder – is highly idiosyncratic in Aegean-type wares on Cyprus, and ultimately may have derived from Levantine types (Kling 2000, 282, 286, 285, fig. 14.3a).

Sherratt (1994, 37–38) calls attention to a one-handled semi-globular bowl, decorated in simple bands, from a tomb at Kouklia *Mantissa* (Karageorghis 1965, 159–160, fig. 38.10). In this case, it is the shape that is of interest. Derived from what are termed 'Levanto-Helladic' forms, such bowls are attested not just in Cyprus but also at Tarsus in Cilicia, and at several coastal sites in Naxos, Euboea and Attica. Taking into account various aspects of shape and decoration on this bowl and several other LC IIIA pottery wares and shapes, usually thought to be of Aegean origin, Sherratt suggests that these hybridised products may have originated either on Cyprus or in the Dodecanese.

Most ceramic specialists involved in the study of these

Type/item no.	Site	Area/Room	Context	Date BCE
Sword, greaves, helmet	Enkomi	Tomb 18	mortuary	13th–12th century
4-sided bronze stands	Kourion ?	Unknown	mortuary ??	12th century
Horned 'god' figurine	Enkomi	Ashlar Bldg/10	ceremonial/feasting	12th century
Ingot 'god' figurine	Enkomi	Quartier 5E/'north adyton'	ceremonial/feasting	12th century

Table 5.3: Context, date and find-spot of bronze metalwork.

enigmatic examples (and there are hundreds more like them) are fully aware of their eclectic qualities. Kling (1988, 272), for example, feels that the strainer jug from Kouklia tomb KA T1 '... displays a hybridization of strains operating in Cypriot ceramics at that time'. I would say that these vessels (see Table 5.2) reveal that quality of 'in-betweenness' that characterises the meetings and mixing of diverse socio-cultural groups during the late 13th–11th centuries BCE on Cyprus. In Sherratt's (1998, 298) opinion, the growing use of geographically diverse Aegean pottery shapes and decorative motifs on 12th century BCE Cyprus '... gives the impression of selective eclecticism mixed with a healthy dose of local improvisation, rather than the transferred ceramic packages of any discrete groups of people'. Those potters who were designing and making ceramics in this particular contact situation seem to have recombined in their products a mixture of diverse elements, thus giving material expression to new social practices that emerged in a changing demographic situation.

During this dynamic period of transition and change that lasted throughout the 12th and into the 11th century BCE, new typological and decorative elements continuously enhanced the Cypriot pottery repertoire; we thus get a glimpse of the active material practices of potters embracing more than one current cultural tradition. The largely impressionistic contextual analysis carried out here, with reference primarily to those objects previously itemised in discussing hybridisation practices during the late 13th–early 11th centuries BCE, reveals little beyond a prominence of mortuary contexts. Nonetheless, these hybridised products also occurred frequently in industrial and domestic contexts (especially at Enkomi) and at least occasionally in ceremonial (or 'ritual') contexts. Before we can draw any, even preliminary conclusions from such an analysis, however, it is essential to look beyond pottery at other classes of material culture from the same era.

Metalwork in bronze

During the 12th century BCE (LC IIIA), we find evidence of a new complex of what might be called 'warrior equipment': metal weapons that had appeared earlier in the Aegean (13th century BCE), and whose origins have been sought in northern Europe (Desborough 1964, 69–72; Muhly 1984, 41–43). These new weapons include socketed spears, bronze greaves and the Naue II type, cut-and-thrust sword (Molloy 2005). A sword of this type, along with greaves and a helmet found in the upper level of Tomb 18 at Enkomi (Catling 1955; Dikaios 1969, 406–408; Table 5.3) is regarded by Karageorghis (1990, 19) as the equipment of an Aegean warrior involved in the destruction of the site at the end of the 13th century BCE (end LC IIC). As Steel (2004b, 196) cautioned, however, all this new weaponry might simply reflect the material response by Cypriot warriors to changing military tactics, or the appropriation of exotic weaponry by elites to enhance their military prowess. Like most of the metal objects described here, these weapons and armour come from mortuary deposits. They serve as examples of the hybridised material and social practices typical of this era and at the same time reflect the ideological and cultural syncretism of Late Cypriot society (Steel 2004b, 205).

Several other, more symbolic bronze objects of probable 12th century BCE date – notably four-sided bronze stands and rod- or cast-tripod stands – reveal pervasive foreign elements (Catling 1964, 192–211; 1984, 78; Papasavvas 2001). The four-sided stands portray ingot bearers and lyre players, antithetic sphinxes, chariot scenes, and bulls fighting with lions and griffins – all motifs that engage and mix Aegean, Levantine and Cypriot elements (see, for example, the stand published in Karageorghis 1979, and discussed in Knapp 2008, 274). Unfortunately, most bronze stands have no known provenance, but were almost certainly looted from tombs during the 19th or early 20th century. Papasavvas (2001), however, has demonstrated the Cypriot basis of the technology, typology and design of most four-sided bronze stands (see also Karageorghis and Papasavvas 2001, 348, 351; Catling 1984, 71), so once again we have uniquely Cypriot artefacts with diverse, 'foreign' stylistic and iconographic features reflecting hybridisation practices.

Two well-known, 12th century BCE bronze anthropomorphic figurines from Enkomi – the so-called Horned God and Ingot god – also show clear signs of hybridisation practices (full discussion of both figurines in Knapp 2008, 221–224). The Horned God portrays a narrow-waisted, broad-shouldered male dressed in a fringed kilt and a two-horned conical cap. There are stylistic similarities between this 54.2 cm tall statuette and Aegean ivories, whilst other aspects – cap, horns, kilt, posture – might be seen as Syrian in origin (Dikaios 1962). Negbi (2005, 26) felt that the Horned God displayed mixed influences from Syrian, Anatolian and Aegean art, but she ultimately regards it as a representation of a local deity of Cypro-Aegean origin. Although Dikaios (1962) argued that it belonged to an Aegean stylistic tradition, Webb (1999, 227–228) – acknowledging these Aegeanising influences – felt that whilst its attributes and attitude were more Near Eastern than Aegean, its origin was, ultimately, to be found in '... the combination of Aegean stylistic features and Near Eastern attributes ... characteristic of Cypriot iconography in LC IIC–III' (*i.e.* late 13th–12th centuries BCE).

A similar fusion of Aegean and Levantine elements is evident in the appearance of the Ingot God. This 34.5 cm high bronze statuette portrays a bearded male attired in a long kilt, v-necked upper garment, a conical horned helmet, and standing on a base in the shape of a miniature ox-hide ingot. The figure holds a small, round shield in his left hand and a spear in his right. Whilst Seeden (1981, 102–23) compares his pose to that of various Levantine 'standard armed' figurines, at the same time we can see elements of Hittite (shield) and Sardinian (headgear) iconography (Negbi 2005, 25; Webb 1999, 223, with further references.). The absence of specifically Aegean features (*contra* Catling 1971, 29–32) and similarities with Levantine 'smiting' or 'standing armed' figurines point toward Syrian overtones or influences. Webb (1999, 225–226) thus suggests that this figurine represents either an assimilation of a local deity akin to the Syrian god Resheph, or the impact of what she calls 'Near Eastern groups' on Late Cypriot society. Papasavvas (2011), intriguingly, suggests that the 'greaves' (actually a second layer of metal wrapped round the bottom of the figurine), the shield and the miniature ingot were cast onto an existing figurine and thus transformed into an entirely new, Cypriot product.

Most scholars who have examined these figurines closely recognise an eclectic mixture of stylistic elements but typically assign origins based on their own area of training and expertise (*i.e.* the Aegean or the Levant), or on the features they believe to be most striking (Knapp 1986, 9–14; 2008, 277; Webb 1999, 225–228). Equating these figurines with divinities from the Aegean or the Levant, however, not only ignores local agency and maintains the cultural division between local Cypriotes and intrusive groups, it also typically assumes their divine status and their involvement in unknown religious or cultic practices, thus precluding any consideration of other, equally likely uses. Given the elaborate mix of stylistic and iconographic elements evident on these figurines, they should probably both be regarded as Cypriot in origin and design, perhaps all the more likely since the Ingot God, at least, is made of pure copper (Papasavvas, personal comm., April 2010).

Equally interesting, however, and more pertinent to the present discussion, are the contexts of both metal figurines (Dikaios 1969, 197–199; Courtois 1971; Knapp 2008, 220–224 for summary). The Horned God was found in the Ashlar Building at Enkomi, originally a residential and administrative structure grouped around a central hall with a large, formal hearth that Dikaios (1969, 175) found reminiscent of a Mycenaean megaron. When this level IIIA Ashlar Building was eventually destroyed (first half of the 12th century BCE) and immediately rebuilt, the large central hall (Room 14) was divided up and lost its official character. Whilst sectors in the north and west were given over to residential usage (Webb 1999, 92), the focus of social interaction seems to have shifted to the southern end of the complex, where two suites of rooms in the south – the 'sanctuaries' of the Horned God and Double Goddess – were given over to 'cultic' activities (Webb 1999, 92–99). The main architectural components of the Level IIIB Horned God sanctuary (or 'West Megaron') and the placement of the figurine in Room 10 of that complex have been described at some length elsewhere (Webb 1999, 98–99, fig. 40; Knapp 2008, 221–223, fig. 45; Fisher 2009, 194). The statue itself, found with its back against the east wall of Room 10, was probably viewed through a portal in Room 9. Fisher (2009, 191, fig. 3) regards Rooms 9 and 10 as a private and exclusive elite context, just off Room 45, which was now the main public hall with central hearth. Based on the finds recovered from Room 10 (267 cups, an alabaster jug and lid – Dikaios 1969, 316, pls. 35–36) or in the immediately surrounding area (animal and bird bones, bronze ornaments and tools), we may suggest that some sort of ceremonial activity involving feasting was conducted here.

Some 50 m southeast of the Ashlar Building, on the opposite side of the main north-south road running through the site of Enkomi (see Knapp 2008, 217, fig. 42), lay the 'sanctuary' of the Ingot God, in Quartier 5E (Courtois 1971, figs. 1–2). Unlike the Ashlar Building, the walls of this structure were built of rubble, and its special-purpose nature is based more on its contents and associations than on its size and construction materials. At some point during the 12th century BCE (Sol III, for which see Webb 1999, 102), perhaps contemporary with the changes seen in the Ashlar Building (Mountjoy 2005, 166, 209), this building comprised a large rectangular hall or courtyard with a small, nearly square room in its northeast corner. In this room ('Northeast Adyton'), the statue of the Ingot God was found in an upright

Type/item no.	Site	Area/Room	Context	Date BCE
pyxis lid	*Evreti*	Well TE III 165	mortuary	12th century
pyxis lid	*Evreti*	Pit KD 137	mortuary	12th century
plaque	Kition	Area III, Floor II	ceremonial	12th century
mirror handle	Enkomi	Tomb 17	mortuary	12th century
mirror handle	*Evreti*	Tomb 8	mortuary	12th century
mirror handle	Enkomi	Swedish Tomb 19	mortuary	12th century
flat disc	Kition	Tomb 9 (lower)	mortuary	12th century
bathtub-shaped *pyxis*	Kition	Tomb 9 (upper)	mortuary	12th century
pyxis	Enkomi	Tomb 24	mortuary	12th century
plaque	Kition	'Temple' 4	ceremonial	12th century
rhyton	Athienou	Pit 637	ceremonial OR industrial	13th century 12th century
gaming box/996	Enkomi	British Tomb 58	mortuary	12th century

Table 5.4: Context, date and find-spot of hybridised ivory objects.

position, immediately inside and to the right of the entrance (Webb 2001, 74, fig. 5a; 76). A large stone block near the structure's centre and a pierced block just to its northwest could have been used for tethering and butchering sacrificial animals. One of the largest and most diverse array of objects ever found in a ceremonial structure on Bronze Age Cyprus came from Sol III: local and imported pottery, a cylinder seal, bronze and iron objects, gold leaf, and an array of animal bones – ox skulls and horns, and the bones and teeth of many smaller animals. Nearby, in the West Adyton, were found hundreds of small, mainly female terracotta figures with cylindrical torsos and upraised arms (Webb 2001, 76). All these materials and objects, alongside solid evidence for animal sacrifices, point to ceremonial practices, including food preparation, feasting activities and the conspicuous display of several unique human representations. Whether they have anything to do with deities, and who those deities might be (Webb 1999, 112–113; Kassianidou 2005, 133–134), remains an irresolvable issue.

Monumental buildings serve as powerful expressions of identity and human memory, and are intimately tied to a specific place (Knapp 2009). In both of the monumental structures discussed here, objects of indisputably hybridised design if not manufacture were recovered in contexts suggesting some sort of ceremonial activity or performance, including feasting. Other architectural features – megara-like halls, hearths and bathrooms – uncovered at Kition, Alassa *Palaeotaverna*, Kouklia *Palaepaphos* and Maa *Palaeokastro* are widely believed to have served as places where élites gathered for feasting and associated activities (Fisher 2009). At Maa *Palaeokastro* they were found in context with large numbers of bones and pottery vessels suitable for consuming food and drink (Karageorghis and Demas 1988, 60–61), at Alassa with extensive storage facilities (at least 16 large storage *pithoi*) and impressive ashlar masonry (Hadjisavvas 2009, 129–131). Such places helped to define the identity of the participants and to mark out the events held within them as memorable, sensual, social experiences. As Fisher (2009, 204) and Knapp (2009, 49) both point out, however, the same qualities of monumentality that imbue structures with permanence in times of stability render them as targets for appropriation in times of stress or upheaval. During the 12th century BCE on Cyprus, the deliberate alterations of the central hall (Room 14) and the destruction of its hearth in the 'sanctuary' of the Horned God in the Ashlar Building, alongside the reconfiguration of the 'sanctuary' of the Ingot God in Quartier 5E at Enkomi, surely signal both material and social changes, including the likely re-negotiation of island identities. In both cases, the actual find contexts are associated with ceremonial, and perhaps feasting activities.

Ivory

Ivory provides some striking cases of hybridisation practices, mixing Aegean, Levantine and local Cypriot elements (Knapp 2008, 269–272). As elsewhere in this study, however, I am concerned more with the contexts of these objects than with their iconography and design elements. For example, two ivory *pyxis* lids found at Kouklia *Evreti* – in Well TE III 165 and Pit KD 137 – were decorated in a mixed style, showing both Levantine and Mycenaean influences (Maier and Karageorghis 1984, 70, 77, figs. 59–60). Their find-spots, a pit and a well, are not domestic contexts but rather form part of the sumptuous mortuary deposit in *Evreti*'s Tomb 8 (Table 5.4). As Catling (1968, 165) pointed out in his brief report on this tomb, although the *Evreti* area had been used as a necropolis in the Late Bronze Age, it was built over during the Archaic and Classical periods. The result was taphonomic chaos: many tombs were disturbed and/or broken into, whether by foundation trenches, rubbish pits, well shafts, or holes dug by tomb looters. The graves at *Evreti* were all chamber tombs, and the wealth of the material goods found in Tomb 8 led Catling (1968, 169) to conclude: 'there is no other LC IIIA tomb of remotely comparable importance'.

From Well TE III 165 at *Evreti*, then, came an ivory *pyxis* lid showing a lion attacking a bull. The same motif – seen on a fragmentary ivory plaque from Kition (Area II, Floor II, Bothros 20 in 'Temple' 5–Karageorghis 1985, 151, 332–333, pl. 175.4097) and on the ivory handle of a mirror from Tomb 17 at Enkomi (Murray *et al.* 1900, 31–32, pl. II.872b) – is well known from Minoan art (Kantor 1947, 98). The other *pyxis* lid, from *Evreti* Pit KD 137, depicts a griffin in front of a tree, recalling Levantine prototypes. An ivory mirror handle, also from *Evreti* Tomb 8 (Maier and Karageorghis 1984, 68, 74–75, figs. 55m, 58), and another handle from Tomb 17 at Enkomi (on the other side of the ivory mirror already noted – Murray *et al.* 1900, 31, pl. II.872a) depict armed warriors in Aegean-style kilts striking a resting lion (*Evreti*) and a griffin (Enkomi). The theme of warriors slaying real or mythical animals has a long tradition in Near Eastern art (Feldman 2006, 73–81). Yet another ivory mirror handle in a mortuary deposit from Enkomi (Swedish Tomb 19–Gjerstad *et al.* 1934, vol. I, 565 no. 91, pls. 92.2, 152.7) was made in the form of a nude woman grasping her breasts, a thematic element seen in both west Asian and Egyptian art (Åström 1972, 612; Kantor 1947, 89–90). Technically and typologically, this handle points to Aegean inspiration, but may have been the product of a Levantine school of carving. All of these objects and several more – a flat ivory disk (Karageorghis 1974, 44 no. 8; 61; pls. 65, 150 no. 19) and an ivory, bathtub-shaped *pyxis* (Karageorghis 1974, 91 no. 354, pls. 87, 170) from Tomb 9 at Kition; an ivory *pyxis* from Enkomi Tomb 24 (Poursat 1977, 159; pl. XVI.6); an ivory plaque from 'Temple' 4 at Kition (Karageorghis 1985, 329–331, pl. 124) – not only portray hybridisation in action, they also derive exclusively from 12th century BCE mortuary (mainly) or ceremonial contexts.

Two other, well known ivory objects must be noted here. The first is a rhyton from Athienou *Bamboulari tis Koukounninas* (Dothan and Ben-Tor 1983, 123–125, fig. 56). Like Aegean rhyta, this vessel has four bands of decoration displaying diverse Mycenaean, Levantine and Syrian elements. Although the local inspiration of this vessel seems clear enough, it embraces many elements of Aegean and Levantine iconography; the whole has been transformed into a unique, hybridised Cypriot product. Although the excavators assigned the pit (637) in which this object was found to their Stratum III (13th century BCE), they noted that the outlines of this pit were already discernible in Stratum II (12th century BCE) (Dothan and Ben-Tor 1983, 15 plan D, 20). Within the main structure of Stratum III (defined as a 'sanctuary'), thousands of pottery vessels (mostly miniature votives) were found together with an offering stand, the leg of a large (bull-shaped?) zoomorphic vessel, other bull-related paraphernalia and the bronze model of a chariot. The rhyton came from a series of pits to the east of the main complex; these pits also contained a perforated, tube-shaped ceramic object, cylinder seals, an Egyptian scarab, a fibula and a situla handle, and beads of faience, carnelian and steatite (amongst many others). Although the chronological placement of these pits, as well as their purpose, are problematic, we may at least posit (with the excavators and others) that the main structure at Athienou served a ceremonial function, perhaps involving feasting (Åström 1987), during the 13th century BCE. By the 12th century BCE, however, it was converted to more specifically industrial purposes (Webb 1999, 25–29, 285). Thus, although the actual dating of the rhyton remains uncertain, if it belongs to the 13th century BCE levels, its function was likely ceremonial in nature.

The second object is the ivory gaming box from British Tomb 58 at Enkomi (Murray *et al.* 1900, 12–15, fig. 19; 31; pl. I). This well-known and widely illustrated item (*e.g.* Karageorghis 2002, 100, fig. 205) portrays several different vignettes: a hunting scene with various horned and hoofed animals pursued by an archer in a chariot – a large bull with lowered horns confronts the chariot. While the chariot scene is Near Eastern in derivation, all animals are shown in the 'flying gallop' style, an Aegean motif. The bull and a small scene depicting a hunter killing a lion have similarities with certain details on a gold bowl and gold plate from Ugarit (Feldman 2006, 65–66). Two bulls lying beneath a tree on one of the side panels recall Aegean traditions.

Like all the other ivory pieces discussed here, this unique object incorporates a mixture of styles indicative of hybridised cultural practices on Cyprus. Some of these ivories – the Athienou rhyton, the Enkomi gaming box, the Kition bathtub-shaped *pyxis* – are unique. Along with many other objects discussed above, they demonstrate how hybridisation practices impacted on a range of different arts and technologies on 12th century BCE Cyprus, giving new forms and meanings to materiality. Although the examples discussed here derive exclusively from mortuary or ceremonial contexts, most of the ivories Antoniadou (2007, 494) documented from the 13th–12th centuries BCE (LC IIC–IIIA) were found in domestic contexts; in only two cases were they found in ritual contexts. Overall, then, ivories may have had a privileged but not restricted usage, and were not regarded as prestigious objects in the same way that precious metals were.

Faience vessels

Faience vessels appear widely throughout the Levant, Egypt and Cyprus, in contexts ranging from royal tombs to common households (Peltenburg 2002; 2007, 379, with references; Antoniadou 2004, 153–155). During the Late Bronze Age, most faience vessels are found in either tombs or 'temples' (Peltenburg 2002, 93); on Cyprus, there are concentrations

Type/item no.	Site	Area/Room	Context	Date BCE
Stirrup vase or juglet/36	Kition *Chrysopolitissa*	Tomb 1	Mortuary	14th–13th century
Hole-mouth bowl/4	Kition *Chrysopolitissa*	Tomb 9/lower burial	Mortuary	14th–13th century
Blossom bowl/5	Kition *Chrysopolitissa*	Tomb 9/lower burial	Mortuary	14th–13th century
Pyxis/230	Kition *Chrysopolitissa*	Tomb 9/upper burial	Mortuary	14th–13th century
Juglet//294	Kition *Chrysopolitissa*	Tomb 9/upper burial	Mortuary	13th century
Rhyton/special series 1	Kition *Chrysopolitissa*	Outside Tombs 4+5	Mortuary	13th century
Jar/KEF-63	Kition *Bamboula*	Sondage L-N 13	Mortuary	13th century
Pomegranate bottle	Enkomi	Tomb 43 (British)	Mortuary	13th century
Tripod plate	Enkomi	Tomb 66 (British)	Mortuary	13th century
Tripod plate	Enkomi	Tomb 7 (Cypriot)	Mortuary	13th century

Table 5.5: Context, date and find-spot of hybridised faience objects.

in Kition Tomb 9 and Enkomi British Tomb 66. Egyptian faience bowls, however, appear in several other sites on Cyprus during the 13th–12th centuries BCE, including Hala Sultan Tekke, Klavdhia, Maroni, Kalavasos *Ayios Dhimitrios*, Episkopi *Bamboula*, Kouklia, Ayios Sozomenos and near Idalion (Peltenburg 2007, 384–385). The contexts are quite varied: fully half of the 18 bowls known from Kition were deposited in what are likely to be ceremonial contexts whereas at Enkomi deposition in tombs predominates. Stylistically, faience containers – like several from Kition depicting everything from lion and bull hunts to heraldic designs – are regarded as luxury objects exemplifying an international artistic koiné that admits of no single source (Feldman 2006, 41–43). Whatever their ultimate origin(s) may be, here I confine myself to presenting only a few faience vessels from Late Bronze Age Cyprus that have reliable contextual evidence as well as diverse stylistic or iconographic elements linked to hybridisation practices.

Excavations in Tombs 1 and 9 at Kition *Chrysopolitissa* uncovered 12 faience vases of various shapes – juglets, bowls, flasks, a pyxis (Table 5.5) – that may be either Egyptian or western Asiatic in origin (Peltenburg 1974, 105–144). From Tomb 1 came the lower half of a small stirrup vase or juglet, which betrays Aegean inspiration in its shape; Peltenburg (1974, 107–108) suggests that this vessel and others like it are Cypriot or north Syrian products. Other faience vessels that may have been produced either in northern Syria or Cyprus include: (1) a spouted (with duck's neck?) hole-mouth bowl from Tomb 9 (lower); (2) a blossom bowl, also from the lower burial in Tomb 9, whose sharp relief work recalls metal prototypes known from both Egypt and the Levant (Peltenburg (1974, 109, 115, fig. 1a); (3) a blue-glazed *pyxis* from the upper burial in Tomb 9, whose shape is common in the Levant but rare in Egypt. Likewise, from the upper burial in Tomb 9 came a handleless juglet that recalls the ovoid shape of Cypriot Base-ring juglets; it has a greenish-white (originally blue?) glazing that compares more closely to Levantine than Egyptian examples (Peltenburg 1974, 135). Finally, from the area just outside Tombs 4+5 came the well known conical faience rhyton, inspired by an Aegean shape, decorated in a Levantine style and produced in a technical manner that is arguably Egyptian (Peltenburg 1974, 116–13, pl. XCIV). It depicts hunting scenes, bulls, a goat, stylised flowers and two hunters with short kilts and tassled headdresses. Although the combination of Egyptian technique and Levantine style precluded attempts to pinpoint its origin, Peltenburg (1974, 134) suggested it was most likely produced either along the Syrian coast or in the southern part of Cyprus.

From a sounding along the rampart wall at Kition *Bamboula* that seems to have cut into one or more burials of the late 13th century BCE came a polychrome faience vessel that depicts hunting scenes with lions and gazelles (?) on the shoulder, and goats flanking a series of voluted palmettes on the body (Yon 1985, 222–223, fig. 2b; Yon and Caubet 1985, 68–69, 77, fig. 35). Both the technique of manufacture and decorative motifs are essentially Egyptian, but the shape has counterparts in both Egypt and the Levant (Ras Shamra).

In addition to the concentration of faience bowls at Enkomi British Tomb 66 (Murray *et al.* 1900, 35–36, fig. 63), I mention here a striking faience bottle in the form of a pomegranate from Tomb 43 of the 1896 British excavations at Enkomi (Buchholz and Karageorghis 1973, 157, 456 no. 1678; Smith 2009, 98–99 suggests this is a representation of a poppy, not a pomegranate). Such vessels are typically made of glass and usually found in Late Cypriot II tombs (Åström and Åström

1972, 524, type 5). Whilst the shape is very distinctive, the horizontal bands of zigzags may betray Aegean influences (Karageorghis 1968, 44 and pl. XL.3). Finally, in this purely mortuary category, mention must be made of tripod plates, found in tomb deposits from both the British (Tomb 66) and Cypriot (Tomb 7) excavations at Enkomi (Murray *et al.* 1900, 35, fig. 63.1045; Dikaios 1969, 355 no. 2, pls. 199.22, 200.17). Given the primarily Cypriot provenance of most tripod plates, and the strong Egyptianising aspects in their design (bulls in marsh-scape, horned animals), it is likely that this style was either produced locally or else made in Egypt for export to Cyprus (Peltenburg 1986, 159).

With regard to faience vessels recovered from settlement contexts, Antoniadou (2004, 153–155) has catalogued 28 examples of vessels or vessel fragments from the 13th–12th centuries BCE at Kition, Enkomi, Maa *Palaeokastro* and Myrtou *Pigadhes* (both the latter with only one bowl each). Most of these are bowls, along with a few jars or goblets, and one example of an animal-headed rhyton, most were found in an industrial context in Kition's Area I. In general, faience vessels from primary deposits occur in domestic and industrials contexts during the 13th century BCE, whilst during the 12th century BCE they also appear in ceremonial contexts. Whether imported or locally produced, it would seem that faience vessels were associated with a variety of different activities and social needs: mortuary, industrial, domestic. Faience amulets and scarabs, widely agreed to be imported items, occur at both Kition and Enkomi, also in diverse contexts. Faience beads and necklaces, however, which may have been produced locally on Cyprus, turn up at those sites as well as at Maa *Palaeokastro* and Athienou, mainly in ceremonial contexts.

Cylinder seals

The final class of objects treated in this study, albeit summarily, is the cylinder seal, in particular those that belong to the 'elaborate' and 'derivative' styles (see Webb 2002, 117–126 for a useful summary). The very concept of such seals is, of course, foreign in derivation, and many of them bear Levantine, Near Eastern or Aegean elements. Keswani (1989, 69–70) maintained that several examples from Enkomi – engraved with sphinxes, real animal motifs, hieroglyphic signs and other cosmic symbols – were associated with Near Eastern ideologies of kingship. Webb (2002, 114) estimates that the total number of known cylinder and stamp seals is close to 1000, fewer than 400 of which have a recorded find-spot. Moreover, many of the best known cylinder seals lack secure provenance, and even those that do must be treated with caution, not least because they were in use (and sometimes reworked) over a long period of time, and would have moved in and out of various contexts, having different usages and meanings. Finally, the high rate at which cylinder seals were curated means that, even when the provenance is known, it is often in the latest known deposits from a site, *e.g.* at Enkomi where most cylinder seals come from 13th–12th century BCE levels (Courtois and Webb 1987, 26).

Over 60% of all provenanced, imported cylinder seals were found at Enkomi, and over 50% of all cylinder seals that have a site provenance come from settlement, mortuary or surface deposits (Courtois and Webb 1987, 25 no. 1; Webb 2002, 114–117; tabs. 1– 2). Most seals from non-mortuary contexts were lost or discarded during the 12th century BCE. Given such statistics and the limitations they imply, as well as the detailed publications on seals and sealings by Webb (Courtois and Webb 1987; Webb 1999, 243–247, 262–283; 2002) and Smith (1994; 2003; 2007), and because I have discussed elsewhere the hybridised Aegean, Levantine and Cypriot elements found on several 13th–12th century BCE cylinder seals (Knapp 2008, 274–277), for my purposes here it must suffice to say that hybridised cylinder seals appear mainly in mortuary or settlement contexts. At least some examples of locally made, 13th century BCE seals come from domestic and industrial, less so from ceremonial contexts at Myrtou *Pigadhes*, Athienou, *Ayios Dhimitrios*, Maroni, Kourion *Bamboula* and Kition (Webb 1999, 247; 2002, 114–115, no. 23–24, with references).

This brief presentation of the glyptic evidence cannot begin to do it justice. A more focused, contextual analysis of all the relevant (hybridised, provenanced) evidence is crucial, but impossible to carry out within the scope of this study. The only conclusion to be drawn here is that the wide array of possible origins, different styles and intermixing of Aegean and Levantine with local Cypriot iconographic elements represents well the 'in-betweeness' and ambiguity expected in any social framework that involves hybridisation practices. As is the case with the various examples of pottery, ivory objects, faience vessels and bronze artworks presented above, we can see that many and diverse aspects of non-local iconography, design and technology were adapted and assimilated into the glyptic repertoire, clearly showing hybridisation practices in the use of local and imported motifs.

Context and meaning

Overall, then, what can context tell us about the meaning and use of the objects presented in this study? Handmade Burnished Wares, at least some of which may have been produced locally, were recovered from what have been defined as domestic, industrial, ceremonial and destruction-level contexts at five Late Cypriot sites dated mainly to the 12th–11th centuries BCE. Contextually indiscriminate, they appear to have been used in a variety of everyday practices, most likely for cooking and related activities. Mycenaean wares, in turn, were found widely distributed in diverse contexts at all sites and so could not have served as exotic items of restricted circulation. Technologically, typologically and contextually, they are very similar to their Cypriot counterparts. The association of this pottery with domestic, industrial, craft-working and ceremonial contexts suggests that it, too, had become integrated into the everyday routines of people living in the towns of Cyprus during the 13th–early 12th centuries BCE. Vessels typically associated with domestic contexts have also been found in ritual contexts, indicating a wide acceptance and usage of locally made Mycenaean wares.

With respect to the hybridised pottery wares used during the transitional period and treated here, we can see that new typological and decorative elements penetrated the Cypriot pottery repertoire. Contextually, these objects were most prominent in the mortuary realm, but they also appeared frequently in industrial and domestic contexts (especially at Enkomi) and at least occasionally in ceremonial contexts. In other words, like the other pottery types discussed here, they should not be seen as exotic products accessible only to a few members of society, but rather as reflections of the everyday circumstances of Late Cypriot society.

Most of the metal objects described in this study, including weapons and armour, come from mortuary deposits. The find contexts of the Horned and Ingot gods, by contrast, are associated with ceremonial contexts and perhaps feasting activities. At least some of the hybridised metal objects found within and beyond these contexts, not just at Enkomi but at other sites large and small throughout the island, may have been in use over a long period of time, from at least the 13th if not 14th century BCE (Muhly 1980, 156–161; Knapp 1986, 86–87). The fluidity of meanings attached to them, and the ways they were appropriated and used in this period of transcultural engagements, must have differed significantly.

The hybridised ivory objects treated in this study derive exclusively from 12th century BCE mortuary (mainly) or ceremonial contexts, with the possible exception of the Kition ivory rhyton (industrial context). Most other ivories known from the 13th–12th centuries BCE derive from domestic contexts. Overall, then, despite the strong affinities these ivories reveal with Near Eastern and Aegean iconography, highlighting hybridised practices on Cyprus, their usage does not seem to have been restricted. Indeed, ivory carving workshops have been postulated for several 13th–12th century BCE sites: Kition, Kouklia, Hala Sultan Tekke and perhaps Enkomi (Knapp 2008, 272, with further references). Several ivory disks from Cyprus bear the same unusual decorative motifs, and may have come from these workshops (Pierides 1973, 276–277); Poursat (1977, 144 no.1, 157, 164–165) actually wonders whether some ivory objects found in Mycenaean sites might actually have been produced on Cyprus. The styles of these intricately carved objects are as eclectic as the people who made and used them, and several from Enkomi, Kition and Paphos form part of the international koiné of luxury goods defined by Feldman (2006, 43–45).

All the hybridised faience bowls discussed here came from mortuary contexts and thus might be seen as prestige objects reflecting some special social status. Within contemporary settlements, however, faience vessels – whether imported or locally produced – were also associated with industrial and domestic contexts, whilst faience amulets and scarabs occur at both Kition and Enkomi in diverse contexts. Faience beads and necklaces that may have been produced locally turn up mainly in ceremonial contexts. These objects thus seem to point to diverse activities and social situations, and some at least were clearly imports (amulets and scarabs). It is also worth noting that the distribution of these objects changes over time: during the 13th century BCE (LC IIC), faience vessels occur in industrial and domestic contexts, while during the 12th century BCE (LC IIIA) they occur in industrial, ceremonial, domestic and working contexts (Antoniadou 2007, 491–492). Whilst the earlier deposition of various faience items in industrial or even domestic contexts might suggest the selection of foreign symbols in acts of self-representation (Antoniadou 2007, 490), by the 12th century BCE faience vessels no longer had a limited distribution, but rather served people's everyday needs.

The extremely limited sample of hybridised cylinder seals presented in this study occurred mainly in mortuary or settlement contexts, but at least some examples of locally made, 13th century BCE seals come from domestic and industrial, less so from ceremonial contexts. At Enkomi, where over 60% of the cylinder seals known on Cyprus have been found, and despite biases of deposition and discovery associated with that site, raw counts of seals associated with rooms indicate they were linked more closely to domestic than to administrative or ceremonial contexts. Seals therefore may have been used mainly as personal ornaments, rather than for official purposes (Webb 2002, 128).

One of the major differences that becomes apparent between mortuary and settlement contexts is the deposition of certain metal objects, ivories and faience bowls in some of the more elaborate tombs excavated in the urban coastal centres, especially at Enkomi and Kition. This stands in some contrast to their restricted appearance in settlement contexts. Antoniadou (2007, 497) also noted a decrease in the number and variety of both imports and hybridised objects in mortuary and settlement contexts at Enkomi during the late 13th–early 12th centuries BCE. By that time, we can no longer regard Mycenaean pottery, metal weapons and figurines, ivory or faience personal goods and vessels as prestige imports or products destined for social elites. Some of the locally produced goods, of course, may constitute an example of Sherratt's (1998, 295–296, 298) 'import substitution', *i.e.* value-added products found in 'sub-elite' contexts and associated with feasting or drinking rituals. The people who lived on Cyprus during this transitional era (LC IIC–III) can be seen to have re-contextualised, transformed or created anew many of these hybridised objects, adjusting them to their own needs and using them as a means of representing themselves.

Social groups continually draw upon and alter their material world, at least in part to demarcate their own social identities (Hendon 2007, 308). All the objects discussed here have complex biographies and social entanglements; they will have changed meanings frequently as they passed from their locus of production to site of consumption to their ultimate point of deposition. I have portrayed them as reflective of hybridisation practices associated with new social identities emerging on Cyprus at this time. Many of these objects were produced locally, albeit with the use of what are widely agreed to be non-local ideas, designs and meanings. Some of them must have been used as items for display and/or conspicuous consumption in certain contexts. We need to assess these objects not simply as indicators of trade and exchange, or in terms of their presumed ethnic affiliation, but rather as hybridised objects – things and materials actively manipulated in specific contexts and for specific purposes, as part of individual or wider social strategies. In order to grapple with the meanings of materiality in complex social arenas such as those that confront us here, it is crucial to ponder what might be called the 'second life of imported objects' (Diamantis Panagiotopoulos, pers. comm.), to consider how material culture was used as part of such strategies, and how the hybridisation practices and transcultural entanglements reflected in material goods constituted key features of new social identities.

Transitions, transcultural contacts and island identity

During the 13th century BCE, Cypriot elites displayed or wore objects of faience, gold or ivory exhibiting Levantine, Egyptian or Aegean artistic and iconographic elements. They made use of imported Aegean pottery and developed the means to produce it themselves. They created metal goods and cylinder seals using ideas and designs from both the Aegean and the Levant. And they did so, not just to emulate their overseas counterparts, but to mark out their own identity and to legitimise new power differentials that emerged toward the end of the Bronze Age.

With the collapse of the international exchange system(s) of the Late Bronze Age and the concomitant loss of state control over trade (Sherratt 1998), elite groups or individuals on Cyprus no longer had easy access to foreign luxury goods. Despite the severity of this collapse elsewhere, on Cyprus there is remarkable continuity in material and social practices (Sherratt 1998, 293–294, with further references). In many respects, the internal situation on the island became more stable and coherent by the end of the 12th century BCE (LC IIIB, *c.* 1125–1050 BCE), conventionally regarded as the beginning of Cyprus's early Iron Age (Iacovou 1999a; 2002). Despite the homogeneity seen in early Iron Age Cypriot material culture, however, there was clearly a break in tradition, from the site level through tomb types and mortuary practices, to individual categories of material goods.

There was no break, however, in the hybridisation practices seen throughout the 13th–12th centuries BCE. Proto-White Painted pottery, for example, reveals a striking amalgamation of local Cypriot, Aegean and Levantine traditions (Iacovou 1988, 84; 1991, 204; Sherratt 1991, 193; 1992, 329–38), whilst new terracotta zoomorphic vessels (bulls, horses, dogs, birds, bicephalous human-animals) nicely complement the Proto-White Painted tradition in their style, fabric and decoration (Courtois 1971, 287–308; Webb 1999, 216–219). The Aegean-type 'goddess with upraised arms' and its local variants were often executed in this same Proto-White Painted tradition (Webb 1999, 213–14, fig. 75). Whatever their iconographic differences, this new 'Aegean-type' figurine also became integrated into the local repertoire in a typically Cypriot manner. In terms of mortuary practices, both cremated and inhumed individuals accompanied by numerous grave goods were now placed in hybridised, 'Mycenaean type' chamber tombs with both long and narrow as well as short and wide *dromoi* (Leriou 2007, 575). Many of these burials contained new status symbols such as gold jewellery, imported Levantine unguent vessels and Canaanite amphorae (Coldstream 1989; 1994; Rupp 1989).

From approximately 1100 BCE onward, the material record of early Iron Age Cyprus bears little resemblance to that of its Bronze Age antecedent. During this transitional time that witnessed widespread human movements throughout the eastern Mediterranean, both indigenous and immigrant peoples transformed the material and social practices of the island of Cyprus. The appearance of some Aegean-type features (*e.g.*, pottery, figurines, chamber tombs) on Cyprus during the 12th century BCE and the fact that Cyprus eventually became – by the Cypro-Archaic period – a mainly Greek-speaking island, has led many scholars to conclude that Cyprus became 'hellenised' during the 12th and 11th centuries BCE.

Those who support a large-scale migration of Aegean people to Cyprus, or even to the Levant, at this time have stressed the Aegean features of several classes of material whose character is, at best, ambivalent (*e.g.* Stager 1995; Karageorghis 2000). Whilst the continuities in architecture, pottery and mortuary practices tend to be overlooked by these scholars, emphasis is given to individual features (cult symbols, weaponry, *etc.*) whose interpretation is, at best, equivocal. The Cypriotes of the 12th–11th centuries BCE were neither 'hellenised' nor 'enculturated' by an influx of superior Greek-speakers, and nor did they passively absorb specific features of Aegean material culture. Nobody had to teach them how to use the pottery-wheel or how to produce carburised iron (Sherratt 1994, 61–62). This does not mean that Aegean people never came to Cyprus, nor made any contribution to the island's material culture. But if we want to understand the Aegean *and Levantine* presence on Cyprus, as well as the impact of materiality and connectivity upon island identity, we have to consider how migrants and others entangled in contact situations might have met and mixed, and in this mixing of social and cultural traditions became transformed.

The concept of hybridisation facilitates our understanding of the ways in which the material representations of these groups became transformed into something entirely new and distinctive. Hybridization practices imprinted on a wide range of objects demonstrate the cultural entanglement of diverse 'social actors' of differing origins (van Dommelen 2005, 117–118). These meetings and mixings had crystallized by the 11th century BCE when fairly homogeneous material and technological traditions blending elements of local, Levantine and Aegean ancestry are seen over the entire island. People from the Aegean or the Levant, possibly even from Anatolia, introduced social as well as material diversity, established new connections between distant areas and different peoples, and in the process developed their own distinctive identity. The journeys of newcomers to Cyprus, in other words, also included the ticket to a new identity shaped by new social and material connections, new customs and new means of representation.

As the editors of this volume contend, the material correlates of socio-cultural entanglements created by the flows of goods and ideas between societies formed one of the constituting features of a culture's socio-political framework. In the Cypriot case, the active negotiation, manipulation and mediation of material practices by social actors led to the emergence of 'third-space' phenomena, new patterns of social interaction and new, hybridised material forms, ultimately to the formation of a new island identity that held meaning for all the inhabitants of early Iron Age Cyprus. At the same time, new elite groups coalesced in the different polities, the so-called city-kingdoms of this period: Phoenicians in towns like Kition or Palaepaphos, indigenous Cypriotes in Amathus, and a mixture of native Cypriot and intrusive Aegean and Levantine elements elsewhere, and probably everywhere. All these social and material entanglements between natives and newcomers ultimately led to what would become the 'pan-Cyprian koine culture' (Iacovou 1999b, 150) of the 11th–10th centuries BCE.

Acknowledgements

I am grateful to Philipp Stockhammer and Joseph Maran for the invitation and support that enabled me to take part in the conference *Materiality and Practice: Transformative Capacities of Intercultural Encounters* that took place in Heidelberg (25–27 March 2010), where I presented an earlier version of this paper. Comments at the conference from both of them, as well as from Reinhard Jung, Diamantis Panagiotopoulos, Assaf Yasur-Landau and Peter van Dommelen helped me to rethink the present paper. Toward the same end, I also wish to thank the research students in Classical and Near Eastern Archaeology at Bryn Mawr College (Bryn Mawr, Pennsylvania) for their comments and views on hybridisation and contextual analysis (given in a seminar following the C. Densmore Curtis Lecture at Bryn Mawr, 16 April 2010). I also wish to thank Philipp Stockhammer for a copy of his forthcoming paper (cited in the references), and especially Sophia Antoniadou, whose previous papers and unpublished PhD thesis were instrumental in helping me to attempt the 'contextual' analysis presented in this study.

References

Åström, L. and Åström, P. (1972) *The Swedish Cyprus Expedition IV: 1D. The Late Cypriote Bronze Age*. Lund, Swedish Cyprus Expedition.

Åström, P. (1972) *The Swedish Cyprus Expedition IV: 1C. The Late Cypriote Bronze Age. Architecture and Pottery*. Lund, Swedish Cyprus Expedition.

Åström, P. (1987) Votive deposits in the Late Cypriote Bronze Age. In T. Linders and G. C. Nordquist (eds), *Gifts to the Gods*. Acta Universitatis Upsaliensis, Boreas 15, 177–199. Uppsala, Uppsala University Press.

Antoniadou, S. (2004) The Impact of Trade on the Society of Cyprus during the Late Bronze Age: Settlements, Artefacts and Social Change. Unpublished PhD thesis. Edinburgh, Department of Archaeology.

Antoniadou, S. (2005) The Impact of Trade on Late Cypriot Society: A Contextual Study of Imports from Enkomi. In J. Clarke (ed.), *Archaeological Perspectives on the Transmission and Transformation of Culture in the Eastern Mediterranean*, 66–77. Oxford, Oxbow.

Antoniadou, S. (2007) Common Materials, Different Meanings: Changes in Late Cypriot Society. In Antoniadou and Pace 2007, 483–508.

Antoniadou, S. and Pace, A. (2007) *Mediterranean Crossroads.* Athens & Oxford, Pierides Foundation & Oxbow Books.

Barlow, J., Bolger, D. and Kling, B. (1991) *Cypriot Ceramics: Reading the Prehistoric Record.* University Museum Monograph 74. Philadelphia, University of Pennsylvania, University Museum Monographs.

Bhabha, H. K. (1994) *The Location of Culture.* London, Routledge.

Boileau, M.-C., Badre, L., Capet, E., Jung, R. and Mommsen, H. (2010) Foreign Ceramic Tradition, Local Clays: The Handmade Burnished Ware of Tell Kazel (Syria). *Journal of Archaeological Science* 37, 1678–1689.

Buchholz, H.- G. and Karageorghis, V. (1973) *Prehistoric Greece and Cyprus.* London, Phaidon Press.

Catling, H. W. (1955) A Bronze Greave from a 13th Century BC Tomb at Enkomi. *Opuscula Atheniensia* 2, 21–36.

Catling, H. W. (1964) *Cypriot Bronzework in the Mycenaean World.* Oxford, Oxford University Press.

Catling, H. W. (1968) Kouklia: Evreti Tomb 8. *Bulletin de Correspondance Héllenique* 92, 162–169.

Catling, H. W. (1971) A Cypriot Bronze Statuette in the Bomford Collection. In Schaeffer 1971, 15–32.

Catling, H. W. (1979) The St. Andrews-Liverpool Museums Kouklia Tomb Excavation. *Report of the Department of Antiquities, Cyprus*, 270–275.

Catling, H. W. (1984) Workshop and Heirloom: Prehistoric Bronze Stands in the East Mediterranean. *Report of the Department of Antiquities, Cyprus*, 69–91.

Coldstream, J. N. (1989) Status Symbols in Cyprus in the Eleventh Century BC. In E. J. Peltenburg (ed.), *Early Society in Cyprus*, 325–335. Edinburgh, Edinburgh University Press.

Coldstream, J. N. (1994) What Sort of Aegean Migration? In V. Karageorghis (ed.), *Proceedings of the International Symposium: Cyprus in the 11th Century BC*, 143–147. Nicosia, Leventis Foundation.

Courtois, J.-C. (1971) Le sanctuaire du dieu au lingot d'Enkomi-Alasia. In Schaeffer 1971, 151–362.

Courtois, J.-C. and Webb, J. M. (1987) *Les Cylindres-Sceaux d'Enkomi (Fouilles Francaises 1957–1970).* Nicosia, Mission Archeologique Francaise d'Alasia, Zavallis Press.

Cusick, J. G. (1998a) *Studies in Culture Contact: Interaction, Culture Change and Archaeology.* Center for Archaeological Investigations Occasional Paper 25. Carbondale, Southern Illinois University Press.

Cusick, J. G. (1998b) Historiography of Acculturation: An Evaluation of Concepts and Their Application in Archaeology. In Cusick 1998a, 126–145.

DeMarrais, E., Gosden, C. and Renfrew, C. (2005) *Rethinking Materiality: Engagement of Mind with Material World.* Cambridge, Macdonald Institute.

Desborough, V. R. D' A. (1964) *The Last Mycenaeans and their Successors.* Oxford, Clarendon Press.

Dietler, M. (1998) Consumption, Agency, and Cultural Entanglement: Theoretical Implications of a Mediterranean Colonial Encounter. In Cusick 1998a, 288–315.

Dietler, M. (2005) The Archaeology of Colonization and the Colonization of Archaeology: Theoretical Challenges from an Ancient Mediterranean Colonial Encounter. In Stein 2005, 33–68.

Dikaios, P. (1962) The Bronze Statuette of a Horned God from Enkomi. *Archäologischer Anzeiger*, 1–39.

Dikaios, P. (1969–1971) *Enkomi. Excavations 1948–1958.* 3 Volumes. Philip von Zabern, Mainz.

Dothan, T. and Ben-Tor, A. (1983) *Excavations at Athienou, Cyprus.* Qedem 16. Jerusalem, Hebrew University, Institute of Archaeology.

Feldman, M. H. (2006) *Diplomacy by Design: Luxury Arts and an 'International Style' in the Ancient Near East, 1400–1200 BCE.* Chicago, University of Chicago Press.

Fisher, K. D. (2009) Elite Place-Making and Social Interaction in the Late Cypriot Bronze Age. *Journal of Mediterranean Archaeology* 22, 183–210.

Franken, H. J. (1992) *Excavations at Tell Deir 'Alla: The Late Bronze Age Sanctuary.* Peeters, Louvain.

Friedman, J. (1997) Global Crises, the Struggle for Cultural Identity and Intellectual Porkbarrelling: Cosmopolitans Versus Locals, Ethnics and Nationals in an Era of Dehegemonisation. In P. Werbner and T. Modood (eds), *Debating Cultural Hybridity: Multi-cultural Identities and the Politics of Anti-racism*, 70–89. London, Zed Books.

Furumark, A. (1944) The Mycenaean IIIC Pottery and its Relation to Cypriot Fabrics. *Opuscula Archaeologica* 3, 194–265.

Gjerstad, E., Lindos, J., Sjöqvist, E. and Westholm, A. (1934) *Swedish Cyprus Expedition I, II: Finds and Results of the Excavations in Cyprus 1927–1931.* Stockholm, Swedish Cyprus Expedition.

Hadjisavvas, S. (2009) Aspects of Regionalism in Late Cypriot Architecture. In I. Hein (ed.), *The Formation of Cyprus in the 2nd Millennium B.C. Studies in Regionalism during the Middle and Late Bronze Ages.* Österreichische Akademie Der Wissenschaften, Denkschriften Der Gesamtakademie 52, 127–133. Wien, Österreichische Akademie Der Wissenschaften.

Hendon, J. A. (2007) Memory, Materiality, and Practice: House Societies in Southeastern Mesoamerica. In R. A. Beck, Jr. (ed.), *The Durable House: House Society Models in Archaeology.* Center for Archaeological Investigations, Occasional Paper 35, 292–316. Carbondale, Illinois, Southern Illinois University Press.

Horden, P. and Purcell, N. (2000) *The Corrupting Sea: A Study of Mediterranean History.* Oxford, Blackwell.

Iacovou, M. (1988) *The Pictorial Pottery of Eleventh Century B.C. Cyprus.* Studies in Mediterranean Archaeology 79. Göteborg, P. Åström's Förlag.

Iacovou, M. (1991) Proto-White Painted Pottery: A Classification of the Ware. Cypriot Sequence. In Barlow, Bolger and Kling 1991, 199–205.

Iacovou, M. (1999a) The Greek Exodus to Cyprus: The Antiquity of Hellenism. *Mediterranean Historical Review* 14(2), 1–28.

Iacovou, M. (1999b) Excerpta Cypria Geometrica: Materials for a History of Geometric Cyprus. In M. Iacovou and D. Michaelides (eds), *Cyprus: The Historicity of the Geometric Horizon*, 141–166. Nicosia, Archaeological Research Unit, University of Cyprus; Bank of Cyprus Cultural Foundation, Ministry of Education and Culture.

Iacovou, M. (2002) From Ten to Naught: Formation, Consolidation and Abolition of Cyprus' Iron Age polities. *Cahier du Centre d'Études Chypriotes* 32, 73–87.

Jung, R. (2009) Pirates of the Aegean: Italy – the East Aegean – Cyprus at the End of the Second Millennium BC. In V. Karageorghis and O. Kouka (eds), *Cypus and the East Aegean: Intercultural Contacts from 3000 to 500 BC*, 72–93. Nicosia, Leventis Foundation.

Kantor, H. J. (1947) *The Aegean and the Orient in the Second Millennium B.C.* Archaeological Institute of America, Monograph 1. Bloomington, Indiana, Archaeological Institute of America.

Karageorghis, V. (1965) *Nouveaux documents pour l'étude du Bronze Récent a Chypre*. Paris, Éditions E. de Boccard.

Karageorghis, V. (1968) *Mycenaean Art from Cyprus*. Nicosia, Department of Antiquities, Cyprus.

Karageorghis, V. (1974) *Excavations at Kition I. The Tombs*. Nicosia, Department of Antiquities.

Karageorghis, V. (1979) Kypriaka IV: A 12th Century Bronze Stand from Cyprus. *Report of the Department of Antiquities, Cyprus*, 203–208.

Karageorghis, V. (1985) Kition Ivories and Various Bone Objects. In V. Karageorghis, *Excavations at Kition V (2). The Pre-Phoenician Levels*, 329–339. Nicosia, Department of Antiquities.

Karageorghis, V. (1986) 'Barbarian' Ware in Cyprus. In V. Karageorghis (ed.), *Acts of the International Archaeological Symposium: Cyprus between the Orient and the Occident*, 246–264. Nicosia, Department of Antiquities.

Karageorghis, V. (1990) *The End of the Late Bronze Age in Cyprus*. Nicosia, Pierides Foundation.

Karageorghis, V. (2000) Cultural Innovations in Cyprus Relating to the Sea Peoples. In Oren 2000, 255–279.

Karageorghis, V. (2002) *Early Cyprus: Crossroads of the Mediterranean*. Los Angeles, J. Paul Getty Museum.

Karageorghis, V., Coldstream, J. N., Bikai, P. M., Johnston, A. W., Robertson, M. and Jehasse, L. (1981) *Excavations at Kition IV. The Non-Cypriote Pottery*. Nicosia, Department of Antiquities, Cyprus.

Karageorghis, V. and Demas, M. (1985) *Excavations at Kition V. The Pre-Phoenician Levels*. Nicosia, Department of Antiquities, Cyprus.

Karageorghis, V. and Papasavvas, G. (2001) A Bronze Ingot-bearer from Cyprus. *Oxford Journal of Archaeology* 20, 339–354.

Kassianidou, V. (2005) Was Copper Production under Divine Protection in Late Bronze Age Cyprus? Some Thoughts on an Old Question. In V. Karageorghis, H. Matthäus and S. Rogge (eds), *Cyprus: Religion and Society from the Late Bronze Age to the End of the Archaic Period*, 127–141. Möhnesee-Wamel, Biblipolis.

Keswani, P. S. (1989) Dimensions of Social Hierarchy in Late Bronze Age Cyprus: An Analysis of the Mortuary Data from Enkomi. *Journal of Mediterranean Archaeology* 2, 49–86.

Keswani, P. S. (2004) *Mortuary Ritual and Society in Bronze Age Cyprus*. Monographs in Mediterranean Archaeology 9. London, Equinox.

Kling, B. (1987) Pottery Classification and Relative Chronology of the LCIIC–LCIIIA Periods. In D. A. Rupp (ed.), *Western Cyprus: Connections*. Studies in Mediterranean Archaeology 77, 97–113. Göteborg, P. Åström's Förlag.

Kling, B. (1988) The Strainer Jug from Kouklia Tomb KA1: A Stylistic Hybrid. *Report of the Department of Antiquities, Cyprus*, 271–274.

Kling, B. (1989a) Local Cypriot Features in the Ceramics of the Late Cypriot IIIA Period. In Peltenburg 1989, 153–159.

Kling, B. (1989b) *Mycenaean IIIC:1b and Related Pottery in Cyprus*. Studies in Mediterranean Archaeology 87. Göteborg, P. Åström's Förlag.

Kling, B. (1991) A Terminology for the Matte-painted, Wheel-made Pottery of Late Cypriot IIC–IIIA. In Barlow, Bolger and Kling 1991, 181–184.

Kling, B. (2000) Mycenaean IIIC:1b and Related Pottery in Cyprus: Comments on the Current State of Research. In Oren 2000, 281–295.

Knapp, A. B. (1986) *Copper Production and Divine Protection: Archaeology, Ideology and Social Complexity on Bronze Age Cyprus*. Studies in Mediterranean Archaeology, Pocketbook 42. Göteborg, P. Åström's Förlag.

Knapp, A. B. (2008) *Prehistoric and Protohistoric Cyprus: Identity, Insularity and Connectivity*. Oxford, Oxford University Press.

Knapp, A. B. (2009) Monumental Architecture, Identity and Memory. *Proceedings of the Symposium: Bronze Age Architectural Traditions in the East Mediterranean Diffusion and Diversity (Gasteig, Munich, 7–8 May, 2008)*, 47–59. Weilheim, Verein zur Förderung der Aufarbeitung der Hellenischen Geschichte.

Leriou, A. (2007) Locating Identities in the Eastern Mediterranean during the Late Bronze Age–Early Iron Age: The case of 'Hellenised' Cyprus. In Antoniadou and Pace, 2007, 563–591.

Maeir, A. M. and Miroschedji, P. (2006) *'I Will Speak the Riddle of Ancient Times': Archaeological and Historical Studies in Honor of Amihai Mazar on the Occasion of his Sixtieth Birthday*. Winona Lake, Indiana, Eisenbrauns.

Maier, F.-G. and Karageorghis, V. (1984) *Paphos: History and Archaeology*. Nicosia, Leventis Foundation.

Manning, S. W. and Hulin, L. (2005) Maritime Commerce

and Geographies of Mobility in the Late Bronze Age of the Eastern Mediterranean: Problematizations. In E. Blake and A. B. Knapp (eds), *The Archaeology of Mediterranean Prehistory*, 275–307. Oxford, Blackwell.

Mattingly, D. J. (2002) Vulgar and Weak 'Romanization', or Time for a Paradigm Shift? *Journal of Roman Archaeology* 15, 536–540.

Meskell, L. (2005) *Archaeologies of Materiality*. Blackwell, Oxford.

Molloy, B. (2005) Naue II Swords and the Collapse of the Aegean Bronze Age. In C. Briault, J. Green, A. Kaldelis and A. Stellatou (eds), *SOMA 2003: Symposium on Mediterranean Archaeology*. British Archaeological Reports, International Series 1391, 115–117. Oxford, Archaeopress.

Mountjoy, P. A. (2005) The End of the Bronze Age at Enkomi, Cyprus: The Problem of Level IIIB. *Annual of the British School at Athens* 100, 125–214.

Muhly, J. D. (1980) Bronze Figurines and Near Eastern Metalwork. *Israel Exploration Journal* 30, 148–161.

Muhly, J. D. (1984) The Role of the Sea Peoples in Cyprus during the LCIII Period. In V. Karageorghis and J. D. Muhly (eds), *Cyprus at the Close of the Late Bronze Age*, 39–55. Nicosia, Leventis Foundation.

Murray, A. S., Smith, A. H. and Walters, H. B. (1900) *Excavations in Cyprus*. London, British Museum Publications.

Nederveen Pieterse, J. (1995) Globalization as Hybridization. In M. Featherstone, L. Lash and R. Robertson (eds), *Global Modernities* (Theory, Culture and Society), 45–68. London, Sage.

Negbi, O. (2005) Urbanism on Late Bronze Age Cyprus: LC II in Retrospect. *Bulletin of the American Schools of Oriental Research* 337, 1–45.

Oren, E. D. (2000) *The Sea Peoples and Their World: A Reassessment.* University Museum Monograph 108, University Museum Symposium Series 11. Philadelphia, University Museum, University of Pennsylvania.

Papasavvas, G. (2001) *Bronze Stands from Cyprus and Crete*. (in Greek, with English Summary) Nicosia, Leventis Foundation.

Papasavvas, G. (2011) From Smiting into Smithing: The Transformation of a Cypriot God. In P. P. Betancourt and S. C. Ferrence (eds), *Metallurgy: Understanding How, Learning Why. Studies in Honor of James D. Muhly*. Philadelphia, Institute for Aegean Prehistory Press.

Peltenburg, E. J. (1974) The Glazed Vases (Including a Polychrome Rhyton). Appendix I. In V. Karageorghis (ed.), *Excavations at Kition I. The Tombs*, 105–144. Nicosia, Department of Antiquities.

Peltenburg, E. J. (1986) Ramesside Egypt and Cyprus. In V. Karageorghis (ed.), *Cyprus between the Orient and the Occident*, 149–179. Nicosia, Department of Antiquities, Cyprus.

Peltenburg, E. J. (1989) *Early Society in Cyprus*. Edinburgh, Edinburgh University Press.

Peltenburg, E. J. (2002) East Mediterranean Faience: Changing Patterns of Production and Exchange at the End of the 2nd Millenniuim BC. In E. A. Braun-Holzinger and H. Matthäus (eds), *Die nahöstlichen Kulturen und Griechenland an der Wende vom 2 zum 1 Jahrtausend v. Chr.*, 75–107. Möhnesee, Bibliopolis.

Peltenburg, E. J. (2007) Hathor, Faience and Copper on Late Bronze Age Cyprus. *Cahier du Centre d'Études Chypriotes* 337, 375–394.

Pierides, A. (1973) Observations on Some Mycenaean Ivories from Cyprus. In V. Karageorghis (ed.), *Acts of the International Archaeological Symposium: The Mycenaeans in the Eastern Mediterranean*, 274–277. Nicosia: Department of Antiquities.

Pilides, D. (1991) Handmade Burnished Wares of the Late Bronze Age: Toward a Clearer Classification System. In Barlow, Bolger and Kling 1991, 139–150.

Pilides, D. (1994) *Handmade Burnished Wares of the Late Bronze Age in Cyprus*. Studies in Mediterranean Archaeology 105. Jonsered, P. Åström's Förlag.

Poursat, J.-C. (1977) *Les ivoires myceniens*. Athens, Paris, École Française d'Athènes.

Rupp, D.W. (1989) Puttin' on the Ritz: Manifestations of High Status in Iron Age Cyprus. In Peltenburg 1989, 336–362.

Russell, A. (2011) In the Middle of the Corrupting Sea: Cultural Encounters in the Sicily and Sardinia between 1450–900 BC. Unpublished PhD dissertation, Department of Archaeology, University of Glasgow.

Schaeffer, C. F. A. (1971) *Alasia I*. Mission Archéologique d'Alasia 4. Paris, Klincksieck.

Seeden, H. (1981) *The Standing Armed Figurines in the Levant*. Praehistorische Bronzefunde, Abteilung 1, Band 1. Munich, Beck.

Sherratt, E. S. (1991) Cypriot Pottery of Aegean Type in LCII–III: Problems of Classification, Chronology and Interpretation. In Barlow, Bolger and Kling 1991, 185–198.

Sherratt, E. S. (1992) Immigration and Archaeology: Some Indirect Reflections. In P. Åström (ed.), *Acta Cypria* 2, *Acts of an International Congress on Cypriote Archaeology held in Goteborg (22–24 August 1991).* Studies in Mediterranean Archaeology and Literature, Pocketbook 117, 316–347. Jonsered, P. Åström's Förlag.

Sherratt, E. S. (1994) Patterns of Contact Between the Aegean and Cyprus in the 13th and 12th Centuries BC. *Archaeologia Cypria* 3, 35–46.

Sherratt, E. S. (1998) 'Sea Peoples' and the Economic Structure of the Late Second Millennium in the Eastern Mediterranean. In S. Gitin, A. Mazar and E. Stern (eds), *Mediterranean Peoples in Transition: Thirteenth to Tenth Centuries BCE*, 292–313 Jerusalem, Israel Exploration Society.

Sherratt, E. S. (1999) E pur si muove: Pots, Markets and Values in the Second Millennium Mediterranean. In J. P. Crielaard, V. Stissi and G. J. van Wijngaarden (eds), *The Complex Past of Pottery: Production, Circulation and Consumption of Mycenaean and Greek Pottery (sixteenth to early fifth centuries BC)*, 163–211. Amsterdam, J.C. Gieben.

Sjöqvist, E. (1940) *Problems of the Late Cypriote Bronze Age.* Swedish Cyprus Expedition, Stockholm.

Smith, J. S. (1994) Seals for Sealing in the Late Cypriot Period. Unpublished PhD dissertation, Bryn Mawr College, Bryn Mawr, Pennsylvania.

Smith, J. S. (2003) Writing Styles in Clay of the Eastern Mediterranean Bronze Age. In N. C. Stampolidis and V. Karageorghis (eds), *Ploes.. Sea Routes...: Interconnections in the Mediterranean, 16th–6th c. BC*, 277–290. Athens, University of Crete, Leventis Foundation.

Smith, J. S. (2007) Theme and Style in Cypriot Wooden Roller Impressions. *Cahier du Centre d'Études Chpriotes* 337, 347–374.

Smith, J. S. (2009) *Art and Society in Cyprus from the Bronze Age into the Iron Age*. Cambridge, Cambridge University Press.

Stager, L. (1995) The Impact of the Sea Peoples in Canaan (1185–1050 BCE). In T. E. Levy (ed.), *The Archaeology of Society in the Holy Land*, 332–348. Leicester, Leicester University Press.

Steel, L. (1998) The Social Impact of Mycenaean Imported Pottery on Cyprus. *Annual of the British School at Athens* 93, 285–296.

Steel, L. (2001) The British Museum and the Invention of the Cypriot Late Bronze Age. In V. Tatton-Brown (ed.), *Cyprus in the Nineteenth Century AD: Fact, Fancy and Fiction*, 160–167. Oxford, Oxbow Books.

Steel, L. (2004a) A Reappraisal of the Distribution, Context and Function of Mycenaean Pottery in Cyprus. In J. Balensi, J.-Y. Monchambert and S. Müller-Celku (eds), *La Ceramique Mycénienne de l'Egée au Levant*. Travaux de la Maison de l'Orient 41, 69–85. Lyon, Travaux de la Maison de l'Orient.

Steel, L. (2004b) *Cyprus Before History: From the Earliest Settlers to the End of the Bronze Age*. London, Duckworth.

Stein, G. J. (2005) *The Archaeology of Colonial Encounters.* Sante Fe, School of American Research Press.

Stockhammer, P. (2012) Conceptualizing Cultural Hybridization in Archaeology. In P. W. Stockhammer (ed.), *Conceptualizing Cultural Hybridization: A Transdisciplinary Approach*. Heidelberg Studies on Asia and Europe in a Global Context, 43–58. Berlin & Heidelberg, Springer Verlag.

Thomas, N. (1991) *Entangled Objects: Exchange, Material Culture, and Colonialism in the Pacific*. Cambridge, Massachusetts, Harvard University Press.

van Dommelen, P. (2005) Colonial Interactions and Hybrid Practices: Phoenician and Carthaginian Settlement in the Ancient Mediterranean. In Stein 2005, 109–141.

van Dommelen, P. (2006a) Colonial Matters: Material Culture and Postcolonial Theory in Colonial Situations. In C. Tilley, W. Keane, S. Küchler, M. Rowlands and P. Spyer (eds), *Handbook of Material Culture*, 104–124. London, Sage.

van Dommelen, P. (2006b) The Orientalising Phenomenon: Hybridity and Material Culture in the Western Mediterranean. In C. Riva and N. Vella (eds), *Debating Orientalization: Multidisciplinary Approaches to Change in the Ancient Mediterranean.* Monographs in Mediterranean Archaeology 10, 135–152. London, Equinox.

van Dommelen, P. and Knapp, A. B. (2010) *Material Connections in the Ancient Mediterranean. Mobility, Materiality and Identity*. London, Routledge.

van Wijngaarden, G. J. (2002) *Use and Appreciation of Mycenaean Pottery in the Levant, Cyprus and Italy*. Amsterdam, Amsterdam University Press.

van Wijngaarden, G. J. (2007) Sharing Material Culture? Mycenaeans in the Mediterranean. In Antoniadou and Pace 2007, 453–482.

Vives-Ferrándiz Sánchez, J. (2007) Colonial Encounters and the Negotiation of Identities in South-East Iberia. In Antoniadou and Pace 2007, 537–562.

Voskos, I. and Knapp, A. B. (2008) Cyprus at the End of the Late Bronze Age: Crisis and Colonization, or Continuity and Hybridization? *American Journal of Archaeology* 112, 659–684.

Webb, J. M. (1999) *Ritual Architecture, Iconography and Practice in the Late Cypriote Bronze Age.* Studies in Mediterranean Archaeology and Literature, Pocketbook 75. Jonsered, P. Åström's Förlag.

Webb, J. M. (2001) The Sanctuary of the Ingot God at Enkomi: A New Reading of its Construction, Use and Abandonment. In P. M. Fischer (ed.), *Contributions to the Archaeology and History of the Bronze and Iron Ages in the Eastern Mediterranean: Studies in Honour of Paul Åström.* Österreichisches Archäologisches Institut, Sonderschriften Band 39, 69–82. Wien, Österreichisches Archäologisches Institut.

Webb, J. M. (2002) Device, Image and Coercion. The Role of Glyptic in the Political Economy of Late Bronze Age Cyprus. In J. Smith (ed.), *Script and Seal Use on Cyprus in the Bronze and Iron Ages*. Archaeological Institute of America, Colloquia and Conference Papers 4, 111–154. Boston, American Institute of Archaeology.

Yannai, E. (2006) The Origin and Distribution of the Collared Rim Pithos and Krater: A Case of Conservative Pottery Production in the Ancient Near East from the Fourth to the First Millennium BCE. In Maeir and de Miroschedji 2006, 89–111.

Yon, M. (1985) Mission archéologique française de Kition-Bamboula 1976–1984. In V. Karageorghis (ed.), *Archaeology in Cyprus, 1960–1985*, 219–226. Nicosia, Leventis Foundation.

Yon, M. and Caubet, A. (1985) *Le Sondage L-N13. Bronze Récent et Géometrique*. Volume 1. Kition Bamboula III. Paris, Recherche sur les Civilisations.

6.

Encountering the foreign. (De-)constructing alterity in the archaeologies of the Bronze Age Mediterranean

Diamantis Panagiotopoulos

Introduction

In the thought-provoking comedy *The Gods Must Be Crazy* from 1980, a Coke bottle thrown from a passing plane lands in the middle of a San village in the Kalahari Desert that had hitherto no contact with the civilized world. This totally alien intruder becomes a one-of-a kind object and despite the fact that it acquires several different functions retains its absolute otherness until it is expelled from the village as an evil thing – and this is where the story actually begins. The short life of the Coke bottle in the San village exemplifies the way archaeologists – in most cases implicitly – have historically perceived foreign objects in the material record of a given culture. In traditional archaeological narratives, the perception of foreign imports in ancient cultures is reconstructed in a way that very much corresponds to a pattern of total alterity (or otherness): Imports are understood as alien objects, maintaining the value of their otherness from the very beginning to the very end of their use. As a result, they are regarded as clear testimonies for a transcultural attitude of their possessors or users.

The main objective of my paper is to show that this conventional wisdom is a very one-sided and simplistic approach that cannot reflect the manifold ways in which foreign items were sensed in their new cultural context. In the discussion that follows, I will attempt to take what seems to be a logical path from the general to the specific. At the very beginning, a cursory look at the history of research seems essential to identifying the advances and deficiencies of previous scholarship. The main part of my paper seeks, as a first step, to demonstrate that there are two different ways of dismantling the aforementioned traditional assumption concerning the status of 'total alterity' of imported objects. These two ways are related to a general and specific/contextual perspective. Next, I will focus on the second, specific level and deal with the two decisive stages in the biography of a foreign item: a) the moment of its entry into a new culture and b) its 'second' life after its cultural dislocation. In the brief treatment of both stages, and by putting an emphasis on the aspects of materiality and practice, I will attempt to show to what extent imported items emanated otherness. The key point of my approach will be that once foreign objects entered into the realm of a new culture, recognition of their otherness is often avoided and they become absorbed into people's lives, where they are no longer 'foreign' things, but part of an individual's personal possessions or expression of indigenous collective beliefs. Since this is nothing terribly new, I would like furthermore to argue that otherness is primarily not a matter of shape or function, but a matter of matter, *i.e.* the material of manufacture. My overall aim will thus be not to deny the alien character of foreign imports but to put them into a more proper perspective by suggesting that things are a bit more complicated than the traditional scholarly opinion has shown.

I must stress at the outset that this hypothesis refers to a specific matrix of historical factors and may, therefore, have a restricted theoretical validity: it is situated in the cultural context of maritime (and not land-based) interaction in the Late Bronze Age Eastern Mediterranean and is primarily related to objects and not images. As to the cultural context, the distance between foreign regions, the narrow and fragile channels of maritime contacts, and the very low percentage of a local population able to travel and experience a foreign culture created a very distinct field of possibilities with many limitations. Despite the desire for, and regular importation of, alien objects, knowledge of their original function and social significance must have been in many cases rather limited or even irrelevant, as argued below. As to the materiality of the 'foreign', my paper focuses not on images but on objects, because the tangible physical thingness of the latter played a significant role in the perception and treatment of foreign artifacts.

A brief retrospective

For the majority of the last century, the historical evaluation of foreign imports was based on the implication that a 'foreign' thing was a cultural intruder whose otherness was clearly distinguishable within a more or less homogeneous material culture. The identification of imports as such was based on visual analysis (raw material, technique, shape, decoration, and style). Inventories of foreign objects became very popular in Aegean archaeology providing a very solid foundation for the study of foreign contacts (Pendlebury 1930; Lambrou Phillipson 1990; Cline 1994; Phillips 2008). The main problem is, however, that these inventories have established a very simplistic frame of reference for the appraisal of cultural interaction. Most archaeologists compiling or using them adhered to the silent hypothesis that ancient people had the same sensitivity and awareness towards foreign objects as themselves. The definition of the term 'foreign' was, in principle, a matter of archaeological classification and not of ancient social practices. Bryan Burns (1999) was one of the first scholars who explicitly questioned the validity of these catalogues and their formal criteria by stressing the importance of ancient perception as a key factor for understanding the impact of foreign things in a given culture. A few years later, Eric Cline (2005) took up Burns' argument and attempted to explore what he described as the multivalent nature of imported objects. Cline raised some important issues, trying to take full advantage of Burns' critical remarks, for instance the questions of at what point in its journey does an export become an import, how its status and value can change, or whether there is an overlap between its old and new function or meaning. An attempt to arrive at more precise definition of an 'import' has been also undertaken by Robert Laffineur (1990–1991; 2005) who questioned the simplistic dichotomy between imports and local production in favor of a wider and more varied classification dependent on the individual components of an object, such as material, technique, shape and decoration, style and meaning or function. The recent awareness towards the issue of how foreign objects were actually experienced after their cultural dislocation coincides with a major shift of interest in the field of social disciplines from the production/creation to the perception, appreciation and consumption/use of objects, craftwork, and images. This new concern about the phenomenological aspects of material culture, which is nourished by the concepts of materiality and practice, has already had a tangible impact on Aegean archaeology (Cline 2005, 49; van Wijngaarden 2003; Barrett 2009; Burns 2010) making the one-sidedness of the aforementioned traditional approach even more apparent. There are actually two ways to attack the conventional understanding of foreign objects: on a general and on a specific level.

On a general level, the conventional understanding of imports is founded on a series of highly problematic terms such as identity (Meskell 2001; Diaz-Andreu *et al.* 2005; Gamble 2007; Insoll 2006; Leerssen 2007), ethnicity (Jones 1997; MacSweeney 2009; Eriksen 2010), alterity (Welz 2005) and hybridity (Bhabha 1994; Burke 2009; Kapchan and Strong 1999). Their definition as constant and static categories rests not on historical facts but rather on modern constructs. The normative construction of identity as a homogeneous, self-contained entity at a personal or communal level does not reflect the historical reality, it distorts it. The underlying assumption that, at some fundamental level, there must have been ideal-typical groups whose identity was internally undifferentiated and homogeneous, is highly problematic. Recent research in quite different fields of social sciences has shown however that identity is not a static, but rather a dynamic value, a life-long project of coming to terms with constantly changing situations. The essentialist idea of a single identity for one culture or the related notion of ethnicity tends *per definitionem* to connote a category that is unchangeable and permanent through time. A dynamic conception of group identity (MacSweeny 2009, 105; Burns 2010, 70–72) putting an emphasis on its highly volatile character provides a much more sensitive theoretical model. This has been aptly posited by Joep Leerssen (2007, 337, 338):

> 'Group identity is at all times the result of a balancing process, where the internal cohesion and external distinctness of the group outweigh the group's internal diversity and its external similarities... A group's identity changes over time and contains within itself potential or actual diversities'.

In spite of being an individual, one can associate with or participate in a diversity of groups (Leerssen 2007, 338). The rejection of identity or single culture as fixed categories unavoidably makes the notions of alterity and hybridity obsolete, or at least not very fruitful (Welz 2005, 1, 20). Nothing can better illustrate the problems which arise from a normative construction of identity and culture in the Aegean context than the rich burial assemblages of the Shaft Graves at Mycenae (Karo 1930; Mylonas 1972–1973; Vermeule 1975; Laffineur 1990–1991; Burns 2010, 88–94). In this case, it would be very naïve to assume that the archaeologists'

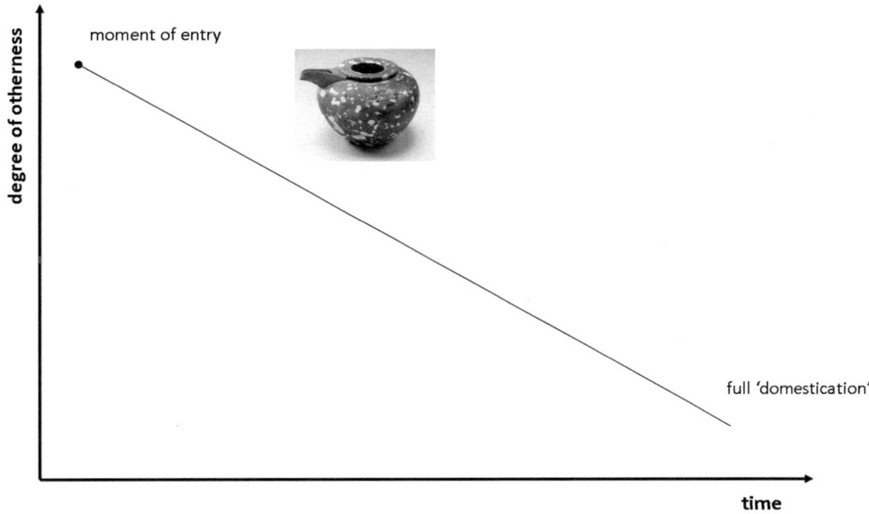

Fig. 6.1: An imaginary curve of otherness.

classification of these prestige items as local vs. foreign can reflect the various ways in which they were experienced by the local audience, even if this classification is correct, which is at least in some cases doubtful (Laffineur 1990–1991, 287–289). These objects, which were either imported from abroad or locally manufactured under foreign influence, expressed – as a whole – a transient group identity in the formative period of what we call Mycenaean culture.

These general observations challenging the methodological validity of some monolithic sociological concepts can be supplemented by a contextual approach, focusing on a specific cultural setting. A straightforward statement by Burns (1999, 48) provides a good starting point for the further exploration of the manifold ways in which Late Bronze societies in the Eastern Mediterranean experienced alterity:

> 'The items that are "foreign" enough to persuade the modern scholar are likely to have been recognised as such in antiquity as well. Although the parties involved in the actual transport of an object might know its origin, it is the perception of an object as foreign that was essential to its operation as an import. But not all imported items are so easily recognized by their material or style'.

Even if it is – at least in my view – very likely that the modern scholar can more easily distinguish between 'local' and 'foreign' than any ancient consumer (who had only limited knowledge of the artistic production of neighbouring cultures), we must concede that the latter were in most cases able to recognise an import as something 'non-local'. Burns' emphasis on the dichotomy between reality and perception, as well as on the low visibility of specific imports as alien objects, provides a solid basis for a closer look at the biography of these exotica in their new cultural frame. By discussing these issues, I would like to focus on the two aforementioned stages: the objects' entry into a new cultural sphere, and their 'second' life in their new environment.

Crossing cultural borders

There can be no doubt that imports possessed the highest possible degree of visibility as foreign things at their time of entry into a new culture. In this liminal stage, the import was still a foreign object, neither embedded into a local system of things and practices, nor invested with a new indigenous function and symbolic meaning. In an imaginary graph of otherness, the moment of the import's entry into a new culture would represent the absolute peak of the graph (Fig. 6.1). From there, the graph would fall continuously – and maybe sharply – down to its bottom indicating the stage of the complete 'domestication' of the object in terms of perception and social practice. Burns (2010, 192) has rightly emphasised that the only short-lived appeal of some foreign goods was due to their regular importation in substantial quantities. A further, almost self-evident, yet decisive reason for the gradual fading of an import's magnetism must have been their intensive use in indigenous social practices. This process is more tangible in the case of images rather than objects. A very telling example for the gradual 'domestication' of an import provides the development of the Egyptian Taweret into the Minoan Genius (Weingarten 1991; 2000; Rehak 1995; Panagiotopoulos 2004, 41; Phillips 2008, 156–167). There can be no doubt that from a certain point onward,

Fig. 6.2: Arrival of Syro-Palestinian ships in the port of Thebes. Tomb of Kenamun, TT 162 (after Davies and Faulkner 1947, pl. VIII).

this fantastic creature was perceived as a totally indigenous demon whose origins lay not in a foreign country, but in local religious tradition. Similar assimilation processes must have been experienced by many imported objects, which, through a long history of use, became part of Aegean realities. One cannot deny, of course, that at the same time they maintained at least a portion of a foreign object's mysticism. Therefore, the gradient of our imaginary graph was obviously determined by the constant tension between the import's integration into local social practices and its alien virility.

The peak and the downward slope of this imaginary graph deserve a closer look. There were at least three different ways of entry that produced quite different circumstances for the visual perception and consciousness of a foreign import. The vast majority of the goods circulating among different cultures and crossing their borders were mobilised through the economic, non-ceremonial channels of commercial exchange. It is worthwhile to attempt a more detailed reconstruction of the possible context of their first appearance in a new culture. In long-distance maritime trade, we deal with two different patterns of exchange: 1) a well organised directional trade operating at long distances and conducted only by major political or mercantile institutions and 2) a small scale down-the-line trade that was a ubiquitous phenomenon in every Mediterranean port throughout the ages. Both types of commercial exchange are possibly illustrated in the famous scene of the arrival of Syro-Palestinian ships in the port of Thebes in the tomb of Kenamun (Fig. 6.2), who served as Mayor of Thebes and Superintendent of the Granaries of Amun probably under Amenhotep III (Davies and Faulkner 1947; Kemp 2006, 324; Wachsmann 1998, 42–47). The bulk of the ships' cargo, including several Canaanite jars, bowls, metal vases, two women with a boy, and two humped bulls, was obviously mobilised in the context of directional trade, or alternatively, as annual 'contributions', *i.e.* as fulfilment of a vassal's material obligation to his king (Davies and Faulkner 1947, 45, pl. VIII; Panagiotopoulos 2000, 141–144, 147–152; 2006, 373–376). Despite the fact that the economic or administrative context of this shipment cannot be defined with certainty, there can be no doubt that its final destination must have been the storehouse of the palace or the temple. The part of the discharged cargo that passed the pier was purchased by Kenamun and disappeared into the magazines of one of the two aforementioned institutions for which the tomb owner acted as agent or representative. It is important to stress here that imported foreign goods that arrived at their destination in the course of an organised trade – and that must have been a considerable amount of seaborne commercial exchange – reached their future owner directly and made their first appearance in their new cultural frame in the possession of a local person, group, or authority, already embedded in indigenous social practices. The same applies for the Syro-Palestinian goods that reached Egypt as part of the annual 'contributions'. The wall painting in Kenamun's tomb illustrates, however, another method of entry. The Syro-Palestinian merchants and sailors engaged themselves in commercial transactions with Egyptians shopkeepers, who sat behind small shelters and offered for sale a range of local goods including textiles, sandals, and food (Davies and Faulkner 1947, 45–46). In the vibrant Mediterranean ports, this act of exchange was undoubtedly a spectacle witnessed by merchants, sailors, potential buyers, and probably also artists and craftsmen, who were eager to gaze at the exotica as a potential source of inspiration. These foreign items certainly enjoyed high visibility, even if they were mixed with objects manufactured locally or in less distant regions. However, most of these objects had dubious biographies. The still popular belief that the transmission of cultural knowledge was heavily determined by the explicit or tacit knowledge of the individuals actively involved in cultural interaction (in this case sailors and merchants) is a rather romantic view, since the primary motivation of these persons was nothing other than profit. Given the fact that obviously none of these goods bore a sealing or 'brand' (Wengrow 2008; 2010; Bevan

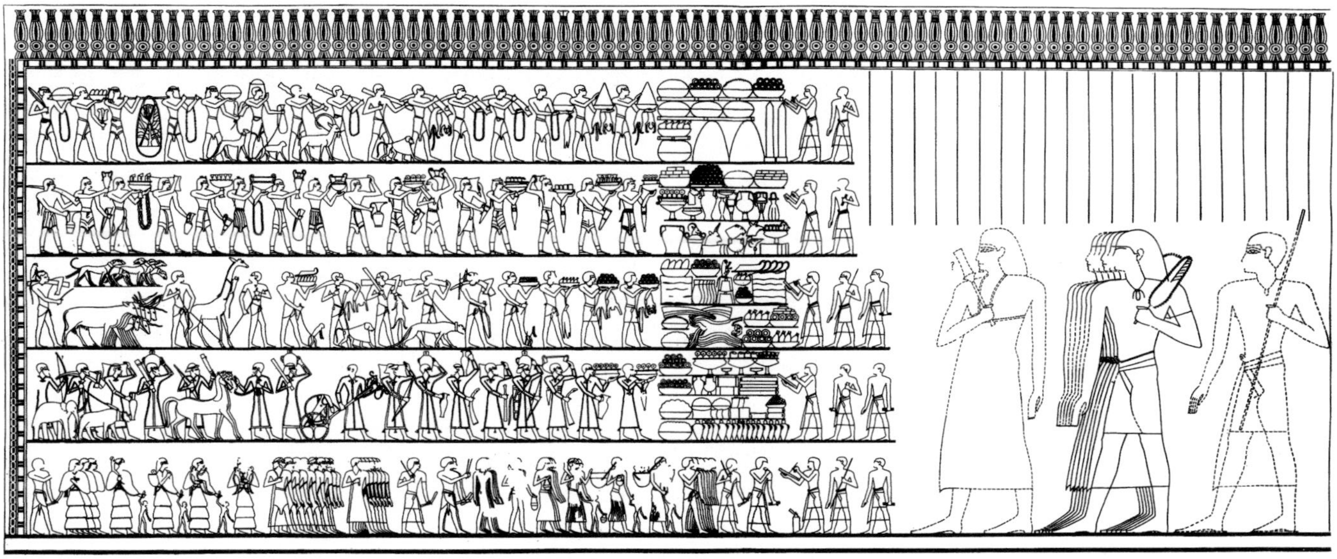

Fig. 6.3: Presentation of foreign gifts in the tomb of Rechmire, TT 100 (after Wachsmann 1987, pl. 40).

2010) documenting the producer or place of manufacture, their price depended largely on the stories the sellers not only knew but also fabricated. Oscar Wilde's definition of a cynic might reflect in a certain way the doubtful competence and coarse motives of these agents of commercial exchange: 'A man who knows the price of everything and the value of nothing'. The dubious competence of sailors and merchants in transmitting cultural knowledge must have determined, to a certain degree, the reaction of the local audience to a foreign object. To sum up, the specific conditions at the moment of entry of foreign goods into a new culture affected in several ways their inherent value of otherness. Many of these either had low or no visibility during their importation or possessed obscure biographies and thus a more abstract value of alterity.

The foreign objects that formed the core of the diplomatic gift-exchange reached the highest possible degree of visibility at the moment of their entry into a new culture, since they were the focus of the dazzling state ceremonies in Late Bronze Age royal courts. These ceremonies are illustrated with great wealth of detail in the Theban private tombs of the 18th Dynasty (Fig. 6.3) and several kindred written documents (Panagiotopoulos 2001; Panagiotopoulos 2008; Hallmann 2006). During these ceremonial acts, the foreign gifts were not only carried, but properly exposed and demonstrated as the pertinent images and texts make apparent. The atmosphere of these audiences is vividly illustrated in a model letter of the Papyrus Koller dating in the Ramesside period. Here, the Egyptian viceroy of Nubia writes to a subordinate official:

> 'Remember the day of bringing the gifts (*inw*), when you pass into the Presence beneath the Window, the nobles in two rows in the presence of His Majesty (may he live, be prosperous, be healthy), the chiefs and envoys of every foreign land standing dazzled at seeing the gifts (*inw*)' (following Caminos 1954, 438–439, 5:1–3; further Panagiotopoulos 2001, 269).

It is striking, however, that even at this moment equivalent to the absolute peak in our imaginary graph of alterity, the alien character of these objects was compromised by the presence of local valuables. In some cases, the foreign embassies are carrying not only their own products, but also Egyptian items (Wachsmann 1987, 67–68, 75–76). According to traditional archaeological opinion, this mixing of foreign goods with Egyptian objects was due to artistic conventions and thus not meaningful. I am not quite sure whether this is true: this is a rather convenient solution to explain what we think to be an Egyptian mistake or incautiousness as a matter of artistic expression and not a matter of cultural attitude. There can be only two possibilities to explain this phenomenon: the Egyptians were either incapable of distinguishing between foreign and indigenous objects or indifferent to doing so. In either case, the mixing of both groups of objects was meaningful, since the foreign objects lost a significant portion of their otherness. The levelling of foreign and local valuables could be furthermore an indication that the act of giving was more significant than the prestige objects themselves or their place of origin.

A similar explanation can be given to the regular depiction of culturally hybrid objects in the same tomb scenes. In several cases, artistic elements taken from different sources are combined for the creation of non-existing vessels of mixed ethnic origin (Wachsmann 1987, 4, 5, 49–77). Behind this apparent case of iconographical convention, we may again suspect an Egyptian incapability or indifference to distinguishing clearly between foreign artistic traditions. An intriguing text from the 18th Dynasty seems, at first glance, to provide clear contradictory evidence to this arbitrary mixing of different cultural elements, implying a thorough knowledge of the artistic production of foreign countries. In an entry from the 37th Year of the 'Annals' of Thutmose III the gifts from Tanaja, very probably Mycenaean Greece or a single Mycenaean centre, are registered as follows:

> 'Gifts (*inw*) from the prince of Tanaja: a silver shawabti-vessel in *Keftiu* workmanship together with four bowls of iron (copper?) with handles of silver. Total: 56 *deben* 4 *kite'* (following Cline 1994, 114, A.32)

The surprising aspect in this brief entry is the indication that the vases brought by the representative of a Greek mainland centre were manufactured in *Keftiu* (Cretan) style. Is it plausible to ascribe this precise stylistic attribution to the educated eyes of an Egyptian official who was responsible for the registration of the foreign goods delivered to the Egyptian court? Did he indeed recognise in these vessels a Minoan origin or influence? Even if this option cannot be fully excluded, I am rather inclined to believe that the Egyptian scribe was very probably copying this list of Mycenaean gifts from a letter of the king of *Tanaja* to his Egyptian partner. In the letter, an indispensible prerequisite of diplomatic gift-exchange, the Mycenaean gifts must have been already mentioned as manufactured in '*Keftiu* style', what seems to have been a *terminus technicus* that survived in its Greek version (*ke-re-si-jo we-ke* = 'of Cretan manufacture') till the age of the Linear B tablets (Ventris and Chadwick 1973, 336). Should this be true, then the precise stylistic attribution of imported items by an Egyptian scribe must not necessarily imply good knowledge of foreign artistic traditions.

The 'second' life of an object

As it has been already indicated, the experience, possession, and use of objects that archaeologists habitually classify as foreign imports did not necessarily evoke the idea of otherness. Most of these objects were, from the beginning of their 'second' life in a new culture, embedded in indigenous codices of communication and practice. Through this embedding, their alien character was superseded by further roles, qualities, and functions and gradually faded. Therefore, otherness can be in many cases determined as an only ephemeral quality of foreign goods.

Let us again pick up the thread of the prestige objects that stood in the centre of the state ceremonies at the Egyptian royal court and try to follow their track within Egypt. It is obvious that most of these prestige items either remained stored in the royal magazines as part of the Pharaoh's symbolic capital, or circulated in channels of exclusively ceremonial character (gifts to other rulers, or the Egyptian high officials, offerings to temples). There can be little doubt that these items were appreciated at their final destination (in a temple or in the possession of a high official) not as exotic objects but mainly as royal gifts demonstrating the recipient's high status and bond with the Pharaoh. Their value of otherness was obviously superseded by another symbolic value that in the Egyptian context was apparently much more significant. The distribution of foreign stone vases in the elite houses of Knossos (Warren 1991) may be linked with a similar social practice. Only in this way is it possible to offer a plausible explanation for the context of the alabaster amphora of Thutmose III in the Katsambas tomb near Knossos (Karetsou 2000, 220–221; Phillips 2008, 67, no. 114). If we assume that at least some of these vases were gifts from the Knossian ruler to the members of his elite, then they must have been experienced first and foremost as royal offerings and only additionally as goods of exotic provenance. To put it in very simple words, these exotica must have been regarded primarily as precious and not alien. Their possession and use denoted high status but not necessarily a transcultural attitude.

The second life of an object in a new culture was determined by the aforementioned tension between compatibility (or the need for compatibility) and otherness (or the desire for otherness). I am certainly not suggesting something new here but reiterating the self-evident by arguing that the need for compatibility with domestic practices affected the design and use of an import, whereas the sustained visibility of its otherness derived from its material. Despite the popular belief among archaeologists that imported objects induced their new users to adapt the acts of consumption in which these objects were embedded in their place of origin, it seems to me more plausible that, in most cases, it was not the thing dictating a new behaviour to the local user, but the user giving the thing a new function and symbolic value. The self-acting subject proceeded inventively in his reuse of a foreign artefact driven by his desire to solve a problem or to adjust the import to a local need. There are two main types of this transformative behaviour towards imported objects: reversible and an irreversible use. In the case of reversible use, we deal with an object that is temporarily or permanently used in a new context, without being converted of its original condition and function. Two good illustrations from modern every life are a jam jar used as a pencil holder or a chair – one of the most multivalent object of everyday

Fig. 6.4: Egyptian alabaster vase from Shaft Grave V at Mycenae (after Karo 1930, pl. CXXXVII).

life – used as hallstand, TV stand, table *etc* . Reversible use is unfortunately virtually invisible in the archaeological record. The second type refers to an irreversible use, *i. e.* an object that has to be permanently changed to suit the new taste or new application. The irreversible redesign of imported items is well documented in the archaeological evidence, for example, the imported ostrich egg rhyta that were embellished with faience fittings by Aegean artists (Sakellarakis 1990; Laffineur 2005, 54–55; Phillips 2008, 80–88; Burns 2010, 94). The same transformative impulse in the encounter of Aegean artists with exotic design also left its traces on some imported stone vessels. They converted them to shapes that better suited local needs and/or aesthetic demands by modifying the vessel's mouth, surface, and base, removing handles, and giving them new attachments (Warren 1997; Karetsou 2000, 207–209, nos. 207–208; Bevan 2007, 125, fig. 6.16). In the case of an Egyptian alabaster vessel from Mycenae (Fig. 6.4), the import's original design was literally turned upside down: the original base was cut out to form the new mouth, the original mouth was plugged to create a solid base, and wooden handles and a separate spout were attached (Warren 1997, 211; Panagiotopoulos 2004, 41–41, fig. 13; Laffineur 2005, 55; Burns 2010, 94). In these instances, the otherness of the foreign import gradually faded through redesign and regular use. Its exotic character was covered, or, better still, tamed by local acts of display and consumption. But even if the design of a foreign import remained unmodified, it is legitimate to assume that its alien character gradually diminished. In Late Bronze Age Eastern Mediterranean societies, in an age lacking registered trademarks, design had no clear pedigrees. Local craftspeople imitated willingly foreign design, not always driven by a mimetic attitude, but striving to create something new, innovative, different, and thus appealing for the local market. One may further imagine that in a sort of a reflexive process the mimesis of the original through the regular production of local copies affected the original itself, leading to the domestication of its alien design and gradually transforming the foreign shape into something familiar. There can be no doubt that after some years, the local manufacture of 'Egyptianising' amphorae in Minoan Crete (Cucuzza 2000; Karetsou 2000, 227–231, nos. 224–227 b; Phillips 2008, 56–58) lead to a different perception of their Canaanite prototypes, which must have gradually appeared as less exotic to local consumers. Given the decisive influence of such perceptual parameters, one may assume that the otherness of imports was reduced to their essential aspect, which was not their transformable and reproducible design but their material. It resisted domestication and thus formed the kernel of the import's alien character (*contra* Burns 2010, 192–193).

Epilogue

In my approach, I have attempted to demonstrate that the perception of imports as alien objects was not as straightforward as previous scholarship tended to believe, but more subtle and subject to several factors. Objects that were re-contextualised into a new cultural frame could gradually lose their alien visibility – or a part of it – to become part of the everyday. Their evident incorporation into local practices forces us to expand the vocabulary of alterity with terms that go beyond the monolithic concept of 'foreign,' such as 'new,' 'rare,' 'different,' 'precious,' and 'powerful'. The gradual deterioration of alterity through the object's embedment into local systems of practices and values was a process affecting primarily their design and function. The latter were ephemeral qualities that could be modified to suit local needs. The inventive reaction of local populations could, on the one hand, disguise, conceal, copy, transform, and develop a foreign design or, on the other hand, change, improve, or extend the function of a foreign import. In the course of such transformative processes, imports lost a significant portion of their otherness. As for the function, it was in most cases the subject, *i.e.* the local consumers, who forced the objects to change their 'attitude', and not vice versa. What remained unaffected, constituting the heart of otherness, was the exotic material. Therefore, I would like to suggest that in this specific cultural context, alterity did not adhere to the design or style but to the physical thingness of an import.

A last issue that is crucial for evaluating the importance and impact of foreign things in an ancient society relates to the real motives of transcultural attitudes. It seems very likely that the cosmopolitanism of Mediterranean elites that was materially expressed through the acquisition of foreign objects or ideas was primarily motivated not by the willingness of their members to participate in an international community sharing common tastes or attitudes (Feldman 2006, 6–17), but of their desire to acquire an additional cultural identity. Through the conscious crossing of their own cultural borders manifested in the acquisition and use of exotica, they actually strived to enhance their high prestige and cement social inequality (Panagiotopoulos 2010, 44). Cosmopolitanism can thus be perfectly explained within a very local and not international frame of reference. The Amarna letters, this corpus of 'classified' documents from the Late Bronze Age, give us a very unequivocal statement for this attitude that was clearly driven by purely domestic concerns. When the Egyptian king refused to give one of his daughters as bride to the Babylonian king, the latter sent him the following barefaced answer:

> '[Someone's] grown daughters, beautiful women, must be available. Send me a beautiful woman as if she were [you]r daughter. Who is going to say, "She is no daughter of the king!"?' (Moran 1992, 9, EA 4).

Can transculturality be explained as an element of local strategies? Maybe yes, since this is only an ostensible ambiguity, as a look at modern politics makes apparent. The cruel fact that foreign policy is nothing more than domestic policy has been shaping the international attitudes of societies and states for several millennia. But that is another story.

References

Barrett, C. E. (2009) The Perceived Value of Minoan and Minoanizing Pottery in Egypt. *Journal of Mediterranean Archaeology* 22/2, 211–234.

Bevan, A. (2007) *Stone Vessels and Values in the Bronze Age Mediterranean*. Cambridge, Cambridge University Press.

Bevan, A. (2010) Making and Marking Relationships. Bronze Age Brandings and Mediterranean Commodities. In A. Bevan and D. Wengrow (eds), *Cultures of Commodity Branding*, 35–85. Walnut Creek, California, Left Coast Press, Inc.

Bhabha, H. K. (1994) *The Location of Culture*. London, Routledge.

Burke, P. (2009) *Cultural Hybridity*. Cambridge, Polity Press.

Burns, B. E. (1999) *Import Consumption in the Bronze Age Argolid (Greece). Effects of Mediterranean Trade on Mycenaean Society*. Unpublished thesis, University of Michigan.

Burns, B. E. (2010) *Mycenaean Greece, Mediterranean Commerce, and the Formation of Identity*. Cambridge, Cambridge University Press.

Caminos, R. A. (1954) *Late Egyptian Miscellanies*. Brown Egyptological Studies 1. London, Oxford University Press.

Cline, E. H. (1994) *Sailing the Wine-Dark Sea: International Trade and the Late Bronze Age Aegean*. British Archaeological Reports, International Series 591. Oxford, Hadrian Books Ltd.

Cline, E. H. (2005) The Multivalent Nature of Imported Objects in the Ancient Mediterranean World. In Laffineur and Greco 2005, 45–51.

Cucuzza, N. (2000) "Egyptianizing" Amphorae in Minoan Crete. In A. Karetsou (ed.) *Κρήτη – Αίγυπτος. Πολιτισμικοί Δεσμοί Τριών Χιλιετιών. Μελέτες*, 101–106. Athens, Kapon Editions.

Davies, N. de G. and R. O. Faulkner (1947) A Syrian Trading Venture to Egypt. *Journal of Egyptian Archaeology* 33, 40–46.

Diaz-Andreu, M., S. Lucy, S. Babic and D. N. Edwards (2005) *The Archaeology of Identity: Approaches to Gender, Age, Status, Ethnicity and Religion*. London and New York, Routledge.

Eriksen, T. H. (2010) *Ethnicity and Nationalism. Anthropological Perspectives*. 3rd ed. London, Pluto Press.

Gamble, C. (2007) *Origins and Revolutions: Human Identity in Earliest Prehistory*. Cambridge, Cambridge University Press.

Hallmann, S. (2006) *Die Tributszenen des Neuen Reiches*. Ägypten und Altes Testament 66. Wiesbaden, Harrassowitz Verlag.

Insoll, T. (ed.) (2006) *The Archaeology of Identities. A Reader*. London and New York, Routledge.

Jones, S. (1997) *The Archaeology of Ethnicity. Constructing Identities in the Past and Present*. London and New York, Routledge.

Kapchan, D. A. and P. T. Strong (1999) Theorizing the Hybrid. *Journal of American Folklore* 112, 239–253.

Karetsou, A. (2000) *Κρήτη – Αίγυπτος. Πολιτισμικοί Δεσμοί Τριών Χιλιετιών. Κατάλογος*. Ηράκλειο, Υπουργείο Πολιτισμού.

Karo, G. (1930) *Die Schachtgräber von Mykenai*. München, F. Bruckmann AG.

Kemp, B. J. (2006) *Ancient Egypt. Anatomy of a Civilization*. 2nd ed. London, Routledge.

Laffineur, R. (1990–1991) Material and Craftsmanship in the Mycenae Shaft Graves: Imports vs Local Production. *Minos* 25–26, 245–295.

Laffineur, R. (2005) Imports/Exports in the Eastern Mediterranean: For a Specific Methodology. In Laffineur and Greco 2005, 53–58.

Laffineur, R. and Greco, E. (2005) *Emporia: Aegeans in the Central and Eastern Mediterranean. Proceedings of the 10th International Aegean Conference, Athens, Italian School of Archaeology, 14–18 April 2004*. Aegaeum 25. Liège and Austin, Université de Liège, Histoire de l'art et archéologie de la Grèce antique and University of Texas at Austin, Program in Aegean Scripts and Prehistory.

Lambrou-Phillipson, C. (1990) *Hellenorientalia: The Near Eastern Presence in the Bronze Age Aegean, c. 3000–1100 BC plus Orientalia: A Catalogue of Egyptian, Mesopotamian, Mitannian, Syro-Palestinian, Cypriot and Asia Minor Objects from the Bronze Age Aegean*. Göteborg, Paul Åströms Förlag.

Leerssen, J. (2007) Identity/Alterity/Hybridity. In M. Beller and J. Leerssen (eds), *Imagology. The Cultural Construction and Literary Representation of National Characters. A Critical Review*, 335–342. Studia Imagologica 13. Amsterdam and New York, Rodopo Publishers.

MacSweeney, N. (2009) Beyond Ethnicity: The Overlooked Diversity of Group Identities. *Journal of Mediterranean Archaeology* 22/1, 101–126.

Meskell, L. (2001) Archaeologies of Identity. In I. Hodder (ed.), *Archaeological Theory Today*, 187–213. Cambridge, Polity Press.

Moran, W. L. (1992) *The Amarna Letters*. Baltimore and London, John Hopkins University Press.

Mylonas, G. E. (1972–1973) *Ο Ταφικός Κύκλος Β των Μυκηνών*. Βιβλιοθήκη της εν Αθήναις Αρχαιολογικής Εταιρείας 73. Αθήνα, Αρχαιολογική Εταιρεία.

Panagiotopoulos, D. (2000) Tributabgaben und Huldigungsgeschenke aus der Levante. Die ägyptische Nordexpansion in der 18. Dynastie aus strukturgeschichtlicher Sicht. *Ägypten und Levante* 10, 139–158.

Panagiotopoulos, D. (2001) Keftiu in Context: Theban Tomb-paintings as a Historical Source. *Oxford Journal of Archaeology* 20/3, 263–283.

Panagiotopoulos, D. (2004) Der ferne Nachbar. Der Einfluß Ägyptens auf das minoische Kreta und das mykenische Griechenland. In P. Bol (ed.), *Fremdheit – Eigenheit. Ägypten, Griechenland und Rom: Austausch und Verständnis*. Städel Jahrbuch 19, 33–46. Frankfurt, Städel Museum.

Panagiotopoulos, D. (2006) Foreigners in Egypt in the Time Hatshepsut and Thutmose III. In E. Cline and D. O'Connor (eds), *Thutmose III: A New Biography*, 370–412. Ann Arbor, University of Michigan Press.

Panagiotopoulos, D. (2008) Geschenk oder Handel? Zu den Gaben der ägäischen Prozessionen in den thebanischen Privatgräbern. In A. Kyriatsoulis (ed.), *Austausch von Gütern, Ideen und Technologien in der Ägäis und im östlichen Mittelmeer von der prähistorischen bis zu der archaischen Zeit*, 167–176. Weilheim, Verein zur Förderung und Aufarbeitung der Hellenischen Geschichte, e.V.

Panagiotopoulos, D. (2010) The Stirring Sea. Conceptualising Transculturality in the Late Bronze Age Eastern Mediterranean. In K. Duistermaat and I. Regulski (eds), *Intercultural Contacts in the Ancient Mediterranean*, 31–51. Orientalia Lovaniensia Analecta 202. Leuven, Peeters.

Pendlebury, J. D. S. (1930) *Aegyptiaca. A Catalogue of Egyptian Objects in the Aegean Area*. Cambridge, Cambridge University Press.

Phillips, J. (2008) *Aegyptiaca on the Island of Crete in their Chronological Context: A Critical Review*. Vols. 1–2. Contributions to the Chronology of the Eastern Mediterranean XVIII. Wien, Verlag der Österreichischen Akademie der Wissenschaften.

Rehak, P. (1995) The 'Genius' in Late Bronze Age Glyptic: The Later Evolution of an Aegean Cult Figure. In W. Müller (ed.), *Sceaux minoens et mycéniens: IVe symposium international, 10–12 septembre 1992, Clermont-Ferrand* 215–231. Corpus der Minoischen und Mykenischen Siegel, Beiheft 5. Berlin, Gebr. Mann Verlag.

Sakellarakis, J. A. (1990) The Fashioning of Ostrich-egg Rhyta in the Creto-Mycenaean Aegean. In D. Hardy *et al.* (eds), *Thera and the Aegean World III. Vol 1: Archaeology. Proceedings of the Third International Congress, Santorini, Greece, 3–9 September 1989*, 285–308. London, The Thera Foundation.

van Wijngaarden, G. J. (2003) *Use and Appreciation of Mycenaean Pottery in the Levant, Cyprus and Italy (ca. 1600–1200 BC).* Amsterdam Archaeological Studies Series 8. Amsterdam, Amsterdam University Press.

Ventris, M. and J. Chadwick (1973) *Documents in Mycenaean Greek.* Cambridge, Cambridge University Press.

Vermeule, E. T. (1975) *The Art of the Shaft Graves of Mycenae.* Oklahoma, The University of Oklahoma Press.

Wachsmann, S. (1987) *Aegeans in the Theban Tombs.* Orientalia Lovaniensia Analecta 20. Leuven, Peeters.

Wachsmann, S. (1998) *Seagoing Ships and Seamanship in the Bronze Age Levant.* London, Chatham Publishing.

Warren, P. (1991) A Merchant Class in Bronze Age Crete? The Evidence of Egyptian Stone Vessels from the City of Knossos. In N. H. Gale (ed.), *Bronze Age Trade in the Mediterranean. Papers Presented at the Conference held at Rewley House, Oxford, in December 1989*, 295–301. Studies in Mediterranean Archaeology 90. Jonsered, Paul Åströms Förlag.

Warren, P. (1997) The Lapidary Art – Minoan Adaptions of Egyptian Stone Vessels. In R. Laffineur and Ph. P. Betancourt (eds) *TEXNH. Craftsmen, Craftswomen and Craftsmanship in the Aegean Bronze Age. Proceedings of the 6th International Aegean Conference, Philadelphia, Temple University, 18–21 April 1996*, Aegeaum 16, 209–223. Liège and AUstin, Université de Liège, Histoire de l'art et archéologie de la Grèce antique and University of Texas at Austin, Program in Aegean Scripts and Prehistory.

Weingarten, J. (1991) *The Transformation of Egyptian Taweret into the Minoan Genius. A Study of Cultural Transmission in the Middle Bronze Age.* Studies in Mediterranean Archaeology 88. Partille, P. Åströms Förlag.

Weingarten, J. (2000) The Transformation of Egyptian Taweret into the Minoan Genius. In A. Karetsou (ed.), *Κρήτη – Αίγυπτος. Πολιτισμικοί Δεσμοί Τριών Χιλιετιών. Μελέτες*, 114–119. Athens, Kapon Editions.

Welz, F. (2005) Rethinking Identity: Concepts of Identity and 'the Other' in Sociological Perspective. *The Society. An International Journal of Social Sciences* 1, 1–25.

Wengrow. D. (2008) Prehistories of Commodity Branding. *Current Anthropology* 49, 7–34.

Wengrow, D. (2010) Introduction: Commodity Branding in Archaeological and Anthropological Perspectives. In A. Bevan and D. Wengrow (eds), *Cultures of Commodity Branding*, 11–33. Walnut Creek, California, Left Coast Press, Inc.

7.

Trade goods reproducing merchants? The materiality of Mediterranean Late Bronze Age exchange

Gert Jan van Wijngaarden

The concept of *materiality* is by no means clear and undisputed, either in social theory or in archaeology (Hoogsteyns 2008). The central idea seems to be that the material world shapes human actions. A materiality approach means taking an interest in the ways objects influence, or, indeed, manipulate, human practice. Objects are not simply vehicles, or symbols, for meaning and identity, but they determine behaviour through their material characteristics. However, scholars differ enormously in their ideas about *how* the material world influences human action. There are fundamental differences, for example, in approaches based on Daniel Miller's objectification compared with the symmetrical approaches inspired by the work of Bruno Latour in particular.

An important characteristic of the ways objects are able to shape human action is that they do so collectively. Categories of objects influence groups of people. As an example, consider the automobile: a world without cars is fundamentally different from a world with cars (Miller 2010, 59). The technical development of the automobile has changed patterns of human mobility and irreversibly affected the physical landscape. Mobile telephones are another good example of collective material action: by their material properties, these devices have fundamentally changed the ways in which people communicate and behave (*cf.* Ihde 1993, 116; Verbeek 2000, 57; Hoogsteyns 2008, 38). Of course, individual items can be endowed with multiple meanings and they can be reinterpreted to act specific cultural roles in different contexts (Hodder 1987; Thomas 1991). On a collective level, however, objects affect social and cultural practices by exercising influence on human behaviour through material properties and technical possibilities. The collective power of goods implies that collections of objects are particularly significant. In archaeological terms, this means that particular attention should be given to situations where assemblages appear to have been meaningfully constituted.

Our material environment is often inconspicuous and familiar (Miller 2010, 50–51). The whole system of things and goods, the internal order of collections of objects, are part of people's *habitus*. The important influence of objects on human behaviour becomes apparent in situations where changes take place in the established material order (Latour 2005, 79–80). When objects and/or people move into a different cultural context, a crisis in the established material order occurs, leading to new associations among objects and people. Foreign and exotic objects are particularly able to upset existing material relations and create new ones.

In this article, I will focus on assemblages of exotic objects, which have been found in different parts of the eastern Mediterranean (see Fig. 7.1 for location of sites). Such assemblages, characteristically, have their own internal structure, consisting of dependent and hierarchical positions of objects towards one another (Robb 2004, 134). These dependencies and hierarchies within material assemblages are object of study here. They vary according to cultural context and, consequently, their effect on the social world will also be different in different societies. Hopefully, these variations in the social impact of collections of exotica will shed light on the ways in which they allowed social groups to express identity. This article should be considered exploratory and experimental for reasons that are outlined below.

Exotic objects in the eastern Mediterranean

Long distance communications and the exchange of goods in the eastern Mediterranean during the second part of the

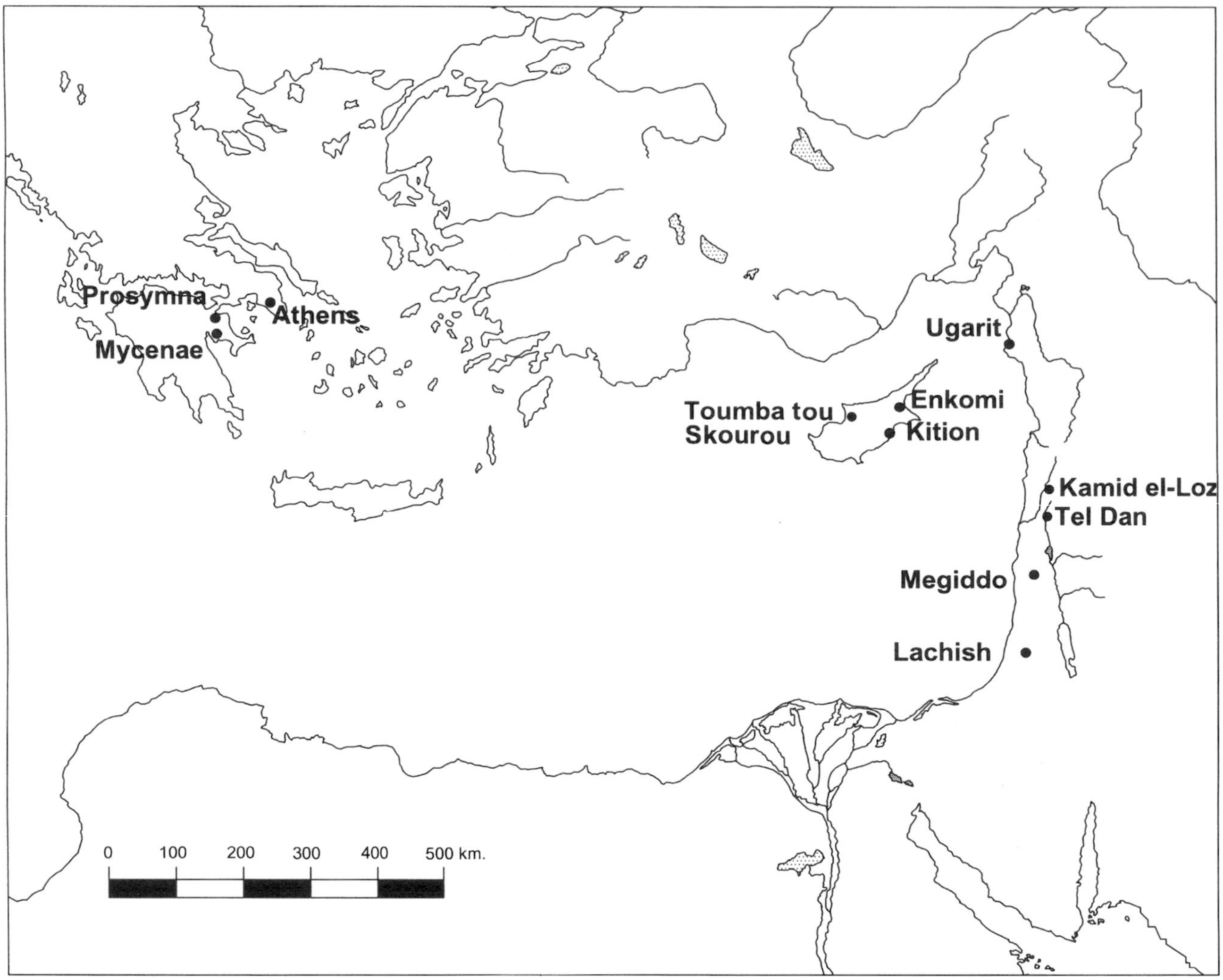

Fig. 7.1: Map indicating places mentioned in the text.

Late Bronze Age, was a highly complex affair. Epigraphic as well as archaeological sources show that a wide variety of goods circulated in extensive networks (Zaccagnini 1973; Liverani 2008, 161–168). Large amounts of goods were involved, both raw materials and manufactured items. The ceremonial language used in the available correspondence between rulers indicates the diplomatic nature of many of these transactions (Liverani 1972; 2000). However, it is also clear that, by the Late Bronze Age, economic motives played a major role even in the ceremonial exchanges between rulers (Zaccagnini 1973, 117–121). The archaeological distribution of goods and objects, which are not (often) mentioned in the epigraphic records, suggests that exchanges also took place outside the formal control of state powers. The extent of the exchange system is such that many people must have participated in it: kings and rulers, emissaries and merchants, artisans and sailors, all participated in a system that surpassed their actions to an extent unknown to them.

The excavations at the Ulu Burun shipwreck have provided us with a view of the actual transport within these networks (Pulak 2001; 2008). The fact that the ship's cargo originated in a wide variety of regions in and beyond the Mediterranean has often been commented upon. Of equal importance, in my opinion, is the fact that large quantities of raw materials were shipped together with clear prestige objects and with a range of manufactured items made of less-valuable raw materials, such as pottery. Objects that could be considered to belong to separate 'spheres of exchange' (*cf.* Knapp and Cherry 1994, 152–155; Artzy 1997, 9) obviously were transported together.

One of the results of these exchange networks is cross-cultural consumption of manufactured items. This is archaeologically visible in the existence of a class of so-called *international objects*: objects that occur frequently in different geographical parts of the Mediterranean (Heymans and van Wijngaarden 2011). Among these international objects are imports and exports (*cf.* Cline 2005; Laffineur 2005), but also so-called imitations and derivatives (*cf.* Papadopolous 1997, 450; Åström 1998), as well as objects in native traditions incorporating foreign stylistic or material elements. Several objects from different parts of the Mediterranean show a convergence of stylistic and material traits up to the point that it is impossible to identify the cultural source of manufacture (Crowley 1989; Feldman 2006). This so-called *International Style* in artistic production is an indication of the high degree of appropriation of foreign cultural elements in many parts of the Mediterranean during this period. Although these international objects are proportionally a very small part of the archaeological record in all areas (Manning and Hulin 1995, 282–286), their wide occurrence in a large area and over a long period of time shows their cultural significance.

Among these international items are a range of manufactured objects, which occur relatively frequently (van Wijngaarden 2007, 467; Heymans and van Wijngaarden 2011): Mycenaean dinner and storage vessels, Cypriot Base Ring ware and White slip II bowls, but also wall-brackets, Egyptian faience or stone scarabs and faience or alabaster vases, cylinder seals from Syria and Mesopotamia, many worn and antique, bone or ivory combs and other implements. Some of these items were produced at specific locations within the Mediterranean and could be transported over large distances (Knapp and Cherry 1994). However, many objects were also imitated and varieties of them were produced in different parts of the Mediterranean. Egyptian style faience scarabs, for example, were produced in the Levant and possibly on Cyprus (McGovern, Fleming and Swann 1993). Imitations, or, rather, foreign interpretations, could also occur in different materials, as is, for example the case for the faience and stone versions of Mycenaean stirrup jars (Hankey 1995, 117–123; Matoïan 2004). Such material derivatives from exotic objects could themselves circulate, as is evident from the presence of Syrian-made faience stirrup jars of Mycenaean shape on Cyprus (Peltenburg 1976, 105). The degree to which the cultural origin of these objects was of relevance for the way they were appreciated is difficult to assess (van Wijngaarden 2008).

In terms of materiality, it should be noted that these objects are, for the most part, not made from very precious materials, nor do they require highly specific artisan skills. In terms of function, it is worthy of note that many of these objects are associated with cultural practices that are culturally highly specific and variable according to practice: bodily adornment (combs, beads, unguent-containers, containers for perfumed oil), dining and drinking (fine drinking, pouring and eating pottery) and symbolic referencing (seals, scarabs). In other words, these objects are exceptionally suited to be culturally reinterpreted and assigned with new meanings (Antoniadou 2005). However, the prime material characteristic of these objects is their foreign raw material, technique, or style. They are exotics, with connotations of luxury and a wider world of long-distance contacts (Heymans and van Wijngaarden 2011, 125).

Tomb assemblages

Low value manufactured items are often found together in assemblages, notably in tombs. Funerary contexts are, of course, highly specific in the sense that they constitute intersections between life and death (Parker Pearson 1993, 203–205). Rituals surrounding death and burial create connections between material objects and living and dead human actors and the supernatural world. Through these rituals funerary assemblages are meaningfully constructed, even though they may constitute different material realities than those in everyday life.

The majority of the tombs with exotics considered in this paper were used for multiple burials. In the Levant, Cyprus and Greece, the use of built tombs during the Late Bronze Age often spanned several generations (Gonen 1992a, 9–15; 1992b; Keswani 2004, 31–36; Mee and Cavanagh 1998). These collective burial practices often resulted in earlier burials being disturbed by later internments and it is extremely difficult to relate individual finds to single burials or individuals. To complicate matters, it is possible that rituals of exhumation and/or secondary burial took place, during which new material items were added or removed from the funerary assemblages (Gallou 2005, 112–117). Assemblages of objects in a tomb are the result of human actions but, taken as a whole, they are not consciously constructed. They are the outcome of slow processes, which span generations and involved a number of different episodes of selection. It is unclear to what extent the assemblages as a whole were perceived as such in antiquity, whether anyone ever was conscious of the full range of the assemblage. The fact that most of the tombs discussed here have been subject to looting adds to the character of these assemblages as open archaeological contexts. One reason why this paper should be considered as experimental is because I will use these open contexts for archaeological analysis.

The open character of the assemblages is counterbalanced by the fact that they are associated with single tombs. The precise ways in which the tombs in the three areas are relating to the societies of the living is not altogether clear. At Ras Shamra-Ugarit in Syria, the tombs are situated below the houses (Salles 1995; Marchegay 2007; 2008). Even though not all houses have a funerary cellar, we may assume a relation between the inhabitants of the house and the occupants of the tomb. At various other sites in the Levant and Cyprus, tombs are also associated with houses in an urban settlement. However, a large number of Late Bronze Age collective graves in the areas under consideration are situated outside of settlements. Since the use of funerary spaces is a highly ritualized activity (Bloch 1971; Laneri 2007), it is likely that there are strictly regulated ties among the living and the dead subjects and the material objects, which are connected to the tomb. It is assumed here that all tombs under consideration can be associated to specific groups in society, most likely kin-based groups (*cf.* Keswani 2004, 33–34; Gallou 2005, 135–137). The rituals by which individual members and material items are placed in (or removed from) the tomb serve to reproduce the collective identity of a group over a long period of time. By placing deceased individuals among his or her ancestors, continuity within the group is created (*cf.* Boyd 2002, 94–95). Rather than static representations of social status, our tomb assemblages should be considered as dynamic sets of material relations between objects and dead and living actors that shape diachronic collective cultural strategies.

In order to assess material relations among individual elements within tomb assemblages incorporating international objects, various points will be taken into account here: the presence of clear wealth indicators, notably gold and silver jewellery and metals; the presence of exotica and the quantities in which they were present with regard to the tomb assemblage as a whole; and the presence of locally made prestige items and/or pottery. The objective of this analysis is to establish structural associations and hierarchies among materials by noting which items frequently occur together. This will provide clues about the ways in which tomb assemblages acquire internal structure, which is the origin of the collective impact on the social world. An additional reason to consider this article as experimental is the large area that will be covered: tombs in the Levant, Cyprus and the Aegean will be included in the study. Hopefully, the comparative perspective adopted here will reveal variations in the transformative capacities of material assemblages of exotics.

The Levant

Ras Shamra-Ugarit in Syria and its harbour town Minet el-Beida are critical sites with respect to our understanding of Late Bronze Age Mediterranean interconnections (Caubet 2007; Calvet and Yon 2008; Routledge and McGeough 2009). Since the discovery of Ugarit in 1929 by Claude Schaeffer, much emphasis has been put on the cosmopolitan character of the town. Tombs, as well as settlement contexts, have yielded a wide variety of artefacts imported from many different areas or imitations thereof. Cross-cultural consumption of exotics seems particularly well established at Ugarit. Nevertheless, it is important to stress that imports and exotica are a very small part of the total material record, even at Ugarit: less than one percent (Monchambert 1983, 25–45). Cross-cultural consumption is primarily a qualitative aspect.

A notable feature of Ugarit and its harbour town are the funerary cellars, which were mostly situated below the houses (Marchegay 2007; 2008). The archaeological analysis of these tombs is seriously hindered by the fact that almost all had been looted and because the publication of the funerary inventories of the earlier campaigns is fragmentary. It is clear that in all Late Bronze Age tombs local pottery, both coarse and painted, is most abundant in a quantitative sense. However, small numbers of imports and exotica are widely distributed. Many Late Bronze Age tombs at Ugarit contain small quantities of imported items or exotics, very often Cypriot and Mycenaean pottery and Egyptian alabaster vases. A typical example is tomb no. 13 in Ras Shamra, which was excavated in 1936 and which was, according to the excavator, undisturbed (Schaeffer 1936a, 139). In addition to a large quantity of Syrian bowls and jugs, a few Cypriot and Mycenaean pots were found, as well as an Egyptian alabaster jug. Considering that in this tomb the remains of 44 individuals have been identified (Vallois and Ferembach 1962, 566), the number of exotics can be considered to be low indeed.

Including small quantities of exotics in burials was a widespread custom in Late Bronze Age Ugarit. In itself, the inclusion of exotics is not a reliable indicator of social status. Some tombs with many valuables, such as the recently excavated grave 1008 at Minet el-Beida, yielded relatively few exotics (Marchegay 2004), whereas some relatively poor tombs, such as tomb 13 or 36, did have exotics (Schaeffer 1938, 201). Including small numbers of exotics in tombs was a widely shared practice among different social groups in Ugaritic urban society during the Late Bronze Age (Marchegay 2008, 109).

A small minority of tombs appears to deviate from the general pattern of tomb assemblages comprising a limited number of exotics only. In particular at Minet el-Beida, ancient Ma'hadou, some tombs contained very large quantities of exotic objects (Marchegay 2008, 112). The large tomb VI, which was excavated in 1930, contained large numbers of Mycenaean and Cypriot pots and even a possible Anatolian Grey ware krater (Courtois 1979, 262). Tomb III in Minet el-Beida (Table 7.1, below) also yielded large quantities of Cypriot and Mycenaean pottery, but also faience stirrup jars, Egyptian faience objects, gold pearls, a hematite cylinder seal and the famous ivory pyxis lid with a seated goddess (Schaeffer 1936b, 19–21; 1949, 144–149).

There are at least four of these exceptional tombs in

Minet el-Beida: tombs III, IV, V, and VI. It should be noted that other tombs in Minet el-Beida yielded smaller quantities of exotics, as was, for example, the case with the tomb that marked the discovery of Ugarit in 1929 (tomb I; Albanèse 1929) and in tomb 1008, which was excavated in 1998 (Marchegay 2004). The inventory of tomb 2698 at Ugarit has only been fragmentarily published (Courtois and Courtois 1978, 342–345), but included remarkably many Mycenaean pots, indicating that, perhaps, it too is one of these tombs with exceptional quantities of exotic objects. In these exceptional tombs exotics appear to have been collected in large quantities. It may be of significance that these tombs are not situated in or near the royal palace of Ugarit, but in the harbour town. In spite of their wealth, these tombs did not necessarily belong to the upper élites in the society of Ugarit. Collecting large quantities of exotic goods in funerary ritual appears to have been a practice of specific groups in the urban population of ancient Ugarit.

Elsewhere in the Levant, we find a similar pattern in the Late Bronze Age II period: many tombs with small numbers of exotics, often not more than one or two scarabs and some faience beads. An example is tomb 501 at Tell ed-Duweir, ancient Lachish (Tuffnell *et al.* 1958, 236), which contained a few bronze objects; some pottery imports and imitations, beads, and a series of scarabs and seals. The somewhat wealthier tomb 216 at the same site yielded Mycenaean and Cypriot pottery, and small quantities of exotic objects, among which were ivory artefacts (Tuffnell *et al.* 1958, 232–234). However, at various sites in the Levant Late Bronze Age tombs have been discovered that can be compared to the funerary cellars III–VI at Minet el-Beida in the presence of large quantities of exotics. Examples are the cave at Sarepta in Lebanon (Baramki 1956–1958), the so-called 'Mycenaean tomb' at Tel Dan (Biran and Ben-Dov 2002, 33–228) and tomb 912B at Megiddo in Israel (Guy 1938, 69–72, pls. 124–132).

An interesting clue about the social groups, which can be associated with these exceptional tombs may come from Tell es-Saidiyeh in Jordan, where fifteen Late Bronze Age II graves were discovered (Pritchard 1980, 28–30). The wealthiest of the tombs, number 101, yielded objects in silver, electrum, carnelian, bronze and ivory. This tomb was in the centre of the necropolis and had some special architectural features. Somewhat away from this tomb was grave 117, which was special because it contained a number of imports: Mycenaean and Cypriot pottery, an alabaster goblet, a faience bowl. Even though the quantities are much lower than in a large centre such as Ugarit, tomb 117 also seems to constitute one of those tombs with a special role for imports and exotics. It is of significance that this is not the wealthiest grave *strictu sensu*, but a tomb somewhat distinguished, with a highly specific material assemblage.

With regard to tomb assemblages of exotics, the general pattern in the Late Bronze Age II Levant is one of many tombs with small numbers of exotics and a few in which they appear to have been collected in large quantities. In social anthropology, a distinction is made between *things of quality* on the one hand and *quantifiable things* on the other (Thompson 1979; Gell 1998, 17–20; Gosden 2004, 36–39). Things of quality are heavily embedded in social relations and acquire value through immaterial aspects such as origin, previous owners *etc* . Quantifiable things are largely disembedded from the social universe and have a more economic value, which can be manipulated through quantity and variety. In all the tombs that have been discussed, exotic objects have the quality to refer to other worlds and far-away contacts. In some tombs, this symbolic significance is enhanced firstly through quantity and, secondly, through the combination of different types of exotics. This practice indicates that, in a social sense, some people were able to quantify exotic objects.

The specific pattern of quantification of exotic goods in a limited number of tombs appears to be characteristic of the Late Bronze Age II period. With the possible exception of the so-called *Schatzhaus* in Kamid el-Loz (Adler 1994), such quantification cannot be recognized in earlier tombs. The evidence from Minet el-Beida and from Tell es-Saidiyeh shows that this type of quantification is related to specific groups among the urban elites of the Levant. For the identification of these groups, it may be of significance that in Akko, several sets of weights were found in a funerary chamber with many imports (Ben Arieh and Edelstein 1977, 8). The extraordinary tomb 912B in Megiddo also yielded weights (Guy 1938, 69–72), while in Minet el-Beida, weights were found in a funerary pit associated with one of our exceptional tombs (Schaeffer 1931, 2).

To assess the collective power of objects, the internal structure of the assemblages is of importance. There is great repetition in the type of exotics that occur in the Levantine Late Bronze Age tombs (see also Heymans and van Wijngaarden 2011 125–127): Cypriot and Mycenaean pottery and figurines; Egyptian alabaster vases, faience beads and faience or glass vessels, stone and faience scarabs; stone cylinder seals, often old and worn and, finally, a range of ivory implements. In tombs in which clear valuables, such as gold and silver or bronze vessels, are present, ivory implements, such as plaques, pyxides or boxes are present as well. When valuables are not present in tombs, usually only faience and glass beads, scarabs and amulets and Egyptian alabaster vases have been found, in addition to imported pottery: Mycenaean and Cypriot vessels occur together. The material dependencies and hierarchies within funerary assemblages in Late Bronze Age Levant are summarized in Table 7.1.

- Ivory implements (boxes etc)
- Cylinder seals
- Alabaster vessels
- Stone and faience Scarabs
- Faience beads and vessels
- Cypriot Base Ring pottery
- Cypriot White Slip II pottery
- Mycenaean drinking and storage pottery

Table 7.1: Material relations and hierarchies among exotics in Late Bronze Age Levantine tombs.

Mycenaean Greece

If we look at the presence of imports and exotica in mainland of Mycenaean Greece, the first thing that strikes us is that there are far fewer such objects than in the Levant and that their distribution shows a concentration in, and around, the Argolid and near Thebes and Pylos, not surprisingly, in the general area of the palaces (Heymans and van Wijngaarden 2011). One reason for this quantitative difference with the Levant is the fact that Mycenaean pottery, obviously, cannot be considered as exotic on the Greek Mainland. But even allowing for this difference, it is clear that absolute numbers of exotica in Mycenaean Greece are much lower than in the contemporary Levant. Interestingly, Cypriot pottery is also quite scarce, especially in tombs.

Despite their relative scarcity, exotics do occur in several Mycenaean tombs, and not only in tombs that can directly be associated with the Mycenaean centres of power. Indeed, small quantities of low-value manufactured exotics occur in tombs with little or no indications for wealth, such as in tombs VII and XXIII in the Athenian Agora (Immerwahr 1971, 183–190, 218–221). Interestingly, the few conspicuously wealthy tombs in the Agora, tombs with much metal and precious jewellery, do not seem to contain substantially more manufactured exotics than modest tombs. Tomb III, for example, is a very wealthy tomb, without exotics (Immerwahr 1971, 170–177). Tomb I, also very wealthy, contained two intricately worked and unique ivory pyxides, in addition to a single large Canaanite jar (Immerwahr 1971, 158–169).

More detailed information about the role of exotics in Mycenaean Greek tombs is obtained from Prosymna, near Argos. The cemetery, excavated in the 1920s by the American School of Classical Studies under the direction of C. Blegen, is the largest of Mycenaean Greece, which has been fully published (Blegen 1937). Most of the LH (Late Helladic) IIIA–LH IIIB tombs at Prosymna contain some metal goods, and low-value manufactured exotics. Of particular interest is that almost all tombs contain glass paste beads or beads of semi-precious stones, often carnelian. Such glass beads could very well have been produced locally or elsewhere on the Greek mainland (Hughes-Brock 1999, 289–290), but the technique is supposed to have come originally from Egypt (Higgins 1980, 40).

Two conspicuously wealthy tombs (II and III), characterized by their many gold and bronze artefacts, contained a wider variety of exotics, among which was a carnelian hippopotamus figurine from Egypt found in tomb III (Cline 1994, cat. 32). However, there are several explicitly wealthy tombs, for example tomb XXXVII, with many wealth indicators and only a few exotics (Blegen 1937, 123–128). And there is a group of tombs at Prosymna without specific wealth indicators but with exotics. An example is tomb XXXVIII, which contained a few bronzes and a large number of exotics, of which some of high quality (Blegen 1937, 71–74).

In Late Helladic III tombs on Mainland Greece, there is not a clear correlation between the presence of low-value manufactured exotics and wealth indicators such as gold and silver jewellery or quantities of metals (Heymans and van Wijngaarden 2011). Exotic objects are present in a wide variety of tombs. Obviously, various social groups within Mycenaean society were associated with the symbolical expression of distant worlds through exotics in funerary assemblages. There are various wealthy LH III tombs without imports or exotics, but when they do have them, they are usually exceptional, notably elaborate sets of ivory (Konstantinidi 2001, 250–253). A larger variety and quality of exotics appears to have been related to some groups among the Mycenaean elites. Interestingly, in the period before the Mycenaean palaces, manufactured exotics in tombs do appear to correlate with the presence of wealth indicators. The Shaft Graves at Mycenae contained a wide range of exotics (Voutsaki, in press), while the tholos tomb at Vapheio also contained valuables in association with manufactured exotics, such as Egyptian stone vases and a Levantine axe (Kilian Dirlmeier 1987, 198–201). Interestingly, the Vapheio tomb also contained a set of led weights. The relatively widespread social role of exotics in Mycenaean funerary ritual appears to be characteristic of the Mycenaean palatial period.

The exotic objects in Mycenaean Greek tombs during the palatial period show various archaeological associations (Heymans and van Wijngaarden 2011, 127–129). Glass, faience and stone beads are most abundant. Seals are less common. Possibly, many of these were made in the Aegean, sometimes from exotic raw materials. Others were worn and clearly old by the time they were deposited in the grave. Single bone and ivory objects do occur repeatedly, but elaborate sets of ivory are limited to tombs with wealth indicators. The internal hierarchy within the funerary assemblages (Table 7.2) resembles that in the Levant (Table 7.1). However, the repertoire of artefacts is much more limited in the Aegean and imported pottery did not serve as an exotic element in Mycenaean funerary rituals. What is altogether

- Elaborate sets of ivory
- Small ivory implements
- Stone cylinder seals
- Scarabs and faience amulets
- Glass, faience stone beads

Table 7.2: Material relations and hierarchies among exotics in Mycenaean Greek tombs.

lacking in Mycenaean Greece, is the type of quantification of exotic goods by specific social groups that we could see in the Levant.

Cyprus

In the archaeological record of Late Bronze Age Cyprus exotic goods appear to have had a prominent role (Steel 2004, 169–171; Bevan 2007, 152–156). The quantity and the diversity of such items are much higher than in the Aegean or in many areas of the Levant. In particular, there are many faience and stone vessels, imported from Egypt and the Levant, but also produced locally (Peltenburg 1974). And there is a substantial amount of Mycenaean pottery on the island (Steel 1998; van Wijngaarden 2002, 125–202), both imported and, towards the end of the thirteenth century, produced locally. Of course, exotics are a very small percentage of the total material record at Late Bronze Age Cyprus, but their wide geographical and contextual distribution shows that their significance derives not from quantities.

During the LC (Late Cypriot) IIC period many burials in the large urban centres of Cyprus were equipped with imported valuables and other prestige goods. It is of interest to note that there is a very clear correlation in the occurrence of manufactured imports and exotics with wealth indicators. Tombs that can be considered as very wealthy because of the presence of metals and jewellery, generally, also yielded a large quantity and wide variety of exotics. An example is the upper burial layer of tomb 9 in Kition, which contained large quantities of gold and silver, as well as a large quantity and wide range of exotics from different parts of the Mediterranean (Karageorghis 1974, 42–94).

The tombs at Enkomi *Ayios Iakovos,* varied considerably in the presence of wealth indicators and the presence of exotics. Fairly simple tombs, such as Swedish tomb 7A and Swedish tomb 13 still contained imports and exotica, often pottery, faience vessels and seals (Gjerstad *et al.* 1934, 498–500). Some of the less distinguished tombs had nice arrays of glass bottles, ivory boxes or faience containers and bowls. Wealthier tombs at Enkomi, such as Swedish tomb 3 (Gjerstadt *et al.* 1934, 475–487) show a larger quantity and a wider variety of exotics. Tombs that can be considered as very wealthy, such as Swedish tombs 11 and 18 (Gjerstadt *et al.* 1934, 546–559) and Dikaios' tomb 10 (Dikaios 1969, 357–394) showed a remarkable variety of exotics, including unique specimens such as ostrich eggs or gold-capped cylinder seals (Keswani 1989, 58–59, 63–64, 77–79; Aruz 2008, 144).

- Elaborate sets of ivory
- Small ivory implements
- Mycenaean pictorial kraters
- Stone cylinder seals (often imported, but reworked locally, such as gold-capping)
- Stone and faience scarabs
- Faience flasks, beads
- Mycenaean containers and Egyptian alabaster vases

Table 7.3: Material relations and hierarchies in Late Cypriot tombs.

The important role for imports and exotics in tombs in Cyprus and the clear association between exotics and wealth indicators originates already in the beginning of the Late Bronze Age. A number of LC I tombs at Dromolaxia and Klavdhia have yielded rare finds of imported Syrian and Egyptian pottery and Near Eastern cylinder seals (Keswani 2004, 98). At Toumba tou Skourou, the wealthy tomb 1, dating to LC I–IIA, contained silver objects, as well as a range of exotic imports, for example LM (Late Minoan) IB dinner vessels (Vermeule and Wolsky 1978, 381–383). Although the absolute numbers of exotics and imports in LC I–II tombs are lower than in later periods, it is clear that such objects were collected and included in tombs by quantity and in wide varieties. The conclusion is that the practice of quantification of exotics in funerary ritual occurred in Cyprus much earlier than in the Levant, and was more widespread socially during LC IIB–C.

The internal archaeological associations of the funerary assemblages of LC II–IIIA, indicate a material hierarchy in which ivories were highly valued (Table 7.3). The same can also be said for Mycenaean pictorial kraters (Van Wijngaarden 2001). However, Mycenaean pottery in general is used widely in tombs on Cyprus, especially small closed vessels. There appears to be a difference between the distribution of Mycenaean drinking sets and storage vessels in Late Cypriot tombs (van Wijngaarden 2002, 201–202). Cylinder seals, especially imported ones, often antique and frequently reworked on Cyprus, are found in substantial quantities in the richer tombs. They may occur in fewer numbers also in tombs with few exotics. Faience beads, scarabs, Egyptian alabaster vases and Mycenaean containers, occur in many tombs, even in relatively poor ones.

The material hierarchy of the Late Cypriot tomb assemblages resembles that of the Levant closely. The wealthier tombs on Cyprus contain quantities and varieties of exotics and imports that equal or even supersede those of the exceptional tombs at Minet el-Beida or elsewhere in the Levant. However, while the quantification of exotics in tombs was a limited practice in the Levant, the correlation between exotics and wealth indicators in Cypriot tombs shows that many different social groups on the island can be related to such quantification practices.

Merchants in the Mediterranean

The overview above shows that the presence of a wide variety of manufactured exotics during the Late Bronze Age resulted in material expressions in tomb assemblages, which were similar but not identical, for various groups of people in different parts of the Mediterranean. By including elements from a coherent range of artefacts in funerary rituals, social groups associated with these tombs were identified with long-distance communication and exchange. Because of the long duration of tomb use, these choices were made by different people in successive generations. Tomb assemblages serve to connect individual actors of different generations into identifiable social groups. The resulting assemblages of exotics constitute highly specific material 'fingerprints' for such groups.

The groups of people that can be associated with these tombs in which international connections are expressed may have had different positions in the Levant, Greece and Cyprus, but they were not (only) among the ruling elites in each area. It is logical to think of the people, who were themselves involved in international communication and the exchange of goods. Merchants are well represented in the epigraphic record of the Late Bronze Age Near East (Knapp and Cherry 1994). Most of the kings had their own merchants who left the palace with a royal endowment and had to bring back raw materials and merchandise unavailable at home (Zaccagnini 1973). In the Amarna letters, these merchants also act as ambassadors and messengers for their king.

The relation of these Near eastern merchants with the state/king has been widely debated, especially with regard to the possibilities for private enterprise in long-distance exchange (Knapp and Cherry 1994, 125–155; Routledge and McGeough 2009). In recent research, the sharp distinction between state- and private trade is increasingly put into question (Schloen 2001, 254; Monroe 2009, 151–206). Instead, we should see a chain of command from rulers downwards, in which there is ample space for private enterprise. Interesting in this respect is the case of the trader Sinnaranu at Ugarit, who is mentioned on several tablets (Libolt 1985, 236–242). In one of the available texts a ship of his is returning from Crete (Kapturi), an expedition for which he is exempted from paying taxes. Even though he is also known to be associated to the palace, the tax exemption shows a form of private enterprise at the same time.

The case of Sinnaranu at Ugarit reveals a complex organization of maritime exchange, with distinct roles for merchants, traders, sailors, investors, emissaries, *etc* . Merchants are usually identified in the archaeological record by sets of weights and/or by scaling pans (Hafford 2001; Alberti 2003). Considering the complex organisation of exchange in the Late Bronze Age eastern Mediterranean, we should rather expect a range of varying material relations to the international world of communications and exchange. The varying patterns of material associations within the tomb assemblages of exotics that have been investigated here, show the capabilities of these objects to represent collectively the specific social role of international contacts for different groups of people

The practice of collecting large quantities of exotics in tombs in the Levant and Cyprus discussed in this paper is significant. The large quantities of exotics found in association with wealth indicators and prestige items highlight the increasing wealth and power of some of the groups of people involved in maritime exchange. This practice is most marked in Cyprus, where it was widespread among different social groups and originated at the beginning of the Late Bronze Age. The widespread quantification of exotics in tomb assemblages highlights the important role of international objects in the social representation of the Cypriot people (Antoniadou 2007, 499–501). Trade and traders appear to have occupied a central place in Late Cypriot society. In the Levant, the practice of collecting exotics in large quantities is also visible, but it is much less common and it appears to be restricted to specific groups among the urban elites. This may indicate that even though many different social groups were involved in trade and international exchange (Bell 2009), mostly sub-elites regarded this involvement as a source of group identity and status. Similar practices of collecting by quantity did not occur in Greece, which suggests that international trade and exchange were not as prominent as a label for group identity and status in Mycenaean society. Perhaps, this is the result of a more peripheral position of merchants and trade in the Mycenaean world in comparison to the Levant and, especially, Cyprus.

Concluding remarks

The experimental approach of this article was emphasized at the outset. If only for the sheer scale and diversity of the area dealt with, the conclusions of this paper must be treated as indicative and hypothetical at this stage. Nevertheless, it is clear that the availability of a wide variety of low-value manufactured items enabled various groups of people in the Late Bronze Age eastern Mediterranean to identify themselves with the world of international communications and exchange. Through the wide range of available artefacts, different groups of people were able to select (and exclude) specific items to be included in collective tomb assemblages. The results of such selection processes, which took place over many generations, are material expressions highly specific to particular social groups.

The material hierarchies that are visible in the tomb assemblages that we have looked at appear roughly similar in the Levant, Cyprus and the Aegean. Ivory implements and seals are to be more closely associated with wealth indicators than alabaster vessels and imported pottery. Faience and glass beads and scarabs were most common. The repeated occurrence of similar material combinations in the assemblages is evidence of a shared material culture (van Wijngaarden 2007). However, the tomb assemblages do show some geographical differences in material hierarchies. In Cyprus, for example, there was a particular appreciation for Mycenaean pictorial kraters. Local values and practices were able to differentiate within the general framework of material hierarchies to make assemblages more culturally specific.

The major observed difference among the three areas concerns the practice of collecting exotic goods in tombs in large quantities. It is postulated here that the collection of large quantities of exotics in funerary assemblages may be a practice of people who were themselves involved in the complex organization of overseas communications and contacts. The fact that these assemblages of exotics were constructed during successive funerary rituals spanning several generations, indicates that they were instrumental in providing identity to these traders as recognizable social groups. Since the assemblages vary considerably from tomb to tomb, it is logical to assume that these groups were hereditary and probably kin-based. The degree to which these social groups were able to quantify exotics varies in the three areas under investigation, suggesting a different social role for traders and trade in the respective societies.

The wide availability of small quantities of low-value manufactured exotics in the LBA eastern Mediterranean had an impact on funerary practices in the area. The material and functional characteristics of many of these objects depended highly on social practices, which made them suitable for cultural reinterpretations in many different contexts. The inclusion of small numbers of such exotics in collective tombs became a widespread practice in the eastern Mediterranean during this period. The objects related groups of people to a wider world of international contacts. Even though for many of these people such contacts may not have been real or frequent, the wide range of objects available allowed them to be specific in their associations by selecting and avoiding certain items.

The collective power of these international objects becomes visible especially in cases where they were quantified. The elaborate assemblages of exotics in Cyprus and the Levant contained objects from multiple regions of the Mediterranean. Through the practice of collective burial, these assemblages also covered a wide chronological range. The variations in the individual elements from which the assemblages were constituted created social differentiations according to the various ways in which people were involved in long-distance exchange and communication. The material, geographical, and temporal dimensions of the assemblages of exotics transformed and strengthened the social role of trade and traders in their respective societies.

Acknowledgements

This paper benefited much from the discussions during a workshop on "Theories of value", which was organized at the Goethe Universität of Frankfurt, Germany in November 2010. I would also like to thank S. Voutsaki (Groningen University) for providing me with the text of an unpublished article. Jacob Eerbeek and Elon Heymans gave valuable comments to a preliminary version of this paper, as did two anonymous reviewers. Naturally, I am solely responsible for errors and mistakes that may occur.

References

Adler, W. (1994) *Kamid el-Loz 11. Das 'Schatzhaus' im Palastbereich. Die Befunde des Königsgrabes*. Bonn, Habelt.

Albanèse, L. (1929) Note additionelle (sur Ras Shamra). *Syria* 10, 16–21.

Alberti, M. E. (2003) Weighting and Dying between East and West: Weighing Materials from LBA Aegean Funerary Contexts. In K. P. Foster and R. Laffineur (eds), *METRON: Measuring the Aegean Bronze Age*, Aegaeum 24, 277–284. Liège/Austin, Univ. de Liége, Histoire de l'Art et Archéologie de la Grèce Antique.

Antoniadou, S. (2005) The Impact of Trade on the Society of Cyprus during the Late Bronze Age: Towards a Contextual Approach. In J. Clarke (ed.), *Archaeological Perspectives on the Transmission and Transformation of Culture in the Eastern Mediterranean,* 66–77. Oxford, Oxbow.

Antoniadou, S. (2007) Common Materials, Different Meanings: Changes in Late Cypriot Society. In Antoniadou and Pace 2007, 483–508.

Antoniadou, S and Pace, A. (2007) *Mediterranean Crossroads.* Athens, Pierides Foundation.

Artzy, M. (1997) Nomads of the Sea. In S. Swiny, R. L. Hohlfelder and H. W. Swiney (eds), *Res Maritimae. Cyprus and the Eastern Mediterranean from Prehistory to Late Antiquity Proceedings of the Second International Symposium 'Cities on the Sea': Nicosia, Cyprus, October 18–22, 1994*, 1–16. Cyprus American Archaeological Research Institute Monograph series 1, Atlanta.

Aruz, J. (2008) *Marks of Distinction: Seals and Cultural Exchange Between the Aegean and the Orient.* Corpus der Minoischen und Mykenischen Siegel, Beiheft 7. Mainz, Zabern.

Aruz, J., Benzel, K. and Evans, J. M. (2008) *Beyond Babylon. Art, Trade and Diplomacy in the Second Millennium BC.* New York/New Haven/London, Yale Univ. Press.

Åström, P. (1998) Ceramics: Influences East and West. In E. H. Cline and D. Harris-Cline (eds), *The Aegean and the Orient in the Second Millennium*, 257–263. Liège, Université de Liège, Histoire de l'Art et Archéologie de la Grèce Antique.

Bachhuber, C. and Roberts, G. (2009) *Forces of Transformation: The End of the Bronze Age in the Mediterranean.* Oxford, Oxbow Books.

Baramki, D. C. (1956–1958) A Late Bronze Age Tomb at Sarafend, Ancient Sarepta. *Berytus* 12/1, 129–142.

Bell, C. (2009) Continuity and Change: the Divergent Destinies of LBA Ports in Syria and Lebanon Across the LBA/Iron Age Transition. In Bachhuber and Roberts 2009, 30–38.

Ben Arieh, S. and Edelstein, G. (1977) Akko. Tombs Near the Persian-Garden, *'Atiqot* English Series XII. Jerusalem, Department of Antiquities and Museums.

Bevan, A. (2007) *Stone Vessels and Values in the Mediterranean.* Cambridge, Cambridge University Press.

Biran, A. and Ben-Dov, R. (2002) *Dan II. A Chronicle of the Excavations and the Late Bronze Age "Mycenaean Tomb".* Jerusalem, Nelson Glueck School of Biblical archaeology.

Blegen, C. W. (1937) *Prosymna: The Helladic Settlement Preceding the Argive Heraeum.* Cambridge, University Press.

Bloch, M. (1971) *Placing the dead.* New York, Seminar Press.

Boyd, M. J. (2002) *Middle Helladic and Early Mycenaean Mortuary Practices in the Southern and Western Peloponnese.* Oxford, Archaeopress.

Calvet, Y. and Yon, M. (2008) *Ougarit au Bronze Moyen et au Bronze Récent.* Lyon, Maison de l'Orient.

Caubet, A. (2007) A propos des arts de luxe à Ougarit. In Michaud 2007, 267–283.

Cline, E. H. (1994) *Sailing the Wine-dark Sea. International Trade and the Late Bronze Age Aegean.* Oxford, Tempus Reparatum.

Cline, E. H. (2005) The Multivalent Nature of Imported Objects in the Ancient Mediterranean World. In Laffineur and Greco 2005, 45–51.

Courtois, J. C. and Courtois, L. (1978) Corpus céramique de Ras Shamra-Ugarit. Niveaux historique d'Ugarit. In C. F. A. Schaeffer (ed.), *Ugaritica VII,* 192–370. Paris.

Courtois, J. C. (1979) Ras Shamra – Archéologie. *Supplement au dictionnaire de la Bible*, 1126–1295. Paris, Letouzey et Ané.

Crowley, J. (1989) *The Aegean and the East: an Investigation into the Transference of Artistic Motifs between the Aegean, Egypt and the Near East in the Bronze Age.* Jonsered, Paul Åströms Förlag.

Dikaios, P. (1969) *Enkomi: Excavations 1948–1958. Volume I: The Architectural Remains, the Tombs.* Mainz, Zabern.

Feldman, M. H. (2006) *Diplomacy by Design: Luxury Arts and an "International Style" in the Ancient Near East, 1400–1200 BC.* Chicago, University of Chicago.

Gell, A. (1998) *Art and Agency: Towards a New Anthropological Theory*, Oxford.

Gallou, C. (2005) *The Mycenaean Cult of the Dead.* Oxford, Archaeopress.

Gjerstad, E., Lindros, J., Sjöqvist, E. and Westholm A. (1934) *The Swedish Cyprus Expedition: Finds and Results of the Excavations in Cyprus 1927–1931.* Stockholm.

Gonen, R. (1992a) *Burial Patterns and Cultural Diversity in Late Bronze Age Canaan.* Winona Lake, Eisenbraun.

Gonen, R. (1992b) Structural Tombs in the Second Millennium BC. In A. Kempinski and R. Reich (eds), *The Architecture of Ancient Israel from the Prehistoric to the Persian Periods.* Jerusalem, Israel Exploration Society.

Gosden, C. (2004) *Archaeology and Colonialism. Cultural Contact from 5000 BC to the Present,* Cambridge, University Press.

Guy, P. L. O. and Engberg, R. M. (1938) *Megiddo Tombs.* Chicago, University of Chicago.

Hafford, W. B. (2001) *Merchants in the Late Bronze Age Mediterranean: Tolls Texts and Trade.* Unpublished dissertation, University of Pennsylvania.

Hankey, V. (1995) Stirrup Jars at el-Amarna. In W. Vinian Davies and L. Schofield (eds), *Egypt, the Aegean and the Levant. Interconnections in the Second Millennium BC*, 116–124. London, British Museum Press.

Heymans, E. and van Wijngaarden, G. J. (2011) Low-value Manufactured Exotics in the Eastern Mediterranean in the Late Bronze and Early Iron Ages. In A. Vianello (ed.), *Exotica in the Prehistoric Mediterranean.* Oxford, Oxbow.

Higgins, R. A. (1980) *Greek and Roman jewellery.* London.

Hodder, I. (1987) The Contextual Analysis of Symbolical Meanings. In I. Hodder (ed.), *The Archaeology of Contextual Meanings*, 1–10. Cambridge, Cambridge University Press.

Hoogsteyns, M. (2008) *Artefact mens. Een interdisciplinair onderzoek naar het debat over materialiteit binnen de material culture studies.* Alphen aan de Maas.

Hughes-Brock, H. (1999) Mycenaean Beads: Gender and Social Contexts. *Oxford Journal of Archaeology* 18/3, 277–296.

Ihde, D. (1993) *Philosophy of Technology – an Introduction.* New York.

Immerwahr, S. A. (1971) *The Neolithic and Bronze Ages*. The Athenian Agora, vol. XIII. Princeton, American School of Classical Studies at Athens.

Karageorghis, V. (1974) *Excavations at Kition: 1. The Tombs*. Nicosia, Leventis.

Keswani, P. S. (1989) Dimensions of Social Hierarchy in Late Bronze Age Cyprus: an Analysis of the Mortuary Data from Enkomi. *Journal of Mediterranean Archaeology* 2, 49–86.

Keswani, P. S. (2004) *Mortuary Ritual and Society in Bronze Age Cyprus*. London/Oakville, Equinox.

Kilian-Dirlmeier, I. (1987) Das Kuppelgrab von Vapheio: die Beiganeausstattung in der Steinkiste. Untersuchungen zur Sozialstruktur in späthelladischer Zeit. *Jahrbuch des Römisch-Germanischen Zentralmuseums Mainz* 34/1, 197–212.

Knapp, A. B. and Cherry, J. F. (1994) *Provenience Studies and Bronze Age Cyprus: Production, Exchange and Politico-economic Change*. Madison/Wisconsin, Prehistory Press.

Konstantinidi, E. M. (2001) *Jewellery in the Burial Contexts of the Aegean Bronze Age*. Oxford, BAR.

Laffineur, R. (2005) Imports/Exports in the Eastern Mediterranean: For a Specific Methodology. In Laffineur and Greco 2005, 53–58.

Laffineur, R. and Greco, E. 2005 *Emporia. Aegeans in the Central and Eastern Mediteranean.* Aegeum 16. Liège, Univ. de Liège, Histoire de l'Art et Archéologie de la Grèce Antique.

Laneri, N. (2007) An Archaeology of Funerary Rituals. In N. Laneri (ed.), *Performing Death. Social Analyses of Funerary Traditions in the Ancient Near East and Mediterranea*n, 1–14. Chicago, Oriental Institute Publications.

Latour, B. (2005) Reassembling the Social. An Introduction to Actor-Network-Theory. Oxford, Oxford University Press.

Libolt, C. G. (1985) *Royal Land Grants from Ugarit*. AnnArbor, University of Michigan.

Liverani, M. (1972) Elementi 'irrazionali' nel commercio amarniano. *Oriens Antiquus* 11, 297–317.

Liverani, M. (2000) The Great Powers' Club. In R. Cohen and R. Westbrook (eds), *Amarna-Diplomacy: The Beginnings of International Relations*, 15–27. Baltimore, Johns Hopkins Univ. Press.

Liverani, M. (2008) The Late Bronze Age: Materials and Mechanisms of Trade and Cultural Exchange. In Aruz, Benzel and Evans 2008, 161–168.

Manning, S. W. and Hulin, L. (2005) Maritime Commerce and Geographies of Mobility in the Late Bronze Age of the Eastern Mediterranean: Problematizations. In E. Blake and A. B. Knapp (eds), *The Archaeology of Mediterranean Prehistory*. Blackwell studies in global archaeology 6, 270–302. Malden, Blackwell.

Marchegay, S. (2004) La tombe no 1008 de Minet el-Beida. In G. Galliano (ed.), *Le royaume d'Ougarit : Aux origines de l'alphabet* 246–255. Catalogue de l'exposition du Musée des Beaux-Arts de Lyon.

Marchegay, S. (2007) Les pratiques funéraires à Ougarit à l'Age du Bronze. In Michaud 2007, 423–447.

Marchegay, S. (2008) Les pratiques funéraires à Ougarit au IIe millénaire. Bilan et perspectives des recherché. In Y. Calvet and M. Yon (eds), *Ougarit au Bronze Moyen et au Bronze Récent* 97–118. Lyon, Maison de l'Orient.

Matoïan, V. (2004) Influence des productions mycéniennes à Ougarit (Syrie): l'exemple des vases à etrier. In J. Balensi, J.-Y. Monchambert and S. Müller Celka (eds), *La céramique mycénienne de l'Égée au Levant. Hammag a Vronwy Hankey*, 105–124. Lyon, maison de l'Orient et de la Méditerranee.

McGovern, P. E., Fleming, S. J. and Swann, C. P. (1993) The Late Bronze Age Egyptian Garisson at Beth Shean: Glass and Faience Production and Importation in the Late New Kingdom. *Bulletin of the American School of Oriental Research* 290–291, 1–27.

Mee, C. and Cavanagh, W. (1998) *A Private Place: Death in Prehistoric Greece*, SIMA 125. Jonsered, Paul Åströms Förlag.

Michaud, J. M. 2007, *Le Royaume d'Ougarit de la Crètè à l'Euphrate. Nouveaux axes de recherché*. Sherbrooke, GGC.

Miller, D. (2010) *Stuff.* Cambridge, Polity.

Monchambert, J.-Y. (1983) La céramique de fabrication locale à Ougarit à la fin du Bronze Récent: quelques exemples. *Syria* 60, 25–45.

Monroe, C. M. (2009) *Scales of Fate. Trade, Tradition, and Transformation in the Eastern Mediterranean c. 1350–1175 BCE*. Münster, Ugarit Verlag.

Papadopoulos, J. K. (1997) Innovations, Imitations and Ceramic Style: Modes of Production and Modes of Dissemination. In R. Laffineur and P. P. Betancourt (eds), *TEXNH Craftsmen, Craftswomen and Craftsmanship in the Aegean Bronze Age*, 449–462. Liège/Austin, Univ. de Liège, Histoire de l'Art et Archéologie de la Grèce Antique.

Parker Pearson, M. (1993) The Powerful Dead: Archaeological Relationships between the Living and the Dead. *Cambridge Archaeological Journal* 3/2, 203–229.

Peltenburg, E. J. (1974) The Glazed Vases. In V. Karageorghis (ed.), *Excavations at Kition I. The Tombs*. Appendix I, 105–144. Nicosia, Zavallis Press.

Peltenburg, E. J. (1976) The Faience Vases from Tomb 1 and 2 at Hala Sultan Tekke. In P. Åström, D. M. Bailey and V. Karageorghis (eds), *Hala Sultan Tekke I, Excavations 1897–1971,* 104–109. SIMA 15. Göteborg, Engvig.

Pritchard, J. B. (1980) *The Cemetery at Tell es-Saidiyeh, Jordan*. Philadelphia, Univ. Museum, Univ. of Pennsylvania.

Pulak, C. (2001) The Cargo of the Uluburun Ship and Evidence for Trade with the Aegean and Beyond. In L. Bonfante and V. Karageorghis (eds), *Italy and Cyprus in Antiquity, 1500–450 BC: Proceedings of an International Symposium Held at the Italian Academy for Advanced Studies in America at Columbia University, November 16–18, 2000*, 13–60. Nicosia, Costakis and Leto Severis Foundation.

Pulak, C. (2008) The Uluburun Shipwreck and Late Bronze Age Trade. In Aruz, Benzel and Evans 2008, 89–310.

Robb, J. (2004) The Extended Artifact and the Monumental Economy: A Methodology for Material Agency. In E. DeMarrais, C. Gosden and C. Renfrew (eds), *Rethinking Materiality. The Engagement of Mind with the Material World*, 131–140. Cambridge, McDonald Institute for Archaeological Research.

Routledge, B. and McGeough, K. (2009) Just What Collapsed? A Network Perspective on 'Palatial' and 'Private' Trade at Ugarit. In Bachhuber and Roberts 2009, 22–29.

Salles, J. F. (1995) Rituel mortuaire et rituel social à Ras Shamra/Ougarit. In S. Campbell and A. Green (eds), *The Archaeology of Death in the Ancient Near East*, 171–184. Oxbow Monographs 51, 171–184. Oxford, Oxbow.

Schaeffer, C. F. A. (1931) Les fouilles de Minet el-Beida et de Ras Shamra. Deuxième campagne (printemps 1930). Rapport sommaire. *Syria* 12, 1–14.

Schaeffer, C. F. A. (1936a) Les fouilles de Ras Shamra-Ugarit. Septième campagne (printemps 1935). Rapport Sommaire. *Syria* 17, 105–149.

Schaeffer, C. F. A. (1936b) *The Cuneiform Texts of Ras Shamra-Ugarit*. London, British Academy.

Schaeffer, C. F. A. (1938) Les fouilles de Ras Shamra-Ugarit. Neuvième campagne (printemps 1937). Rapport sommaire. *Syria* 19, 313–327.

Schaeffer, C. F. A. (1949) *Ugaritica II*. Paris, Libraire orientaliste Paul Geuthner.

Schloen, J. D. (2001) *The House of the Father as Fact and Symbol. Patrimonialism in Ugarit and the ancient Near East.* Winona Lake, Eisenbrauns.

Steel, L. (1998) The Social Impact of Mycenaean Imported Pottery in Cyprus. *Annual of the British School at Athens* 93, 285–296.

Steel, L. (2004) *Cyprus Before History.* London, Duckworth.

Thomas, N. (1991) *Entangled Objects.* Cambridge/Mass., Harvard University Press.

Thompson, M. (1979) *Rubbish Theory: The Creation and Destruction of Value.* Oxford, University Press.

Tufnell, O. (1958) *Lachish IV (Tell ed-Duweir): The Bronze Age.* Oxford, University Press.

Vallois, H. V. and Ferembach, D. (1962) Les restes humain de Ras Shamra et de Minet el-Beida: étude anthropoligique. In C. F. A. Schaeffer (ed.), *Ugaritica IV*, 565–622. Paris, Geuthner.

van Wijngaarden, G. J. (2001) The Cultural Significance of Mycenaean pictorial kraters. *Pharos. Journal of the Netherlands Institute in Athens* 9, 75–96.

van Wijngaarden, G. J. (2002) *Use and Appreciation of Mycenaean Pottery in the Levant, Cyprus and Italy.* Amsterdam, Amsterdam University Press.

van Wijngaarden, G. J. (2007) Sharing Material Culture? Mycenaeans in the Mediterranean. In Antoniadou and Pace 2007, 453–482.

van Wijngaarden, G. J. (2008) The Relevance of Authenticity. Mycenaean Pottery in the Mediterranean. In P. F. Biehl and Y. Rassamakin (eds), *Import and Imitation in Archaeology,* 125–145. Langenweißbach, Beier & Beran.

Verbeek, P. P. (2000) *De daadkracht der dingen. Over techniek, filosofie en omgeving.* Amsterdam.

Vermeule, E. and Wolzky, F. Z. (1978) New Aegean Relations with Cyprus: The Minoan and Mycenaean Pottery from Toumba tou Skourou. *Proceedings of the Philosophical Society* 122, 294–317.

Voutsaki, S. (in press) From Value to Meaning, from Things to Persons. In G. Urton and J. Papadopoulos (eds), *The Construction of Value in the Ancient World.* Los Angeles, Kotsen Institute.

Zaccagnini, C. (1973) *Lo scambio dei doni nel Vicino Oriente durante i secoli X.* Roma, Centro per le antichità e la storia dell'arte del vicino oriente.

8.

Migrant drinking assemblages in Aegean Bronze Age settings

Jeremy B. Rutter

Introduction

This paper explores the transfer from one culture to another of groups of containers connected with the activity of social drinking – that is, the dispensing and consumption of liquids by small to medium-sized human groups in regularly occurring social gatherings.[1] Precisely *what* was being consumed at these gatherings, though undeniably an important question, cannot at present be meaningfully addressed due to a simple lack of data. Presumably, the beverages would have included, although not necessarily been restricted to, alcoholic ones, principally wine or beer (*e.g.* Jung 2006b, 412 and note 39).

The region under consideration comprises the southern and central portions of the western Aegean, specifically the island of Crete, the southern and central Greek mainland, and the central Aegean islands of the Cyclades. I have chosen three chronologically and spatially discrete examples of the transmission of drinking assemblages that date between the middle of the third millennium and the end of the second and are more or less equidistant from one another in time. Two of these involve the introduction of new forms from outside the region of direct concern, while the third consists of what may be termed an 'internal transfer' from one southern Aegean cultural sphere to another. During the periods concerned, the *southern* Aegean is conventionally considered to have encompassed at least four distinct Bronze Age traditions of material culture: the Minoan culture of Crete, the Helladic culture of the central and southern Greek mainland; the Cycladic culture of the central Aegean islands; and the western Anatolian culture of the Turkish mainland. A central purpose of this paper is to sketch a series of considerations in terms of which the individuality of specific transfers of a *functionally* comparable artefactual set – in this case, a drinking assemblage – within a single well-connected region can be highlighted. By stressing the particular characteristics of each such transfer, while at the same time noting when the absence of specific categories of data prevents us from describing it as thoroughly as we might like, we can move beyond vague expressions of one culture's 'influencing' another to a fuller and more nuanced understanding of what specific instances of material cultural transmission may signify or alternatively to a heightened realisation of what kinds of information are still needed before its significance can become readily apparent.

Example 1

Around the middle of the third millennium – let us simply say *c.* 2500 BCE – five new ceramic forms make what might have been a relatively sudden, and with one possible exception perhaps even synchronous, appearance in the Cycladic islands at more than a dozen sites located on at least ten different islands, including both settlement and funerary contexts: from east to west, Markiani on Amorgos, Daskalio on Keros, Panormos and other sites on Naxos, Paroikia on Paros, Akrotiri on Thera, Mt. Kynthos on Delos, Kastri and Chalandriani on Syros, Akrotiraki on Siphnos, Phylakopi on Melos, and Ayia Irini on Keos, and much further to the north in the Sporades, Palamari on Skyros (Fig. 8.1; Wilson 1999, 97–100, fig. 3.6; Broodbank 2000, 312, fig. 103; Angelopoulou 2008; Kouka 2009). These shapes (Fig. 8.2) include three readily differentiable drinking vessels, usually termed the tankard, the bell-shaped cup, and the *depas*, a narrow-necked beaked jug (often made more distinctive by way of a lentoid body), and a very shallow, lipless

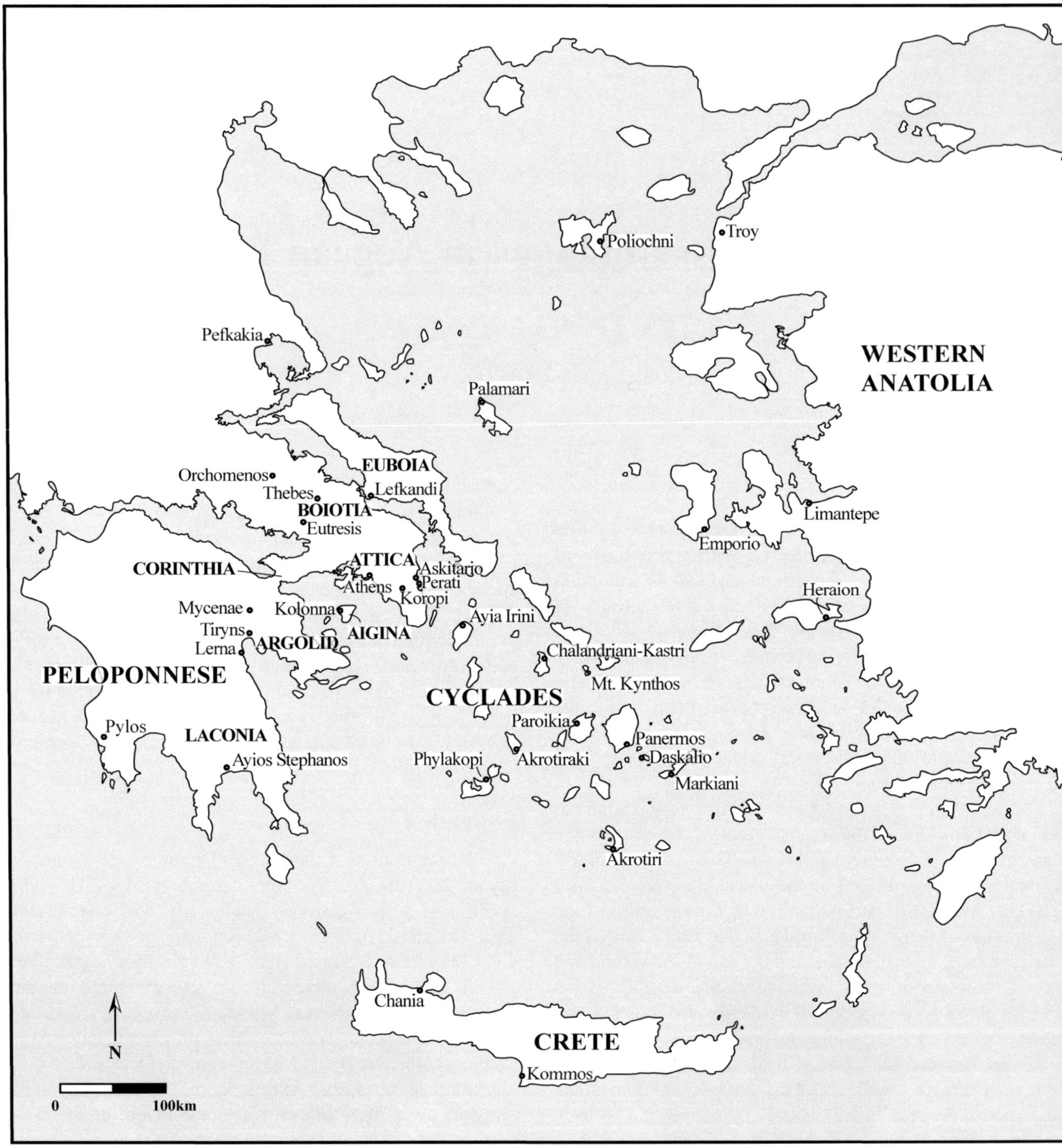

Fig. 8.1: Map of the Aegean showing locations of sites and regions mentioned in the text.

bowl, often described as a plate, especially when straight-sided and wheel-made. All authorities are agreed that this group of shapes was originally at home along the western Anatolian coast and spread from there, beginning well after the start of the EB (Early Bronze) 2 period, to sites situated on such large eastern Aegean islands as Lemnos, Chios, and Samos that shared a common material culture with the northwest Anatolian assemblage termed by Korfmann

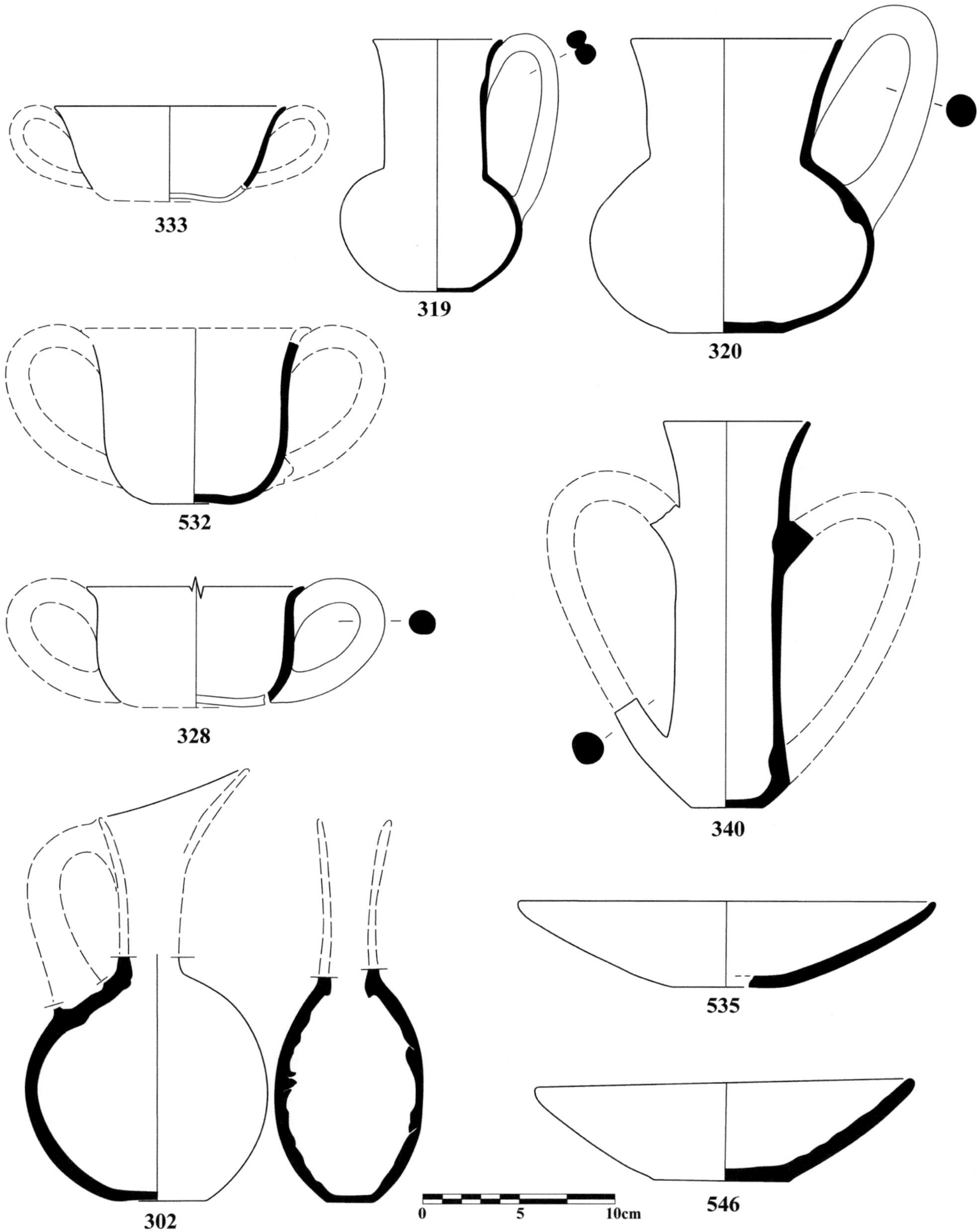

Fig. 8.2: The five shapes considered diagnostic of the Kastri Group (in the Cyclades) and Lekandi I (on Euboea, Aigina, and the central Greek mainland) ceramic assemblages.

the 'Maritime Troia-Culture' characteristic of cities I–III at Troy (Korfmann 2001; Çalis-Sazci 2006). Whether these shapes were transmitted to the Cyclades from northwestern Anatolia or from some region further south along the coast in the vicinity of such major Early Bronze centers as Limantepe, Emporio on Chios, and the Heraion on Samos is still something of an open question, but sites on northern Aegean islands such as Poliochni on Lemnos and Palamari on Skyros are more likely to have acquired their versions of these shapes by contacts with Troy. Such analyses as have so far been applied to examples of these shapes from Cycladic sites have confirmed that the drinking vessels, exclusive of the wheelmade plates, were in most cases locally produced as well as imported when they occur in substantial numbers (Wilson 1999, 119, 125; Broodbank 2000, 312–313).[2] But relatively few of these sites – in fact, only Kastri on Syros, Daskalio on Keros, and Ayia Irini on Keos – have produced examples of all four of the drinking shapes (Broodbank 2000, 312, fig. 103). Several authors have suggested that the *depas* is indicative of a chronologically later stage within late EB 2 but this has not yet been conclusively demonstrated. Certainly this particular form is considerably rarer in island settings than the other two open forms, the tankard and the bell-shaped cup, but this could be the result of its having had status implications in the central and western Aegean that we have failed to perceive at, for example, Troy, where it is exceedingly common in deposits within the royal citadel (MacGillivray 1984, 74–75; Mellink 1986, 147, pl. 16; *contra* Wilson 1999, 100–101). In the Cyclades, the cultural phase represented by the local adoption of these Anatolianising forms is termed the Kastri Group. At all sites where this cultural phase is represented, with the single and very recently claimed exception of Daskalio on Keros (Renfrew *et al.* 2009, 31–35), it constitutes a final period of occupation immediately preceding either a substantial hiatus in settlement or else the final abandonment of the site. But, as Broodbank has stressed, the *introduction* of the novel Anatolianising shapes is an island-wide phenomenon that precedes the subsequent horizon of abandonment by a lengthy time, possibly as long as a couple of centuries (Broodbank 2000, 309–319).

Aside from the shapes themselves, aspects of the decoration, technology of production, and frequency of these Anatolianising forms in Cycladic contexts merit consideration. At Ayia Irini on Keos, the site that has so far produced by far the largest and most fully published and carefully contextualised collection of this material, all examples are handmade, with surfaces being either the same reddish-brown as the fracture or coated with a streaky black wash and smoothed, or alternatively burnished, either directly over the reddish-brown fabric or after the application of a slip that has fired either black or reddish-brown. Decoration other than the overall coating with coloured slips is limited to the horizontal ribbing that appears on some tankard necks (Wilson 1999, 120 III–253/255, pl. 83; 126 III–324/326, pls. 33, 86). The Anatolian prototypes of these shapes are frequently wheel-made, so it is perhaps not surprising to encounter a form of decoration on a few handmade tankards that might be mimicking wheel-ridging, but this ribbing is arguably more likely to imitate metalwork. At Ayia Irini, only a handful – six, to be precise – fine pinkish-buff plates are wheel-made and these are all considered to be imported, possibly from Euboea where closely comparable examples have been found at Lefkandi (Wilson 1999, 141–142, III–546/551, pls. 37, 92–93). Possibly imported from the same source are red-slipped-and-polished examples of bell-shaped cups, shallow bowls, and beaked jugs. If the source of these imports is accurately identified as Euboea, we are confronted with the fact that versions of these shapes that are closer to the Anatolian originals than any of the local imitations, both technologically and decoratively, are reaching Keos from regions further west than from the original source of these shapes in the east. Thanks to David Wilson's attempts at quantification of over 4200 vessels from undisturbed Phase III contexts at Ayia Irini, we learn that tankards are three times as popular as bell-shaped cups and over twenty times as popular as *depa*;[3] very shallow bowls are extremely common, but only one out of 200 of them is a wheelmade import. Beaked jugs are as numerous as the bell-shaped cups, but unfortunately highly fragmentary and thus difficult to assign to specific types; only one can be identified as having had a lentoid body, a feature that because of its rarity is taken to mark this vessel as an import (Wilson 1999, 123 III–302, pls. 32, 85).

The very same new, Anatolianising shapes that characterise the Kastri Group phase in the Cyclades show up at a significant number of mainland Greek sites distributed principally along the coast between Thessaly in the north (at Pefkakia in the Bay of Volos) and eastern Attica in the south, including several sites on Euboea and one on Aigina in the middle of the Saronic Gulf, both islands that fall within the mainland rather than Cycladic cultural orbit throughout most of the Bronze Age. A fair number of sites further inland, in the region of Boeotia, have also produced examples of these new shapes, notably Thebes, Orchomenos, and Eutresis. At both Pefkakia and the Euboean site of Lefkandi, these shapes are found stratified in a number of superposed architectural levels, demonstrating that they enjoyed a lengthy *floruit* in these mainland settings, where they are the diagnostic shapes of what is known as the Lefkandi I assemblage, a sub-phase of Early Helladic II that probably corresponded quite closely to the duration of the Kastri Group in the islands. But these mainland sites were not abandoned in the same way as those in the Cyclades (except for Daskalio), so the developmental history of these shapes and their evolution into new forms is documented only in these Helladic and, in the case of

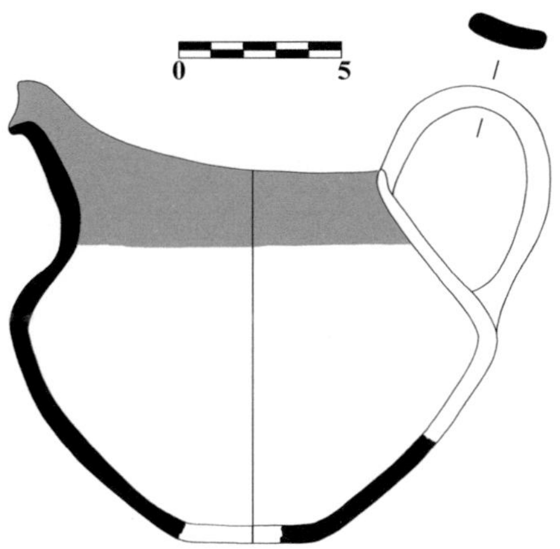

Fig. 8.3: Hybrid sauceboat from Kolonna III (Ceramic Phase C) on Aigina: Walter and Felten 1981, 155 no. 125 (Courtesy of Lydia Berger).

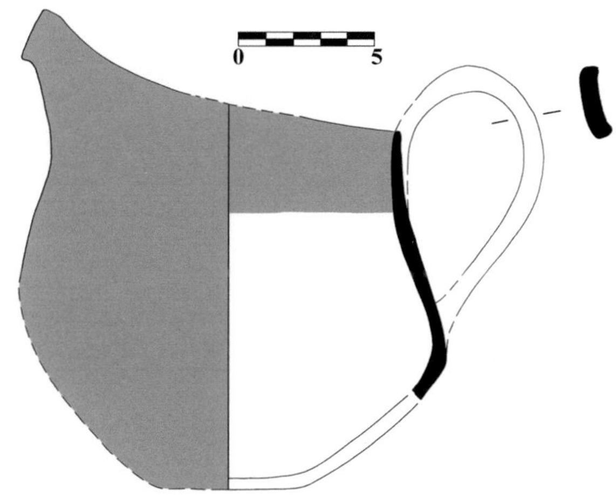

Fig. 8.5: Hybrid sauceboat from Kolonna III (Ceramic Phase C) on Aigina 155: Walter and Felten 1981, no. 127 (Courtesy of Lydia Berger).

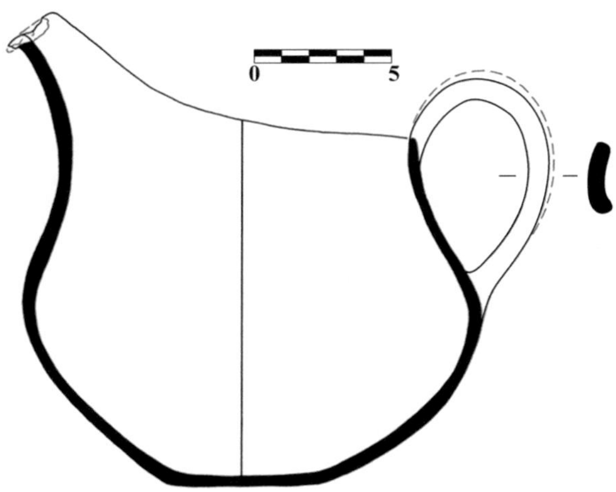

Fig. 8.4: Hybrid sauceboat from Kolonna III (Ceramic Phase C) on Aigina: Walter and Felten 1981, 155 no. 126 (Courtesy of Lydia Berger).

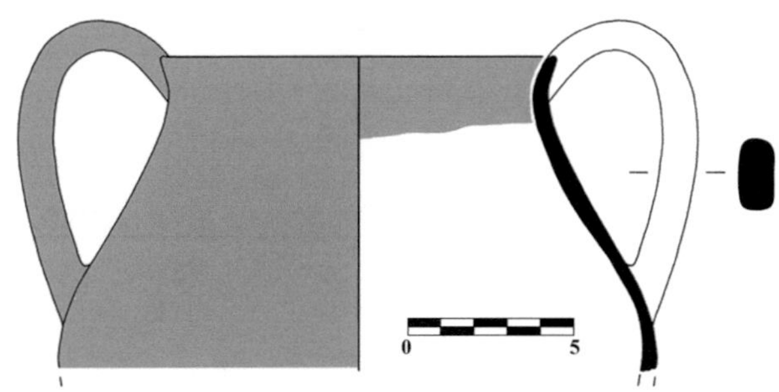

Fig. 8.6: Hybrid tankard from Kolonna III (Ceramic Phase C) on Aigina: Walter and Felten 1981, 156 no. 136 (Courtesy of Lydia Berger).

Pefkakia, Thessalian contexts. Unfortunately, only the sites of Kolonna on Aigina and Pefkakia in Thessaly have been both recently and carefully enough excavated, as well as fully enough published, to provide the kinds of data useful in the present context. What emerges clearly from these mainland Greek sites is that the wheel was more extensively used at these sites than at any locale so far identified in the islands, certainly for unslipped and unburnished plates, and also for some of the other shapes. Also noteworthy, and most clearly exemplified at Kolonna, is the appearance of altogether new shapes that represent hybrid forms manifesting features adopted from both the indigenous Early Helladic II ceramic repertoire and the novel Anatolianising forms. Thus the spouted, ring-footed, and small-handled form known as the sauceboat, by far the most popular indigenous shape in fine ware and one that had presumably served as the standard drinking vessel at this site for centuries, now occurs in Phase III at Kolonna in a flat-based, stubby-spouted, and high-handled version that is barely recognisable as a sauceboat variant; its flat base and high-swung vertical strap handle have been taken over from the Anatolianising drinking shapes (Figs. 8.3–8.5; Walter and Felten 1981, 155 nos. 125–127, pl. 84; Berger 2004, 1099–1100; forthcoming, fig. 2).[4] At the very same time, a modified form of the Anatolianising bell-cup or *depas* appears at Kolonna, which features a piriform rather than cylindrical body shape and has substituted a pair of vertical strap handles, roughly rectangular in section, for the two loop handles, round in section, that were standard on the two-handled Anatolianising shapes (Figs. 8.6–8.8; Walter and Felten 1981, 156 no. 136, fig. 99; 157 no. 163, fig. 98, pl. 88; Rutter 1983, 343–345 and notes 53–55; 1995, 300–301; Berger 2004, 1100, pl. 7.34, 36; forthcoming, fig. 2).[5] Thus

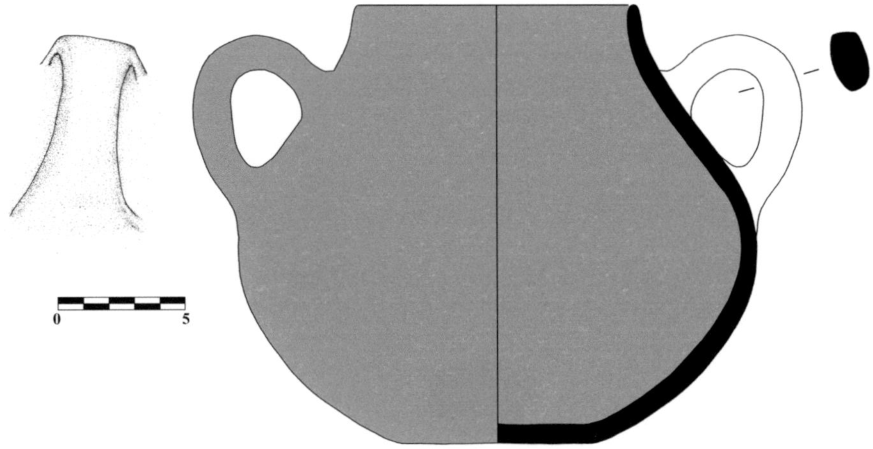

Fig. 8.7: Hybrid tankard from Kolonna III (Ceramic Phase C) on Aigina: Walter and Felten 1981, 157 no. 163 (Courtesy of Lydia Berger).

Fig. 8.8: Hybrid tankard from Kolonna III (Ceramic Phase C) on Aigina: Walter and Felten 1981, 1100, pl. 7.34 (Courtesy of Lydia Berger).

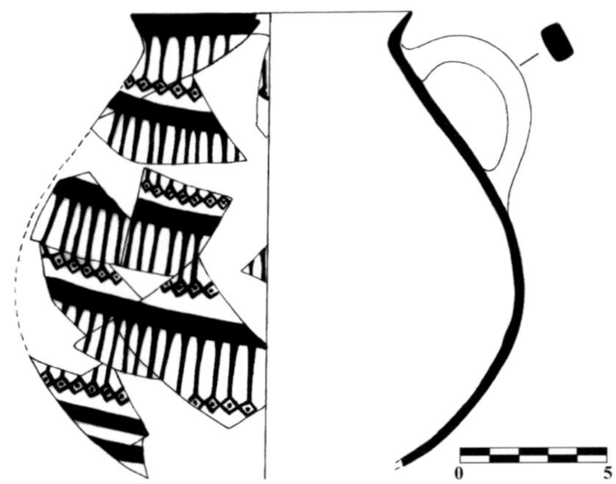

Fig. 8.9: Hybrid tankard from Koropi (Attica). Brauron Museum (Courtesy of Kerasia Douni).

a new pair of drinking vessels came into existence on Aigina that enjoyed a comparatively brief lifespan, possibly restricted to this one site in the case of the modified sauceboat, before the sauceboat disappeared entirely and the modified bell-cup/*depas* morphed once more into the shoulder-handled tankard typical of the ensuing Early Helladic III period at Kolonna (Phase V) and throughout adjacent regions of the Greek mainland.

An even more striking version of such a ceramic hybrid form is a shoulder-handled tankard from Koropi in Attica (Fig. 8.9; Kakavogianni 1993, 166, pl. 18a, six fragments at lower left) that features pattern-painted decoration employing Cycladic motifs in a style that discoveries at the nearby coastal site of Askitario suggest may have been at home in this particular region of central Greece at the end of the Early Helladic II period. But this vase clearly betrays in its three-zoned decorative syntax that it is ancestral to the standard decoration on vessels of this shape in the Early Helladic III Argolid and Corinthia (Rutter 1995, 290, 487–490). An additional feature of this same vase from Koropi connects it with yet another kind of short-lived hybrid product that is reasonably common in Boeotia, eastern Attica, and Locris, but to my knowledge nowhere else at this time: namely, its crinkled or petal-shaped rim. Restricted ordinarily to solidly coated or partially coated tankards, this feature has always been associated with the influence of metalwork on ceramics. In this instance, the connection with metalwork once again suggests influence from western Anatolia and the well-known vessels in gold and silver found in amazing numbers by Schliemann in the ruins of Troy II. These Trojan precious metal vessels exhibit a number of the other features of the Anatolianising ceramic vessels that we have been focusing on: for example, the shapes of the Kastri Group tankard and bell-shaped cup in silver (albeit lacking the tubular handles characteristic of the ceramic types, but these could be easily enough soldered on: Tolstikov and Treister 1996, 36, nos. 6–7; 96–97, nos. 102–103) or the famous gold double-sauceboat that is actually itself a hybrid in being a combination of a sauceboat and a bell-shaped cup (Tolstikov and Treister 1996, 32–35, no. 5).

Such clear associations of our migrating ceramic forms with precious metal prototypes have suggested a plausible scenario for why these western Anatolian drinking shapes were being adopted in a variety of different regions where they had previously been unknown: they represent imitations of metallic originals (Nakou 2007, 228–240), all but a few of which were melted down and re-used long ago, but which may once have been circulating widely throughout the Aegean and coastal Anatolia thanks to the maritime contacts of Troy and other western Anatolian centres, the introduction of new metallurgical practices into the Aegean such as the use of tin bronzes from Troy in particular, and the capabilities of the jewellers and smiths working for royal masters at sites such as Troy and Liman Tepe. Potentially caught up in this wide-ranging dissemination of precious metal drinking vessels may have been artisans working in other materials such as clay, with the result that potters exploiting the technology of the wheel for the first time in the Aegean during the Troy II era may also have migrated to select sites on the other side of the Aegean. Such a reconstruction would account for the application of the wheel to the production of plates in particular, a shape that lent itself especially well to this mode of manufacture and one that may not have been produced often in metal, and perhaps only in copper or bronze when it was (*e.g.* Tolstikov and Treister 1996, 28–29, no. 1).

Only some time *after* the arrival of the new ceramic technology in central Greece in the second half of the Early Helladic II period was it further extended, in combination with controlled reduction firing that had been experimented with on several previous occasions in Greece as early as the Neolithic, to produce the fine gray-burnished class of pottery that is known to us in its Middle Bronze Age incarnation as Gray Minyan, a passable imitation of silver plate that became popular, and was probably initially developed, in Boeotia before being exported as an idea to the northeast Peloponnese and other regions of mainland Greece (Rutter 1983; Nakou 2007, 231–232). As Georgia Nakou has made clear in a brilliant analysis of ceramic change on the Greek mainland at the end of the third millennium BCE, this second and later series of ceramic developments that characterise the Early Helladic III period involve not only continuing inspiration from metalwork and variable applications of the new technology of the wheel to pottery production but also altogether new decorative preferences derived from basketry (Nakou 2007, 235–240, fig. 13.7; Choleva, forthcoming; Rutter 1988). Nevertheless, however much we may have learned over the past three decades about the when, where, and even how of the transmission of this suite of Early Bronze Anatolian drinking shapes across the Aegean, we can still say very little about who orchestrated it at either end. What are needed are more helpful contexts in which the usage of these new ceramic types can be investigated and compared in greater detail from site to site and generation to generation. Even at those sites where the distinctive Kastri Group and Lefkandi I forms have been recovered in the greatest quantities and have been most extensively published (*e.g.* Ayia Irini, Pefkakia), the vast majority of examples derive from building fills and miscellaneous dumps rather than from floor deposits or burials.[6]

Example 2

Five to six hundred years later, the remarkable collection of precious metal vessels recovered from Grave Circles A and B at Mycenae and contemporary changes in mainland Greek ceramics at the dawn of the Mycenaean era allow us to examine once again, but under quite different historical circumstances, the connection between metalwork and ceramics involving what is in functional terms largely, although not entirely,[7] a drinking assemblage. Whether this second case study is to be dated to the 17th century following Manning and others, or to the 16th century as Warren, Bietak, Wiener, and the traditional chronology would have it, is fortunately an irrelevant concern: a relative chronological scheme will serve satisfactorily for the purposes of ordering the sequence of events, even if we should recognise from the outset that the overall timeframe of this second case study is much shorter than the several centuries occupied by the first. The periods now of concern, Late Helladic I and IIA, are usually given roughly a century and a half (from roughly 1600 to 1450, *e.g.* Warren and Hankey 1989, 169, tab. 3.1), and even with Manning's higher chronology will have lasted for a maximum of no more than two (Rutter 2001, 106, tab. 2, from 1680 to 1520/1480 BCE). The source of prototypes in precious metal has now shifted from western Anatolia to Crete, and the area directly affected initially has moved from the Cyclades and east-central Greece to the southern and eastern Peloponnese, with a special focus on the Argolid. Crete and these areas of the Greek mainland had been in regular contact for centuries during the Middle Bronze Age – that is, the Middle Helladic era in the Peloponnese – and mainlanders living at major coastal sites such as Lerna, Ayios Stephanos (Zerner 2008, especially 178–188, 201–206), and Kolonna (Hiller 1993; Kilian-Dirlmeier 1997, 136–154; Gauss 2006) had been exposed to substantial numbers of Minoan ceramic imports of all kinds, albeit chiefly tablewares, with no significant impact on local ceramic production in the Argolid and only modest impact on that of coastal Laconia and Aigina. But within a very short space of time in LH (Late Helladic) I , regions of the mainland from Messenia and Laconia in the south through the Argolid and Corinthia and on into Attica, Boeotia, and even Locris in central Greece all of a sudden adopted Minoan drinking shapes in whatever the finest of locally produced tablewares happened to be. In the south, these wares actually resembled Minoan products quite closely because of the very close relationship that southern Laconia appears to have enjoyed at this time with the culturally Minoan inhabitants of Kythera, just off their southern coast.[8] But the further north one proceeds, the less the local fine wares resemble Minoan ones, especially north of the Argolid. Regardless of where one goes during LH I in southern and east-central Greece, however, one encounters local production of Minoan drinking shapes, especially the straight-sided or Vapheio cup and to some degree also the semiglobular cup with a sharply everted lip: in the Argolid, in so-called Lustrous Decorated ware, the direct ancestor of decorated Mycenaean pottery;[9] in the Corinthia, in Light-on-Lustrous-Dark-slipped-and-Burnished; in Boeotia and Locris, in Gray Minyan and Polychrome Matt-painted (more recently termed Boeotian Bichrome: Lindblom, Mommsen, and Whitbread, forthcoming); and in virtually all regions in the local version of fine monochrome matt-painted ware. What has caused this sudden, widespread but regionally variable adoption of Minoan cup types, and is it really only fine ware cup types that are changing at this time?

Two developments in particular seem to be responsible for, or at the very least closely connected with, this phenomenon. First of all, it is precisely at this time that the first vessels in gold and silver begin to appear in the sequence of shaft graves spanning the terminal Middle Helladic through Late Helladic IIA periods at Mycenae (Graziadio 1988; 1991). Metalwork of this kind appears only with the latest burials of Grave Circle B – in Tombs Alpha, Gamma, Delta, Iota, and Nu. Though present in all of the graves of the generally later Circle A, the numbers of precious metal vessels in the earliest tombs – Graves II and VI – are comparable to what one finds in Circle B – one or at most two such vessels per tomb. It is not until close to the end of the series of graves in Circle A that the number and morphological range of such vessels explodes in the richest graves – V, IV, and III in chronological order – before tapering off to the levels of one or less per burial in the latest grave, I, that is said to have contained three women. Thanks to the first-rate study of these vessels published by Ellen Davis in 1977, building on the monumental 1930 work of Georg Karo, it is possible to trace developments in the introduction of new types and techniques within this assemblage of over 70 precious metal vessels in considerable detail (Karo 1930; Davis 1977; Wright 2004, 22–23, tabs. 4–5).

The elites who were buried in Circles B and A at Mycenae are likely to have been emulating the example of other elites in their choices of burial form (that is, the shaft grave) and in the ranges of activities that their grave goods emphasised (namely hunting, warfare, and the pouring of high-end liquids from exotic containers into equally exotic drinking vessels for the purposes of consumption at exclusive, one imagines, social gatherings). That is, these particular elite groups at Mycenae did not themselves invent the shaft grave form, nor were they the first to draw particular attention to their prowess as hunters, warriors, and drinkers. With respect to all of these traits, in my opinion, they were following the earlier example established by the elite at the supremely important Middle Helladic site of Kolonna on Aigina, and perhaps also to some extent of other island-based elites at such sites as Ayia Irini, Phylakopi, and maybe even Akrotiri. But the elite of Circles B and A at Mycenae, presumably the rulers of whatever polity Mycenae controlled at that time, do appear to have been pioneers in introducing metal vessels as a mark of their societal dominance. And one reason that they were moved to do so appears to have been their control of a metallic resource that none of their fellow rulers possessed to a comparable degree – *gold* (Davis 1983; *cf.* also Nakou 2007 for Troy at an earlier period). With this material, if not also with others, they were able to hire artisans to produce objects of constantly increasing sophistication at the same time as they traded for functionally equivalent finished artefacts in a metal to which they did not have such exclusive access, namely silver. As they began to display their power by way of locally produced gold vessels and imported silver vessels embellished with gold accents, they set off an explosion of emulation that resulted in the production of ceramic lookalikes of their precious metal cups and pouring vessels – initially, all straight-sided cups and ewers or beaked jugs (Wright 2004, 23, tab. 5). These are precisely the shapes that are the first metallic forms to be imitated in ceramic, and these imitations are typically decorated in a fashion that is as close to the metallic original as possible. The earliest straight-sided cups in gold and silver from Circles B and A are decorated with vertical fluting or slightly more evolved arcade patterns, and these are what are being imitated by ceramic straight-sided and Vapheio cups decorated with Ripple.

The extensive exchange in decorated tablewares that is documented during the LH I period presumably reflects the consumption by local elites all over the Greek mainland, above all by persons aspiring to *become* elite, of the most handsome regional products, all of which were themselves modelled to at least some degree after the precious metal prototypes initially put into play at Mycenae. The rapid dissemination of the new shapes and their associated decoration reflects the second important factor that was operative at the time when these metal drinking vessels were initially produced and displayed, namely a spirit of intense competition for status in mainland Greek culture between established as well as aspiring elites. This competitive milieu explains not only the rapid adoption by individuals of the latest advances in drinking equipment[10] but also, in spatial terms, the sudden rise in the LH I period of a series of competing tableware assemblages, each seemingly characteristic of a particular region – the wares that I have already mentioned as the vehicles of the new Minoan-inspired drinking shapes such as Gray Minyan, various schools of fine matt-painted, Mainland Polychrome Matt-painted, and Light-on-Dark-slipped-and Burnished, in addition to the Lustrous Decorated ancestor of pattern-decorated Mycenaean pottery. The more distinctive such wares were, apparently, the better – how else to explain the sudden proliferation of so many visually distinct wares producing examples of what are effectively the same shapes?

Within the short lifetime of the LH I period, this intense competition for dominance among these regional tablewares had been settled in favour of the lustrous-decorated style that by the end of the period appears to have been at home in the Argolid, whether or not this is where the style actually originated – that is, the production of this style was taken over by the region where the whole competition was kicked off in the first place by the elite of Mycenae. And why was everyone imitating Minoan drinking shapes, the straight-sided cup and various beaked jugs? The answer must be because the initial products in gold were produced at Mycenae by local craftsmen imitating the only precious metal vessels they could get their hands on at this time as models – namely, Minoan Neopalatial drinking vessels in silver. But in the highly competitive atmosphere of the Argolid at this time, and especially at Mycenae, it was a matter of very few years indeed before the next stage in the competition for enhanced status began, with the introduction of new shapes, new motifs, and ultimately altogether new techniques by not only local artisans but now also by immigrant Minoan craftsmen and perhaps even metalworkers from further afield. The resulting experiments with materials, modes of decoration, and novel shapes are familiar to Aegean prehistorians as some of the artistic masterpieces of the Shaft Grave era: the Silver Siege rhyton (Athens NM 477, 504), the silver Battle krater (Athens NM 605–607), the gold stemmed cup with repoussé rosettes once elaborated with white and blue inlays (Athens NM 351), to name only a few. A significant feature of these masterpieces, which distinguishes them sharply from the earliest precious metal vessels recovered from Circle B and the earlier Circle A tombs, is their uniqueness. At some point, sheer creativity in morphology or decoration or the combination of both became a value of preeminent importance to the elite with regard to these gold and silver containers, albeit a short-lived one.

Mycenaean potters could only follow this trail of metallurgical inventiveness so far. During the LH IIA period, the comparatively small number of different pattern-decorated ceramic types was dramatically expanded by a class of vessels to which Oliver Dickinson originally gave the name 'palatial', a term that has unfortunately stuck even though Mycenaean culture at this time could boast nothing remotely resembling a palace, at least not in the Argolid (Dickinson 1972; Mountjoy 1999, 21–22).[11] Dickinson's 'palatial' forms tend to be elaborately decorated and comparatively rare – rhyta and pouring vessels of various kinds, usually of well-established Minoan types of the Late Minoan IB phase (bridge-spouted jugs and jars, in-and-out bowls, one- and two-handled stemmed cups, *etc*.). They are typically *not* the kinds of new metal vessels being invented at this time by the smiths working for the elite at Mycenae. As a consequence, virtually none of the advanced pictorial work that appears on the metal vessels of the shaft graves makes its way into ceramics, in pronounced contrast to what had happened on Thera in the late Middle Bronze Age only a couple of generations earlier (Papagiannopoulou 2008). The close connection between metalwork and ceramics in the early Mycenaean era was a very short-lived phenomenon; Dickinson's 'palatial' class of pottery, itself imitating metallic models of the LH I and early LH IIA phases, has disappeared by the end of LH IIA. The spirit of Mycenaean competition had moved on to other spheres of activity (such as tomb architecture, once again especially at Mycenae: Wright 1987), with the result that Mycenaean pottery of the subsequent LH IIB phase is much simpler and much less indebted to Minoan models: indeed, it represents the earliest phase during which Mycenaean pottery becomes essentially independent of Minoan models and begins to exert some influence on Cretan products for the first time (Furumark 1972, 495–497; Mountjoy 1986, 37). Mycenaean plate likewise becomes simpler in every way during the LH IIB and subsequent periods, as the finds from such tombs as the Kokla tholos and Dendra tomb 10 show (Wright 2004, 23, tab. 5; 25 and fig. 4).

The case study offered by the Shaft Graves has allowed far greater insights into the human agency operating at various levels in this particular example of the interaction between metallic and ceramic forms than could be derived from the preceding analysis of the earlier Kastri Group/Lefkandi I assemblage. Artisans as well as their elite patrons both played a major role, and it is even possible to distinguish between the impacts of multiple craftsmen trained in different traditions as well as several spatially discrete groups of elites. Thanks to the chronological fine-tuning possible in the cases of this specific series of burials, it is also possible to isolate at least two distinct stages in the interaction between metallic and ceramic forms and to appreciate how astonishingly quickly such outbursts of stylistic and technological innovation and emulation can both arise as well as subside.

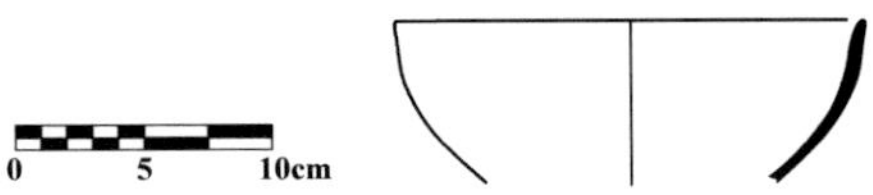

Fig. 8.10: Sardinian bowl and jar type imported to LM IIIB Kommos (Crete): Kommos C6710. After Rutter 2006, pl. 3.86.

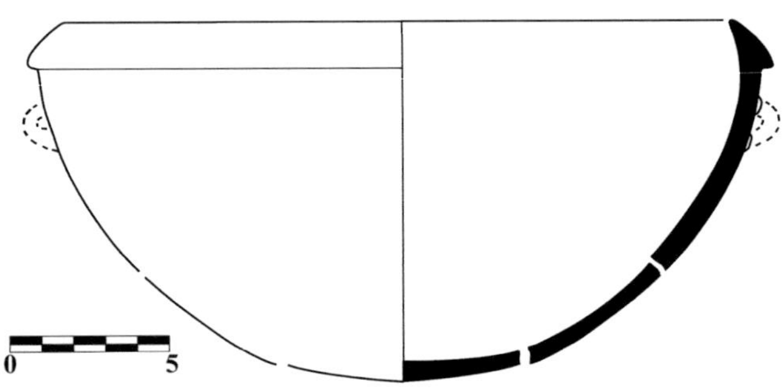

Fig. 8.11: Sardinian bowl and jar type imported to LM IIIB Kommos (Crete): Kommos C6694. After Rutter 2006, pl. 3.86.

Example 3

A third and last case study, from near the end of the Bronze Age, involves ceramic forms moving into the Aegean from further west in the central Mediterranean. The shapes in question, never produced in metal, were introduced into the Aegean during the 13th and 12th century BCE in the form of handmade and burnished pots produced usually in medium coarse to coarse fabrics; that is, the vessels that in this case inspired Aegean lookalikes in fine wheelmade and painted wares were materially as well as technologically inferior to the imitations they provoked. At least four comparatively recent and comprehensive assessments of these intrusive dark-surfaced, handmade, and burnished wares provide for the first time extensive and well-illustrated corpora of this distinctive ceramic class from sites on both the Greek mainland and Crete (Jung 2006a, 21–47; Strack 2007, 25–111; Kilian 2007; Lis 2009). The focus here, as in the previous two case studies, is on the impact that the introduction of these novel forms

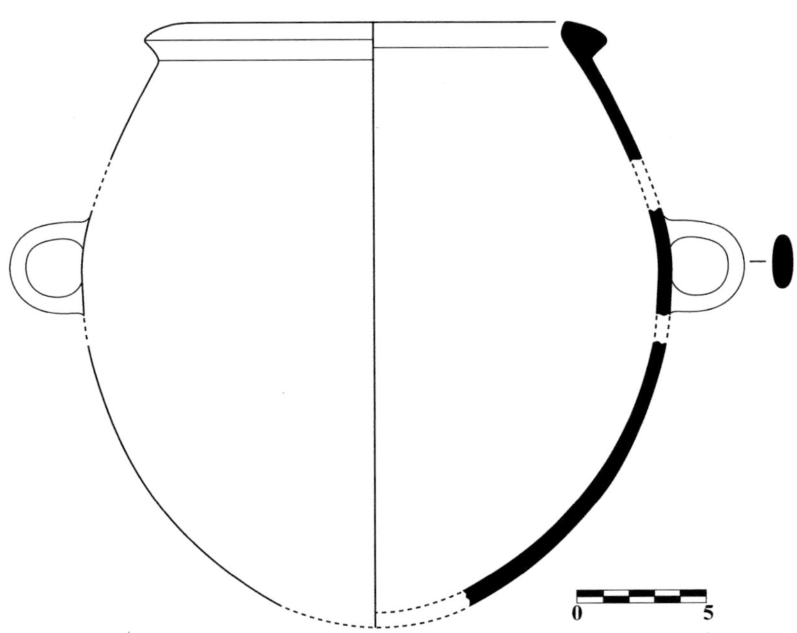

Fig. 8.12: Sardinian bowl and jar type imported to LM IIIB Kommos (Crete): Kommos C3310. After Watrous 1992, figs. 74, 76.

had on local ceramic production at those Aegean sites where substantial quantities of these alien wares appear.

The series of Sardinian jars and bowls that were imported to the south Cretan harbour town of Kommos in some numbers during the 13th century appear to have had either minimal or altogether no impact on local ceramic production of any kind (Figs. 8.10–8.13; Watrous 1992, 163–168, figs. 73–76, pls. 56–58; Watrous, Day, and Jones 1998; Rutter 2006, 674–678, pls. 3.86, 3.90).[12] The reasons for this are likely to be twofold: first of all the pots in question were exclusively imported rather than locally made; and secondly, the pots functioned as transport vessels, the jars as the containers of bronze scrap and the bowls as lids for the jars, a usage that appears to have been as peculiarly Sardinian as their fabric. Among the bowls, the smaller examples could in theory have been used as drinking vessels, but there is nothing in their circumstances of discovery to suggest that they functioned in this way in a Cretan environment.

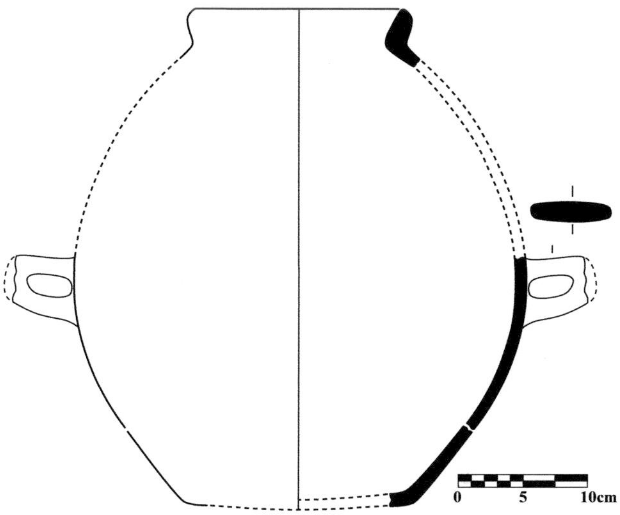

Fig. 8.13: Sardinian bowl and jar types imported to LM IIIB Kommos (Crete): Kommos C5348. After Watrous 1992, figs. 74, 76.

A second series of handmade and burnished dark-surfaced vessels recovered in roughly equivalent numbers from the west Cretan harbour town of Chania are formally quite different and have been identified as local products on the basis of limited chemical analyses, although they were unquestionably modelled after southern Italian prototypes of the Subappenine Late Bronze Age, or Bronzo Recente (Hallager 1983; 1985; Hallager and Hallager 2003, 253–254, pls. 84–85; Strack 2007, 37–39). The most popular shapes here are three varieties of very deep bowls, two with horizontal handles and one seemingly hole-mouthed and handleless, each termed an *olla* according to its Italian pedigree, and a carinated one-handled cup, or *ciotola carenata* (Figs. 8.14–8.17). Other shapes of this handmade Italianising class, such as a shallow convex-bodied cup (or *scodella*) and

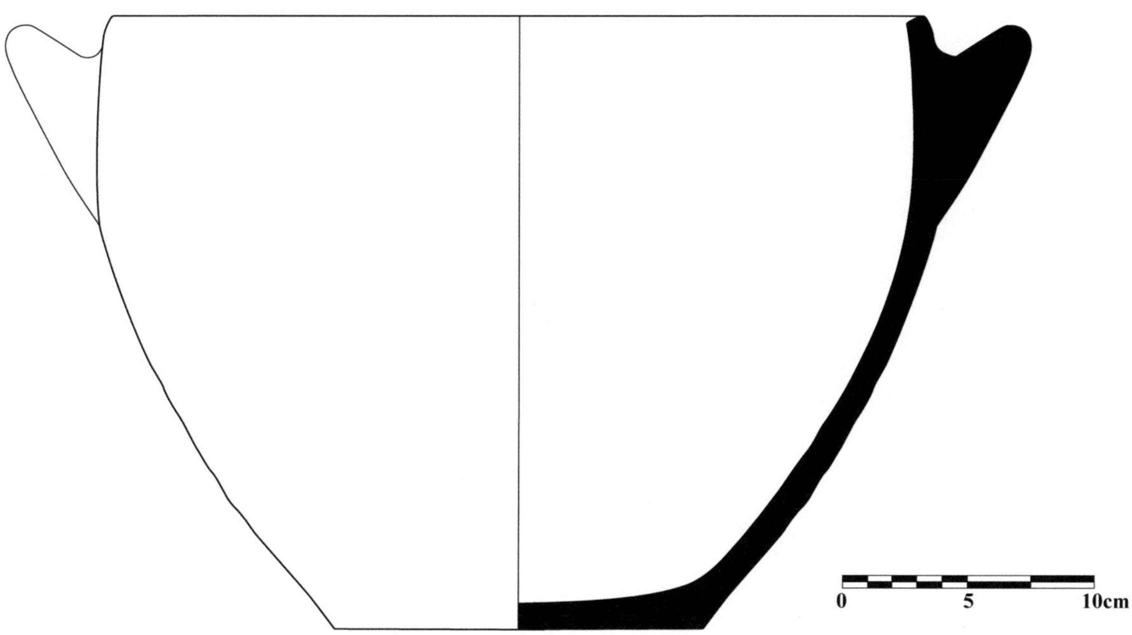

Fig. 8.14: Italianizing handmade and burnished pottery from LM IIIB2 Chania (Crete): olla 71-P0941. After Hallager and Hallager 2003, pls. 84–85.

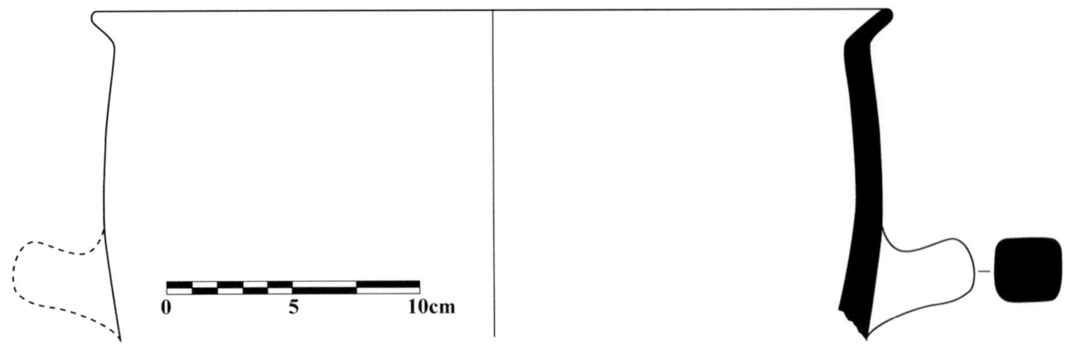

Fig. 8.15: Italianizing handmade and burnished pottery from LM IIIB2 Chania (Crete:) olla 71-P0230/1477/1494. After Hallager and Hallager 2003, pls. 84–85.

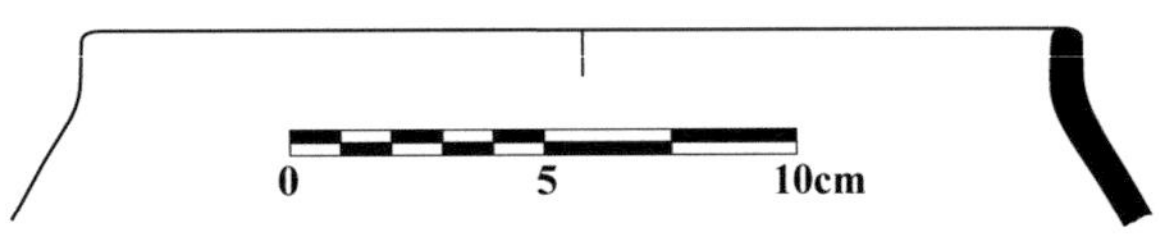

Fig. 8.16: Italianizing handmade and burnished pottery from LM IIIB2 Chania (Crete): olla 80–P0811. After Hallager and Hallager 2003, pls. 84–85.

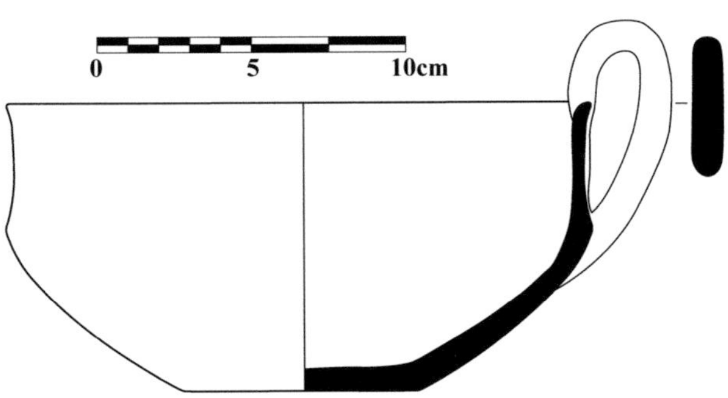

Fig. 8.17: Italianizing handmade and burnished pottery from LM IIIB2 Chania (Crete): ciotola carenata 71-P0182. After Hallager and Hallager 2003, pls. 84–85.

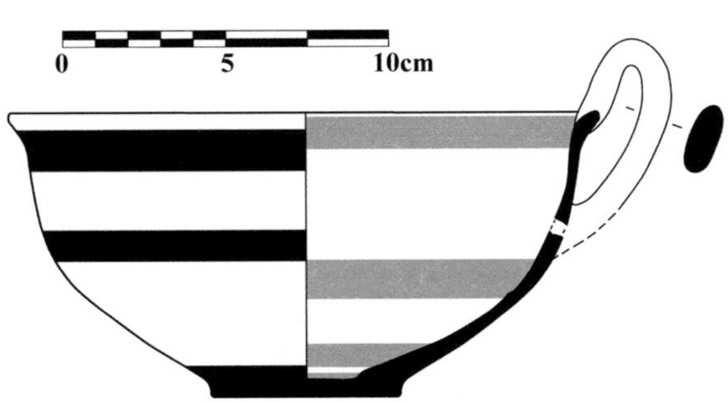

Fig. 8.18: Linear 'banded cup' inspired by the ciotola carenata: banded cup 83-P0369. After Hallager and Hallager 2003, pl. 47.

a bowl with a horizontal handle rising vertically from the rim (or *vaso situliforme*), are conspicuously rare, as is a larger than usual deep bowl or jar termed a *dolio* rather than an *olla*. The larger of the two principal forms – the *olla* – seems to have had absolutely no impact on or interaction with the local ceramic repertoire, within which the functional equivalent in painted fine ware is the horizontal-handled krater, typically raised on a low conical or higher flaring foot. But the *ciotola carenata*, a drinking cup, inspires a large number of wheel-made, high-handled lookalikes that are virtually all decorated in a purely linear fashion (so-called 'banded cups': Fig. 8.18; Hallager and Hallager 2003, 201, 204, pl. 47), in a manner quite different from the patterned décor that is characteristic of the two indigenous pattern-decorated drinking forms, the semiglobular cup (deeper-bodied, with a handle rising barely if at all above the rim) and the high-stemmed kylix.[13]

On the Greek mainland, among the most popular handmade and burnished shapes that appear at sites in the eastern Peloponnese in particular (Laconia, the Argolid, and the Corinthia) are the carinated cup along with a series of deep, convex-sided bowls or jars, most often supplied with either flat-topped and incurving or else flaring and tapered rims as well as with horizontal lugs, in addition to occasional hole-mouthed, handleless, and rather smaller jars – in other words, more or less the same suite of shapes already familiar from Chania, namely, several versions of the *olla* form plus the *ciotola carenata*. As at Chania, other shapes are certainly also part of the handmade and burnished repertoire, but they are comparatively rare and include very few closed forms, except at the site of Tiryns where a much wider range of handmade and burnished shapes of all kinds, including numerous lids, is attested (Kilian 2007; Strack 2007, 32–37). Again as at Chania, these handmade vessels in the Peloponnese all appear to be locally made at the sites where more than a handful have been recovered – that is, *not* at such central Greek sites as Perati or Athens or perhaps even Lefkandi, where only a small number of these handmade vessels have been found and are thus suspected of being imports (Popham, Schofield, and Sherratt 2006, 141, 215–218, fig. 2.42, pls. 49–50). Finally, once again as at Chania, the carinated cups in the Peloponnese and at Lefkandi soon inspire painted and wheel-made imitations, here either solidly coated or, as at Chania, linearly decorated on the exterior (Popham, Schofield, and Sherratt 2006, 181–182; Mountjoy 1986, 147, fig. 185; 1999, 156; Strack 2007, 70–71 and note 149). These imitation cups at mainland sites, however, are noticeably smaller initially than the contemporary Minoan imitations, and indeed smaller even than their handmade burnished models. What differentiates the mainland Mycenaean response to these intrusive, but locally produced, Italianising shapes is the impact that the jars have on indigenous kraters. Not as quickly as the carinated cups, to be sure, but still within a generation or two of the introduction of the handmade material in any quantity, local kraters begin to feature a diagonally impressed band or two below the rim (Mountjoy 1986, 174–175, fig. 225; 1999, 170; Popham, Schofield, and Sherratt 2006, 191, 193), a feature unmistakably derived from the deeper ollas with flaring or flat-topped rims and horizontal lugs – that is, the functional equivalents of the Mycenaean kraters (Rutter 1990, 37–39; Strack 2007, 70–71). At essentially this same time, the wheel-made versions of the carinated cups begin to bear decoration derived either from standard Mycenaean ceramic patterns or from the impressed decoration that appears on some handmade and burnished cups; the imitation carinated cups also become bigger at this time, matching the sizes of their handmade prototypes (Mountjoy 1986, 171–172, fig. 200; 1999, 170). Finally, it seems as though the quantities of handmade material may decline in quantity at roughly the same time as these handmade and burnished decorative features are being adopted on wheel-made Mycenaean painted vessels. Although it may be grossly oversimplified, the conclusion that the intrusive population element considered responsible for the production of the handmade and burnished dark-surfaced class is being absorbed into the mainstream of Mycenaean post-palatial culture in much the same way as are some of the more noticeable elements of its pottery has some obvious appeal.

What this rather sketchy overview of the impact of handmade and burnished pottery on regular wheelmade Mycenaean drinking vessels reveals are a couple of elements missing from the preceding case studies with their focus on the influence of metallic containers on ceramics. First, the influence of culturally foreign materials can be bottom-up rather than top-down: there is no denying the technological inferiority of the handmade and burnished pottery relative to the Aegean wheel-made containers of the Minoan and Mycenaean traditions. Moreover, even if one accepts that this intrusive handmade pottery is the product of an immigrant population element, as increasingly appears to be the *communis opinio* among Aegean prehistorians, no one seriously imagines the intrusive groups in question to have been numerically, militarily, or in any other way dominant within the regions or at the sites where they settled, whether temporarily or permanently. Second, the impact of very similar intrusive ceramic sub-assemblages may be quite different on the indigenous ceramic repertoire at home in any particular site or region: the response of Chaniote potters to the Italian-derived ceramic novelties diverges appreciably from that of their Peloponnesian contemporaries. And thirdly, the importance of the intrusive ceramic types being locally produced as a prerequisite to their having any impact at all on the indigenous assemblage may be suggested by the evidence of the Sardinian imports to Kommos, although it is also possible that the Sardinian material's function as transport vessels may be partially responsible for its lack of impact. Tablewares, and especially drinking equipment, even when made of fired clay rather than from an exotic material such as a precious metal, are more prone to be copied in a foreign environment than are transport or storage containers.

Acknowledgements

I am extremely grateful to the following for assistance with the following aspects of this paper: to Lydia Berger for providing me with the line drawings reproduced here as Figs. 8.3–8.8 and for consultation on matters relating to Kolonna III, ceramic phase C; to Kerasia Douni for providing me with the line drawing reproduced here, in slightly modified form, as Fig. 8.9, an image of one of the EH (Early Helladic) II finds from Koropi for whose final publication she is responsible; to Bartek Lis, Stepan Rückl, and Zoe Zgouleta for making me aware of the Koropi tankard as reconstructed in Fig. 8.9 and for helping to put me into contact with Ms. Douni; and to Tina Ross for producing the map (Fig. 8.1) and the layouts in which Figs. 8.3–8.18 have been arranged. I would also like to thank Dr Hans Peter Hahn for his assistance in identifying some relevant readings in the pages of the *Journal of Material Culture*.

Postscript

For a provocative, and very recent examination of the dramatic changes taking place at the very end of the Middle Bronze Age on the Greek Mainland that serves as a helpful theoretical introduction to some of the points made here about the origins of Lustrous Decorated Mycenaean pottery, see Petrakis 2010.

Notes

1. Consumption of liquids by single individuals, or alternatively consumption on a massive scale by large numbers of

participants, is explicitly omitted. Although the details of the social gatherings envisioned here cannot be specified in any detail in most cases, there is no reason to consider them to be exceptional in any recurring way.

2. P. Day (pers. comm. 3/17/2010) informs me that sites at which such Kastri Group forms are numerous and have been examined petrologically, *e.g.* Ayia Irini and Akrotiri, have yielded both locally produced and imported varieties. At Panormos on Naxos, the very small number of Kastri Group types all appear to be local. By contrast, those from Daskalio-Kavos may have been largely or entirely imported (Broodbank 2000, 233–236, fig.72).
3. In Phase IV at Markiani, a total of 32 Kastri Group ceramic types were identified: 31 examples of tankards (almost all of them locally produced) and a single *depas*, a ratio of the former to the latter that is broadly commensurate with the ratio of the two shapes at Ayia Irini. No Kastri Group jugs or bell-shaped cups at all were recognised, but shallow bowls, albeit none of them wheel-made or perfectly conical in profile, were common enough (Eskitzioglou 2006, 143–146, 165–168, tabs 7.16–18).
4. Berger notes resemblances between this new sauceboat form and the typical EH II askos, but also recognises that several of its more distinctive features are shared by the new form of strap-handled tankard that appears in the same horizon at Kolonna.
5. As the examples illustrated here show, the handles of these hybrid tankards actually vary quite a bit typologically, ranging from the flat-backed vertical loops of Fig. 8.8 through the narrow and thick vertical straps of Fig. 8.7 to the broader but still quite thick vertical straps of Fig. 8.6.
6. A review of the stratified Phase III contexts in which Lefkandi I ceramic types appear in the western sector at Ayia Irini reveals no obvious patterning in how these forms are distributed either spatially or chronologically (Wilson 1984, 184–208). The architecture and stratigraphy of this phase at Ayia Irini, however, have yet to be published in final form.
7. Conspicuously *not* associated with drinking behavior are a series of small closed shapes in gold – piriform jars and pyxides with simple flat lids – that were recovered from the latest of the two shaft graves in Circle A, IV (Davis 1977, no. 61, figs. 144–145) and III (*ibid.*, nos. 93–96, figs. 188–190, 192–193); these probably all belonged to women and may represent a rather different phenomenon in which metal vessels were mimicking prototypes in ceramic toward the end of the Shaft Grave phase.
8. For the debate over what 'Minoan' means when applied to various southern Aegean human groups, see Broodbank 2004, Davis and Gorogianni 2008, and Momigliano 2009.
9. For an up-to-date review of the continuing difficulties in identifying how and where Mycenaean decorated pottery began to be produced, see Dickinson (forthcoming). The thesis proposed here, that Mycenaean decorated pottery is so closely connected with a similar range of shapes and decorative motifs in precious metal vessels as to suggest that this class of pottery may have been inspired by these prototypes in gold and silver, is a subject that cannot be explored in detail here. Note that the few examples of closed vessel forms in gold and silver from the Shaft Graves correspond to the few small closed forms current in the LH I decorated ceramic repertoire (see also note 7 above).
10. One might logically have expected the elite at Mycenae to have pioneered an equivalent range of creatively designed weaponry to be used in hunting and warfare, and this is presumably precisely what one is seeing in the niello-inlaid daggers, the innovative design of Type B swords, and the novel kinds of ornament applied to Type A swords lavishly decorated with pictorial art in the form of engraved horses, birds, *etc* . Once again, the sources of these new developments, and presumably also of many of the artisans who were responsible for them, were Minoan, but the encouragement these artisans received for designing novelties, both functional and decorative, came from their elite patrons at Mycenae, whose examples were then widely adopted by elites at other mainland Greek sites.
11. As Michael Nelson has made clear (2001; 2007), the Mycenaean ruling class resident at Pylos in Messenia was already constructing large buildings in cut stone in LH I, and by LH II were building walls employing ashlar orthostates. But emulation by other mainland Greek elites of these sophisticated building techniques did not occur for some time, in marked contrast to the rapid emulation of the metalwork being produced at Mycenae. The reasons for this no doubt have to do with the portability of the Mycenae products and the fact that they could function satisfactorily as display pieces in both settlement and funerary contexts.
12. Opinions on the identification, provenience, and chronology of these imported dark-burnished wares from Kommos have changed considerably from their initial detection by Watrous (1992) to their most recent evaluation by Rutter (2006); the last was published too late to be taken into consideration by Strack (2007).
13. The excavators at Chania evidently do not see any particular connection between the contemporary introduction of handmade and burnished carinated cups with high-swung strap handles (*e.g.* Hallager and Hallager 2003, pl. 85.71–P0182 = Fig. 8.17) and the wheelmade, linearly decorated 'banded cups' (sometimes, in fact, solidly coated or pattern-decorated with a horizontal wavy band on the exterior shoulder), presumably because the 'banded cups' rarely have carinated body profiles (as Hallager and Hallager 2003, 201, pl. 47.84–P0545). The derivation of the wheelmade and decorated form from the handmade, dark-burnished, and carinated model seems to me a logical inference.

References

Angelopoulou, A. (2008) The Kastri Group: The Evidence from Korphari ton Amygdalion, Panormos, Naxos, Dhaskaleio Kavos, Keros and Akrotiri, Thera. In Brodie, Doole, Gavalas and Renfrew 2008, 149–164.

Berger, L. (2004) Ägina-Kolonna 2: Neue Ergebnisse zur FH II-Keramik aus der prähistorischen Innenstadt. In E. Alram-Stern, *Die ägäische Frühzeit 2.Serie: Forschungsbericht 1975–2002* II,2: *Die Frühbronzezeit in Griechenland mit Ausnahme von Kreta*, 1093–1103. Vienna, Verlag der Österreichischen Akademie der Wissenschaften.

Berger, L. (forthcoming) The Late Early Helladic II Pottery of Aegina Kolonna. In D. Katsonopoulou (ed.), *The Early Helladic Peloponnesos*. Helike IV, 121–130. Athens, Helike Society.

Brodie, N., Doole, J., Gavalas, G. and Renfrew, C. (2008), *ORIZON. A Colloquium on the Prehistory of the Cyclades*. Cambridge, Cambridge University Press

Broodbank, C. (2000) *An Island Archaeology of the Early Cyclades*. Cambridge, Cambridge University Press.

Broodbank, C. (2004) Minoanisation. *Proceedings of the Cambridge Philosophical Society* 50, 46–91.

Çalis-Sazci, D. (2006) Die Troianer und das Meer: Keramik und Handelsbeziehungen der sog. 'Maritimen Troia-Kultur'. In M. O. Korfmann (ed.), *Troia: Archäologie eines Siedlungshügels und seiner Landschaft*, 201–207. Mainz, Philipp von Zabern.

Choleva, M. (forthcoming) The First Wheel-made Pottery in the Aegean: Wheel-thrown or Wheel-fashioned? The Case of the Site of Lerna IV. *Hesperia*, forthcoming.

Davis, E. N. (1977) *The Vapheio Cups and Aegean Gold and Silver Ware*. New York, Garland.

Davis, E. N. (1983) The Gold of the Shaft Graves: the Transylvanian Connection. *Temple University Aegean Symposium* 8, 32–38.

Davis, J. L. and Gorogianni, E. (2008) Potsherds from the Edge: the Construction of Identities and the Limits of Minoanized Areas of the Aegean. In Brodie, Doole, Gavalas and Renfrew 2008, 339–348.

Dickinson, O. T. P. K. (1972) Late Helladic IIA and IIB: Some Evidence from Korakou. *Annual of the British School at Athens* 67, 103–112.

Dickinson, O. T. P. K. (forthcoming) Late Helladic I Revisited. In D. Nakassis, J. Gulizio and S. A. James (eds), *KE-RA-ME-JA: Studies Presented to Cynthia Shelmerdine*.

Eskitzioglou, P. 2006. The Pottery of Markiani Phase IV. In Marangou, Renfrew, Doumas and Gavalas 2006, 139–157.

Furumark, A. (1972) *Mycenaean Pottery* I: *Analysis and Classification*. Stockholm, Svenska Institutet i Athen.

Gauss, W. (2006) Minos auf Ägina – Beobachtungen zu den Beziehungen Äginas zu Kreta. In E. Czerny, I. Hein, H. Hunger, D. Melman and A. Schwab (eds), *Timelines: Studies in Honour of Manfred Bietak* II, 437–448. Leuven, Uitgeverij Peetersen Departement Oosterse Studies.

Graziadio, G. (1988) The Chronology of the Graves of Circle B at Mycenae: A New Hypothesis. *American Journal of Archaeology* 92, 343–372.

Graziadio, G. (1991) The Process of Social Stratification at Mycenae in the Shaft Grave Period: a Comparative Examination of the Evidence. *American Journal of Archaeology* 95, 403–440.

Hallager, B. P. (1983) A New Social Class in Late Bronze Age Crete: Foreign Traders in Khania. In O. Krzyszkowska and L. Nixon (eds), *Minoan Society*, 111–119. Bristol, Bristol Classical Press.

Hallager, B. P. (1985) Crete and Italy in the Late Bronze Age III Period. *American Journal of Archaeology* 89, 293–305.

Hallager, E. and Hallager, B. P. (2003) *Greek-Swedish Excavations at the Agia Aikaterini Square: Kastelli, Khania 1970–1987 III: The Late Minoan IIIB:2 Settlement*. Stockholm, Paul Åströms Förlag.

Hiller, S. (1993) Minoan and Minoanizing Pottery on Aigina. In Zerner, Zerner and Winder, 197–199.

Jung, R. (2006a) *CHRONOLOGIA COMPARATA: Vergleichende Chronologie von Südgriechenland und Süditalien von ca. 1700/1600 bis 1000 v. u. Z.* Vienna, Verlag der Österreichischen Akademie der Wissenschaften.

Jung, R. (2006b) Εὔποτον ποτέριον: Mykenische Keramik und mykenische Trinksitten in der Ägäis, in Syrien, Makedonien und Italien. In *Studi di Protostoria in Onore di Renato Peroni*, 407–423. Borgo San Lorenzo, All'Insegna del Giglio.

Kakavogianni, O. (1993) Οι έρευνες Πρωτοελλαδικό οικισμό στο Κορωπί. In Zerner, Zerner and Winder 1993, 165–167.

Karo, G. (1930) *Die Schachtgräber von Mykenai*. München, Bruckmann.

Kilian, K. (2007) *Die handgemachte geglättete Keramik mykenischer Zeitstellung. Tiryns* XV. Wiesbaden, Reichert.

Kilian-Dirlmeier, I. (1997) *Alt-Ägina* IV, 3: *Das mittelbronzezeitliche Schachtgrab von Ägina*. Mainz, Philipp von Zabern.

Korfmann, M. O. (2001) Troia als Drehscheibe des Handels im 2. und 3. vorchristlichen Jahrtausend. Erkenntnisse zur troianischen Hochkultur und zur maritimen Troia-Kultur. In J. Latacz (ed.), *Troia. Traum und Wirklichkeit*, 355–368. Stuttgart, K. Theiss.

Kouka, O. (2009) Third Millennium BC Aegean Chronology: Old and New Data from the Perspective of the Third Millennium AD. In S. W. Manning and M. J. Bruce (eds), *Tree-Rings, Kings, and Old World Archaeology and Environment: Papers Presented in Honor of Peter Ian Kuniholm*, 133–148. Oxford, Oxbow Books.

Lindblom, M., Mommsen, H. and Whitbread, I. K. (n.d.) Bichrome Pottery in the MBA–LBA Central Aegean. In I. Hein (ed.), *Potters' Art in Red and Black. The Manual of Cypriote Bichrome Wheel-made Ware II*. Vienna, forthcoming.

Lis, B. (2009) Handmade and Burnished Pottery in the Eastern Mediterranean at the End of the Bronze Age: Towards an Explanation for its Diversity and Geographical Distribution. In G. Bachhuber and G. Roberts (eds), *Forces of Transformation: The End of the Bronze Age in the Eastern Mediterranean*, 152–163. Oxford, Oxbow Books.

MacGillivray, J. A. (1984) The Relative Chronology of Early Cycladic III. In J. A. MacGillivray and R. L. N. Barber (eds), *The Prehistoric Cyclades*, 70–77. Edinburgh, Department of Classical Archaeology, University of Edinburgh.

Marangou, L., Renfrew, C., Doumas, C. and Gavalas, G. (2006) *Μαρκιανη Αμοργου – Markiani, Amorgos: An Early Bronze Age Fortified Settlement*. British School at Athens Supplement 40. London, British School at Athens.

Mellink, M. J. (1986) The Early Bronze Age in West Anatolia: Aegean and Asiatic Correlations. In G. Cadogan (ed.), *The End of the Early Bronze Age in the Aegean. Cincinnati Classical Studies* 6, 139–152. Leiden, E. J. Brill.

Momigliano, N. (2009) Minoans at Iasos? In C. F. Macdonald, E. Hallager and W.-D. Niemeier (eds), *The Minoans in the Central, Eastern and Northern Aegean – New Evidence.* Monographs of the Danish Institute at Athens 8, 121–140. Athens, Danish Institute at Athens.

Mountjoy, P. A. (1986) *Mycenaean Decorated Pottery: A Guide to Identification.* Studies in Mediterranean Archaeology 73. Göteborg, Paul Åströms Forlag.

Mountjoy, P. A. (1999) *Regional Mycenaean Decorated Pottery.* Rahden, M. Leidorf.

Nakou, G. (2007) Absent Presences: Metal Vessels in the Aegean at the End of the Third Millennium. In P. M. Day and R. C. P. Doonan (eds), *Metallurgy in the Early Bronze Age Aegean.* Sheffield Studies in Aegean Archaeology 7, 224–244. Oxford, Oxbow Books.

Nelson, M. C. (2001) *The Architecture of Epano Englianos, Greece.* Unpublished PhD dissertation, University of Toronto.

Nelson, M. C. (2007) Pylos, Block Masonry and Monumental Architecture in the Late Bronze Age Peloponnese. In J. Bretschneider, J. Driessen and K. van Lerberghe (eds), *Power and Architecture: Monumental Public Architecture in the Bronze Age Near East and Aegean*, 143–159. Leuven, Peeters.

Papagiannopoulou, A. (2008) From Pots to Pictures: Middle Cycladic Figurative Art from Akrotiri, Thera. In Brodie, Doole, Gavalas and Renfrew 2008, 433–449.

Petrakis, V. P. (2010) Diversity in Form and Practice in Middle Helladic and Early Mycenaean Elaborate Tombs: An Approach to Changing Prestige Expression in Changing Prestige Expression in Changing Times. In A. Philippa-Touchais, G. Touchais, S. Voutsaki and J. Wright (eds), *MESOHELLADIKA: The Greek Mainland in the Middle Bronze Age.* Bulletin de Correspondance Héllenique Supplément 52, 403–416. Athens, École Française d'Atheès.

Popham, M., Schofield, E. and Sherratt, S. (2006) The Pottery. In D. Evely (ed.), *Lefkandi IV: The Bronze Age. The Late Helladic IIIC Settlement at Xeropolis.* BSA Supplementary Vol. 39, 137–231. London, British School at Athens.

Renfrew, C., Philaniotou, O., Brodie, N. and Gavalas, G. (2009) The Early Cycladic Settlement at Dhaskalio, Keros: Preliminary Report of the 2008 Excavations Season. *Annual of the British School at Athens* 104, 27–47.

Rutter, J. B. (1983) Fine Gray-burnished Pottery of the Early Helladic III Period: The Ancestry of Gray Minyan. *Hesperia* 52, 327–355.

Rutter, J. B. (1988) Early Helladic III Vasepainting, Ceramic Regionalism, and the Influence of Basketry. In E. B. French and K. A. Wardle (eds), *Problems in Aegean Prehistory*, 73–89. Bristol, Bristol Classical Press.

Rutter, J. B. (1990) Some Comments on Interpreting the Dark-surfaced Handmade Burnished Pottery of the 13th and 12th Century B.C. Aegean. *Journal of Mediterranean Archaeology* 3, 29–49.

Rutter, J. B. (1995) *Lerna. A Preclassical Site in the Argolid* III: *The Pottery of Lerna IV.* Princeton, Princeton University Press.

Rutter, J. B. (2001) Review II: The Prepalatial Bronze Age of the Southern and Central Greek Mainland. In T. Cullen (ed.), *Aegean Prehistory: A Review*, 95–155. Boston, Archaeological Institute of America.

Rutter, J. B. (2006) Ceramic Evidence for External Contact: Neopalatial and Postpalatial. In J. W. and M. C. Shaw (eds), *Kommos* V: *The Monumental Buildings at Kommos*, 646–688. Princeton, Princeton University Press.

Strack, S. (2007) *Regional Dynamics and Social Change in the Late Bronze and Early Iron Age: A Study of Handmade Pottery from Southern and Central Greece.* Unpublished Ph.D. dissertation, University of Edinburgh.

Tolstikov, V. and Treister, M. (1996) *The Gold of Troy: Searching for Homer's Fabled City.* New York, H. N. Abrams.

Walter, H. and Felten, F. (1981) *Alt-Ägina III,1: Die vorgeschichtliche Stadt: Befestigungen, Häuser, Funde.* Mainz, Philipp von Zabern.

Warren, P. and Hankey, V. (1989) *Aegean Bronze Age Chronology.* Bristol, Bristol Classical Press.

Watrous, L. V. (1992) *Kommos* III: *The Late Bronze Age Pottery.* Princeton, Princeton University Press.

Watrous, L. V., Day, P. M. and Jones, R. E. (1998) The Sardinian Pottery from the Late Bronze Age Site of Kommos in Crete: Description, Chemical and Petrographic Analysis, and Historical Context. In M. S. Balmuth and R. H. Tykot (eds), *Sardinian and Aegean Chronology: Towards the Resolution of Relative and Absolute Dating in the Mediterranean*, 337–340. Oxford, Oxbow Books.

Wilson, D. E. (1999) *Keos* IX*: Ayia Irini: Periods I–III. The Neolithic and Early Bronze Age Settlements.* Mainz, Philipp von Zabern.

Wright, J. C. (1987) Death and Power at Mycenae: Changing Symbols in Mortuary Practice. R. Laffineur (ed.), *THANATOS. Les coutûmes funéraires en Égée à l'âge du Bronze.* Aegaeum 1, 171–184. Liège, Université de l'Etat, Histoire de l'art et archéologie de la Grèce antique.

Wright, J. C. (2004) A Survey of Evidence for Feasting in Mycenaean Society. In J. C. Wright (ed.), *The Mycenaean Feast*, 13–58. Princeton, American School of Classical Studies at Athens.

Zerner, C. (2008) The Middle Helladic Pottery, with the Middle Helladic Wares from Late Helladic Deposits and the Potters' Marks. In W. D. Taylour and R. Janko (eds), *Ayios Stephanos. Excavations of a Bronze Age and Medieval Settlement in Southern Laconia.* British School at Athens Supplementary Vol. 44, 177–298. London, British School at Athens.

Zerner, C., Zerner, P. and Winder, J. (1993) *Wace and Blegen: Pottery as Evidence for Trade in the Aegean Bronze Age 1939–1989.* Amsterdam, J. C. Gieben.

9.

Entangled pottery: phenomena of appropriation in the Late Bronze Age Eastern Mediterranean

Philipp W. Stockhammer

While the search for 'entangled histories' in Google offers around 13 million hits, fewer than 2,000 are offered for 'entangled object' and just a handful for 'entangled pottery'. Obviously, histories can be entangled, but so far, material objects – or more specifically pottery – are difficult to consider as entangled. Taking this as starting point, I will begin with conceptualizing processes of appropriation and entanglement of objects within archaeology. I will then focus on some of those processes concerning the Aegean-type pottery found in the Late Bronze Age Southern Levant. My aim is to show the integration of the Aegean-type pottery into local practices and to analyze which actors were willing to appropriate this pottery and which groups intentionally refrained from acquiring these objects.

Methodological approach

The relevant processes are often termed as 'hybridization' by modern academics. However, the term 'hybridity' is mostly used as a political metaphor in postcolonial discourse (Bhabha 2007). Moreover, we have to deal with its pejorative biological background (*cf.* Papastergiadis 1997; Stewart 1999, 45; Weißköppel 2005, 317–319). In order to avoid the associations of this biological metaphor I would like to use a different term, namely 'entanglement' in English and '*Geflecht*' and '*Verflechtung*' in German (*cf.* Stockhammer 2012). In both languages, these terms encapsulate aspects of agency, processualism and the creation of something new that is more than just the sum of its parts. In order to analyze phenomena of entanglement, I will focus on the liminal spaces of our etically defined entities and, therefore, etically defined liminal spaces, which were probably never perceived as being liminal by prehistoric man. The creative potential of these liminal spaces often results in what I would like to call 'entanglement'. There is no doubt that the whole world is completely entangled and every culture has to be thought as 'trans-cultural'. However, I believe it is possible to develop this metaphor into an epistemologically useful concept by restricting the use of the term 'entanglement' and connected terms like 'liminal spaces' to the analysis of distinct processes. These processes emerge from the dialectical relationship of acceptance and resistance after the encounter with otherness. Igor Kopytoff (1986, 67) has already stated: 'What is significant about the adoption of alien objects – as of alien ideas – is not the fact that they are adopted, but the way they are culturally redefined and put to use'. The ethnologist can observe those practices. Archaeologists, however, are lucky to find evidence for what practices might have been connected with a certain object. Consequently, I would like to differentiate between the appropriation of objects and the appropriation of social practices and meanings (*i.e.* symbols, traditions *etc.*), as this makes a significant epistemological difference for archaeological sources.

In order to analyze archaeological evidence, it is necessary to structure the processes of appropriation and entanglement into several stages in order to assess their potential to be visible in the material record (Stockhammer 2012): the process starts with the 'encounter' of at least two different etically defined entities. Instead of falling back to ideas of essentialism and purity, we have to be aware of the etic character of these entities. They are mental templates only created for analytical purposes. Therefore, it is not material, if both entities interacted before. However, the etic recognition of difference supposes that this difference might also have been perceived by past individuals – perhaps only in the brief moment of the first encounter. This moment of encounter, the perception of otherness and difference, is the central trigger, taking place in liminal spaces, which I visualize as situations and spaces that are not limited to a certain geographical area. I define liminal space as space of encounter, irrespective where this confrontation happens. This encounter can trigger a process, which results in what I would like to call the state of 'relational entanglement'. This transition from encounter to relational entanglement is characterized by appropriation, incorporation, objectification, and transformation as defined by Hans P. Hahn (Hahn 2004a, 64–67; 2004b, 218–220; 2005, 102–104; 2007, 209–210): The object becomes a personal possession, and is classified within local classification systems, connected with certain practices, and attributed with a new meaning. Nevertheless, it is important to acknowledge that an appropriated artefact is not an entangled artefact. If one excavated an appropriated foreign object in a local context, the object in its materiality is most often unchanged.[1] It is only the context that has changed, such as the social practices, meanings and traditions connected with the object (*cf.* Hahn 2004b, 226; 2005, 101). All the creative powers of liminal spaces are first invested in creating new practices connected with the object. In the moment of first encounter we do not trigger a change of the object, but the object changes us. Merely its material presence changes perceptions of social space and movements. Therefore, the state of relational entanglement is a state of entanglement of social practices and meanings, as these are newly created, whereas the object is, at most, only manipulated.

It is only the next step that leads to the creation of entangled objects. I would like to call this next step 'material entanglement' which is achieved by the process of 'material creation'. At this point the creative energies originally released by the encounter and broadened within the process of appropriation, result in the creation of a new object that combines the familiar with the formerly foreign. Its materiality exhibits that it is not the result of local continuities, but of changes triggered by encounter with otherness. It is more than just a sum of the entities from which it originated. It is an indissoluble combination of all of them – a cultural '*Geflecht*' – and might be seen as a new entity.

Even if such an object has lost its functional context over time, we can still identify it as an entangled artefact in the archaeological evidence from an etic perspective. This kind of decontextualized material entanglement is the most common evidence of entanglement in archaeology. We are excavating the final embodiment or result of a multitude of appropriation and creation processes without being able to document the specific process of material entanglement. We are confronted with the material uniqueness of an entangled object and are unable to explain how and why it was created, because the social practices and meanings are barely materialized. And most often, we are unable to understand if and how this object was perceived (*e.g.* local *vs.* foreign), or even if there was one overriding perception at all.

One has to take into consideration that it is impossible to determine the end result of such processes of appropriation and creation. These processes can result in continuous re-interpretations, incorporations, manipulations, and creations (Hahn 2005, 106–107), but for the sake of analysis, I would like to fix the end of a certain process of entanglement with the creation of an entangled object. This entangled object may be a unique specimen and forgotten after its deposition, but it may happen that a flourishing local production of entangled objects is triggered. It is possible that these products were never perceived as being the product of a former process of entanglement by prehistoric man, but only by us archaeologists.

It is also necessary to acknowledge that processes of appropriation are not governed by anthropologically predefined social units like 'the elite' or 'the migrants', but by individual actors. Thus, it is important to draw the Actor-Network-Theory (ANT) with its seminal works by Bruno Latour (1986; 2005) and John Law (1992) into consideration. In their line of thought, society has to be seen as a network of actors that consists of human and non-human actors (*e.g.* objects). The driving force behind their action is considered to be a 'source of uncertainty' and given the name '*actant*' by Latour (2005, 52–55). Due to this uncertainty, Latour refrains from using the term agency, whereas he is willing to admit that Pierre Bourdieu's (1982) concept of *habitus* 'once it is freed from its social theory, remains such an excellent concept' (Latour 2005, 209 n. 280). In my view, it is necessary to read ANT and Bourdieu's concept of *habitus* together in order to understand why different actors were driven by seemingly similar actants to act. This similarity of actants can at least partly be explained with the similar habitus of the individuals. Thus, when I use terms like 'the elite', I am aware of the difficulty to explain individual action with scientifically created entities. In order to avoid this problem, I take contextual studies as a basis for further reflections and to analyse actors and their individual practices. With terms like 'the elite' I want to name a group of actors that are characterized by similar actions and thus possibly similar actants, which I would explain as the result of a common social habitus.

Previous contextual studies

Having defined this methodological approach, I would now like to analyse several different processes of entanglement of Aegean-type pottery in the Levant by evaluating contexts from Hazor, Megiddo, Tell el-ᶜAjjul and the tomb of Nahalat

Ahim in Jerusalem in the Late Bronze and Early Iron Age (*cf.* Stockhammer, in prep.). All sites are situated inland in modern Israel. The settlement sites of Hazor (Yadin *et al.* 1958; 1960; 1961; Ben-Tor 1997; Ben-Tor and Zuckerman 2008; Zuckerman 2007a; 2007b; 2007d; 2008) and Megiddo (Guy and Engberg 1938; Loud 1939; 1948; Finkelstein, Ussishkin and Halpern 2000; 2006) have been excavated for decades. The settlement and the graves of Tell el-ᶜAjjul were primarily excavated by Sir William Matthew Flinders Petrie in the 1930s (Flinders Petrie 1931; 1932; 1933; 1934; Flinders Petrie, Makay and Murray 1952) with some recent activity by Peter M. Fischer and Moain Sadeq in 1999 and 2000 (Fischer and Sadeq 2000; 2002; Fischer 2001a; 2001b; 2004). The grave inventory from Nahalat Ahim was published in 1960 by Ruth Amiran (1960).

A contextual analysis of the Aegean-type pottery from the old excavations in Hazor has been conducted by Gert Jan van Wijngaarden (2002, 75–97) and that from Megiddo by Albert Leonard and Eric H. Cline (1998). The Aegean-type pottery from Flinders Petrie's excavations in Tell el-ᶜAjjul has been the topic of a study by Louise Steel (2002).

As a result of his research on the shapes and contexts of Aegean-type pottery from Hazor, van Wijngaarden (2002, 82–83, 86, 96) postulates that closed Aegean-type vessels were 'widely used among the inhabitants' and 'an integral part of the everyday life', whereas open feasting vessels of Aegean type had a special role within rituals including burial rituals. In his view, 'high-level social groups' and the temples tried to monopolize those open vessels so that 'the possession and use of these vessels was of social significance' (van Wijngaarden 2002, 95–96). Sharon Zuckerman (2007a, 626) and Kristina Josephson Hesse (2008, 135, 144, 202, 211) interpret the evidence of sherds from Aegean-type vessels from the Upper Tell of Hazor as a clear indication for its integration into elite ritual practices. In their evaluation of the contexts in Megiddo, Leonard and Cline observe a concentration of Aegean-type pottery in palatial and domestic contexts, but 'not a single Aegean import has been found at Megiddo in any secure religious or cult context' (Leonard and Cline 1998, 16). Therefore, while van Wijngaarden postulates an important role of Aegean-type feasting dishes in elite and cultic performances, Leonard and Cline's evidence seems to support only the elite practices. Steel (2002, 39, 43) considers the Aegean-type pottery from the Tell el-ᶜAjjul as 'luxury imported exotica' which use 'was strictly controlled in Egypt's major stronghold in the southern Levant'. This was suggested by the rarity of Aegean-type sherds from the settlement (mostly amphoroid kraters) and the quantity of small closed transport containers of Aegean type in the rich so-called 'Governor's Tomb'. In her view, the kraters possibly reached the settlement 'as rare examples of internal gift exchange between the Canaanite city kingdoms ...; however, they were not commonly integrated within local dining customs, nor were they carefully curated', the fragmentary state of preservation being an indicator of this lack of care (Steel 2002, 38).

Notwithstanding these contradictory results, all the aforementioned studies underestimate the crucial role of site-formation processes in any contextual approach, although Steel (2002, 28–29) even explicitly elaborates on this issue. Potsherds are easily and often systematically mixed into the mud for the brick architecture (Blum 2003, 76, 237; Stockhammer 2008, 73), consciously or unconsciously re-located, and sometimes even collected for special purposes.[2] Other than tomb contexts, there are only a few instances of complete or largely preserved Aegean-type vessels found in Hazor and Megiddo for which a secondary context of find is unlikely. Thus, I will take a minimalist approach and evaluate only those contexts, where complete or restorable vessels have been found, thus suggesting a primary position of the vessel in the context.

Hazor

During the recent excavations of the Late Bronze Age 'Royal Precinct/Ceremonial Palace' on the Upper Tell of Hazor, 781 completely preserved vessels were found together with a considerable number of exceptional small finds (Zuckerman 2007b; 2008; pers. comm.). There is no doubt that this complex provides a unique insight into the role of material culture within rituals performed by high-status individuals and can be seen as representative of elite ritual performances in Late Bronze Age Hazor. Despite this exceptionally well-preserved context, not one Aegean-type vessel has been found complete or at least as multiple sherds. Around 90 single Aegean-type sherds – often very fragmented and badly worn – were discovered which were clearly found in a secondary position, often in Iron Age layers (Zuckerman 2007a, 623, 624, fig. 2; 626; Josephson Hesse 2008, 135, 144, 202, 211). However, complete vessels were excavated in non-palatial residential contexts. In my view, there is no doubt that the Aegean-type sherds from the Upper Tell in Hazor were all relocated by being within mud bricks. Therefore, those sherds cannot be taken as evidence for the use of Aegean-type vessels in elite performances. This interpretation is supported by the absence of Aegean-type pottery in the princely tomb of Qatna that was buried under the debris of the destroyed palace around 1340 BCE. Although the ruler of Qatna had Aegean-type frescoes in his palace with some motifs showing strong links to vase painting (Pfälzner 2008; von Rüden 2009), there appears to have been no interest in placing similarly painted Aegean vessels into the ruler's tomb even though the contemporary Mycenaean LH (Late Helladic) IIIA2 pottery was widely available at the Levant and was also found in Qatna itself (Du Mesnil du Boisson 1928, pl. 18; Mühlenbruch 2009, 67–68). I have no doubt that if the individuals ruling these city-states of the Late Bronze Age Canaanite hinterland wanted to integrate Aegean-type pottery into their practices, they would have been able to acquire them, but clearly they refrained from appropriating Aegean-type pottery despite their possibly even daily encounters with it. However, we always have to take into consideration that strategies of appropriation are based on individual decisions and landscapes of consumption, or 'consumptionscapes' as Güliz Ger and Russel W. Belk (1996) call it following Arjun Appadurai's (1990) terminology. Therefore, I do not want to propose an overriding rule for actants driving high-status individuals after the encounter with Aegean-type pottery. If there is evidence of completely or largely preserved Aegean-type pottery from high-status contexts within the huge inland Canaanite city states, it often seems to be restricted to surprisingly old Aegean – predominantly Cretan – pottery of the 16th to early14th century, *e.g.* a LM (Late Minoan) IB bridge-spouted jar in the *Schatzhaus* in Kamid el-Loz (Penner 2006, 180–182, 181 fig. 107) or two LM IIIA1 conical cups in a newly found elite building in Tell Beth-Shemesh, Level 9 (Ziffer, Bunimovitz and Lederman 2009; Bunimovitz and Lederman, pers. comm.). This, again, fits very well contextually with the Qatna paintings, as they have their best parallels in early Mycenaean and early Late Minoan vase painting.

If it were not high-status individuals, which elements of society were acquiring Aegean-type pottery and which actors chose to appropriate those vessels? Different patterns of use seem to emerge from a contextual analysis among a myriad of other possible and probable relational entanglements of those vessels. First, Aegean-type pottery was often chosen as a burial offering and was already of importance in the ritual practices accompanying a burial. Second, Aegean-type pottery seems to be connected with households that also exhibit interregional interactions in other material correlates.

Aegean-type pottery was frequently used as a burial offering. Small closed vessels like stirrup jars, piriform jars, and alabastra were especially favoured. This is also true for the tombs discovered in Hazor and at the other sites that I am going to discuss. However, we have to keep in mind that Aegean-type pottery should not be taken as a clear indicator for the high status of the buried person. In Hazor, the huge number of Aegean-type vessels from tomb 8144–8145 (Yadin *et al.* 1960, 140–142, 145–153, pl. 137.1–13) has been taken as an argument for their use as an indicator of high-status individuals buried there (van Wijngaarden 2002, 95; Zuckerman 2007a, 626). However, the tomb was continuously used for burials from the early 14th until the mid 13th century BCE, and although the number of burials is unclear due to the bad preservation of bone material (Yadin *et al.* 1960, 141), the long period of use and more than 500 pottery vessels from the grave indicate a huge number of burials. Thus, only a small number of the probably high-status individuals buried in the tomb were given an Aegean-type vessel as a burial offering. On the other hand, the unusual burial of a young woman in cistern 9027 in Hazor contained two Aegean-type alabastra, a Cypriot milk bowl, and several vessels of Canaanite origin. Apart from the pottery, no other burial goods were found that might support an interpretation as an elite burial. Thus, this woman was better equipped with Aegean-type vessels than most of the deceased from tomb 8144–8145. It is therefore difficult to deduce an elite status from the imported pottery. Moreover, it is of special interest to look at the role of Aegean-type pottery within the practices of preparation of a burial.

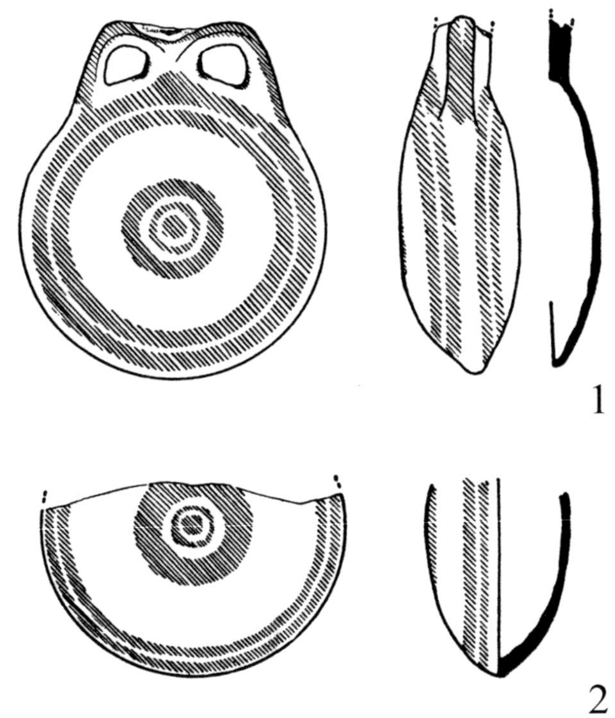

Fig. 9.1: Aegean-type pottery from Hazor (Yadin et al. *1960, pl. 148. 5, 6; with permission from the Israel Exploration Society).*

Of particular interest is the primary depositional context of two nearly identical Aegean-type flasks in room 8024 of house 8068 in Hazor, Area F (Fig. 9.1; Yadin *et al.* 1960, 128–129, 137, 153, pl. 148.5, 6; pl. 195.4). To judge from the illustrations, one of the two flasks is preserved up to ca 80%, whereas only 20–30% of the second vessel was found. They were found together with a huge pithos, a bowl, a miniature bowl, and two amphorae of local origin and a grinding stone (Yadin *et al.* 1960, 137, pl. 141.9, pl. 142.8, pl. 144.1, pl. 145.3, 9; pl. 146.19; *cf.* van Wijngaarden 2002, 85 for a slightly different description of the findings). This room also connected the so-called cultic place 8019 with an altar and an inner courtyard, where a beheaded statue of a goddess was found. Within the room, but reaching into the inner courtyard, a large stone bench was situated, where another flask of local origin was found that had fallen from the bench into the courtyard. According to Sharon Zuckerman (pers. comm.), the whole building complex has to be seen in connection with the tomb 8144–8145 in its immediate vicinity. van Wijngaarden (2002, 86) interprets the context as a place of daily food preparation and storage, which does not account for the special architectonical position of the room as passageway between areas where clearly cultic practices took place. In contrast to van Wijngaarden, the excavators already considered the room as place for the preparation of food and drinking for the rituals conducted nearby (Yadin *et al.* 1960, 140). However, the rituals conducted in room 8024 clearly differed from those in the 'Royal Precinct/Ceremonial Palace' as flasks are totally missing from the impressive ceramic inventory of this high-status building complex (Zuckerman 2007b). Normal sized flasks are also missing in the so-called Podium Complex (Area M) where only three miniature flasks were found (Zuckerman, pers. comm.). There is no doubt that the lack of flasks from the Areas A and M on the Upper Tell cannot be explained by mere chance only. It seems most likely that the flasks contained perfumed oil used for the embalming of the dead body. As recent scientific analysis from the human remains found in the Qatna grave indicates, the deceased was anointed with oils mixed with earth pigments, then covered with textiles, and then dried over an open fire at a temperature of 200 to 250°C in order to stop the decay of the body (Pfälzner 2009, 242; Witzel 2009, 210).

Megiddo

Similar to Hazor, single sherds of Aegean-type vessels were found in the Late Bronze Age palace (Leonard and Cline 1998, 9 fig. 4; 16), but complete vessels are missing (*cf.* Stockhammer 2011 for a reevaluation of the Aegean-type pottery from Megiddo). However, only a few complete Canaanite and Cypriot vessels were discovered in the palace so that the evidence is less significant than that from Hazor with its great number of vessels preserved *in situ*. Similar to Hazor, complete vessels are documented from non-palatial residential contexts and the Aegean-type sherd material from the palace appears to be entirely relocated. Already the excavator mentions that one of the Aegean-type sherds was found inside a mud brick used for the palace (Loud 1948, pl. 137.5; Leonard and Cline 1998, 5–6, 21 no. 5).

There is interesting evidence from Megiddo, Area AA, that supports the association of Aegean-type flasks with burial preparations: In Locus 2131, a room between the palace and the city gate, the excavator Gordon Loud discovered *c.* 40 complete vessels in situ on a floor (Fig. 9.2; for a compilation of all vessels from Locus 2131 *cf.* Finkelstein and Zimhoni 2000, 237, fig. 10.10; 238, fig. 10.11), one of them being an Aegean-type flask (Fig. 9.2b.4; Leonard and Cline 1998, 23 No. 16) – probably a LH IIIA2/B import from the Argolid. The vessel inventory seems unusual for a residential context. Together with the flask, five cups-and-saucers, one scoop and an incense burner were found Fig. (9.2a.13–16, Fig. 9.2b.5), which are also usually connected with cultic or ritual practices (*cf.* Zuckerman 2007b, 193; 2007c; Uziel and Gadot 2010). Moreover, the inventory comprised two local imitations of Aegean type straight-sided alabastra, which are rare in settlement contexts (Fig. 9.2b.7). However, local imitations of alabastra are first evidenced in burials in the late 14th or early 13th century BCE in Nahalat Ahim (Amiran 1960, 37 fig. 3.54) and become a very frequent burial good later on, especially in the 12th century (*e.g.* Megiddo, Tomb 912D (Guy and Engberg 1938, pl. 35.21), Tell Beth-Shemesh, Tomb 1 (Grant 1929, 191, fig. 386), Lachish, Tomb 532 (Tufnell 1958, pl. 55.49, pl. 82. 9299), Aphek, Tomb 1200 (Gadot 2009a; 2009b fig. 8.47, 4; fig. 8.48, 4, 5). Together with the Canaanite and Aegean-type vessels, the excavators encountered an imported large neckless storage jar with rolled rim of Egyptian origin, a shape that is otherwise restricted to Egyptian centres, fortresses, or necropolis in Canaan (Fig. 9.2b.8). This type of Egyptian storage jar, *i.e.* type JR13 in Mario A. S. Martin's taxonomy, was also discovered in Tel Beth-Shean, Tel Mor, Tel Sera^{c}, Askhelon and Deir el-Balah, as well as in the necropolis of Tell es-Sa^{c}idiyeh (Martin 2004, 271; 2005, 132–135; 2008, 248, 255), but also in Tel Dan, a site with less strong relations to Egypt (Martin and Ben-Dov 2007, 196, fig. 5.5–7; 199–200). This distribution indicates that it was only relevant for Egyptian practices, but appears to have been hardly ever appropriated by the local Canaanites. It is interesting to see that the ceramic inventory of Locus 2131 points to local burial rituals as well as to the presence of Egyptians in Megiddo. However, it must remain open, whether the ceramic inventory thus points to the preparation of a burial by Egyptians living in Megiddo.

Another highly interesting context with Aegean-type pottery is Room 1817 in Area CC in Megiddo, which is thought to be part of an average residential building. This room is constituted by Locus W=1817 and Locus 1817.[3] In the remaining discussion, I will leave aside most of the finds from the room (including a considerable number of Aegean-type sherds) and concentrate on two amphoroid kraters (Fig. 9.3). One of the vessels survives as five sherds, the other one as 20 sherds. The large number of sherds suggests an *in*

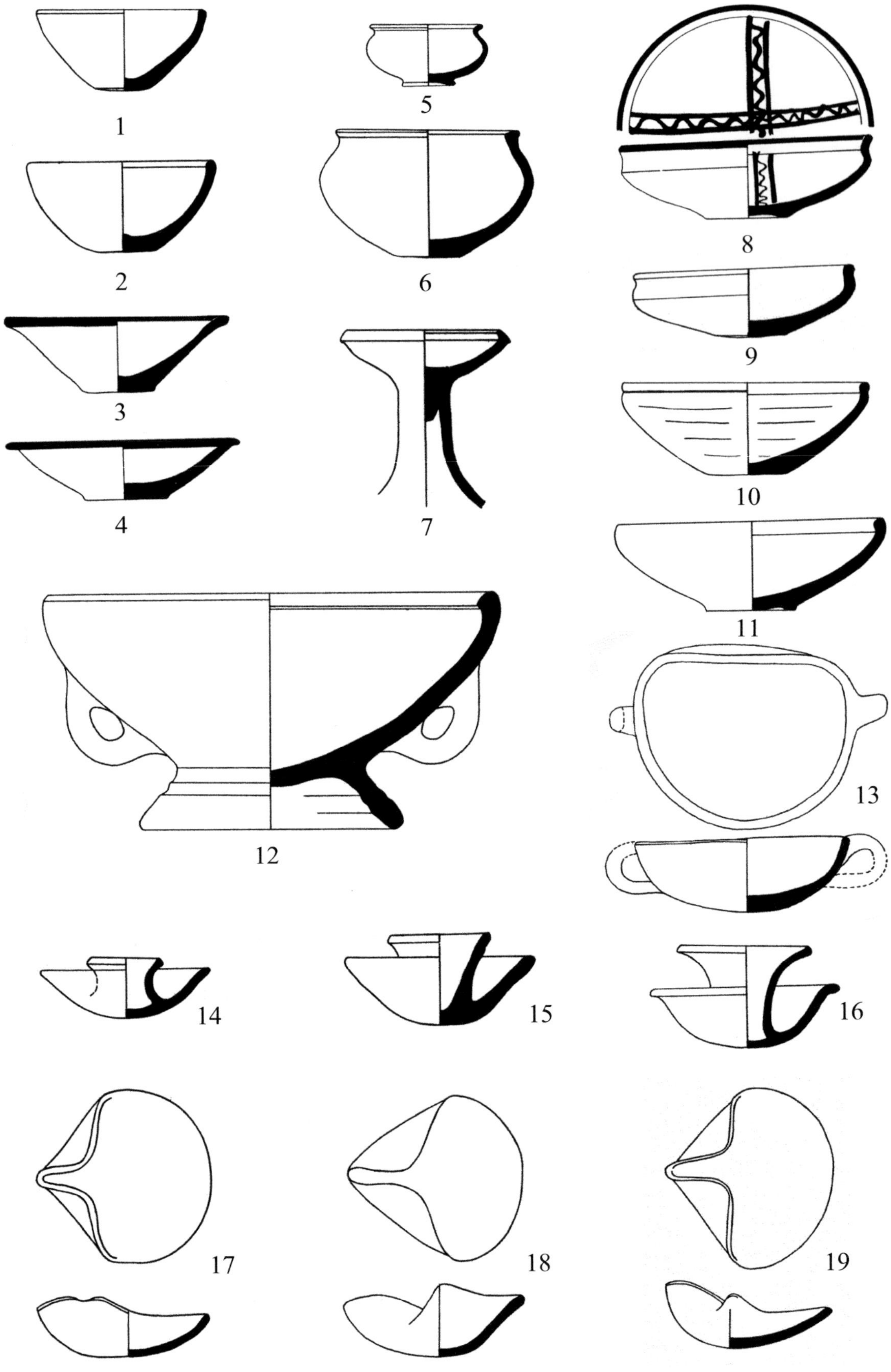

Fig. 9.2a: Pottery from Megiddo, Area AA, Locus 2131 (Loud 1948, pl. 63–67; with permission from the Oriental Institute Chicago) (continued on the opposite page).

Fig. 9.2b.

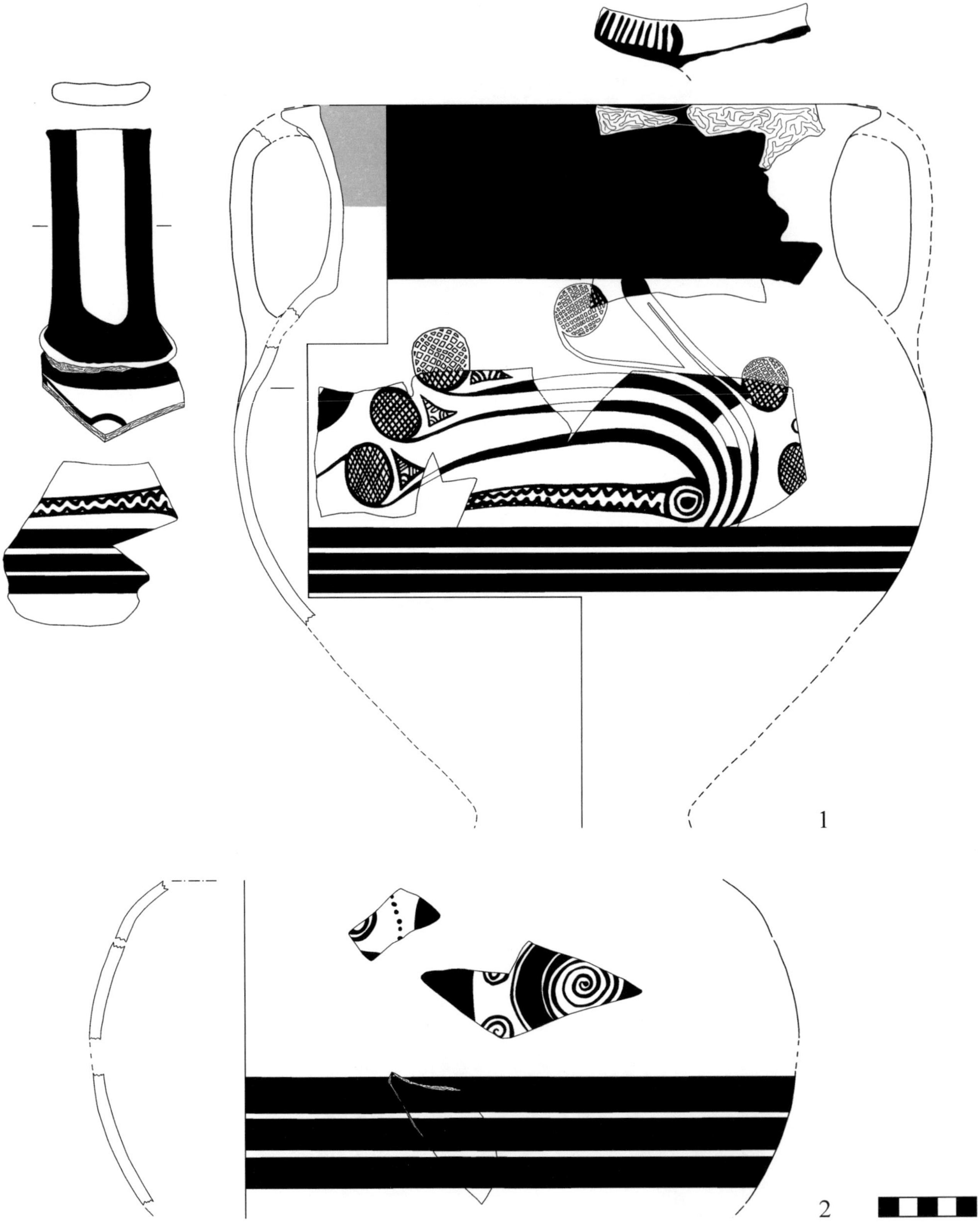

Fig. 9.3: Amphoroid kraters from Megiddo, Area CC, Locus 1817 (Drawings by the author).

situ position of deposition, at least for the better-preserved krater. This krater depicts stylized argonauts FM (Furumark Motif) 22, whose arms are filled with a net pattern FM 57, rather than the usual spiral (Fig. 9.3.1). Unfortunately, fabric, surface finish, and the quality of paint do not allow a closer identification of the place of production of the vessel, other than mainland Greece or Cyprus. The best – and mostly unpublished – parallels for the argonaut motif can be found in Tiryns between LH IIIB1 and LH IIIC Early 2 (Fig. 9.4): a body sherd from a krater (Fig. 9.4.1) found in Stratum *SH (Späthelladisch) IIIB Früh* (LXII 41/82 XIIIa), *i.e.* LH IIIB1, depicts an argonaut with a crescent shaped body with dot fill. Another krater sherd (Fig. 9.4.2) from a base-ring krater FS (Furumark Shape) 281 was found in a slightly later context in Stratum 17a3–a4 or *SH IIIB Entwickelt* (LXI 40/18 *Oberfläche* XIX), which can be equated with the pottery phase LH IIIB2 Late (French and Stockhammer 2009). On this sherd, the argonaut's body has virtually disappeared and only the arms are depicted. A deep bowl FS 284 (Fig. 9.4.3) with a very similar motif was found on the surface of the *Unterburg* in LXIII 45 and can therefore be LH IIIB or IIIC. As only one sherd is preserved from these vessels, we should not rule out secondary depositional processes. This is not the case for a large and very heavy sherd of a large closed vessel (Fig. 9.4.4), which can most probably be attributed to the floor of Room 208 (LXII 42/98 XI) of *SH IIIB Mitte*, thus dating to LH IIIB2 Early. The only published parallel is a nearly complete krater with stylized argonauts (Fig. 9.4.5) that was found *in situ* on the floor of Room 8/00 in the Northeastern Lower Town and dates to LH IIIC Early 2 (Stockhammer 2008, 160–164, 169–170, pl. 50.1196). The only other evidence for this motif known to me is from a bowl found in Kalavasos-Ayios Dhimitrios on Cyprus that is most likely of Argolid origin (South 1988, pl. 35.4). The krater from the Northeastern Lower Town of Tiryns and the ones from Megiddo were all found in an early 12th century BCE context, and in both cases they were found together with a Cypriot style wall bracket (Loud 1948, pl. 249.2; Maran 2004, 16, fig. 4). A Simple Style stirrup jar from the context of Room 8/00 enforces this Cypriot connection (Stockhammer 2008, pl. 57.1219), as does the fragment of a milk bowl from Room 1817 (Loud 1948, pl. 140.7). However, like the considerable number of single sherds from Aegean-type vessels from Room 1817, also this milk bowl fragment is very likely in a secondary context of find. The use of Cypriot wall brackets clearly indicates a strong relation to Cypriot cultic practices and Nava Panitz-Cohen connects these wall brackets with Cypriot inhabitants in Megiddo and Tiryns (Panitz-Cohen 2006). Whether Cypriots or people with close contacts to Cypriots lived in Room 1817, the inhabitants of these spaces doubtlessly had a broad network of contacts. The wall bracket from Room 1817 is the only one that also depicts an Egyptian motif, thus combining Cypriot practices with Egyptian iconography (Panitz-Cohen 2006, 627). Be it the Cypriot origin of the inhabitants or their permanent encounter with otherness that supported their appropriation of Aegean-type vessels, rather than the local elites, these families with strong international contacts, whether or not they were migrants, had no problems in integrating foreign pottery into their local practices. Following my methodological approach, the state of relational entanglement is documented in this instance, but not material entanglement, as the Megiddo kraters are unchanged in their materiality.

Tell el-ᶜAjjul

Although no Aegean-type vessels have been found complete and *in situ* during the excavations in the settlement of Tell el-ᶜAjjul, Louise Steel's (2002) interpretation of the role of the Aegean-type pottery at the site has been very influential (*cf.* Zuckerman 2007a, 626; Yasur-Landau 2010, 197). One of her basic arguments is that the rarity of this ware in the settlement contexts can be interpreted as evidence for elite controlled consumption (Steel 2002, 34–39). However, she does not take into consideration that Flinders Petrie concentrated on publishing only the complete vessels that were found in the tombs. In contrast to that, the Aegean-type sherd material from the settlement remained largely unpublished (*e.g.* unpublished sherd material in the University College London, Archaeology Collection Catalogue Nos. EXIII.67/89–91, EXIII.99/88–90, EXIII.78/99–101 and in the Rockefeller Museum Jerusalem, Israel Antiquities Authority Nos. 1935–4321/2, –4322, –4325, –4328 and –4331; with kind permission by the Israel Antiquities Authority), and was therefore not included in her analysis. Since Aegean-type sherd material is not rare in the settlement, as supposed by Steel, it cannot be taken as an indicator for an elite controlled consumption of this pottery in daily use.

The large number of 18 Aegean-type vessels from the so-called 'Governor's Tomb'[4] was interpreted by Steel (2002, 43–44) as 'one of a number of means used to demonstrate the high status of the incumbents, and their participation in international maritime commerce'. However, she does not take the long history of this tomb into account that was used for burials from the early or mid 14th century until at least the end of the 13th century BCE. Flinders Petrie documented the number of skeletons only for the last burial layer. Those seven burials were associated with four Simple Style stirrup jars of local or Cypriot production (Flinders Petrie 1933, pl. 11.42A, 43E, 44G, 45I). The number of Aegean-type vessels per burial is therefore less then in the simple single burials of the same cemetery with one or two of such vessels but without other possibly precious grave goods.

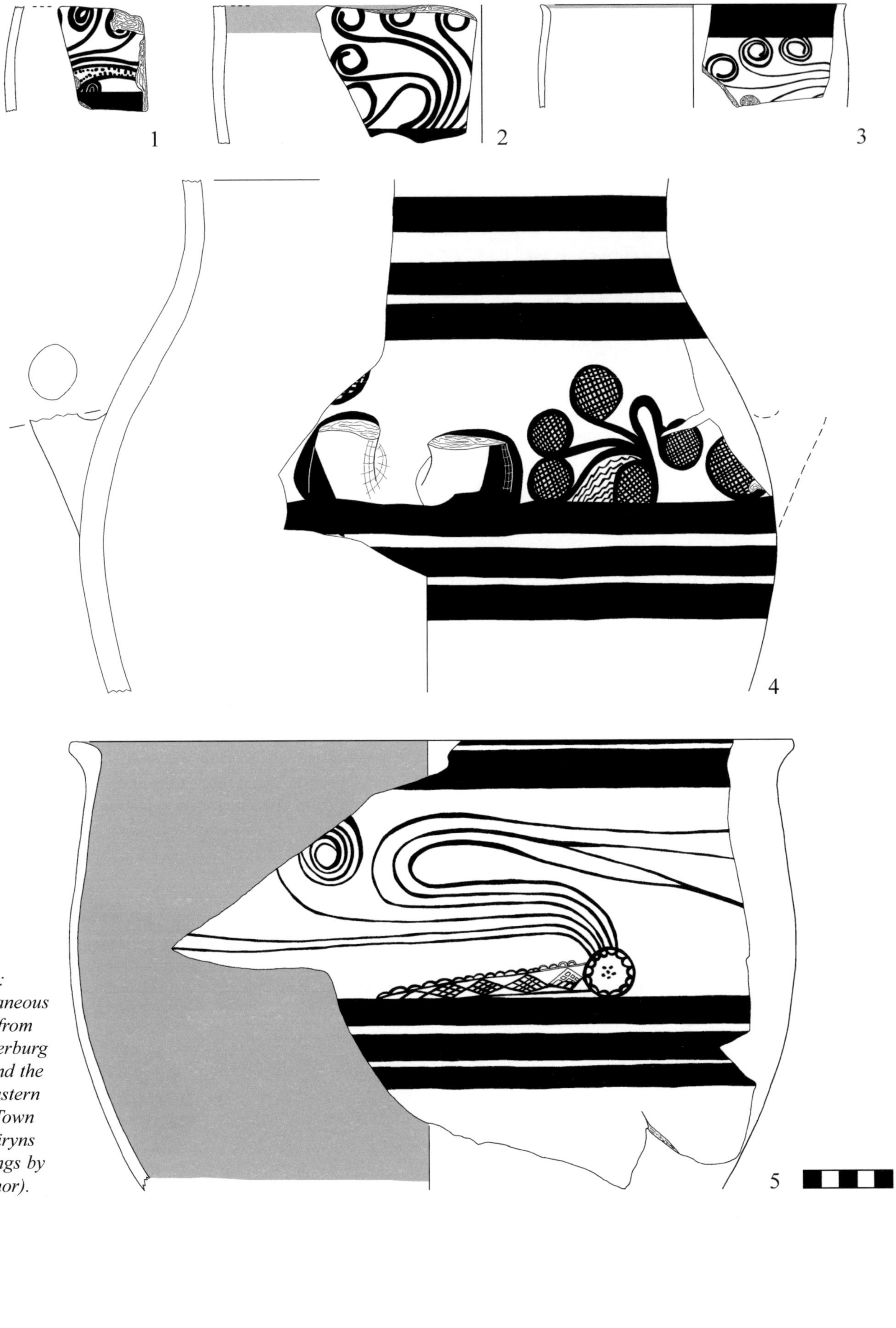

Fig. 9.4: Miscellaneous vessels from the Unterburg (1–4) and the Northeastern Lower Town (5) of Tiryns (Drawings by the author).

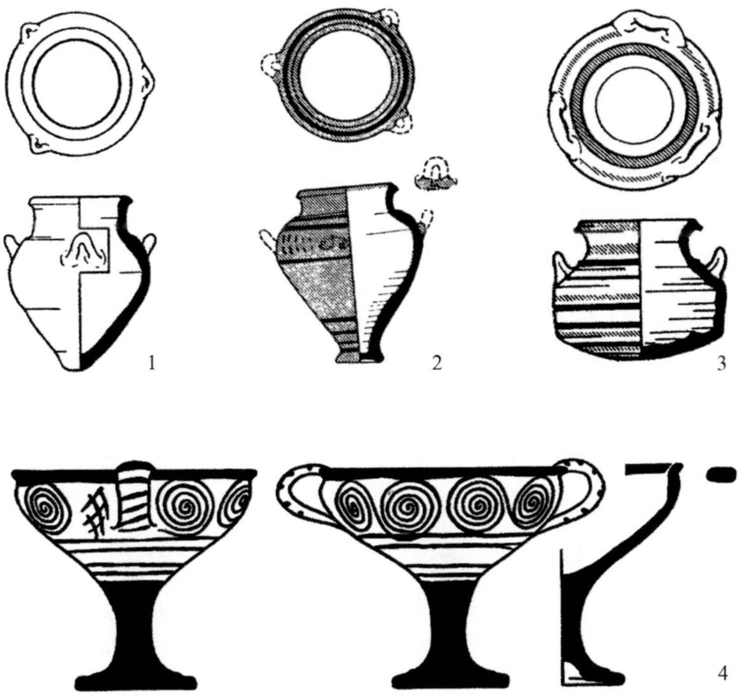

Fig. 9.5: Aegean-type pottery from Nahalat Ahim (Amiran 1960, 35, fig. 1, 1; 37, fig. 3.53–55).

There is no doubt that the deceased buried in Tell el-[c]Ajjul were anointed with what were probably perfumed oils, as it was the habit in Egypt and the Levant. The variety of grave contexts with Aegean-type pottery from the site suggests that deceased of very different status position were embalmed with perfume of Aegean origin, probably due to the individual selection of an adequate fragrance. As it is reported in later Talmudic literature, vessels with perfumed oils were also taken to produce a flavoursome smell in tombs that were used for burials over a longer period of time (Dayagi-Mendels 1989, 130, 132). Thus, the Aegean-type vessels from the 'Governor's Tomb' could also be interpreted as an attempt of the bereaved to make the tombs smell bearable during the reopening of the tomb.

Nahalat Ahim

After having demonstrated case studies of non-appropriation and relational entanglement, let me now illustrate a case of material entanglement from the cave tomb of Nahalat Ahim in Jerusalem. This tomb was used in the 14th and probably also early 13th century BCE (Amiran 1960). As well as many other finds, the tomb contained imported pottery from Cyprus and the Aegean and several local imitations of Aegean-type vessels (Fig. 9.5). The only imported Aegean vessel is a LH IIIA2 Early kylix FS 256 (Fig. 9.5.4; Amiran 1960, 35, fig. 1.1), which means that it reached the Levant before most of the other Mycenaean pottery which left Greece in the late 14th and 13th century BCE. Small Aegean-type container vessels were also found in this burial context, *i.e.* two piriform jars and one alabastron (Fig. 9.5.1–3; Amiran 1960, 37, fig. 3.53–55). However, all three vessels were not imported, but are local imitations of their late 14th century BCE Aegean counterparts. The imported kylix was obviously appropriated and documents the state of relational entanglement. The local imitations of Aegean-type vessels go one step further, as those are not just imitations of imported vessels, but show the creative dialogue triggered by the encounter of the potter with a foreign vessel. The most noticeable evidence for this creative potential of local potters is one of the piriform jars (Fig. 9.5.1; Amiran 1960, 37, fig. 3.53), which copies the imported Aegean piriform jars in its size and upper part. However, the lower part does not show the typical flat base for this shape, but a rounded base, which is typical for local Levantine storage vessels and is totally unusual for such vessels in the Aegean. Why a local potter created this new vessel shape by the combination of an Aegean-type upper part with a Levantine lower part remains unclear. This vessel can doubtlessly be considered entangled in its materiality and presents a singular ceramic creation.

Conclusion

As demonstrated with the contexts from Hazor, Megiddo, Tell el-[c]Ajjul and Nahalat Ahim, it is necessary to focus on single contexts as evidence for individual actor's practices. Their analysis enables us to understand why and by whom Aegean-type pottery was appropriated and to develop some insight into individual practices, worldviews, and ideologies. These are again influenced by the *habitus* and different identity groups one belongs to, be they due to status positions, migration, profession, or gender affiliations. It is, however, clear that Aegean-type pottery was not immediately taken and integrated into local practices as soon as it was offered. It is also obvious that neither the consumption of closed transport vessels nor the feasting dishes of Aegean origin can be associated with a Southern Levantine 'elite behaviour'. In my view, it is the integration of a clear methodological approach and the intense evaluation of significant contexts of find that will enable us to get a better appreciation of past material entanglements.

Acknowledgements

This article is part of my current research project 'Material Entanglements: The Appropriation of Foreign Pottery in the Eastern Mediterranean Late Bronze Age' within the Cluster of Excellence 'Asia and Europe in a Global Context' at the University of Heidelberg. I would like to thank Joseph Maran for intense discussions, Sharon Zuckerman, Galit Litani, Shlomo Bunimovitz and Zvi Lederman for allowing me to quote so far unpublished information and Carol Bell and Christina Sanchez-Stockhammer for proofreading and helpful advice.

Notes

1. I am using the term 'materiality' in the same way as Nicole Boivin (2008, 26): '*Materiality* … is a word that I will use to emphasise the physicality of the material world – the fact that it has dimensions, that it resists and constrains, and that it offers possibilities for the human agent (or organism) by virtue of a set of physical properties.'
2. An early 11th century BCE sherd plaster from the Northeastern Lower Town of Tiryns (settlement phase 5, LHIIIC Late) remains as a cautionary tale: Selected body sherds of at least 37 kraters of different ceramic styles have been collected to create a substructure for a hearth (Stockhammer 2008, 243).
3. Locus W=1817 is the area west of Locus 1817 which is the southeastern edge of a room from which only part of the eastern and southern wall were preserved (Loud 1948, fig. 409). To judge from Loud's architectural plan, it seems very reasonable to consider W=1817 as the western part of the room 1817 therefore consisting of Loci 1817 and W=1817.
4. Steels (2002a, 41–42, 45, tab. 1) analysis of the grave inventory contains several errors due to misunderstandings of the documentation published by Flinders Petrie (1933, 5–6, pl. 6–13). This results in several wrong attributions of vessels to burial levels and an erraneous number of 19 Aegean type vessels from the grave (*cf.* Stockhammer, in prep. for a detailed analysis of the tomb).

References

Amiran, R. (1960) A Late Bronze Age II Pottery Group from a Tomb in Jerusalem. *Eretz-Israel* 6, 25–37 (in Hebrew).

Appadurai, A. (1990) Disjuncture and Difference in the Global Cultural Economy. *Theory, Culture & Society* 7, 295–310.

Ben-Tor, A. (1997) An Account of the Fifth Season of Excavation, 1968. In A. Ben-Tor (ed.), *Hazor* 5. Jerusalem, Israel Exploration Society.

Ben-Tor, A. and Zuckerman, S. (2008) Hazor at the End of the Late Bronze Age: Back to Basics. *Bulletin of the American Schools of Oriental Research* 350, 1–6.

Bhabha, H. K. (2007) *The Location of Culture* (London and New York 2007).

Blum, S. W. E. (2003) *Işıklar. Ethnoarchäologische Untersuchungen zu Formation und Transformation archäologischer Siedlungskontexte*. Studies in Ethnoarchaeology 1. Remshalden, Greiner.

Boivin, N. (2008) *Material Cultures, Material Minds. The Impact of Things on Human Thought, Society, and Evolution.* Cambridge, Cambridge University Press.

Bourdieu, P. (1982) *Die feinen Unterschiede*. Frankfurt a. Main, Suhrkamp.

Dayagi-Mendels, M. (1989) *Perfumes and Cosmetics in the Ancient World*. Israel Museum Katalog 305. Jerusalem, Keter Publishing.

Du Mesnil du Buisson, R. (1928) L'ancienne Qatna: ou les ruines d'el Mishrifé au N.-E. de Homs (Émèse) – Deuxième campagne de fouilles (1927). *Syria* 9, 6–24.

Finkelstein, I. and Zimhoni, O. (2000) The Pottery from the Late Bronze Gate. In I. Finkelstein, D. Ussishkin and B. Halpern (eds), *Megiddo III, 1: The 1992–1996 Seasons*. Monograph Series of the Institute of Archaeology, Tel Aviv University 18, 223–243. Tel Aviv, Emery and Claire Yass Publication.

Finkelstein, I., Ussishkin, D. and Halpern, B. (2000) *Megiddo III, 2: The 1992–1996 Seasons*. Monograph Series of the Institute of Archaeology, Tel Aviv University 18. Tel Aviv, Emery and Claire Yass Publication.

Finkelstein, I., Ussishkin, D. and Halpern, B. (2006) *Megiddo IV: The 1998–2002 Seasons*. Monograph Series of the Institute of Archaeology, Tel Aviv University 24. Tel Aviv, Emery and Claire Yass Publication.

Fischer, P. M. (2001a) Cypriote Bichrome Wheel-Made Ware and Base-Ring Ware from the New Excavations at Tell el-ᶜAjjul: Synchronism and Dating. In P. Åström (ed.), *The Chronology of Base-Ring and Bichrome Wheel-Made Ware. Proceedings of a Colloquium Held in the Royal Academy of Letters, History and Antiquities, Stockholm, 18th–19th May 2000*, 221–230. Stockholm, Almqvist and Wiksell.

Fischer, P. M. (2001b) Cypriote Finds from the Renewed Excavations at Tell el-ᶜAjjul: Statistics and Chronology. In P. M. Fischer (ed.), *Contributions to the Archaeology and History of the Bronze and Iron Ages in the Eastern Mediterranean. Studies in Honour of Paul Åström*. Sonderschriften des Österreichischen Archäologischen Institutes Wien 39, 159–170. Wien, Österreichisches Archäologisches Institut.

Fischer, P. M. (2004) Coast Contra Inland: Tell el-ᶜAjjul and Tell Abu al-Kharaz during the Late Middle and Late Bronze Ages. *Ägypten und Levante* 14, 249–263.

Fischer, P. M. and Sadeq, M. (2000) Tell el-ᶜAjjul 1999. A Joint Palestinian-Swedish Field Project: First Season Preliminary Report. *Ägypten und Levante* 10, 211–226.

Fischer, P. M. and Sadeq, M. (2002) Tell el-ᶜAjjul 2000. Second Season Preliminary Report. *Ägypten und Levante* 12, 109–153.

Flinders Petrie, W. M. (1931) *Ancient Gaza I: Tell el Ajjūl*. Publications of the British School of Archaeology in Egypt 53. London, British School of Archaeology in Egypt and Bernard Quaritch.

Flinders Petrie, W. M. (1932) *Ancient Gaza II: Tell el Ajjūl*. Publications of the British School of Archaeology in Egypt 54. London, British School of Archaeology in Egypt and Bernard Quaritch.

Flinders Petrie, W. M. (1933) *Ancient Gaza III: Tell el Ajjūl*. Publications of the British School of Archaeology in Egypt 55. London, British School of Archaeology in Egypt and Bernard Quaritch.

Flinders Petrie, W. M. (1934*) Ancient Gaza IV: Tell el Ajjūl*. Publications of the British School of Archaeology in Egypt 56. London, British School of Archaeology in Egypt and Bernard Quaritch.

Flinders Petrie, W. M., Makay, E. J. H. and Murray, A. (1952) *City of Shepherd Kings and Ancient Gaza V*. Publications of the British School of Archaeology in Egypt 64. London, British School of Archaeology in Egypt and Bernard Quaritch.

French, E. and Stockhammer, P. W. (2009) Mycenae and Tiryns: The Pottery of the Second Half of the 13th Century BC: Contexts and Definitions. *The Annual of the British School at Athens* 104, 175–232.

Gadot, Y. (2009a) Late Bronze Age Stone-Built Tomb. In Gadot and Yadin 2009, 84–87.

Gadot, Y. (2009b) Late Bronze and Iron Age Pottery. In Gadot and Yadin 2009, 182–341.

Gadot, Y. and Yadin, E. (2009) *Aphek-Antipatris II. The Remains on the Acropolis. The Moshe Kochavi and Piryia Beck Excavations*. Monograph Series of the Institute of Archaeology, Tel Aviv University 27. Tel Aviv, Emery and Claire Yass Publication.

Ger, G. and Belk, R. W. (1996) I'd like to buy the World a Coke. Consumptionscapes of the 'Less Affluent World'. *Journal of Consumer Policy* 19, 271–304.

Grant, E. (1929) *Beth Shemesh (Palestine). Progress of the Haverford Archaeological Expedition*. Haverford, Biblical and Kindred Studies.

Guy, P. L. O. and Engberg, R. M. (1938) *Megiddo Tombs*. Oriental Institute Publications 33. Chicago, University of Chicago.

Hahn, H. P. (2004a) Globale Güter und lokales Handeln in Afrika. Einige methodische Vorbemerkungen. *Sociologus* 53, 51–77.

Hahn, H. P. (2004b) Global Goods and the Process of Appropriation. In P. Probst and G. Spittler (eds), *Between Resistance and Expansion. Explorations of Local Vitality in Africa*. Beiträge zur Afrikaforschung 18, 211–229. Münster *et al.*, LIT.

Hahn, H. P. (2005) *Materielle Kultur. Eine Einführung*. Berlin, Reimer.

Hahn, H. P. (2007) Zur Ethnologie des Konsums in Afrika. *Paideuma* 53, 199–220.

Josephson Hesse, K. (2008) *Contacts and Trade at Late Bronze Age Hazor: Aspects of Intercultural Relationships and Identity in the Eastern Mediterranean*. Diss. Umeå 2008. <http://urn.kb.se/resolve?urn=urn:nbn:se:umu:diva-1816> 04.10.09

Kopytoff, I. (1986) The Cultural Biography of Things. In A. Appadurai (ed.), *The Social Life of Things. Commodities in Cultural Perspective*, 64–91. Cambridge, Cambridge University Press.

Latour, B. (1986) The Powers of Association. In J. Law (ed.), *Power, Action and Belief: A New Sociology of Knowledge?* Sociological Review Monograph 32, 264–280. London, Boston and Henley, Routledge and Kegan.

Latour, B. (2005) *Reassembling the Social: An Introduction to Actor-Network-Theory*. Oxford, University Press.

Law, J. (1992) Notes on the Theory of the Actor-Network: Ordering, Strategy and Heterogeneity. *Systems Practice* 5, 379–393.

Leonard, A. and Cline, E. H. (1998) The Aegean Pottery at Megiddo: An Appraisal and Reanalysis. *Bulletin of the American Schools of Oriental Research* 309, 3–39.

Loud, G. (1939) The Megiddo Ivories. *Oriental Institut Publications* 52. Chicago, University of Chicago.

Loud, G, (1948) Megiddo II: Seasons of 1935–39. *Oriental Institut Publications* 62. Chicago, University of Chicago.

Maran, J. (2004) The Spreading of Objects and Ideas in the Late Bronze Age Eastern Mediterranean: Two Case Examples from the Argolid of the 13th and 12th Centuries B. C. *Bulletin of the American Schools of Oriental Research* 336, 11–30.

Martin, M. A. S. (2004) Egyptian and Egyptianized Pottery in Late Bronze Age Canaan. Typology, Chronology, Ware Fabrics, and Manufacture Techniques. Pots and People? *Ägypten und Levante* 14, 265–284.

Martin, M. A. S. (2005) *Aspects of the Egyptian Involvement in Late Bronze and Early Iron Age Canaan: The Egyptian and Egyptianstyle Pottery. A Case Study.* Unpublished thesis, University of Vienna.

Martin, M. A. S. (2008) Egyptians at Ashkelon? An Assemblage of Egytpian and Egyptian-Style Pottery. *Ägypten und Levante* 18, 245–274.

Martin, M. A. S. and Ben-Dov, R. (2007) Egyptian and Egyptian-Style Pottery at Tel Dan. *Ägypten und Levante* 17, 191–203.

Mühlenbruch, T. (2009) *Die Synchronisierung der nördlichen Levante und Kilikiens mit der ägäischen Spätbronzezeit.* Denkschriften der Gesamakademie/Österreichische Akademie der Wissenschaften 55. Wien, Österreichische Akademie der Wissenschaften.

Panitz-Cohen, N. (2006) 'Off the Wall': Wall Brackets and Cypriots in Iron Age I Israel. In A. M. Maeir and P. de Miroschedji (eds), *'I Will Speak the Riddles of Ancient Times'. Archaeological and Historical Studies in Honour of Amihai Mazar on the Occasion of His Sixtieth Birthday* 2, 613–636. Winona Lake, Eisenbrauns.

Papastergiadis, N. (1997) Tracing Hybridity in Theory. In P. Werbner and T. Modood (eds), *Debating Cultural Hybridity. Multi-Cultural Identities and the Politics of Anti-Racism,* 257–281. London, Zed Books.

Penner, S. (2006) *Die Keramik der Spätbronzezeit. Tempelanlagen T3 bis T1, Palastanlagen P5 bis P1/2, Königsgrab ('Schatzhaus') und 'Königliche Werkstatt'. Kamid el-Loz 19.* Saarbrücker Beiträge zur Altertumskunde 6. Bonn, Habelt.

Pfälzner, P. (2008) Between the Aegean and Syria: The Wall Paintings from the Royal Palace of Qatna. In D. Bonatz, R. M. Czichon and F. J. Kreppner (eds), *Fundstellen. Gesammelte Schriften zur Archäologie und Geschichte Altvorderasiens ad honorem Hartmut Kühne,* 95–118. Wiesbaden, Harrassowitz.

Pfälzner, P. (2009) Die Bestattungsrituale der Könige von Qatna. *In Schätze des Alten Syrien. Die Entdeckung des Königreichs Qatna.* Ausstellungskatalog, 240–243. Stuttgart, Landesmuseum Württemberg.

South, A. K. (1988) Kalavasos-Ayios Dhimitrios 1987: An Important Ceramic Group from Building X. *Report of the Department of Antiquities Cyprus*, 223–228.

Steel, L. (2002) Consuming Passions: A Contextual Study of the Local Consumption of Mycenaean Pottery at Tell el-[c]Ajjul. *Journal of Mediterranean Archaeology* 15, 1, 25–51.

Stewart, C. (1999) Syncretism and its Synonyms. Reflections on Cultural Mixture. *Diacritics* 29/3, 40–62.

Stockhammer, P. W. (2008) *Kontinuität und Wandel – Die Keramik der Nachpalastzeit aus der Unterstadt von Tiryns.* Thesis, University of Heidelberg. <http://www.ub.uni-heidelberg.de/archiv/8612/>

Stockhammer, P. W. (2011) An Aegean Glance at Megiddo. In W. Gauß, M. Lindbolm, R. A. K. Smith and J. C. Wright (eds), *Our Cups are Full: Pottery and Society in the Aegean Bronze Age. Papers Presented to Jeremy B. Rutter on the Occasion of his 65th Birthday.* British Archaeological Reports, International Series 2227, 282–296. Oxford, Archaeopress.

Stockhammer, P. W. (2012) Conceptualizing Cultural Hybridization in Archaeology. In P. W. Stockhammer (ed.), *Conceptualizing Cultural Hybridization: A Transdisciplinary Approach. Papers of the Conference, Heidelberg, 21st–22nd September 2009. Transcultural Research.* Heidelberg Studies on Asia and Europe in a Global Context, 43–58. Berlin/Heidelberg, Springer.

Stockhammer, P. W. (in preparation) *Materielle Verflechtungen – Zur lokalen Einbindung fremder Keramik in der ostmediterranen Spätbronzezeit.* PostDoc-Thesis, University of Heidelberg.

Tufnell, O. (1958). *Lachish (Tell ed-Duweir) IV: The Bronze Age.* London, Oxford University Press.

Uziel, J. and Gadot, Y. (2010) The 'Cup-and-Saucer' Vessel: Function, Chronology, Distribution and Symbolism. *Israel Exploration Journal* 60, 41–57.

van Wijngaarden, G. J. (2002) *Use and Appreciation of Mycenaean Pottery in the Levant, Cyprus and Italy (1600–1200 BC).* Amsterdam Archaeological Studies 8. Amsterdam, University Press.

von Rüden, C. (2009) Ein Hauch von westlichem Luxus – Die Wandmalerei. In *Schätze des Alten Syrien. Die Entdeckung des Königreichs Qatna.* Ausstellungskatalog, 176–181. Stuttgart, Landesmuseum Württemberg.

Weißköppel, C. (2005) 'Hybridität' – die ethnografische Annäherung an ein theoretisches Konzept. In R. Loimeier, D. Neubert and C. Weißköppel (eds), *Globalisierung im lokalen Kontext. Perspektiven und Konzepte von Handeln in Afrika.* Beiträge zur Afrikaforschung 20, 311–347. Münster, LIT.

Witzel, C. (2009) Was die Toten erzählen – Eine anthropologische Untersuchung. In *Schätze des Alten Syrien. Die Entdeckung des Königreichs Qatna.* Ausstellungskatalog, 208–211. Stuttgart, Landesmuseum Württemberg.

Yadin, Y., Aharoni, Y., Amiran, R., Dothan, T., Dunayevsky, I. and Perrot, J. (1958) *Hazor 1: An Account of the First Season of Excavations, 1955.* Jerusalem, Magnes.

Yadin, Y., Aharoni, Y., Amiran, R., Dothan, T., Dunayevsky, I, and Perrot, J. (1960) *Hazor 2: An Account of the Second Season of Excavations, 1956.* Jerusalem, Magnes.

Yadin, Y., Aharoni, Y., Amiran, R., Dothan, T., Dothan, M., Dunayevsky, I. and Perrot, J. (1961) *Hazor 3–4: An Account of the Third and Fourth Season of Excavations, 1957–1958.* Jerusalem, Magnes.

Yasur-Landau, A. (2010) *The Philistines and Aegean Migration at the End of the Late Bronze Age.* Cambridge, Cambridge University Press.

Ziffer, I., Bunimovitz, S. and Lederman, Z. (2009) Divine or Human? An Intriguing Late Bronze Age Plaque Figurine from Tel Beth-Shemesh. *Ägypten und Levante* 19, 333–341.

Zuckerman, S. (2007a) Dating the Destruction of Canaanite Hazor without Mycenaean Pottery? In M. Bietak and E. Czerny (eds), *The Synchronisation of Civilisations in the Eastern Mediterranean in the Second Millennium B.C. III. Proceedings of the Second Euro Conference of SCIEM 2000 Held at the Austrian Academy, Wien, 28. Mai–1.*

Juni 2003, 621–629. Wien, Österreichische Akademie der Wissenschaften.

Zuckerman, S. (2007b) ' ...Slaying Oxen and Killing Sheep, Eating Flesh and Drinking Wine...': Feasting in Late Bronze Age Hazor. *Palestine Exploration Quarterly* 139/3, 186–204.

Zuckerman, S. (2007c) Late Bronze Age Scoops: Context and Function. In S. W. Crawford (ed.), *Up to the Gates of Ekron. Essays on the Archaeology and History of the Eastern Mediterranean in Honor of Seymour Gitin,* 313–330. Jerusalem, Israel Exploration Society/W. F. Albright Institute of Archaeological Research.

Zuckerman, S. (2007d) Anatomy of a Destruction: Crisis Architecture, Termination Rituals and the Fall of Canaanite Hazor. *Journal of Mediterranean Archaeology* 20/1, 3–32.

Zuckerman, S. (2008) Fit for a (not-quite-so-great) King: A Faience Lion-Headed Cup from Hazor. *Levant* 40/1, 115–125.

10.

Can we say, what's behind all those sherds? Ceramic innovations in the Eastern Mediterranean at the end of the second millennium

Reinhard Jung

Introduction

Various methodological models that aim to interpret the archaeological record of regions at the intersection of different social and political entities in the Mediterranean are currently being debated. Inasmuch as those entities are characterised by recognisable differences in their material cultures, their presence and influence in the Mediterranean zone of interaction can be described by archaeology. In the second half of the second millennium BCE, people in many regions outside Greece imported Mycenaean pottery in an earlier phase, while local production of Mycenaean and Mycenaeanizing pottery started only subsequently. The 12th century BCE saw the peak of local Mycenaean pottery production in Italy, Macedonia, western Asia Minor, Cyprus and on the Levantine coast, although in some of these areas the local workshops had reached a high output even 100 or 200 years earlier (*e.g.* in western Asia Minor at Troy, *cf.* Mountjoy 2006). At about the same time, other pottery classes of western origin started to be produced in various regions of the eastern Mediterranean. These phenomena found expression in a multitude of different production lines and usage of these new types of pottery in the various eastern Mediterranean microregions and at individual settlement sites. To variable degrees, the new vessel classes were integrated with pre-existing pottery traditions or replaced those earlier traditions, while all gradations between these two extremes were possible. This highlights the need to treat separately each situation where people from different regions came in contact and created new forms of material culture thereby shaping the social relationships between them. Two sites from Cyprus and Syria will serve as case studies to demonstrate the contribution pottery studies can make for historical interpretation of such contact situations.

1. Typology

The subject of this conference is the material archaeological record at places of intense intercommunity contacts, which is characterised by phenomena that have been called international style (Feldman 2006), hybridisation (van Dommelen 2006; Voskos and Knapp 2008), creolisation (Webster 2001) or entanglement (Stockhammer, this volume). In order to analyse such phenomena, it is necessary to disentangle elements of different origin that were combined in creating a new material culture. The archaeological analysis of finds from sites located at the intersection of different systems of material culture poses specific problems. These problems occur on different levels of processing and analysis of finds, and concern the identification and classification, as well as the descriptive and interpretative terminology that can be employed.

In the case of a site with locally produced vessels that depend on manufacturing traditions brought from another region, those locally made pots often exhibit certain typological and stylistic details, which distinguish them from the production series in their region of derivation. In the case of Aegean-style pottery produced outside of the Aegean, such situations often led to the definition of specific typological categories and terminologies for these local pottery classes, in which their relationship with the original models they depend on sometimes became blurred. In addition, in those terminologies criteria of typology, fabric classification and chronology were frequently mixed, which, unsurprisingly, led to confusion regarding production locations and chronology. In the Levant and Cyprus scholars traditionally tend to use the term 'Mycenaean pottery' only with reference to the imported wares, while they use different terms such as 'White Painted Wheel-made III' in Cyprus or 'Philistine Pottery (monochrome and bichrome)' in the southern Levant and 'Mycenaean IIIC:1b' in both areas for designating local products with Mycenaean typological characteristics. I agree with Barbara Kling's plea for the 'abandonment of terms that carry chronological and historical meaning' (Kling 1991, 183). Indeed, pottery terminology should refer to type, style and fabric only while remaining neutral in every other respect. We should use clear typological and technological categories, which leave any wider social and historical interpretation to a second step *after* pottery classification.

In the regions outside the Aegean, it is essential for both chronological and culture-historical analyses to differentiate between the ceramic classes that follow the Aegean style closely and others that exhibit the influence of other, non-Mycenaean traditions of pottery manufacture. Those local products that follow the Aegean developments closely, should be termed 'local Mycenaean pottery' – even if found far from Greece (*e.g.* in Syria or in Italy). In this definition 'Mycenaean' has no historical connotation, but refers only to the technological and typological characteristics of the pottery, which link it to the ceramic repertoire of the Aegean.

In many eastern Mediterranean regions other pottery classes were produced by combining Aegean and local elements in their shapes, decorations and technological features. These are mixed creations, which result from an intense interplay between foreign and local traditions of pottery production and consumption. My proposal is to include these mixed products in a typological category named 'Mycenaeanising pottery'. Alternatively 'Aegeanising' might be used, in order to be neutral about some possible Minoan influence. Numerous examples around the central and eastern Mediterranean could be cited, but two from Cyprus and Syria may serve to illustrate the issue. One illustrates how a local shape was painted in a way that was inspired by Mycenaean linear decoration (Fig. 10.1.1–3). The other one shows the possibility to produce a Mycenaean shape, but decorate it according to local conventions (Fig. 10.1.4–6).

In a second step of pottery analysis, it may prove useful to look at the typologically defined groups as a whole and also to examine these groups with regard to other collected data such as those on ceramic ware or fabric. Wares or fabrics (Horejs 2010) are understood here as technological categories, which have to be treated separately from typological categories. Each ware or fabric is defined by the combination of recurrent technological characteristics (colours, surface treatment, inclusions *etc* .) that can be observed in every sherd or vessel assigned to that fabric or ware. It may be instructive to examine whether the typological categories coincide with the fabric groups, or if the same fabrics occur in several different typologically defined pottery classes.

In the two case studies that follow, pottery data assembled according to the principles outlined above are interpreted from two points of view: the viewpoint of pottery production and the viewpoint of pottery use (or consumption, as it is often called somehow misleadingly). Both viewpoints can contribute to a holistic historical conclusion.

2. Production viewpoint

Case study 1

Tell Kazel, situated in the northern Akkar Plain of southern Syria, is strategically located on the main route between the Mediterranean coast and inland Syria, at the major break between the mountain chains of Mt Lebanon and Jebel Ansariyeh (Al-Maqdissi 2008, 43, fig. 17). In the LBA the settlement belonged to the region called *Amurru*, which was constituted as a kingdom during the 14th century BCE. Initially contested by Egyptians and Hittites, it eventually became a Hittite vassal and remained in the sphere of influence of the Great Kingdom of Hatti until the fall of that kingdom early in the 12th century BCE (Singer 1991; Klengel 1992, 160–174). Excavations in two areas have brought to light an extensive habitation quarter and a temple complex in use during the course of the 13th century. The whole settlement was destroyed by fire at the Late Bronze–Iron Age transition. This destruction can be ascribed to the Sea Peoples' incursion mentioned in the inscription of the 8th regnal year of Ramesses III with an explicit reference to the destruction of Amurru (Badre 2006, 92–93; Jung 2006a, 203–207; 2009a, 41–45). In the levels of that destruction in the early 12th century, small quantities of locally produced Mycenaean and Mycenaeanising ceramics were found, alongside with handmade and burnished pottery (traditionally called Handmade Burnished Ware or HMBW). These pottery categories were new at the time of the destruction, while the importation of Mycenaean pottery from the Argolid had already stopped some time before the catastrophic event. In the following Iron Age I settlement phase, the two pottery

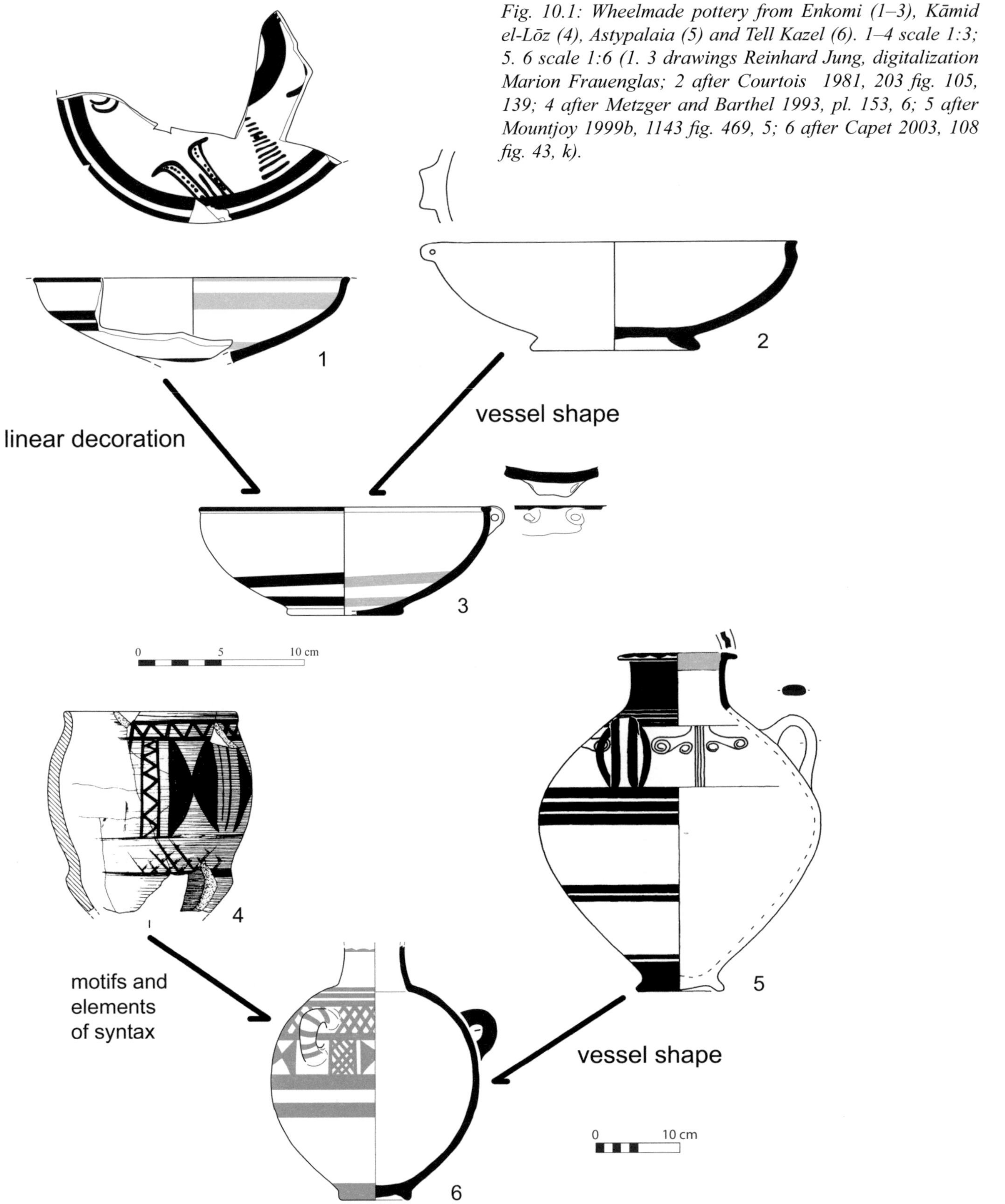

Fig. 10.1: Wheelmade pottery from Enkomi (1–3), Kāmid el-Lōz (4), Astypalaia (5) and Tell Kazel (6). 1–4 scale 1:3; 5. 6 scale 1:6 (1. 3 drawings Reinhard Jung, digitalization Marion Frauenglas; 2 after Courtois 1981, 203 fig. 105, 139; 4 after Metzger and Barthel 1993, pl. 153, 6; 5 after Mountjoy 1999b, 1143 fig. 469, 5; 6 after Capet 2003, 108 fig. 43, k).

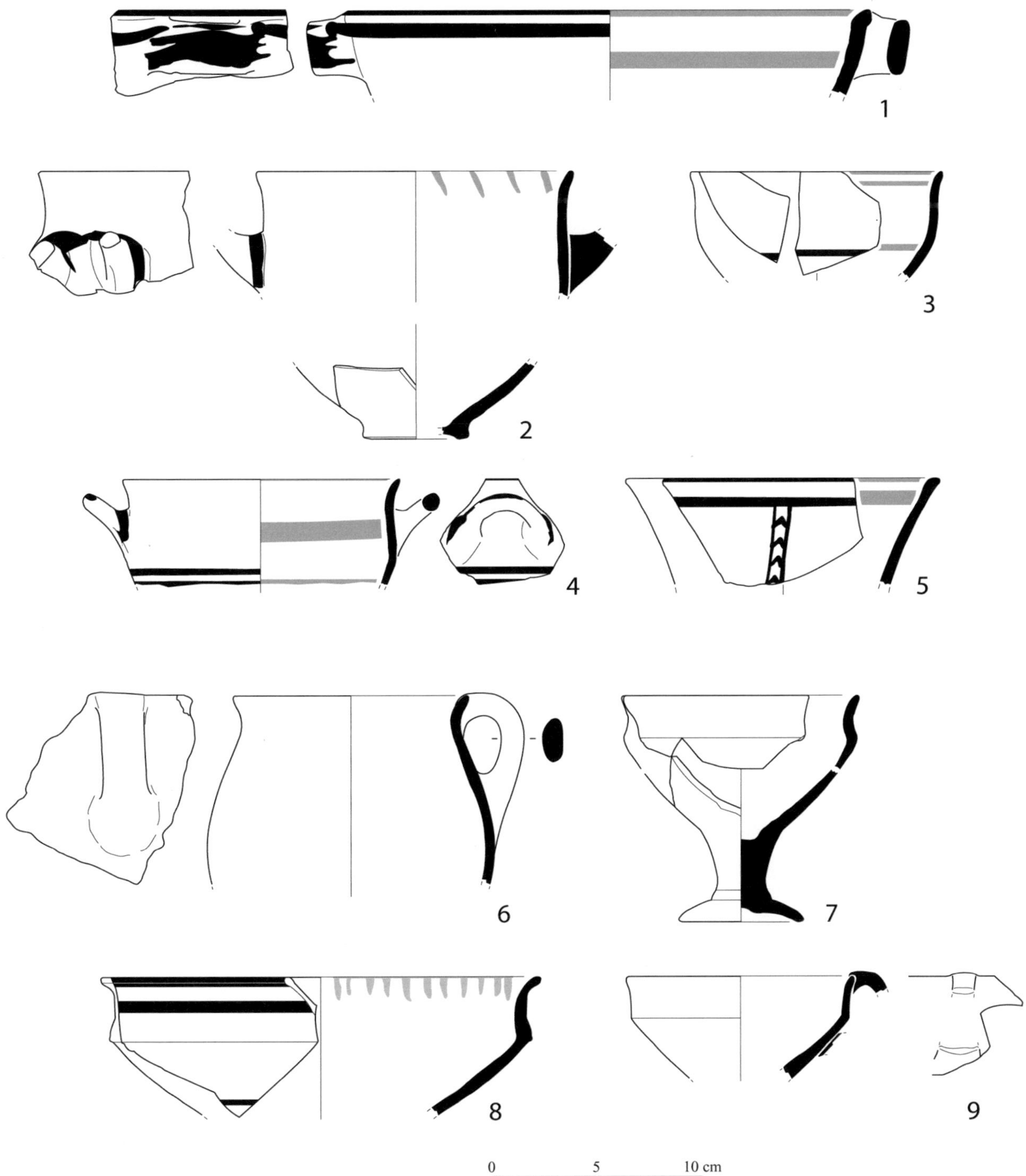

Fig. 10.2: Local Mycenaean pottery (except for no. 8) from Tell Kazel. 1. 3. 5–7 LBA II/IA I transition; 2. 4. 8 IA I. Scale 1:3 (drawings Reinhard Jung and Rami Yassine, digitalization Rami Yassine).

classes of western derivation continued to be produced, while there was yet a third one, a Grey Ware class, which again originated from regions in the west.

In order to learn more about pottery production at Tell Kazel, two chemical and petrographic analysis programs were conducted[1] and the results were compared to the macroscopic

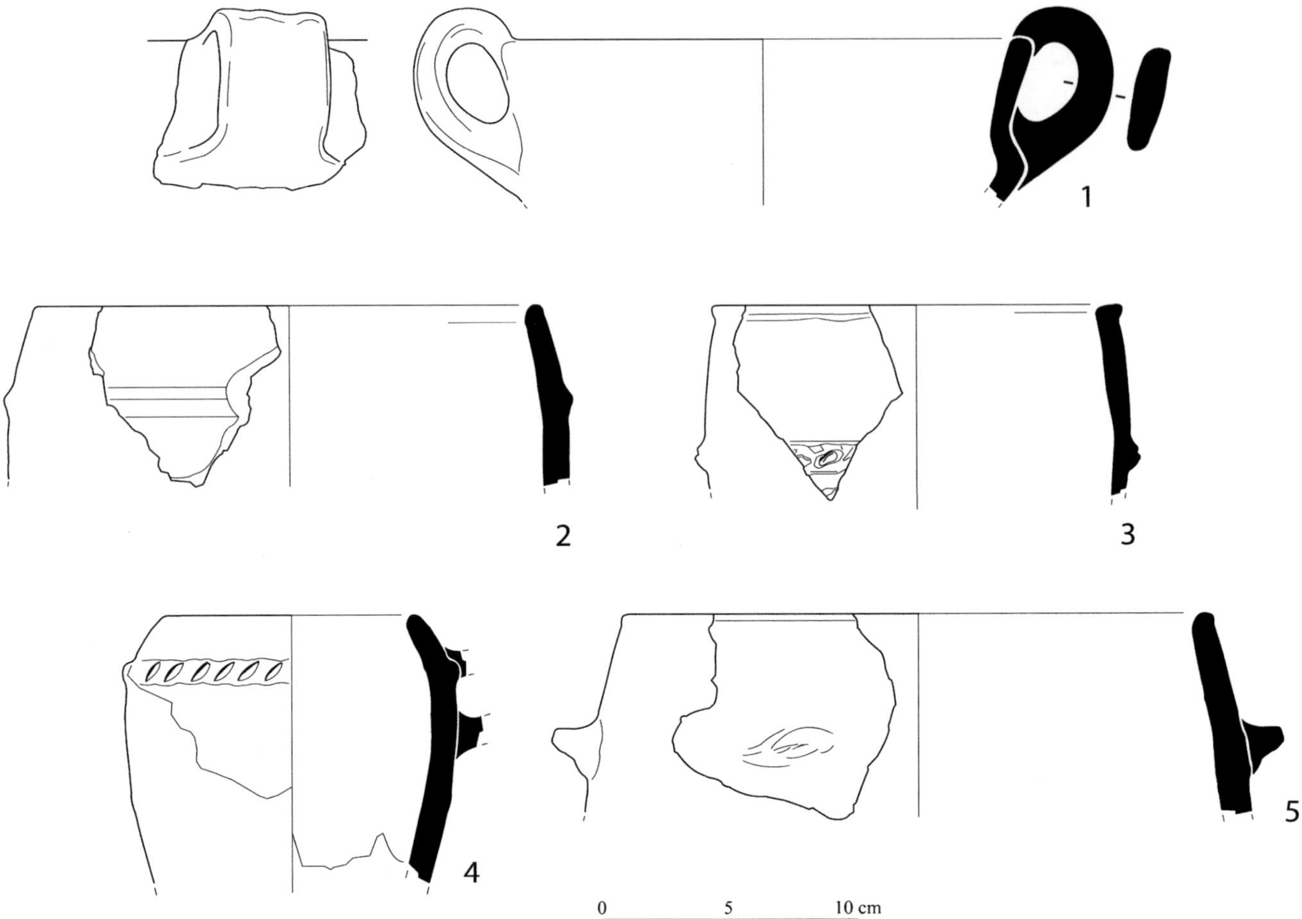

Fig. 10.3: Handmade and burnished pottery from Tell Kazel. 4 LBA II/IA I transition; 1–3. 5 IA I. Scale 1:3 (1–3. 5 after Badre 2006, 88 fig. 88, 1.4–6; 4 after Capet 2003, 95 fig. 31, m).

fabric categories defined before. Hans Mommsen was responsible for NAA, while petrographic analyses were undertaken by Marie-Claude Boileau. Both methods gave clear evidence for including most fabrics of the supposedly local Mycenaean pottery (Fig. 10.2) into one group, named TKaA or Calcareous Petrofabric (Badre *et al.* 2005, 17, fig. 1; 20–23; 27–29, tab. 5). Chemical and petrographic comparisons with samples of red marls, which were taken close to the banks of the Nahr al-Abraš river, confirmed its production in the plain and most probably close to the tell settlement itself (Boileau *et al.* 2010, 1679, 1682, fig. 3a; 1685–1686, tab. 4). Interestingly, there is almost no overlap of the local Mycenaean pottery group with pottery of Syrian type. Some of the analysed Syrian-type pots are petrographically similar to the local Mycenaean ones, but not identical (Badre *et al.* 2005, 27, 29).[2]

A second interesting result from the analytical programs is a group named TKaD or IRF/Chert Sand Petrofabric (Badre *et al.* 2005, 17, fig. 1; 23). It includes not only various Syrian-type vessels such as trefoil-mouthed jugs, jars ('Canaanite jars') and bowls (Badre *et al.* 2005, 28, fig. 4.2, 4, 5), but also vessels with a whitish slip and red paint, which show mixed typological characteristics of Aegean and Levantine origin (Badre *et al.* 2005, 28, fig. 4; 30, fig. 5.1). The latter category consists basically of amphoroid kraters and piriform jars, the production of which commenced in the last phase before the Sea Peoples' destruction of the settlement and continued in the following Iron Age I.[3] Mycenaeanising amphoroid kraters and piriform jars of similar fabrics are also known from contemporaneous sites in the neighboring kingdom of Ugarit (see *e.g.* Monchambert 2004, 226, 230, 233, fig. 94.1280; 239, fig. 100.1347; Vansteenhuyse in press, fig. 12). They may be interpreted in terms of adapting Mycenaean vessel shapes to local consumption habits by painting them in a Syrian manner – at a time when these vessel shapes could not be imported anymore from the Argolid.

Thus, two different clay recipes are attested: one used (nearly) exclusively for pottery of Mycenaean type, the other one for pottery of Syrian type and of mixed Mycenaean and Syrian type as well. This suggests that Mycenaean-type pottery was treated as a category of its own and set apart from Syrian and from Mycenaeanising ceramics by the potters in Amurru. Moreover, the analyses show that both finer and coarser vessels of Mycenaean type (including also one cooking pot) were made in the same Calcareous petrofabric. This is a hint at a standardised production.

However, Dean Arnold reminds us that the first factor influencing the variability of clay pastes is the local geology of the production region (Arnold 2000, 342, 363, 369–370). The Akkar Plain is a zone in which different geological formations are found rather close together. According to worldwide ethnoarchaeological studies, 7 km is the maximum distance that most traditional potters would travel in order to obtain clay (Arnold 2000, 343). When considering Tell Kazel, even within a radius of 7 km around the site, a high geological diversity can be observed (*cf.* Boileau *et al.* 2010, 1679, 1682, fig. 2). This geological heterogeneity is reflected also in the Syrian-type pottery of Tell Kazel for which Marie-Claude Boileau defined seven different petrofabrics (Boileau *et al.* 2010, 1685). Therefore, the homogeneity of the local Mycenaean-type vessels in chemical and petrographic terms surely reflects a conscious clay selection by their potters. When compared to contemporary products from the Aegean, the quality of the local Mycenaean pottery can be described as medium to low (Jung, in press). However, the Mycenaean pots produced in the Akkar Plain show fewer and smaller inclusions than the products of Levantine type from the same region (Badre *et al.* 2005, 21–23, fig. 1.e–f). The uniform style and the lack of care for surface finishing add to the picture of homogeneity and suggest a standardisation of production with not much care invested for the single vessel.

This standardised pottery of Aegean derivation stands in marked contrast to the heterogeneity of the HMBW (Fig. 10.3, see Badre 2006), a second ceramic category of foreign origin, which is of south Italian Recent Bronze Age type (for its comparison to the handmade so-called *impasto* pottery from Italy see Jung 2006b, 26, 51 n. 370, pls. 25–26; 2009b, 144–146, figs. 9–10). For a number of reasons, this last group of pottery is a unique ceramic category of very poor craftsmanship in comparison to the local (wheelmade) pottery classes: the manufacture without the use of the potter's wheel, the use of very coarse and poorly sorted temper, a very porous texture, a dark external surface, which is burnished in variable degrees, and a varied low firing in a mainly reducing, and rarely oxidising, atmosphere as the result of bonfire firing. A main petrographic group, a minor petrographic group and a number of petrographic loners were identified among the 44 analysed samples. This grouping accords well with the results of the NAA on 12 HMBW samples (Badre *et al.* 2005; Boileau *et al.* 2010). Thus the HMBW of Tell Kazel shows a considerable variability of petrofabrics and surface finishing techniques attesting to a technological heterogeneity, which can be interpreted in terms of non-standardised manufacture on the level of small social units, that is a domestic production (Boileau *et al.* 2010, 1686). The presence of grog temper in many of the HMBW vessels is a technological feature not seen amongst any of the other pottery classes from the site, but it is attested in a considerable portion of the related *impasto* pottery from Recent Bronze Age settlements in southern Italy (Boileau *et al.* 2010, 1682–1684, 1686; *cf.* Levi 1999, 131–133, fig. 85; 241–242, fig. 251; Gorgoglione *et al.* 2006, 1138). The contrast in technology between the local Syrian and Aegean-type wares on the one hand, and the HMBW pots on the other hand, is striking. The new technology must have been introduced from Italy, either directly or via the Aegean.

There is yet another group of pottery, numerically much smaller than the HMBW, which is related to pottery production of Recent Bronze Age southern Italy. That pottery class is a kind of Grey Ware, which was made on the wheel, slipped and burnished and fired under reducing conditions (fabric no. G 1, see Badre *et al.* 2005, 42). Most of the finds in this Grey Ware category were found in contexts of IA I date.[4] The production technology of this class cannot be derived from any local pot-making tradition at Tell Kazel. Being wheelmade and grey, one might think that the fabric was related to the Troad in north-western Asia Minor. The Troad is a well known pottery exporting region of the Late Bronze Age, from which Grey Ware ceramics reached many Cypriot and Levantine sites (Mommsen and Pavúk 2007), among which Tell Kazel itself is also included (Badre *et al.* 2005, 17–19, 31–32). However, according to the NAA results the samples of fabric G 1 do not match any of the numerous pottery samples of Trojan Grey Ware in the Bonn database. In fact, this non-Trojan Grey Ware, as it has provisionally been called, could not be related to any known pottery production centre by means of NAA, but its local production seems possible based on the petrographic analyses (Boileau *et al.* 2010, 1684–1687, fig. 7).

Among the non-Trojan Grey Ware vessels, the deep bowl is obviously a Mycenaean shape (FT (Furumak Type) 284/285, Fig. 10.4.10). However, deep bowls FT 284/285 in wheel-made Grey Ware were not only produced in Mycenaean Greece (Belardelli 1999, 452–455, figs. 1.2, 16.2, 28, 31, 37), but also at Troy VIIb1 and VIIb2 (Blegen *et al.* 1958, 20, tab. 9; 156–157, tab. 18; Pavúk 2002, 61) and in Recent Bronze Age southern Italy (Fig. 10.4.9, see Castagna 2002, 234–235, fig. 100.3). By contrast, the carinated bowls reproduce Grey Ware vessel shapes from southern Italy, which in turn depend on the Recent Bronze Age *impasto* pottery tradition (*cf.* Fig. 10.4.5 with 10.4.4 and Fig. 10.4.8 with 10.4.6–7; for the interdependency of *impasto* and Grey Ware bowls see Castagna 2006).[5] Based on these Italian parallels, the carinated Grey Ware bowls from Tell Kazel can be reconstructed as carinated cups with high-swung strap handles (*cf.* Fig. 10.4.4; see also Castagna 2006, 359, fig. 5). A Grey Ware handle fragment from Tell Kazel belongs to yet another southern Italian vessel type, a small carinated cup with high-swung round handle, (*cf.* Fig. 10.4.3 with 10.4.1; see also Castagna 2002, 235, fig. 100.6–7). The fragment from Tell Kazel is provided with two cylindrical protrusions on the handle apex, for which there is a parallel in Grey Ware from Taranto, Scoglio del Tonno (Gorgoglione 2002, 129, 132, fig. 4.3; 136). Moreover, such cylindrical protrusions are not rare among the *impasto* versions of those cups in southern Italy, while one parallel also exists among the HMBW pots from LH (Late Helladic) IIIC Early Dhimíni in Thessaly (Fig. 10.4.2, see Jung 2006b, 202, pls. 8.9, 10; 17.6; Pagliara *et al.* 2008, 255, 257, figs. 13 A, 16). The Trojan footed cup with high-swung handle (Blegen type A 100) does not offer a good morphological *comparandum* for the Kazel handle, as its horns are always pointed (Blegen *et al.* 1953, 55–56, figs. 292b, A 100; 318.35; 627.36; 704; 385.10, 11; 391.3; 396.12, 14). Moreover, that shape was in use until the end of Troy VI, *i.e.* until the transition from LH IIIA to LH IIIB (Mountjoy 1999a, 264–265, figs. 3, 17; Pavúk 2002, 53–54, fig. 12; 47, 48, 60), while the Italian horn-handled cups date to the phase Recent Bronze Age 2, that is contemporaneous with LH IIIC Early–Advanced. Thus, the Italian Grey Ware cups are not only closer morphological parallels for the Kazel handle fragment, but also fit better chronologically with the Syrian evidence. A fragmentary large jug (Badre 2006, 88, fig. 17) demonstrates that there were also closed Grey Ware vessels in use at Tell Kazel. Although this is a rather unspecific shape, again a find from southern Italy can be named as a parallel (Castagna 2002, 240, figs. 103.29; 243 no. 29). Summarising the Grey Ware evidence from Tell Kazel, one can say that fabric G 1, the non-Trojan Grey Ware, presents a range of vessel types that matches best the Grey Ware repertoire of southern Italy during Recent Bronze Age 2. Especially along the Ionian coast wheelmade Grey Ware was a recurrent part of the local pottery assemblage (S. T. Levi and M. Bettelli in Bettelli 2002, 96–97, fig. 44.A, B). Some shapes are Mycenaean in origin, but most are related to handmade *impasto* types (*ibid.*, 101–105, figs. 48–49). A combination of Mycenaean shapes and Italian ones can also be observed at a few coastal sites in the Aegean such as Tiryns in the Argolid (Belardelli 1999) and Dhimíni in Thessaly (Adrimi-Sismani 2006a; 2006b; Jung 2006b, 47–51, 203), both of which produced some quantity of Grey ware. Finally, this mixture of Aegean and south Italian types characterises the non-Trojan Grey Ware of Tell Kazel itself. Therefore its presence in the Akkar Plain may be either explained by direct contacts to the Ionian coast of southern Italy, or rather – given its contemporaneity with HMBW and local Mycenaean pottery – with contacts to Italian pottery manufacturing traditions via Aegean coastal sites.

3. Consumption viewpoint

Let us turn now to the use of pottery. At Tell Kazel, all the western-derived pottery classes described so far were found in very small quantities, when compared to the amount of the dominant Syrian-type pottery. They were found at different locations within the settlement, sometimes forming concentrations of several vessels in the same room. The local Mycenaean pots do not continue the vessel repertoire of the earlier Mycenaean imports from the Argolid. Rather, they represent a totally new set, which basically consists of serving and drinking vessels (Jung 2006a, 191–203; in press). These include deep bowls FT 284/285 (painted, Fig. 10.2.2–4, and unpainted), conical kylikes FT 274–275 (painted and unpainted), unpainted carinated kylikes FT 267 (Fig. 10.2.7; 10.2.9), painted mugs FT 226 (Fig. 10.2.5), painted kraters FT 281/282, painted basins FT 294 (Fig. 10.2.1) or with spout FT 302, shallow angular bowls FT 295C (painted and unpainted) and closed vessels (amphorae and hydriae, painted and unpainted). So far, Tell Kazel is the only Levantine site with a high percentage of unpainted local Mycenaean fine ware (more than one third of the whole local Mycenaean repertoire by rim count, see Jung, in press). A unique exception among the vessels made in the local Mycenaean fabrics is a large carinated bowl shape that seems to be a local creation, which is not Mycenaean but does not relate to any Syrian vessel type either (Fig. 10.2.8; this is the only non-Mycenaean vessel type made in one of those fabrics that are otherwise restricted to Mycenaean types). It is attested in very few examples only. Apart from this shape, the repertoire of types is not very different from contemporary Aegean assemblages, be it on the Greek mainland or on the Cyclades (Jung 2006a, 191–203; in press). However, an important difference is the rarity of Mycenaean cooking pots FT 65/66 at Tell Kazel (Fig. 10.2.6). The typical cooking pot of the settlement at the end of LBA (Late Bronze Age) II and at the beginning of IA I still had the traditional round-bottomed shape of the Levantine coastal regions, although, of course, a typological development of this shape can be observed (Badre in Badre and Gubel 1999–2000, 182, 188, fig. 41.a, b; Capet 2003, 81, 86, fig. 23.e; 89, fig. 26.b–d; 94–95, fig. 30.a; 103–106, figs. 37. a, 38.b, 40.a–b).

By contrast, the corpus of Tell Kazel HMBW is dominated by storage and preparation vessels, among which the so-called hole-mouthed jars of different sizes are most prominent (Fig.

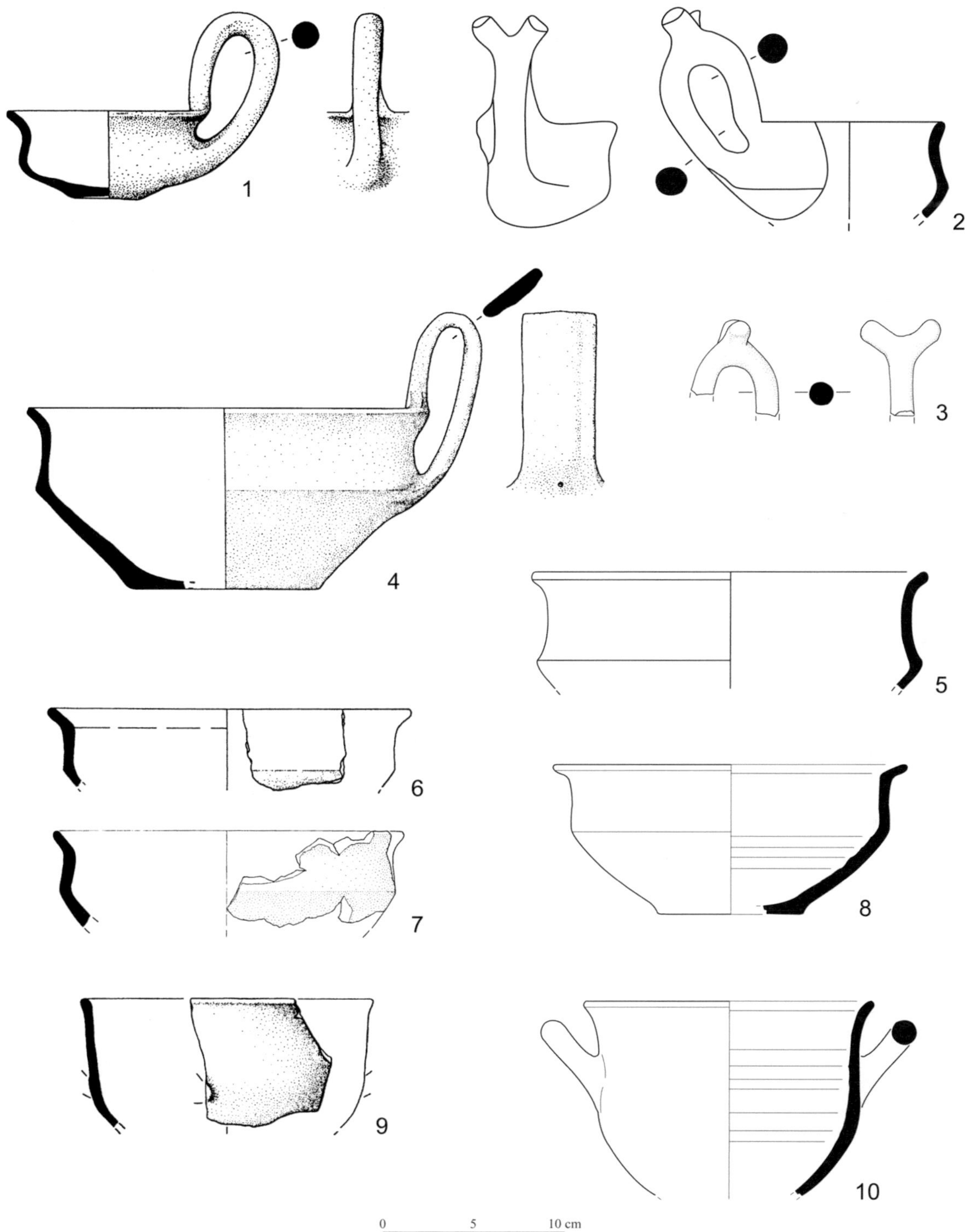

Fig. 10.4: Wheelmade Grey Ware from Broglio di Trebisacce, Recent Bronze Age 2 (1. 4. 9); wheelmade Grey Ware from Tell Kazel, IA I (3. 5. 8. 10); impasto pottery dated to Recent Bronze Age 2 from Broglio di Trebisacce (6) and Torre Mordillo (7); handmade and burnished pottery from Dhimini, LH IIIC Early (2). Scale 1:3 (1. 4. 9 after Castagna 2002, 235 fig. 100, 3.7; 240 fig. 103, 26; 2 after Adrimi-Sismani 2006a, 108 fig. 13, BE 36013; 3 drawing Reinhard Jung, digitalization Marion Frauenglas; 5. 8. 10 after Badre 2006, 88 fig. 17, 7. 9. 10; 6 after Capoferri and Giardino 1984, 67 pl. 2,5; 7 after Arancio et al. *2001, 100 fig. 50, 5).*

10.3.2–3, 5). There are some shapes that may have been used for consumption (Fig. 10.3.1), but it is striking that the finer class of consumption and serving shapes known from Italian settlements is underrepresented (for the function of *impasto* vessels in Italy see Evans and Recchia 2001–2003). Carinated cups and bowls were not found at the site so far, while they do appear side by side with hole-mouthed jars at contemporary Tell 'Arqa situated *c.* 20 km to the south as the crow flies (Charaf 2006, 169, pl. 1.a–b; 174, fig. 3; 2008, 147–149, figs. 43–44, pl. 4.a–b). At Tiryns, in the most extensive published HMBW corpus from Greece, storage and preparation vessels form the largest group, while consumption vessels are present, but rare (Kilian 2007, 49–50; Stockhammer 2008 I, 150–151, 203). The recent final publication of the HMBW finds from the Menelaion at Sparta reveals a similar picture: again storage and preparation vessels outnumber consumption vessels by far (Catling 2009, 381–382). The systematic publication of the pottery from Broglio di Trebisacce on the Ionian side of Calabria allows an evaluation of the difference in vessel frequencies between a southern Italian settlement and those eastern Mediterranean sites where HMBW was used in some quantity: bowls and cups represent between one third and half of the vessels in the various Recent Bronze Age find assemblages at Broglio (Moffa 2002, 112, fig. 64).

Coming back to the Tell Kazel HMBW, one may suppose that the Grey Ware cups and the Grey Ware jug at least partly filled the mentioned functional gap, as they were found together with a considerable number of HMBW vessels (Fig. 10.3.1–3, 5; 10.4.5, 8, 10). This means that one can reconstruct fully functional sets of Mycenaean-type dinnerware (*cf.* Jung, in press) as well as other sets of Italian type, which combine *impasto* and wheelmade Grey Ware vessels. Such combined sets of different pottery classes were observed also at Recent Bronze Age settlements in southern Italy (Castagna 2002, 248; 2004). Finally, the food was prepared in cooking pots of local type, to a lesser degree in *impasto* cooking pots, and only occasionally in Mycenaean cooking jugs/amphorae.

Case study 2

My second case study for the consumption viewpoint is Enkomi, a city that is located in eastern Cyprus. Let us focus on a much-debated break in the material culture of the city, chronologically placed between the Levels IIB and IIIA according to Porphyrios Dikaios' stratigraphy. At the end of the use period of Level IIB, a fortification wall was erected around the city. Soon afterwards, however, this phase ended in a violent destruction, which Dikaios ascribed to an enemy attack (Dikaios 1969/71, 82, 89–92, 168–170, 457, 513–514). Based on the Mycenaean pottery finds, this destruction can be dated in Aegean terms to the beginning of LH IIIC Early. A new city was built on the ruins and the fortification was reinforced (Dikaios 1969/71, 92–95, 171–173, 517). This is Enkomi Level IIIA. In this phase of the city, Mycenaean type pottery of LH IIIC Early (2) and LH IIIC Developed date was in use (Mountjoy 2007). Profound changes in Level IIIA affected the architecture with the introduction of ashlar masonry for house architecture and the invention of elaborate hearth platforms (Dikaios 1969/71, 514–517, pls. 19.4, 20, 33.5). Another cultural break can be observed in the burial customs with the abandonment of the majority of collectively used chamber tombs (Dikaios 1969/71, 419, 428–434; Keswani 2004, 96–97, 113).

A re-examination of the ceramic finds offers new data for other aspects of cultural changes in this crucial period. At the outset, it is important to stress that my study confirms the opinion of the excavator that architectural Levels IIB and IIIA follow each other synchronously in both Areas, I and III (in contrast to diverging opinions, according to which Level IIIA in Area I is earlier than Level IIIA in Area III, *cf.* the overview of those opinions given by Crewe 2007, 73, tab. 11.1; 81).

Some change in pottery production at Enkomi appears gradual and continuous over time. An example is the steady rise of wheelmade and the decline of handmade vessels, which can be observed through the later phases of the LBA since Level IIA. Additionally, the number of pots with painted decoration rose from 35% in Level IIB to 62% in Level IIIA. It has been proposed that such developments should be understood in terms of an enhancement of pottery production by making wheelmade pottery with cheaper unit costs (Sherratt 1982, 185–186; 1998, 298–299). If this were the case, one should expect a similarly steady change in vessel classes and types. New wheelmade and painted types should be related in some way to older handmade and unpainted types, or alternatively they should imitate previously imported pots. These hypotheses might find some verification at Enkomi Level IIB with wheelmade versions of Cypriot unpainted pottery (Fig. 10.5.2, the so-called Plain White Wheelmade pottery of the Swedish Cyprus Expedition), with local versions of some Mycenaean shapes (mainly shallow strap-handled bowls, cf. Jung 2009c, 79, 90, fig. 3.5) and with Mycenaeanising vessels typologically connected to Cypriot shapes (Fig. 10.1.3).

However, the changes occurring with Enkomi Level IIIA are of an entirely different nature. Let us compare first the painted wheel-made pottery of Levels IIB and IIIA. In Level IIB the most common shapes were Mycenaean-type shallow strap-handled bowls FT 295/296 (imported, Fig. 10.1.1, and locally made) and Mycenaeanising bowls of Cypriot shapes (Fig. 10.1.3). By Level IIIA the percentage of these two categories has dropped to insignificant numbers, though they did not go completely out of use (for a Mycenaeanising bowl see Mountjoy 2007, 588, fig. 5.9). Instead, Mycenaean-type deep bowls FT 284/285 and shallow angular bowls with marked carination FT 295C have become the dominant shapes.

Turning to the unpainted pottery the break with previous material culture is even more marked. At the time of Level IIB only handmade cooking pots were in use at Enkomi, made in traditional round-bottomed shapes (*cf.* Fig. 10.5.1).[6] Right from the start of Level IIIA these handmade pots were almost totally replaced by wheel-made cooking pots, the vast majority of which are Mycenaean cooking jugs FT 65 and cooking amphorae FT 66 (Fig. 10.5.4). The few small sherds of handmade cooking pots are small and are most probably residual. In addition, there are very few Levantine cooking pots (Jung 2009c, 80, 92 fig. 6.3). This does not simply mean a change in production technique, but also in food preparation, for the Cypriot handmade pots were directly set into the charcoals (similarly to the Levantine round-bottomed wheelmade cooking pots, *cf.* Ben-Shlomo *et al.* 2008, 235–236), while the Mycenaean ones with their raised or flat, often slightly concave bases stood on hearth platforms (Ben-Shlomo *et al.* 2008, 236; Stockhammer 2008 I, 319–321). Carefully built hearth platforms of clay and lime mortar, sometimes with a sherd layer underneath, were introduced at Enkomi at the same time as the Mycenaean cooking pots, *i.e.* during Level IIIA (Dikaios 1969/71, 106, 112, 119, 175, 183, 186, pls. 33.5, 34.1; 254; 273; 280.7). Earlier hearth locations outside workshops are only characterised by a burnt zone of the clay floor, sometimes with a few additional stones next to them (Level IIB: Dikaios 1969/71, 49, 165, pls. 251, 271). Elsewhere on the island a similar development can also be reconstructed. In settlements contemporary with Enkomi IIB such as Kalavassós *Áyios Dhimítrios* there are no carefully built hearth platforms (Karageorghis and Demas 1988, 60). They are only found in later settlements, *e.g.* at Maa *Palaeókastro*, and are most probably typologically related to Mycenaean hearth platforms (Karageorghis 1998, 277–279).

Three of the best preserved Mycenaean cooking pots from Enkomi (for an example of FT 65 see Fig. 10.5.3) were found *in situ* next to a hearth platform in Room 12 of Area I in Level IIIB as a result of the destruction at the end of Enkomi Level IIIB, together with a whole set of Mycenaean drinking, eating, and serving vessels (Dikaios 1969/71, 200, pls. 105, 106.1–3; 124.1–19) . The whole assemblage in this room shows the continuity in Mycenaean pottery production and use in the city and dates to the Submycenaean phase in terms of Aegean chronology (Mountjoy 2005, 165, tab. 7; 166–210). The hearth consists of a circular clay platform built over a sherd layer and, on the western half of the platform, the actual fire place, a rectangular enclosure of mud walls, within which ashes and charcoal were found (Dikaios 1969/71, 200 pl. 41.2). This would allow the cooking pots to be positioned on the even surface of the platform next to the fire. One may wonder, if this two-part hearth construction is in any way related to post-palatial hearth platforms at Tiryns, which regularly have a circular space in the middle of the underlying sherd pavement, where no sherds were laid out (*cf.* Maran and Papadimitriou 2006, 116–117, figs. 21–23; Maran, this volume).

This change in food preparation at Enkomi is analogous to the one in southwestern Palestine, but even more radical than there, because round-bottomed cooking pots of Canaanite type were not fully replaced by those of Mycenaean type in the so-called Philistine cities (Ben-Shlomo 2005, 70, 74; Dothan *et al.* 2006, 78, 87–88; Ben Shlomo *et al.* 2008, 226; Yasur Landau, this volume). Stratum VII of the rural site of Qubur al-Walaydah south of Gaza has yielded cooking pots that were exclusively of Mycenaean derivation, constituting the only exception to this rule so far (Lehmann *et al.* 2010, 151–152, fig. 12.1–3).

However, these dramatic changes in the use of pottery vessels for food preparation and for food and drink consumption did not bring about a total abandonment of Cypriot pottery forms. Some unpainted fineware shapes remained in use, but their percentage was low in Enkomi Level IIIA. By Enkomi Level IIIB, a certain revival of a number of Cypriot plain ware types can be observed, but at present the statistical analysis of the pottery from that Level is not completed. It is clear, however, that there was no return to Cypriot cooking pot types. Two sanctuary contexts show that certain Cypriot vessel shapes were used specifically in religious contexts. Room 10 of the Sanctuary of the Horned God (Floor III, Level IIIB Late) contained three large piles of bowls turned upside down, which were obviously deposited there during the ritual (Dikaios 1969/71, 196, pls. 35–35.A, 36.1–3). These 276 vessels are almost exclusively wheel-made bowls of Base Ring shape (Fig. 10.5.5), which was in its handmade version a typical local shape of LBA Cyprus, while there is only a single Mycenaean-type bowl (Fig. 10.5.6). It has already been noted (Karageorghis 1985, 242; Knapp 1986, 22; Webb 1999, 189–192) that this assemblage has a counterpart in the contemporary sanctuary of the Ingot God, Floor III (Courtois 1971, fig. 2; 242, fig. 83; 244–245, figs. 85–86B; 247–248, figs. 88–89; 278, fig. 113). Jennifer Webb has postulated that wheelmade Base Ring bowls had a specialised function for religious rituals during LC (Late Cypriot) III (Webb 1999, 189, 192), but a negative selection, the exclusion of vessel shapes that had no long tradition on the island, is also a possible explanation for those sanctuary assemblages. It may be that, during a time when Mycenaean-type pottery dominated every day life, rituals for certain gods had to be performed using traditional Cypriot vessel shapes.

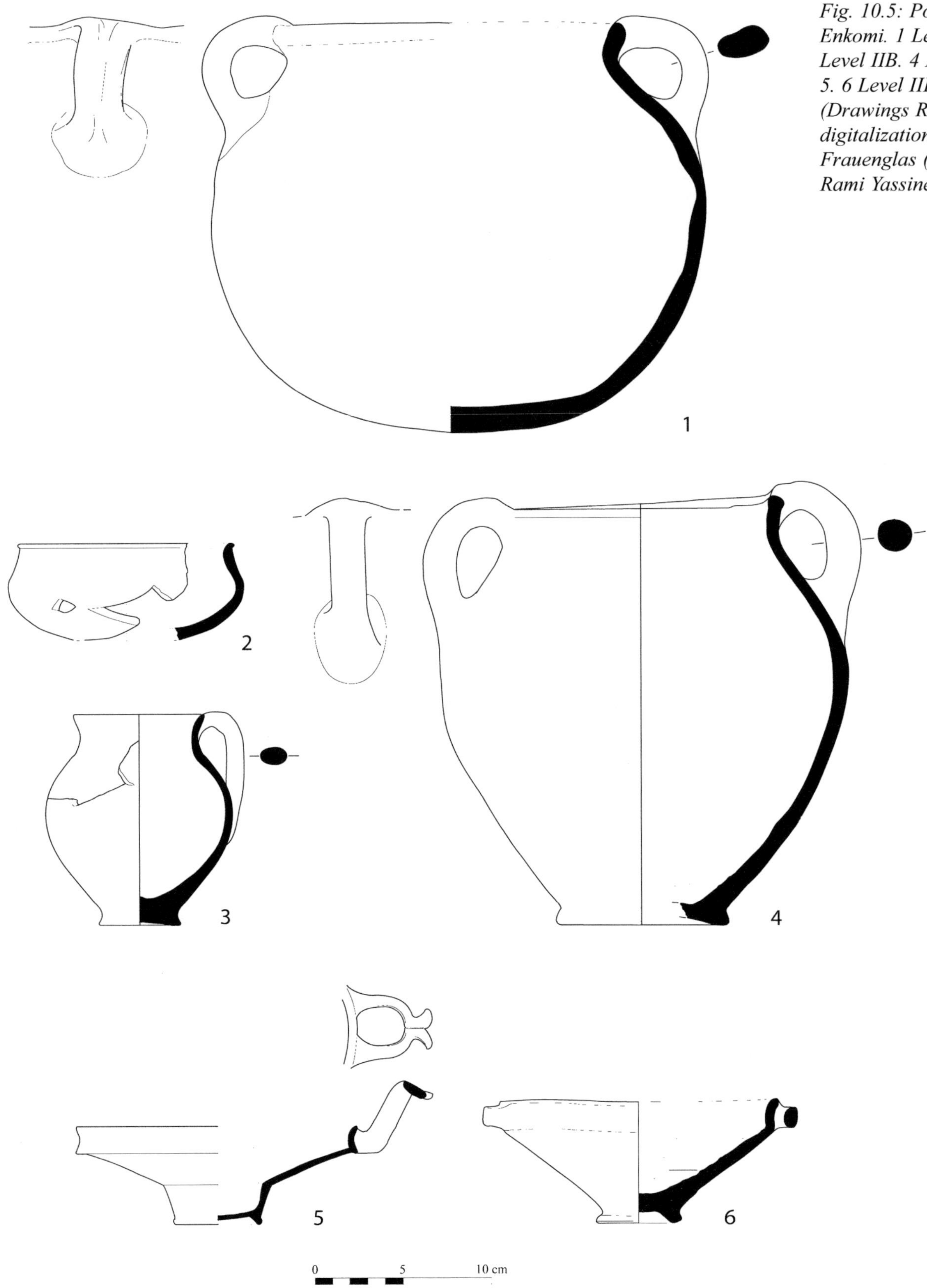

Fig. 10.5: Pottery from Enkomi. 1 Level IIA. 2 Level IIB. 4 Level IIIA. 3. 5. 6 Level IIIB. Scale 1:3 (Drawings Reinhard Jung, digitalization Marion Frauenglas (3. 4) and Rami Yassine (1. 2. 5. 6).

However, it cannot be determined whether a functional aspect also underlaid this preference, *e.g.* that a libation movement could be easier performed with a bowl with whishbone handle (Fig. 10.5.5) rather than with one with two small strap handles (Fig. 10.5.6).

The contrast between the vessel depositions in the sanctuaries of the Horned God and the Ingot God and the pottery use in other areas of life at the end of Enkomi IIIB becomes clear when looking at the banqueting assemblage in Room 12, which did not communicate by doors with the sanctuary complex. Here, vessels of Cypriot type are absent (I was not able to locate all of the unpainted vessels of this assemblage in the storerooms of the Department of Antiquities in Cyprus, but most of them).

3. Conclusions

In this paper I have presented a very short survey of two roughly contemporary cases of changes in the material culture in the eastern Mediterranean. In both cases external factors are strongly involved in those changes, but in different ways and at different levels.

The pottery record at Tell Kazel immediately prior to the Sea Peoples' destruction reminds me of a community where different languages are spoken. The dominant language is a local one, but two languages of foreign origin can be heard, too. One of the foreign languages has two dialects or separate sets of vocabulary. One of these dialects includes borrowed words from the second foreign language. The local language interacts with the two foreign languages only to a minimal extent. To stay in this illustrative analogy, at Enkomi in the earlier phase one foreign language largely supersedes the local one, without borrowing many of its words. However, the traditional local language was not extinct and regained some of its importance over time, while it was spoken at other occasions than the new language. By some, at least, the local language is spoken with the gods, although in a slightly more modern dialect.

At Tell Kazel two (possibly three) pottery classes of western origin were introduced contemporaneously shortly before the destruction of the site by the Sea Peoples (it is possible, but not certain that the non-Trojan Grey Ware class already made its first appearance before this destruction). They were locally produced according to manufacturing techniques for two of which at least there were no local predecessors. None of the new elements of their manufacturing techniques were adopted in the continuing and quantitatively much more important production of Syrian-type pottery. Even the clay selection for the Mycenaean-type pottery was independent from the clay selection for the Syrian-type and for the Mycenaeanising pottery. The Mycenaeanising pottery consists of a much smaller number of examples than the local Mycenaean pottery. Typologically, it is instead related to the earlier Argive imports, rather than to the contemporaneous local Mycenaean pots. Finally, the new ceramic classes were in use as complete or mixed vessel sets, not unlike the vessel sets in their regions of origin, although with some local preferences and selections. Regarding the local Mycenaean pottery, it is important to note that its painted and unpainted vessel repertoire is not related to the imported Mycenaean vessel sets of the preceding settlement phases. Rather the whole assemblages of local Mycenaean pottery, HMBW and Italian-type Grey Ware were completely new inventions. They had no relationship to earlier pottery from the settlement, from the viewpoint of production as well as from the viewpoint of consumption. Furthermore, it is important to note that they did not fill any functional gap in the local pottery repertoire, if we look at basic functions of storing, cooking, mixing, serving, drinking and eating. Pots for all of these functions did exist in the settlement, but the Italian- and Mycenaean-type vessels were made to provide new ways of performing those activities.

In order to understand the introduction such western-type pottery at Tell Kazel, one has to take into consideration the long history of goods exchange between Amurru and Mycenaean Greece, which we can grasp in the archaeological record by means of imported Argive pottery of LH IIIA Late to LH IIIB date (Jung 2006a, 152–186; Badre *et al.* 2005, 17, fig. 1; 18, tab. 1; 21). However, the archaeological record seems only to indicate a continuous familiarity with the routes of contact rather than a direct continuation of those exchange relationships into the final phase of LBA II, given the breaks in the material culture at the site that were outlined above. The way to go was known to the actors of change, but the kind of cultural contact those actors brought about was a new one. Taken together, these factors argue in favour of interpreting the mentioned ceramic innovations in terms of movements of people from the west to Syria, rather than in terms of knowledge transfer by means of goods exchange and hospitality. This is of course only a possible explanation and not a proof. Continuity can be observed in other parts of material culture such as the quantitatively dominating pottery of Syrian type and the architecture. The architecture is characterised by an impoverishment at the transition from Bronze to Iron Age (Badre and Gubel 1999–2000; Capet 2003), but not by a radical alteration of the settlement plan contemporaneous to the introduction of the pottery classes of western derivation. The archaeozoological and archaeobotanic evidence is still under study. Unfortunately, we can make no statements about the burial customs as the burial places of the LBA II and IA I are still unknown. To my mind, on the basis of the evidence presented above, the most plausible interpretation is that prior to the large

Sea Peoples' destruction, smaller groups of people arrived by ship at Tell Kazel and settled together within the local population. Some brought with them alien techniques of pot making and usage.

Accepting this hypothesis of small-scale immigration the question emerges, which routes the newcomers had taken? Here, one has to keep in mind several points:

1. The contemporaneous introduction of locally made HMBW and locally made Mycenaean pottery at Tell Kazel;
2. The peculiarity that so far the Akkar Plain is the only Levantine region that has yielded Italian-type pottery of Recent Bronze Age date (at Tell Kazel and Tell 'Arqa);
3. The fact that such pottery is very rare in Cyprus (Jung 2009c, 78; Borgna 2009, 300);
4. The lack of archaeological evidence at southern Italian sites of Recent Bronze Age date that would point to direct contacts to Syria;
5. The presence of Italian-type pottery at several coastal sites of the Aegean at the same time as at Tell Kazel and at some sites even earlier (from LH IIIB Developed–Final onwards).

These points suggest that we are dealing with immigrants who had a variety of personal histories of migration, as they were bringing in elements of both Aegean and Italian origin. For those people with an Italian background, a direct immigration from the Ionian coast of Italy appears to be a hypothesis of lower probability than a reconstruction in which those people spent some time in the Aegean prior to settling down in Amurru.

Regarding the local Mycenaean pottery, it is astonishing that the predominance of the dinnerware seems to reflect vessel usage in the Aegean. This is suggested among other ways by the comparatively large percentage of unpainted kylikes and deep bowls, which is unparalleled elsewhere in the eastern Mediterranean. In late palatial Greece especially, unpainted kylikes were used in banquets characterised by social inequality (Jung 2006c, 408–416). One may wonder if this was the kind of use also at Tell Kazel or whether the users of those pots came from the exploited classes of the fallen palace system (see in greater detail Jung, in press).

The archaeological record of Tell Kazel at the end of the Bronze Age can thus be interpreted in terms of an immigration of smaller groups of people who started from the Aegean, but who themselves had a variety of migratory biographies, part of which began in southern continental Italy. Furthermore, it is interesting to note that these routes of migration reconstructed from the pottery record coincide geographically and chronologically with the spread of bronze weapons of Recent Bronze Age type from Italy to the Aegean and farther to the east, as it is now understood on the basis of archaeometallurgical research (Jung *et al.* 2008; Jung and Mehofer 2008; Jung 2009c, 72–75). There is geographical and chronological coincidence also with written sources from Egypt and Ugarit dating to the later 13th and the early 12th centuries BCE, which report hostile coalitions of different peoples of unknown precise origin, who moved across the Mediterranean. Some confederated against Egypt, others attacked the coastal areas of Cyprus, Ugarit and Amurru itself as pirates (Sandars 1985; Noort 1994). Such movements may have led to the settlement of smaller groups of foreign warriors in the Levant prior to the great destruction under the reign of Ramesses III.

By contrast, at Enkomi Level IIIA after the destruction of the preceding Level IIB, many parts of the archaeological record attest to marked cultural discontinuity. Most of these may be interpreted in terms of an immigration of larger groups of people from the Aegean, while other parts of the archaeological record hint at some population continuity of uncertain extent. For example, the introduction of ashlar masonry in house architecture at Level IIIA is an innovation at the site, but building with ashlar blocks was practiced of course earlier at other settlements in Cyprus (Knapp 2008, 260), and Lindy Crewe makes a good case for the early introduction (during Level IIA or IIB) of ashlar masonry in tomb architecture at Enkomi itself, as a result of contacts with Ugarit (Crewe 2009). Thus, this architectonic innovation can also be interpreted in terms of cultural continuity, especially when seen from an island-wide viewpoint. However, the new hearth installations of Enkomi Level IIIA had no predecessors on the island and form part of the new cultural package of Aegean origin. The interpretation of the abandonment of most Late Bronze Age chamber tombs during the time of Enkomi Level IIIA has been controversial. Priscilla Keswani interpreted the phenomenon as the result of economic and social changes leading to loosening of traditional kinship bounds and a decline of their importance (Keswani 2004, 159–160), but Dikaios' initial interpretation, according to which the immigration of new population groups was responsible for this discontinuity (Dikaios 1969/71, 434), is at least equally plausible. Keswani also notes the possibility that part of the inhabitants of Enkomi IIIA 'may have come from communities elsewhere on the island or even beyond,' and thus had no relationships of ancestral descent in the city (Keswani 2004, 160). When taken together, the contemporary break with traditional burial places, the abandonment of many traditions in pottery production in favour of adopting Mycenaean ways of pot-making, and the total break with local cooking traditions again in favour of Mycenaean cooking habits accompanied with the introduction of a new type of kitchen installations – these support the interpretative hypothesis that quite a substantial number of immigrants from the Aegean inhabited Enkomi IIIA. However, the implementation of Cypriot architectural models for the new settlement of these immigrants reveal a local component in these processes of change, which seems to have been important as well and which became even more important over time – namely during Level IIIB.

Anthropological research suggests that behavioural patterns in a 'private', household context – such as the preparation and consumption of food and drink, as discussed for Enkomi and Tell Kazel – may hint at cultural traditions of groups of people, which in a migration context can be maintained for quite some time (Burmeister 1996, 15–17). Such group traditions may play a role in forming and maintaining an ethnic consciousness, but this needs not be so (Müller-Scheeßel and Burmeister 2006, 33). Thus, they may offer arguments for tracing the movement of people, but they cannot prove the existence of any ethnic group identity. Ethnic identity can be totally independent from certain patterns of (material) culture, and different people can view the same objects as related in different ways or not at all related to ethnic identity (*e.g.* Hahn 2009). Moreover, there are innumerable examples for the possibility that external definitions of ethnic identities (which all archaeological attempts to define ethnic groups inevitably are) do not coincide with the self-definitions of those individuals that are subsumed under certain ethnic group names by outsiders, other groups, states *etc* . Thus, in my understanding, it is not possible to uncover ethnic identities by interpreting the archaeological record. However, the archaeological record can be used to unravel actions, which were consciously related to specific traditions by people in one community as characterised by a variety of traditions and personal origin. At Enkomi IIIB, in the case of the sanctuaries of the Horned God and the Ingot God we glimpse a conscious decision to continue traditional worship in the city. Such a decision probably had an ideologically integrative function and thereby also the effect of political stabilisation among the heterogeneous population of Enkomi, whoever may have been the rulers and who the ruled and exploited.

Acknowledgements

For illuminating discussions and information I wish to express my gratitude to Marie-Claude Boileau, Stefanos Gimatzidis, Eleftheria Kardamaki, Florian Ruppenstein and Jeremy Rutter.

Notes

1. Both studies were mainly financed by the Institute for Aegean Prehistory [INSTAP] in Philadelphia and additionally supported by The Fitch Laboratory at the British School at Athens and the Special Research Programme SCIEM2000 in Vienna.
2. The sherd sample TK 86 grouped with the TKaA can now definitedly be assigned to a Mycenaean-type cooking pot (FT 65–66, see Badre *et al.* 2005, 28, fig. 4.1), as a better preserved example proves the use of Mycenaean cooking pots in the settlement (Fig. 10.2.6).
3. *Cf.* Capet 2003, 84, fig. 21, n; 108–109, figs. 43k and 44a (the last two of Early Iron Age I date); Badre 2006, 82–83, fig. 13.3; Jung 2006a, 189.
4. This is the result of my re-examination of the relevant find contexts, which is still preliminary due to the pending stratigraphic analysis of the most recent excavations in this sector of the settlement.
5. At Troy VIIa and VIIb the local carinated one-handled cup A 93 in Grey Ware resembles the carinated bowl from Tell Kazel, but it does not show the everted and carinated rim of the Syrian examples, *cf.* Pavúk 2002, 59, fig. 16.57; 61.
6. This well-preserved handmade cooking pot is representative for the shape of the Level IIB cooking pots. However, it was found in a context of the preceding Level IIA (Dikaios 1969/71, 38. 554, pl. 60.31).

References

Adrimi-Sismani, V. (2006a) Η γκρίζα ψευδομινύεια και η στιλβωμένη χειροποίητη κεραμική από τον μυκηναϊκό οικισμό Διμηνίου. In *Αρχαιολογικό Έργο Θεσσαλίας και Στερεάς Ελλάδας 1. Πρακτικά επιστημονικής συνάντησης, Βόλος 27.2–2.3.2003*, 85–110. Vólos, Laboratory of Archaeology of the University of Thessaly and Ministry of Culture.

Adrimi-Sismani, V. (2006b) The Palace of Iolkos and its End. In S. Deger-Jalkotzy and I. Lemos (eds), *Ancient Greece: from the Mycenaean Palaces to the Age of Homer*. Edinburgh Leventis Studies 3, 465–481. Edinburgh, Edinburgh University Press.

Al-Maqdissi, M. (2008) The Development of the Trade Routes in the Early Second Millennium BC. In J. Aruz, K. Benzel and J. M. Evans (eds), *Beyond Babylon. Art, Trade, and Diplomacy in the Second Millennium BC*, 42–43. New York, Yale University Press.

Arancio, M. L., Buffa, V., Damiani, I. and Trucco, F. (2001) Catalogo delle unità stratigrafiche e dei reperti. In F. Trucco and L. Vagnetti (eds), *Torre Mordillo 1987–1990. Le relazioni di una comunità protostorica della Sibaritide*. Incunabula Greca CI, 61–153. Roma, Istituto per gli Studi Micenei ed Egeo-Anatolici.

Arnold, D. E. (2000) Does the Standardization of Ceramic Pastes Really Mean Specialization? *Journal of Archaeological Method and Theory* 7/4, 333–375.

Badre, L. (2006) Tell Kazel–Simyra: A Contribution to a Relative Chronological History in the Eastern Mediterranean during the Late Bronze Age. *Bulletin of the American Schools of Oriental Research* 343, 65–95.

Badre, L., Boileau, M.-C., Jung, R. and Mommsen, H. (2005) The Provenance of Aegean- and Syrian-type Pottery Found at Tell Kazel (Syria). *Ägypten und Levante* 15, 15–47.

Badre, L. and Gubel, E. (1999–2000) Tell Kazel, Syria. Excavations of the AUB Museum, 1993–1998. Third Preliminary Report. *Berytus* 44, 123–203.

Belardelli, C. (1999) Produzioni artigianali tardoelladiche dall'Italia meridionale in Argolide: la ceramica pseudominia di Tirinto. In V. La Rosa, D. Palermo and L. Vagnetti (eds), *επί πόντον πλαζόμενοι. Simposio italiano di studi Egei dedicato a Luigi Bernabò Brea e Giovanni Pugliese Carratelli, Roma, 18–20 febbraio 1998*, 451–460. Athens, Scuola Archeologica Italiana di Atene.

Ben-Shlomo, D. (2005) Material Culture. In M. Dothan and D. Ben-Shlomo, *Ashdod VI. The Excavations of Areas H and K (1968–1969)*. IAA Reports 24. Jerusalem, Israel Antiquities Authority.

Ben-Shlomo, D., Shai, I., Zukerman, A. and Maier, A. M. (2008) Cooking Identities: Aegean-Style Cooking Jugs and Cultural Interaction in Iron Age Philistia and Neighbouring Regions. *American Journal of Archaeology* 112, 225–246.

Bettelli, M. (2002) *Italia meridionale e mondo miceneo. Ricerche su dinamiche di acculturazione e aspetti archeologici, con particolare riferimento ai versanti adriatico e ionico della penisola italiana*. Grandi contesti e problemi della Protostoria italiana 5. Firenze, All'Insegna del Giglio.

Blegen, C. W., Caskey, J. L. and Rawson, M. (1953) *Troy III. The Sixth Settlement*. Princeton, Princeton University Press.

Blegen, C. W., Boulter, C. G., Caskey, J. L. and Rawson, M. (1958) *Troy IV. Settlements VIIa, VIIb and VIII*. Princeton, Princeton University Press.

Boileau, M.-C., Badre, L., Capet, E., Jung, R. and Mommsen, H. (2010) Foreign Ceramic Tradition, Local Clays: the Handmade Burnished Ware of Tell Kazel (Syria). *Journal of Archaeological Science* 37, 1678–1689.

Borgna, E. (2009) Patterns of Bronze Circulation and Deposition in the Northern Adriatic at the Close of the Late Bronze Age. In Borgna and Cassola Guida 2009, 289–309.

Borgna, E. and Cassola Guida, P. (2009), *Dall'Egeo all'Adriatico: organizzazioni sociali, modi di scambio e interazione in età postpalaziale (XII–XI sec. a. C.) / From the Aegean to the Adriatic: Social Organisations, Modes of Exchange and Interaction in Postpalatial Times (12th–11th c. BC). Atti del Seminario internazionale (Udine, 1–2 dicembre 2006)*. Studi e ricerche di protostoria mediterranea 8. Roma, Edizioni Quasar.

Burmeister, S. (1996) Migration und ihre archäologische Nachweisbarkeit. *Archäologische Informationen* 19, 13–21.

Capet, E. (2003) Tell Kazel (Syrie), Rapport préliminaire sur les 9e–17e campagnes de fouilles (1993–2001) du Musée de l'Université Américaine de Beyrouth, Chantier II. *Berytus* 47, 63–121.

Capoferri, B. and Giardino, C. (1984) I materiali dell'età del bronzo media e recente. In R. Peroni (ed.), *Nuove ricerche sulla protostoria della Sibaritide*, 46–123. Roma, Paleani Editrice.

Castagna, M. A. (2002) La ceramica grigia tornita dalla 'casa centrale' (campagne di scavo 1980–82): una messa a punto. In M. Bettelli (ed.), *Italia meridionale e mondo miceneo. Ricerche su dinamiche di acculturazione e aspetti archeologici, con particolare riferimento ai versanti adriatico e ionico della penisola italiana*. Grandi contesti e problemi della Protostoria italiana 5, 233–249. Firenze, All'Insegna del Giglio.

Castagna, M. A. (2004) Servizi da simposio in ceramica d'impasto e depurate dalla 'casa centrale' di Broglio di Trebisacce. In D. Cocchi Genick (ed.), *L'età del bronzo recente in Italia. Atti del Congresso Nazionale di Lido di Camaiore, 26–29 ottobre 2000*, 263–267. Viareggio, Mauro Baroni editore.

Castagna, M. A. (2006) Variazioni dimensionali e variabilità tipologica del vasellame da mensa del Bronzo recente in Italia meridionale. In *Studi di protostoria in onore di Renato Peroni*, 354–360. Firenze, All'Insegna del Giglio.

Catling, H. W. (2009) *Sparta: Menelaion I. The Bronze Age*. The British School at Athens Supplementary Volume 45. Athens, The British School at Athens.

Charaf, H. (2006) La céramique Hand Made Burnished Ware (HMBW). Nouvelles découvertes à Tell Arqa. *Bulletin d'Archéologie et d'Architecture Libanaises* 10, 167–181.

Charaf, H. (2008) Arqa during the Bronze Age: Connections with the West. In C. Doumet-Serhal (ed.), *Networking Patterns of the Bronze Age and Iron Age Levant. The Lebanon nd its Mediterranean Connections*. Archaeology and History in the Lebanon Special Edition, 122–166. Beirut, The Lebanese British Friends of the National Museum.

Courtois, J.-C. (1971) Le sanctuaire du dieu au lingot d'Enkomi-Alasia. In C. F.-A. Schaeffer (ed.), *Alasia I*, 151–362. Mission Archéologique d'Alasia 4. Paris, Mission Archéologique d'Alasia, E. J. Brill.

Courtois, J.-C. (1981) *Alasia II. Les tombes d'Enkomi. Le mobilier funéraire (fouilles C.F.-A. Schaeffer 1947–1965*. Paris, Mission Archéologique d'Alasia, Diffusion de Boccard.

Crewe, L. (2007) *Early Enkomi. Regionalism, Trade and Society at the Beginning of the Late Bronze Age on Cyprus*. British Archaeological Reports, International Series 1706. Oxford, Hadrian Books.

Crewe, L. (2009) Feasting with the Dead? Tomb 66 at Enkomi. In Th. Kiely (ed.), *Ancient Cyprus in the British Museum. Essays in honour of Veronica Tatton-Brown*. British Museum Research Publication 180, 27–48. Oxford, Oxbow Books.

Dikaios, P. (1969–1971) Enkomi. Excavations 1948–1958. Mainz, Verlag Philipp von Zabern.

Dothan, T., Gitin, S. and Zukerman, A. (2006) The Pottery: Canaanite and Philistine Traditions and Cypriote and Aegean Imports. In M. W. Meehl, T. Dothan and S. Gitin (eds), *Tel Miqne-Ekron Excavations 1995–1996. Field INE East Slope. Iron Age I (Early Philistine Period)*, 71–175. Jerusalem, W. F. Albright Institute of Archaeological Research and Institute of Archaeology, Hebrew University of Jerusalem.

Evans, J. and Recchia, G. (2001–2003) Pottery Function: Trapped Residues in Bronze Age Pottery from Coppa Nevigata (southern Italy). *Scienze dell'Antichità* 11, 187–201.

Feldman, M. H. (2006) *Diplomacy by Design. Luxury Arts and an 'International Style' in the Ancient Near East, 1400–1200 BCE*. Chicago and London, University of Chicago Press.

Gitin, S., Mazar, A. and Stern, E. (1998) *Mediterranean Peoples in Transition Thirteenth to Early Tenth Centuries BCE*. In Honor of Professor Trude Dothan. Jerusalem, Israel Exploration Society.

Gorgoglione, M. (2002) Lo Scoglio del Tonno. Problematiche precoloniali nel II millennio. In M. Gorgoglione (ed.), *Strutture e modelli di abitati del Bronzo tardo da Torre Castelluccia a Roca Vecchia. Rapporti ed interrelazioni sull'arco ionico da Taranto al canale d'Otranto e sul versante adriatico. Atti del Convegno di Studio 28–29 novembre 1996, Pulsano (TA) – Castello De Falconibus*, 125–140. Mandria, Filo editore.

Gorgoglione, M., Jones, R. E. and Levi, S. T. (2006) Lo Scolgio del Tonno. La ceramica domestica di tipo egeo: produzioni locali e modelli egei. In *Materie prime e scambi nella preistoria italiana. Atti della XXXIX Riunione Scientifica, Firenze, 25–27 novembre 2004*, 1129–1143. Firenze, Istituto Italiano di Preistoria e Protostoria.

Hahn, H. P. (2009) Keramische Produktion, interethnische Beziehungen und soziale Identitäten in der westafrikanischen Savane. In P. Stockhammer (ed.), *Keramik jenseits von Chronologie. Beiträge der Arbeitsgemeinschaft 'Theorie in der Archäologie' bei der Tagung des West- und Süddeutschen Verbandes für Altertumsforschung e.V. in Xanten, 7.–8. Juni 2006*, 146–165. Rahden/Westf., Verlag Marie Leidorf.

Horejs, B. (2010) Possibilities and Limitations in Analysing Ceramic Wares. In B. Horejs, R. Jung and P. Pavúk (eds), *Pottery Analysis. Processing – Classification – Publication*. Studia Archaeologica et Medievalia 10, 15–27. Bratislava, Comenius University.

Jung, R. (2006a) Die mykenische Keramik von Tell Kazel (Syrien). *Damaszener Mitteilungen* 15, 147–218.

Jung, R. (2006b) *Χρονολογία comparata. Vergleichende Chronologie von Südgriechenland und Süditalien von ca. 1700/1600 bis 1000 v. u. Z.* Veröffentlichungen der Mykenischen Kommission 26. Vienna, Verlag der Österreichischen Akademie der Wissenschaften.

Jung, R. (2006c) ΕΥΠΟΤΟΝ ΠΟΤΕΡΙΟΝ: Mykenische Keramik und mykenische Trinksitten in der Ägäis, in Syrien und Italien. In *Studi di protostoria in onore di Renato Peroni*, 407–423. Firenze, All'Insegna del Giglio.

Jung, R. (2009a) "Sie vernichteten sie, als ob sie niemals existiert hätten" – Was blieb von den Zerstörungen der Seevölker? In H. Meller (ed.), *Schlachtfeldarchäologie/Battlefield Archaeology. 1. Mitteldeutscher Archäologentag vom 09. bis 11. Oktober 2008 in Halle (Saale)*. Tagungen des Landesmuseums für Vorgeschichte Halle 2, 31–48. Halle (Saale), Landesamt für Denkmalpflege und Archäologie Sachsen-Anhalt, Landesmuseum für Vorgeschichte.

Jung, R. (2009b) I 'bronzi internazionali' ed il loro contesto sociale fra Adriatico, Penisola balcanica e coste levantine. In Borgna and Cassola Guida 2009, 129–157.

Jung, R. (2009c) Pirates of the Aegean. Italy – East Aegean – Cyprus at the End of the Second Millennium BCE. In V. Karageorghis and O. Kouka (eds), *Cyprus and the East Aegean: Intercultural Contacts from 3000 to 500 BC. An International Archaeological Symposium held at Pythagoreion, Samos, October 17th–18th 2008*, 72–93. Nikosia, A.G. Leventis Foundation.

Jung, R. (2011) Mycenaean Vending Cups in Syria? Thoughts about the Unpainted Mycenaean Pottery from Tell Kazel. In W. Gauss, M. Lindblom, R. A. K. Smith and J. C. Wright (eds), *Our Cups are Full: Pottery and Society in the Aegean Bronze Age. Papers Presented to Jeremy B. Rutter on the Occasion of his 65th Birthday*. British Archaeological Reports, International Series 2227, 121–132. Oxford, Archaeopress.

Jung, R., Moschos, I. and Mehofer, M. (2008) Φονεύοντας με τον ίδιο τρόπο: Οι ειρηνικές επαφές για τον πόλεμο μεταξύ Ελλάδας και Ιταλίας κατά τη διάρκεια των όψιμων μυκηναϊκών χρόνων. In S. A. Paipetis and Ch. Giannopoulou (eds), *Πρακτικά/Proceedings: Πολιτισμική αλληλογονιμοποίηση νότιας Ιταλίας και δυτικής Ελλάδας μέσα από την ιστορία/Cultural Cross Fertilization of Southern Italy and Western Greece through History*, 85–107. Pátra, Region of Western Greece.

Jung, R. and Mehofer, M. (2008) A Sword of Naue II Type from Ugarit and the Historical Significance of Italian-type Weaponry in the Eastern Mediterranean. *Aegean Archaeology* 8, 111–135.

Karageorghis, V. (1985) Religious Aspects. In V. Karageorghis and M. Demas, *Excavations at Kition V. The Pre-Phoenician Levels, Part I*. Nicosia, Department of Antiquities, Cyprus.

Karageorghis, V. (1998) Hearths and Bathtubs in Cyprus: A 'Sea Peoples' Innovation? In Gitin, Mazar and Stern 1998, 276–282.

Karageorghis, V. and Demas, M. (1988) *Excavations at Maa-Palaeokastro 1979–1986*. Nicosia, Department of Antiquities, Cyprus.

Keswani, P. (2004) *Mortuary Ritual and Society in Bronze Age Cyprus*. Monographs in Mediterranean Archaeology. London, Oakville, Equinox Publishing.

Kilian, K. 2007. *Die handgemachte geglättete Keramik mykenischer Zeitstellung*. Tiryns XV. Wiesbaden, Reichert Verlag.

Klengel, H. (1992) *Syria 3000 to 300 BC. A Handbook of Political History*. Berlin, Akademie Verlag.

Kling, B. (1991) A Terminology for the Matte-Painted, Wheelmade Pottery of Late Cypriot IIC–IIIA. In J. A. Barlow, D. Bolger, and B. Kling (eds), *Cypriot Ceramics: Reading the Prehistoric Record*. University Museum Symposium Series 2, 181–184. Philadelphia, The University Museum.

Knapp, A. B. (1986) *Copper Production and Divine Protection: Archaeology, Ideology and Social Complexity on Bronze Age*

Cyprus. Studies in Mediterranean Archaeology Pocket-book 42. Göteborg, Paul Åströms Förlag.

Knapp, A. B. (2008) *Prehistoric and Protohistoric Cyprus. Identity, Insularity and Connectivity*. Oxford, University Press.

Lehmann, G., Rosen, S. A., Berlejung, A., Neumeier, B.-A. and Niemann, H. M., Excavations at Qubur al-Walaydah (2010). *Die Welt des Orients* 40, 137–159.

Levi, S. T. (1999) *Produzione e circolazione della ceramica nella Sibaritide protostorica I. Impasto e dolii*. Grandi contesti e problemi della Protostoria italiana 1. Firenze, All'Insegna del Giglio.

Maran, J. and Papadimitriou, A. (2006) Forschungen im Stadtgebiet von Tiryns. *Archäologischer Anzeiger* 2006/1, 97–162.

Metzger, M. and Barthel, U.-R. (1993) *Kāmid el-Lōz 8. Die spätbronzezeitlichen Tempelanlagen. Die Kleinfunde*. Bonn, Dr Rudolf Habelt.

Moffa, C. (2002) *L'organizzazione dello spazio sull'acropoli di Broglio di Trebisacce. Dallo studio delle strutture e dei manufatti in impasto di fango all'analisi della distribuzione dei reperti*. Grandi contesti e problemi della Protostoria italiana 6. Firenze, All'Insegna del Giglio.

Mommsen, H. and Pavúk, P. (2007) Provenance of the Grey and Tan Wares from Troia, Cyprus and the Levant. *Studia Troica* 17, 25–41.

Monchambert, J.-Y. (2004) *La céramique d'Ougarit. Campagnes de fouilles 1975 et 1976*. Ras Shamra-Ougarit XV. Paris, Éditions Recherche sur les Civilisations.

Mountjoy, P. A. (1999a) The Destruction of Troia VIh. *Studia Troica* 9, 253–293.

Mountjoy, P. A. (1999b) *Regional Mycenaean Decorated Pottery*. Rahden/Westf., Verlag Marie Leidorf.

Mountjoy, P. A. (2005) The End of the Bronze Age at Enkomi, Cyprus: The Problem of Level IIIB. *The Annual of the British School at Athens* 100, 125–214.

Mountjoy, P. A. (2006) Mykenische Keramik in Troia – Ein Überblick. In M. O. Korfmann (ed.), *Troia. Archäologie eines Siedlungshügels und seiner Landschaft*, 241–252. Mainz, Philipp von Zabern.

Mountjoy, P. A. (2007) The Dating of the Early LC IIIA Phase at Enkomi. In M. Bietak and E. Czerny (eds), *The Synchronisation of Civilisations in the Eastern Mediterranean in the Second Millennium BC. III. Proceedings of the SCIEM 2000 – 2nd EuroConference, Vienna, 28th of May–1st of June 2003*, 583–594. Vienna, Verlag der Österreichischen Akademie der Wissenschaften.

Müller-Scheeßel, N. and Burmeister, S. (2006) Einführung: die Identifizierung sozialer Gruppen. Die Erkenntnismöglichkeiten der Prähistorischen Archäologie auf dem Prüfstand. In S. Burmeister and N. Müller-Scheeßel (eds), *Soziale Gruppen – kulturelle Grenzen. Die Interpretation sozialer Identitäten in der Prähistorischen Archäologie*. Tübinger Archäologische Taschenbücher 5. Münster, New York, München, Berlin, Waxmann.

Noort, E. (1994) *Die Seevölker in Palästina*. Kampen, Pharos.

Pagliara, C., Guglielmino, R., Coluccia, G., Malorgio, I., Merico, M., Palmisano, D., Rugge, M. and Minonne, M. (2008) Roca Vecchia (Melendugno, Lecce), SAS IX: relazione stratigrafica preliminare sui livelli di occupazione protostorici (campagne di scavo 2005–2006). *Rivista di Scienze Preistoriche* 58, 239–280.

Pavúk, P. (2002) Troia VI and VIIa. The Blegen Pottery Shapes: Towards a Typology. *Studia Troica* 12, 35–71.

Sandars, N. K. (1985) *The Sea Peoples. Warriors of the Ancient Mediterranean*. London, Thames and Hudson.

Sherratt, E. S. (1982) Patterns of Contact: Manufacture and Distribution of Mycenaean Pottery, 1400–1100 BC. In J. G. P. Best and M. W. de Vries (eds), *Interaction and Acculturation in the Mediterranean II*. Proceedings of the Second International Congress of Mediterranean Pre- and Protohistory, Amsterdam, 19–23 November 1980, 179–195. Amsterdam, B. R. Grüner Publishing.

Sherratt, E. S. (1998) 'Sea Peoples' and the Economic Structure of the Late Second Millennium in the Eastern Mediterranean. In Gitin, Mazar and Stern 1998, 292–313.

Singer, I. (1991) A Concise History of Amurru. In S. Izre'el, *Amurru Akkadian: a Linguistic Study*. Atlanta, Scholars Press.

Stockhammer, P. W. (2008) *Kontinuität und Wandel – Die Keramik der Nachpalastzeit aus der Unterstadt von Tiryns*. Ph.D. Dissertation, Heidelberg University, http://www.ub.uni-heidelberg.de/archiv/8612.

van Dommelen, P. (2006) The Orientalizing Phenomenon: Hybridity and Material Culture in the Western Mediterranean. In C. Riva and N. C. Vella (eds), *Debating Orientalization. Multidisciplinary Approaches to Change in the Ancient Mediterranean*, 135–152. London, Oakville, Equinox Publishing.

Vansteenhuyse, K. (in press) La céramique du chantier A. In M. al-Maqdissi, K. van Lerberghe, J. Bretschneider, and M. Badawi, (eds), *Tell Tweini. Onze campagnes de fouilles syro-belges (1999–2010)*. Damascus, Ministère de la Culture, Direction Générale des Antiquités et des Musées.

Voskos, I. and Knapp, B. (2008) Cyprus at the End of the Late Bronze Age: Crisis and Colonization or Continuity and Hybridization? *American Journal of Archaeology* 112, 659–684.

Webb, J. M. (1999) *Ritual Architecture, Iconography and Practice in the Late Cypriot Bronze Age*. Studies in Mediterranean Archaeology and Literature Pocket-book 75. Jonsered, Paul Åströms Förlag.

Webster, J. (2001) Creolizing the Roman Provinces. *AJA* 105, 209–225.

11.

Ceremonial feasting equipment, social space and interculturality in Post-Palatial Tiryns

Joseph Maran

Introduction

The attempt to understand the complexity and variety of acts of appropriation of new cultural traits necessitates going beyond a perception of society as a neatly circumscribed and homogenous entity.[1] Instead, the social world should be perceived as dynamic and fluid, a 'social space' in the sense of Pierre Bourdieu (1984, 99–168), in which agents with different *habitus*, resources and interests are relationally linked to one another (Bourdieu 1977, 76–95; Knapp and van Dommelen 2008, 678; van Dommelen 2005, 117–118). In broadening the spectrum of agents envisioned by Bourdieu, non-human agents, the latter encompassing not only social goods, but also natural materials and phenomena as well as even supernatural forces, if those are thought to be part of the social world, should be included in the definition of the relational networks constituting the Social (*cf.* Latour 1986; 2005; Law 1992). From this point of view, society and culture are generative principles (Friedman 1997, 82) that have to be re-assembled over and over again in thought, discourse and practice (Latour 2005).

The necessity to apply a fluid and dynamic model of the Social when analyzing forms of appropriation (Friedman 1991; Spittler 2002; Hahn 2004; Voskos and Knapp 2008) especially arises in times of intense intercultural entanglement brought about by the unfolding of trade relations, such as the Mediterranean during the Late Bronze Age. In nodes of long-distance exchange such as harbor towns, we must reckon with the presence of groups of peoples originating from more or less distant areas and living at the place for different lengths of time (Voskos and Knapp 2008, 678). This is a 'contact zone' (Pratt 1991) *par excellence* for which the idea of an 'indigenous' population coming into contact with foreign cultural traits needs to be rejected as overly simplistic. Not only does it disregard the heterogeneity of the social space of any given society (Voskos and Knapp 2008, 678; Hodos 2010, 13–15), but it is also based on the flawed assumption that a clear-cut division between the 'indigenous' and the 'outside' is possible. Since in a contact zone identities, values, and meanings were negotiated between groups of different origin, the forms and the content of appropriation must have differed significantly from group to group. For those who had recently arrived, the subjects of appropriation were above all elements of the local majority culture, while in the case of those who had lived there for a long time appropriation meant engaging with unknown cultural forms received either through direct exchange with distant outside partners, or indirectly, through the mediation of groups of foreign ancestry living at the same site or in its surrounding region. As these are only two idealised extremes with many possible trajectories of personal biography and identity in-between, appropriation is likely to have had many facets, with a whole series of processes of merging the local with the global occurring at the same time and place.

The Tiryns Treasure – a key find for understanding post-palatial ceremonial feasting

Around 1200 BCE, a period of an unprecedented degree of interconnectedness of elites in the East Mediterranean came to an end. The character of this period is encapsulated in the luxury goods of the 'international style', whose cultural ambiguity, as suggested by Marian Feldman (2006), was based on the wish to make them suited as gifts in exchange networks linking rulers of different cultural backgrounds. That the 'International Style' must indeed have been rooted to a significant degree in the specific political structures of the centuries between *c.* 1400 and 1200 BCE is reflected by its disappearance after the former political landscape had been swept away. For a long time the opinion prevailed that after 1200 BCE long-range contacts largely came to a standstill. In recent years, there has been increasing evidence that this was not the case and that, under very different political and social circumstances, again through intercultural entanglements, novel material forms and practices were created. Thanks especially to the contributions of Susan Sherratt (*cf.* 1994; 2003) and A. Bernard Knapp (1994; 2006), it was realised that the political upheaval around 1200 BCE in a way opened up new opportunities for peoples in specific zones of the East Mediterranean, and that societies on Cyprus played a crucial role in the transformation of trade contacts from the 13th to the 12th centuries BCE.

I regard metal ceremonial feasting equipment as the most clear expression of these new forms of entanglement. This equipment is encountered especially in the centuries after 1000 BCE, when during the Early Iron Age bronze vessels like the tripod cauldron, the tripod stand and the cauldron as well as metal spits and firedogs for the roasting of meat appear in elite contexts from Etruria in the West to Cyprus in the East (Karageorghis 1974; 2003; Scheffer 1981; Kohler and Naso 1991; Stary 1994; Hoffman 1997, 141–146; Crielaard 1998; Strøm 2001; Stampolidis 1998). It is long known that bronze tripod stands are found on Cyprus already in the late 13th century, with their frequency increasing in the following centuries (Matthäus 1985, 332; Papasavvas 2001, 116–119, 212–215). As Knapp (1986, 66–69, 77–84; 2006, 54–59) has suggested, such vessels, which were true-masterpieces of bronze-casting (Papasavvas 2001, 18–27, 152–157), were employed by Cypriote elites to amplify their social position. This contribution to the present volume will ascribe also the emergence of the tradition of spit roasting on metal firedogs to the late 2nd millennium BCE and attribute the origin of the whole set of metal ceremonial feasting equipment to a combination of intercultural exchange with specific social values of the communities introducing and appropriating these novel objects.

The starting point of my investigation is Tiryns, a site that in the 12th century BCE underwent a breathtaking development. At a time when all other former Mycenaean palatial centers declined in size, or were even abandoned, Tiryns exhibits astonishing signs of the restoration of a central political authority and of processes of reconstruction and even expansion (Maran 2006; 2008; 2010). The extraordinary role of the site is further exemplified by the Tiryns treasure (Arvanitopoulos 1915; Karo 1930) which I recently interpreted as the *keimelia* of a prominent post-palatial family (Maran 2006). At that time, my focus was on proposing the first reconstruction of the treasure and interpreting it as a sign that post-palatial elites tried to gain legitimacy by appropriating and displaying political symbols of the palatial period. In this article the focus will lie on other aspects that are related to the composition of the treasure.

Contrary to a long-standing research opinion, the treasure does not represent a motley collection of heaped-up valuables, but instead follows carefully chosen patterns (see Maran 2006, 132–141). Its components can be subdivided into two principal categories: On the one hand jewelry, among which there are also political or religious insignia, and on the other hand, a set of bronze ceremonial feasting equipment consisting of various open vessels (bowls, basins, a mug and a chalice) for the consumption of food and/or beverages, as well as utensils for the preparation or serving of food, like a large cauldron, both a tripod cauldron and tripod basin as well as a tripod stand (Fig. 11.1) and a pair of bronze

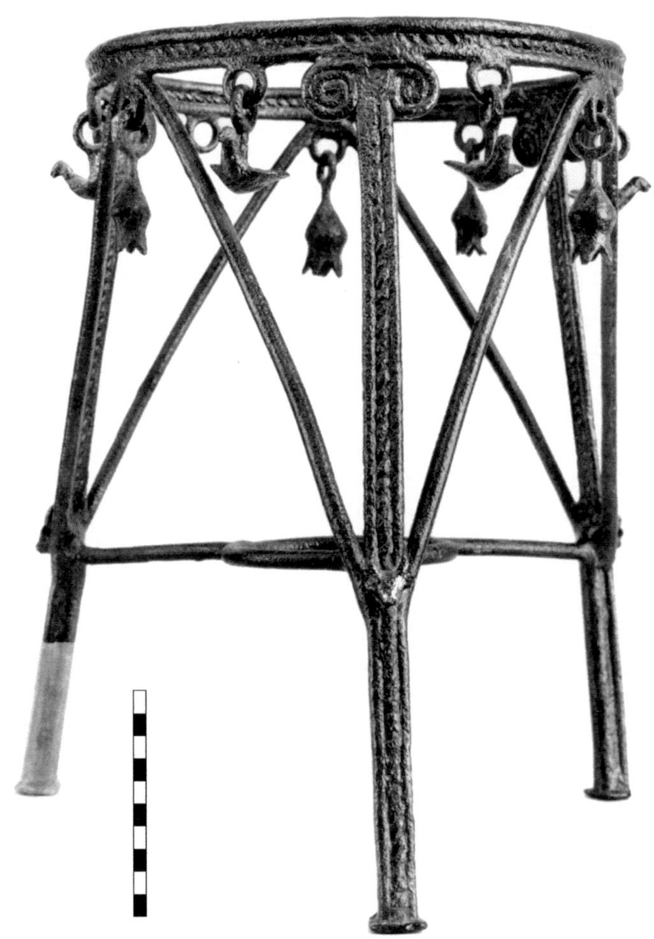

Fig. 11.1: Bronze tripod stand from the Tiryns treasure with reconstructed leg (after Jantzen 1975, fig. 81).

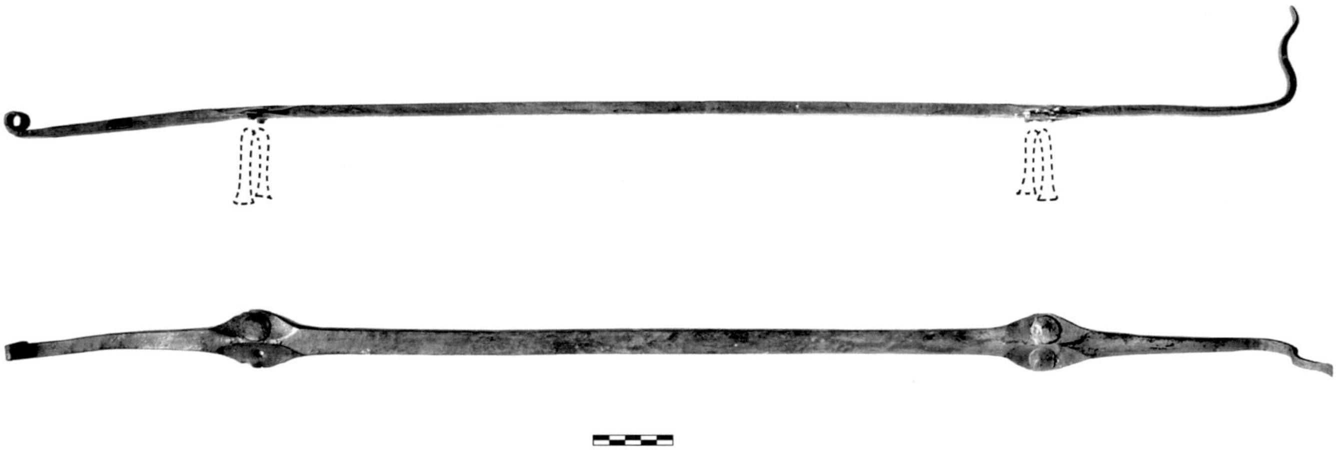

Fig. 11.2: Two firedogs from the Tiryns treasure with legs added (German Archaeological Institute, Neg.-Nr. NM 3497, Photograph: H. Wagner).

firedogs (Fig. 11.2). To the same category of implements for food preparation or serving in the context of feasting I would assign two bent cutting instruments, one made of iron, the other of bronze (Karo 1930, 135–136, fig. 6; Maran 2006, 134, fig. 8.4b), which, despite their usual designation as 'sickles', may instead have been used for cutting and apportioning meat.[2] Such a function is suggested by the massive blade of the iron instrument, which prompted already Georg Karo (1930, 135–136) to consider a use as a chopping knife ('*Hackmesser*'). Given the number of utensils linked to the consumption and preparation of food and drinks, the absence of bronze vessels related to the serving of beverages, i.e. jugs or ewers, is noteworthy, especially since they are so prominently depicted on the signet ring (Fig. 11.3).

Fig. 11.3: Image on the golden signet ring of the Tiryns treasure (after Sakellariou 1964, 202 No. 179).

Practices, images and objects – an 'interactive' relation

Of particular interest are signs for a close interlinkage of components of the Tiryns treasure. The cauldron and a basin fit into the opening of the tripod stand (Karo 1930, fig. 4).[3] In their depositional context, the vessels for consumption were densely packed together and held the cutting instruments possibly employed for preparing and apportioning the meat (Maran 2006, 134, fig. 8.1) that would have been spit-roasted on the firedogs. Finally, the subject of the image on the famous gold signet-ring (Fig. 11.3) may be interpreted as creating a multiple semantic link between the jewelry and the feasting equipment. In addition to the goddess being depicted participating in feasting (Wright 2004b, 44–45), she also holds a chalice resembling the one that seems to have served as the container for that signet ring and the rest of the jewelry (Fig. 11.4) (Karo 1930, 120; Maran 2006, 132–134, fig. 8.1). The unique bronze chalice of the Tiryns treasure has the astonishing height of approximately 21 cm and, not only was it found without a handle, but it probably never had one,[4] since the only metal vessel vaguely resembling it is a much smaller and also handle-less chalice from Perati, again dating to LH (Late Helladic) IIIC (Matthäus 1980, 257, pl. 43.365). Of course, we know that the vessel shown on the signet-ring was supposed to be a high-footed chalice, of the kind found since the Neopalatial period and usually manufactured from special kinds of stone (Warren 1969, 36–37; Dickers 1990, 141–143; Wright 2004b, 44–45; Marthari 2008, 381–383; but see Sakellariou 1964, 202 for an identification as a rhyton). At the time of the deposition

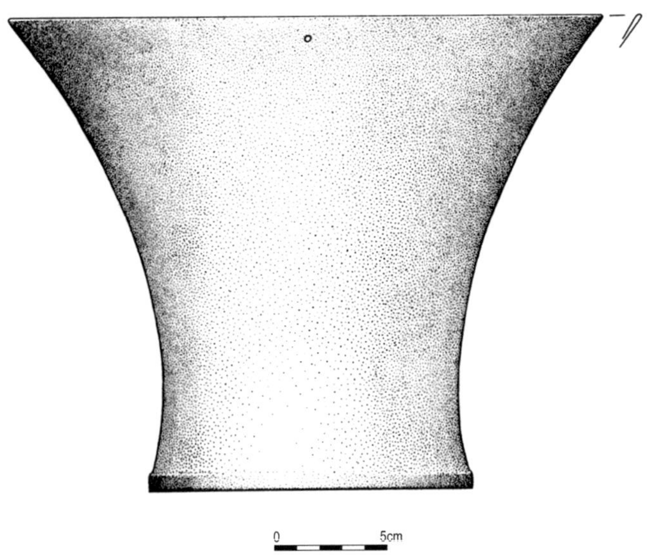

Fig. 11.4: Bronze chalice from the Tiryns treasure (after Matthäus 1980, pl. 4.:364).

of the Tiryns treasure, however, this knowledge may have been already lost, thereby leading to an identification of the vessel with a bronze chalice with a flat base. Similar cases of the transfer of a 'biography' from an object that was lost, or known only from narratives, to a similar looking artifact are historically attested. Perhaps the best documented case of an object which at one point in time may have become the substitute of an earlier one with a rich and religiously charged 'biography' is that of the 'holy lance' in the treasury of the Vienna Hofburg (Kirchweger 2005).

An even more intriguing semantic interrelation between the image on the signet ring and specific objects in the treasure may derive from the wheel-shaped astral symbol, probably designating the sun (Müller-Karpe 2009, 92–99; Marinatos 2010, 28, 69, 161), in the centre of the 'sky' above the cult scene on the ring. This symbol is reminiscent of the two wheels of woven and wound gold wire with bronze spokes bearing the eponymous amber beads of the 'Tiryns type' (Karo 1930, 127, Beilage XXXA, XXXI; Harding 1984, 82–85, fig. 22). Although the number of spokes of the depicted symbol and the gold wheels differ, the similarity of the form together with the choice of combining the brightly shining materials gold and amber, the latter's Greek name 'electron' being even etymologically linked to its quality to shine (Geerlings 1996, 395; Hughes-Brock 1993, 223–224), point to the likelihood that the term 'sun wheels' proposed by Helen Hughes-Brock (1993, 221) and Oliver Dickinson (1994, 255; 2006, 205) for the enigmatic and unique objects may indeed capture very well what they were meant to be.[5]

If indeed the image on the signet ring and actual objects were semantically interrelated, the strong religious connotations of the feasting ceremonies, in which the constituents of the Tiryns treasure were used, would be emphasised. Moreover, it would mean that in Mycenaean times images, even on small objects like seals and signet rings, were carefully studied and interpreted to gain insights into the realm of the supernatural, an interpretation that is also suggested by the case of the association of a extremely rare Near Eastern fenestrated axe with the depiction of such an axe on a seal in the central grave of the tholos tomb of Vapheio (Boulotis 2008). In this way the perceived meaning of the scenes was integrated into discourses explaining the special significance of certain objects. This contributed significantly to the possibility to provide objects with 'biographies' (Appadurai 1988; Mills and Walker 2008b; Hoskins 2002; 2006; Knapp 2006), linking them with religious or mythical beings and to display such objects on certain occasions. In turn, the ability to 'prove' the supernatural character of objects by referring to an image served to enhance the positions of the persons who employed items like the signet ring, the chalice and the 'sun wheels' in ritual. The Tiryns treasure may thus serve as a reminder that, in ritual communication practices, objects and images may have been 'interactively' related, thereby connecting realms usually treated by archaeological research separately.[6]

The notion of a religious context of the usage of the objects of the Tiryns treasure (Jung 2007) is further supported by additional observations concerning the two firedogs, two swords and the tripod stand that were found outside of the cauldron (Arvanitopoulos 1915, 212; Maran 2006, 134, fig. 8.1). In retrospect, my proposal to interpret these objects as 'scrap metal' due to their broken state[7] may have been premature in light of indications pointing to the intentional damage to at least two key components of the ceremonial feasting equipment of the Tiryns treasure, namely the tripod stand and the firedogs. The latter (Fig. 11.2) were found without their legs and the same applies to the lowermost part of one of the legs of the otherwise perfectly preserved tripod stand (Fig. 11.1) (Papasavvas 2001, 235). Neither the four legs of the firedogs nor the missing piece of the leg of the tripod stand were among the deposited objects thereby provoking the possibly erroneous assignment to the category 'scrap metal'. However, it is inconceivable that regular usage of the objects may have led to such kind of damage and, rather, it must be assumed that the legs of the firedogs were intentionally removed, while the leg of the tripod stand is likely to have been detached by a directed blow. I therefore now propose that the objects were damaged, and the detached legs removed, to render any further use impossible in the course of the dedication of the whole treasure after a specific religious ceremony.[8] Whether the same interpretation of an intentional damaging may also apply to the two swords found in the treasure together with the firedogs underneath the cauldron (Karo 1930, 135, Beilage XXXVII; Maran 2006, fig. 8.1) could possibly be clarified by a careful inspection of the originals. The hilts of both swords, as well as the blade of one sword, were found in a broken state, and again the missing pieces were not part of the treasure. While arguably these breakages could have been caused by usage, the rich evidence from late 2nd and early 1st millennia BCE contexts in Central Europe for intentionally inflicted damage of the hilts and blades of deposited swords points to the possibility that also the two swords from the Tiryns treasure may have been ritually destroyed (Čivilytė 2009, 47–66, fig. 6; see also Pollard 2008, 55–56).

The origins of spit roasting on metal firedogs

In interpreting parts of the Tiryns treasure as an interrelated set of ceremonial feasting equipment, the striking conclusion emerges that we are confronted with basically the same range of forms that gained a wide distribution during the Iron Age. For this reason the chronological position of the treasure is of special significance. According to the analysis of Hartmut Matthäus (1980, 56–58) the treasure contains a number of objects that are or could be earlier than the 12th century BCE while the majority of objects can be assigned to LH IIIC which commences in the 12th Century BCE. There is, however, not a single object unequivocally pointing to a date later than that, which is quite remarkable given the fact that the variety of artifacts of widely differing object groups provides a broad and diverse basis for comparison. The parallels for the metal vessels without exception date to the period between 1300 and 1100 BCE and suggest, as Matthäus (1985, 328) and Giorgos Pappasavas (2001, 160–163, 230, 235) have argued, that at least the tripod stand was imported from Cyprus. A similar date is suggested by the comparisons of the jewelry. It is certainly not a coincidence that the gold wheels find their closest comparisons in the early Urnfield culture of Eastern Central Europe dating exactly to the same chronological range (Marinatos 1960; Bouzek 1985, 172–173; Plesl 1993; Jung 2007, 234 with footnote 101). Even the iron 'sickle' cannot be used to substantiate a post-Mycenaean dating of the deposition of the treasure, because the object probably belonged to the earliest horizon of such iron cutting instruments appearing during the last centuries of the 2nd millennium BCE in the East Mediterranean (Sherratt 1994, 69–71; 2003, 44; Maran 2006, 140 with footnote 31). Since there are no objects in the Tiryns treasure unequivocally postdating LH IIIC, I regard a deposition of the treasure as late as Submycenaean times as unlikely (*pace* Jung 2007, 238 with footnote 130).[9]

Accordingly, there is not the slightest reason not to extend a LH IIIC-date also to the pair of bronze firedogs. That the objects should indeed be identified as such implements for spit roasting is borne out by several observations. The shape and 80 cm length of the two identical objects conform to the size and format of later firedogs, and, just as in the case of the Early Iron Age examples (Boardman 1971), the ends of the elongated horizontal bar are shaped in a way to prevent spits from falling down. While one end is flaringly bent upwards, the other end is simply rolled up. Finally, the elongated bars of both objects are each furnished with two widened parts of oval form that hold two rivets to attach legs. All these morphological features are consistent with their identification as firedogs, which makes these objects the hitherto earliest metal implements of that kind anywhere. Demonstrably, equipment for spit roasting can be traced back in Greece at least to the beginning of the Late Bronze Age. From the time of the Neopalatial period in Crete and the Cyclades pairs of simple terracotta spit supports are known (Scheffer 1984; Georgiou 1986, 23–24; Doumas 2004, 409–410, figs. 10–11; for Early Iron Age examples of similar spit supports see W. D. E. Coulson in McDonald, Coulson and Rosser 1983, 89, 95, 108, fig. 3–47), while ceramic trays used for spit roasting ('souvlaki trays') are attested during the Mycenaean palatial period (Blegen and Rawson 1966, 418; Wardle 1969, 294; Scheffer 1984, 158; E.B. French in Tzedakis and Martlew 1999, 134, fig. 17; Baumann 2007, 162; Hruby 2008, 154; Catling 2009, 429–430). In light of this long tradition, it is striking that prior to ca. 1200 BCE there is so little evidence for the existence of metal roasting equipment in the East Mediterranean. The allegedly earliest example of a metal spit is a bronze object that was stored together with finds from the central grave of the Tholos tomb of Vapheio (Kilian-Dirlmeier 1987, 200 with footnote 50, fig. 6; Karageorghis 1974, 171; Sherratt 2004, 192), but not mentioned by the excavator as belonging to this context. Accordingly, the attribution to the grave is uncertain (Kilian-Dirlmeier 1987, 200). An identification of metal spits is more secure in the case of bronze examples from the Cape Gelidonya shipwreck and the Anthedon hoard (Bass 1967, 109; Spyropoulos 1972, 200, pl. 17.27; Sherratt 2004, 192 with footnote 37; Catling 1964, 297), but these find complexes are unlikely to date earlier than the end of the 13th century BCE and could easily be later than that. Regarding metal firedogs in the East Mediterranean, however, no evidence for a date prior to 1200 BCE can be brought forward. The earliest pairs of metal firedogs from Cyprus and Crete are all made of iron and date to the 10th century BCE (Karageorghis 1974, 168–171; 2003, 341–343; Hoffman 1997, 143–146; Stampolidis 1998, 258). They make their appearance approximately at the same time as the first iron spits (Haarer 2001, 262). Possibly already during the 11th century BCE the first metal firedogs appeared in Atlantic Europe which, however, followed a different principle of construction than both the Tirynthian examples and the Early Iron Age firedogs from Greece and Cyprus (Needham and Bowman 2005, 95, 120–126, fig. 9; for examples of this Atlantic type in the Mediterranean see Karageorghis and Lo Schiavo 1989, 17; Crielaard 1998, 191–192). Indeed, the firedogs from the Tiryns treasure show features that lend additional support to a date earlier than the Early Iron Age examples from Cyprus and Greece. In contrast to all Iron Age firedogs known from Greece, they were not given the form of a warship with a ram bow (Courbin 1957; Boardman 1971; Snodgrass 1996, 591–592; Stampolidis 1998), although the one upturned and flaring end of both firedogs from the Tiryns treasure may already anticipate the ship symbolism, inasmuch as it could allude to the design of a ship's stempost terminating in a birdhead, as the one depicted on ships on LH IIIC pictorial pottery (Wachsmann 1998, 131–142, 190–193; Wedde 1999, 466, pl. 88.A4–5).[10] Moreover, the firedogs from Tiryns are not made of iron, but instead of bronze, which makes them, to my knowledge, the only such implements of that material from the East Mediterranean.[11]

Ceremonial feasting and transformations in social space

The question is why the set of ceremonial feasting equipment ranging from metal vessels to firedogs and iron knives evidently makes its appearance only after the fall of the Mycenaean palaces? It is generally accepted that a research approach linking the creation of meaning of foreign cultural traits to their integration into practices and discourses reaches its limits in the case of such luxury objects, since, in contrast to pottery, they are usually not found where they had been used, but rather in graves or hoards. This explains why most attempts to gain insight into post-palatial feasting have been based on pottery groups. The masterful analysis of the LH IIIC pottery from the excavation in the Northeastern Lower Town of Tiryns by Philipp Stockhammer (2008, 295–310; 2009) suggests that the disappearance of the more consolidated hierarchies of the palatial period led to a new importance of feasting, since it gave individuals the opportunity to bolster or alter their position in social space by strengthening ties with some members of society, while setting themselves apart from others (For similar observations on feasting on Crete during the 12th century BCE see Borgna 2004). In using the absence of certain open pottery shapes in contexts otherwise clearly related to feasting, Stockhammer (2008, 320–325; 2009) was even able to present a case for indirectly deducing that metal vessels are likely to have been part of such practices of feasting during the post-palatial Mycenaean period.

It is relevant to the question of how ceremonial feasting equipment may have been employed in the social space of LH IIIC Tiryns that its main components like the firedogs, the cauldron, the tripod cauldron, the tripod basin and probably also the cutting instruments are all *hearth implements* (Hägg 1994), that is they were exclusively or occasionally used at the hearth. That is why changes in hearth construction from the 13th to the 12th centuries BCE in the domestic environment as well as in the centre of political power deserve special attention. Undoubtedly, the most striking case is the abandonment of the palatial ceremonial hearth in the building succeeding the Great Megaron, Building T (Maran 2001; 2008). About the same time, a similar transformation leading to the abandonment of a central hearth occurred in the megaron of nearby Midea. While the central hearth may indeed have lost its importance as an interior feature of the megaron (Walberg 1995; 2007, 67), this does not mean a general loss of the significance of the hearth as a central focus of ritual practice. Thus, parallel to the construction of Building T the palatial period round altar in the Great Court was rebuilt. At least one row of stones of the round altar was removed and used as building material in Building T, thereby creating an important linkage between the construction of the building and the transformation of the altar (W. Dörpfeld in, Schliemann 1886, 234–235; Müller 1930, 137–138; Maran 2001, 115 with footnote 15). After the removal of the stones, the altar was converted into a square platform in which the outline of the round altar remained visible without rising significantly above the uppermost level of stones of the platform (Figs. 11.5–11.6). Recent excavation results may shed new light on the motive of the reconstruction of the altar. In the excavation in the Northeastern Lower Town we encountered a hearth construction which appeared frequently in the LH IIIC-contexts, but was previously unknown (Maran and Papadimitriou 2006, 117, figs. 21–23). The clay hearths of a rectangular or roundish shape with a sherd or pebble pavement consistently exhibited a round part in the centre that was left open probably to put in firewood, charcoal[12] and/or hearth implements (Figs. 11.7–11.8). One such hearth in a courtyard was rebuilt four times within a few decades thus underlining the intensity of food-preparation under open sky (Maran and Papadimitriou 2006, 117, figs. 20, 27). It is here argued that the remodeled platform in the Great Court was a monumental version of such a hearth and that the ceremonial hearth of the Great Megaron was given up, because the central LH IIIC ceremonial hearth-altar was shifted to a hypaethral space.[13] It cannot be proven, but I suppose that in such an elevated social context the valuable components of the ceremonial feasting equipment were used (for the strong religious connotation of the use of firedogs see Hägg 1995, 231).

Within the social space of post-palatial Tiryns, different

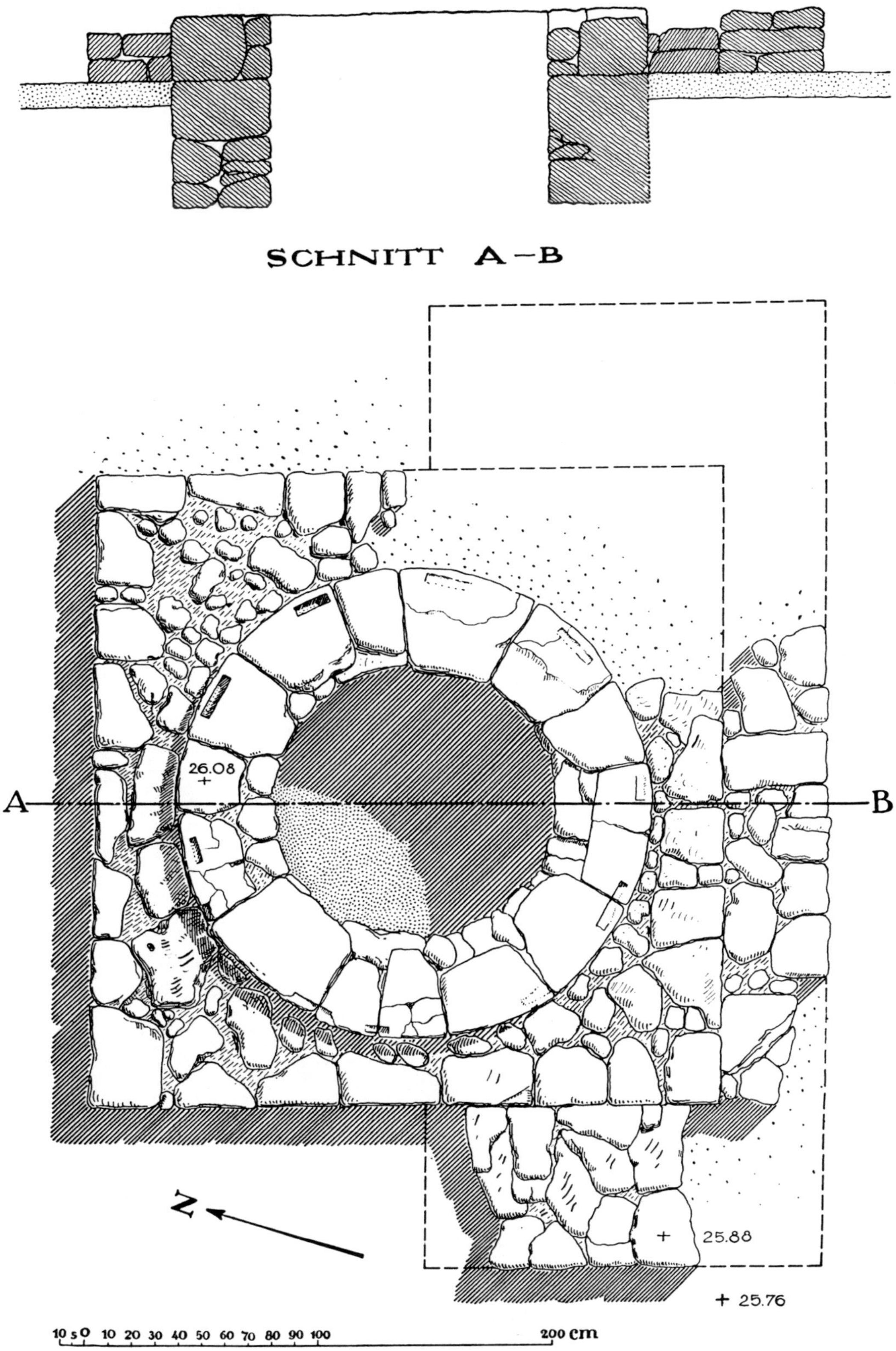

Fig. 11.5: Plan of the altar in the Great Court of Tiryns with LH IIIC phase of square platform and later addition (after Müller 1930, fig. 64).

Fig. 11.6: Altar in the Great Court of Tiryns with LH IIIC phase of square platform and excavated palatial round altar in the middle, from south (German Archaeological Institute, Neg.-Nr. TIR 14. Photograph: unknown).

Fig. 11.7 Remnants of LH IIIC clay platform of hearth in the Northeastern Lower Town of Tiryns with segment of round opening in the middle (Tiryns Archive. Photograph: J. Maran).

sorts of capital, in the sense of Bourdieu, are likely to have augmented economic capital as the predominant forms of resources. Symbolic capital was gained on the one hand by creating a link for oneself and one's group to the palatial past and to supernatural powers (Maran 2011, 174–175), on the other hand, as Knapp (2006, 55–59) has suggested for Cypriote elites, through the display of novel cultural traits and the reference to their 'social life'. Social capital arose through relations that were established on occasions like ritualised feasting ceremonies. In my opinion, the role of the 'warrior-barbecue feast' (Sherratt 2004, 194) with its distinctive equipment as a deliberate form of elite differentiation, which was highlighted by Susan Sherratt for Early Iron Age Cyprus, took its start already in the 12th century BCE and provided the background for the rapid adoption of the first iron knives. The use of such instruments displayed the right of specific persons to split and distribute the meat to the gods and to participants of the feasts, a practice that in turn reified and re-created the differences among the members of a group, as was already described by Susan Sherratt (2004, 188–190) for 'Homeric feasting'. The mentioned absence of ewers or jugs in the Tiryns treasure, on the other hand, may signify that the serving of beverages did not belong to the duties expected from a person of high status involved in such ceremonies.

Clearly, visibility of social communication must have attained a new importance in post-palatial Tiryns. While in the 13th century BCE ritual practices were carried out in the heart of the palace, screened by high walls in near-total seclusion by the innermost circle of dignitaries (Maran, forthcoming), after the destruction of the palace, the walls

Fig. 11.8 Sherd pavement of LH IIIC clay hearth in the Northeastern Lower Town of Tiryns with round opening in the middle (Tiryns Archive. Photograph: J. Maran).

Fig. 11.9 Model of Tiryns during LH IIIC. View of the Upper Citadel with Building T from a southerly direction. (Photograph: ARW-Modellbau, T. Weber; remastered by Dipl.-Arch. M. Kostoula).

surrounding the Great Court were not rebuilt. This, together with the transfer of the central ceremonial hearth/altar from an interior to a hypaethral space, allowed more people to attend the ceremonies and opened up the view from the outside of the citadel on what was happening in front of Building T (Fig. 11.9) (Maran, forthcoming). Like in 'Homeric feasting' (Sherratt 2004, 181–187), the practices of food preparation carried out on the hearth/altar just as much involved sacrifice to supernatural forces as they allowed the distribution of roasted meat to the participants of the ceremony assembled in Building T and in front of it.[14]

In the case of the post-palatial Upper Citadel of Tiryns the interplay of a network of human and non-human entities (Callon 1986; Law 1992; Walker 2008) comprising the architectural setting of Building T rising from the ruins of the former palace, the hearth/altar, the fire, the cult participants, the sacrificial animals and their meat, the knives, the firedogs and other hearth implements together with different scents,[15] sights, movements and sounds (Hamilakis and Konsolaki 2004, 146; Hitchcock 2008; Fox 2008) provided the opportunity to draw on the integrative power of social communication (Connerton 1989, 72–73) and at the same time to reify one's position in social space. The Tiryns treasure in my opinion signifies that after ceremonies of a special nature the used paraphernalia became objects to be sacrificed and some of the implements were even manipulated to prevent further usage.

Interculturality and the emergence of ceremonial feasting equipment

By finally addressing the origins of the ceremonial feasting equipment, I wish to demonstrate how problematic this question is. While most metal vessels, and possibly also the iron cutting instruments, derive from Cypriote metalwork, an origin of spit roasting on Cyprus has been, in my opinion rightly, questioned by Vassos Karageorghis.[16] The firedogs of the Tiryns treasure and the long tradition of spit roasting equipment in the Aegean are instead indications that the first metal firedogs are likely to have emerged in Greece. On the other hand, there can be little doubt that, as rightly emphasised by Susan Sherratt (2004, 193), only as of the 'Dark Ages' was this way of preparing meat elevated to the status of an elite practice. Before that, in palatial times, boiling or stewing seems to have been the predominant form of elite food preparation (Sherratt 2004, 194). But even if we could neatly disentangle the origin of each component of ceremonial feasting equipment, this would say very little about how such special objects became closely intertwined. It seems to me that after the upheaval around 1200 BCE certain forms of material culture of heterogenous origin, some of which were already known for several centuries, were gradually merged to form an interrelated assemblage that had not existed anywhere before. This came about through a combination of the interaction between groups in different parts of the Mediterranean and the agency of peoples as manifested by the integration of the new forms into local patterns of practice. Tellingly, the ceremonial feasting assemblage was not taken-up by societies in all zones of the Mediterranean, but specifically by such societies as those of regions like Cyprus, the Greek Mainland, Crete and later also the Central Mediterranean, that already in palatial times had been in intense contact. These intercultural networks of the 13th century BCE were crucial for the emergence of ceremonial feasting equipment. During that last century of palatial rule we encounter in Tiryns an unusually high number of Cypro-Minoan graffiti on imported and local pots (Hirschfeld 1996; 1999, 55–60), as well as a concentration of objects of Cypriote or Levantine derivation in specific areas (Maran 2004; Maran and Kostoula, forthcoming; Cohen *et al.* 2010). This suggests the presence of people with strong ties, probably of genealogical character, to these areas (Sherratt 2003, 42; 2009, 48–50). It can be assumed that the relations of this group to the East persisted beyond the destruction of the palace (Maran 2004), and that these persons had an important share in the influx of valuable Cypriote goods like tripod stands and iron knives. This was a group that may not have been at the site long enough to bolster its position by referring to a deep local ancestry, and they may have instead turned to gaining symbolic capital by becoming mediators, translators and multipliers of distant cultural knowledge (Voskos and Knapp 2008, 678; Stockhammer 2008, 327; 2009; Maran 2011, 173–175) who appropriated exquisite foreign goods and combined them with other material forms in new practices, which in turn were appropriated by other groups and so on. In all likelihood it was the creative potential of such an intercultural situation that led to the transformation of the rather modest roasting equipment of the Mycenaean palatial period into the first firedogs made of metal.

In summary, ceremonial feasting equipment above all prevailed, because it ideally suited communities whose relatively unconsolidated hierarchies necessitated the constant re-assembling and re-negotiating of their social space and system of value in various forms of social communication (see also Needham and Bowman 2005, 125–128 for similar phenomena in Atlantic Europe). However, for such equipment to become widely distributed in the Mediterranean, an additional factor had to be involved, namely the intercultural situation created by the co-presence of people of different origin in 'contact zones' such as the community of Tiryns. The peculiarities of the social space in such a community motivated people of foreign descent to use their contacts within networks linking distant exchange partners to acquire and appropriate novel forms of material culture, to combine these with other objects, and to adjust them to local practices. What I am thus suggesting is that the networks of exchange between elite persons in different parts of the Mediterranean, which Crielaard (1998, 194–199) has described as a decisive prerequisite for the spreading of exclusive forms of material culture during the beginning of the Early Iron Age, had already come into being earlier than that, during the 12th cent BCE. Just as the 'International Style' would have been unthinkable without the dynastic relations before 1200 BCE, the intercultural situation and the systems of value in communities of the 12th century BCE created the precondition for a cross-linkage of different Mediterranean regions and the emergence of a common understanding between groups of people about combining certain material forms in social practice in a way that was hitherto unknown.

Notes

1. For helpful discussions and important information on various topics related to the article I am indebted to Ann Brysbaert, Elizabeth French, Andrea Babbi, Hartmut Matthäus and David Wengrow. I would like to thank Maria Kostoula for preparing and remastering the digital images used in this article.
2. For the linkage of knives with metal firedogs and spits during the Geometric and Archaic periods see Kilian (1983, 133).
3. Papasavvas 2001, 128 has rightly pointed out that the tripod stands were probably used as supports for different vessels.
4. It cannot be clarified whether a hole directly under the rim of the large chalice was used for repairing the vessel or for fastening a rivet of a handle (Matthäus 1980, 256–257).
5. For the religious solar symbolism of the gold wheels and their relation to the symbol of the wheel cross see Jung (2007, 234–240).
6. For an 'interactive' relation between image and ritual action

in the case of the wall-paintings in Minoan and Mycenaean throne rooms see Reusch (1958, 352, 356); Niemeier (1986, 88); and Bennet (2001, 34).

7. Maran 2006, 140 with footnote 30; there, I also erroneously stated that the Cypriote tripod stand was found unbroken. I am indebted to Hartmut Matthäus for discussing with me the breakage pattern of this tripod stand.
8. An attempt to make the objects useless may also explain why no metal spits were included in the treasure. Indications for an intentional damage of components of the jewelry of the Tiryns treasure were already recognised by Jung (2007, 236).
9. Tellingly, the furnishings of Grave 28, the most outstanding Submycenaean find complex from Tiryns (Verdelis 1963, 10–17), show no similarities to the objects from the Tiryns treasure. The unusual array of weapons found in that grave serves as a reminder that inhabitants of Tiryns even during the height of the alleged 'Dark Ages' were able to obtain the latest state of the art forms of material culture.
10. Clear evidence for metal firedogs with both ends terminating in stylised bird's heads comes from Etruria (Scheffer 1981, 57, 62).
11. During the Iron Age in Italy bronze firedogs are very rarely found (Kohler and Naso 1991, nos. 4 [Praeneste], 53 [Cerveteri], 88–89 [Populonia], 151 [Bologna]). I would like to thank Andrea Babbi for advice on literature about metal roasting equipment in Iron Age Italy.
12. Since in roasting a direct exposure to the flames of an open fire involved the danger of burning the meat, the usage of terracotta or metal firedogs which are characterized by a close distance between spits and fuel, probably required an availability of charcoal and thus the knowledge of how to produce it. It seems to be generally assumed that charcoal was readily available in the 2nd millennium BCE Aegean (*cf.* terms like 'coal scuttle'), but when the production of this fuel may have started and what technologies were employed remain problems warranting scientific research; for the problem of the possible usage of charcoal in copper smelting on Cyprus see W. Fasnacht (in discussion of Fasnacht 2004, 131). I am grateful to Ann Brysbaert for discussions about the problem of the production and availability of charcoal, and to Elizabeth French for information on literature about terracotta roasting trays in Mycenaean Greece.
13. Dörpfeld did not mention any signs of burning on the platform, which led S. Lupack (2008, 479) to assume that the structure may not have been used for burning offerings. Dörpfeld, however, was sure that it served that purpose, since he emphasised that the platform was large enough to burn a whole sacrificial animal (W. Dörpfeld in Schliemann 1876, 234). The lack of traces of burning is not surprising, because, as Dörpfeld mentions, the layer of clay or stucco that had originally covered the platform was not preserved. On the LH IIIC hearths excavated in the Northeastern Lower Town of Tiryns the effects of fire were only visible when the actual thin clay layer of the hearth was preserved. Usually, no impact of fire was recognized on the sherd or pebble pavement beneath that clay layer. This may be an indirect indication of a controlled usage of fire possibly accomplished by using charcoal as a fuel.
14. The mounting evidence for burnt animal sacrifice during the Mycenaean palatial period (Hamilakis and Konsolaki 2004; Isaakidou *et al.* 2002; Halstead and Isaakidou 2004; Ekroth 2009, 145) raises the question whether already these sacrificial practices may have involved the consumption of the meat of sacrificial animals by the cult participants. The evidence of later Greek cult practices provides examples in which after such kinds of sacrifices the meat was either cooked (Ekroth 2008, 88) or roasted (Ekroth 2008, 93) to be consumed by cult participants.
15. For supernatural connotations attributed to the smoke rising from roasting meat see Hamilakis and Konsolaki (2004); Fuller and Rowlands (forthcoming); and Wengrow (forthcoming). I am grateful to David Wengrow for stimulating discussions about this aspect.
16. Karageorghis (2001; 2007, 258–259) has opted for an introduction of spit roasting on Cyprus from the Aegean, without excluding the possibility that it may have been the other way around (Karageorghis 2003, 343).

References

Alram-Stern, E. and Nightingale, G. (2007) *KEIMELION. The Formation of Elites and Elitist Lifestyles from Mycenaean Palatial Times to the Homeric Period. Akten des internationalen Kongresses vom 3. bis 5. Februar 2005 in Salzburg*. Vienna, Austrian Academy of Sciences

Appadurai, A. (1988) *The Social Life of Things: Commodities in Cultural Perspective*. Cambridge, University Press.

Arvanitopoulos, A. S. (1915) 'Ανασκαφαί και έρευναι εν Τιρύνθι'. *Πρακτικά της εν Αθηναίς Αρχαιολογικής Εταιρείας*, 201–236.

Bass, G. F. (1967) *Cape Gelidonya: A Bronze Age Shipwreck*. Transactions of the American Philosophical Society, New Series 57. Philadelphia, American Philosophical Society.

Baumann, M. (2007) The Late Helladic Coarse Wares. In G. Walberg (ed.), *Midea: The Megaron Complex and Shrine Areas. Excavations on the Lower Terraces 1994–1997*. Prehistory Monographs 20, 154–162. Philadelphia, INSTAP Academic Press.

Bennet, J. (2001) Agency and Bureaucracy: Thoughts on the Nature and Extent of Administration in Bronze Age Pylos. In S. Voutsaki and J. Killen (eds), *Economy and Politics in the Mycenaean Palace States. Proceedings of a Conference Held on 1–3 July 1999 in the Faculty of Classics, Cambridge*, 25–37. Cambridge Philological Society Suppl. Vol. 27. Cambridge, Philological Society.

Blegen, C. W. and Rawson, M. (1966) *The Palace of Nestor at Pylos in Western Messenia. Volume 1: The Buildings and Their Contents*. Princeton, University Press.

Boardman, J. (1971) Ship Firedogs and Other Material from Kavousi. *Κρητικά Χρονικά* 23, 1–8.

Borgna, E. (2004) Aegean Feasting: A Minoan Perspective. In Wright 2004a, 127–159.

Boulotis, C. (2008) From Mythical Minos to the Search for Cretan Kingship. In M. Andreadaki-Vlazaki, G. Rethemiotakis and N. Dimopoulou-Rethemiotaki (eds), *From the Land of the Labyrinth: Minoan Crete, 3000–1100 BC. Essays*, 44–55. New York, Onassis Foundation.

Bourdieu, P. (1977) *Outline of a Theory of Practice*. Cambridge Studies in Social and Cultural Anthropology 16. Cambridge, University Press.

Bourdieu, P. (1984) *Distinction: A Social Critique of the Judgment of Taste*. Cambridge, Mass.

Bouzek, J. (1985) *The Aegean, Anatolia and Europe: Cultural Interrelations in the Second Millennium BC*. Studies in Mediterranean Archaeology 29. Göteborg, Åström.

Callon. M. (1986) Some Elements of a Sociology of Translation: Domestication of the Scallops and the Fishermen of St Brieuc Bay. In J. Law (ed.), *Power, Action and Belief: A New Sociology of Knowledge?* Sociological Review Monograph 32, 196–233. London, Boston and Henley, Routledge and Kegan.

Catling, H. W. (1964) *Cypriot Bronzework in the Mycenaean World*. Oxford, Clarendon Press.

Catling, H. W. (2009) *Sparta: Menelaion I. The Bronze Age*. Supplementary Volume 45. London, British School at Athens.

Čivilytė, A. (2009) *Wahl der Waffen. Studien zur Deutung der bronzezeitlichen Waffendeponierungen im nördlichen Mitteleuropa*. Universitätsforschungen zur Prähistorischen Archäologie 167. Bonn, Habelt.

Cohen, C., Maran, J. and Vetters, M. (2010) An Ivory Rod with a Cuneiform Inscription, Most Probably Ugaritic, from a Final Palatial Workshop in the Lower Citadel of Tiryns. *Archäologischer Anzeiger* 2010, 1–22.

Connerton, P. (1989) *How Societies Remember*. Cambridge, University Press.

Courbin, P. (1957) Une tombe géométrique d'Argos. *Bulletin de Correspondance Hellénique* 81, 322–386.

Crielaard, J. P. (1998) Surfing on the Mediterranean Web: Cypriot Long-distance Communications during the Eleventh and Tenth Centuries BC. In V. Karageorghis and N. C. Stampolidis (eds), *Eastern Mediterranean: Cyprus, Dodecanese, Crete 16th–6th century. BC.*, 187–206. Athens, University of Crete and A.G. Leventis Foundation.

Dickers, A. (1990) Spätbronzezeitliche Steingefässe des griechischen Festlands. *Studi Micenei ed Egeo-Anatolici* 28, 125–223.

Dickinson, O. (1994) *The Aegean Bronze Age*. Cambridge, University Press.

Dickinson, O. T. P. K. (2006) *The Aegean from Bronze Age to Iron Age: Continuity and Change between the Twelfth and Eighth Centuries BC*. London and New York, Routledge.

Doumas, C. (2004) Οι εφαρμογές της φωτιάς στη Θήρα (Σαντορίνη) της Εποχής του Χαλκού. In Kyriatsoulis 2004, 405–428.

Ekroth, G. (2008) Burnt, Cooked or Raw? Divine and Human Culinary Desires at Greek Animal Sacrifice. In E. Stavrianopoulou, A. Michaels and C. Ambos (eds), *Transformations in Sacrificial Practices: From Antiquity to Modern Times*, 87–111. Berlin, LIT.

Ekroth, G. (2009) Thighs or Tails? The Osteological Evidence as a Source for Greek Ritual Norms. In P. Brulé (ed.), *La norme en matière religieuse en Grèce ancienne*. Kernos Supplèment 21, 125–151. Liège, Centre International d'Étude de la Religion Grecque Antique.

Fasnacht, W. (2004) Antike Kupfertechnologie: Das Beispiel der Kupferverhüttungsstätte Agia Varvara – Almyras auf Zypern. In Kyriatsoulis 2004, 121–131.

Feldman, M. H. (2006) *Diplomacy by Design. Luxury Arts and an 'International Style' in the Ancient Near East, 1400–1200 BCE*. Chicago and London, University of Chicago.

Fox, R. (2008) Tastes, Smells and Spaces: Sensory Perceptions and Mycenaean Palatial Feasting. In Hitchcock, Laffineur and Crowley 2008, 133–140.

Friedman, J. (1991) Consuming Desires: Strategies of Selfhood and Appropriation. *Cultural Anthropology* 6, 154–163.

Friedman, J. (1997) Global Crises, the Struggle for Cultural Identity and Intellectual Porkbarelling: Cosmopolitans versus Locals, Ethnics and Nationals in an Era of De-hegemonisation. In P. Werbner and T. Modood (eds), *Debating Cultural Hybridity: Multi-Cultural Identities and the Politics of Anti-Racism*, 70–89. London and New Jersey, Zed Books.

Fuller, D. and Rowlands, M. (forthcoming) Ingestion and Food Technologies: Maintaining Differences over the Long-term in West, South and East Asia. In T. C. Wilkinson, S. Sherratt and J. Bennet (eds), *Interweaving Worlds: Systemic Interactions in Eurasia, 7th to 1st Millennia BC*. Oxford, Oxbow.

Geerlings, W. (1996) Die Tränen der Schwestern des Phaethon – Bernstein im Altertum. In M. Ganzelewski and R. Slotta (eds), *Bernstein: Tränen der Götter*. Katalog der Ausstellung des Deutschen Bergbau-Museums Bochum in Zusammenarbeit mit dem Ostpreußischen Landesmuseum Lüneburg und dem Siebenbürgischen Museum Gundelsheim, 395–400. Bochum, Bergbau-Museum.

Georgiou, H.S. (1986) *Ayia Irini: Specialized Domestic and Industrial Pottery. Keos VI*. Mainz, Zabern.

Haarer, P. (2001) Problematising the Transition from Bronze to Iron. In A. J. Shortland (ed.), *The Social Context of Technological Change: Egypt and the Near East, 1650–1550 BC*. Proceedings of a Conference Held at St Edmund Hall, Oxford, 12–14 September 2000, 255–273. Oxford, Oxbow.

Hägg, I. (1994) Kultgebräuche im Alpenraum und in der Ägäis. Zur Frage der Funktion der Feuerböcke aus Eschenz. In B. Schmid-Sikimić and P. Della Casa (eds), *Trans Europam. Beiträge zur Bronze- und Eisenzeit zwischen Atlantik und Altai. Festschrift für Margarita Primas*. Antiquitas, Reihe 3, Band 34, 211–234. Bonn, Habelt.

Hahn, H.-P. (2004) Global Goods and the Process of Appropriation. In P. Probst and G. Spittler (eds), *Between Resistance and Expansion: Explorations of Local Vitality in Africa*. Beiträge zur Afrikaforschung 18, 211–230. Münster, LIT.

Halstead, P. and Isaakidou, V. (2004) Faunal Evidence for Feasting: Burnt Offerings from the Palace of Nestor at Pylos. In P. Halstead and J. C. Barrett (eds), *Food, Cuisine and Society in Prehistoric Greece*. Sheffield Studies in Aegean Archaeology 5, 136–154. Oxford, Oxbow.

Hamilakis, Y. and Konsolaki, E. (2004) Pigs for the Gods: Burnt Animal Sacrifices as Embodied Rituals at a Mycenaean Sanctuary. *Oxford Journal of Archaeology* 23, 135–151.

Harding, A. F. (1984) *The Mycenaeans and Europe*. London, Orlando, San Diego, Academic Press.

Hirschfeld, N. E. (1996) Cypriots in the Mycenaean Aegean. In E. de Miro, L. Godart, and A. Sacconi (eds), *Atti e Memorie del Secondo Congresso Internazionale di Micenologia, Roma-Napoli, 14–20 Ottobre 1991*, 289–297. Rome, Gruppo Editoriale Internazionale.

Hirschfeld, N. E. (1999) *Potmarks of the Late Bronze Age Eastern Mediterranean*. PhD Dissertation, University of Texas at Austin.

Hitchcock, L. (2008) Architectures of Feasting. In Hitchcock, Laffineur and Crowley 2008, 317–326.

Hitchcock, L. A., Laffineur, R. and Crowley, J. (2008) *DAIS. The Aegean Feast*. Proceedings of the 12th International Aegean Conference, University of Melbourne, Centre for Classics and Archaeology, 25–29 March 2008. Aegaeum 29. Liège and Austin, Université de Liège and University of Texas at Austin.

Hodos, T. (2010) Local and Global Perspectives in the Study of Social and Cultural Identities. In S. Hales and T. Hodos (eds), *Material Culture and Social Identities in the Ancient World*, 3–31. Cambridge, University Press.

Hoffman, G. (1997) *Imports and Immigrants: Near Eastern Contacts with Iron Age Crete*. Ann Arbor, University of Michigan Press.

Hoskins, J. (2002) *Biographical Objects. How Things Tell the Stories of People's Lives*. London, Routledge.

Hoskins, J. (2006) Agency, Biography and Objects. In C. Tilley, W. Keane, S. Küchler, M. Rowlands and P. Spyer, *Handbook of Material Culture*. Los Angeles, London, New Delhi, Singapore, Washington DC, Sage.

Hruby, J. (2008) You Are How You Eat: Mycenaean Class and Cuisine. In Hitchcock, Laffineur and Crowley 2008, 151–157.

Hughes-Brock, H. (1993) Amber in the Aegean in the Late Bronze Age: Some Problems and Perspectives. In C. W. Beck and J. Bouzek (eds), *Amber in Archaeology*. Proceedings of the Second International Conference on Amber in Archaeology, Liblice 1990, 219–229. Prague, Institute of Archaeology.

Isaakidou, V., Halstead, P., Davis, J. and Stocker, S. (2002) Burnt Animal Sacrifice in late Bronze Age Greece: New Evidence from the Mycenaean 'Palace of Nestor', Pylos. *Antiquity* 76, 86–92.

Jantzen, U. (ed.) (1975) *Führer durch Tiryns*. Athen, Deutsches Archäologisches Institut.

Jung, R. (2007) Goldene Vögel und Sonnen. Ideologische Kontakte zwischen Italien und der postpalatialen Ägäis. In Alram-Stern and Nightingale 2007, 219–255.

Karageorghis, V. (1974) Pikes or Obeloi from Cyprus and Crete. In *Antichità cretesi: studi in onore di Doro Levi, Vol. II*. Cronache di archeologia 13, 168–172. Catania, Istituto di Archeologia.

Karageorghis, V. (2001) Some Innovations in the Burial Customs of Cyprus (12th–7th Centuries BC). *Eulimene* 2, 53–65.

Karageorghis, V. (2003) Heroic Burials in Cyprus and Other Mediterranean Regions. In N. C. Stampolidis and V. Karageorghis (eds), *ΠΛΟΕΣ...Sea Routes...Interconnections in the Mediterranean 16th–6th c. BC*. Proceedings of the International Symposium Held at Rethymnon, Crete, September 29th–October 2nd 2002, 339–351 Athens, A. G. Leventis Foundation.

Karageorghis, V. (2007) Eating and Drinking in Cyprus, 13th–6th Centuries BC. In Alram-Stern and Nightingale 2007, 257–262.

Karageorghis, V. and Lo Schiavo, F. (1989) A West Mediterranean Obelos from Amathus. *Rivista di Studi Fenici* 17, 15–29.

Karo, G. (1930) Schatz von Tiryns. *Mitteilungen des Deutschen Archäologischen Instituts Athenische Abteilung* 55, 119–140.

Kilian, K. (1983) Weihungen aus Eisen und Eisenverarbeitung im Heiligtum zu Philia (Thessalien). In R. Hägg (ed.), *The Greek Renaissance of the Eighth Century BC.: Tradition and Innovation*. Proceedings of the Second International Symposium at the Swedish Institute in Athens, 1–5 June, 1981, 131–147. Lund, Åströms Förlag.

Kilian-Dirlmeier, I. (1987) Das Kuppelgrab von Vapheio: Die Beigabenausstattung in der Steinkiste Untersuchungen zur Sozialstruktur in späthelladischer Zeit. *Jahrbuch des Römisch-Germanischen Zentralmuseums* 34, 197–212.

Kirchweger, F. (ed.) (2005) *Die heilige Lanze in Wien. Insignie, Reliquie, 'Schicksalsspeer'*. Schriften des Kunsthistorischen Museums 9. Wien, Kunsthistorisches Museum.

Knapp, A. B. (1986) *Copper Production and Divine Protection: Archaeology, Ideology and Social Complexity on Bronze Age Cyprus*. Studies in Mediterranean Archaeology Pocket-Book 42. Göteborg, Åström.

Knapp, A. B. (1994) Emergence, Development and Decline on Bronze Age Cyprus. In C. Mathers and S. Stoddart (eds), *Development and Decline in the Mediterranean Bronze Age*. Sheffield Archaeological Monographs 8, 271–304. Sheffield, J. R. Collins.

Knapp, A. B. (2006) Orientalization and Prehistoric Cyprus: The Social Life of Oriental Goods. In C. Riva and N. C. Vella (eds), *Debating Orientalization: Multidisciplinary Approaches to Processes of Change in the Ancient Mediterranean*. Monographs in Mediterranean Archaeology, 48–65. London, Equinox.

Knapp, A. B. and van Dommelen, P. (2008) Past Practices: Rethinking Individuals and Agents in Archaeology. *Cambridge Archaeological Journal* 18, 15–34.

Kohler, C. and Naso, A. (1991) Appunti sulla funzione di alari e spiedi nelle società arcaiche dell'Italia centro-meridionale. In E. Herring, R. Whitehouse and J. Wilkins (eds), *Papers of the Fourth Conference of Italian Archaeology. Volume 2: The Archaeology of Power, Part 2*, 41–63. London, Accordia Research Centre.

Kyriatsoulis, A. (2004) *Althellenische Technologie und Technik, Tagung 21.–23.3.2003 Ohlstadt*, 121–131. Weilheim, Verein zur Förderung der Hellenischen Geschichte e.V.

Latour, B. (1986) The Powers of Association. In J. Law (ed.), *Power, Action and Belief: A New Sociology of Knowledge?* Sociological Review Monograph 32, 264–280. London, Boston and Henley, Routledge and Kegan.

Latour, B. (2005) *Reassembling the Social: An Introduction to Actor-Network-Theory*. Oxford, University Press.

Law, J. (1992) Notes on the Theory of the Actor-Network: Ordering, Strategy and Heterogeneity. *Systems Practice* 5, 379–393.

Lupack, S. (2008) The Northeast Building of Pylos and An 1281. In A. Sacconi, M. del Freo, L. Godart and M. Negri (eds), *Colloquium Romanum. Atti del XII Colloquio Internazionale di Micenologia, Roma, 20–25 Febbraio 2006*. Pasiphae 2, 467–484. Pisa and Rome, Fabrizio Serra Editore.

Maran, J. (2001) Political and Religious Aspects of Architectural Change on the Upper Citadel of Tiryns: The Case of Building T. In R. Laffineur and R. Hägg (eds), *POTNIA. Deities and Religion in the Aegean Bronze Age,* Proceedings of the 8th International Aegean Conference Göteborg, Göteborg University, 12–15 April 2000. Aegaeum 22, 113–122. Liège and Austin, Université de Liège and University of Texas at Austin.

Maran, J. (2004) The Spreading of Objects and Ideas in the Late Bronze Age Eastern Mediterranean: Two Case Examples from the Argolid of the 13th and 12th Centuries BC. *Bulletin of the American Schools of Oriental Research* 336, 11–30.

Maran, J. (2006) Coming to Terms with the Past: Ideology and Power in Late Helladic IIIC. In S. Deger-Jalkotzy and I. S. Lemos (eds), *Ancient Greece: From the Mycenaean Palaces to the Age of Homer*. Edinburgh Leventis Studies 3, 123–150. Edinburgh, University Press.

Maran, J. (2008) Nach dem Ende. Tiryns – Phönix aus der Asche. In *Zeit der Helden. Die 'dunklen Jahrhunderte' Griechenlands 1200–700 v. Chr.* 63–73. Darmstadt, Primus.

Maran, J. (2010) Tiryns. In E. H. Cline (ed.), *The Oxford Handbook of the Bronze Age Aegean*, 722–734. Oxford, University Press.

Maran, J. (forthcoming) Architektonischer Raum und soziale Kommunikation auf der Oberburg von Tiryns – Der Wandel von der mykenischen Palastzeit zur Nachpalastzeit. In F. Arnold, R. Haensch and U. Wulf-Rheidt (eds), *Orte der Herrschaft. Charakteristika antiker Machtzentren von der babylonischen Zeit bis in den Frühislam. Menschen – Kulturen – Traditionen.* Studien aus den Forschungsclustern des Deutschen Archäologischen Instituts.

Maran, J. (2011) Contested Pasts – The Society of the 12th c. BCE. Argolid and the Memory of the Mycenaean Palatial Period. In W. Gauss, M. Lindblom, R. A. K. Smith and J. C. Wright. (eds), *Our Cups are Full: Pottery and Society in the Aegean Bronze Age. Papers Presented to Jeremy B. Rutter on the Occasion of his 65th Birthday*. British Archaeological Reports, International Series 2227, 169–178. Oxford, Archaeopress.

Maran, J. and Kostoula, M. (forthcoming) A Group of Animal-headed Faience Vessels from Tiryns. In G. Lehmann, Z. Talshir, M. Gruber and S. Ahituv (eds), *All the Wisdom of the East: Studies in Near Eastern Archaeology and History in Honor of Eliezer D. Oren*. Orbis Biblicus et Orientalis. Fribourg: Fribourg Academic Press.

Maran, J. and Papadimitriou, A. (2006) Forschungen im Stadtgebiet von Tiryns 1999–2002. *Archäologischer Anzeiger*, 97–169.

Marinatos, N. (2010) *Minoan Kingship and the Solar Goddess: A Near Eastern Koine*. Urbana, Chicago, and Springfield, University of Illinois Press.

Marinatos, Sp. (1960) Lausitzer Goldschmuck in Tiryns. In F. Eckstein (ed.), *Theoria. Festschrift für W.-H. Schuchhardt*. Deutsche Beiträge zur Altertumswissenschaft 12, 151–157. Baden-Baden, Grimm.

Marthari, M. (2008) Αγροτική οικονομία και αγροτική λατρεία στό Ακρωτήρι Θήρας. Στοιχεία από την εξέταση μιάς θηραϊκής κεραμικής κατηγορίας. In C. G. Doumas (ed.), Ακρωτήρι Θήρας. Τριάντα χρόνια έρευνας 1967–1997. Επιστημονική συνάντηση, 19–20 Δεκεμβρίου 1997. Βιβλιοθήκη της εν Αθηναίς Αρχαιολογικής Εταιρείας 257. Athens, Αρχαιολογική Εταιρεία.

Matthäus, H. (1980) *Die Bronzegefäße der kretisch-mykenischen Kultur*. Prähistorische Bronzefunde II,1. München, C. H. Beck.

Matthäus, H. (1985) *Metallgefäße und Gefäßuntersätze der Bronzezeit, der geometrischen und archaischen Periode auf Cypern*. Prähistorische Bronzefunde II, 8. München, C. H. Beck.

McDonald, W. A., Coulson, W. D. E. and Rosser, J. (1983) *Excavations at Nichoria in Southwest Greece. Volume III: Dark Age and Byzantine Occupation*. Minneapolis, University of Minnesota Press.

Mills, B. J. and Walker, W. H. (2008a) *Memory Work: Archaeologies of Material Practices*. Santa Fe, School for Advanced Research Press.

Mills, B. J. and Walker, W. H. (2008b) Introduction: Memory, Materiality, and Depositional Practice. In Mills and Walker 2008a, 3–23.

Müller, K. (1930) *Tiryns III. Die Ergebnisse der Ausgrabungen des Instituts. Die Architektur der Burg und des Palastes*. Augsburg, Filser.

Müller-Karpe, H. (2009) *Religionsarchäologie. Archäologische Beiträge zur Religionsgeschichte*. Frankfurt on Main, Lembeck.

Needham, S. and Bowman S. (2005) Flesh-Hooks, Technological Complexity and the Atlantic Bronze Age Feasting Complex. *European Journal of Archaeology* 8, 93–136.

Niemeier, W.-D. (1986) Zur Deutung des Thronraumes im Palast von Knossos. *Mitteilungen des Deutschen Archäologischen Instituts Athenische Abteilung* 101, 63–95.

Papasavvas, G. (2001) *Χάλκινοι υποστάτες από την Κύπρο και την Κρήτη. Τριποδικοί και τετράπλευροι υποστάτες από την Ύστερη Εποχή του Χαλκού έως την Πρώιμη Εποχή του Σιδήρου.* Lefkosia, A. G. Leventis Foundation.

Plesl, E. (1993) Zur Frage des Bernsteinvorkommens während der Urnenfelderperiode in der Tschechoslowakei. In C. W. Beck and J. Bouzek (eds), *Amber in Archaeology*. Proceedings of the Second International Conference on Amber in Archaeology, Liblice 1990, 164–170. Prague, Institute of Archaeology.

Pollard, J. (2008) Deposition and Material Agency in the Early Neolithic of Southern Britain. In Mills and Walker 2008a, 41–59.

Pratt, M.L. (1991) Arts of the Contact Zone. *Profession*, 33–40.

Reusch, H. (1958) Zum Wandschmuck des Thronsaales in Knossos. In E. Grumach (ed.), *Minoica. Festschrift zum 80. Geburtstag von Johannes Sundwall*, 334–358. Berlin, Akademie-Verlag.

Sakellariou, A. (1964) *Die minoischen und mykenischen Siegel des Nationalmuseums in Athen*. Corpus der Minoischen und Mykenischen Siegel 1. Berlin, Gebrüder Mann.

Schliemann, H. (1886) *Tiryns – Der prähistorische Palast der Könige von Tiryns*. Leipzig, Brockhaus.

Scheffer, C. (1981) Etruscan Firedogs. *Opuscula Romana* 13, 57–62.

Scheffer, C. (1984) Aegean, Bronze Age, Spit Supports with Scalloped Tops. *Opuscula Atheniensia* 15, 155–162.

Sherratt, S. (1994) Commerce, Iron and Ideology: Metallurgical Innovation in 12th–11th Century. In V. Karageorghis (ed.), *Cyprus in the 11th century BC.* Proceedings of the International Symposium Organized by the Archaeological Research Unit of the University of Cyprus and the Anastasios G. Leventis Foundation, Nicosia, 30–31 October 1993, 59–106. Nicosia, A. G. Leventis Foundation.

Sherratt, S. (2003) The Mediterranean Economy: Globalization at the End of the Second Millennium BCE. In W. G. Dever and S. Gitin (eds) *Symbiosis, Symbolism, and the Power of the Past. Canaan, Ancient Israel, and Their Neighbors from the Late Bronze Age through Roman Palaestina.* Proceedings of the Centennial Symposium W.F. Albright Institute of Archaeological Research and American Schools of Oriental Research, Jerusalem, May 29–31, 2000, 37–62. Winona Lake, Eisenbrauns.

Sherratt, S. (2004) Feasting in Homeric Epic. In Wright 2004a, 181–217.

Sherratt, S. (2009) The Aegean and the Wider World: Some Thoughts on a World-Systems Perspective. In W. A. Parkinson and M. L. Galaty (eds), *Archaic State Interaction – The Eastern Mediterranean in the Bronze Age*, 81–106. Santa Fe, School for Advanced Research Press.

Snodgrass, A.M. (1996) Iron. In J. N. Coldstream and H. W. Catling (eds), *Knossos North Cemetery: Early Greek Tombs.* Supplementary Volume 28, 575–597. London, British School at Athens.

Spittler, H.-P. (2002) Globale Waren – Lokale Aneignungen. In B. Hauser-Schäublin and U. Braukämper (eds), *Ethnologie der Globalisierung: Perspektiven kultureller Verflechtungen*, 15–30. Berlin, Reimer.

Spyropoulos, T.G. (1972) *Υστερομυκηναϊκοί Ελλαδικοί θησαυροί.* Βιβλιοθήκη της εν Αθηναίς Αρχαιολογικής Εταιρείας 72. Athens, Αρχαιολογική Εταιρεία.

Stampolidis, N. C. (1998) Ζεύγος σιδερένιων κρατευτών με οβελούς. In N. Stampolidis and A. Karetsou (eds), Ανατολική Μεσόγειος. Κύπρος – Δωδεκάνησα – Κρήτη, 16ος – 6ος αι. π. Χ, 258–259. Heraklion, University of Crete.

Stary, P. F. (1994) Metallfeuerböcke im früheisenzeitlichen Grabritus. In C. Dobiat (ed.), *Festschrift für Otto-Herman Frey zum 65. Geburtstag.* Marburger Studien zur Vor- und Frühgeschichte 16, 603–624. Hitzeroth, Vorgeschichtliches Seminar Marburg.

Stockhammer, P. W. (2008) *Kontinuität und Wandel – Die Keramik der Nachpalastzeit aus der Unterstadt von Tiryns.* Ph.D. Dissertation, Heidelberg University, http://www.ub.uni-heidelberg.de/archiv/8612.

Stockhammer, P. (2009) The Change of Pottery's Social Meaning at the End of the Bronze Age: New Evidence from Tiryns. In C. Bachhuber and R. G. Roberts (eds), *Forces of Transformation: The End of the Bronze Age in the Mediterranean.* Themes from the Ancient Near East BANEA Publication Series 1, 164–169. Oxford, Oxbow.

Strøm, I. (2001) Cypriote Influences on Early Etruscan Banqueting Customs. In L. Bonfante and V. Karageorghis (eds), *Italy and Cyprus in Antiqity 1500–450 BC*, 361–376. Nicosia, Severis Foundation.

Tzedakis, Y. and Martlew, H. (1999) *Minoans and Mycenaeans: Flavours of Their Time. National Archaeological Museum, 12 July– 27 November 1999.* Athens, Kapon editions.

Van Dommelen, P. (2005) Colonial Interactions and Hybrid Practices. Phoenician and Carthaginian Settlement in the Ancient Mediterranean. In G. J. Stein (ed.), *The Archaeology of Colonial Encounters. Comparative Perspectives*, 109–141. Santa Fe: School of American Research.

Verdelis, N. M. (1963) Neue Geometrische Gräber in Tiryns. *Mitteilungen des Deutschen Archäologischen Instituts Athenische Abteilung* 78, 1–62.

Voskos, I. and Knapp, A. B. (2008) Cyprus at the End of the Late Bronze Age: Crisis and Colonization or Continuity and Hybridization. *American Journal of Archaeology* 112, 659–684.

Wachsmann, S. (1998) *Seagoing Ships and Seamanship in the Bronze Age Levant.* London, Chatham Publishing.

Walberg, G. (1995) The Midea Megaron and Changes in Mycenaean Ideology. *Aegean Archaeology* 2, 87–91.

Walberg, G. (2007) *Midea: The Megaron Complex and Shrine Area. Excavations on the Lower Terraces 1994–1997*. Prehistory Monographs 20. Philadephia, INSTAP Academic Press.

Walker, W. H. (2008) Practice and Nonhuman Social Actors. The Afterlife Histories of Witches and Dogs in the American Southwest. In Mills and Walker 2008a, 137–157.

Wardle, K.A. (1969) A Group of Late Helladic IIIB 1 Pottery from within the Citadel at Mycenae. *Annual of the British School at Athens* 64, 261–297.

Warren, P. (1969) *Minoan Stone Vases*. Cambridge, University Press.

Wedde, M. (1999) War at Sea: The Mycenaean and Early Iron Age Oared Galley. In R. Laffineur (ed.), *POLEMOS. Le context guerrier en Égée à l'âge du Bronze,* Actes de la 7e Rencontre égéenne internationale, Université de Liège, 14–17 avril 1998. Aegaeum 19, 465–476. Liège and Austin, Université de Liège and University of Texas at Austin.

Wengrow, D. (forthcoming) 'Fleshpots of Egypt': Rethinking Temple Economy in the Bronze Age Mediterranean. In E. Frood, A. McDonald and R. Parkinson (eds), *Essays for John Baines*. Oxford, Griffith Institute.

Wright, J. C. (2004a) *The Mycenaean Feast.* Athens, American School of Classical Studies.

Wright, J. C. (2004b) A Survey of Evidence for Feasting in Mycenaean Society. In Wright 2004a, 13–58.

12.

From Minoan Crete to Mycenaean Greece and beyond: the dissemination of ritual practices and their material correlates in ceremonial architecture

Elisabetta Borgna

For several years scholars have been exploring in some detail the themes of banqueting, feasting, and ritual consumption in Mediterranean prehistory; in doing this, they have focused, on the one hand, on the role of food manipulation and consumption as constitutive practices in the shaping of cultural behaviours and social identities of human groups; they have outlined, on the other hand, discrete typologies of feasts and banquets – either religious within communal public contexts or mundane in private and exclusive settings – as well as their functions within strategies of social control and political legitimisation, and even within politics of acculturation and interaction at a distance.[1]

In dealing with feasting in the context of Minoan-Mycenaean interaction in LM (Late Minoan) Crete on the basis of some relevant archaeological evidence, such as pottery style and its social use (Borgna 1997; 1999; 2003, 354–371; 2004a; 2004b), I was prompted to contrast the multifaceted range of Minoan convivial practices to a Mainland pattern of feasting which seemed to be shaped more overtly and univocally by such factors as selectivity and exclusivity. Stemming from the Middle Helladic ideological background of private mutual hospitality as a means of constructing networks of alliances and partnerships, banquets in the Mycenaean world were mostly instruments of individual, exclusionary power-strategies proper to small-scale societies, based on highly competitive social and ideological practices aimed at the control of resources (Borgna 2004a, in part 146; *cf.* Galaty and Parkinson 2008, 27; for the classification of society see Blanton *et al.* 1996).

Some aspects of the structured and formalised scenario of Mycenaean feasts have been recently illuminated in the topography of the palace of Pylos (Bendall 2004). There, the available textual documentation made it clear that feasts of a somehow more unrestricted nature, including communal banqueting (Killen 1994; Palaima 2004; 2008; Stocker and Davis 2004; Shelmerdine 2001; 2008, with literature), played a role also in the Mainland palace ideology, and not only at the core of the Minoan palaces, where public feasts were clearly ruled by inclusive ideological strategies well-suited to a corporate or group-oriented social and political organisation (Borgna 2004a, 146).

Exploring in more detail the theme of cultural encounters in the field of ritual, I believe the time is ripe for conducting a comparative analysis of the architectural settings of feasts. Thus far, mainly evidence related to material culture such as ceramic sets and special assemblages of artefacts discarded according to structured patterns – together with iconographic sources – have been used for identifying feasting contexts. The field of architecture meanwhile has identified open spaces and courts as definite markers of ceremonial settings.[2]

My contention is that in the framework of the highly centralised palatial societies, structured principles of architectural planning could indeed have played a role in the materialisation of power ideologies in the ritual domain by creating built spaces well apt to incorporate relevant social practices and promote the social relations that were negotiated and sanctioned by those practices (for architecture as 'incorporative practice' in the Aegean and for the contextual analysis of forms and social functions see recently Wright 2006b, with literature; for the concept of materialisation *cf.* DeMarrais, Castillo and Earle 1996). Were such built spaces formalised according to shared patterns also in the communicative strategies of societies at a distance? One of the aims of the present analysis is to verify whether spatial patterns travelled together with the ritual activities and the social practices shared by Mediterranean Bronze Age interacting agents (for agency within interaction studies, see in particular Stejn 2002, 907 with literature).

In a preliminary contribution (Borgna 2009–2010, 176–180), I have attempted to locate public Mycenaean religious feasts, as they are believed to have taken place according to the written texts, in a concrete environmental, topographical and architectural setting. I believe I have identified such characteristics in the architecture of the South Enclosure of Gla, in Boeotia (Fig. 12.1; Iakovidis 1989; 1998; 2001; *cf.* Wright 2006a, 27–28): there, formalism, symmetry, repetition, and redundancy seem to give a special emphasis to the built space, as recent developments in the archaeology of ritual permit us to suggest (Kyriakidis 2005, 28–49; *cf.* Borgna 2009–2010, note 55). In particular, the twin long buildings B and K (Figs. 12.1–12.2), which Pascal Darcque (2005, 358) has recently mentioned as examples of the largest single buildings in the Mycenaean world, appear to play a special role in sheltering not only goods but also people, in addition to delimiting space useful for gathering and communal consumption. I have discussed several aspects of this argument by conducting a contextual analysis of the various classes of evidence – beginning with fragments of wall decoration and pottery used for food preparation and consumption. This evidence made me doubt that the buildings of the South Enclosure could be exclusively devoted to utilitarian aims, such as those of granaries and storehouses (Iakovidis, *e.g.* 2001, 80–84; *cf.* Hiesel 1990, 168–169). For this kind of building, no useful comparanda appear to exist in the Aegean world, although some intriguing, albeit late, evidence, such as the plan of some Archaic temples/*hestiatoria* (*e.g.* in the layout of the archaic temple/*hestiatorion* of Apollo at Halieis, Argolis: Borgna 2009–2010 with literature; for the interpretation of this building see Bergquist 1990; 1998 [*hestiatorion*], and Mazarakis Ainian 1997, 162–164 [temple/*hestiatorion*]), show interesting similarities raising the possibility of some continuity between the Bronze Age and historic times in relation to the politics of hospitality and commensality.

For the purposes of this contribution, I would like to concentrate on a functional analysis of the architecture, adopting the view introduced by John Coulton (1976) in his masterly research on the origin of the Greek *stoa*. A *stoa* is an elongated building with a row of central supports. This is nothing more than a special, simpler version of the large hall, where constraints are set by the necessity of ensuring both lighting and ease of access as well as a large unitary space for accommodating many people or goods; multiple openings on the long walls are indeed normal devices when buildings must be large enough for communal attendance indoors but are also planned for promoting the exploitation of the outdoor space. Building B (Fig. 12.2) – provided with central supports – and possibly Building K at Gla, with their elongated plan, their multiple rooms ordered in a linear paratactic sequence onto an open space centred on a large road and their exceptionally wide openings in the long side-walls figure as special versions of the large hall, namely a building normally devoted to prominent public activities in ancient societies. In such versions communication, mobility and interaction with the outside are major constitutive principles than seclusion and restriction of access, normally emphasised in storerooms.

I therefore believe that we should consider the buildings of Gla as kinds of *stoai*, namely buildings originally planned for communal activities and functions. These functions would include the possible sheltering of people, as well as providing temporary storage, housing the manipulation and preparation of goods, and facilitating participation in outdoors events and consumption activities. As is well-known, however, Mycenaean architects do not seem to have constructed ceremonial buildings similar to the later Greek *stoa*. Possible analogues have only been identified in Minoan Crete, as Coulton already noted (Coulton 1976, 18–19; on Minoan *stoai* see also Hayden 1982; 1984; Driessen 1989–1990; Shaw 1987; Shaw and Shaw 2006, 91–94).

Before addressing Minoan architecture, I would like to take into consideration another building where the same principles of topographical and architectural planning as at Gla might have been applied: the much debated North-Eastern Building (NEB) at Pylos (Blegen and Rawson 1966, 299–325; Kilian 1984, 42–43; Tegyey 1984; Westerburg 2001; Bendall 2003; Lupack 2008, 131–138; *cf.* also Flouda 2000) (Fig. 12.3). This is a very long rectangular built space, divided by inner partitions into at least three rooms, all possessing particularly large openings in the long southwestern side; the central room (99), one of the largest of the whole palace complex, is possibly provided with a row of central supports (Blegen and Rawson 1966, 320; Westerburg 2001, 5) and opens onto court 92 throughout a deep pillared portico (94). This seems to have constituted a conspicuous setting for the ceremonies performed in the court and centred on the altar in front of the small room or shrine 93. Although I fully accept the results of the thorough analysis of Lisa Bendall (2003), which dismisses the possibility that the NEB was a workshop, I would support the religious connotation for the court-altar-shrine system, as has been reasserted by several scholars and recently by Susan Lupack (2007, 58–59; 2008,

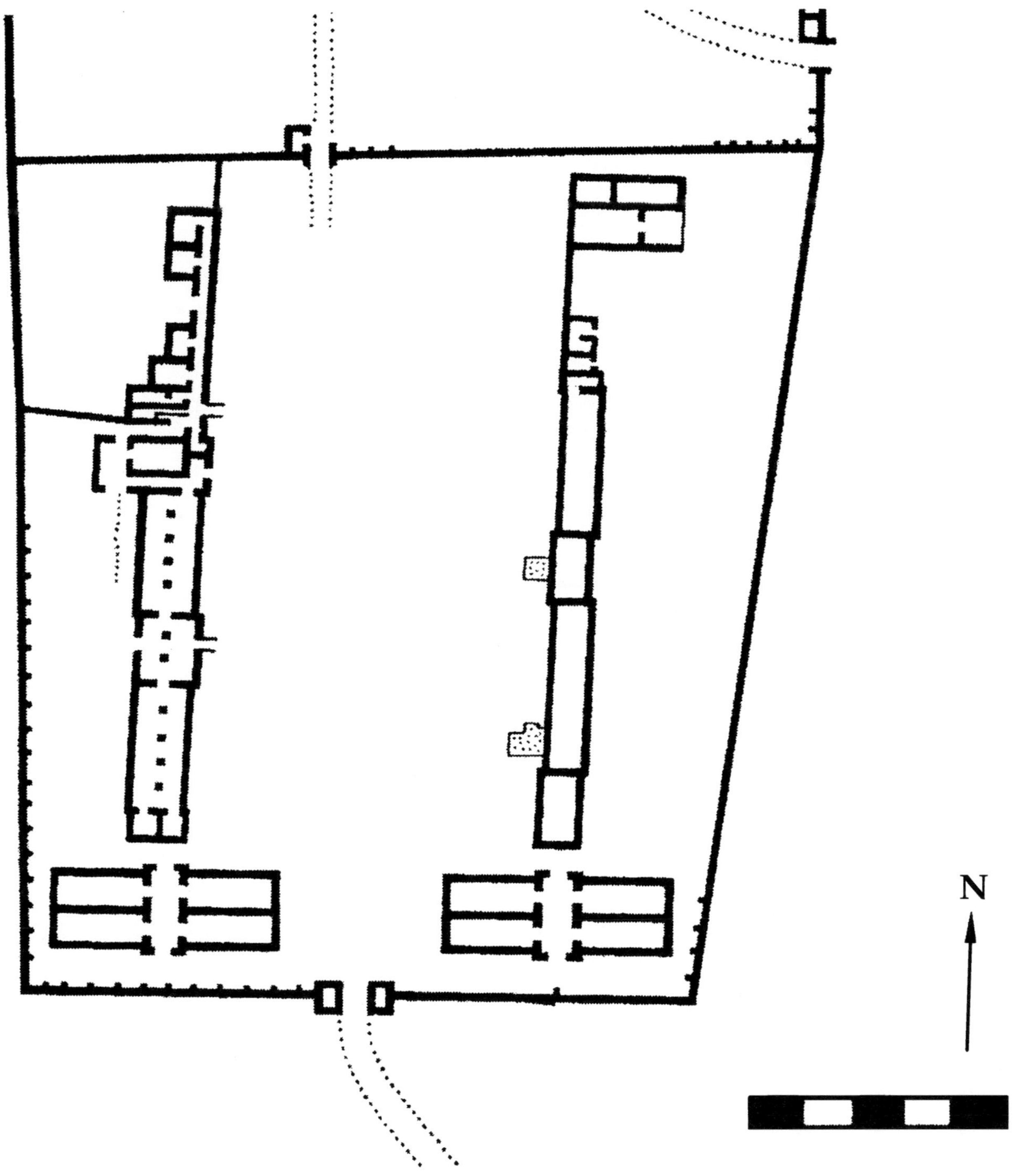

Fig. 12.1: Plan of the South Enclosure at Gla (redrawn after Iakovidis 2001, 43 plan 16).

136–138; *cf.* Whittaker 1997, 179–180). Such a role is supported not only by the axial layout of the whole system, but in particular by the evidence of the decorated block/altar and by meaningful, albeit rare, artifacts consisting of a number of *kylikes* including a well-known miniature exemplar.

Focusing now on the rear building, in the sequence of

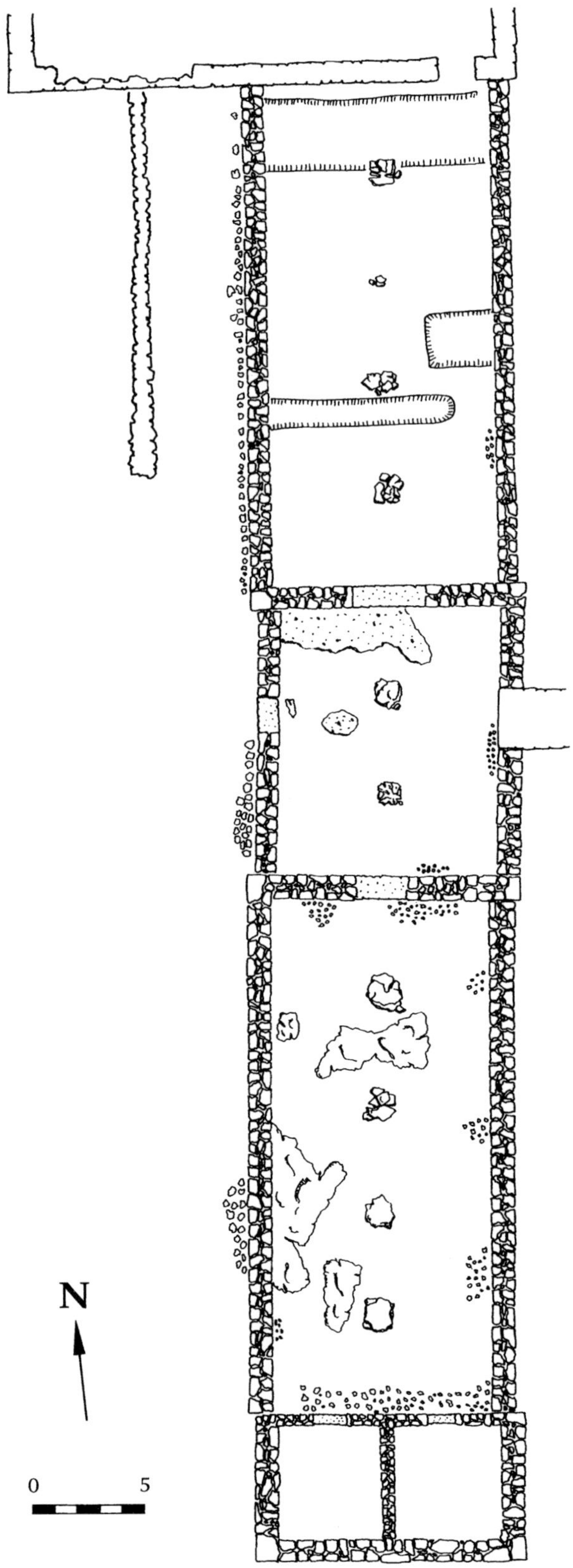

Fig. 12.2: Plan of Building B at Gla (redrawn after Iakovidis 2001, 45 plan 18a).

rooms 98-99-100 it is possible to visualise a long hall provided with easy access from an outer open space by means of very large multiple doors in the long sides.[3] Such a hall seems to match the functional domain described as occurring at Gla, but all the more so, as emphasis on the in-and-out circulation is given here by the front portico, which Carl Blegen (Blegen and Rawson 1966, 306) has already interpreted as a space useful for providing shade and/or shelter for people attending to ceremonies in the court. I find it difficult to accept that the activities performed in the NEB were completely unrelated to what was happening outdoors, and although I do not rule out the role as a clearing house proposed by Bendall for the complex, I would add to the processing and distribution of goods the functions of housing, receiving and organising people within the framework of ritual activities and practices including communal participation and dining.

The NEB has been excluded from the many areas devoted to feasting in the Pylos palace mainly on the basis of its humble architecture, consisting of a simple one-storey building made mainly of mud-bricks, and also for the diverse finds pointing to storage and administration, namely obsidian, ivory and bronze fragments, arrowheads and tablets. Bendall has also specified that the quantity of *kylikes* – normally a marker of ritual contexts – recorded in the NEB (at least 1000 examples from the whole area) does not equate the higher numbers detected in other contexts determined to be well-suited for banqueting.[4] It is worth remembering that, on the one hand, the ritual architecture in the Mycenaean world is very often characterised by the use of humble materials and techniques, as the shrines of Mycenae, Phylakopi and Tiryns testify (*cf.* Wright 1994, 61–62; for literature on the cult buildings see Whittaker 1997). On the other hand, some evidence exists that supports the possibility that the NEB had had a ritual function involving communal participation. Hints of possible drinking sets retrievable from several groups of sherds from floor deposits (corridor 95; Blegen and Rawson 1966, 307, fig. 339), fragments of kitchenware belonging also to a few special vessels, such as spit-stands, tripods, baking pans, (corridor 95, rooms 96, 97 and 98), many kylikes, including a miniature version from room 98 that matches the one from shrine 93 (Blegen and Rawson 1966, 318; miniature kylikes are considered to be univocally linked to ritual contexts by Stocker and Davis [2004, 70–71]), and a few figurines (95, 96, 97) also constitute evidence that fits well with a ritual setting where food and drink were processed and consumed. This function is suggested by the interpretation of room 98 as a 'pantry' for materials useful for reception, a point reasserted by Bendall (2004, 116, quoting Hofstra 2000).

While the presence of fragments of obsidian, ivory, and bronze do not contradict a ritual interpretation, as data from many sanctuaries allow us to assert, the large quantity of arrowheads carefully kept in wooden-cases in both rooms 99

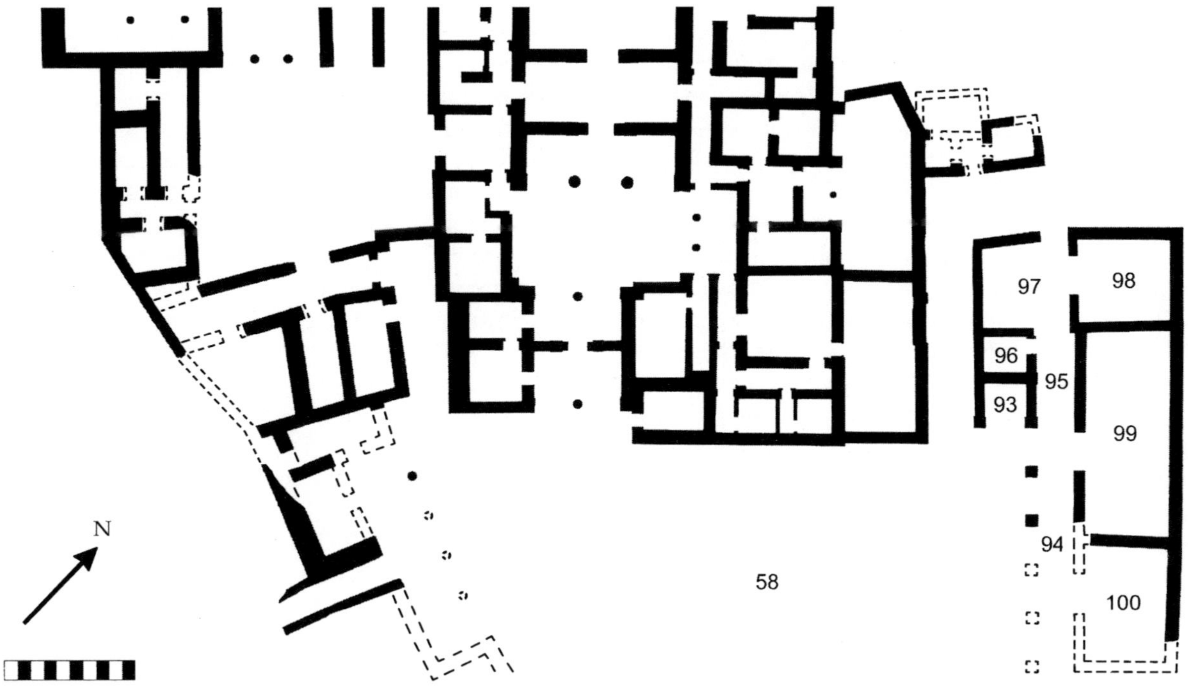

Fig. 12.3: Plan of the Palace of Nestor at Pylos (redrawn after Thaler 2007, pl. 15).

and 100 deserves special consideration. Both the shape and dimensions of these objects fully justify Blegen's terminology of 'diminutive arrowheads' (Blegen and Rawson 1966, 321–322, 324). Included in the class 1a of Avila's classification (1983, 82*ff.*, in part, p. 86, nos. 197–473 and 474–515), these arrowheads range from less than 1 cm to a maximum of 2.5 cm in length. They have been cut from a very thin bronze sheet (1 mm) and do not present the usual holes that arrowheads without a tang normally have for connection to the shaft. Avila admits that these objects could be useful for hunting small animals (Avila 1983, 88; for an overview of dimensions and typologies of arrowheads in Late Mycenaean Greece see Borgna 1992, 32–42).

I believe, however, that such a large concentration of small arrowheads that apparently had no, or only a very restricted, function could have been assembled for ritual offering or for use as ritual items in some special activity, such as hunting, sacrifice or ritual games. The role of hunting for ritual ceremonies is stressed at Pylos itself in the well-known fresco with dogs and men with tripods (Immerwahr 1990, 132–133, pls. 73–74, 76; for the context *cf.* Wright 2004b, 38–39, figs. 10–11, with literature). Furthermore, some cult assemblages such as the deposit by the altar in the court of the Cult Centre at Mycenae bring to light the importance of birds and small game for cult activities (Whittaker 1997, 146–149; French and Taylour 2007, 102; *cf.* Bendall 2007, 275, note 31). But even if we maintain the military connotation of the NEB arrowheads in addition to the military prowess communicated by the chariots – which seem to have been the subject of several NEB tablets (Schon 2007) – a ceremonial setting cannot be easily dismissed. This is all the more so as chariots and weapons take part in many ritual arenas going from the religious to the mundane sphere,[5] as some evidence suggests at different level of reliability. It is worth noting the reference to 'ka-ko na-wi-jo pa-ta-jo-i-qe e-ke-si-qe a-ka-sa-ma' ('temple bronze for arrow- and spearheads') in the well-known Pylian tablet (Jn 829) made by Tegyey (1984, 77) in this connection.

I would also mention the recurrent discovery of weapons and bronze instruments in cult buildings such as temples and *hestiatioria* in historical times (see *e.g.* knives, swords, spearheads in the mentioned complex of Apollo at Halieis (see above): Mazarakis Ainian 1997, 163; *cf.* Kilian-Dirlmeier 2002 (Athena Sanctuary, Philia, Thessaly); Felsch 2007 (Kalapodi); see also Stocker and Davis 2004, 70), as well as the famous passage from the Odyssey (XXI–XXII), where Odysseus is using bow and arrows in the banqueting hall during the competition against the suitors. A new discovery from Nestor's palace seems now to strengthen the association between bow and arrows on the one hand and ritual performances on the other, as the archer recently identified from the stored pieces of wall-painting has been tentatively interpreted as a divine figure, most probably in the context of a hunting scene (Brecoulaki *et al.* 2008).

As for the important evidence of the NEB tablets and sealings, in her careful survey Bendall (2003, 203*ff.*) calls our attention to the various texts dealing with the mobilisation of people, which seems to have been recorded more often than the transport and distribution of goods. Furthermore, some documents related to personnel and men may be related, in her opinion, to other texts from the main archive dealing with the organisation of banquets. In the main archive, remains of banqueting including long animal bones were carefully kept. This means that strong connections existed between administrative and ritual activities (Stocker and Davis 2004, with literature). Most sealings from NEB are ultimately compared to the well-known documents from Thebes referring to food and animal contributions for religious feasts, and Bendall herself admits that some NEB texts dealing with the movement of animals might belong to the same ritual sphere. I wonder whether the mention of bedding could have to do with an activity related to reception and hospitality.[6]

In conclusion, I propose that the NEB complex would have served not only as a clearing house or place of distribution for various goods, but also as a kind of reception hall or *hestiatorion*, where people coming from afar or those who shared common social status (work groups, strangers, guests, subelite components) could have gathered and shared food, drink and shelter during ceremonies celebrated outdoors. Shape and function would assign the NEB, as is the case for the Gla buildings, to a typological group including long halls, galleries, and possibly *stoai*, a type well-known in Minoan Crete.

A connection between the NEB and Cretan *stoai* has been already suggested by Jörg Westerburg (2001, 5–8), who envisaged in an early phase of NEB the existence of a true, pillared *stoa*, according to a pattern of noble architecture very much alike the ones known at Neopalatial and Late Palatial Kommos, Tylissos and Ayia Triada.[7]

In order to find a closer connection to Crete it is worth taking into consideration the wider context of the southern area of Pylos outside the main *propylon*, where ritual banqueting has been supposed to have taken place in large court 58. This court was possibly framed by two opposing porticoes: portico 94 to the NE and a similar one to the SW (Fig. 12.3; see Blegen and Rawson 1966, 228; *cf.* Thaler 2006, 99, pl. 15; for court 58: Bendall 2004, 120–122; for a combination of practical and ceremonial use of court 58, see also Cavanagh 2001, 127–128).

A similar layout can be found at Kommos in southern Crete, in the recently published Civic Centre, where the North and the South *stoai* faced each other on the opposite sides of the large court in a layout that seems to anticipate what we have just seen at Pylos (Shaw and Shaw 2006, 27ff., 56ff.). The recent detailed analysis of pottery groups and their contexts by Jeremy Rutter (2004; 2006) has clearly demonstrated that both *stoai* were important settings of communal feasting. During an earlier Neopalatial phase (MM (Middle Minoan) III/LM IA), the North *stoa* in particular might have materialised the ideological programme of the elites, which is suggested by some evidence of fine and exclusive cultural elements, including frescoes. In the later phases – from an advanced Neopalatial phase to LM II early and possibly later – the area was devoted to the activities of preparing, cooking, and consumption on a large scale, as is attested in particular by installations for grain-grinding, hearths and ovens, pieces of kitchenware, as well as fine tableware, most probably used in the context of public feasting. A certain ritual function has also been detected in the LM III layout in Tylissos in the combination of the columnar *stoa* with the courtyard provided with an altar (Hayden 1984, 41–43).

Mycenaean long buildings, such as B-K at Gla and NEB at Pylos, and Minoan *stoai* could have shared, therefore, principles not only of formal layout but also of function as for both the use of space at the interface of indoor/outdoor public areas and the encoding of social values. If Mycenaeans really adopted such an architectural pattern, it is highly probable that, by adapting it to their needs, they deeply transformed the original prototype, which underwent a major restriction of the built space due to the construction of both external walls and inner partitions. A similar shift can possibly be seen at LM III Ayia Triada in Crete, where the 'grande stoa' is characterised by an inner subdivision into small rooms of equal size.[8] The history of excavations at this site makes it impossible to reconstruct the function of the architecture from the available stratigraphic contexts, but it should be mentioned, as regards a possible ritual function, that some groups of pottery for drinking and serving have been identified as coming from layers related to the life-cycle of the building, according to the new investigations by Vincenzo La Rosa (1977, 331, 337: *strato VII*; 1979–1980 [1986], 53*ff.*). Further evidence might be added by the most recent proposal of Nicola Cucuzza and Nils Hellner (2009) to envisage a monumental *propylon,* which, by giving access to the paved court in front of the *stoa*, clearly enhanced a ceremonial exclusive role for the area.

In summary, I am tempted to suggest that the Mycenaeans, in their strategies of legitimising their new identities and, in particular, in their attempt to disguise themselves as Minoans, could have adopted in Crete – or elaborated there – some architectural patterns that were widespread in the Minoan built environment in the context of communal ceremonies, such as the *stoa* – but also portico and loggia. These patterns, which would have been strategic in the ceremonial arena promoted by elite competition in an early phase (LH [Late Helladic] II–IIIA), in the developed palatial age would have become

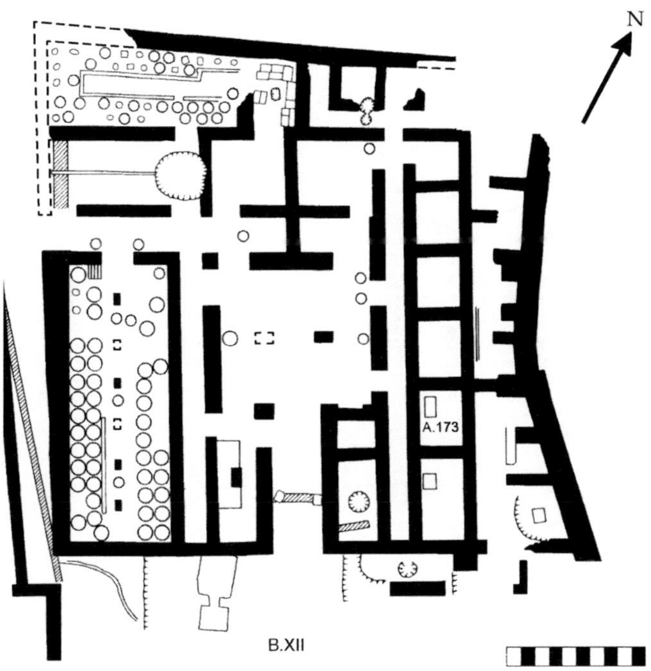

Fig. 12.4: Plan of Ashlar Building X at Kalavasos-Ayios Dhimitrios, Cyprus (redrawn after Steel 2004, 160, fig. 6.6).

useful for exercising social control, legitimising power and recruiting manpower. Meanwhile, in the formal layout of elongated buildings with inner partitions, the Mycenaeans would have materialised and reproduced their exclusive ideology founded on the perception of a very close social structure, articulated in several peer corporate groups, which had possibly eminent roles at local and regional level.

We could try to get more information on the role of architecture within dynamics of interaction by widening our perspective towards both the eastern and the western edge of the Aegean world. In search of comparisons, my attention was captured by the evidence from area 173 of Ashlar Building X at Kalavasos-Ayios Dhimitrios in Cyprus, which has been recently discussed in the context of banqueting (South 2008; Steel 2004, 170–171; Borgna 2009–2010, 180) (Fig. 12.4). There, feasting debris consisting mostly of Mycenaean fine tableware has been retrieved together with animal bones and vegetal remains, which had been discarded in a deep shaft located in one of the small rooms of the long building on the eastern side of the central court – a room possibly provided with a door giving access, through a corridor, to the court itself. The presence of Mycenaean components in the feasting practices of a Cypriot community is not a novelty: Mycenaean ceramics and banqueting traditions were at home in Cyprus, as has been pointed out by several scholars (*cf.* Steel 2004), and served Cypriot elites in their strategies of legitimisation of social status as well as in their politics of identity assertion (*cf.* Antoniadou 2007, 495–497). It is possible that, beyond the contents of pottery and organic remains, also the physical setting of feasting was encoded in a kind of international language serving interaction strategies. It is fair to say that the Kalavasos building is not exactly comparable to our Aegean structures in particular because access to the inner space there seems much more limited, and for this it resembles several other Cypriot buildings in the context of storerooms or warehouses; we cannot nevertheless rule out the possibility that an intentional mixture of cultural and functional patterns was created by Cypriot elites in the monumental settings of ritual feasting. Selection, adaptation, and hybridisation might be seen as choices proper to local elites, not only in pottery and other artefacts, but also in built space (*cf.* Knapp 2008; Voschos and Knapp 2009, with literature).

Meanwhile, if a Mycenaean palatial component was really at work in the planning of monumental architecture, this could be considered but a sign of an important role of Mycenaean elites in the dynamics of cultural diffusion: when we take into consideration the impressive quantities of fine tablewares that were imported from the Argolid, we can only think of the existence of a kind of organised trade, handled by either palatial elites or subelites on behalf of the palaces.

Substantially different was the situation in the central Mediterranean, where convivial habits and ritual practices seem nevertheless to have been central at the interface of cultural encounters, as the recent impressive data from Rocavecchia, in Apulia, point out (Guglielmino 2007; Pagliara *et al.* 2008, in part. 241–247, 276; Guglielmino *et al.* 2010; *cf.* Bietti Sestieri 2009, 27*ff.*). On the present occasion, I will limit myself to a short survey of a couple of remarkable sites, beginning with Thapsos in Eastern Sicily, a main coastal settlement at the crossroads of many interlocking networks including the Aeolian Islands, peninsular Italy, Malta and the Aegean, and which, according to some scholars, was a special emporial centre or even a colonial enclave of Aegean people (Fig. 12.5).[9] In particular, the sudden transformation of the settlement towards a regular layout in the second phase of its life – the local Middle Bronze Age (14th–13th) – has been related to a pervasive Aegean influence (for architecture related to Gla (main building) see Tomasello 1996; 2004; *cf.* Doonan 2001, who considers Pylos, NEB; for a Cypriot connection see firstly Ross Holloway 1981, 85: courtyard building of Enkomi, Level IIA). What I would like to stress here is that the linear sequence of rooms ensuing from a well-conceived unitary plan, giving rise to one or more long buildings provided with many openings onto a paved court, may be interpreted as evidence of ritual architecture in the field of feasting and ceremonial consumption, as has been already suggested (Doonan 2001, 180; Militello

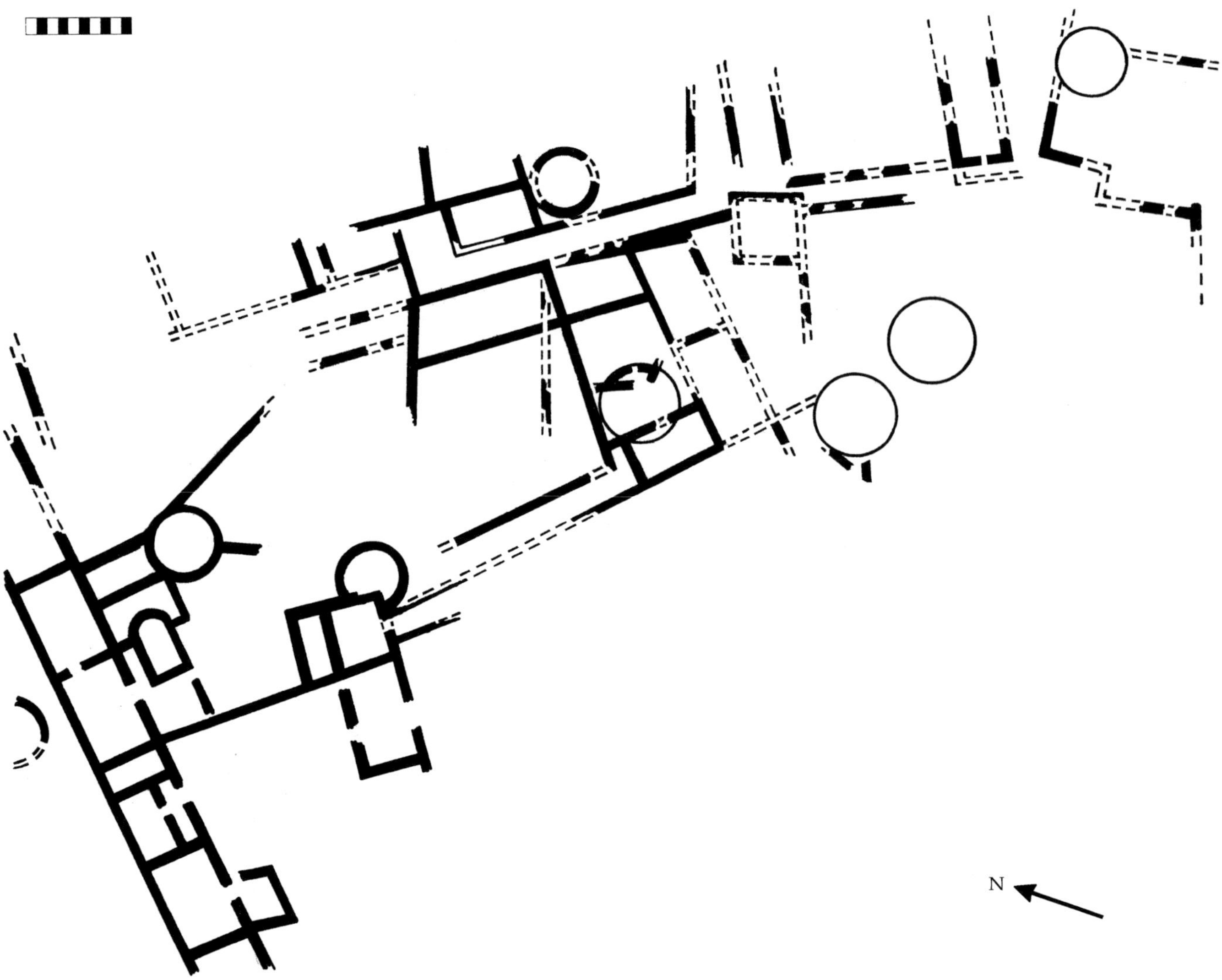

Fig. 12.5: Plan of the Thapsos settlement (Siracusa, Sicily) (redrawn after Militello 2004, 314, fig. 5).

2004, 315–318). Hearths associated with benches in most rooms, together with querns, deer horns, and other faunal remains, and additionally some pottery evidence, such as the monumental *lebes*/cauldron from Complex B (D'Agata 1987; 2000, 67–70, fig. 2), are all evidence pointing to this direction. The Thapsos buildings, which have been already compared from a formal point of view with the architecture of both Gla and the NEB of Pylos, as well as with East Mediterranean patterns (see above), might represent a 'western' version of ritual architectures of long halls and *stoai*, figuring, as in Cyprus, as a result of the diffusion of an interactive international language related to 'feasting'; such a language was possibly created through the agency of several interacting, not exclusively Mycenaean, cultural components.

Further Aegean elements in the Thapsian culture – implying knowledge in the field of specialised craftsmanship and the diffusion of ideological elite behaviours and symbols – are represented by the well-known rock-cut tholoi (Tomasello 1995–1996; 2004, 189–195) as well as by the rich grave furniture including Aegean pottery, jewellery, and weapons (Alberti 2006 with literature; *cf.* Militello 2004, 305*ff.*). Material culture, however, and in particular pottery production, does not seem to have been affected by Mycenaean influence. Only very limited evidence, consisting in the incised pictorial patterns on some tablewares at Thapsos itself *(cf.* Vagnetti 2000–2001, 113–114), seems to point to the emulation of the Aegean decorative style in the field of social and ideological communication, within a topographic and monumental framework, which according to Owen Doonan (2001, 181) would have been 'a formal setting for the interaction of outside and local components'.

A similar setting may also possibly be suggested for the central building at Pantalica, in the Thapsian hinterland, at the end of the Bronze Age (12th), though the *anaktoron* of Pantalica (Bernabò Brea 1990; Tomasello 1996) seems to be typologically far from the architectural patterns so far considered. However, the complex, characterised by a regularly linear modular plan, is striking for the lack, in particular in its early phase, of any inner communication device between the individual rooms, which are accessed only from the outside, from a paved open space. As Luigi Bernabò Brea observed, a residential or domestic function for rooms marked by the absence of any inner circulatory pattern is difficult to accept, while a different use of the whole building, depending upon the need of interaction and participation in communal activities performed in the court, is much more possible. What little evidence of tableware there is, including a huge *lebes*/cauldron on a high foot (Bernabò Brea 1990, 78), might be useful in this framework.

Once we have verified the presence in Sicily of Aegean components at a very high, exclusive level of interaction – including architectural and urban planning drawing upon palatial patterns – we are obliged to stress once more that Mycenaean elements are here much more rare and subject to a more discontinuous distribution than in Cyprus, either geographically or socially: they are at home at some places and some regions and not in the neighbouring ones; with regard to richness and social visibility they enter contexts and furniture at different social levels, not just the most prominent ones, as is clear from a look at the tombs; they affect certain sectors of production and not others, as seems to be the case with pottery.

From such a picture we can infer, on the one hand, what has been already asserted by other scholars (*e.g.* Bietti Sestieri 2002, 423, 429), namely that real forms of ideological and symbolic integration may take place in the dynamics of interaction at a distance when the contact societies are structurally similar and are both characterised by the presence of eminent competing groups independent enough to take on autonomous behaviours of selection and emulation, which do not engage the whole community, as is the case of both Cyprus and Sicily. On the other hand, we may suggest that the discontinuity of Mycenaean elements in Middle Bronze Age Sicily was a result of a low degree of internal integration of local societies, shaped by a multifocal self-perception in the interaction with various partners of exchange (*cf.* Doonan 2001; in the new paradigms of interaction studies see Stejn 2002, 907). Furthermore, if a definitely homogeneous and structured socio-economic upper class had not yet developed and social organisation was multifocal and heterarchical rather than centralised and hierarchical, then only a particular group or faction would have managed to interact with the Mycenaeans. Such a group was possibly formed by mixed social components following one or more chiefs or aggrandisers, who had prerogatives over only certain resources and were interpreters of only one of the many identities that were negotiated in the framework of the multidirectional relationships that Sicilian communities were engaged in.

What seems to me rather certain is that we do not have to postulate any political or colonial Aegean presence at Thapsos, though some sort of participation by the Mycenaeans has to be considered in the interactive dynamics. In the attempt at constructing an interaction model between Sicily and the Aegean in the Late Bronze Age, active strategies of diffusion of ideological patterns by Aegean elites have to be considered in addition to the careful adoption, emulation and adaptation of these patterns by restricted local groups.

A different pattern must be conceived for southern Italy, and in particular the Ionian region with the main settlement of Broglio di Trebisacce (Bettelli 2002, 30–31 no. 67, with literature; for settlement pattern *cf.* Vanzetti 2000). Here, during local Bronzo Recente, the 'Casa centrale' (Peroni *et al.* 2004, 173–175) is nothing more than a hut a little bigger than normal and located in a prominent position on the so-called acropolis; material culture from this building has been interpreted as evidence not so much of domestic residential activities and more of communal ritual practices, as seems to be suggested by the meaningful association of local and so-called Italo-Mycenaean pottery (Castagna 2002, in part. 248; 2004; *cf.* Borgna and Cassola Guida 2006, 157–158). Ritual consumption seems to have been, however, only marginally affected by Aegean component – though visible in the huge amount of Italo-Mycenaean vessels – and the ideology of banqueting seems to have been shaped by such constraints as local autonomy and resistance, as indicated by the evidence of a preponderance of local shapes among the individual open vessels suitable for consumption.

In the field of pottery production, as in other spheres, technological, economical, and generally utilitarian elements seem to have been almost exclusively involved in the dynamics of Aegean interaction (for a summary, Bietti Sestieri 2009, 2–24, with literature): The inhabitants of Broglio learned from their trade partners how to produce good pottery according to specialised Aegean patterns, which they used particularly for closed shapes suitable for storing and transporting goods. Most probably they also learned to adapt their subsistence economy through the introduction of such specialised activities as wine and oil production; furthermore, pithoi manufactured according to Aegean and Cypriot prototypes might point to Aegean patterns affecting storing activities (Borgna and Cassola Guida 2006, with literature). Meanwhile the inhabitants of Broglio seem to have remained unaffected by Aegean patterns in the field of symbolic and ideological behaviour, as is clear especially in funerary practices, which were not touched at all by the Mycenaean influence (Bietti Sestieri 2002, 422–423).

In this case strategies of interaction seem to have been less emulative and more selective than in the case of Thapsos; they would have prompted, however, a deep integration in a number of everyday activities implying long-lasting relationships most probably founded on patterns of residential interaction. In my view, the demographic perspective cannot be ruled out in this case, though the immediate presence of people from the Aegean does not mean a planned transfer of crafters, as has been sometimes suggested, but rather a non-systematic and unofficial, unrestricted flow of people moving under the pressure of social motivation in the context of a symmetric interaction (*cf.* Stejn 2002, 908). We could possibly infer that the structure of the local community, not consisting of independent peer groups and instead characterised by a central emerging elite, may have conditioned the modes of interaction: in this framework, Aegean elites would have interacted not so much with single members of the local community, as with the whole community gathered around one shared authority, which was not engaged in internal struggles and confrontation with peers. Selection of external cultural components would have been activated far from both competitive and emulative strategies and innovations would have been exploited for local purposes and possibly in the dialogue with the population of the hinterland.

In conclusion, I would propose the following points for discussion:

- Interaction seems to have been intense and mainly active in the field of ideology, when in the local communities existing structured elites, as in Cyprus, or independent and competing groups, as in Sicily, receive external components through strategies of emulation. Though not highly selective, such strategies favour the adaptation of the new elements to local contexts through important transformation processes that vary according to the degree of local socio-political complexity and integration;
- In the so-called 'simple' societies, or in 'group-oriented' communities, ideological resistance is much more visible and external components are submitted to drastic selection processes, though local adaptation may be less evident. Exchange and interaction affect more the fields of subsistence and technology than ideology, and favour a kind of integration that may result in being a very deep, well-rooted and permanent phenomenon.

In such a case, a positive feedback loop may affect the ideological domain of the primary counterpart society: partnership and affiliation with the new mixed societies, which developed at the local level, may become objects of competition and contention through the adoption of new status symbols: Italian objects, such as swords, tools, and ornaments, in Late Mycenaean Greece could be interpreted as symbols of display of special social and economic partnership and, finally, as markers of new mixed cultural identities (*cf.* Borgna and Cassola Guida 2006, 160; on Italian bronzes in Greece see Bettelli 2002, 117–137; Jung 2006, 51–57, with literature).

Acknowledgements

I would like to thank Joseph Maran and Philipp Stockhammer for inviting me to speak at Heidelberg, where, while enjoying a warm hospitality, I had the opportunity to benefit from a stimulating conference and many useful comments which I have tried to take into account in my contribution. I am also grateful to Dimitris Grigoropoulos for revising my English.

Notes

1. For the Aegean world, see recently Wright (2004a); Halstead and Barrett (2004); Mee and Renard (2007); Hitchcock, Laffineur and Crowley (2008, with previous literature); for anthropological accounts, see for instance Dietler and Hayden (2001); Jones (2007); in the field of interaction studies *cf.* Dietler (1998).
2. For the centrality of courts in the Minoan human landscape see *e.g.* Driessen (2002); in the Mycenaean architectural layout Cavanagh (2001); for the function of the courts in the Mycenaean citadels *cf.* Maran (2006 with literature); on the theme of feasting see now Hitchcock (2008).
3. If the wide doors served as access for chariots according to an opinion that has been supported for instance by Darcque (2005, 361–366) in the case of Gla, this argument can not ne used to explain why an opening 2.50 m large would have served also the small room 98 which was surely not large enough to house chariots; the front portico would also have been an obstacle to the movement of chariots.
4. Furthermore, she (2003, 185 and n. 23; 2004, 116) relates at least a some of the many sherds from kylikes to possibile inclusions from mud-bricks. Apart from tiny and worn sherds, which Blegen himself considered as possibly coming from mud-brick inclusions, I believe the depositional, dimensional and preservation data should help in identifying pottery that is in its original depositional context and even filling deposits which, though not *in situ*, are mostly originated by discard and sealing of pottery belonging, in some way, to the life-cycle of the structures where they were found.

   In my view, the case of sealings and tablets is more ambiguous, all the more so when we consider the observations by Blegen (Blegen and Rawson1966, 316, 320: Rooms 98 and 99), who claimed to have found pieces of tablets mixed to the 'reddish clay of disintegrated mud-bricks'.

5. For the dominant ritual setting in the iconography of chariots *cf.* in particular the representation of a procession of chariots towards a shrine on a well-known krater from Kalavasos-Ayios Dhimitrios, Cyprus (Steel 1994; Rystedt 2001) and the feasting framework of the chariot racing on a much-debated pictorial fragment from Tiryns: Kilian (1980); Wright (2004b, 45 fig. 17); see also the Enkomi krater with a chariot associated with a drinking set (Wright 2004b, 49 fig. 18; Müller-Celka 2005).
6. Among the many stone bases near the inner walls of room 99 that have been interpreted as supports for shelves, some are placed at a distance of 1.35–1.40 from the walls (Blegen and Rawson 1966, 319–320) and could rather indicate the presence of benches for sitting or reclining; for a row of central supports in an early phase of the building, see Westerburg (2001, 5).
7. A ritual use can be suggested during the early phase of occupation as a result of the so-called 'shaft-grave' under Room 97, which included precious materials and pottery dating to the early Mycenaean periods and even the Middle Bronze Age. The small number of associated bones, however, were 'not identified as humans' (Blegen and Rawson 1966, 313) and might suggest a ritual use very much alike the one of shaft 173 in Kalavasos-Ayios Dhimitrios (see below).
8. For this and for *stoa* FG see Cucuzza (2001; 2003, with literature); in general on the Ayia Triada *stoai* including Neopalatial *stoa* 10 see also Halbherr, Stefani and Banti (1977, 204*ff.*); Puglisi (2003, 165–172); a progressive restriction of the circulation may be inferred also at Kommos where the North stoa seems to have been closed by a wall substituting the columns towards the end of the Neopalatial or the beginning of the Late Palatial period (Shaw 1986, phase 3a; Shaw and Shaw 2006, 35–38).
9. On excavations of the settlement: Voza (1972; 1973; 1980–1981, 675–680; 1984–1985, 666–668); for interpretation see, with literature, Militello (2004; 2005); in the context of Aegean interaction, see furthermore van Wijngaarden (2002, 229–236; 2007); on the problem of colonisation see Kilian (1990, 455–456 (trading port); *cf.* Karageorghis 1990, 26); in terms of acculturation see Tanasi (2009, 51–52, with recent literature).

References

Alberti, G. (2006) Per una 'gerarchia sociale' a Thapsos: analisi contestuale delle evidenze funerarie e segni di stratificazione. *Rivista di Scienze Preistoriche* 56, 369–427.

Antoniadou, S. (2007) Common Materials, Different Meanings: Changes in Late Cypriot Society. In S. Antoniadou and A. Pace (eds), *Mediterranean Crossroads*, 483–508. Athens, Pierides Foundation.

Avila, R. A. J. (1983) *Lanzen- und Pfeilspitzen der griechischen Spätbronzezeit*. Prähistorische Bronzefunde Abteilung 5, 1. München, Beck.

Bendall, L. (2003) A Reconsideration of the NE Building at Pylos: Evidence for a Mycenaean Redistributive Center. *American Journal of Archaeology* 107, 181–231.

Bendall, L. (2004) Fit for a King? Hierarchy, Exclusion, Aspiration and Desire in the Social Structure of Mycenaean Banqueting. In Halstead and Barrett 2004, 105–135.

Bendall, L. (2007) *Economics of Religion in the Mycenaean World. Resources Dedicated to Religion in the Mycenaean Palace Economy.* Oxford, Oxford University School of Archaeology.

Bergquist, B. (1990) Primary or Secondary Temple Function: the Case of Halieis. *Opuscula Atheniensia* 18, 23–37.

Bergquist, B. (1998) Feasting of Worshippers or Temple and Sacrifice? The Case of the Herakleion on Thasos. In R. Hägg (ed.), *Ancient Greek Cult Practice from the Archaeological Evidence, Proceedings of the Fourth International Seminar on Ancient Greek Cult at the Swedish Institute at Athens, 22–24 October 1993*, 57–72. Stockholm, Åströms.

Bernabò Brea, L. (1990) *Pantalica. Ricerche intorno all'Anaktoron*. Naples, Centre J. Berard.

Bettelli, M. (2002) *Italia meridionale e mondo miceneo. Ricerche su dinamiche di acculturazione e aspetti archeologici, con particolare riferimento ai versanti adriatico e ionico della penisola italiana*. Firenze, All'Insegna del Giglio.

Bietti Sestieri, A. M. (2002) Mediterranean Interaction in the Second and Early First Millennium BC. In B. Cunliffe, W. Davies and C. Renfrew (eds), *Archaeology. The Widening Debate*, 411–438. Oxford, Oxford University Press.

Bietti Sestieri, A. M. (2009) L'età del bronzo finale nella penisola italiana. *Padusa* 44, 7–54.

Blanton, R. *et al.* (1996) A Dual-Processual Theory for the Evolution of the Mesoamerican Civilization. *Current Anthropology* 37, 1–14.

Blegen, C. W. and Rawson, M. (1966) *The Palace of Nestor at Pylos in Western Messenia, I: The Buildings and their Contents*. Princeton, Princeton University Press.

Borgna, E. (1992) *L'arco e le frecce nel mondo miceneo*. Roma, Accademia Nazionale dei Lincei.

Borgna, E. (1997) Kitchen-ware from LM IIIC Phaistos. Cooking Tradition and Ritual Activities in Late Bronze Age Cretan Society. *Studi Micenei ed Egeo-Anatolici* 39/2, 189–217.

Borgna, E. (1999) Circolazione e uso della ceramica nello scambio cerimoniale tra mondo miceneo palaziale e Creta tardominoica: la prospettiva di Festòs nel TM III. In V. La Rosa, D. Palermo and L. Vagnetti (eds), *Epì ponton plazomenoi. Simposio Italiano di Studi Egei dedicato a L. Bernabò Brea e G. Pugliese Carratelli, Roma, 18–20 febbraio 1998*, 199–205. Roma, Scuola Archeologica Italiana di Atene.

Borgna, E. (2003) *Il complesso di ceramica Tardominoico III dell'Acropoli mediana di Festòs*. Padova, Aldo Ausilio.

Borgna, E. (2004a) Native Traditions of Drinking at Phaistos during the Mycenaean Period. In Wright 2004a, 127–159.

Borgna, E. (2004b) Social Meanings of Drink and Food Consumption at LM IIIC Phaistos. In Halstead and Barrett 2004, 174–195.

Borgna, E. (2009–2010) Osservazioni su forme e luoghi di

culto in età micenea. *Annuario della Scuola Archeologica di Atene e delle Missioni italiane in Oriente* 87, serie III, tomo I, 168–189.

Borgna, E. and Cassola Guida, P. (2006) Note sui modi e sulla natura dello scambio tra Italia peninsulare e mondo egeo alla fine dell'età del bronzo. *Annuario della Scuola Archeologica Italiana di Atene e delle Missioni italiane in Oriente* 82, 2004 (2006), 149–180.

Brecoulaki, H., Zaitoun, C., Stocker, S. R. and Davis, J. L. (2008) An Archer from the Palace of Nestor. A New Wall-Painting Fragment in the Chora Museum. *Hesperia* 77, 363–397.

Castagna, M. A. (2002) La ceramica grigia tornita dalla 'Casa centrale' (campagne di scavo 1980–82): una messa a punto. In M. Bettelli (ed.), *Italia meridionale e mondo miceneo. Ricerche su dinamiche di acculturazione e aspetti archeologici, con particolare riferimento ai versanti adriatico e ionico della penisola italiana*, 233–248. Firenze, All'Insegna del Giglio.

Castagna, M. A. (2004), I servizi da simposio in ceramica d'impasto e depurata dalla 'Casa centrale' di Broglio di Trebisacce. In D. Cocchi Genick (ed.), *L'età del bronzo recente in Italia, Atti del Congresso Nazionale di Lido di Camaiore, 26–29 ottobre 2000*, 263–267. Viareggio, Mauro Baroni.

Cavanagh, W. (2001) Empty Space? Courts and Squares in Mycenaean Towns. In K. Branigan (ed.), *Urbanism in the Aegean Bronze Age*, 119–140. London and New York, Oxbow, Sheffield Academic Press.

Coulton, J. J. (1976) *The Architectural Development of the Greek Stoa*. Oxford, Oxford University Press.

Cucuzza, N. (2001) Religion and Architecture: Early LM IIIA 2 Buildings in the Southern Area of Haghia Triada. In Laffineur and Hägg 2001, 169–174.

Cucuzza, N. (2003) Il volo del grifo: osservazioni sulla Haghia Triada 'Micenea'. *Creta Antica* 4, 199–272.

Cucuzza, N. and Hellner, N. (2009), A LM III propylon at Haghia Triada, *Creta Antica* 10/2, 501–518.

D'Agata, A. L. (1987) Un tipo vascolare della cultura di Thapsos. *Studi Micenei ed Egeo-Anatolici* 26, 187–198.

D'Agata, A. L. (2000) Interactions between Aegean Groups and Local Communities in Sicily in the Bronze Age. The Evidence from Pottery. *Studi Micenei ed Egeo-Anatolici* 42, 41–83.

Darcque, P. (2005) *L'habitat mycénien. Formes et fonctions de l'éspace bati en Grèce continentale à la fin di IIe millénaire avant J.-C.* Athènes, École Française d'Athènes.

DeMarrais, E., Castillo, L. J. and Earle, T. (1996) Ideology, Materialization, and Power Strategies. *Current Anthropology* 31, 15–31.

Dietler, M. (1998) Consumption, Agency, and Cultural Entanglement: Theoretical Implications of a Mediterranean Colonial Encounter. In J. Cusick (ed.), *Studies in Culture Contact: Interaction, Culture Change and Archaeology*, 288–315. Carbondale, Center for Archaeological Investigations.

Dietler, M. and Hayden, B. (2001) *Feasts: Archaeological and Ethnographic Perspectives on Food, Politics, and Power*. Washington D.C., Smithsonian Institution press.

Doonan, O. (2001) Domestic Architecture and Settlement Planning in Early and Middle Bronze Age Sicily: Thoughts on Innovation and Social Process. *Journal of Mediterranean Archaeology* 14/2, 159–188.

Driessen, J. (1989–1990) The Proliferation of Minoan Palatial Architectural Style: (I) Crete. *Acta Archaeologica Lovaniensia* 28–29, 3–23.

Driessen, J. (2002) 'The King must Die.' Some Observations on the Use of Minoan Court Compounds. In J. Driessen, I. Schoep and R. Laffineur (eds), *Monuments of Minos. Rethinking the Minoan Palaces*, Proceedings of the International Workshop 'Crete of the Hundred Palaces?' held at the Université Catholique de Louvain, Louvain-la Neuve, 14–15 December 2001, 1–13. Université de Liège – University of Texas at Austin.

Felsch, R. C. S. (ed.) (2007) *Kalapodi II: Ergebnisse der Ausgrabungen im Heiligtum der Artemis und des Apollon von Hyampolis in der antiken Phokis*. Mainz am Rhein, von Zabern.

Flouda, G. S. (2000) Inscribed Pylian Nodules: Their Use in the Administration of the Storerooms of the Pylian Palace. *Studi Micenei ed Egeo-Anatolici* 42/2, 213–245.

French, E. B. and Taylour, W. D. (2007) *The Service Area of the Cult Centre*. Oxford, Oxbow Books.

Galaty, M. L. and Parkinson, W. A. (2007) *Rethinking Mycenaean Palaces II. Revised and Expanded Edition*. Los Angeles, The Cotsen Institute of Archaeology at UCLA.

Guglielmino, R. (2007) Roca Vecchia (Lecce). New Evidence for Aegean Contact with Apulia during the Late Bronze Age. *Accordia* 10, 2004–2006, 87–102.

Guglielmino, R., Maggiulli, G., Pagliara, C. and Rugge, M. (2010) Indizi di comunanza di culti e riti tra genti indigene ed egee. In F. Radina and G. Recchia (eds), *Ambra per Agamennone. Indigeni e Micenei tra Adriatico, Ionio ed Egeo*. Bari, Palazzo Simi e Museo Civico, 28 maggio–16 ottobre 2010, 129–139. Bari, Mario Adda Editore.

Halbherr, F., Stefani, E. and Banti, L. (1977) Haghia Triada nel periodo tardo palaziale. *Annuario della Scuola Archeologica Italiana di Atene e delle Missioni italiane in Oriente* 55, 13–296.

Halstead, P. and Barrett, J. C. (2004) *Food, Cuisine and Society in Prehistoric Greece*. Oxford, Oxbow Books.

Hayden, B. (1982) The Derivation and Architectural Context of Cretan Bronze Age Stoas. *Archaeological News* 11, 1–7.

Hayden, B. (1984) Late Bronze Age Tylissos. *Expedition* 3, 37–46.

Hiesel, G. (1990) *Späthelladische Hausarchitektur. Studium zur Architekturgeschichte des griechischen Festlandes in der späten Bronzezeit*. Mainz am Rhein, von Zabern.

Hitchcock, L. (2008) Architecture of Feasting. In Hitchcock, Laffineur and Crowley 2008, 317–326.

Hitchcock, L. A., Laffineur, R. and Crowley, J. (2008) *Dais. The Aegean Feast*, Proceedings of the 12th International Aegean

Conference, University of Melbourne, Centre for Classics and Archaeology, 25–29 March 2008. *Aegaeum* 29, 317–326. Université de Liège – University of Texas at Austin.

Hofstra, S. U. (2000), *Small Things Considered: the Finds from LH IIIB Pylos*, PhD Thesis, University of Texas at Austin.

Iakovidis, S. (1989) *Γλας. Ανασκαφή 1955–1961*. Αθήναι, Η εν Αθήναις αρχαιολογική Εταιρεία.

Iakovidis, S. (1998) *Γλας. Ανασκαφή 1981–1991*. Αθήναι, Η εν Αθήναις αρχαιολογική Εταιρεία.

Iakovidis, S. (2001) *Gla and the Kopais in the 13th Century B.C.* Athens, The Archaeological Society in Athens.

Immerwahr, S. A. (1990) *Aegean Painting in the Bronze Age*. Princeton, Pennsylvania State University Press.

Jones, M. (2007) *Why Humans share Food*. Oxford, Oxford University Press.

Jung, R. (2006) *CHRONOLOGIA COMPARATA. Vergleichende Chronologie von Südgriechenland und Süditalien von ca. 1700/1600 bis 1000 v.u.Z.* Wien, Verlag der Österreichischen Akademie der Wissenschaften.

Karageorghis, V. (1990) *The End of the Late Bronze Age in Cyprus*. Nicosia, Pierides Foundation.

Kilian, K. (1980) Zur Darstellung eines Wagenrennens aus spätmykenischer Zeit. *Athenische Mitteilungen* 86, 21–31.

Kilian, K. (1984) Pylos – Funktionsanalyse einer Residenz der späten Palastzeit. *Archäologisches Korrespondenzblatt* 14, 37–48.

Kilian, K. (1990) Mycenaean Colonization: Norm and Variety. In J.-P. Descoeudres (ed.), *Greek Colonists and Native Populations*, Proceedings of the First Australian Congress of Classical Archaeology held in Honour of Emeritus Professor A. D. Trendall, Sydney 9–14 July 1985, 445–462. Oxford, Oxford University Press.

Kilian-Dirlmeier, I. (2002) *Kleinfunde aus dem Athena Itonia-Heiligtum bei Philia (Thessalien)*. Mainz, von Zabern.

Killen, J. T. (1994) Thebes, Sealings, Knossos Tablets, and Mycenaean State Banquets. *Bulletin of the Institute of Classical Studies, University of London* 39, 67–89.

Knapp, A. B. (2008) *Prehistoric and Protohistoric Cyprus: Identity, Insularity and Connectivity*. Oxford, Oxford University Press.

Kyriakidis, E. (2005) *Ritual in the Bronze Age Aegean: the Minoan Peak Sanctuaries*. London, Duckworth.

Laffineur, R. and Hägg, R. (2001), *Potnia: Deities and Religion in the Aegean Bronze Age*, Proceedings of the 8th International Aegean Conference/8e Rencontre égéenne internationale. Göteborg, Göteborg University, 12–15 April 2000. *Aegaeum* 22. Université de Liège–University of Texas at Austin.

La Rosa, V. (1977) La ripresa dei lavori ad Haghia Triada: relazione preliminare sui saggi del 1977. *Annuario della Scuola Archeologica Italiana di Atene e delle Missioni italiane in Oriente* 55, 297–342.

La Rosa, V. (1979-1980) Haghia Triada II: relazione preliminare sui saggi del 1978 e 1979. *Annuario della Scuola Archeologica Italiana di Atene e delle Missioni italiane in Oriente* 57–58, 1979–1980, 49–164.

Lupack, S. (2007) Palaces, Sanctuaries, and Workshops: The Role of the Religious Sector in Mycenaean Economics. In Galaty and Parkinson 2007, 54–65.

Lupack, S. (2008) *The Role of the religious Sector in the Economy of Late Bronze Age Mycenaean Greece*. Oxford, Archaeopress.

Maran, J. (2006) Mycenaean Citadels as Performative Space. In Maran, Juwig, Schwengel and Thaler 2006, 75–88.

Maran, J., Juwig, C., Schwengel, H. and Thaler, U. (2006) *Constructing Power. Architecture, Ideology and Social Practice/Konstruktion der Macht – Architektur, Ideologie und soziales Handeln*. Hamburg, Lit.

Mazarakis Ainian, A. (1997) *From Rulers' Dwellings to Temples: Architecture, Religion and Society in Early Iron Age Greece (1100–700 B.C.)*. Jonsered, Paul Åström.

Mee, Ch. and Renard, J. (2007) *Cooking the Past. Food and Culinary Practices in the Neolithic and Bronze Age Aegean*. Oxford, Oxbow Books.

Militello, P. (2004) Commercianti, architetti ed artigiani: riflessioni sulla presenza micenea nell'area iblea. In V. La Rosa (ed.), *Le presenze micenee nel territorio siracusano*, I Simposio siracusano di Preistoria Siciliana in memoria di Paolo Orsi, 295–336. Padova, Aldo Ausilio.

Militello, P. (2005) Mycenaean Palaces and Western Trade: a Problematic Relationship. In R. Laffineur and E. Greco (eds), *Emporia. Aegeans in the Central and Eastern Mediterranean*, Proceedings of the 10th International Aegean Conference/10e Rencontre égéenne internationale, Athens, Italian School of Archaeology, 14–18 April 2004, 585–597. Université de Liège–University of Texas at Austin.

Müller-Celka, S. (2005) Le 'Cratère au Parasol', Chypre et l'Égée. Une histoire de vases. In I. Bradfer-Burdet, B. Detournay and R. Laffineur (eds), *Kris Technitis. L'Artisan Crétois: Recueil d'articles en l'honneur de Jean-Claude Poursat, publié à l'occasion des 40 ans de la découverte du Quartier Mu*, 153–170, *Aegaeum* 25. Université de Liège–University of Texas at Austin.

Pagliara, C., Guglielmino, R., Coluccia, L., Malorgio I., Merico, M., Palmisano, D., Rugge M. and Minnone F. (2008) Roca Vecchia (Melendugno, Lecce), SAS IX: relazione stratigrafica preliminare sui livelli di occupazione protostorici. Campagne di scavo 2005–2006. *Rivista di Scienze Preistoriche* 58, 239–279.

Palaima, T. G. (2004) Sacrificial Feasting in the Linear B Documents. In Wright 2004a, 97–126.

Palaima, T. G. (2008) Mycenaean Religion. In C. W. Shelmerdine (ed.), *The Cambridge Companion to the Aegean Bronze Age*, 342–361. Cambridge, Cambridge University Press.

Peroni, R. *et al.* (2004) Broglio di Trebisacce (Cosenza). In D. Cocchi Genick (ed.), *L'età del bronzo recente in Italia*, Atti del Congresso Nazionale di Lido di Camaiore, 26 – 29 ottobre 2000, 167–176. Viareggio, Mauro Baroni.

Puglisi, D. (2003) Haghia Triada nel periodo Tardo Minoico I. *Creta antica* 4, 145–198.

Ross Holloway, R. (1981) *Italy and the Aegean, 3000 – 700 BC*.

Louvain-La-Neuve – Providence (Rhode Island), Université Catholique de Louvain.

Rutter, J. B. (2004) Ceramic Sets in Context: One Dimension of Food Preparation and Consumption in a Minoan Palatial Setting. In Halstead and Barrett 2004, 63–89.

Rutter, J. B. (2006) Neopalatial and Later Minoan Pottery. In Shaw and Shaw 2006, 377–630.

Rystedt, E. (2001) A New (Old) Mycenaean Scene of Worship. In Laffineur and Hägg 2001, 393–399.

Schon, R. (2007) Chariots, Industry, and Elite Power at Pylos. In Galaty and Parkinson 2007, 133–145.

Shaw, J. W. (1986) Excavations at Kommos (Crete) during 1984–1986. *Hesperia* 55, 219–269.

Shaw, J. W. (1987) A Palatial Stoa. In R. Hägg and N. Marinatos (eds), *The Function of the Minoan Palaces*, Proceedings of the Fourth International Symposium at the Swedish Institute in Athens, 10–16 June 1984, 101–110. Stockholm, Swedish Institute in Athens.

Shaw, J. W. and Shaw, M. C. (eds) (2006) *Kommos. An Excavation on the South Coast of Crete by the University of Toronto under the auspices of the American School of Classical Studies at Athens. Vol V. The Monumental Minoan Buildings at Kommos*. Princeton–Oxford, Princeton University Press.

Shelmerdine, C. W. (2001) Review of Aegean Prehistory VI: The Palatial Bronze Age of Southern and Central Greek Mainland. In T. Cullen (ed.), *Aegean Prehistory. A Review*, 329–381. Boston, The Archaeological Institute of America.

Shelmerdine, C. W. (2008) Host and Guest at a Mycenaean Feast. In Hitchcock, Laffineur and Crowley 2008, 401–410.

South, A. (2008) Feasting in Cyprus: a View from Kalavasos. In Hitchcock, Laffineur and Crowley 2008, 309–315.

Steel, L. (1994) Representations of a Shrine on a Mycenaean Chariot Krater from Kalavasos-Ayios Dhimitrios, Cyprus. *Annals of the British School at Athens* 89, 201–211.

Steel, L. (2004) A Goodly Feast ... a Cup of Mellow Wine: Feasting in Bronze Age Cyprus. In Wright 2004a, 161–180.

Stejn, G. J. (2002) From Passive Periphery to Active Agents: Emerging Perspectives in the Archaeology of Interregional Interaction. *American Anthropologist* 104/3, 903–916.

Stocker, Sh. R. and Davis, J. L. (2004) Animal Sacrifice, Archives, and Feasting at the Palace of Nestor. In Wright 2004a, 59–75.

Tanasi, D. (2009) Sicily at the End of the Bronze Age: 'Catching the Echo'. In Ch. Bachhuber and R. Gareth Roberts (eds), *Forces of Transformation. The End of the Bronze Age in the Mediterranean*, Proceedings of an International Symposium held at St. John's College, University of Oxford 25–6 March 2006, 51–58. Oxford, Oxbow Books.

Tegyey, I. (1984) The Northeast Workshop at Pylos. In C. W. Shelmerdine and Th. G. Palaima (eds), *Pylos Comes Alive: Industry and Administration in a Mycenaean Palace*, 65–79. New York, The Archaeological Institute of America.

Thaler, U. (2006) Constructing and Reconstructing Power. In Maran, Juwig, Schwengel and Thaler 2006, 93–111.

Tomasello, F. (1995–1996) *Le tombe a tholos della Sicilia centromeridionale*. Catania, Consiglio Nazionale delle Ricerche–Università di Catania.

Tomasello, F. (1996) Un caso di progettazione "micenea" in Sicilia: l'anaktoron di Pantalica. In E. De Miro, L. Godart and A. Sacconi (eds), *Atti e Memorie II congresso internazionale di micenologia*, Roma–Napoli, 14–20 nov. 1991, 1595–1602. Roma, Gruppo editoriale internazionale.

Tomasello, F. (2004) L'architettura 'micenea' nel siracusano. TO-KO-DO-MO A-PE-O o DE-ME-O-TE?. In V. La Rosa (ed.), *Le presenze micenee nel territorio siracusano*, I Simposio siracusano di Preistoria Siciliana in memoria di Paolo Orsi, 187–215. Padova, Aldo Ausilio.

Vagnetti, L. (2000–2001) Preliminary remarks on Mycenaean Pictorial Pottery from the Central Mediterranean. *Opuscula Atheniensia* 25–26, 107–115.

van Wijngaarden, G. J. (2002) *Use and Appreciation of Mycenaean Pottery in the Levant, Cyprus and Italy (ca. 1600–1200 BC)*. Amsterdam, Amsterdam University Press.

van Wijngaarden, G. J. (2007) Sharing Material Culture? Mycenaeans in the Mediterranean. In S. Antoniadou and A. Pace (eds), *Mediterraenan Crossroads*, 453–482. Athens, Pierides Foundation.

Vanzetti, A. (2000) Broglio di Trebisacce nel quadro dell'Italia meridionale. In M. Harari and M. Pearce (eds), *Il Protovillanoviano al di qua e al di là dell'Appennino* (Pavia 1995), 133–171. Como, Edizioni New Press.

Voskos, I. and Knapp, A. B. (2009) Cyprus at the End of the Late Bronze Age: Crisis and Colonization or Continuity and Hybridization? *American Journal of Archaeology* 112/4, 659–684.

Voza, G. (1972) Thapsos, primi risultati delle più recenti ricerche. In *Atti della XIV Riunione Scientifica dell'Istituto Italiano di Preistoria e Protostoria in Puglia*, 13–16 Ottobre 1970, 175–205. Firenze, Istituto Italiano di Preistoria e Protostoria.

Voza, G. (1973) Thapsos: resoconto sulle campagne di scavo del 1970/71. In *Atti della XV Riunione Scientifica dell'Istituto Italiano di Preistoria e Protostoria*, Verona–Trento 27–29 ottobre 1972, 133–157. Firenze, Istituto Italiano di preistoria e Protostoria.

Voza, G. (1980–1981) L'attività della Soprintendenza alle antichità della Sicilia orientale. *Kokalos* 26–27, 674–693.

Voza, G. (1984–1985) Attività nel territorio della Soprintendenza alle antichità di Siracusa nel quadriennio 1980–1984. *Kokalos* 30–31, 657–677.

Westerburg, J. (2001) Ein Rekonstruktionsvorschlag zum Nordostbau des 'Nestor Palastes' in Pylos: die erste Stoa auf den griechischen Festland. *Archäologischer Anzeiger*, 1–12.

Whittaker, H. (1997) *Mycenaean Cult Buildings. A Study of their Architecture and Function in the Context of the Aegean and the Eastern Mediterranean*. Bergen, The Norwegian Institute at Athens.

Wright, J. C. (1994) The Spatial Configuration of Belief. In S. E. Alcock and R. Osborne (eds), *Placing the Gods.*

Sanctuaries and Sacred Space in Ancient Greece, 37–78. Oxford, Clarendon Press.

Wright, J. C. (2004a) *Mycenaean Feast* (*Hesperia*). Princeton, The American School of Classical Studies at Athens.

Wright, J. C. (2004b) A Survey of Evidence for Feasting in Mycenaean Society. In Wright 2004a, 13–58.

Wright, J. C. (2006a) The Formation of the Mycenaean Palace. In S. Deger-Jalkotzy and I. S. Lemos (eds), *Ancient Greece: from the Mycenaean Palaces to the Age of Homer*, 7–52. Edinburgh, Edinburgh University Press.

Wright, J. C. (2006b) The Social Production of Space and the Architectural Reproduction of Society in the Bronze Age Aegean during the 2nd Millennium BCE. In Maran, Juwig, Schwengel and Thaler 2006, 49–69.

13.

The intercultural transformative capacities of irregularly appropriated goods

Susan Sherratt

Introduction

Around the end of the second and the beginning of the first millennia BCE, one begins to find examples of what looks like an interesting phenomenon springing up in the Aegean and other parts of the Mediterranean, which may have some interesting implications for intercultural interaction and its mechanisms, as well as for its capacity to transform attitudes and practices, whether in the distant past or in the archaeological present. This is the appearance of what seem to be chronologically and often also geographically out-of-place objects in what might otherwise be supposed to be contemporary contexts, which range in date from the late 13th century to somewhere around the 8th century BCE. Some of these are objects from 10th–9th century graves at Lefkandi in Euboea (Carter 1998; Whitley 2002; Sherratt 2009), to which I shall return briefly below. Another very striking instance is the clay '*kernos*' from Tomb 122 at Perati in eastern Attica (Iakovides 1969–1970, fig. 114.866, pl. 126; 1980, 73, 105, 111, fig. 84): a Cycladic vessel, probably originally from the island of Melos and dating to the late Early Bronze Age or early Middle Bronze Age, but found more than 130 kilometres across the sea from Melos in a tomb whose contents otherwise belong exclusively to the early 12th century BCE. Another is the series of ivory plaques from an 8th century foundation deposit at the Artemision on Delos, the best known of which shows a helmeted and beshielded warrior and is certainly Late Bronze Age and probably Cypriot in manufacture (Krzyszkowska 1991, 116). Then there is the 'Tiryns Treasure', buried in a pit in the lower town at Tiryns, which Joseph Maran has recently argued was deposited in the 12th century (Maran 2006). It contains an extraordinary chronological and geographical mixture of items, including a gold signet ring which probably dates back at least as far as the 15th century BCE (Krzyszkowska 2005, 241–244, fig. 457), gold earrings or pendants in the form of bulls' heads of a type well known in Cyprus (Maran 2006, 137, Fig. 8.4a), and the famous amber and gold 'wheels', which find the best parallels for their amber bead type in Italy, the eastern Alpine region, the Adriatic and as far east as the Ukraine in the 12th–11th centuries, and for their gold wirework in central Europe (Harding and Hughes-Brock 1974, 155, 158; Ślusarska 2007). It also contains, among other things, a Cypriot bronze tripod stand, an iron sickle (or possibly knife) also likely to originate in Cyprus, a Hittite cylinder seal, and two bronze swords of European Urnfield (Naue II) type (Karo 1930, 135, pl. 37; Catling 1964, 195; Maran 2006, 132–134), as well as a bronze slab ingot, a bronze sickle, seven bronze vessels, the broken-off supports of a couple of bronze firedogs and fragments of gold and ivory. Finally, again in the 8th or 7th century, we have the curious phenomenon of bronze weapons (especially spearheads) dedicated at sanctuaries like Olympia and Delphi at a time when one can probably assume that iron versions were the functional military norm in Greece (Snodgrass 1971, 279–281, fig. 98). The mere fact that these are of bronze perhaps need not worry us, since, in the period in which they were dedicated, we can probably assume that bronze was a much more desirable medium for capital accumulation of the sort to which early Greek sanctuaries aspired than iron could ever be in a fully-fledged Iron Age. What is interesting, however, is that, while some of these were probably contemporary imports from Italy or the Alpine region (*cf.* Bettelli 2001), others, in terms of their technique, typology and evidently worn state, appear to be distinctly antique (Snodgrass 1971, fig. 98).

Chronologically out-of-place objects like some of those

mentioned above are often glossed over as 'heirlooms', a term not infrequently used by archaeologists when they recognise what seems to them a chronological anomaly but cannot think of any more specific way of explaining it (Whitley 2002, 226). Its use can thus be something of an interpretational cop-out, not dissimilar to the use of the term 'ritual object'. 'Heirloom', nonetheless, also rings some emotionally or intellectually comforting bells: the continuity of life and culture, and the sense that one is witnessing the transfer of a tangible material and cultural (not to mention personal) inheritance across generations; and a symbol of the long-term stability of populations or kin structures. Recently, 'heirlooms' have also had a tendency to transmogrify into 'symbols of the past', which can be manipulated in self-conscious attempts to incorporate a 'past' (real or imagined) into the present (*e.g.* Maran 2006). They have also become 'entangled' with *keimelia* (treasures, or treasured keepsakes, or 'objects with biographies'; Whitley 2002; Deger-Jalkotzy 2002; Maran 2006; *cf.* Bennet 2004).

Although I do not doubt the ability of antique objects found in a later setting to symbolise continuity with or manipulation of a past, or their potential to act as a 'biographied' memory of illustrious chains of relationships, it seems to me that there are problems in regarding some of the above objects, given their contexts, as 'heirlooms' in any meaningful sense of the word, as obviously or unproblematically forming links with past generations or as possessing readily identified biographies which would not have required a great deal of inventive imagination. In view of the 800 or so years and the distance which separate the Cycladic '*kernos*' from its final resting place at Perati, it is hard to imagine that it could have remained in circulation all that time, or (given its material) that it could ever have been regarded as a 'treasure' rather than a curiosity. And while the ivory plaque from Delos might well be seen as an example of the use of the past, one is left wondering why it was apparently a past which originally belonged somewhere else, and, more importantly, how it got there. Maran (2006) has suggested that the gold signet ring from the 'Tiryns Treasure' should be regarded as an heirloom but – regardless of the purpose of the assemblage as a whole or in part – given the geographically very mixed nature of the 'Treasure' and the very high proportion of metal it contains, some of which is incomplete or broken, one does rather wonder if the heirloom notion really provides an answer to the ring's actual history and how exactly it ended up where it did. Similarly, one might question whether the antique bronze spearheads dedicated in early Greek sanctuaries were handed down as heirlooms, or whether their history lay in something less romantic.

Here we might also consider some of those metal hoards found in both the East Mediterranean and the Aegean, the deposition of which dates from the late 13th–12th centuries and possibly in some cases also later (see *e.g.* Catling 1964, 278–298; Matthäus and Schumacher-Matthäus 1986; Knapp 1988; Knapp, Muhly and Muhly 1988; Borgna 1995). These hoards are exclusively metal, with emphasis particularly on bronze; they often contain an obvious element of scrap and sometimes of castings, and have frequently been regarded with some justification as metalworkers' hoards. One problem with such hoards is not only that they themselves may be difficult to date (and in some cases to authenticate as hoards), but that they have often – especially in the case of some of the Cypriot hoards – served as the main basis by association for dating individual bronze types found within them.

Further afield, it has sometimes been recognised or suspected that seemingly 'utilitarian' hoards from north of the Alps and round the head of the Adriatic as well as in Italy, ranging in date from the late 13th century to Late Hallstatt, may sometimes contain objects that appear to be several generations (or even centuries) older than the latest objects with which they are associated (Borgna 2000–2001, 296–307; Müller-Karpe 1959; Bietti Sestieri 1969, 270; Carancini 1979; Lo Schiavo, Macnamara and Vagnetti 1985, 43, 50, 62; Palincaş 2007; Gerloff 2007, 146; Maggiulli 2009, 211; Fischer 1973). Like several of the Cypriot and Aegean hoards, as well as the 'Tiryns Treasure', they may also contain objects which seem to be 'out-of-region', as we shall see below. Nor does this geographical diversity, at least, apply only to hoards. The late 13th century Gelidonya wreck, which had a noticeable element of bronze scrap (as well as smithing tools) on board, included fragments of Cypriot tripods alongside a Naue II sword of European 'Urnfield' type (Bass *et al.* 1967, 107–108, fig. 116; Bass 1991, 69).

The Makarska Hoard

A particularly intriguing example of a hoard which contains both geographically and chronologically anomalous objects is that known as the Makarska hoard, now in the Ashmolean Museum in Oxford (Fig. 13.1; Ashmolean Museum, accession nos. 1927.1218–1226). It was originally part of the collection of John Evans, and was given to the museum by his son, Arthur Evans, in 1927, almost 20 years after his father's death. The hoard, which consists of two flat axes, two chisels, a spear-butt, a large hammer, two shafthole axes and a miniature oxhide ingot, was in John Evans's possession by 1881, when he referred to three of the objects (the chisels and the hammer – which he called an 'anvil') in his *Ancient Bronze Implements, Weapons and Ornaments of Great Britain and Ireland*, published in that year (Evans 1881, 173, 183). In 1906, Arthur Evans, introducing the miniature ingot as a possible example of a form of early currency, stated that his father acquired the hoard from Makarska on the Dalmatian

Fig. 13.1: The Makarska hoard (Ashmolean Museum 1927.1218-1226. Reproduced courtesy of the Keeper and Department of Antiquities, Ashmolean Museum).

coast in 1880 (Evans 1906, 360); and Arthur himself, in an undated notebook which includes other entries which can be dated to 1883, sketched all the objects from the hoard under the heading 'Illyrian Bronze Age' and alongside sketches of bronze objects from the plain of Canali in Montenegro, the Unnac district in Bosnia, and the island of Cherso (Cres) now in Croatia (Fig. 13.2: Evans n.d. [±1883?]).[1]

John Evans mentioned the chisels and the hammer in *Ancient Bronze Implements* (Evans 1881, 173, 183), Arthur Evans mentioned the hammer and discussed the bronze 'ingot' in 1906 (Evans 1906, 360), and the ingot and hoard were mentioned in a footnote by Hector Catling in 1964 in his *Cypriot Bronzework in the Mycenaean World* (Catling 1964, 269 n.3). The ingot alone was noted by several people, including von Scala (1911, 17), Buchholz (1958, 95; 1959, 37 no. 57 (also for earlier references), pl. 5.5), Bass *et al.* (1967, 61 no. 75), Vagnetti (1967, with further references), with information mainly derived at second-hand from Evans. However, the hoard as a whole was never fully published until 1971, when Lucia Vagnetti described and discussed it thoroughly (Vagnetti 1971). Catling had already expressed doubts about the findplace of the hoard, noting that 'none of the objects would appear out of place in a Cypriot context' (Catling 1964, 269 n. 3). Vagnetti too expressed strong doubts about its Makarskan origin, and in the main body of her article suggested that the hoard derived from excavations of Cypriot tombs in the late 19th century and was brought to Makarska courtesy of the antiquities trade. However, in a postscript to the article she cited a letter written to her by Catling in which he suggested that a small village called 'Makrasyka', just south of Kalopsidha in south-east Cyprus, might have been where the hoard was actually acquired, and that John Evans, confusing his notes, could have assumed that the name of this obscure village was a mistake for the more familiar Makarska (Vagnetti 1971, 214).[2] The likelihood of this would depend largely on the circumstances of its acquisition by John Evans, who, on the whole – though he did undoubtedly occasionally make mistakes with his labelling[3] – was not generally in the habit of acquiring objects without having some clear idea of where they were said to have come from. In addition, there appears to have been very little in any of his collections with a Cypriot provenance (for an exception – a flat axe, see Evans 1881, 40 fig. 1). On the other hand, his son Arthur was based in Ragusa (now known as Dubrovnik), just over 100 km down the coast from Makarska, from 1877 to 1882 (Evans 1943, 182–258; Brown 1993, 20–26). A cryptic note accompanying the Ashmolean accessions register entry for 1927.1218–1226, which reads 'AJE 1879', might well be taken to imply that it was Arthur himself who initially acquired the hoard in 1879.[4] Since there is no suggestion

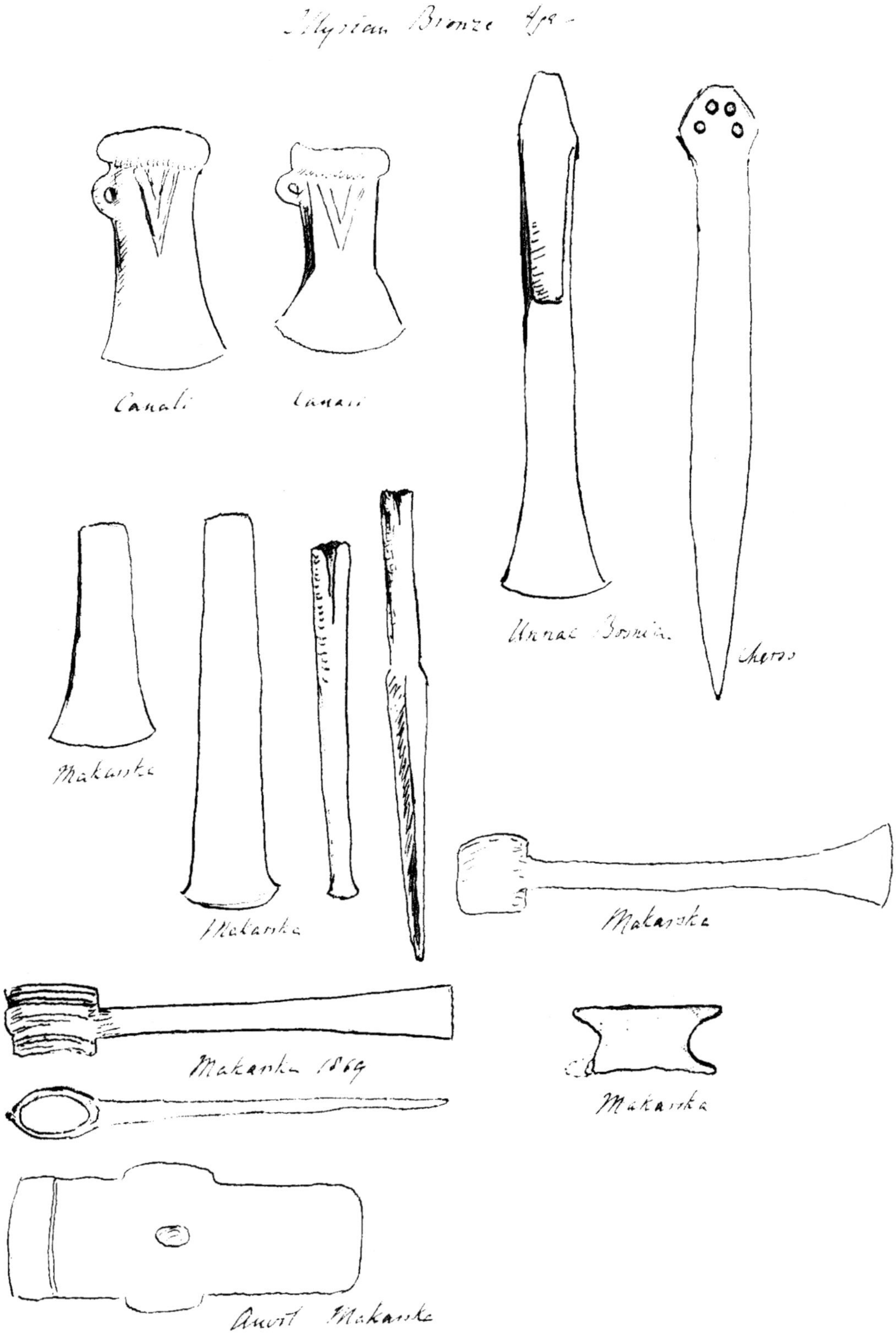

Fig. 13.2: Page from an undated notebook of Arthur Evans, with sketches of Makarska objects and other Illyrian bronzes. (Arthur Evans Archive, Department of Antiquities, Ashmolean Museum. Reproduced courtesy of the Keeper and Department of Antiquities, Ashmolean Museum).

anywhere on the part of either John or Arthur that it was acquired anywhere other than at Makarska, this could perhaps have taken place when Arthur passed through Makarska (as he would almost certainly have had to do) on his way to or from Knin in the Dalmatian hinterland, whither he travelled from Ragusa in January 1879 (Evans 1943, 217), or possibly when he visited Kulen Vakuf in the same region in March the same year (Evans 1943, 218). Although I can find no record of John having visited Ragusa in 1880, there was plenty of coming and going among members of the Evans family in 1879–80, which would have given ample opportunity for the hoard to reach John's hands. Arthur's sister Alice was with Arthur and his wife Margaret in Ragusa from summer 1879 until March 1880, when she and Margaret went back to England together (Evans 1943, 220, 222, 224); but also in summer 1879 Arthur, Margaret and Alice met up with John Evans and his wife at Rimini (Evans 1943, 222). The fact that Arthur knew about, and was obviously interested in, the hoard as early as the early 1880s suggests that he knew all about it from the beginning, and that there was none of the kind of vagueness about its immediate provenance that Catling suggested. Indeed, Arthur states quite categorically in 1906 that it was obtained from Makarska (Evans 1906, 360). Whether it was actually found at Makarska itself and whether it represents a single hoard are perhaps other questions, but there seems little reason to doubt that it was at least obtained there, and that both Evanses believed that it came from that region.[5]

Both Catling (1964, 269 n. 3) and Vagnetti (1971, 213) rightly concluded that most – and arguably all – of the hoard consisted of objects which would look very much at home on Cyprus, and that some of the objects could *only* be Cypriot in origin. In the 1960s and early 1970s it seemed virtually inconceivable that anything so unmistakably 'Cypriot' as the miniature ingot and the shafthole axes could have been found as far away as the Adriatic, and hence the notion either that Makarska was a mistake or that the objects had arrived there in the late 19th century. Those were the days when the idea of finding Cypriot ceramics at Tiryns seemed beyond the bounds of possibility, so that a White Slip II sherd labelled 'Tiryns' and very likely to be from Schliemann's excavations, given to the Ashmolean as part of the Sayce bequest in 1933 (Merrillees 2001, 100), was tucked away among other Cypriot material in a drawer in the Cypriot gallery, as indeed was the Makarska hoard (for Schliemann's friendship with A.H. Sayce, who was his chief intermediary at Oxford, see *e.g.* Traill 1996, esp. 222–223). However, since then, of course, the picture has changed dramatically. Cypriot objects, including ceramics and metalwork, have been identified in southern Italy, Sicily and Sardinia in contexts dating mainly from the 13th century BCE onwards (see *e.g.* Lo Schiavo, Macnamara and Vagnetti 1985; Vagnetti 1986; Ferrarese Ceruti, Vagnetti and Lo Schiavo 1987; Vagnetti and Lo Schiavo 1989; Matthäus 1989; Lo Schiavo 1995; Calcagno 1997, 159–162; Matthäus 1998; Vagnetti 2001; Hirschfeld 2001). These include such things as smithing tools, among them heavy hammers from Sardinia almost identical to ones from Cyprus, with the shape of some of the Cypriot hammers themselves very similar to the example from Makarska.[6] There are also fragments of imported Cypriot bronze stands from Sardinia and from central Italy (Lo Schiavo, Macnamara and Vagnetti 1985, 36–42, fig. 14, pl. II; Vagnetti 1986, 208, fig. 3.1–3). More specifically, metalwork and other connections between the eastern part of the Mediterranean and the Adriatic in the later centuries of the second and the early centuries of the first millennium have been documented and discussed in considerable detail and over a much wider range of artefact types over the last 20–30 years than I can possibly discuss here (see *e.g.* Bietti Sestieri 1969; Càssola Guida 1999; Borgna 1999; 2000; 2003; 2009; Eder and Jung 2005; Teržan 2007; Papadopoulou 2007; Borgna and Càssola Guida 2009 *passim*). Cypriot metalwork in the Adriatic region includes, among other things, a fragment of a Cypriot bronze tripod from a Hallstatt A1 hoard at Udje in Slovenia (Teržan 1996, 250, fig. 4; Borgna 2000, 46) and what E. Borgna has identified as a probable Cypriot bronze hemispherical bowl from a Hallstatt B hoard at Ehingen in Bavaria (Borgna 2000, 42–45, fig. 2). More generally, the pattern of amber distribution in the eastern half of the Mediterranean in the 13th–12th centuries (Harding and Hughes-Brock 1974, 152, fig. 3) tends to suggest that much of it was then reaching the Aegean and further east via the Adriatic, as opposed to its earlier route via South Italy and Sicily (Harding 1984, fig. 16). This includes the distributions particularly of Tiryns and Allumiere bead types, which show a strong Adriatic focus (Teržan 2007, 161–162, pl. XXXVIa; Barbarić 2009, 318). There is also the distribution of a particular design of ivory comb or its bone or horn counterparts, from the head of the Adriatic to Enkomi on Cyprus (Teržan 2007, 158–159, pl. XXXVb). Both of these serve as a reminder of the clear East Mediterranean connections at the site of Frattesina in the Po valley, where unworked ivory, ostrich eggshell and fragments of Cypriot rod tripod from the East Mediterranean combine with indications of silver production and the manufacture of amber and glass beads (Bietti Sestieri 1975; 1982).[7] In addition, there are Pare's arguments, based on a metrological examination of such things as the widespread 'pani a piccone' found in hoards of Final Bronze 2–3 (roughly the 12th–11th centuries) in central and north-east Italy as well as in Slovenia and eastern France, and on the so-called Pannonian 'cushion ingots' from Hallstatt A–B hoards in Hungary and Croatia, that from around 1200 BCE a new weight system, based on an East Mediterranean shekel unit, may have been introduced into the area round the head of the Adriatic (Pare 1999, 493–497, 506–508). And for what it is worth (and I remain unsure what to think about it), a clay spindle whorl with marks incised on it before firing, found with a number of other spindle whorls of Reinecke Bronze C/D to Hallstatt A1 date at Vatin in north-east Serbia, has been compared enthusiastically by E. Masson to the inscribed clay 'boules' from Enkomi of very roughly the same date (Garašanin 1983, 509, pl. LXXIV.2–2a; Masson 1971, 30–31, pl. III). Finally, there is the strong possibility that, when novelty bronzes of selected 'Urnfield' type started reaching the East Mediterranean and Aegean from the later 13th century onwards, many of these travelled down the Adriatic sea routes (*e.g.* Sherratt 2000).[8]

As already mentioned, many of the metal hoards which start to appear in the Aegean and the East and Central Mediterranean from around this time include a distinct element of bronze scrap. Moreover, several of them also combine Cypriot bronzework with bronzework of Central Mediterranean or circum-Alpine origin. Around this time, too, as the evidence from sites such as Enkomi and Kition clearly shows, Cyprus itself was heavily into recycling bronze (Karageorghis and Kassianidou 1999). Leaving aside the question of what individual hoards may represent – whether votive deposits perhaps with the additional effect at an economic level of helping to counter the effects of bronze inflation, or simply bronzeworkers' hoards which for some reason were never recovered, or combinations of both – at the most basic level they are an index of how much bronze there was in circulation over a very wide area of the Mediterranean and further north. The elements of bronze scrap found in hoards over a similarly wide area, together with the indications of the potential for precision weighing (Pare 1999; Ruiz-Gálvez 2000; Ruiz-Gálvez Priego 2008), also suggest that bronze circulation was often taking place in a more highly commoditised form than previously, with the capacity to be exchanged in individual transactions in small weighted units of bronze. The observation that a number of hoards (and the Gelidonya wreck) also contain smithing tools – as well as in some cases 'ingots' of various forms[9] – supports the idea that bronze-circulation, including the working (or 'tinkering') of recycled bronze, over a wide area but potentially on an individually small scale, was a widespread facet of life in the entire eastern half of the Mediterranean in this general period (Borgna 1995).

It seems to me that the Makarska hoard fits extremely well into this background picture. One of the shafthole axes is bent, while the other has an irregular fracture at the tip (Vagnetti 1971, 204–205, 214–15, figs. 2–3; de Jesus 1976, 222), and one of the flat axes shows signs of damage on the cutting edge (Vagnetti 1971, 207, fig. 4), as does the hammer (Vagnetti 1971, 211, 215, fig. 8). The socket of the spear butt is broken just above the cog pin (Vagnetti 1971, 208, fig. 6), and one corner of the miniature ingot has broken off (Vagnetti 1971, 210, fig. 7). All of the objects, moreover, are of tin bronze, with tin contents ranging from around 2% (in the case of one of the flat axes) to over 13% (in the case of one of the chisels) (de Jesus 1976, 221, 232). That apart, the miniature ingot itself (which has over 7% tin content) might also conceivably be interpreted as having been intended as a weighted unit of bronze, since its reconstructed weight, with a bit of good will, fits reasonably comfortably into a system based on a shekel unit of roughly around 9 grams (Evans 1906, 361; Pare 1999, 495–496). As such, it could perhaps be seen as either a product or a facilitator of the circulation of alloyed bronze in small commoditised units.

Given that there no longer seems any overwhelming reason to regard the hammer as a Roman anvil (de Jesus in Vagnetti 1971, 215), the miniature bronze ingot is arguably the latest easily datable object from the hoard, which may give us a *terminus post quem* for its deposition. It fits in with a series of miniature ingots of oxhide shape which appear at the end of the 13th and in the 12th century, above all on Cyprus (with at least 5 and possibly 7 examples from Enkomi alone) (Catling 1964, 268–269, pls. 49.h, 52.b. 37; Dikaios 1969–1971, 691 no. 1995, 729 no. 885, 764 no. 774, pls. 138.1–2,4, 147.35, 148.4–5, 171.14, 176.42; Masson 1971; Courtois, Lagarce and Lagarce 1986, 67, pl. XVIII.11–12; Knapp 1986, 25–29, tab. 1; Hadjisavvas 1986, pl. 18.6; Buchholz 1988), although a few outliers are found outside the island, for example in Egypt (Catling 1964, 269 n.3; Nibbi 1986),[10] and, most recently, a particularly tiny one as a stray find from Yabalkovo in the Maritsa valley in south-central Bulgaria, which has a tin content of just over 4% and weighs just under 4g (Leshtakov 2007, 450–451, pl. CIX.c) – a weight which would make it a little under one twenty-sixth of the weight of the Makarska ingot and approximately two-fifths of a shekel of 9.0–9.5g (*cf.* Pare 1999, 496). The generically not dissimilar Pannonian 'cushion ingots' (Pare 1999, 493–496) from 11th–10th century hoards at Kloštar in north-east Croatia and various places in southern and western Hungary, which have often been referred to as miniature oxhide ingots (Vinski-Gasparini 1983, 661–662, pl. XCIV.37; Mozsolics 1984, 33–34, 50 no. 9, 52 no. 13, 59 no. 47; Ilon 1992, 252–253, table I; *cf.* Borgna 2000, 47), may conceivably have some relationship to these, possibly in terms of metrology and/or function (Pare 1999, 496).[11]

There have been various suggestions about the function or intended purpose of the miniature ingots, ranging from a form of currency or possibly weights (Evans 1906, 360–361; Pare 1999, 495, 507) to votive offerings (Buchholz 1959, 19; Knapp 1986, 25–29), this last suggestion bolstered by the Cypriot inscriptions found on three of those from Enkomi (Masson 1971); another of the examples from Enkomi (Dikaios 1969–1971, 691 no. 1995, pl. 148.5) has a single sign inscribed on it. Although the Makarska ingot and the recent find from Yabalkovo have been shown to be made of tin-bronze, recent X-ray fluorescence spectrometry analysis of 6 examples from Enkomi (or possibly from Enkomi) and one from the Mathiati hoard suggests that these Cypriot examples are of unalloyed copper (Giumlia Mair, Kassianidou and Papasavvas 2010; I am grateful to Bernard Knapp for drawing my attention to this paper). It may well be, therefore, that the miniature ingots represent a range of related but subtly differing end purposes, linked chiefly by date (or at least a *terminus post quem*), by the symbolism embodied in their outward form and possibly also by their adherence to a regular weight system (Pare 1999, 295–296; *contra* Giumlia-Mair, Kassianidou and Papasavvas 2010).[12] Whatever one's views about lead isotope analysis, the suggestion that the Makarska ingot (as also the hammer) was made of Sardinian copper (Knapp and Cherry 1994, 116, 214 table 11) has at least the potential for some interesting implications (see also below), and in general would seem to fit quite well with other indications for the existence of a complex trade in highly commoditised recycled bronze throughout the Mediterranean from the later 13th century onwards (Knapp 2000, 42–45; Lo Schiavo 2003, 23–28).

However, as Vagnetti (1971, 205–206, 213) pointed out – and indeed this was one of the main reasons why she doubted both the integrity of the hoard and its Makarskan provenance – the elegant tin-bronze shafthole axes ought to be something like half a millennium earlier in date than the miniature ingot. They are a type familiar from the Middle Bronze Age in Cyprus, where a number of them are now known from Middle Cypriot tombs, for example at Dhali Kafkallia and Politiko-Chomazoudhia, in the Pera hoard (Åström 1977–1978, 11–12, figs. 7–8), or as objects in older museum collections with only vague locational provenances, most of them places in eastern Cyprus within easy reach of Late Cypriot centres such as Enkomi and Kition (Catling 1964, 66, pl. 2.d; de Jesus 1976, 225–226, pls. I–II; Buchholz 1979; Philip 1991, 80–83; Keswani 2004, 72, 80, 187, tab. 3.1; 2005, 380, fig. 16.a). Similar, but slightly different forms of axes are known from the Levant and elsewhere in the Near East in the Middle Bronze Age, but so far the variant to which the two Makarska examples belong is peculiar to Cyprus (Philip 1991, 81–82). It has very plausibly been suggested that most of the Cypriot axes without preserved excavation contexts originated in tombs (Åström 1977–1978, 39; Philip 1991, 80), and a Middle Cypriot tomb (or tombs) also seems a likely origin for the Makarska two, not least since the 'killing' of weapons by bending them is not unknown among Cypriot tomb material of Middle Bronze Age and later periods (Åström 1977–1978, 40; Buchholz and Karageorghis 1973, no. 1870; Karageorghis 2002, 127, fig. 287; *cf.* Vagnetti 1971, 205 n. 6, 215; de Jesus, Rapp and Vagnetti 1982, 14, 28, fig. 3.18). With the possible exception of the hammer and the miniature ingot (which one might not expect to find in tombs), Cypriot tombs of similar or later date could conceivably have provided most of the other Makarska objects, including the flat axes (with which Vagnetti saw particular parallels in Middle Cypriot III examples), and the (probably Late Cypriot) chisels and spear-butt spike – which, with their wrapped-around sockets, are of typical eastern Mediterranean manufacture.[13]

Vagnetti (1971, 213), indeed, initially concluded that the Makarska hoard must have been a collection of miscellaneous bronze objects rifled from Cypriot tombs of various dates before the end of the 19th century, which somehow found its way to an antiquities dealer in Makarska and was constituted there into a 'hoard'. This is certainly not impossible, but it does not solve the more general problem of chronologically (sometimes vastly) anomalous objects in archaeologically reliable contexts of the kind that we have met elsewhere (see also below). Before giving up on the authenticity of the Makarska hoard and on some other possibly anomalous Cypriot objects in unexpected places to which I shall turn next, it seems worth drawing attention to some observations that have been made about Cypriot tombs.

It is becoming increasingly clear that, particularly perhaps in the later 13th and 12th centuries – but certainly later as well – there was quite a lot of entering of Cypriot tombs for various purposes. Lindy Crewe has recently pointed out the evident importance of long-term accessibility to built tombs (and other tombs) at Enkomi, and the existence of a variety of evidence to indicate that people did indeed enter these tombs, sometimes apparently introducing grave goods from significantly earlier tombs located elsewhere, and very probably also taking others out (Crewe 2009; for possible examples of chronologically earlier objects also in Cypriot Early Iron Age tombs, see Coldstream 1989, 329–330). At Kition, the finding of substantial fragments of pottery, or more or less complete pots, of distinctly earlier date in the contexts of temple courtyards in the 12th century levels leads to suspicions that earlier tombs in the locality (many of which, when excavated, were found to be rich in every sort of material but bronze) may quite regularly have been cleaned out or had objects removed from them, perhaps in the course of new building work but equally possibly in the quest for bronze to feed the Kition recycling industry, much of which took place in those courtyards (see Karageorghis 1976, 28–31; 1981, 10–11; Kling 1989, 76–77; *cf.* Karageorghis and Kassianidou 1999, 172, 175). Part of a Late Bronze Age tomb complex at Palaepaphos-*Teratsoudhia* in south-west Cyprus seems to have been fairly thoroughly looted sometime between the Late Cypriot and the early Cypro-Archaic periods, leaving its one or two unrobbed (and possibly undiscovered) chambers unusually rich in bronze, while the looted chambers were actually knocked together to create a metal workshop (Karageorghis 1990, 18–24; see also Merrillees 1993, 10 for a couple of Cypro-Archaic pots left by 'intruders' in an Early-Middle Cypriot tomb at Bellapais-*Vounous*). Many other Cypriot chamber tombs of all dates also appear to have been robbed in antiquity, and it is evident from textual and other evidence that acquiring (or robbing) objects from tombs was a regular part of life in many periods in the Near East and East Mediterranean (*cf.* Oppenheim 1968, 87; Simpson 2000, 6). In Egypt there is plentiful written and archaeological evidence for the looting of tombs as a profitable way of gaining a livelihood during the 20th Dynasty and Third Intermediate period, some of it condoned or even organised at a high official level (Phillips 1992; Kemp 1993, 242–248); and tomb curses were frequent in the Phoenician world of the early first millennium BCE, implying that tomb robbing figured greatly in the minds of its inhabitants (Paton 1917, 897; Wright 2004, 356; *cf.* Ribichini 2001, 142; Honeyman 1939, 106–107).

Hook-tanged weapons

We could perhaps also glance briefly at the problem of another Cypriot bronze type which has turned up in some unexpected places. These are the notorious hook-tanged weapons (either daggers/swords or spearheads (Catling 1964, 56; *cf.* Philip 1991, 67–68)) found at various places in mainly western Europe, most of which found their way into museums or private collections in the 19th or early 20th century, and none of which have any reliable contexts. They gave rise to some debate during the last century between those who took them as evidence of East Mediterranean contacts with Europe in the early- to mid-second millennium BCE (and possibly as prototypes of the tanged spearheads of Arreton Down type in mid-second millennium south-west Britain) (Clerc 1927, 66–67; Childe 1927, 89; Benoit 1965, 64; Briard 1965, 60–62; Gerloff 1975, 149–152, 255–257, pls. 56.J–K, 64; 1993, 73; Branigan 1983; Harding 1989, 35–36; *cf.* Gallay 1988, 168–169, pls. 52–6) and those who regarded them as antiquities brought from Cyprus in the later 19th century, which were then either sold, or lost or discarded and later found again (Déchelette 1910, 195; Reinecke 1933; Watkins 1976; Csornay-Caprez 2000, 8). Dirk Brandherm (2000) has recently revisited the problem, and divided them into what are considered to be actual imports and local 'imitations'. If we ignore those that arguably have nothing to do with Cypriot hook-tanged weapons, which include the 'imitations' and one or two of the 'imports' (see *e.g.* Royal Society of Antiquaries of Ireland 1910; Lo Schiavo, Macnamara and Vagnetti 1985, 9, fig. 3; Gallay 1988, pls. 55.1633–5, 56.1638; Brandherm 2000, 25–32 nos. 1, 19–20, 22–23, 32–34, 36–41, figs. 1.b, 3, 5–6), we are left with a total of around 31 examples. Of these, the find circumstances of 7 (over 22%) are totally unknown, 5 (just over 16%) are single stray finds (including one supposedly from a river), and 18 (58%) are thought to belong to hoards of uncertain integrity and provenance, concentrated in western France and south-west England, with an outlier in the Carpathian basin (Brandherm 2000, 25–29, map). Typologically and chronologically, in Cypriot terms, they range from Early Cypriot to Late Cypriot I (Gerloff 1975, 255–257, based on Catling 1964, 56–59; *cf.* Csornay-Caprez 2000, 8). Those that have any claimed associations tend to be with flat axes of types that could equally well be Cypriot in origin and fall within a similar date range (*cf. e.g.* Briard 1965, 60–61, fig. 15.A), although one example of a convincingly Cypriot-looking hook-tanged weapon from Dricourt in north-east France was supposedly, according to some accounts, found in a tumulus with a flat-hilted dagger and an 8th century Italian fibula (Watkins 1976, 139; Gallay 1988, 169 no. 1627, pl. 54; Brandherm 2000, 25 no. 10).

Brandherm (2000, 2–5) has demonstrated fairly conclusively that an example in the Bad Dürkheim Museum in the Rhineland, long thought to be from a site near Neustadt-Gimmeldingen, was almost certainly imported from Cyprus in the late 19th century, shortly before it was bought from the same Strassburg antiquarian and prehistorian (Robert Forrer) who sold a number of Cypriot metal objects (including flat axes, a shafthole axe, a chisel and three hook-tanged weapons, several of them with an – albeit vague – eastern Cypriot provenance) to the Art and History Museum in Geneva in the 1890s (de Jesus, Rapp and Vagnetti 1982). It is, of course, quite possible, and Watkins (1976) has indeed argued, that something similar lay behind all the examples of Cypriot hook-tanged weapons which have been found or have turned up in western Europe. However, one cannot help wondering not only about the numbers (*cf.* Harding 1984, 171) but also about the majority of definite or supposed find-spots, which seem to show a distinct bias towards the Atlantic regions and the west generally (*cf.* Brandherm 2000, map). Alternatively, could it be that there are no more of these than of other items of Cypriot metalwork brought to the west in the late 19th century whose provenances were subsequently forgotten, obscured or muddled – and that it is only because 20th century scholars became so excited about the hook-tanged weapons that they have even been noticed?

To step aside from this conundrum, it seems to me that it need not, perhaps, simply be a question of a stark choice between import in the early second millennium BCE and import in the late second millennium CE. If we take the alleged hoard from Plouguernau in north-west France (Briard 1965, 60–62, fig. 15.A; Gerloff 1975, 255 nos. 2–8; Gallay 1988, 168–169 nos. 1624, 1626, 1628, 1633–4, 1637–8, pls. 53–56; Brandherm 2000, 26 nos. 11–13, 19–22), and forget for the moment the doubts about its integrity or findspot (*cf.* Watkins 1976, 137), we can perhaps glimpse something that might be thought of as analogous to the geographical anomaly and possibly to the chronological disparities which have been responsible for the doubt cast on the Makarska hoard, but for which I have tried to argue above that it is now possible to construct a plausble context in antiquity. The Plouguernau hoard (originally said to have been found around 1900 by a peasant in a grave near Aber Vrach in Finistère (Briard 1965, 60)) consists of 4 hook-tanged and 3 straight-tanged weapons, 2 flat axes and 2 flesh-hooks, for all of which a Cypriot origin has been suggested at one time or another. However, two at least of the straight-tanged weapons are not overwhelmingly Cypriot-looking, and in general seem closer to some of the tanged spearheads of Arreton Down or related type from southern Britain for which Gerloff has suggested the Cypriot hook-tanged weapons provided prototypes (Gerloff 1975, 148–152, 252–253, pls. 49.E.6, 8; 50.C.4; 51.4),[14] suggesting that in this case we may not have a hoard or collection of exclusively Cypriot objects.[15] In addition, although one can certainly find two-pronged flesh-hooks in Middle Cypriot tombs (*cf.* Catling 1964, 66, fig. 4.8 from Lapithos), it seems to me that the Plouguerneau examples might equally well be compared with what S. Needham and S. Bowman, in a series of typological studies of Atlantic flesh-hooks, have called their 'Class 1 unsocketed double-prong flesh-hooks', which they date between the 13th and late 9th centuries (Needham and Bowman 2005, 96–8, 108, table 8; Bowman and Needham 2007, 55–56, figs. 3, 22.a). A couple of such flesh-hooks, very similar to the Plouguerneau examples, come, for instance, from an impeccably documented hoard at Langoëlan in Brittany, about 100km inland from Plouguerneau and dated on other grounds to the 9th century (Needham and Bowman 2005, 108–111, 117, figs. 1.2, 7, tab. 1 no. 4). Thus, whether or not the Plouguerneau hoard as a whole preserves genuine ancient associations, it seems possible that its flesh-hooks could just as well be 13th–9th century in date and Atlantic as 19th–16th century and Cypriot, and it would be difficult to tell the difference. More significantly, perhaps, as Needham and Bowman (2005, 117) point out, there are reasons for concluding that this simple type of flesh-hook reached the west towards the end of the second millennium, ultimately from the eastern Mediterranean.

It strikes me that, if we were able to shift some at least of the 31 or so Cypriot hook-tanged weapons found in Europe, and perhaps their handful of accompanying flat axes, into the context of the period between the late 13th century and the end of the 9th century, we might find a third-way solution to the conundrum of the date of their arrival, which is *neither* early second millennium *nor* modern.[16] In the case of the Makarska hoard, crucially, the key to unlocking this kind of chronological and contextual conundrum lies in the *terminus post quem* provided by the miniature ingot and, even more importantly, in the general context of long-distance bronze circulation which links the East Mediterranean (especially perhaps Cyprus) with the Adriatic and Tyrrhenian seas from the 13th–12th century onwards, and for which there is now quite independent evidence. As far as the western hook-tanged blades are concerned, the clue might possibly lie in the flesh-hooks in which some sort of connection between the development of the Atlantic series and earlier East Mediterranean types (and practices) has often been postulated. Increasing signs of links in metal objects, both direct and indirect, between the East and West Mediterranean in the final centuries of the second and the first few centuries of the first millennium are now becoming evident. These include the articulated spits of Atlantic type from both Monte sa Idda in Sardinia and a 10th century tomb at Amathus on Cyprus (Karageorghis and Lo Schiavo 1989), and the growing scatter of East Mediterranean or East Mediterraneanising bronzes from hoards and burials of varied date within this time frame from sites such as Berzocana in Estremadura, La Clota in Aragon and Nossa Senhora da Guia in western Portugal (Mederos Martín 1996; Rafel 2002; Armbruster 2004; *cf.* Torres Ortiz 2008, 80–82; Rafel *et al.* 2008, 251–252; for the suggestion that the Berzocana bronze bowl might have arrived in Spain several centuries later than its date of manufacture, see also Lipínski 2004, 246 n. 94). These should be seen in the context of the increasingly impressive *koine* in metallurgy and metal objects which linked Sicily and Sardinia with Iberia and the Atlantic regions from the final centuries of the second millennium onwards (Giardino 2000; Di Stefano 2004; Lo Schiavo 2003; 2004; 2008; Albanese Procelli 2008; Armada Pita 2008). At the same time, there is the development of the Atlantic Late/Final Bronze Age in which we see common echoes in metal production and metal types all the way along the Atlantic seaboard, from Britain to southern Spain (Burgess and O'Connor 2008, 47–55). The 10th–9th century Huelva hoard (the remains of a shipwreck?) from the Rio Odiel estuary in south-west Spain (Crawford 1927, 106–107; Almagro Basch 1958; Bradley 2005, 157–160; Torres Ortiz 2008, 64; Mederos Martín 2008, 77–79), provides a good example of this long-distance link-up in metal types, since it includes a marvellous mixture of Atlantic swords and spearheads, proto-carp's tongue swords of probable Iberian manufacture and elbow fibulae of East Mediterranean and Sicilian type (Buchholz 1986; Lo Schiavo and D'Oriano 1990, 122–4, fig. 9; Mederos Martín 1996, 98–101; for the date, see Torres Ortiz 2008, 64 with further references). It also contains bronze scrap, and it is tempting to think of this large collection of mixed metalwork as an example in microcosm of the kind of trade and recycling of metal artefacts which characterised much of the Mediterranean and

Europe at this time and itself contributed to the creation of *koinai* in metalworking and metal types, and in many cases accompanying practices, from the Atlantic coasts to the shores of the East Mediterranean (*cf.* Figueiredo *et al.* 2010; Mederos and Harrison 1996; also Catling 1986a, 95; Maran 2004, 26). Now that we have firm indications of the presence at Huelva, by around 900 BCE, of Phoenician seamen, who, to judge from some of the amphorae they brought with them, had probably stopped off at Kommos on Crete and in Sardinia on their way (González de Canales, Serrano and Llompart 2006), it seems to me that we need not think *only* in terms of Middle to early Late Cypriot metalwork travelling west either in a period contemporary with their date of manufacture or in the luggage of a 19th century antiquities collector. Items like hook-tanged weapons could equally well have come out of East Mediterranean tombs several hundred years after they were deposited there, and been carried westward as part of the remarkable multi-directional flows of bronze objects, bronze scrap and itinerant bronzeworkers circulating around the entire Mediterranean from the late 13th century BCE onwards and by the 10th century (at least) articulating directly with Atlantic circuits.[17]

Antique East Mediterranean objects in 10th–9th century contexts: the evidence from Lefkandi

In support of the argument that examples of antique metalwork, perhaps most plausibly garnered from earlier tombs in the east, did indeed travel westward in the period between the end of the second millennium and the early centuries of the first, we can turn to some objects from the Early Iron Age cemeteries at Lefkandi in Euboea, a site which lies at a choke point on an important sea-route which links the southern and northern Aegean along the east coast of central Greece. These, unlike the Makarska hoard or the hook-tanged weapons, have impeccable contexts, since they come from properly excavated graves which can be dated on independent ceramic grounds. One is a bronze krater from the so-called 'heroon' burial in the Toumba cemetery, in which the cremated remains of a male were placed sometime around the mid-10th century (Popham, Touloupa and Sackett 1982, 172–173, pl. XXIV; Catling 1993); another is a granulated gold pendant found around the neck of a woman whose inhumed remains were buried beside him (Popham, Touloupa and Sackett 1982, 172, pl. XXIII.b; Popham, Calligas and Sackett 1993, 15–20); another is a single plate from a suit of bronze scale armour, which was found in an early 9th century grave (S 59) in the Skoubris cemetery, and was evidently worn by its last owner as a pendant (Catling and Catling in Popham, Sackett and Themelis 1979–1980, 251, pl. 239.(l)); others are a couple of bronze jugs with lotus blossom decoration on the handles from 10th and 9th century graves (T 33, T 39) in the Toumba cemetery (Catling and Catling in Popham, Sackett and Themelis 1979–1980, 249–250, pl. 243.(a)–(c); Popham and Lemos 1996, pls. 132, 143.(e)), and parts of a similar jug also from a 10th century Toumba grave (T 70) (Popham and Lemos 1996, pl. 143.(g)–(h)). These are especially interesting, because all of them are of eastern (in the case of the bronze jugs most probably Egyptian) origin, and all appear to have been well and truly antique or obsolete by the time they were deposited in these graves (*cf.* Carter 1998; Whitley 2002, 225–226). Apart from the scale plate, which had long been divorced from the rest of the armour,[18] none of these objects was in the best of conditions by the time it was deposited. The decorated bronze krater, which has been characterised as a Cypriot product of perhaps no later than the 12th century, had had its rim and handles broken and repaired sometime before it went into the grave as a repository for the cremated remains (Catling 1993, 87). Even more curious is the case of the granulated gold pendant, for which it has been argued that the best parallels are to be found in Mesopotamia a whole millennium earlier (Popham, Calligas and Sackett 1993, 15).[19] It, too, was badly damaged, with a large hole in the centre which must have been there before it was buried around the woman's neck. The bronze jugs are best paralleled in Egyptian tombs of the 18th and 19th Dynasties, and as far as one can see not any later than that (Carter 1998, 173–174).[20]

While there is often a temptation to label such objects as 'heirlooms', it seems much more likely that, rather than being carefully curated and cherished for centuries, these old, already damaged or *déraciné* metal items of eastern origin had already had checkered histories by the time their owners in the western Aegean got hold of them (*cf.* Catling 1994, 137–138). Some of the pre-deposition damage is of a sort which might well have been suffered in previous sojourns under the ground or (in the case, perhaps, of the pendant) in the course of hasty extraction from it. In view of this, it does not seem over-imaginative to suggest that they were hauled out of tombs somewhere in the East Mediterranean shortly before they made their way to Lefkandi.

Concluding remarks

Elsewhere, I have outlined the implications that antique oriental objects such as these from well-dated graves at Lefkandi may have for the construction of some aspects of an early Greek stereotype of the people they called Phoenicians, as these appear in the Homeric epics and later Greek literature, which in turn fed into an ideological construction of 'Greek' identity in relation to an eastern 'other' (Sherratt 2009).

Here, I shall confine myself to the more general suggestion that goods (particularly metal goods), irregularly acquired from earlier tombs in the East Mediterranean and possibly also elsewhere, contributed, possibly quite significantly, to intercultural transformative effects of an economic, cultural and technological as well as ideological nature within European and Mediterranean societies during the period from the late 13th century until well down into the early centuries of the first millennium. They contributed to the *mélange* of an increasingly 'globalising' trade in bronze and other metals, which resulted in Mediterranean-wide transformations and indeed in the process of 'Mediterraneanisation' itself. The effects of this included a gradual homogenisation of aspects of material culture and associated practices, as 'Urnfield' bronze types, such as swords, spearheads, pins and fibulae, become 'naturalised' in the eastern half of the Mediterranean, bringing with them new modes of fighting and quite possibly also dress fashions (Sherratt 2000), as incense-using and feasting practices associated with cauldrons and flesh-hooks spread to the west and perhaps those associated with metal spits spread to the east (Mederos and Harrison 1996; Armada Pita 2008; Sherratt 2004, 192), and as sheet-bronze-working spread northwards and westwards over Europe (Sandars 1983, 57). The creation of progressively more direct route- and exchange-linkages between the far east of the Mediterranean and its far west during this period encouraged regions such as Italy, Sardinia and Sicily to increase their manufacturing capacity of such commodities as bronze items or wine, olive oil and textiles, which then began to reach destinations in both directions. Meanwhile, the decentralised circulation of bronze objects in ever-increasing quantities (some of it abstracted from ancient tombs), combined with the circulation of bronze in scrap or recyclable form along with itinerant metal-workers, meant that bronze and bronze goods (including, incidentally, weapons) had become available directly to almost anyone who wanted them, thus subverting the tight control which eastern Mediterranean ruling elites had once attempted to exert over the bulk circulation and centralised redistribution of copper and tin, and contributing to their 'collapse' at the end of the East Mediterranean Bronze Age. What is more, this bronze inflation, which must have affected the value of bronze in the eastern half of the Mediterranean, turned the attention of copper and bronze-producing regions like Cyprus to the increasing production of traditionally highly precious materials like iron. One might also argue that it gave an added impetus to the search for silver, the traditional standard of exchange in the east, with effects which are obvious in Cypriot, followed by Cypro-Phoenician and Phoenician activities further and further west, culminating in the Phoenician arrival at Huelva by the end of the 10th century.

To return to the Makarska hoard, within this context I see no reason why we should not give it the benefit of the doubt and conclude that it may well be a coherent assemblage which was deposited in or some time after the late 13th century somewhere not far from Makarska, that several of its contents may well originally have been extracted from Cypriot tombs possibly in eastern Cyprus and that the whole may well represent the stock-in-trade and tools of an itinerant smith (*cf.* Borgna 1995). Rather more speculatively, we might perhaps also be tempted to suggest that some, at least, of the Cypriot hook-tanged weapons had similar origins and travelled westward and northward through the linked metal exchange networks in the same broad period. It seems extremely likely that the Early/Middle Cycladic '*kernos*' at Perati, and perhaps also the famous gold ring from the Tiryns treasure and the ivory plaque from the Artemision deposit on Delos had also once lain in tombs, the last perhaps in Cyprus; and it has similarly been argued that a handful of considerably earlier (14th–early 13th century) pots found preserved in 12th century contexts in the Unterburg at Tiryns were also abstracted from chamber tombs somewhere in the Argolid (Stockhammer 2009).[21] The same may well be the case with some of the antique and worn-out spearheads eventually deposited at Delphi or Olympia, and – highly speculative though the thought may be – something similar might perhaps account for the mysterious and often debated 'Aegina Treasure'.[22]

While some examples of this putative re-use of tomb-raided antiquities, like items from the Makarska hoard and perhaps the hook-tanged weapons, are perhaps best seen as playing a walk-on part in the systemic economic transformations which arose from the multi-directional, interlinked exchanges of metals which covered a wide area of Europe and the Mediterranean during these centuries and which in turn contributed to the social and cultural changes which accompanied increasingly widespread *koinai* in metalworking and metal types, others, such as the Tiryns ring and the Delos ivory plaque, may well, as Maran (2006) has argued, have helped to transform or actively create retrospective notions of a local or regional 'past'. Yet others, like the old or damaged items of eastern origin in Early Iron Age graves at Lefkandi, may, as I have suggested, have had a hand in shaping collective ideologies, above all, perhaps, in contributing to stereotypes of the 'other' against which an increasingly self-conscious Greek identity was gradually constructed in the early centuries of the first millennium (Sherratt 2009). Finally, such objects may, in some respects, have intercultural transformative implications for us, as archaeologists in relation to the past, not only in the sense that many of our typological chronologies, especially of bronze artefacts, have often previously been based on associations in hoards which, though their findspots and integrity as hoards may be much less suspect than those of Makarska, may nevertheless in some cases also include objects plucked from earlier tombs in distant regions shortly before they were deposited (*cf.* Catling 1986b), but also in the sense that they may remind us that, despite our love of abstract concepts of a generalising nature as vehicles for archaeological interpretation in prehistory, we are for the most part tracking the actions of individual human beings, who were often doing nothing more abstract than trying to find practical solutions to the challenges they encountered in the immediate economic, social and cultural circumstances in which they found themselves. Long-standing anthropological strictures based on observations of the diversity of human cultures have made prehistorians understandably wary of treating the past as too much like the present and of assuming, for instance, that people several millennia ago could have engaged in anything quite as apparently socially 'disembedded' or 'modern' as raiding the tombs of their own or others' 'ancestors' for their own profit or advantage. Yet numerous historical documents, including those of Egypt and the Near East, tell us otherwise. While 'heirlooms' can be regarded in many cases as a form of romantic retreat, recourse to theoretical abstractions derived from other disciplines, though perhaps one way of avoiding the perceived risk of anachronism, may nevertheless sometimes encourage us to leave the possible mechanisms which lie behind our primary archaeological observations unexplored in our haste to get on to more elevated forms of interpretation within an abstract conceptual framework. My aim in this paper has been not to question the validity or appropriateness of concepts such as 'appropriation of a past' or 'entangled' or 'biographied' objects (since one can well imagine that some of the old and damaged objects at Lefkandi, at least, arrived there with probably fictional stories attached to them), but to offer suggestions on contextual, if perhaps somewhat speculative, grounds for a mechanism which may have formed part of the background to a phenomenon which seems to have characterised some of the most transformative centuries in Mediterranean and European prehistory.

Acknowledgements

I am most grateful to Ruprecht-Karls-Universität Heidelberg, and to the organisers of 'Materiality and Practice: Transformative Capacities of Intercultural Encounters' (Prof. Dr Joseph Maran and Dr Philipp Stockhammer) for inviting me to take part in the conference and for their extraordinary hospitality on that and previous occasions, and to its various participants for all I learned from them during the course of the conference. My thanks, too, to Dr Susan Walker, Dr Anja Ulbrich and Dr Yannis Galanakis for permission (yet again) to raid the Ashmolean Museum's Cypriot collection and its Arthur Evans archive, and for permission to reproduce Figs. 13.1–2. I am particularly grateful to Dr Galanakis for providing me with a reproducible version of Fig. 13.2 as well as photocopies and photographs of various other items needed in the course of writing this paper. Responsibility for any errors or perverse conclusions rests, of course, with me.

Notes

1. The date 1869, written below the sketch of one of the shafthole axes from Makarska in the notebook (Fig. 13.2), may be a slip of Evans's pen, and he may have intended to write 1879 (see further below). On the other hand, 1869 might just conceivably denote the year in which the hoard was found or surfaced. Much depends on the date at which (and where) the sketches on this page were done, which we simply do not know – though it seems almost certain that all were sketched at the same time. I have not yet had the opportunity to try to track down the whereabouts of the first four objects sketched. If they were also part of John Evans's collections, then they could have been sketched in England at any time up to and including 1883 or even later. On the other hand, it is perhaps possible that all were sketched while Evans was still in the Balkans (between 1877 and 1882). For Evans's visits to the Unnac district of north-west Bosnia in spring 1877 and his excavation of a Bronze Age barrow in the plain of Canali in May and August of the same year, see Evans 1943, 187, 192, 199; Brown 1993, 21–2; *cf.* Evans 1883, 46, 60.
2. Vagnetti reports that in the same letter Catling went on to suggest that it was possible that some of the objects in the group might originally have come from the ancient (mainly late Early to Middle Bronze Age) site of Kalopsidha (*cf. e.g.* Åström 1966).
3. Though he was assiduous in attaching his distinctive blue-bordered labels to objects, John Evans never seems systematically to have catalogued any part of his collections (Evans 1964, 29).
4. Arthur is known to have collected antiquities for John Evans during his time in Dalmatia. See Evans (1943, 187) for a reference to 'a nice flat celt from Topolje on the Dalmatian-Bosnian frontier' acquired for his father.
5. John Evans (1881, 183) states quite clearly that the bronze 'anvil' and 'other instruments of the same metal' which accompanied it were found at Makarska, and Buchholz (1959, 37) was willing to accept this. Rudolf von Scala's enigmatic remark (1911, 17) that the original findplace of the ingot from Makarska was the island of Issa or Gissa, while interesting and possibly suggestive, has done little other than create confusion, since, although the island of Issa (modern Lissa) is the outer one of the group of islands which lies directly off the coast at Makarska, the island of Gissa (modern Pago) lies considerably further north than this and well out of the ambit of Makarska (see Vagnetti 1967, 29).

   For mention or discussion of the Makarksa ingot and/or hoard after 1971, see *inter alios* Åström 1977–1978, 40; Batović 1983, 276, 344, fig. 21.13; Marović 1984, 59; Lo Schiavo, Macnamara and Vagnetti 1985, 2; Bouzek 1985, 28 n. 9; Parović-Pešikan 1985, pl. 28.5; Knapp 1986, 26–8, pl. 4;

Ilon 1992, 252, tab. I; Borgna 1992, 86 (*non vidi*); Pare 1999, 495; Borgna 2000, 47; Glogović 1999–2000, 15; Csornay-Caprez 2000, 8; Harding 2007, 51–2; Barbarić 2009, 320; Tomas 2010, 201–2, fig. 8.8; Buchholz 2010, 336–338. Of these, Glogović, Barbarić and Buchholz (2010), at least, do not doubt that it was acquired at Makarska.

6. Lo Schiavo, Macnamara and Vagnetti 1985, 22–3, fig. 7.6–8; *cf.* Catling 1964, 99–100, pl. 11.a–c.; Vagnetti 1971, fig. 8. Vagnetti suggests that the scratches on the side and its weight in relation to the size of the shafthole may indicate that the Makarska example, like the one from Gelidonya (Bass *et al.* 1967, 102, figs. 112.B135, 113.B135), was used as an anvil, as John Evans believed. However, she also concluded, on these grounds and because of its similarity to a couple of iron anvils from Heidenberg in the Mainz Museum thought to be of Roman date (Petrie 1917, 40, pl. XLV.92,102), that it was likely to be later in date than the Late Bronze Age (Vagnetti 1971, 212–213; though *cf.* de Jesus in Vagnetti 1971, 215 for the likelihood of its primary function as a hammer). Like examples of hammers from Cyprus and Sardinia, the Makarska example has a round (or slightly oval) shafthole.
7. See Barbarić 2009, 318 for glass beads in Dalmatia (including on the island of Mljet), probably imported from the North Adriatic in Hallstatt A1–A2. For a glass bead from a tomb at Kastri on Thasos in the north Aegean, of apparently the same composition as glass manufactured at Frattesina, see Henderson in Koukouli-Chrysanthaki 1992, 804–806. It may be no coincidence that an iron knife from a contemporary tomb on Thasos has a bronze handle which lead isotope analysis suggests may be consistent with manufacture from Cypriot copper (Muhly 1996, 54). For a glass bead of similar composition and of very roughly similar date from Elateia in Phocis, see Nightingale 2007, 427.
8. For wind and current patterns in the Adriatic, which favoured northward navigation along the eastern Adriatic coast, with its myriad of off-shore islands, see Calcagno 1998, 214–216. See also Barbarić 2009, 318 for a marked increase in fortified settlements situated at strategic points for the control of communication routes in Dalmatia in Hallstatt A1, and for elite use of amber in this region.
9. For (copper) oxhide ingots or fragments thereof in the Central Mediterranean, including Sardinia, Corsica and southern France, see most recently Lo Schiavo 2008, 420–425; for the Oberwilflingen hoard in Baden-Württemberg, see Primas and Pernicka 1998. For bun ingots from Sardinia, see Begemann *et al.* 2001; while the majority of these are of copper, at least one has been found to contain 11% tin (Begemann *et al.* 2001, 51, 78 n. 5; *cf.* Knapp 2000, 43–44). For (bronze) bun and slab ingots from the Gelidonya wreck, see Bass *et al.* 1967, 78–82; and for an ambiguously bronze oxhide ingot fragment from the same wreck, see de Jesus 1976, 230. In the Aegean area, fragments of (presumably copper) oxhide ingots are known, for example, from the Poros Wall hoard, Tsountas' hoard and Mylonas' hoard at Mycenae (Catling 1964, 295; Knapp, Muhly and Muhly 1988, 248, tab. 4).
10. Ashmolean 1892.919 was acquired from G. J. Chester's collection after his death, and is said to have been bought near El Manshah in Egypt and thought to have come from Abydos. It is not clear why Catling (1964, 269 n. 3) says that it was said to be from Tarsus. Four more examples are known from Egypt (*cf.* Bass *et al.* 1967, 62, 172–174; see below, note 12) and one from Tell Beit Mirsim in the southern Levant (Albright 1936–1937, 54, pl. 41.13). The El Manshah example is discussed by Nibbi (1986), who suggests it may have been the base of a statuette, comparable perhaps to the those of the 'ingot god' from Enkomi (Buchholz and Karageorghis 1973, 163 no. 1741) or the bronze 'Astarte' figurine from the Bomford Collection, now in the Ashmolean Museum (Brown and Catling 1986, 34, pl. XIII). For a small (but not really miniature) copper ingot of rather unusual shape from the late 14th century Uluburun wreck, see Pulak 1998, 194, fig. 9.
11. For what has been claimed to be a sandstone mould for one of these 'cushion ingots' from Gór in western Hungary, see Ilon 1992, 244, fig. 6.2. This was found with moulds for a socketed axe, a spearhead and other objects. For a possible mould for a miniature oxhide ingot of indeterminate, but possibly relatively late, date from Sinda on Cyprus, see Buchholz 2003, 128–130, fig. 6.b.
12. The four miniature (or 'model') ingots from Egyptian Thebes, recovered by W. M. F. Petrie in foundation deposits in the funerary temples of Siptah and Twosre, are said to be made of sheet copper – presumably much flimsier (and lighter in weight) than the robust miniature ingots from either Cyprus or Makarska. At least one of them carries the incised cartouches of Siptah on one side (Bass *et al.* 1967, 173–174). They should probably be regarded as manifestations of a quite different phenomenon, as – for other reasons – should the example bought at El Manshah, if indeed it was originally part of a statuette.
13. In addition to two shafthole axes, the Pera hoard, said to have been found in a field near Pera in Cyprus, also contained several flat axes and a chisel (some of these similar to the examples from Makarska: *cf.* Åström 1977–1978, figs. 9.10, 19, 23.89). For the suggestion that the contents of this hoard (which also included a number of hook-tanged weapons and a three-pronged flesh-hook) may have derived from tombs and/or were part of a smith's stock-in-trade, see Åström 1977–1978, 39–40. If the two iron axes (Åström 1977–1978, 11, fig. 6) were part of the original hoard then it was probably deposited in or after the 11th century BCE. Otherwise, the objects are all of Middle or Late Cypriot date (Åström 1977–1978, 37–38).

I find it intriguing that the only two items from the Makarska hoard which lead isotope analysis suggests are of Sardinian copper are the two least likely to be placed in Cypriot tombs (Knapp and Cherry 1994, 214 table 11) as well as the two perhaps most likely to be either a tool used in metal recycling or a product of recycling itself. If I were not somewhat sceptical of the general usefulness of such analyses, I might be tempted to suggest that the results – which include the suggestions that two objects are of Cypriot copper, two of Sardinian, one of dubiously Middle Eastern and the rest of copper from unknown sources – might provide further reasons for believing in complex movements of bronze, including bronze for recycling, along the Mediterranean in the late 13th and subsequent centuries (Knapp 2000), and that the Makarska hoard is indeed a hoard of this period.

14. For some of the potentially confusing typological similarities between the two, which led to the suggestion that they might be related, see Gerloff 1975, 149, 151. The pitfalls of largely subjective classification are not helped by the lack of consistent, detailed illustrations of the Plouguernau examples. Gallay's drawings are taken from – but also seem to differ in several details from – Watkins 1976, fig. 1, which in turn differs somewhat from Briard 1965, fig. 15.A.
15. For results of spectrographic trace-element analyses of one of the 'daggers' and one of the axes from Plouguerneau and of four hook-tanged weapons and two flat axes from the Lhomme collection in Angoulême, see Briard 1965, 60; Gomez and Bourhis 1971, 50 (we do not know which of the Plouguerneau daggers is the one in question); and for neutron activation trace-element analysis of four hook-tanged weapons and seven flat axes from Cyprus in Geneva, see de Jesus, Rapp and Vagnetti 1982, 24 nos. 1–4, 6–8, 14–15, 17–18. While they might appear to suggest that examples known to be from Cyprus may contain substantial traces of zinc, their results are not only not directly comparable, but are most unlikely to be any sort of reliable guide to provenance (*cf.* de Jesus 1976, 223).
16. If the alleged association of the Dricourt example with an 8th century Italian fibula could only be substantiated, it might provide some more concrete backing for this hypothesis. Unfortunately, I have not been able to consult the original report (Fromols 1938).
17. For the Pera hoard, with its numbers of hook-tanged weapons as well as other objects similar to ones in the Makarska hoard, see Åström 1977–1978 and above, note 13. For the curious example of a Middle Cypriot (hook-tanged?) weapon with a Cypro-Syllabic inscription recording a dedication to Astarte by Abdimilk of Paphos, see Merrillees 1993, 10–11, (with reference to Masson 1983, 391, pl. LXXII.5–6).
18. For an overview and discussion of single armour scales from various contexts in the Aegean and East Mediterranean, see Maran 2004, 18–24 with the addition of Maran and Papadimitriou 2006, 118 n. 30. Some of these may well have been originally destined for recycling (*e.g.* most probably the example from the founder's hoard at Pyla-Kokkinokremos on Cyprus, and just possibly also the early 12th century example from the Unterburg at Tiryns which may be linked to a metallurgical installation, and that from the French excavations at Enkomi in the area of the sanctuary of the horned god, near where three of the miniature ingots were found [Giumlia-Mair, Kassianidou and Papasavvas 2010]). Others, however, are found in tombs, such as the three uncovered in Alaas tomb 12 in eastern Cyprus, which – perhaps significantly from the point of view of the later Lefkandi example – had evidently been looted in antiquity (Karageorghis 1975, 6).
19. See Nightingale 2007, 422, 427, pl. CVI.b for two faience beads which formed part of the woman's necklace of which the pendant was also a part. According to him, these two beads are Mycenaean and at least 250 years older than the date of the burial. See also Higgins in Popham, Sackett and Themelis 1979–1980, 225, pls. 173. Tomb 12B.3–4, 235.(b) for two moulded glass seals from a 10th century grave which may date as far back as the 14th century BCE; and Krzyszkowska 2005, 308–9 for other Bronze Age seals, possibly looted from second millennium tombs, in first millennium contexts.
20. Two further examples of these jugs, which Carter considers are also Egyptian and of Eighteenth to Nineteenth Dynasty date, have been found in a 9th–8th century tomb (Tomb P) at Fortetsa near Knossos on Crete, which also contained Cypro-Phoenician black-on-red pottery, a glass bowl and several other metal objects, including a bronze pendant of eastern appearance. Several more have also been identified among the miscellaneous metalwork deposited in the Idaean cave (Carter 1998, 172–173, pl. I.(a)–(b); *cf.* Hoffman 1997, 30–32; Matthäus 2000).
21. My guess is that, if they were removing clay pots from tombs, they were also removing other more immediately valuable items, which have long since disappeared. For the conjunction of metallurgical installations and Cypriots in the Unterburg at Tiryns in the late 13th–12th centuries, see Maran 2004; and for the periodic removal of metal items from Late Minoan IIIB tombs at Armenoi on Crete, albeit probably in more controlled circumstances, see Baboula 2000, 75.
22. The 'Aegina Treasure', acquired by the British Museum in murky circumstances in 1892, has long posed something of a problem, not only as to its date but also because of the markedly Near Eastern and/or Egyptian appearance of many of its items. Indeed, it has been suggested that much of it resembles the jewellery found in the tomb of Khnumet, a princess buried in Amenemhat II's pyramid complex at Dahshur in Egypt in the 19th century BCE (Schiestl 2009, 53; Markowitz and Lacovara 2009, 60; Fitton 2009). Various ideas have been put forward as to the date and circumstances of its deposition on Aegina, with the favourite for the last twenty years or so being that it could have come from one or more early Middle Helladic shaft graves on the island, like that of a richly equipped warrior excavated in 1981 at Kolonna (Higgins 1987; *cf.* Williams 2009, 15). However, Laffineur (2009) regards it as a secondary assemblage of objects of different periods and from different geographical areas, while Hiller (2009, 36) has expressed his belief that not only are the individual pieces heterogeneous in date but that the whole represents a Late Bronze Age tomb robber's cache. I would like to go further and suggest very tentatively that, although the objects themselves might belong to the early or mid-second millennium, they – or at least some of them – might not have reached Aegina until several centuries later. Around the time of its acquisition by the British Museum, a handful of Mycenaean pots also from Aegina were rumoured to be associated with the Treasure (Williams 2009, 14; *cf.* Evans 1893, 195). Four of them were bought by the Ashmolean in 1893 and two others by the British Museum in the same year, along with some bronze tools (Williams 2009, 14 with nn. 35 and 37, fig. 8). Since four of these pots (Forsdyke 1925, nos. A1091–2, *cf.* Williams 2009, fig. 8; and Ashmolean nos. AE 301–2) are of 12th century date, it occurs to me that it might be at least worth considering the possibility that the Treasure might also have been deposited in an Aeginetan chamber tomb or other coherent context in the 12th century, and that some of it, at least, may have been the result of a particularly spectacular haul from an earlier tomb or tombs further east in the Mediterranean. Aegina lies, after all, in a

very suggestive position in the Saronic Gulf, at an articulation point of the long-distance east-west sea route networks along which much of the metal trade was conducted.

References

Åström, P. (1966) *Excavations at Kalopsidha and Ayios Iakovos in Cyprus*. Studies in Mediterranean Archaeology 2. Lund, Åström.

Åström, P. (1977–1978) *The Pera Bronzes*. Scripta Minora Regia Societatis Humaniorum Litterarum Lundensis 4. Lund, Gleerup.

Albanese Procelli, R. M. (2008) La Sicilia tra Oriente e Occidente: interrelazioni mediterranee durante la protostoria recente. In Celestino, Rafel and Armada 2008, 403–415.

Albright, W. F. (1936–1937) *The Excavation of Tell Beit Mirsim. Vol. II. The Bronze Age*. Annual of the American Schools of Oriental Research 17.

Almagro Basch, M. (1958) *Depósito de la Ría de Huelva*. Inventaria Archaeologica, Corpus de Conjuntos Arqueologicos, España fasc. E–1. Madrid, Instituto Español de Prehistoria.

Armada Pita, X.–L. (2008) Carne, drogas o alcohol? Calderos y banquetes en el Bronce Final de la península Ibérica. *Cuadernos de Prehistoria y Arqueologia de la Universidad de Granada* 18, 125–162.

Armbruster, B. (2004) Tradition atlantique et innovation méditerranéenne à la fin de l'âge du bronze: le complexe de Baiões (Viseu, Portugal). In Lehoërff 2004, 45–65.

Baboula, E. (2000) 'Buried' Metal in Late Minoan Inheritance Customs. In Pare 2000, 70–81.

Barbarić, V. (2009) Late Bronze Age in Dalmatia: State of Research. In Borgna and Càssola Guida 2009, 311–323.

Bass, G. F. (1991) Evidence of Trade from Bronze Age Shipwrecks. In N. H. Gale (ed.), *Bronze Age Trade in the Mediterranean. Papers Presented at the Conference held at Rewley House, Oxford, in December 1989*. Studies in Mediterranean Archaeology 90, 69–82. Jonsered, Paul Åströms Förlag.

Bass, G. F., Throckmorton, P., du Plat Taylor, J., Hennessy, J. B., Shulman, A. R. and Buchholz, H.-G. (1967) *Cape Gelidonya: A Bronze Age Shipwreck*. Philadelphia, American Philosophical Society.

Batović, Š. (1983) Kasno brončano doba na istočnom Jadranskom primorju. In D. Basler, A. Benac, S. Gabrovec, M. Garašanin, N. Tasić, B. Čović and K. Vinska-Gasparini (eds), *Praistorija Jugoslavenskih Zemalja IV. Bronzano Doba*, 271–373. Sarajevo, Akademija Nauka i Umjetnosti Bosne i Hercegovine.

Begemann, F., Schmitt-Strecker, S., Pernicka, E. and Lo Schiavo, F. (2001) Chemical Composition and Lead Isotopy of Copper and Bronze from Nuragic Sardinia. *European Journal of Archaeology* 4, 43–85.

Bennet, J. (2004) Iconographies of Value: Words, People and Things in the Late Bronze Age Aegean. In J. C. Barrett and P. Halstead (eds), *The Emergence of Civilisation Revisited*. Sheffield Studies in Aegean Archaeology 6, 90–106. Oxford, Oxbow Books.

Benoit, F. (1965) *Recherches sur l'hellénisation du midi de la Gaule*. Annales de la Faculté des Lettres, Aix-en-Provence, nouvelle série. no. 43. Aix-en-Provence, Editions Ophrys.

Bettelli, M. (2001) A Supposed Mycenaean Spearhead from Eretria. *Studi Micenei ed Egeo-anatolici* 43/2, 189–93.

Bietti Sestieri, A. M. (1969) Ripostigli di bronzi dell'Italia meridionale: scambi fra le due sponde dell'Adriatico. *Bullettino di Paletnologia Italiana* 78, 259–276.

Bietti Sestieri, A. M. (1975) Elementi per lo studio dell'abitato protostorico di Frattesina di Fratta Polesine. *Padusa* 11, 1–14.

Bietti Sestieri, A. M. (1982) Frattesina. In L. Vagnetti (ed.), *Magna Grecia e Mondo Micenei: Nuovi documenti*, 201–207. Naples, Istituto per la Storia e l'Archeologia della Magna Grecia.

Borgna, E. (1992) *Il ripostiglio di Madriolo presso Cividale e i pani a piccone del Friuli-Venezia Giulia*. Roma, Quasar.

Borgna, E. (1995) I ripostigli delle acropoli Micenee e la circolazione del bronzo alla fine dell'età palaziale. *Studi Micenei ed Egeo-anatolici* 35, 7–55.

Borgna, E. (1999) The North Adriatic Regions between Europe and the Aegean World (12th–8th CA): Social Strategies and Symbols of Power in the Long-distance Exchange. In *Eliten in der Bronzezeit: Ergebnisse zweier Kolloquien in Mainz und Athen*, 151–183. Mainz: Römisch-Germanisches Zentralmuseum, Forschungsinstitut für Vor- und Frühgeschichte.

Borgna, E. (2000) Osservazioni sulla presenza Egeo-Cipriota nella metallurgia delle regioni comprese tra l'alto Adriatico e l'Europa centrale. In A. Giumlia-Mair (ed.), *Ancient Metallurgy between Oriental Alps and Pannonian Plain*, 41–51. Aquileia, Associazione nazionale per Aquileia.

Borgna, E. (2000–2001) I ripostigli del Friuli: proposta di seriazione cronologica e di interpretazione funzionale. *Rivista di Scienze Preistoriche* 51, 289–335.

Borgna, E. (2003) Attrezzi per filare nella tarda età del Bronzo italiana: connessioni con l'Egeo e con Cipro. *Rivista di Scienze Preistoriche* 53, 519–548.

Borgna, E. (2009) Patterns of Bronze Circulation and Deposition in the Northern Adriatic at the Close of the Late Bronze Age. In Borgna and Càssola Guida 2009, 289–309.

Borgna, E. and Càssola Guida, P. (2009) *From the Aegean to the Adriatic: Social Organisations, Modes of Exchange and Interaction in Postpalatial Times (12th–11th BC)*. Rome, Quasar.

Bouzek, J. (1985) *The Aegean, Anatolia and Europe: Cultural Interrelations in the Second Millennium BC*. Praha, Academia.

Bowman, S. and Needham, S. (2007) The Dunaverney and

Little Thetford Flesh-hooks: History, Technology and Their Position Within the Later Bronze Age Atlantic Zone Feasting Complex. *Antiquaries Journal* 87, 53–108.

Bradley, R. (2005) *Ritual and Domestic Life in Prehistoric Europe*. Abingdon, Routledge.

Brandherm, D. (2000) *Zyprische Griffangelklingen aus West- und Mitteleuropa? Zur Problematik einer Quellengruppe der frühen und mittleren Bronzezeit*. Kleine Schriftenreihe 4. Freiburg, Freiburger Institut für Paläowissenschaftliche Studien.

Branigan, K. (1983) A Cypriot Hook-tang Weapon from Devon. *Proceedings of the Devon Archaeological Society* 41, 125–128.

Briard, J. (1965) *Les Dépôts bretons et l'Age du Bronze atlantique*. Rennes, Becdelièvre.

Brown, A. (1993) *Before Knossos...Arthur Evans's Travels in the Balkans and Crete*. Oxford, Ashmolean Museum.

Brown, A. C. and Catling, H. W. (1986) *Ancient Cyprus*. Oxford, Ashmolean Museum.

Buchholz, H.-G. (1958) Der Kupferhandel des zweiten vorchristlichen Jahrtausends im Spiegel der Schriftforschung. In E. Grumach (ed.), *Minoica. Festschrift zum 80. Geburtstag von Johannes Sundwall*, 92–115. Berlin, Akademie Verlag.

Buchholz, H.-G. (1959) Keftiubarren und Erzhandel im zweiten vorchristlichen Jahrtausend. *Prähistorische Zeitschrift* 37, 1–40.

Buchholz, H.-G. (1979) Bronzene Schaftrohräxte aus Tamassos und Umgebung. In V. Karageorghis (ed.), *Studies Presented in Memory of Porphyrios Dikaios*, 76–88. Nicosia, Lions Club of Nicosia.

Buchholz, H.-G. (1986) Ein kyprischer Fibeltypus und seine auswärtige Verbreitung. In Karageorghis 1986, 223–245.

Buchholz, H.-G. (1988) Der Metallhandel des zweiten Jahrtausends im Mittelmeer. In M. Heltzer and E. Lipínski (eds), *Society and Economy in the Eastern Mediterranean (c. 1500–1000 B.C.)*, 187–228. Leuven, Orientaliste.

Buchholz, H.-G. (2003) Einige zyprische Gussformen. *Report of the Department of Antiquities, Cyprus* 2003, 113–138.

Buchholz, H.-G. (2010) *Archaeologia Homerica; die Denkmäler und das frühgriechische Epos Bd 1, Kapitel E: Kriegswesen 3: Ergänzungen und Zusammenfassung*. Göttingen, Vandenhoeck & Ruprecht.

Buchholz, H.-G. and Karageorghis, V. (1973) *Prehistoric Greece and Cyprus: an Archaeological Handbook*. London, Phaidon.

Burgess, C. and O'Connor, B. (2008) Iberia, the Atlantic Bronze Age and the Mediterranean. In Celestino, Rafel and Armada 2008, 41–58.

Calcagno, C. (1997) Aspects of Seafaring and Trade in the Central Mediterranean Regions. Unpublished DPhil thesis, Merton College, Oxford.

Carancini, G. L. (1979) I ripostigli dell'età del Bronzo finale. In *Il Bronzo Finale in Italia. Atti della XXI riunione scientifica, Firenze 21–23 Ottobre 1977*, 631–641. Florence, Istituto Italiano di Preistoria e Protostoria.

Carter, J.B. (1998) Egyptian Bronze Jugs from Crete and Lefkandi. *Journal of Hellenic Studies* 118, 172–7.

Càssola Guida, P. (1999) Indizi di presenze egeo-orientali nell'Alto Adriatico alla fine del'età del bronzo. In V. La Rosa, D. Palermo and L. Vagnetti (eds), *Επί πόντον πλαζόμενοι. Simposio Italiano di Studi Egei dedicato a L. Bernabò Brea e G. Pugliese Carratelli (Roma, 18–20 febbraio 1998)* 487–497. Roma, Scuola archeologica italiana di Atene.

Catling, H. W. (1964) *Cypriot Bronzework in the Mycenaean World*. Oxford, Clarendon Press.

Catling, H. W. (1986a) Cypriot Bronzework – East or West? In Karageorghis 1986, 91–103.

Catling, H. W. (1986b) The Date of the Cape Gelidonya Ship and Cypriot Bronzework. *Report of the Department of Antiquities, Cyprus* 1986, 68–71.

Catling, H. W. (1993) The Bronze Amphora and Burial urn. In M. R. Popham, P. G. Calligas and L. H. Sackett, *Lefkandi II.2: the Protogeometric Building at Toumba: the Excavation, Architecture and Finds*. British School at Athens Supplementary volume 23, 81–96. London, British School at Athens.

Catling, H. W. (1994) Cyprus in the 11th Century BC – an End or a Beginning? In V. Karageorghis (ed.), *Cyprus in the 11th Century B.C.*, 133–141. Nicosia, A. G. Leventis Foundation and University of Cyprus.

Celestino, S., Rafel, N. and Armada, X.-L. (2008), *Contacto cultural entre el Mediterráneo y el Atlántico (siglos XII–VIII ane): La precolonización a debate*. Madrid, Consejo Superior de Investigaciones Científicas.

Childe, V. G. (1927) The Danube Thoroughfare and the Beginnings of Civilization in Europe. *Antiquity* 1, 79–91.

Clerc, M. (1927) *Massalia. Histoire de Marseille dans l'antiquité, des origines à la fin de l'Empire romain d'occident (476 ap. J.-C.)*. Marseille, Tacussel.

Coldstream, J. N. (1989) Status Symbols in Cyprus in the Eleventh Century BC. In Peltenburg 1989, 325–335.

Courtois, J.-C., Lagarce, J. and Lagarce, E. (1986) *Enkomi et le Bronze Récent à Chypre*. Nicosie, Fondation A. G. Leventis.

Crawford, O. G. S. (1927) Notes and News. *Antiquity* 1, 96–109.

Crewe, L. (2009) Feasting with the Dead? Tomb 66 at Enkomi. In T. Kiely (ed.), *Ancient Cyprus in the British Museum. Essays in Honour of Veronica Tatton-Brown*, 27–48. London, The British Museum.

Csornay-Caprez, B. (2000) *Cypriote Antiquities*. Rome, 'L'Erma' di Bretschneider.

Déchelette, J. (1910) *Manuel d'archéologie préhistorique, celtique et gallo-romaine, II: Archéologie celtique et protohistorique. Première partie. Age du bronze*. Paris, A. Picard.

Deger-Jalkotzy, S. (2002) Innerägäische Beziehungen und auswärtige Kontakte des mykenischen Griechenland in nachpalatialer Zeit. In E. A. Braun-Holzinger and H. Matthäus (eds), *Die nahöstlichen Kulturen und Griechenland an der Wende vom 2. zum 1. Jahrtausend v.Chr.: Kontinuität und Wandel von Strukturen und Mechanismen kultureller Interaktion. Kolloquium des Sonderforschungsbereiches 295 "Kulturelle und sprachliche Kontakte" der Johannes Gutenberg-Universität Mainz, 11.–12. Dezember 1998*, 47–74. Möhnesee, Bibliopolis.

Dikaios, P. (1969–1971) *Enkomi. Excavations 1948–1958*. Mainz, Philipp von Zabern.

Di Stefano, G. (2004) Importazioni occidentali nel ripostiglio di Castelluccio di Sicilia (Ragusa). Note technice. In Lehoërff 2004, 211–227.

Eder, B. and Jung, R. (2005) On the Character of Social Relations between Greece and Italy in the 12th/11th c. BC. In R. Laffineur and E. Greco (eds), *EMPORIA. Aegeans in the Central and Eastern Mediterranean. Proceedings of the 10th International Aegean Conference*. Aegaeum 25, 485–495. Liège, Université de Liège.

Evans, A. J. (1883) *Antiquarian Researches in Illyricum*. Parts I and II. Westminster, Nichols & Sons.

Evans, A. J. (1893) A Mykênaean Treasure from Aegina. *Journal of Hellenic Studies* 13, 195–226.

Evans, A. J. (1906) Minoan Weights and Mediums of Currency from Crete, Mycenae and Cyprus. In G. F. Hill (ed.), *Corolla Numismatica: Numismatic Essays in Honour of Barclay V. Head*, 336–367. London, H. Frowde.

Evans, A. J. n.d. [±1883?] Notebook Containing Notes and Sketches on Stone Age Greece, Bronze Age Greece, Italy, Illyria, Troy pottery, and Delphi.

Evans, J. (1943) *Time and Chance: The Story of Arthur Evans and his Forebears*. London, Longmans, Green & Co.

Evans, J. (1964) *Prelude and Fugue*. London, Museum Press.

Evans, J. (1881) *Ancient Bronze Implements, Weapons and Ornaments of Great Britain and Ireland*. London, Longmans, Green & Co.

Ferrarese Ceruti, M. L., Vagnetti, L. and Lo Schiavo, F. (1987) Minoici, Micenei e Ciprioti in Sardegna alla luce delle più recenti scoperte. In M. Balmuth (ed.), *Studies in Sardinian Archaeology III. Nuragic Sardinia and the Mycenaean World*. British Archaeological Reports, International Series 387, 7–37. Oxford, B.A.R.

Figueiredo, E., Silva, R. J. C., Senna-Martinez, J.-C., Araújo, M. F., Braz Fernandes, F. M. and Inês Vaz, J. L. (2010) Smelting and Recycling Evidences from the Late Bronze Age Site of Baiões (Viseu, Portugal). *Journal of Archaeological Science* 37/7, 1623–1634.

Fischer, F. (1973) ΚΕΙΜΗΛΙΑ: Bemerkungen zur kulturgeschichtlichen Interpretation des sogenannten Südimports in der späten Hallstatt- und frühen Latène-Kultur des westlichen Mitteleuropa. *Germania* 51, 436–459.

Fitton, J. L. (2009) *The Aigina Treasure: Aegean Bronze Age Jewellery and a Mystery Revisited*. London, British Museum Press.

Fitton, J. L. (2009) Links in a Chain: Aigina, Dahshur and Tod. In Fitton 2009, 61–65.

Forsdyke, E. J. (1925) *Catalogue of the Greek and Etruscan vases in the British Museum. Vol. 1, Part 1, Prehistoric Aegean pottery*. London, British Museum.

Fromols, J. (1938) Découvertes et communications régionales. *Bulletin de la Société archéologique champenoise* 32, 161–2.

Galanaki, I., Tomas, H., Galanakis, Y. and Laffineur, R. (2007) *Between the Aegean and Baltic Seas: Prehistory Across Borders. Proceedings of the International Conference, Bronze and Early Iron Age Interconnections and Contemporary Developments between the Aegean and the Regions of the Balkan Peninsula, Central and Northern Europe, University of Zagreb, 11–14 April 2005*. Aegaeum 27. Liège and Austin: Université de Liège, Histoire de l'art et archéologie de la Grèce antique and University of Texas at Austin, Program in Aegean Scripts and Prehistory.

Gallay, G. (1988) *Die mittel- und spätbronze- sowie ältereisenzeitlichen Bronzedolche in Frankreich und auf den britischen Kanalinseln*. Prähistorische Bronzefunde 6.7. München, C. H. Beck.

Garašanin, M. (1983) Vatinska grupa. In D. Basler, A. Benac, S. Gabrovec, M. Garašanin, N. Tasić, B. Čović and K. Vinska-Gasparini (eds), *Praistorija Jugoslavenskih Zemalja IV. Bronzano Doba*, 504–519. Sarajevo: Akademija Nauka i Umjetnosti Bosne i Hercegovine.

Gerloff, S. (1975) *The Early Bronze Age Daggers in Great Britain and a Reconsideration of the Wessex Culture*. Prähistorische Bronzefunde 6.2. München, C. H. Beck.

Gerloff, S. (1993) Zu Fragen mittelmeerländischer Kontakte und absoluter Chronologie der Frühbronzezeit in Mittel- und Westeuropa. *Prähistorische Zeitschrift* 68, 58–102.

Gerloff, S. (2007) Reinecke's ABC and the Chronology of the British Bronze Age. In C. Burgess, P. Topping and F. Lynch (eds), *Beyond Stonehenge: Essays on the Bronze Age in Honour of Colin Burgess*, 117–161. Oxford, Oxbow Books.

Giardino, C. (2000) Sicilian Hoards and Protohistoric Metal Trade in the Central West Mediterranean. In Pare 2000, 99–107.

Giumlia-Mair, A., Kassianidou, V. and G. Papasavvas (2010) Miniature Ingots from Cyprus. In P. P. Betancourt and S. C. Ferrence (eds), *Metallurgy: Understanding How, Learning Why. Studies in Honor of James D. Muhly*, 11–19. Prehistory Monographs 29. Institute for Aegean Prehistory.

Glogović, D. (1999–2000) Brončanodobne ostave iz Dalmacije. *Opuscula Archaeologica* 23–24, 11–20.

Gomez, J. and Bourhis, J. (1971) Les poignards chypriotes, dits de Taillebourg, du Musée municipal d'Angoulême. *Bulletin de la Société Préhistorique Française* 71, 49–51.

González de Canales, F., Serrano, L. and Llompart, J. (2006) The Pre-colonial Phoenician Emporium of Huelva *c.* 900–770 BC. *BABesch* 81, 13–29.

Hadjisavvas, S. (1986) Alassa. A New Late Cypriote Site. *Report of the Department of Antiquities, Cyprus* 1986, 62–67.

Harding, A. F. (1984) *The Mycenaeans and Europe*. London, Academic Press.

Harding, A. F. (1989) Mycenaean Relations with Central and Western Europe. In *Actes du 113e Congrès national des Sociétés savantes, Strasbourg, 1988. Pré-Protohistoire. Dynamique du Bronze moyen en Europe occidentale*, 33–38. Paris, Comité des travaux historiques et scientifiques.

Harding, A. F. (2007) Interconnections between the Aegean and Continental Europe in the Bronze and Early Iron Ages: Moving beyond Scepticism. In Galanaki, Tomas, Galanakis and Laffineur 2007, 47–55.

Harding, A. and Hughes-Brock, H. (1974) Amber in the Mycenaean World. *Annual of the British School at Athens* 69, 145–172.

Higgins, R. A. (1987) A Gold Diadem from Aegina. *Journal of Hellenic Studies* 107, 162.

Hiller, S. (2009) Ornaments from the Warrior Grave and the Aigina Treasure. In Fitton 2009, 36–39.

Hirschfeld, N. (2001) Cypriots to the West? The Evidence of Their Potmarks. In L. Bonfante and V. Karageorghis (eds), *Italy and Cyprus in Antiquity, 1500–450 BC*, 121–129. Nicosia, Costakis and Leto Severis Foundation.

Hoffman, G. (1997) *Imports and Immigrants: Near Eastern Contacts with Iron Age Crete*. Ann Arbor, University of Michigan Press.

Honeyman, A. M. (1939) The Phoenician Inscriptions of the Cyprus Museum. *Iraq* 6, 104–108.

Iakovides, S. E. (1969–1970) *Περατή. Το Νεκροταφείον* (Βιβλιοθήκη της εν Αθήναις Αρχαιολογικής Εταιρείας αρ. 67. Athens.

Iakovides, S. E. (1980) *Excavations of the Necropolis at Perati*. Los Angeles, Institute of Archaeology, University of California.

Ilon, G. (1992) Keftiubarren Ingot from an Urn Grave Culture Settlement at Gór–Kápolnadomb (C. Vas). *Acta Archaeologica Academiae Scientiarum Hungaricae* 44, 239–259.

Jesus, P. S. de (1976) Report on the Analyses of the 'Makarska' Tools and Some Implications. *Studi Micenei ed Egeo-anatolici* 17, 221–33.

Jesus, P. S. de, Rapp G. Jr, and Vagnetti, L. (1982) Cypriote Bronzes in the Art and History Museum at Geneva. *Studi Micenei ed Egeo-anatolici* 23, 7–29.

Karageorghis, V. (1975) *Alaas. A Protogeometric Necropolis in Cyprus*. Nicosa, Department of Antiquities, Cyprus.

Karageorghis, V. (1976) *Kition: Mycenaean and Phoenician Discoveries in Cyprus*. London: Thames and Hudson.

Karageorghis, V. (1981) *Excavations at Kition IV. The Non-Cypriote Pottery*. Nicosia, Department of Antiquities, Cyprus.

Karageorghis, V. (ed.) (1986) *Acts of the International Archaeological Symposium 'Cyprus between the Orient and the Occident', Nicosia, 8–14 September 1985*. Nicosia, Department of Antiquities, Cyprus.

Karageorghis, V. (1990) *Tombs at Palaepaphos. 1. Teratsoudhia. 2. Eliomylia*. Nicosia, A. G. Leventis Foundation.

Karageorghis, V. (2001) *The White Slip Ware of Late Bronze Age Cyprus. Proceedings of an International Conference Organized by the Anastasios G. Leventis Foundation, Nicosia, in Honour of Malcolm Wiener*. Wien, Österreichische Akademie der Wissenschaften.

Karageorghis, V. (2002) *Κύπρος. Το Σταυροδρόμι της Ανατολικής Μεσογείου*. Athens, Kapon.

Karageorghis, V. and Kassianidou, V. (1999) Metalworking and Recycling in Late Bronze Age Cyprus – the Evidence from Kition. *Oxford Journal of Archaeology* 18, 171–188.

Karageorghis, V. and Lo Schiavo, F. (1989) A West Mediterranean Obelos from Amathus. *Rivista di Studi Fenici* 17, 15–29.

Karo, G. (1930) Schatz von Tiryns. *Mitteilungen des Deutschen Archäologischen Instituts, Athenische Abteilung* 55, 119–140.

Kemp, B. J. (1993) *Ancient Egypt: Anatomy of a Civilization*. London, Routledge.

Keswani, P. (2004) *Mortuary Ritual and Society in Bronze Age Cyprus*. London, Equinox.

Keswani, P. S. (2005) Death, Prestige, and Copper in Bronze Age Cyprus. *American Journal of Archaeology* 109, 341–401.

Kling, B. (1989) *Mycenaean IIIC:1b and Related Pottery in Cyprus*. Studies in Mediterranean Archaeology 87. Göteborg, Paul Åströms Förlag.

Knapp, A. B. (1986) *Copper Production and Divine Protection: Archaeology, Ideology and Social Complexity on Bronze Age Cyprus*. Studies in Mediterranean Archaeology Pocket-book 42. Göteborg, Paul Åströms Förlag.

Knapp, A. B. (1988) Hoards d'Oeuvres: Of Metals and Men on Bronze Age Cyprus. *Oxford Journal of Archaeology* 7, 147–76.

Knapp, A. B. (2000) Archaeology, Science-based Archaeology and the Mediterranean Bronze Age Metals Trade. *European Journal of Archaeology* 3, 31–56.

Knapp, A. B. and Cherry, J. F. (1994) *Provenience Studies and Bronze Age Cyprus: Production, Exchange and Politico-Economic Change*. Monographs in World Archaeology 21. Madison, Prehistory Press.

Knapp, A. B., Muhly, J. D. and Muhly, P. M. (1988) To Hoard is Human: Late Bronze Age Metal Deposits in Cyprus and the Aegean. *Report of the Department of Antiquities, Cyprus* 1988/1, 233–262.

Koukouli-Chrysanthaki, C. (1992) *Πρωτοϊστορική Θάσος: Τα νεκροταφεία του οικισμού Καστρί*. Athens, Ταμείο Αρχαιολογικών Πόρων.

Krzyszkowska, O. (1991) The Enkomi Warrior Head Reconsidered. *Annual of the British School at Athens* 86, 237–242.

Krzyszkowska, O. (2005) *Aegean Seals: An Introduction*. London, Institute of Classical Studies.

Laffineur, R. (2009) The Aigina Treasure: The Mycenaean Connection. In Fitton 2009, 40–42.

Lehoërff, A. (2004), *L'artisanat métallurgique dans les sociétés anciennes en Méditerranée occidentale: techniques, lieux et formes de production*. Rome, Ecole française de Rome.

Leshtakov, K. (2007) The Eastern Balkans in the Aegean Economic System during the LBA. Ox-hide and Bun Ingots in Bulgarian Lands. In Galanaki, Tomas, Galanakis and Laffineur 2007, 447–458.

Lipínski, E. (2004) *Itineraria Phoenicia*. Studia Phoenicia 18. Leuven, Peeters.

Lo Schiavo, F. (1995) Cyprus and Sardinia in the Mediterranean: Trade Routes Toward the West. In V. Karageorghis and D. Michaelides (eds), *Cyprus and the Sea. Proceedings of the International Symposium, Nicosia, 25–26 September 1993*, 45–60. Nicosia, University of Cyprus.

Lo Schiavo, F. (2003) Sardinia Between East and West: Interconnections in the Mediterranean. In N. C. Stampolidis and V. Karageorghis (eds), *ΠΛΟΕΣ...Sea Routes...Interconnections in the Mediterranean 16th–6th c. BC. Proceedings of the International Symposium held at Rethymnon, Crete, September 29th–October 2nd 2002*, 15–34. Athens, University of Crete and A. G. Leventis Foundation.

Lo Schiavo, F. (2004) Produzione, distribuzione e conservazione degli strumenti da lavoro nella Sardegna nuragica. In Lehoërff 2004, 229–261.

Lo Schiavo, F. (2008) La metallurgia sarda: relazioni fra Cipro, Italia e la Penisola Iberica. In Celestino, Rafel and Armada 2008, 417–436.

Lo Schiavo, F. and D'Oriano, R. (1990) La Sardegna sulle rotte dell'Occidente. In A. Stazio (ed.), *La Magna Grecia e il lontano Occidente. Atti del ventinovesimo convegno di studi sulla Magna Grecia, Taranto, 6–11 ottobre 1989*, 99–161. Taranto, Istituto per la Storia e l'Archeologia della Magna Grecia.

Lo Schiavo, F., Macnamara, E. and Vagnetti, L. (1985) Late Cypriot Imports to Italy and their Influence on Local Bronzework. *Papers of the British School at Rome* 53, 1–71.

Maggiulli, G. (2009) I ripostigli di Roca Vecchia (Lecce): analisi dei materiali e problematiche archeologiche. In Borgna and Càssola Guida 2009, 205–218.

Maran, J. (2004) The Spreading of Objects and Ideas in the Late Bronze Age Eastern Mediterranean: Two Case Examples from the Argolid of the 13th and 12th Centuries BC. *Bulletin of the American Schools of Oriental Research* 336, 11–30.

Maran, J. (2006) Coming to Terms with the Past: Ideology and Power in Late Helladic IIIC. In S. Deger-Jalkotzy and I.S. Lemos (eds), *Ancient Greece: from the Mycenaean Palaces to the Age of Homer*, 123–150. Edinburgh, Edinburgh University Press.

Maran, J. and Papadimitriou, A. (2006) Bericht zu den Ausgrabungen in Stadt-Nordost. *Archäologischer Anzeiger* 2006, 99–133.

Markowitz, Y. J. and Lacovara, P. (2009) Egypt and the Aigina Treasure. In Fitton 2009, 59–60.

Marović, I. (1984) Sinjska regija u prahistoriji. In *Cetinska krajina od prethistorije do dolaska Turaka*. Izdanja Hrvatskog arheološkog društva 4, 27–63. Split, Hrvatsko arheološko drustvo.

Masson, E. (1971) *Etude de vingt-six boules d'argile inscrites trouvées à Enkomi et Hala Sultan Tekke (Chypre)*. Studies in Mediterranean Archaeology 31/1. Göteborg, Paul Åströms Förlag.

Masson, O. (1983) *Les inscriptions chypriotes syllabiques*. Paris, Boccard.

Matthäus, H. (1989) Cypern und Sardinien im frühen 1. Jahrtausend v. Chr. In Peltenburg 1989, 244–255.

Matthäus, H. (1998) Zypern und das Mittelmeergebiet: Kontakthorizonte des späten 2. und frühen 1. Jahrtausends v.Chr. In R. Rolle and K. Schmidt (eds), *Archäologische Studien in Kontaktzonen der antiken Welt. Festschrift für Hans Georg Niemeyer*. Veröffentlichung der Joachim Jungius-Gesellschaft der Wissenschaften Hamburg 87, 73–91. Göttingen, Vandenhoeck and Ruprecht.

Matthäus, H. (2000) Crete and the Near East during the Early 1st Millennium BC. In D. Theochares and A. Kalokairinos (eds), *Πεπραγμένα του Η' διεθνούς Κρητολογικού συνεδρίου, Ηράκλειο 1996*, 267–280. Ηράκλειο: Εταιρεία Κρητικών Ιστορικών Μελετών.

Matthäus, H. and Schumacher-Matthäus, G. (1986) Zyprische Hortfunde: Kult und Metallhandwerk in der späten Bronzezeit. In O. H. Frey, H. Roth and C. Dobiat (eds), *Gedenkschrift für Gero von Merhart*. Marburger Studien zur Vor- und Frühgeschichte 7, 129–191. Marburg, Hitzeroth.

Mederos Martín, A. (1996) La conexíon Levantino-Chipriota. Indicios de comercio Atlántico con el Mediterráneo oriental durante el Bronce Final (1150–950 AC). *Trabajos de Prehistoria* 53, 95–115.

Mederos Martín, A. (2008) El Bronce Final. In F. Gracia Alonso (ed.), *De Iberia a Hispania*, 19–91. Barcelona, Ariel.

Mederos, A. and Harrison, R. J. (1996) 'Placer de dioses'. Incensarios en soportes con ruedas del Bronce Final de la península Ibérica. *Complutum Extra* 6/1, 237–253.

Merrillees, R. S. (1993) The Languages of Cyprus. *Cahiers du Centre D'Etudes Chypriotes* 20, 3–17.

Merrillees, R. S. (2001) Some Cypriote White Slip Pottery from the Aegean. In Karageorghis 2001, 89–100.

Mozsolics, A. (1984) Ein Beitrag zum Metallhandwerk der ungarischen Bronzezeit. *Bericht der Römisch-Germanischen Kommission* 65, 19–72.

Müller-Karpe, H. (1959) *Beiträge zur Chronologie der Urnenfelderzeit nördlich und südlich der Alpen*. Römisch-Germanische Forschungen 22. Berlin, de Gruyter.

Muhly, J. D. (1996) The Significance of Metals in the Late Bronze Age Economy of Cyprus. In V. Karageorghis and D. Michaelides (eds), *The Development of the Cypriot Economy from the Prehistoric Period to the Present Day*, 45–60. Nicosia, The University of Cyprus and the Bank of Cyprus.

Needham, S. and Bowman, S. (2005) Flesh-hooks, Technological Complexity and the Atlantic Bronze Age Feasting Complex. *European Journal of Archaeology* 8/2, 93–136.

Nibbi, A. (1986) Some Middle Kingdom Oxhide-shaped Objects in the Egyptian Iconography and their Name: nms and Ashmolean Ingot 1892–919. *Discussions in Egyptology* 4, 41–66.

Nightingale, G. (2007) Lefkandi. An Important Node in the International Exchange Network of Jewellery and Personal Adornment. In Galanaki, Tomas, Galanakis and Laffineur 2007, 421–429.

Oppenheim, A. L. (1968) *Letters from Mesopotamia*. Chicago, University of Chicago Press.

Palincaş, N. (2007) Contacts with the Aegean and Their Social Impact in the Late Bronze Age in the Lower Danube. In Galanaki, Tomas, Galanakis and Laffineur 2007, 231–237.

Papadopoulou, E. (2007) Western Greece and the North in the Late Bronze Age: The Evidence of Metalwork and Objects of Exotic Material. In Galanaki, Tomas, Galanakis and Laffineur 2007, 459–467.

Pare, C. F. E. (1999) Weights and Weighing in Bronze Age Central Europe. In *Eliten in der Bronzezeit. Ergebnisse zweier Kolloquien in Mainz und Athen*, 421–514. Mainz, Römisch-germanisches Zentralmuseum.

Pare, C. F. E. (2000) *Metals Make the World Go Round: the Supply and Circulation of Metals in Bronze Age Europe*. Oxford, Oxbow Books.

Parović-Pešikan, M. (1985) Neki novi aspekti širenja egejske i grčke kulture na centralni Balkan. *Starinar* 36, 19–49.

Paton, L. B. (1917) Phoenicians. In J. Hastings (ed.), *Encyclopedia of Religion and Ethics, vol. 9*, 887–897. Edinburgh, T. & T. Clark.

Peltenburg, E. (1989) *Early Society in Cyprus*. Edinburgh, Edinburgh University Press.

Petrie, W. M. F. (1917) *Tools and Weapons Illustrated by the Egyptian Collection in University College, London*. British School of Archaeology in Egypt Publications 30. London, British School of Archaeology in Egypt.

Philip, G. (1991) Cypriot Bronzework in the Levantine World: Conservatism, Innovation and Social Change. *Journal of Mediterranean Archaeology* 4/1, 59–107.

Phillips, J. (1992) Tomb-robbers and Their Booty in Ancient Egypt. In S. E. Orel (ed.), *Death and Taxes in the Ancient Near East*, 157–192. New York, E. Mellen Press.

Popham, M. R., Calligas, P. G. and Sackett, L. H. (1993) *Lefkandi II.2: the Protogeometric Building at Toumba: the Excavation, Architecture and Finds*. British School at Athens Supplementary volume 23. London, British School at Athens.

Popham, M. R. and Lemos, I. S. (1996) *Lefkandi III. The Early Iron Age Cemetery at Toumba. The Excavations of 1981 to 1994. Plates*. London, The British School at Athens.

Popham, M. R., Sackett, L. H. and Themelis, P. G. (1979–1980) *Lefkandi I. The Iron Age Settlement. The Cemeteries*. The British School of Archaeology at Athens Supplementary Volume 11. London, Thames and Hudson.

Popham, M. R., Touloupa, E. and Sackett, L. H. (1982) The Hero of Lefkandi. *Antiquity* 56, 169–74.

Primas, M. and Pernicka, E. (1998) Der Depotfund von Oberwilflingen. Neue Ergebnisse zur Zirkulation von Metallbarren. *Germania* 76, 25–65.

Pulak, C. (1998) The Uluburun Shipwreck: An Overview. *International Journal of Nautical Archaeology* 27/3, 188–124.

Rafel, N. (2002) Un trípode de tipo chipriota procedente de la Clota (Calaceite, Teruel). *Complutum* 13, 77–83.

Rafel, N., Vives-Ferrándiz, J. Armada, X.-L. and Graells, R. (2008) Las comunidades de la Edad del Bronce entre el Empordà y el Segura: espacio y tiempo de los intercambios. In Celestino, Rafel and Armada 2008, 239–271.

Reinecke, P. (1933) Kyprische Dolche aus Mitteleuropa? *Germania* 17, 256–9.

Ribichini, S. (2001) Beliefs and Religious Life. In S. Moscati (ed.), *The Phoenicians*, 120–144. London, I. B. Tauris.

Royal Society of Antiquaries of Ireland (1910) Bronze Knife from Ardevan, Co. Clare. *Journal of the Royal Society of Antiquaries of Ireland* 40/3, 248.

Ruiz-Gálvez, M. (2000) Weight Systems and Exchange Networks in Bronze Age Europe. In Pare 2000, 267–279.

Ruiz-Gálvez Priego, M. (2008) Writing, Counting, Self-awareness, Experiencing Distant Worlds. Identity Processes and Free-lance Trade in the Bronze Age/Iron Age Transition. In Celestino, Rafel and Armada 2008, 27–40.

Sandars, N. (1983) North and South at the End of the Mycenaean Age: Aspects of an Old Problem. *Oxford Journal of Archaeology* 2, 43–68.

Scala, R. von (1911) Die Anfänge geschichtlichen Lebens in Italien. *Historische Zeitschrift* 108, 1–37.

Schiestl, R. (2009) Three Pendants: Tell el-Dab'a, Aigina and a New Silver Pendant from the Petrie Museum. In Fitton 2009, 51–58.

Sherratt, S. (2000) Circulation of Metals and the End of the Bronze Age in the Eastern Mediterranean. In Pare 2000, 82–98.

Sherratt, S. (2004) Feasting in Homeric Epic. In J. C. Wright (ed.), *The Mycenaean Feast*, 181–217. Princeton, American School of Classical Studies at Athens.

Sherratt, S. (2009) Greeks and Phoenicians: Perceptions of Traders in the Early First Millennium BC. In A. A. Bauer and A. S. Agbe-Davies (eds), *Social Archaeologies of Trade and Exchange*, 119–142. Walnut Creek: Left Coast Press.

Simpson, St J. (2000) Observations on Early Iron Age Beads from Luristan. *Bead Study Trust Newsletter* 36, 6–10.

Ślusarska, K. (2007) Some Remarks on the Possibility that there Existed an 'Eastern Branch' in the System of Amber Routes in the Late Bronze and Early Iron Ages. In Galanaki, Tomas, Galanakis and Laffineur 2007, 371–375.

Snodgrass, A. M. (1971) *The Dark Age of Greece. An Archaeological Survey of the Eleventh to the Eighth Centuries BC*. Edinburgh: Edinburgh University Press.

Stockhammer, P. (2009) The Change of Pottery's Social Meaning at the End of the Bronze Age: New Evidence from Tiryns. In C. Bachhuber and R. G. Roberts (eds),

Forces of Transformation: the End of the Bronze Age in the Mediterranean. Proceedings of an International Symposium Held at St. John's College, University of Oxford, 25–6th March 2006. Themes from the Ancient Near East BANEA Publication Series 1, 164–169. Oxford, Oxbow Books.

Teržan, B. (1996) *Depojske in posamezne kovinske najdbe bakrene in bronaste dobe na Slovenskem II*. Katalogi in monografije 30. Ljubljana, Narodni Muzej.

Teržan, B. (2007) Cultural Connections Between Caput Adriae and the Aegean in the Late Bronze and Early Iron Age. In Galanaki, Tomas, Galanakis and Laffineur 2007, 157–165.

Tomas, H. (2010) The World Beyond the Northern Margin: the Bronze Age Aegean and the East Adriatic Coast. In W. A. Parkinson and M. L. Galaty (eds), *Archaic State Interaction: the Eastern Mediterranean in the Bronze Age*, 181–212. Santa Fe, School for Advanced Research Press.

Torres Ortiz, M. (2008) Los 'tiempos' de la precolonización. In Celestino, Rafel and Armada 2008, 59–91.

Traill, D. (1996) *Schliemann of Troy: Treasure and Deceit*. London, Penguin.

Vagnetti, L. (1967) Il pane di bronzo di Makarska. *Studi Micenei ed Egeo-Anatolici* 3, 128–130.

Vagnetti, L. (1971) Osservazioni sul cosidetto ripostiglio di Makarska (including an appendix by P. S. de Jesus). *Studi Ciprioti e Rapporti di Scavo* 1, 203–216.

Vagnetti, L. (1986) Cypriot Elements Beyond the Aegean in the Bronze Age. In V. Karageorghis (ed.), *Acts of the International Archaeological Symposium, 'Cyprus between the Orient and the Occident'*, 202–214. Nicosia; Department of Antiquities, Cyprus.

Vagnetti, L. (2001) How Far Did White Slip Pottery Travel? Some Evidence from Italy and from the Libyan Coast. In Karageorghis 2001, 101–103.

Vagnetti, L. and Lo Schiavo, F. (1989) Late Bronze Age Long Distance Trade in the Mediterranean: the Role of the Cypriots. In Peltenburg 1989, 217–243.

Vinski-Gasparini, K. (1983) Ostave s područja kulture polja sa žarama. In D. Basler, A. Benac, S. Gabrovec, M. Garašanin, N. Tasić, B. Čović and K. Vinska-Gasparini (eds), *Praistorija Jugoslavenskih Zemalja IV. Bronzano Doba*, 647–667. Sarajevo, Akademija Nauka i Umjetnosti Bosne i Hercegovine.

Watkins, T. (1976) Wessex Without Cyprus: 'Cypriot Daggers' in Europe. In J. V. S. Megaw (ed.), *To Illustrate the Monuments: Essays on Archaeology Presented to Stuart Piggott*, 135–143. London, Thames and Hudson.

Whitley, J. (2002) Objects With Attitude: Biographical Facts and Fallacies in the Study of Late Bronze Age and Early Iron Age Warrior Graves. *Cambridge Archaeological Journal* 12/2, 217–232.

Williams, D. (2009) The Story of the Aigina Treasure. In Fitton 2009, 11–16.

Wright, D. P. (2004) Prayers, Hymns, Incantations and Curses. In S. I. Johnston (ed.), *Religions of the Ancient World: a Guide*, 355–357. Cambridge Mass., Belknap Press.

14.

Lasting impressions. The appropriation of sealing practices in Minoan Crete

Sarah Cappel

Introduction

The function of seals as visual markers of social status and their role in manipulating social identity is widely accepted (*e.g.* Karytinos 1998, 85; Krzyszkowska 2005, 21; Aruz 2008, 1–2; Sbonias 1999, 27). But aside from their function as emblems of elite status or amulets, seals were actively engaged in shaping one important sector of Minoan society, namely administration. This is mainly reflected in sealings, which are closely associated with administrative practices in a socio-economic context (Ferioli and Fiandra 1989, 47; Sbonias 1995, 122). As this conference focuses on materiality and practice, I would like to evaluate the transformative capacity that sealing practices, mediated through seals and sealings, had in Minoan society.[1]

The introduction of sealing practices to Minoan Crete in the Early Bronze Age, long after administrative sealing systems had been established in the Near East, Egypt and Anatolia, has been a matter of debate among Minoan scholars. The alleged sudden appearance of an advanced sealing system in the earliest palaces in Minoan Crete, and elsewhere on the island, in MM (Middle Minoan) IIB without a tangible predecessor in the Prepalatial and the early Protopalatial period has been used to support the idea of a wholesale import from the Near East. The evidence for the use of seals in the preceding period, meanwhile, is mostly not characterised as being administrative in nature due to the scarcity of finds and the lack of evidence for central authorities (Weingarten 1990, 105 n. 2; Poursat 1990, 55). However, while a sphragistic use on a household level is acknowledged for the Prepalatial seals (Sbonias 2010, 350), the idea of an import of the Protopalatial sealing system is upheld, citing the more extensive foreign contacts developing from the MM IA period onwards (Weingarten 1990, 105–107; Schoep 2006, 53 *contra* Schoep 1999, 268–272).

This paper will operate on the premise that the appearance of a sealing system in the Protopalatial period cannot be separated from the evidence for seal use in the Prepalatial period (*cf.* Schoep and Knappett 2004, 25–26), even if the seals were not used 'administratively' before, and that this kind of seal use paved the way for the development of the later system, without excluding an additional stimulus from external contacts shortly before the early Protopalatial period. For a diachronic view of the development of sealing practices, this paper will take a closer look at the evidence for sealing practices in the Prepalatial and early Protopalatial period. These practices, reflected in the seals and sealings, contributed first to Minoan material culture in EM (Early Minoan) II and had to be integrated within it from this time. While seals and sealings are obviously inextricably linked with each other, they are found in quite different contexts – seals in burials and sealings in settlements. To date, no extant sealing can be matched to a seal. Nevertheless, I will attempt to achieve an integrated perspective by considering the role of both object categories in the process of appropriation. In order to provide the basis for an evaluation of the impact of this process on Minoan society, I will present an account of the development of sealing practices structured by the criteria for the process of appropriation, conceptualised for modern consumer societies by Hans-Peter Hahn (2005, 99–107).

Materiality of sealings

Before presenting the material evidence on which the present argument is based, I will begin by discussing the ways in which the material categories of seals and sealings contribute to the study of sealing practices. Material culture studies and the concept of materiality have received growing attention in recent literature and research (*e.g.* Graves-Brown 2000; DeMarrais, Gosden and Renfrew 2004; Miller 2005; Knappett 2005). According to Robb (2004, 133), materiality explicitly takes into account that humans have a material engagement with the world. The concept is based on the assumption that a mutual relationship exists between things and humans and it 'aims to define and redefine the importance of the texture and dimensions of material existence in the cultural contexts that archaeology attempts to reconstruct.' (Taylor 2008, 298). Instead of elaborating further on the general aspects of the concept of materiality, I shall only state what constitutes the materiality of the sealings and how adopting this perspective could be advantageous to achieving the objective outlined above.

Sealing practices can only be inferred from their material manifestations in seals and, especially, sealings. As for the material capacities of the sealings, these are lumps of clay onto which seals were impressed. Those impressed lumps of clay were either directly attached to objects (direct object sealings or flat-based nodules), were hanging from objects by strings (hanging nodules) or the term can refer to so-called noduli or roundels, which were 'independent' devices, *i.e.* sealings, that were not attached to other objects: 'sealings that do not seal' (Weingarten 1986, 4). Sealings, as opposed to seals, were not intended for long term use. Their temporary character can be inferred from the fact that they were not intentionally fired and that most of them would have to be broken before they could be removed from the objects they sealed. The deposits in which they are found, at least in the Proto- and Neopalatial contexts, suggest that the broken sealings were collected and probably kept for at least one administrative cycle for accounting purposes and then discarded (*cf.* Ferioli and Fiandra 1989, 48).

Sealings were communicative devices, which could convey information about transactions across time and space. Through being impressed with a seal, sealings 'provide evidence for the relationship between the procedure of closure and the person responsible for that specific function' (Ferioli and Fiandra 1989, 48). While the active role of seals in such transactions can only be inferred from the impression they left behind, sealings virtually encapsulate the practices they were part of at the same time. Thus, apart from the information we can observe directly from the material capacities of the sealings, they also provide information about the mode of sealing and, thus, about the use of seals (*cf.* Foster 2000, 79; Ferioli, Fiandra, Fissore 2000; *cf.* also Knappett 2002, who discusses the relationship between material culture – in this case pottery – activities and social structures). Through the study of their distribution patterns, their find associations and contexts, statistical analysis of the types and seal impressions found in a given context and the symbolic meanings of the seal motives (through the study of the iconography and its implications *e.g.* for hierarchical structures) as well as their morphology (identification of the objects sealed), they not only supply evidence for their practical use but also help us reconstruct the socio-cultural and socio-economic context with which they are associated (*cf.* Ferioli and Fiandra 1989, 46–47). Most of these criteria are more applicable in the Protopalatial period than in the Prepalatial period in which sealings are few and far between. However, as there is evidence for sealing practices in the Prepalatial period, this must be borne in mind when trying to explain the development of the elaborate Protopalatial sealing system.

Through these non-material capacities of sealings we can begin to understand better the mutual relationship between human agency and material culture. In the case of sealing practices we can observe such mutuality in a diachronic perspective. It is informed not only by Minoan sealings, but also by seals and related finds such as imported goods. We can trace their iconography and other formal criteria, and put them into perspective by means of distribution patterns and contexts, thus gaining insight into administrative practices, the movements of people and the transcultural transfer of ideas (Aruz 2008, 2; Sbonias 1999, 27).

Material evidence

The material that is relevant for the present purpose is mainly the Prepalatial evidence for sealing practices, as this is the period when these practices were introduced to Minoan Crete, and the Early Protopalatial material, shortly before the existence of an advanced sealing system is evident in the MM IIB archives. Seals were introduced to Crete in the EM II period in the middle of the 3rd Millennium BCE. From then onwards they are a constant and constantly developing feature of the material record (Krzyszkowska 2005, 1) and are found mainly in funerary contexts. Sealings also appear as early as EM II but the number of sealings which can be attributed to the Prepalatial period is very small in comparison with the Protopalatial period, when they are discovered in larger numbers at various (palatial) sites.

In Minoan Crete seals are generally found in communal tombs and thus in not closely datable contexts (*cf.* Karytinos 1998, 81) whereas sealings mainly come from settlement contexts. They appear at a time when, in the Near East, Anatolia, and Egypt, sealing administrations had already been firmly established for several millennia (Aruz 2008, 15). Evidence for foreign contacts with these regions is attested by a few imports, again mainly in funerary contexts especially in EM IIA, but it is difficult to say whether contact was direct or indirect (Pini 2005, 777; Schoep 2006, 49; Wilson 2008, 88, 93–94, 99). The EB (Early Bronze) II period is also a time of intense cultural interaction in the Aegean between the Greek Mainland, the Cyclades and Crete, which is inferred from parallels in material culture (Broodbank 2000, 300–309; Wilson 2008, 92; 99; for comprehensive studies on Prepalatial seals see Yule 1980 and Sbonias 1995; for an overview of Minoan glyptic from the Early to the Late Bronze Age see Galanakis 2005; for a general overview of Aegean seals see Krzyszkowska 2005).

The evidence for sealing practices in the Prepalatial period amounts to only a few sealings which are scattered all over the island. Of the 23 seal impressions which can be attributed to the Prepalatial period, only about a dozen count as 'true' sealings, in the sense that they are impressed on lumps of clay which are attached to objects instead of being directly impressed on the objects themselves (*cf.* Sbonias 2010, 349). They include three unusual sealing types found in Sphoungaras and Archanes. These are unusual because of their shape: they look like conical stamp seals and are provided with a string hole but are made of clay and have a positive seal impression instead of a negative seal face CMS II, 6 nos. 149, 150, 155). Their function is not clear. Vlasaki and Hallager (1995, 269, n. 48) see them among the administrative devices and compare them with the later Protopalatial medallions while Pini suggests a simple decorative function (for CMS II, 6 no. 155: Pini 1984, 76–77). The remaining seal impressions of the Prepalatial period are either impressions on pottery or on loom weights (Vlasaki and Hallager 1995; Hallager 2000). These are often only mentioned as a side note, because they could also be interpreted as decoration or potter's marks and because such impressions on objects do not play a role in later sealing administration. However, they may also be significant for the study of sealing practices in the Prepalatial period as they could be indicative of 'some sort of control and organization of the production' (Response Poursat to Pini 1990, 55; *cf.* also Vlasaki and Hallager 1995, 268, 270; Aruz 2008, 24–25), yet exactly what role they would have played is not clear (*cf.* Relaki 2009, 364–365).

The sealings that are found in Crete mostly come from settlement contexts (Schoep 2006, 44), with only two found in cemeteries, and most are direct object sealings, most likely sealing basketry or wooden containers. The sealings are found in EM II contexts in Myrtos Phournou Koriphi and Trypiti, in an EM IIB context in Malia, in an EM II/III context in Chania and Mochlos, an EM IIB/transitional EM III/MM IA context in Psathi, an EM III context in Knossos and an EM IIIA/MM IA context in Khamalevri (Schoep and Knappett 2004, 26; Vlasaki and Hallager 1995; for Malia: Pelon 1993, 545; for Mochlos: Soles and Davaras 2004, 514, no. 345; for Psathi: Hallager 2000, 97–99; *cf.* also Schoep 2006, 44 n. 68: she and Vlasaki and Hallager 1995, 254 also list the two West Court sealings from Knossos for EM IIA which are stylistically later in date, probably MM II, according to Pini 2002, 5). One of the unusual sealing types mentioned above is found in the Neopalatial building at Archanes, but attributed to EM III/MM IA due to its iconography CMS II, 6 no. 149). The other two examples of this group are found in cemeteries, one at Sphoungaras, tentatively dated to MM I and the other at Archanes Phourni in a MM IA context (Vlasaki and Hallager 1995, 253–254).

The most significant of these in terms of possible administrative activity before the palaces might be the Malia sealing, which was found in an EM IIB structure below the EM III/MM IA court building (Pelon 1993, 545–546; see also Schoep 2006, 44–45), and represents the earliest occurrence of a nodulus – a sealing shape which was closely associated with later palatial administration (Weingarten 1986; Krzyszkowska 2005, 102–103).

The sealings are not only distributed widely over the island, but also span a very long period of time. Compared with the great number of seals found in burial contexts over the same period of time, their number is vanishingly small. Therefore, doubts have been expressed as to whether this small sample of sealings is really indicative of administrative use (Weingarten 1990, 105) although more recently a number of scholars have argued in favour of such an idea (see above; Schoep and Knappett 2004, 26; Perna 1999, 67; Krzyszkowska 2005, 78; Relaki 2009, 364, 367). Another factor in the interpretation of this evidence is the chance of survival, as the development on the Greek mainland has shown. Although the existence of administrative activity for the mainland had long been rejected, three sites have yielded important and large groups of sealings within the last 60 years, starting with Lerna and being complemented by the more recent finds at Petri and Geraki (*cf.* Krzyszkowska 2005, 37; Lerna: Heath 1958; Weingarten 2000a; Petri: Kostoula 2000; Geraki: Weingarten 2000b). A great amount of evidence for sealing practices in Prepalatial Crete might thus be lost due to the lack of destruction horizons in settlements, poor excavation techniques, or indeed lack of excavation (*cf.* Ferioli and Fiandra 1989, 41; Schoep 1999, 268). But the greater number of sealings on the mainland could also be due to the fact that there already existed some sort of centralised economic/administrative structure at this time (as suggested by the evidence of the corridor houses, *cf.* Aruz 2008, 31) while on Crete in the early Prepalatial period this was not yet the case.

The Prepalatial pattern of a few stray sealings scattered all over the island is completely reversed in the Protopalatial period. An advanced administrative sealing system is clearly in use with the sealing deposits dating to the last phase of the early Minoan palaces, MM IIB. There are five main deposits of sealings, which can be identified in the Protopalatial period:

The hieroglyphic archives of Knossos, Malia (palace and Quartier Mu) and Petras and the two Linear A archives of Phaistos and Monastiraki.[2] These deposits are attributed to MM IIB, a phase which lasted approximately 50 years (the Protopalatial period in all lasted approximately 150 years and comprises MM IB, MM IIA and MM IIB), and are preserved due to destruction horizons in which the usually unbaked sealings were fired. Although the dating of the archives at the palaces of Knossos and Malia presents some difficulties, they are included in this account as they both contain material which can be ascribed to the Protopalatial period, though they also yielded material from the Neopalatial period, suggesting that both are not true closed deposits (Weingarten 1995, 292; Krzyszkowska 2005, 111, 114). The largest deposit is the one at Phaistos, with approximately 6500 sealing fragments, consisting mainly of direct object sealings sealing doors or chests, found together with a few written documents (Fiandra 1968; 1975).

Particularly significant for the question of continuity from Prepalatial to Protopalatial is the early Protopalatial evidence for sealing practices. Knossos is the only site where sealings are found more or less continuously from EM II–LM IIIA. The first evidence for seal use in the Protopalatial palace are three noduli, all stamped by the same seal, which were found in an MM IB level in Early Magazine A (Weingarten 2007, 134–136). Two further sealings from the Vat Room Deposit can also be attributed to early MM IB (Weingarten 1990, 56). Two noduli and four sealings were found in the Southeast Pillar Room (Schoep 2004, 286 and tab. 23.2), and dated to MM IB (Weingarten 2007, 135). Another two direct object sealings come from Deposit E in the Southwest House, dating to MM IIA, as well as a nodulus from workshop debris in a corner room of the same house (Weingarten 2007, 136–137). Furthermore, seven sealings were found in the Room of the Olive Press, though their context does not allow for a more precise dating than EM–MM IIA/B (Panagiotaki 1993, 35, 39–40)

This evidence together with the Prepalatial sealings suggests some kind of continuity and strengthens the case for a continuous development rather than a complete import in the Protopalatial period (*cf.* Schoep and Knappett 2004, 25–26). Another argument in favour of this interpretation, albeit one out of silence, could be that the deposits are preserved due to destruction at the end of MM IIB and that continuing building activity and the lack of earlier destruction horizons in the palaces might have obscured the picture of the earlier development of sealing administration at these places.

In order to achieve a more systematic picture of the proposed continuous development of sealing practices, the process of appropriation of this practice in Minoan culture will be examined more closely in this paper, as this approach offers a diachronic perspective (see below). For heuristic purposes it is not vital whether it was an import or an indigenous invention: the important point is that a new material trait was integrated. For this reason, primarily the process of appropriation will be evaluated in this paper, as well as the question to what extent this appropriation had an impact on the further development of sealing practices in Minoan Crete.

Criteria for the process of appropriation

In his introduction to material culture (*Materielle Kultur. Eine Einführung* 2005), Hans-Peter Hahn analyses the 'handling' ('*Umgang*') of objects and within this framework delineates the phenomenon of the appropriation of objects in modern consumer societies. One of his main points is that cultures are able to generate new cultural forms instead of becoming homogeneous entities due to the consumption of the same objects (Hahn 2005, 100). Imported goods are integrated into the local material culture and while they undergo changes themselves they in turn also change their surroundings.[3] The increasing consumption of such imported goods has led to a growing importance of these goods for the determination ('*Bestimmung*') of the 'local' within the own culture (Hahn 2005, 88). His arguments are based on ethnological studies concerned with changing consuming habits of societies from the possession of few goods ('*Gesellschaften mit geringem Sachbesitz*') to mass consumption including imported goods ('*Konsumgesellschaften*'). His objective is to describe systematically the process that 'consumption objects' ('*Konsumobjekte*') have to go through in order to eventually qualify as personal goods (Hahn 2005, 102, 107). As the respective steps in the appropriation process are concerned with the 'handling' ('*Umgang*') of objects, the approach focuses not only on the objects but also takes into consideration the active part of the consumer in this process (Hahn 2005, 107). As will become clear, especially in the criterion of incorporation, this approach not only considers the implications of appropriation for the objects but also how the objects in turn affect the persons who appropriate them. Thus, this perspective enables us to explore the mutual relationship between objects and people, which is an important part of the study of sealing practices as outlined above.

Although these criteria were developed for modern consumer societies, they can also be used in a modified form for the description of the appropriation process of objects in prehistoric societies. As ethnographical/ethnological studies have shown, contemporary societies such as those typified in this case as '*Gesellschaften mit geringem Sachbesitz*', have comparable structures with prehistoric societies (*cf.* for example the use of Helms' ethnographical studies in Minoan archaeology; *e.g.* Schoep 2006; Colburn 2008). Thus the stages of the appropriation process as detailed below remain essentially the same. As sealing practices were a new conceptual addition to the material traits of Minoan culture in the Early Bronze Age, the appropriation criteria represent a feasible approach for the evaluation of the adoption of these practices.[4] There are six criteria which are divided into three stages, with the second to fifth criterion belonging to the same stage, designated as 'transformations' (Hahn 2005, 102). The criteria are the following (Hahn 2005, 103–104):

1. Type of acquisition/acceptance[5] (Erwerb/Annahme): The first step in analysing new additions to material culture is to look at how they came to be in their new cultural environment.

Transformations (2.–5.):

2. Material transformation ('*Materielle Umgestaltung*'): Objects that have been acquired become personal goods through being transformed in a number of ways, for example by being newly decorated or even by just being cleaned. This is not a necessary step in the process of appropriation.
3. Designation ('*Benennung*'): By giving them a name in the local language, objects are integrated into an existing framework of meanings, and a specific environment of local material culture.
4. Cultural transformation ('*Kulturelle Umwandlung*'): Assigning new local meanings which transcends the mere re-naming of an appropriated object is encompassed by the term of cultural transformation. As a result, the object is thereafter perceived as local from a local perspective.
5. Incorporation ('*Inkorporierung*'): The aspect of incorporation refers to the way appropriated objects interact specifically with their new user's body. Objects demand a certain way in which they are used and influence the amount of time which is spend with them. Furthermore, they can also change the perception of one's own body as the right handling of the objects is also a question of physical ability.
6. Traditionalisation ('*Traditionalisierung*'): The prerequisites for traditionalisation are a sufficiently long period of time for the appropriation and a societal consensus on the local meaning of the appropriated object.

As already indicated, the criteria were developed for the study of the appropriation of objects in modern consumer societies. In the following, these criteria are applied to the situation in Minoan Crete with regard to the appropriation of sealing practices. In the case of administrative sealing practices, seals and sealings are inextricably linked with each other – the latter could not exist without the former. Thus, sealings are a product of the sphragistic use of seals. But, as already mentioned, seals could also have other functions. Accordingly, the influences or developments that affected the seals might not necessarily be connected to administrative trajectories. When trying to reconstruct administrative sealing practices this ambiguity or rather multivalent nature of seals has to be taken into account, and in the following discussion of Hahn's criteria it will become apparent that it is not possible to clearly separate the various functions of the seals from each other, especially as they are often closely entangled with administrative sealing practices, as for example the function of seals as markers of social status. Although sealings are more unambiguously associated with the administrative domain, the fact that sealing practices are mediated through both object categories means that they both have to be taken into account in an evaluation of the appropriation of this practice and its impact on Minoan society in the Pre- and early Protopalatial periods. As it is not possible to deal with the complete evidence for sealing practices during the respective periods in the scope of this paper, the application of the criteria will be illustrated below with the help of case studies involving both object categories.

Type of acquisition/acceptance

Seals seem to have been readily accepted into Minoan material culture to judge by the large number of seals found in funerary contexts since their first appearance in EM II. As for the question of how sealing practice was transmitted, only general comments can be ventured on the basis of the material evidence and the general accounts of trade in the Early Bronze Age Aegean (*cf.* Pini 2005, 777 on the lack of consensus in the study of Aegean and Near Eastern exchange).

Cultural traits travel with people – and seals are easily portable objects. A receiving group can copy materials, decorative styles and iconography with relative ease. According to Clarke, these types of cultural transmissions are commonly found in the archaeological record, not least because they are easily identified. The transmissions of technologies and ideologies, or of a social practice as in this case, are more difficult to identify archaeologically, as they require greater human involvement in the transmission process, which has to be inferred from the material evidence (Clarke 2005, 138). In the case of the sealings, we are able to identify the practices associated with them due to the information we can infer from their materiality and their inextricable entanglement with practice. As for the way these practices were transmitted, we have to assume that they came with the seals or rather the persons, the seals travelled with.

Although it may not be possible to determine the exact origin of sealing practices or the influences that led to their development in Minoan Crete, it is possible to observe several foreign influences after they had been accepted into Minoan society. Imported seals, such as the Near Eastern cylinder seals found in Prepalatial burials already mentioned, may be considered as luxury items and 'emblems of elite identity' (Colburn 2008, 210). They were small, made of precious materials, with carvings that would have been perceived as charged with meaning of one sort or another, and they were easily transported (*cf.* also Krzyszkowska 2005, 30; Schoep 2006, 51). As Postgate remarks in his study on Mesopotamian trade in the third and second millennia BCE, such luxury items were tacked on to the transport of what he calls semi-staples – raw metals and textiles – and travelled with them (Postgate 2003, 9; such a scenario might also apply to the trade with raw materials in the EB II Aegean, *e.g.* the metal trade from non-Aegean sources, *cf.* Broodbank 2000, 293). Thus, even though the quantities of foreign objects, including cylinder seals, are small in Prepalatial Crete, their very presence may hint at more regular contacts (*cf.* Broodbank 2000, 284).[6] It is conceivable that sealing practices were transmitted in this way (*cf.* also Cosmopoulos 1991, 162–163) – whether as a general idea or as an entire concept is, however, difficult to determine. The few instances of sealing practices in the Prepalatial period might argue for the former, but it could also mean that Minoan Crete was not yet ready to adopt a complete system at that time, as there was not yet a need for a complex system.

It seems almost certain that there was no single source of influence for the development of sealing practices on Crete and that influence could have come from almost every direction. The evidence of seal iconography, seal use, and seal types, as well as sealing types is so far inconclusive; nonetheless foreign influence is evident. The impulse that reached Crete might have already been a conglomerate of merged traditions, which was further shaped and adapted by the Minoans, making Minoan sealing practices an entirely transcultural phenomenon.

Material transformation

Material transformation encompasses the ways in which newly acquired objects might be modified, *e.g.* through cleaning, decoration *etc* . Although we cannot exactly determine the source from which sealing practices were inspired, it is possible to compare the evidence for seals and sealings with contemporary sealing administrations. As Olga Krzyszkowska has remarked with respect to the glyptic development (2005, 57): 'Crete has always been different.' Seals and sealings are both object categories which show a wide variety of shapes and can have many varying features. As already mentioned above, the original inspiration for the seals and sealings is missing, thus it is difficult to say something about material transformation. But from their very first appearance, Minoan seals display specific characteristics in seal shape, as well as motives ('[...] while inspiration from elsewhere in the Aegean and beyond is entirely likely, from the start Minoan glyptic seems a largely indigenous phenomenon.' Krzyszkowska 2005, 57).

This is perhaps best illustrated by a phenomenon of the later Prepalatial period, when the scarab was introduced to the Minoan repertoire of seal shapes: Shortly after its introduction in MM IA, either directly from Egypt or through Syria-Palestine (Krzyszkowska 2005, 74) they were imitated by Minoan workshops in a material thought to imitate Egyptian faience. Apart from a cruder carving technique, the Minoan scarabs are very similar to the Egyptian originals in shape and material (Krzyszkowska 2005, 73–74; Phillips 2004, 163). Cynthia Colburn has argued recently that such imitation suggests a context of emulation, placing the adoption of such objects in the context of elite (distinction) strategies (Colburn 2008, 220; also Weingarten 2005, 761). While the Minoans seem to have established such links through the adoption of these artefacts or through the use of foreign imagery either in seal shape, *e.g.* lions or apes (Krzyszkowska 2005, 67–68, fig. 113, 116), or on the seal face, *e.g.* the Egyptian goddess Taweret transformed into the Minoan Genius (Weingarten 1991), at the same time they tend to adapt it to their own needs (*cf.* also Panagiotaki 2008, 66).

Designation

The local designation of the seals and sealings is something we are not able to determine for the periods concerned, as we have either no or only undeciphered written sources. It would be interesting to know whether the seals were primarily referred to as administrative objects (as we do today by referring to their functional aspect) or whether they were referred to with a term for adornment, for example. This would be of considerable importance when considering in which capacity the Minoans saw them primarily but this question will have to remain unanswered for the time being. However, as we are primarily concerned with the functional aspects of seals and sealings, this criterion is not particularly relevant for our current purpose.

Cultural transformation

Cultural transformation, *i.e.* the attribution of local meaning, can be determined through detailed analysis of the find contexts and the materiality of the sealings, *i.e.* the local contexts are decisive. In Minoan Crete seals generally come from funerary contexts and are found in their hundreds mainly in communal tombs, whereas sealings come from settlement contexts (see above). The sealings primarily come from settlement contexts and are direct object sealings, probably sealing basketry or wooden containers, with the one exception of the nodulus found at Malia which not only differs from the other sealings in function but is also associated with a large building with a court below the later palace (see above; Schoep 2006, 44).

Thus, the situation in the Prepalatial period is characterised by a plethora of seals, which argues for their distinct relevance in this period. The fact that they mainly come from burial contexts implies a status-relevant function (*cf.* also Relaki 2009, 361). However, the presence of sealings in the material record of the settlements from the introduction of the seals onwards, strongly suggests that these were already used at least for basic administrative purposes in the Prepalatial period in addition to any other form of use: 'The practice of sealing, even at the simplest level of the household, reflects further the control of the seal-owner of unauthorized access, showing a developed notion of property, depersonalization of economic relations, and growing complexity of economic life.' (Sbonias 1999, 44; *cf.* also Schoep and Knappett 2004, 25–26 and Relaki 2009, 367). The nodulus from Malia might imply an even more sophisticated, probably administrative aspect of sealing practice (Schoep 2006, 44–45).

Both in the Prepalatial and Protopalatial periods sealings seem to be associated with specific local contexts, in the Prepalatial period with house contexts in settlements (Schoep 2006, 44) and in the Protopalatial with buildings controlled by elites. These are not only palaces, but also distinct elite residences, as has been argued by Ilse Schoep for the evidence of sealing activity for example at the so-called Quartier Mu at Malia (Schoep 2002a; 2006, 49–50; *cf.* also Branigan 1989, 66–67).

Thus, the use of sealings in the Prepalatial period contexts, combined with the function of seals as markers of social identity and status, might be taken as an indication of the intentional application of such practices by emerging elites (*cf.* Schoep 2006, 57–58; Relaki 2009, 367–368; Sbonias 2010, 358–361). The presence of sealings complements the picture of social complexity in the Prepalatial period, which also involves competitive consumption and strategies for the consolidation and legitimisation of power through the use of prestige objects and 'differential access to commodities' (*cf.* Schoep 2006, 51), which is suggested by the use of sealings (Sbonias 1999, 44). Sealings as reflections of sealing practices might represent 'an expression of such a strategy, without *per se* implying the presence of a centralised (hierarchical) authority' (Schoep 2004, 284), the lack of which has been cited as an argument against the administrative use of sealings in the Prepalatial period (Weingarten 1990, 105 n. 2; see also Schoep 2006, 45 n. 70).

These aspects of the seals and sealings – the former being a prestige object denoting status and rank, the latter restricting access to certain commodities for certain groups – tie in with the notion included in Hahn's discussion of the effects of appropriation of objects, that it can generate social diversity, as the objects could be exploited for exactly such purposes (Hahn 2005, 104). Thus, it might be said that the appropriation of sealing practices not only reflects a strategy of elites, but also contributed to the establishment of the elites.

In terms of cultural transformation the local meaning attributed to sealing practices within the general sphere of elites and administration does not differ at all from the meaning attributed to sealing practices in those cultures which could possibly have transmitted these practices (*cf.* Aruz 2008, 15; Ferioli, Fiandra and Fissore 2000, 354). Only the scale and the design changes, while the basic idea behind the sealing practices remains the same.

Incorporation

The criterion of incorporation is better applicable to the seals than to the sealings as the former could be bodily adornment, personal belongings, or used as amulets. With regard to this criterion, it can be stated that seals are closely associated with the body through their sphragistic function, which requires them to be handled regularly. However, this is not the only way in which Minoan seals were incorporated. They were also intended to be worn on the body, as they were invariably either provided with string-holes or could be worn as rings (Krzyszkowska 2005, 21). This would also have made them highly visible. As they were often made from imported and precious materials, when the 'acquisition and display of exotic materials is a common sign of growing social diversity' (Kzryszkowska 2005, 76) it may well be said that incorporated seals (and their impressions) served indeed as 'marks of distinction' (Aruz 2008; *cf.* also Aruz 2005, 756). Cynthia Colburn (2008, 217–219) discusses the indication of social status through bodily adornment, claiming adornment to be 'a key social function in a dynamic system of communication within societies' (Colbourn 2008, 218). The adornment of the body with seals would thus have been significant as a means of denoting status and expressing difference between social groups (*cf.* Schoep 2006, 57–58). Sbonias (1999, 35) argues in a similar way: 'They were meant as a means of identification, and thus it is quite probable that they played a role as emblems of personal identity or group affiliation. Their appropriateness for transmitting symbolic messages is reflected also in the fact that they were worn during life and were used as grave goods after death.'

Though we cannot attribute seals to specific individuals in the communal tombs, their presence in these funerary assemblages also indicates a function of the seals as communicating social status and group identity, as funerals 'are arenas within which material culture can be actively used [...] material culture in mortuary contexts [can be regarded] as an active statement made about the status, social and other identities of the deceased, and possibly of the living involved in the mortuary ritual' (Papadatos 2007, 434–435; *cf.* also Blasingham 1983, 17–18). With their close links to sealing practices this might be a further indication that even in the Prepalatial period the patchy evidence for these practices is not arbitrary but to be evaluated in the context of emerging elites.

As regards the incorporation of sealings, their production and their 'correct' handling, *i.e.* their application to other objects and their being impressed by seals is evident early on in the material record. Thus the Minoans were aware of their function and the way in which they were to be employed and used them for their purposes which were probably of an administrative nature.

Traditionalisation

The last one of Hahn's criteria, traditionalisation, is something we can infer from a diachronic overview of the Early, Middle and Late Bronze Age, or even within these periods. The patchy evidence for sealing practices in the Prepalatial period was for a long time taken to confirm the view that there was no social complexity in this period (see above). Then again, evidence for a sudden administrative complexity shortly after the palaces were built, seemed to argue for the interpretation of a wholesale import at this time (*e.g.* Weingarten 1990, 105). Recent research has led to a more detailed picture of the Prepalatial period, with increasing evidence of social complexity emerging in respect to almost every aspect of Minoan society (see above; Day and Wilson 2004, 58–59; Schoep and Knappett 2004, 25–30). The more or less continuous occurrence of sealings, albeit very few over a period of approximately 700 years, and the use of the same sealing types – direct objects sealings and noduli – in Prepalatial and Protopalatial sealing practices (Schoep and Knappett 2004, 26) as well as the continuous development of the seals for over 1000 years (Krzyszkowska 2005, 1) indicate a traditionalisation of sealing practices in Minoan culture. Unfortunately, sufficient contextual evidence in the Prepalatial period is missing and the patchy pattern of sealing practices does not suggest the existence of administrative practices at first glance, but the fact that there already are sealings, argues for at least a basic administrative use of seals.[7] The strongest argument for this view might be the nodulus found in an EM IIB level at Malia (see above), a distinct sealing device, which was later closely associated with palatial administration (Weingarten 1986).

Ilse Schoep has already made the case for the use of seals in a wider social network than just on a household level in the Prepalatial period, arguing from the growing evidence for social complexity in this period (Schoep 2004, 284; see also above). However, she sees the 'selective adoption of technologies borrowed from the East during EM III–MM II' as something different from the 'wholesale importation of a cultural package in MM IB that included a new social order, the institution of kingship and kingly regalia, administrative practices using scripts, monumental architecture, and other crafts' (Schoep 2006, 53). While I would not contest that the development of administrative practices might have received an additional impetus through more intense overseas contacts from MM IA onwards, I would argue that we can observe a continuous development in the material record. As outlined above, sealing practices are mediated through two material components and we certainly have a consistent and rich record of seals from the Early Bronze Age onwards.

The presence of sealing practices – even if their potential was not fully explored in the Prepalatial period – must, at least partially, have shaped the way in which administrative structures were organised in the Protopalatial period. Thus, the mutual aspect of the materiality of the sealings as outlined above manifests itself in the shaping of the administrative characteristics, while the sealings themselves were adapted and acquired culture-specific shapes and functions in the course of this development.

Institutionalisation

The criterion of institutionalisation, which is not discussed by Hahn, might be added as a subcategory of traditionalisation. Such a process can also be ascertained by a diachronic perspective but even more so by a detailed study of the find contexts. Similar to the arguments in favour of traditionalisation, the institutionalisation of sealing practices can be observed in the Protopalatial centres with their almost simultaneous establishment and the use of very similar sealing types in the elaborate sealing administrations at the respective sites (Sbonias (1999, 45) already sees an institutionalisation of seal use in MM IA with the appearance of the hieroglyphic script on seal stones). This is carried further in the Neopalatial period, when Minoan sealing administration continues and becomes more widespread, now using only Linear A and specific types of sealing devices, though practices vary slightly from site to site.[8]

Conclusion

In the present paper I have applied the heuristic categories of the process of appropriation to the case of Minoan sealing practices in the Early and Middle Bronze Age. To sum up, the criteria for the process of appropriation can be applied to the development of Minoan sealing practices with some limitations. This is due to the fact that the appropriation in this case concerns not an object but a social practice whose characteristics have to be inferred from its material manifestation in two different object categories found in diverse social contexts. Not all of the criteria could be applied to both object categories.[9] On the other hand, this forces us to aim at reconciling evidence from different contexts, so that such an analysis can make a virtue out of necessity, achieving a truly integrative perspective. In the particular case of Minoan sealing practices, Hahn's approach offers a methodological tool to capture the emphasis on the active manipulation of objects or ideas and the mutual influence of humans and objects underlying the integration of foreign traits into a local context. Thus, the criteria for the process of appropriation offer a more systematic perspective for the development of administrative sealing practices in Minoan Crete. Having undergone a long phase of traditionalisation, the transformative capacities of the appropriated sealing practices are then revealed in the shape of the Protopalatial sealing system. For this paper, the exact origin of the sealing practices was not of such great relevance as was the fact that a new cultural trait arrived and the manner in which it was integrated.[10] The question, whether the sealing practices were imported directly from the Near East or 'down the line' via the Greek Mainland and the Cyclades needs to be evaluated through more thorough analysis. Both scenarios would carry weight for the question, not only of emulation of foreign elites in Crete (*cf.* also Schoep 2006, 51–52), but also for the concept of the transcultural character of sealing practices (*cf.* Ferioli, Fiandra and Fissore 2000, 354).

The introduction of seals and sealing practices can be seen within the framework of Papadatos' view that Aegean cultures in the Early Bronze Age are created by flows of people, goods and information (2007, 419–420, 440). The use of material culture in such a network has to be analysed in terms of the strategies and intentions of the interacting groups. The appropriation of seals in Minoan Crete and the subsequent development of sealing practices, albeit patchy and infrequent at first, might be attributed to the efforts of an emerging elite to manipulate the existing social structures. The procurement of imported artefacts and technologies holds great social potential and can be used to 'establish, maintain, increase and legitimise social differentiation' (Papadatos 2007, 438; *cf.* also Schoep 2006, 49–52). The appropriation of seals and the application of sealing practices might have been a part of such a strategy as '[...] specific seals can mark, maintain, and further social differentiation' (Weingarten 2005, 764). Kostas Sbonias (1999, 36–39 and 2010, 358) and Judith Weingarten (2005, 763–765) have both argued for the significance of the iconographic seal groups emerging in EM III/MM IA, with regard to group affiliation and social differentiation, especially for the Parading Lions/Spiral group, impressions of which are also found on the Prepalatial sealings, namely on the stopper from Knossos (CMS II, 8.1 no. 6), the conoid sealing from the Neopalatial building at Archanes (CMS II, 6 no. 149), as well as on a jar handle from Myrtos Pyrgos (CMS II, 6 no. 223).

As suggested by the use of seals as prestige objects in elite strategies (*e.g.* in funerary contexts), the introduction of sealing practices might originally rather have been part of such a strategy, instead of being an administrative necessity. Though sealing practices might not have been consciously employed in an elite strategy as were prestige objects, their close connection with the seals – made of precious materials and with symbolic iconography – certainly places these practices in such a context. The restriction of access to commodities or the obligation to submit goods as can be inferred from the existence of such a system should also be seen in the context of elite strategies (*cf.* Papadatos 2007, 423; Sbonias 1999, 45).

The introduction of sealing practices in the Early Bronze Age certainly had an impact on the development of the administrative system. It is probably safe to assume that an administrative system would have developed in some form or other but the appropriation of sealing practices in the Prepalatial period must have contributed towards the way in which administrative structures were organised. In my view, the 'sudden' appearance of the elaborate Protopalatial sealing system is an argument in favour of the profound and long term integration of these practices in the periods leading up to the formation of the palaces rather than for the need to import such a system from outside.[11] Thus, the mutual aspect of the materiality of the sealings manifests itself in the shaping of the administrative characteristics while the sealings themselves were adapted and acquired new shapes and functions in the course of this development.

Notes

1. This study is part of my doctoral research at the Institute of Archaeology, University of Heidelberg, in affiliation with the Cluster of Excellence 'Asia and Europe in a global context. Shifting asymmetries in cultural flows'. My PhD project is part of subproject D2 'Materiality and practice. Cultural entanglements in 2nd millennium BC East Mediterranean societies' and is concerned with the administrative aspects of cross-cultural exchange in the Aegean Bronze Age using Minoan Crete as a case study.
2. No roundels or tablets with Linear A inscriptions were found in Monastiraki, mainly direct object sealings and only one nodulus, but seal-types compare well with geometric and decorative motifs represented in the Phaistos deposit; furthermore, the architecture, pottery and other finds show similarities with Phaistos (Kanta and Tzigounaki 2000)
3. For a discussion of the status and nature of imported goods in the Bronze Age Aegean see Cline 2005; he is, however, more concerned with the exact moment of introduction and the

definition of the status as 'import' rather than the subsequent process of appropriation.

4. *Cf.* also Broodbank (2000, 287): 'In social terms, what we need to consider is how the arrival of orientalia and eastern customs and technologies (their significance much refracted by successive transmissions) made exotic objects, materials and ways of doing things a part of at least some Aegean people's cultural perceptions, thereby widening the repertoire of means for local leaders to advertise status, technological skill and economic power'.
5. The English terms are translations made by the author. The original German terms Hans-Peter Hahn uses are added in brackets for clarification.
6. Pini (2005, 777) sees these few 'isolated foreign objects' as an indicator of 'small-scale exchange of some kind' and differentiates between this 'casual trade' and 'controlled intentional wholesale trade'. With regard to the latter he suggests a regular trade with hippopotamus tusk from Egypt or Palestine at the beginning of the second millennium BCE based on the amount of excavated material (779). Connected to this regular contact he sees the introduction of Egyptian scarabs to Crete in MM IA. Such a scenario would support the argument made above about the ways in which seals could have been transmitted – probably travelling with the raw materials exchanged during this time of intensive contact.
7. Vlasaki and Hallager (1995, 268–270); Hallager (2000, 99); Sbonias (1999, 44); Pini (1990, 34–37); Schoep and Knappett (2004, 25–26); Palaima (response to Pini, 1990, 57) has argued that even if only one sealing is found in a settlement, the seal user is likely to have used his seal in this way more than just once as the impulse to seal will have had a specific purpose.
8. *Cf.* Schoep (2002b); while the use of seals in Minoan Crete for administrative purposes ends with the late sealings at Knossos in LM (Late Minoan) II–III, the use of seals for sealing purposes on the Mainland is secured from LH (Late Helladic) IIIB onward. The sealing practices of the mainland palaces are similar to those of the late Knossian palace (Krzyszkowska 2005, 279) and the inspiration is undoubtedly the Minoan island.
9. As was exemplified with the criterion of designation, it is generally difficult to apply all criteria to archaeological objects, as there is a lot of (contextual) information missing.
10. *Cf.* also Broodbank (2000, 285): '[...] it is best to focus attention not so much on whether external stimuli were working on Aegean societies at this time (they clearly were) but rather on how they were transferred and what impact they had'.
11. *Cf.* also Schoep (1999, 268–272) and Perna (1999); Cline (2005, 50) makes a related point in his discussion on the nature of foreign objects. He discusses the import of foreign objects after an object category had already been introduced. If an object was already known to the receiving society, the 'degree of reaction and response will be based upon the amount of previous experience that they have had with that type of object.'

References

Aruz, J. (2005) Unravelling the Mysteries of the Well-Travelled Seal. In Laffineur and Greco 2005, 751–758.

Aruz, J. (2008) *Marks of Distinction. Seals and Cultural Exchange Between the Aegean and the Orient (c. 2600–1360 BC).* Corpus der minoischen und mykenischen Siegel (CMS), Beiheft 7. Mainz, Verlag Philipp von Zabern.

Blasingham, A. C. (1983) The Seals From the Tombs of the Messara: Inferences as to Kinship and Social Organization. In O. Krzyszkowska and L. Nixon (eds), *Minoan Society. Proceedings of the Cambridge Colloquium 1981*, 11–21. Bristol, Bristol Classical Press.

Branigan, K. (1989) Minoan Foreign Relations in Transition. In R. Laffineur (ed.), *Transition. Le monde égéen du Bronze moyen au Bronze récent. Actes de la deuxième Rencontre égéenne internationale de l'Université de Liège, 18–20 avril 1988,* 65–71. Liège, Universitè de l'Etat à Liège.

Broodbank, C. (2000) *An Island Archaeology of the Early Cyclades.* Cambridge, Cambridge University Press.

Clarke, J. (2005) Crossing Cultural Divides: Transmissions and Transformations in Space. In J. Clarke (ed.), *Archaeological Perspectives on the Transmission and Transformation of Culture in the Eastern Mediterranean,* 137–139. Oxford, Oxbow Books.

Cline, E. H. (2005) The Multivalent Nature of Imported Objects in the Ancient Mediterranean World. In Laffineur and Greco 2005, 45–51.

Colburn, C. S. (2008) Exotica and the Early Minoan Elite: Eastern Imports in Prepalatial Crete. *American Journal of Archaeology* 112, 203–224.

Cosmopoulos, M. B. (1991) Exchange Networks in Prehistory. The Aegean and the Mediterranean in the Third Millennium B.C. In R. Laffineur and L. Basch (eds), *Thalassa. L'égée prehistorique et la mer. Actes de la troisième Rencontre égéenne internationale de l'Université de Liège, Station de recherches sous-marines et océanographiques (StaReSO), Calvi, Corse (23–25 avril 1990),* 155–168. Liège, Université de Liège.

Day, P. and Wilson, D. E. (2004), Ceramic Change and the Practice of Eating and Drinking in Early Bronze Age Crete. In P. Halstead and J. C. Barrett (eds), *Food, Cuisine and Society in Prehistoric Greece,* 45–62. Oxford, Oxbow Books.

DeMarrais, E., Gosden, C. and Renfrew, C. (2004) *Rethinking Materiality. The Engagement of Mind with the Material World.* Cambridge, McDonald Institute for Archaeological Research.

Ferioli, P. and Fiandra, E. (1989) The Importance of Clay Sealings in the Ancient Administration. In I. Pini (ed.), *Fragen und Probleme der bronzezeitlichen ägäischen Glyptik. Beiträge zum 3. Internationalen Marburger Siegel-Symposium 5.–7. September 1985.* Corpus der minoischen und mykenischen Siegel (CMS), Beiheft 3, 41–53. Berlin, Gebr. Mann Verlag.

Ferioli, P., Fiandra, E. and Fissore, G. G. (2000) Research into the Use of *Cretulae* in Ancient Administrative Systems: Problems Regarding Orientation and Methods. In Perna 2000, 353–364.

Fiandra, E. (1968) A che cosa servivano le cretule di Festòs. In *Pepragmena tu B' Diethnus Kritoloyiku Sinedriu 1*. Filoloyikos Sillogos 'O Hrisostomos', 383–397. Athens.

Fiandra, E. (1975) Ancora a proposito delle cretule di Festòs: connessione tra i sistemi amministrativi centralizzati e l'uso delle cretule nell'età del bronzo. *Bollettino d'arte del Ministero della Pubblica Istruzione* 60, 1–25.

Foster, A. L. (2000) Administrative Functions of Seals on Sealings at Phaistos: A Comparative View from Egypt. In Pini 2000, 79–94.

Galanakis, K. (2005) *Minoan Glyptic: Typology, Deposits and Iconography from the Early Minoan Period to the Late Minoan IB Destruction in Crete.* Oxford, John and Erica Hedges Ltd.

Graves-Brown, P. M. (2000) Introduction. In P. M. Graves-Brown (ed.), *Matter, Materiality and Modern Culture,* 1–9. London, Routledge.

Hahn, H. P. (2005) *Materielle Kultur. Eine Einführung.* Berlin, Dietrich Reimer Verlag.

Hallager, E. (2000) New Evidence for Seal Use in the Prepalatial and Protopalatial Periods. In Pini 2000, 97–105.

Heath, M. C. (1958) Early Helladic Clay Sealings from the House of Tiles at Lerna. *Hesperia* 27, 81–121.

Kanta, A. and Tzigounaki, A. (2000) The Protopalatial Multiple Sealing System. New Evidence from Monastiraki. In Perna 2000, 193–205.

Karytinos, A. (1998) Sealstones in Cemeteries: A Display of Social Status? In K. Branigan (ed.), *Cemetery and Society in the Aegean Bronze Age*, 78–86. Sheffield, Sheffield Academic Press.

Knappett, C. (2002) Mind the Gap: Between Pots and Politics in Minoan Studies. In Y. Hamilakis (ed.), *Labryrinth Revisited. Rethinking Minoan Archaeology,* 167–188. Oxford, Oxbow Books.

Knappett, C. (2005) *Thinking Through Material Culture.* Philadelphia, University of Pennsylvania Press.

Kostoula, M. (2000) Die frühhelladischen Tonplomben mit Siegelabdrücken aus Petri bei Nemea. In Pini 2000, 135–148.

Krzyszkowska, O. (2005) *Aegean Seals. An Introduction.* London, Institute of Classical Studies.

Laffineur, R. and Greco, E. (2005) *Emporia: Aegeans in the Central and Eastern Mediterranean.* Proceedings of the 10th International Aegean Conference, Athens, Italian School of Archaeology, 14–18 April 2004. Liège and Austin, Université de Liège.

Miller, D. (2005) Materiality: An Introduction. In D. Miller (ed.), *Materiality,* 1–50. Durham and London, Duke University Press.

Panagiotaki, M. (1993) Sealings from the Olive Press Room, Knossos: New Information from the Unpublished Notes of Sir Arthur Evans. *The Annual of the British School at Athens* 88, 29–47.

Panagiotaki, M. (2008) Exchange of Prestige Technologies as Evidence of Cultural Interactions and Integration Between the Aegean and the Near East in the Bronze Age. In C. Papageorgiadou-Banis and A. Giannikouri (eds), *Sailing in the Aegean. Readings on the Economy and Trade Routes,* 55–76. Athens, De Boccard.

Papadatos, Y. (2007) Beyond Cultures and Ethnicity: A New Look at Material Culture Distribution and Inter-regional Interaction in the Early Bronze Age Southern Aegean. In S. Antoniadou and A. Pace (eds), *Mediterranean Crossroads,* 419–451. Athens, Pierides Foundation Publications.

Pelon, O. (1993) La salle à piliers du palais de Malia et ses antecedents: recherches complémentaires. *Bulletin de correspondance hellénique* 117, 523–546.

Perna, M. (1999) Il sistema amministrativo minoico nella Creta prepalaziale. In V. LaRosa, D. Palermo and L. Vagnetti (eds), *Epi ponton plazomenoi. Simposio italiano die Studi Egei dedicato a Luigi Bernabò Brea e Giovanni Pugliese Carratelli, Roma, 18–20 febbraio 1998,* 63–68. Athens, Scuola Archeologica Italiana di Atene.

Perna, M. (2000) *Administrative Documents in the Aegean and their Near Eastern Counterparts.* Proceedings of the International Colloquium Naples, February 29–March 2, 1996. Rome, Ministero per i beni e le attività culturali, Ufficio centrale per i beni archivistici.

Philipps, J. (2004) The Odd Man Out. Minoan Scarabs and Scaraboids. In M. Bietak and E. Czerny (eds), *Scarabs of the Second Millennium BC from Egypt, Nubia, Crete and the Levant: Chronological and Historical Implications. Papers of a Symposium, Vienna, 10th–13th of January 2002,* 161–170. Vienna, Verlag der Akademie der Österreichischen Wissenschaften.

Pini, I. (1984) Minoische und helladische Tonsiegel. In Centre G. Glotz (ed.), *Aux origins de l'Hellénisme. La Crète et la Grèce. Hommage à Henri van Effenterre,* 73–81. Paris, Publications de la Sorbonne.

Pini, I. (1989) *Fragen und Probleme der bronzezeitlichen ägäischen Glyptik. Beiträge zum 3. Internationalen Marburger Siegel-Symposium 5.–7. September 1985.* Corpus der minoischen und mykenischen Siegel (CMS), Beiheft 3. Berlin, Gebr. Mann Verlag.

Pini, I. (1990) The Hieroglyphic Deposit and the Temple Repositories at Knossos. In T. Palaima (ed.), *Aegean Seals, Sealings and Administration. Proceedings of the NEH-Dickson Conference of the Program of Aegean Scripts and Prehistory of the Department of Classics, University of Texas at Austin, January 11–13, 1989,* 33–54. Université de Liège.

Pini, I. (ed.) (1999) *Iraklion. Archäologisches Museum. Corpus der minoischen und mykenischen Siegel (CMS)* II, 6. Berlin, Gebr. Mann Verlag.

Pini, I. (2000) *Minoisch-mykenische Glyptik. Stil, Ikonographie, Funktion. Corpus der minoischen und mykenischen Siegel (CMS)*, Beiheft 6. Berlin, Gebr. Mann Verlag.

Pini, I. (2002) In I. Pini (ed.) *Iraklion, Archäologisches Museum. Corpus der minoischen und mykenischen Siegel (CMS)* II, 8.1, 1–23. Mainz, Verlag Philipp von Zabern.

Pini, I. (ed.) (2004) *Kleinere griechische Sammlungen. Neufunde aus Griechenland und der westlichen Türkei. Corpus der minoischen und mykenischen Siegel (CMS)* V, Supplementum 3,2. Mainz, Verlag Philipp von Zabern.

Pini, I. (2005) Seals as an Indicator of Trade? In Laffineur and Greco 2005, 777–784.

Pini, I. and Poursat, J.-C. (1995) *Sceaux minoens et mycéniens.* Corpus minoischer und mykenischer Siegel (CMS), Beiheft 5. Berlin, Gebr. Mann Verlag.

Postgate, J. N. (2003) Learning the Lessons of the Future: Trade in Prehistory through a Historian's Lens. *Bibliotheca Orientalis* 60, 5–26.

Poursat, J.-C. (1990) Response to I. Pini (1990) *The Hieroglyphic Deposit and the Temple Repositories at Knossos.* In T. Palaima (ed.), *Aegean Seals, Sealings and Administration. Proceedings of the NEH-Dickson Conference of the Program of Aegean Scripts and Prehistory of the Department of Classics, University of Texas at Austin, January 11–13 1989.* Aegaeum 5, 55. Université de Liège, Histore de l'Art et Archéologie de la Grèce Antique.

Relaki, M. (2009) Rethinking Administration and Seal Use in Third Millennium Crete. *Creta Antiqua* 10/2, 353–372.

Robb, J. (2004) The Extended Artefact and the Monumental Economy: A Methodology for Material Agency. In DeMarrais, Gosden and Renfrew 2004, 131–139.

Sbonias, K. (1995) *Frühkretische Siegel. Ansätze für eine Interpretation der sozial-politischen Entwicklung auf Kreta während der Frühbronzezeit.* Oxford, Tempus Reparatum.

Sbonias, K. (1999) Social Development, Management of Production, and Symbolic Representation in Prepalatial Crete. In A. Chaniotis (ed.), *From Minoan Farmers to Roman Traders: Sidelights on the Economy of Ancient Crete,* 25–51. Stuttgart, Franz Steiner Verlag.

Sbonias, K. (2010) Diversity and Transformation. Looking for Meaning in the Prepalatial Seal Consumption and Use. In W. Müller (ed.), *Die Bedeutung der minoischen und mykenischen Glyptik.* Corpus minoischer und mykenischer Siegel Beiheft 8, 349–362. Mainz, Verlag Philipp von Zabern.

Schoep, I. (1999) The Origins of Writing and Administration on Crete. *Oxford Journal of Archaeology* 18, 265–276.

Schoep, I. (2002a) Social and Political Organization on Crete in the Proto-Palatial Period: The Case of Middle Minoan II Malia. *Journal of Mediterranean Archaeology* 15, 101–132.

Schoep, I. (2002b) *The Administration of Neopalatial Crete. A Critical Assessment of the Linear A Tablets and Their Role in the Administrative Process.* Salamanca, Ed. Univ. de Salamanca.

Schoep, I. (2004) The Socio-Economic Context of Seal Use and Administration at Knossos. In G. Cadogan, E. Hatzaki and A. Vasilakis (eds), *Knossos: Palace, City, State,* 283–293. Athens, The British School at Athens.

Schoep, I. (2006) Looking Beyond the First Palaces: Elites and the Agency of Power in EM III–MM II Crete. *American Journal of Archaeology* 110, 37–64.

Schoep, I. and Knappett, C. (2004) Dual Emergence: Evolving Heterarchy, Exploding Hierarchy. In J. C. Barrett and P. Halstead (eds), *The Emergence of Civilisation Revisited,* 21–37. Oxford, Oxbow Books.

Soles, J. and Davaras, C. (2004) Sitia. Mochlos, Siedlung. In I. Pini (ed.) *Kleinere griechische Sammlungen. Neufunde aus Griechenland und der westlichen Türkei. Corpus der minoischen und mykenischen Siegel (CMS)* V, Supplementum 3,2, 514. Mainz, Verlag Philipp von Zabern.

Taylor, T. (2008) Materiality. In R. A. Bentley, H. D. G. Maschner and C. Chippindale (eds), Handbook of Archaeological Theories, 297–320. Lanham, Altamira Press.

Vlasaki, M. and Hallager, E. (1995) Evidence for Seal Use in Pre-Palatial Western Crete. In Pini and Poursat 1995, 251–270.

Weingarten, J. (1986) Some Unusual Minoan Clay Nodules. *Kadmos* 25, 1–21.

Weingarten, J. (1990) Three Upheavals in Minoan Sealing Administration: Evidence for Radical Change. In T. Palaima (ed.), *Aegean Seals, Sealings and Administration. Proceedings of the NEH-Dickson Conference of the Program of Aegean Scripts and Prehistory of the Department of Classics, University of Texas at Austin, January 11–13, 1989,* 105–120. Université de Liège.

Weingarten, J. (1991) *The Transformation of Egyptian Taweret into the Minoan Genius: A Study in Cultural Transmission in the Middle Bronze Age.* Partille, Paul Åströms Förlag.

Weingarten, J. (1995) Sealing Studies in the Middle Bronze Age, III: The Minoan Hieroglyphic Deposits at Mallia and Knossos. In Pini and Poursat 1995, 285–311.

Weingarten, J. (2000a) Lerna: Sealings in a Landscape. In Perna 2000, 103–123.

Weingarten, J. (2000b) Early Helladic II Sealings from Geraki in Laconia: Evidence for Property, Textile Manufacture, and Trade. In Pini 2000, 317–329.

Weingarten, J. (2005) How Many Seals Make a Heap? Seals and Interconnections on Prepalatial Crete. In Laffineur and Greco 2005, 759–766.

Weingarten, J. (2007) Noduli, Sealings and a Weight from Deposits A and E. In C. F. MacDonald and C. Knappett (eds), *Knossos. Protopalatial Deposits in Early Magazine A and the South-West Houses,* 134–139. Athens, The British School at Athens.

Wilson, D. 2008, Early Prepalatial Crete. In C. W. Shelmerdine (ed.), *The Aegean Bronze Age,* 77–104. Cambridge, Cambridge University Press.

Yule, P. (1980) *Early Cretan Seals. A Study in Chronology.* Mainz, Verlag Philipp von Zabern.

15.

Hyperculture, tradition and identity: how to communicate with seals in times of global action. A Middle Bronze Age seal impression from Kamid el-Loz

Marlies Heinz and Julia Linke

In general, archaeological research focuses on tracking processes of cultural development under very dissimilar conditions and in very diverse contexts. It deals with a variety of forms of interaction – war, trade, diplomacy, contact through migration as well as encounters between societies with sedentary, mobile and seasonally mobile ways of life, sustained by an equally diverse range of stakeholders and participants.

The reasons behind these encounters and the 'nature' of the actors are expected to have a considerable influence on social, political, cultural and religious life when the actors have been exposed to the influence of the outside, of the 'other'. Critical comments on the influence of globalisation, colonisation and/or intercultural encounters raise the question of whether global cultural contacts do lead to the homogenisation of cultural expression – and, as such, to the diminution of cultural plurality? Or, on the contrary, do they promote the diversity of cultural, political, and economical modes of expression and organisation? Closely related to this complex of interests is the examination of the initially immaterial world of humans, their ideas, their self- and worldviews, as well as their values of life and the direct or indirect expressions these mental fields leave behind – expressed in the material heritage.

Similar questions are fundamental considerations when we deal with the cultural contacts and intercultural encounters between the ancient Near Eastern societies in the Levant during the Bronze Age and their neighbours. We are interested in finding out what they understood by their 'self' and the 'other' with respect to those living in neighbouring communities, how they imagined 'themselves and the others' and how these conceptualisations might have been expressed in the material terms. The logical next question is whether it was important to differentiate between 'us' and 'them' at all, or, furthermore, to materialise the difference? If so: why, and for whom in society were those differences intended to be meaningful? Research on cultural encounters in ancient societies thus concentrates on the many ways of constructing identities, *i.e.* whether a common history, a common tradition and the remembering of a common past had been important, for whom it was important and why?

From the archaeological research, it may then be possible to find out who kept which memory in the past and who had the means at hand to express the materialised memory, the imaginations about 'us' and 'them', about here and there – especially in matters of intercultural encounters. We furthermore consider to what extent the intercultural encounters result in continuities or breaks, modifications or innovations, in differentiation or, alternatively, in homogenisation of the materialised cultural record. By taking this approach, our objective is to uncover the transformative potential of intercultural relations and what the results, *i.e.* the materialised cultural characteristics, for those societies, are. Did these societies adopt cultural expressions of 'the others' from the outside, appropriating them and possibly reinterpreting them? In short – what does materiality tell us?

A transformation initially can denote nothing more than the change of form or shape of an object. A change of this kind does not necessarily mean that content, function, or method of using an object has changed too. At the same time, it is exactly this change that we also have to take into consideration: a transformation of the form may well be accompanied by a transformation of the idea behind the form, of the meaning, of the immaterial connotations that originally belonged to the materialised evidence. Additionally, even if the shape of an object remains the same, it is still possible that the meaning behind it could change, which would not be recognised by archaeologists in the first place.

The example that may try to illustrate *pars pro toto* the possible impact of intercultural encounters in the Levant is a seal-impression from Kamid el-Loz in Lebanon that we excavated during our 2009 season. The model that will be referred to in reconstructing the conjunction between intercultural encounters and their transformative capacities in the field of the material culture is that of Byung-Chul Han, a philosopher who was born in Korea, who studied in Germany and who today is a Professor in Karlsruhe, Germany. Byung-Chul Han designed an interesting concept, entitled 'Hyper culture – Globalisation and Culture' (Han 2005), in which he describes and elucidates the effects of globalisation on global cultural development. Hyper culture, according to Han, is product and result of global contacts, a global cultural mélange of anything with everything. Hyper culture, according to Han, is characterised through dissolution (*Entgrenzung*) Rather than having boundaries and limitations, a globally linked and networked world characterises the hyper-room of culture (Han 2005, 16–17). Hyper culture arises from a mixture of very different traits of cultural elements and expressions, life styles, worldviews, beliefs and convictions rather than being descended or inherited from a recognisable ancestral tradition. As such, hyper culture does not have a tangible place of origin or a history of development and cannot be identified as growing from an original source. In principle, hyper-culture is structured by conjunctions, it is not an 'either ... or', but an 'all things considered'. Hyper culture is the coherence of the incoherent, the coexistence of the disparate, the closeness of the remote (see Han 2005, 35).

Referring to the German philosopher Hegel (cited by Han 2005, 10) culture always arises from contact with the 'other'. Han integrates this view into his reflections and extends it. His model, therefore, does not present one individual cultural authenticity. It is rather the opposite: the integration of all possible global origins (Han 2005, 16). Hyper culture originates from accumulation, from the interaction between and the influence of cultural areas on each other. That is to say, hyper culture emerges through the process of disaggregating elements of cultural expression from their original contexts and recombining them into a new form – the hyper cultural form. As mentioned above, hyper culture exists as cultural pattern for which it is impossible to identify the historical origins from which it stemmed. Hyper culture creates a new basis for identity through the mixture of traditions, and hence it creates new forms of communal organization. It establishes identity by using cultural elements and expressions from the 'other' in order to establish the 'self' (Han 2005, 29). As an intentional creation, hyper culture can be fabricated at any time – and possesses the potential of being a powerful political instrument. Without being rooted in local traditions or cultural meanings and, as a consequence of the global mixture of cultural elements within it, hyper culture makes the global actor at home all over the world.

In such a hyper cultural system, according to Han, the completely 'other' does not exist and does not threaten anyone anymore! This new identity offers an understanding of a 'we' without regional, cultural or chronological limitations, creating a reality without history (Han 2005, 17). Hyper culture changes the self-conception of the people involved: the other is no longer exotic, but part of the own. The Self is generated through the acquisition of the other. Hyper culture thus produces an acute plurality of life styles and forms of perceptions of the world (Han 2005, 68) and is, at the same time, not based upon a common horizon of experience. Hyper culturality creates a colourful collage-society of different influences and no longer represents the tradition of a historical evolved common destiny bound through a common handed down history. Hyper culture has the potential to create smooth transitions between a centre and a periphery (Han 2005, 33–34). However, this potential does not exclude the facility for establishing a dominating cultural formation.

In short: globalisation and intercultural encounters create new forms of cultural expressions and new self-conceptions, or rather identities, for those involved into and affected by global activities. This new identity is characterised by an understanding of a 'we' without regional and cultural limitations, generated through the acquisition of the other or of elements of the other. Globalisation or intercultural encounters create a reality that is not based upon a common horizon of experience and without any common history.

With that model of Han in mind we should turn to Kamid el-Loz and the global relationships during the Middle Bronze Age. Middle Bronze age Lebanon (*c.* 2000–1550 BCE) can be characterised as an urban culture that was integrated into a wide ranging network of connections. The political and religious elites of these urban communities are represented through material evidence, be it the so-called palaces and temples, cuneiform tablets (containing information about the economic activities), and cylinder seals as tools of administration, representation and communication, as well as imported goods made of various materials and imported pottery. Both material and textual evidence verify the integration of modern-day Lebanon in this period through a variety of intercultural encounters that included the regions of Egypt in the southwest, Palestine in the south, Syria in the east and north as well as Cyprus and Crete in the west. Texts from Egypt and Mari contain details about the economic exchange with the area of Lebanon, texts from Egypt and Byblos inform in addition about political contacts and local forms of political organization, and texts from Kamid el-Loz about local economical aspects. Material evidence from Arqa, Byblos, Beirut, Burak, Sidon and Kamid el-Loz proves the existence of the intercultural encounters for which we are looking. We can also be sure that Mesopotamian neighbours were aware of the urban and economic development in the area covered today by Lebanon. Relevant information reached Mesopotamia via connections to Mari. The verification of intercultural encounters between Cyprus and Crete in the west with the urban sites in Lebanon during the MBA (Middle Bronze Age) has been demonstrated through the pottery finds from Sidon, Beirut, Byblos and Kamid el-Loz. As one of the urban sites on a major trade route, Kamid el-Loz was also involved in these intercultural encounters. From the MBA in Kamid el-Loz ,a palace and a temple-building as well as a domestic area including burials are known.

During the season 2009 we found, in the filling of room 3 of the Middle Bronze Age palace, a seal impression, placed on the handle of a storage jar. Based on our current interpretation, we believe this find spot represents an entrance room into the palace. The seal-illustration contains a main and a secondary scene (see Fig. 15.1). The main scene depicts three male (?) figures and one female figure as well as several filling motives. The secondary scene renders a sphinx and a lion, separated by an interwoven band. Parallels to single elements of this image are known from the area of today's Lebanon, Syria, Palestine, Iraq, Turkey and Egypt.

The naked female, represented frontally with her head turned to her right hand side and crossing her arms in front of her chest, is a common motif in MBA seals in Syria, and here well known for example from Ugarit (*e.g.* R.S. 24.363: Otto 2000, no. 53) or Mari (ME 242: Otto 2000, no. 94). It is also common in Palestine (*e.g.* Megiddo: Otto 2000, no. 153), from Anatolia (*e.g.* Kültepe: Otto 2000, no. 154), and also from Mesopotamia where, different from the illustration here, the female protagonist is usually depicted with her head *en face*. According to current research in the field of seal iconography in this geographic region, a naked female depicted in this manner should be identified as a goddess (*cf.* Winter 1983). Additionally, the figure on the Kamid el-Loz seal impression may be wearing a headdress that looks like a horned crown, as would be typical for a goddess.

Three figures are approaching the naked goddess, separated from her by an incense burner or altar. The first is wearing a coat with a rolled fringe and is facing the female. His right hand is upraised and maybe he's holding some kind of vessel or offering it to the goddess (*cf.* Otto 2000, no. 21). Above his hand a vulture is depicted as is underneath the incense burner. These vultures have parallels in Egypt with the so-called Nḫbet, which in that culture have protective features (Otto 2000, 260).

This composition is well known from contemporary seals from Syria and Palestine: namely, the man in front of the goddess would represent a king or high official. The first person is followed by a second (probably male) figure, depicted smaller than the first one and holding a *lituus* – well known from the Syrian (*e.g.* Mari, TH 82.245: Otto 2000, no. 383) and Anatolian (*e.g.* Kültepe, Kt. p/k 134: Otto 2000, no. 185) seal iconography and in those places being a sign of royal rank. On the seal from Kamid el-Loz, the carrier of the sign would not be the king himself but rather, according to the composition of the scene and due to his significantly smaller size, a high official.

The third male participant may be characterised, on the one hand, as a bearer of gifts and is identified as such by his action: carrying and presenting an animal to the goddess, a motive again well known for example from the seals of Emar (*cf.* Beyer 2001, *e.g.* D16, D17, E9, E10). At the same time this figure matches the type of the so-called 'athlete warrior,' and is characterised as such by his posture, the walking stance, the long hair falling over his back and his slender waist. These athletes are typical for the so-called Lebanese seals, a problematic designation (*cf.* Nagel and Eder 1992), as before we found the seal in Kamid el-Loz, this designation referred solely to a group of unprovenanced seals from the Beirut art market. Within this one figure we thus may find the depiction of two functions: the bearing of gifts and fighting! According to Dominique Collon (1994), the motive of the athlete-warrior developed first in Syria (early second millennium), then in Crete (MM (Middle Minoan) III, 1700–1550/MB II) and, as we see with the Kamid el-Loz sample, found its way into 'Lebanese' glyptic tradition during the early second millennium BCE

The secondary scene shows a seated winged sphinx with an upraised paw, a striding lion and the interwoven band. The sphinx motif comes from Egypt, where the character with an upraised paw is usually shown standing and with snakes lying at her feet, which the sphinx either crushes or fights. The sphinx displayed in this way is currently only known from the so-called 'Lebanese' glyptic tradition. Another modification from the Egyptian original can be seen in the presentation of its wings, which are depicted in every detail including the reproduction of the individual feathers, a mode of representation, which is typical for the Levantine depictions. In Egypt, winged sphinxes are very rare. The lion,

Fig. 15.1: The Kamid el-Loz seal impression (drawing: M. Leicht / photography: Chr. Krug).

walking, looking to the right, the mouth open, the tail spirally twisted inwards, is a typical execution of the motive known from the western Syrian seal-iconography. The seal, therefore, incorporates single individual elements of iconography that come from Anatolia, several areas of modern-day Syria, Cyprus, Crete, Egypt, Palestine, Mesopotamia and Lebanon.

Whether this composition of the seal image represents the homogenisation of cultural expression or, on the contrary, the creation of cultural diversity, seems to be a matter for discussion. Also deserving of reflection is whether the transformation of the iconographic composition was accompanied by a transformation of the ideas and the immaterial connotations behind the image that originally belonged to the dis-integrated and re-integrated elements.

All motifs, but especially those of the naked goddess, the 'athlete warrior' and the sphinx are taken out of their original context and transferred into a new one (one could of course discuss whether the motifs, well-known in the mentioned areas, had been independently 'invented' also in the area of Lebanon, a reflection that we consider less likely). The female figure with the unusual attitude of her head is clearly different from her Mesopotamian origins but still certainly the same motif. The sphinx with her upraised paw is totally taken out of her original context where she would be fighting against snakes. Shown without the snake, whose presence in the original context explains her upraised paw, means that this depiction seems illogical. Above all the 'athlete warrior', originally derived from Crete, where he is only depicted in fighting or athletic actions, is here transformed into a bearer of gifts. Thus the composition represents a classic example of hyper culture according to Han's definition. We see the coherence of the incoherent, the coexistence of the disparate and the closeness of the remote. We see a mixture of iconographical elements that had the potential to create a new basis for identity. The image of the seal impression from Kamid el-Loz affirms in an amazing way the model Han developed and in which globalisation or intercultural encounters appeared first and foremost as a highly creative and, for certain circles of the involved societies, a highly integrative power. A power, which by disaggregating elements of cultural expressions from its original contexts and re-integrating them into a new form, creates new self-conceptions and identities for those involved in and affected by cross-regional activities. This new identity which could be created through this mixture of iconographical elements in one seal offered an understanding of a 'we' without regional or cultural limitations, a reality without one common history or tradition, in which the 'other' was no more the exotic, but part of the own. The totally other thus did not exist anymore.

When we take up now the question stated at the outset of who the protagonists were in this 'brave new world', then the context of the seal impression in Kamid el-Loz and its visual theme strongly point to the upper class, that is, the world of the local elite that represented the 'global players' of that time. For this segment of society, the intercultural encounter created a specific 'language', an iconography that was thought for and read by a circle of elite members of the involved societies, an imagery that created the new form of social identity and possibly a new community form – that Byung-Chul Han is referring to – an elite identity, that became effective through the transgression, by leaving the local cultural tradition behind, and by expressing itself as the new 'we' via the hyper cultural images.

Byung-Chul Han generated a highly valuable tool for describing the effects of intercultural encounters on the material heritage. He describes what hyper culture is and how it emerges, but he does not offer an explanation for the reasons that cause these encounters. The model of Han seems a remarkable creative heuristic model to reflect possible impacts of global action or intercultural encounters on the material heritage and the social order of those societies involved – thus, on the transformative capacities of intercultural encounters that we are looking for. Nevertheless, at the moment there should be certain reservations about applying Han's ideas to the seal impression of Kamid el-Loz, which do not result from doubts on the model of hyper culture but on the term 'intercultural encounter' and its applicability to the cultural background in the Levant, the traditions and the 'local' in the areas that we call today Syria, Israel, Palestine and Lebanon (to which we should also add Jordan). The idea of the intercultural encounters – as well as the idea of hyper-culture – is based on the premise that a clearly recognisable local exists. But what are local traditions and local cultural meanings, what is the materiality of one individual cultural authenticity, what was the expression of the "other" and what had been the common horizons of experience in these areas? Do we capture intercultural or intra-cultural encounters when we are dealing with the above-mentioned areas? We still have to clarify *en detail* what we mean when we are talking about a local society in the Levant and about the types and range of identities – on the elite level and on the levels of the other community members. And if it was not the local culture, tradition and history that held at least the elite-circle together – but the fusion of the 'other' with the 'self' – what meaning did the 'self', *i.e.* the local culture and traditions, have besides this 'global own'? How did the local elite show proof of legitimacy if not via a common tradition? The 'global parallels' in the material heritage are evident, intercultural encounters have been demonstrated, but the identification of the 'local,' and thus the answer to whether we are dealing with intercultural or intra-cultural encounters when it comes to shared cultural expressions within the Levant, still presents a wide field for future cultural research.

Acknowledgements

This paper focuses on the model of hyper culture. A colleague in the group of the peer-reviewer mentioned, that there is a difference 'between hyper culture and hybridization, acculturation or creolization', aspects not reflected in the present contribution. We thank our colleague for the valuable advice and we consider it very worthwhile to integrate these aspects in a future contribution.

References

Beyer, D. (2001) *Les sceaux*. Emar IV. Orbis biblicus et orientalis 20. Friburg, Edition Université Fribourg.

Collon, D. (1994) Bull-Leaping in Syria. *Ägypten und Levante* 4, 81–88.

Han, B.-C. (2005) *Hyperkulturalität: Kultur und Globalisierung*. Berlin, Merve.

Heinz, M, Kulemann-Ossen, S., Linke, J. and Wagner, E. (2010) *Kamid el-Loz – Intermediary between Cultures. More than 10 Years of Archaeological Research in Kamid el-Loz (1997–2007).* Beirut, BAAL Hors Série.

Heinz, M., Cantazaretti, A., Linke,S., Müller, J.-M., Wagner, E., Walther, A. and Weber, M., (2010) *Kamid el-Loz. Report on the Excavations in 2008 and 2009*. Beirut, BAAL Hors Série.

Nagel, W. and Eder, C. (1992) Altsyrien und Ägypten. *Damaszener Mitteilungen* 6, 3–108.

Otto, A. (2000) *Die Entstehung und Entwicklung der klassisch-syrischen Glyptik.* Berlin and New York, De Gruyter.

Winter, U. (1983) *Frau und Göttin. Exegetische und ikonographische Studien zum weiblichen Gottesbild im Alten Israel und in dessen Umwelt*. Fribourg, Edition Université Fribourg.

16.

The role of the Canaanite population in the Aegean migration to the Southern Levant in the late second millennium BCE

Assaf Yasur-Landau

It will be argued that the Canaanite inhabitants of the southern coastal plain and the Shephela area had an active role in the foundation or in the rebuilding of the of the *Pentapolis* sites of Ashkelon and Tel Miqne Ekron, and as a result, Canaanite material culture traits appear side by side with Aegean ones. The domestic behavioural patterns of food preparation and food consumption continue in both Aegean-style and local tradition, and such Canaanite cult symbols as the ibex and palm tree, continue to appear in the 12th century, side by side with the newly introduced Aegean-style figurines. This reconstruction challenges the existing, prevalent paradigm of violent conquest of the Canaanite sites by the Philistines and colonial, asymmetrical power relations between the Aegean newcomers and the local population.

Introduction

After decades of careful excavations at Tel Miqne/Ekron, Ashdod and Ashkelon and a rapidly growing number of publications, the appearance of 12th century Aegean material culture traits in southern Canaan may be one of the poster-children for the identification of migration in the archaeological record, thanks to overwhelming evidence for a profound Aegean impact on domestic behavioural patterns. Indeed, the 12th century brought sudden and multiple changes in the domestic assemblages of Ashdod, Ashkelon and Tel Miqne/Ekron, which can only interpreted as a change in the *habitus* of the residents formed by the arrival of new migrant population from the Aegean and not by the impact of any previous mercantile activity (*e.g.* Dothan 1989; Killebrew 1998; Barako 2000; Dothan and Zukerman 2004; Ben Shlomo 2006; Yasur-Landau 2010). These changes included the introduction of house forms centred around the rectangular or circular hearth and a large array of domestic behavioural patterns stemming from an Aegean origin: food was cooked on the hearths using Aegean-style cooking jugs or amphorae, displaying the same burn marks on their sides as they show in the Aegean area (Ben-Shlomo *et al.* 2008; Yasur-Landau 2010, 130–131, 228–234). Food and drinks were served in a complete assemblage of locally made LH (Late Helladic) IIIC-Style pottery which included skyphoi, shallow angular bowls and kraters, as well as various closed forms as strainer jug, feeding bottle, and trefoil mouth jugs. Stirrup jugs, pyxides and hydriae were used for small and medium scale storage (Yasur-Landau 2010, tab. 7.2; 243–255). Pottery production was transformed with the introduction of new clay recipes and kiln types (Yasur-Landau 2010, 264–266). Textile production was also transformed with the introduction of the imperforated spool-shaped loom weights (Yasur-Landau 2010, 267–270), and the world of domestic cult was enriched with the introduction of 'Ashdoda' and 'mourner' type figurines (Ben-Shlomo and Press 2009), as well as by the use of incised bovid scapulae (Zukerman *et al.* 2007; Yasur-Landau 2010, 303).

However, the innovative forms, striking though they may be and manifesting what I termed as a *deep change* (Yasur-Landau 2010, 14–33) in behavioural patterns that are indicative of the arrival of a migrant population, are not the complete story of the 12th century BCE domestic assemblages in Philistia. In every house and assemblage in Ashkelon, Ashdod, and Ekron, local Canaanite pottery forms are found in large quantities, sometimes surpassing the quantity of locally made Aegean-style pottery. Despite the fact that this pottery was published together with the Aegean pottery types in the final reports of Ashdod (Dothan 1971, Dothan and Porath 1993), local Canaanite-style pottery was neglected or mentioned only in passing by many scholars when analyzing the Philistine phenomenon until very recently. They do not appear in Dothan's *The Philistines and their Material Culture* (1982), or in Stager's (1995) seminal synthesis on the Philistines. In the 2004 landmark article by Dothan and Zukerman (2004, tab. 1) which both defined the earliest Aegean-style ceramic repertoire from 12th century Philistia and presented the results of a quantitative study by Mazow, the authors show that Aegean and Canaanite styles were equally represented (around 50% of each pottery tradition; see below) in field IV at Ekron. They also stressed the important role of the Aegean-style pottery as archaeological proof of an Aegean migration; however they did not relate to the astonishing fact that half of the assemblage was non-Aegean. Perhaps as a symptom of the focus on the Aegean material culture traits, Killebrew (2005, 225) sees the Canaanite pottery types from Ekron stratum VII as background noise – the cooking pots were interpreted as intrusive, and the storage jars and lamps are really an international form.

To my mind, the focus on Aegean-style traits did not only result from the desire of many archaeologists (myself included) to present the archaeological background of the historical scenario of the Philistine migration, but also from a prevailing paradigm concerning the power relations between the Philistine migrants and the local Canaanite population. Many scholars would argue that following the defeat of the Sea Peoples by the Egyptians in year 8 of Ramses III, the Philistines had forcefully settled in the southern coastal plain, after destroying the unfortunate Canaanite sites they chose to inhabit. Stager (1995, 348) is very clear in this matter, arguing that 'during stage I of settlement, the Philistines destroyed indigenous cities and supplanted them with their own in the four corners of the territory they conquered'. Moreover, he uses the term 'urban imposition' to describe the establishing of Philistine cities atop the ruined Canaanite towns.

Very similarly, Killebrew (2005, 200) names the Philistine migrants 'urban colonists' and adopts van Dommelen's 1997 definition of colonialism with its explicit component regarding the power relations between newcomers and local populations: '... the existence of asymmetrical socioeconomic relationships of dominance or exploitation between the colonizing groups and the inhabitants of the colonized region' (van Dommelen 1997, 136).

This predominant scholarly theory of the settlement of the Philistines in the southern coastal plain is remarkably consistent in defining the power relations between the Canaanites and arriving Philistines, strongly suggesting that a strict *separation or segregation* acculturation strategy was taken by the Philistine newcomers, who maintained colonial asymmetrical power relations with the Canaanite population.

Bunimovitz (1998, 108) is a clear exception, arguing that 'the strong Canaanite cultural traditions, prevailing in all the major Philistine cities, are the best proof that these urban centres were inhabited no less by Canaanites then by new immigrants'. However, he too believes power relations between Canaanites and Philistines are clear: 'I would not hesitate to credit the local Canaanites for the continuation of urbanism in Philistia at least as much as their new masters'. For him, the presence of Canaanite material culture traits in the Philistines cities is an attestation of the passive role played by the Canaanites in the grand scheme of the Philistines' urban ambitions. Thus, he stated that that the Philistines '... adopted a purposeful policy of urban nucleation, displacing the Canaanite rural population from their own territory and relocating them in the *Pentapolis*' (Bunimovitz 1998, 107–108).

I have no doubt that this view of the power relations between the Aegean migrants and the local Canaanite population does not have much to do with the archaeological reality, but has everything to do with the tyranny of the text. The image of the Philistines and the other Sea Peoples as formidable enemies in Egyptian royal propaganda has no doubt combined with the well-embedded Biblical narrative, recounting the Philistines as militarily superior to the Israelites, who are forced into submission before the rise of monarchy. If the Egyptian couldn't prevent the Philistine settlement, and the Israelites could not defeat them before the days of Saul and David, what could the Canaanites do?

Migration, colonization and explanation of change and variability in domestic behavioural patterns

A starting point for the understanding of the household assemblages in Philistia, which seem to contain, in almost equal parts, Aegean and Canaanite behavioural patterns, is Burmeister's (2000, 542) discussion of the archaeological identification of migration. He argues for a dichotomy in elements of the identity of migrant societies: those belonging to the external public sphere, in which there is much interaction with the local population, and those belonging to the internal, domestic domain. The *habitus* is affected by changes occurring in the external sphere, inflicted by the social and economic environment of the target society. The *habitus* is likely to persist in its original form in the internal domain, which is less exposed to external conditions. Therefore, according to Burmeister (2000), the social system of family and household, as well as the organization of private life, are less prone to change than behavioural patterns connected with the 'outside world'. Migrants will import their domestic behavioural patterns to their new countries, and locals will continue to maintain their behavioural patterns even in situations of close intercultural contact and acculturation.

Further insights into the mechanisms active in determining the material culture assemblages within houses of migrants can be found in Berry's (1992; 1997, 9–11) work on acculturation strategies. Berry, working in the field of applied psychology, offers a simple system of acculturation strategies taken by migrants that is based on two factors: the will of the migrants to maintain their cultural identity and the importance given to maintaining relationships with other groups. *Integration* is the result of the will of the migrants to maintain their identity while having daily interactions with other groups. *Assimilation* is a strategy taken by migrant groups who do not wish to maintain their culture of origin. *Separation or segregation* will occur when migrants prefer to have no connection with other cultures while protecting their own heritage. *Marginalization* is the situation in which the migrant group loses both its own culture and the ability to contact other cultures. Following Berry's model, migrants who follow the acculturation strategies of integration and separation will be easier to identify by their material culture assemblages than those who choose the strategies of assimilation and marginalization. The balance of power between the cultures involved in the interaction is also considered an important factor in determining the strategy of acculturation (Burmeister 2000, 545–546; Berry 1997, 9). Thus it may be assumed that asymmetrical power relations, of the type seen in a colonial situation, will have a strong impact on the material culture in the houses of locals, as well as the material culture change seen in the houses of the migrants.

The sophisticated recent studies of Greek and Phoenician colonization (*e.g.* van Dommelen 2005; Hodos 2006; Dietler and López-Ruiz 2009) have gone far beyond the focus on the colonists and their material culture, to explore the entangled relationships between migrants and locals, often followed by a deconstruction of previous assumptions on colonial situations and superiority of the migrants. Furthermore, these, as well as other recent studies on intercultural contacts, have stressed the caution necessary when using post-colonial terminology, pre-eminently *creolisation* and *hybridisation*, to describe ancient interactions. Michael Dietler (2009) expressed 'considerable ambivalence' concerning the celebration of the terms *creolisation* and *hybridisation* in archaeology. To him, these terms may be used only to describe specific situations: Creolisation is to be used in contexts of indigenous vernacular representation of identity, such as in the Caribbean. Hybridisation, following Homi Bhabha, is originally a specific form of intentional, strategic, political form of cultural subversion a strategy practiced by the colonised (Dietler 2009, 30).

Indeed, the concept of hybridisation is useful when discussing ancient colonisation, *i.e.*, situations of asymmetrical power relations between the colonisers and the colonised. As put by van Dommelen (1997, 307): 'In this sense, hybridization refers to the ways in which social, economic or ethnic groups of people construct a distinct identity within the colonial context and situate themselves with respect to the dominant, *i.e.* colonial culture' (see also van Dommelen 2006). This, however, is not true for any interaction between two cultures. For example, *hybridisation* cannot be used to describe the result of each and every form of intercultural interaction, without altering the meaning of this concept beyond the point of being useful (Stockhammer 2012). The term *entanglement* points to a more sophisticated investigation of the past – one that deals with 'complex webs of economic, political and social linkage that can result from consumption of alien material culture' (Dietler 2009, 31). However, although *entanglement* points in the right direction of acknowledging the complexity in intercultural interaction, this term hardly explains which form of interaction resulted in which specific material culture assemblage. It is still a catchall category that needs to be further defined in order for it to be a useful tool for describing interaction process. It is therefore not surprising that Stockhammer (2012) recently chose to elaborate on *entanglement*, referring to the specific entanglement of objects, as well as to the entanglement of social practices.

It is rather surprising that, despite these demonstrations of variability in intercultural interactions, the predominant scholarly theory for the settlement of the Philistines in the southern coastal plain is still characterized by the notion of colonial asymmetrical power relations between migrants and the Canaanite population. The assumption of Philistine domination strongly suggests that a strict *separation or segregation* acculturation strategy was taken by the Philistine newcomers.

Towards a re-evaluation of Philistine and Canaanite interactions

I would argue that the Canaanites played a critical role in the settlement of the Aegean migrants, and that material culture can well attest to a balance of power between migrants and locals very different from the one currently perceived.

First, the circumstances of the settlement do not reflect

a violent incursion. Recent discoveries at Ashkelon show that the migrants settled on a deserted site, on top of the unfinished remains of an Egyptian garrison (Master 2005; Stager *et al.* 2008, 256–261). There are no clear signs for any violent destruction at Ashdod, and there seems to be a peaceful transition between strata XIV and XIII in area G, with the signs of destruction described by the excavators may be no more than evidence for cooking, while destruction deposits yielding complete vessels and fallen walls are absent (Dothan and Porath 1995, 53; Yasur-Landau 2010, 220–222). At Ekron, the small Canaanite village of stratum IX was indeed destroyed by fire, but, according to Killebrew (1998), replaced by another Canaanite village of stratum VIII, before the arrival of the migrants and the construction of the large town of stratum VII.

Second, the names of the Philistine *Pentapolis* are without exception Semitic. One would expect in a violent or asymmetrical colonial environment to find Aegean, rather than Canaanite place names (Yasur-Landau 2010, 288–289; Shai 2009)!

Third, the varied headdresses of the women in the Land Battle relief in Medinet Habu indicate that the women who accompanied the Philistine warriors did not belong to a single ethnic group, in contrast with the uniform feather hats of the men, suggesting that inter-cultural marriages occurred already along the migration route (Sweeney and Yasur-Landau 1999). The presence of Syrian men on the same carts further hints that the philistines began to be ethnically diverse even before their settlement.

Fourth, and perhaps the most neglected form of evidence to date, is that each and every house excavated in Philistia contained what seems to be a complete assemblage of Canaanite bowls, jugs, jars, and cooking pots, which typologically continue the local Late Bronze Age traditions. A comparison between the functional categories of the Aegean-style and Canaanite pottery at Ashdod and Tel Miqne/Ekron (Yasur-Landau 2010, tab. 7.3; the Ashkelon ceramic assemblage is still under study) points to the coexistence of two complete functional repertoires in the same assemblage. The most common household activities of preparing, serving, and storing food and drink in small and medium-sized containers could have been practiced in either Aegean-style or Canaanite vessels.

This is not only a qualitative observation, as it is also backed by statistical analysis of the existing data for pottery from Philistia. Thus in Ashdod area H, stratum XIII, 73% of the pottery was termed 'Canaanite' (based on rim count) 18% was classified as 'Mycenaean IIIC and Aegean', 6% as 'Philistine Bichrome', and 3% as 'LB imports' (Ben-Shlomo 2006, fig. 3.4). In the later stratum XII 52% were classified as 'Canaanite', 27% was classified as 'Mycenaean IIIC and Aegean', 20% 'Philistine Bichrome' and 1% 'LB imports' (Ben-Shlomo 2006, fig. 3.35). A similar picture is seen at Tel Miqne/Ekron field IV (Dothan and Zuckerman 2004, tab. 1, data collected by L. Mazow). In stratum VII the earliest stratum of Philistine settlement, 52% of the pottery is defined as 'Mycenaean IIIC:1 pottery and coarse ware cooking jugs', and 48% as 'Canaanite Tradition Pottery'. The situation remains similar in stratum VIB, after Bichrome 'Philistine' pottery makes its appearance, with 50% 'Mycenaean IIIC:1' and 'Later Philistine Types' and 50% 'Canaanite Tradition Pottery'. This same picture of close numerical ratios between Aegean-style and local Canaanite-style pottery is seen in Field X at the same site. At stratum VIIB, diagnostic 'Mycenaean IIIC:1b' comprises 5.7% of the assemblage, while coarseware (presumably contemporary local forms) is 6.6% (the rest is 76% body sherds, 10.5% pre-Iron Age, and 1.2% intrusive 'Philistine'; Dothan 1998, fig. 1). The situation remains similar in stratum VIB, with 3.1% 'Mycenaean IIIC:1b', 2% 'Philistine' and 6.3 coarseware (Dothan 1998, fig. 3).

The continuation of Canaanite cooking habits is evident not only in the round base cooking pots, which were used in each and every Philistine house, but also in the *tabuns*, round bread ovens, existing in all Philistine settlements from their early stages, for example at Ashkelon Phase 20 (Stager *et al.* 2008, fig. 15.10), and at Tel Miqne/Ekron field X stratum VIIB (Bierling 1998, stratum VIIB plan).

A most illuminating case for the simultaneous conduct of both Aegean-style and local foodways can be found at Ashdod area G, stratum XIIIb, where both Canaanite and Aegean cooking pots were found by the Aegean style hearth (Dothan and Porath 1993, figs. 17.4–6), and the same is true for Ekron field IV stratum VII (Mazow 2005, 156).

This apparent duality in household behavioural patterns was not limited to the realm of food preparation and consumption alone. Much scholarly attention has been dedicated to the religious practices of the Philistine migrants, with Aegean inspired female figurines, the 'Ashdoda' figurines and the 'mourner' figurines – a version of the Aegean psi-figurines (Yasur-Landau 2001; Ben-Shlomo and Press 2009). These were found mostly in domestic contexts, indicating that the domestic behavioural patterns migrants have brought with them included also domestic cult of an Aegean goddess. However, these traits are rare in the first phase of Philistine settlement, and become common only 50–100 years after the initial arrival.

In the 12th centruy BCE, however, the cultic iconography of Philistia includes not only the few Aegean-style figurines, but also representations of the ibex and palm tree motif. This and related motifs connected with the sacred tree are arguably the most common figural motifs on 14th and 13th century pottery from Canaan, an image of sacred fertility directly connected with the Canaanite goddess Asherah or Elat (the goddess) (Keel 1998, 30–41; Keel and Uehlinger

1998, 56–58; Yasur-Landau 2008, 216). While this symbol disappears during the early Iron Age in Philistia (Yasur-Landau 2008, 216–217), it seems that at least in the first phase of Philistine settlement, Canaanite and Aegean cultic symbolism co-existed (*e.g.* from Ekron: Dothan, Gitin and Zuckerman 2006, figs. 3.3, 18; Ashdod: Dothan and Porath 1993, fig. 13.12; Ben-Shlomo 2005, figs. 3.5, 12, 17, 20, 21). Two of the most telling cases of inclusion of Canaanite symbolism into the new Aegean repertoire are the those of two ring base kraters from Ekron, which are decorated with palm trees, a theme not appearing elsewhere in the Aegean-style pottery repertoire, and one that must have been borrowed from the Canaanite iconographic tradition (Dothan 1998, pl. 2.2, stratum VIIB; Dothan and Zukerman 2004, fig. 18.8).

Conclusions: beyond asymmetry?

How can we explain the co-occurrence of Canaanite and Aegean repertoires for the preparation, serving and storage of food, not to mention the co-existence of both Canaanite and Aegean cultic iconography? Indeed, this may be seen an indication of hybridity in domestic behavioural patterns, yet hybridity or creolization, with their emphasis on the creation of new behavioural patterns by 'mixing' old and new traditions, cannot account for what appears to be two distinct sets of behavioural patterns seen in each and every house in Philistia. This situation seems to echo van Dommelen's (2006, 115) observations concerning historical case studies from North America, in which colonial situations are manifested in domestic assemblages: 'It also makes it patently clear that the colonial situations were far more complex than initially suggested and that, most of all, in both cases, despite the apparent differences, people of very different cultural and ethnic background lived together very closely without entirely losing their own traditions.' This concept of people from different cultural backgrounds residing closely may well be the explanation for the domestic assemblages in Philistia.

The domestic arena, inseparable from concepts of family and kinship, is where socialising starts; by participating in group activity, observing the behaviour of others, and assimilating behavioural patterns, one establishes some of the most important elements of one's identity, among them kinship (lineage), place of birth, and language. It is therefore clear that the *habitus* of the people residing in the houses of the *Pentapolis* maintained during the first stage of settlement both Aegean and Canaanite behavioural patterns. Such a situation, to my mind, is possible only when processes of cultural transmission of both traditions are carried out within the domestic unit- in other words, the common existence of intercultural marriages and intercultural families, who considered it important to maintain both cultural traditions.

Rather than colonial asymmetry, material remains from early Iron Age Philistia reveal intricate, and predominantly peaceful, interactions between migrants and locals. Within the *Pentapolis* sites, the settlement process was accompanied by the creation of multi-cultural families. It may be possible to argue that such unions were meant to strengthen alliances between migrant and local kinship groups, alliances that would ensure intergroup collaboration in the difficult and uncertain times of the 12th century. It thus seems that the balance of power between migrants and locals made it important to preserve both cultural traditions, resulting in the amazing picture of two distinct sets of domestic behavioural patterns, which coexisted in each and every house excavated in Philistia. This status quo was largely maintained throughout the 12th and the 11th centuries, doubtlessly through socialization and cultural transmission within the family unit.

Foundation stories of the Greek colonization in the Archaic period point to the varied strategies, mostly peaceful, in relating to local population, and reflecting careful cost/benefit calculations. The distinctively local and non-Aegean character of the choice of sites for settlement by the Philistines calls to mind situations from the Greek Colonization in which local populations guide the migrants into a favourable location- thus is the case of the local Lybians, who showed the Theran settlers to a better place in which they finally built Cyrene (Herodotus 4.158), or of king Hyblon, who directed the Megarians to a good place to settle in, possibly within his own kingdom, and naming the city Megara Hyblaia after him (Malkin 1985, 117–118; Thucydides 6.4.1), or even in the case of the foundation of Massalia (Justin 43.3.4–12). Whether reflecting ancient reality or legend, they attest that peaceful settlement was a conceivable option in antiquity.

Similarly, the lack of asymmetrical power relations between Phoenicians, Greeks and locals in Iberia had caused Dietler (2009, 22) to conclude that, '... most of the interactions that took place ... in Iberia did not involve *colonization* ...' (Italics in original text). I would therefore venture to suggest that the general lack of violence connected with the foundation of the Philistine cities, their Semitic names, and the co-existence of both Aegean and local cultural traditions indicate that these were joint foundations of Aegean migrants and local populations, rather than colonial enterprises.

References

Barako, T. J. (2000) The Philistine Settlement as Mercantile Phenomenon? *American Journal of Archaeology* 104, 513–530.

Ben-Shlomo, D. (2006) *Decorated Philistine Pottery: An Archaeological and Archaeometric Study.* British Archaeological Reports International Series 1541. Oxford, Archaeopress.

Ben-Shlomo, D. and Press, M. D. (2009) A Reexamination of Aegean-style Figurines in Light of New Evidence from Ashdod, Ashkelon, and Ekron. *Bulletin of the American Schools of Oriental Research* 353, 39–74.

Ben-Shlomo, D., Shai, I., Zukerman, A. and Maeir, A. (2008) Cooking Identities: Aegean-style and Philistine Cooking Jugs and Cultural Interaction in the Southern Levant during the Iron Age. *American Journal of Archaeology* 112, 225–246.

Berry, J. W. (1992) Acculturation and Adaptation in a New Society. *International Migration* 30, 69–85.

Berry, J. W. (1997) Immigration, Acculturation, and Adaptation. *Applied Psychology: An International Review* 46, 5–34.

Bierling, N. (1998) *Report on the 1995–1996 Excavations in Field XNW: Areas 77, 78, 79, 89, 101, 102. Iron Age I. Text and Data Base (Plates, Sections, Plans).* Ekron Limited Edition Series 7. Jerusalem, Albright Institute and the Hebrew University.

Bunimovitz, S. (1998) Sea Peoples in Cyprus and Israel: A Comparative Study of Immigration Processes. In Gitin, Mazar and Stern 1998, 103–113.

Burmeister, S. (2000) Archaeology and Migration: Approaches to an Archaeological Proof of Migration. *Current Anthropology* 41, 539–667.

Dietler, M. (2009) Colonial Encounters in Iberia and the Western Mediterranean: An Exploratory Framework. In M. Dietler and C. López-Ruiz (eds), *Colonial Encounters in Ancient Iberia. Phoenician, Greek and Indigenous Relations*, 3–48. Chicago and London, Chicago University Press.

Dietler, M. and López-Ruiz, C. (2009) *Colonial Encounters in Ancient Iberia. Phoenician, Greek and Indigenous Relations*. Chicago and London, Chicago University Press.

Dommelen, P. van (1997) Colonial Constructs: Colonialism and Archaeology in the Mediterranean. *World Archaeology* 28, 305–323.

Dommelen, P. van (2005) Colonial Encounters and Hybrid Practices: Phoenicians and Carthaginian Settlement in the Ancient Mediterranean. In G. J. Stein (ed.), *The Archaeology of Colonial Encounters: Comparative Perspectives*, 109–141. Santa Fe, NM, School of American Research.

Dommelen, P. van (2006) Colonial Matters: Material Culture and Postcolonial Theory in Colonial Situations. In C. Tilley, W. Keane, S. Küchler, M. Rowlands and P. Spyer (eds), *Handbook of Material Culture*, 104–124. London, SAGE.

Dothan, M. (1971) *Ashdod II–III: The Second and Third Season of Excavations 1963, 1965, Sounding in 1967. Text and Plates* (Atiqot 9–10). Jerusalem, Dept. of Antiquities and Museums, Israel.

Dothan, M. and Porath, Y. (1993) *Ashdod V: Excavations of Area G: The Fourth–Sixth Seasons of Excavations 1968–1970.* Atiqot 23. Jerusalem, Dept. of Antiquities and Museums, Israel.

Dothan, T. (1982) *The Philistines and Their Material Culture.* New Haven, Yale University Press.

Dothan, T. (1989) The Arrival of the Sea Peoples: Cultural Diversity in Early Iron Age Canaan. *Annual of the American Schools of Oriental Research* 49, 1–22.

Dothan, T. (1998) The Pottery. In N. Bierling (ed.), *Report on the 1995–1996 Excavations in Field XNW: Areas 77, 78, 79, 89, 101, 102. Iron Age I. Text and Data Base (Plates, Sections, Plans).* Ekron Limited Edition Series 7, 20–48. Jerusalem, Albright Institute and the Hebrew University.

Dothan, T. and Zukerman, A. (2004) A Preliminary Study of the Mycenaean IIIC:1 Pottery Assemblages from Tel Miqne-Ekron and Ashdod. *Bulletin of the American Schools of Oriental Research* 333, 1–54.

Dothan, T., Gitin, S. and Zukerman, A. (2006) The Pottery: Canaanite and Philistine Traditions and Cypriote and Aegean Imports. In M. W. Meehl, T. Dothan and S. Gitin (eds), *Tel Miqne-Ekron Excavations 1995–1996: Field INE East Slope – Iron Age I (Early Philistine Period)*.Tel Miqne Ekron Final Field Report Series 8, 71–179. Jerusalem, Albright Institute and the Hebrew University.

Gitin, S., Mazar, A. and Stern, E. (1998) *Mediterranean Peoples in Transition: Thirteenth to Early Tenth Centuries BCE.* Jerusalem, Israel Exploration Society.

Hodos, T. (2006) *Local Responses to Colonization in the Iron Age Mediterranean.* London and New York, Routledge.

Keel, O. (1998) *Goddesses and Trees, New Moon and Yahweh: Ancient Near Eastern Art and the Hebrew Bible.* Journal for the Study of the Old Testament Supplement 261. Sheffield, Sheffield Academic Press.

Keel, O. and Uehlinger, C. (1998) *Gods, Goddesses and Images of God in Ancient Israel.* Minneapolis, Fortress Press.

Killebrew, A. E. (1998) Ceramic Typology and Technology of Late Bronze II and Iron I Assemblages from Tel Miqne-Ekron: The Transition from Canaanite to Philistine Culture. In Gitin, Mazar and Stern 1998, 379–405.

Killebrew, A. E. (2005) *Biblical Peoples and Ethnicity: An Archaeological Study of Egyptians, Canaanites, Philistines, and Early Israel, 1300–1100 BCE.* Atlanta, Society of Biblical Literature.

Malkin, I. (1985) What's in a Name? The Eponymous Founders of Greek Colonies. *Athenaeum* 63, 114–130.

Master, D. M. (2005) Iron I Chronology at Ashkelon: Preliminary Results of the Leon Levy Expedition. In T. E. Levy and T. Higham (eds), *The Bible and Radiocarbon Dating*, 337–348. London, Equinox Publishing.

Mazow, L. B. (2005) *Competing Material Culture: Philistine Settlement at Tel Miqne-Ekron in the Early Iron Age.* Unpublished dissertation, University of Arizona.

Shai, I. (2009) Understanding Philistine Migration: City Names and Their Implications. *Bulletin of the American Schools of Oriental Research* 354, 15–27.

Stager, L. E. (1995) The Impact of the Sea Peoples in Canaan (1185–1050 BCE). In T. E. Levy (ed.), *The Archaeology of Society in the Holy Land*, 332–348. London, Leicester University Press.

Stager, L. E., Schloen, J. D., Master, D. M. and Press, M. D.

(2008) Stratigraphic Overview. In L. E. Stager, J. D. Schloen and D. M. Master (eds), *Ashkelon 1: Introduction and Overview (1985–2006)*, 213–323. Winona Lake, IN, Harvard Semitic Museum and Eisenbrauns.

Stockhammer, P. W. (2012) Conceptualizing Cultural Hybridization in Archaeology. In P. W. Stockhammer (ed.), *Conceptualizing Cultural Hybridization: A Transdisciplinary Approach. Papers of the Conference, Heidelberg, 21–22 September 2009.* Transcultural Research. Heidelberg Studies on Asia and Europe in a Global Context, 43–58. Berlin and Heidelberg, Springer Verlag.

Sweeney, D. and Yasur-Landau, A. (1999) Following the Path of the Sea Persons: The Women in the Medinet Habu Reliefs. *Tel Aviv* 26, 116–145.

Yasur-Landau, A. (2001) The Mother(s) of all Philistines: Aegean Enthroned Deities of the 12th–11th Century Philistia. In R. Laffineur and R. Hägg (eds), *Potnia: Deities and Religion in the Aegean Bronze Age*. Aegaeum 22, 329–343. Liège, Université de Liège.

Yasur-Landau, A. (2008) A Message in a Jug: Canaanite, Philistine and Cypriot Iconography and the 'Orpheus Jug'. In A. Fantalkin and A. Yasur-Landau (eds), *Bene Israel: Studies in the Archaeology of Israel and the Levant during the Bronze and Iron Ages in Honour of Israel Finkelstein.* Culture and History of the Ancient Near East 31, 213–229. Leiden and Boston, Brill.

Yasur-Landau, A. (2010) *The Philistines and Aegean Migration in the Late Bronze Age*. Cambridge and New York, Cambridge University Press.

Zukerman, A. H., Lev-Tov, L. K. J. and Maeir, A. (2007) A bone of Contention? Iron Age IIA Notched Scapulae from Tell es-Safi/Gath, Israel. *Bulletin of the American Schools of Oriental Research* 347, 57–81.

17.

The practical logic of style and memory in early first millennium Levantine ivories

Marian H. Feldman

This contribution explores the role of style and stylistic continuity in the collective memory and community identities of the emerging Iron Age city-states of greater North Syria from around 1200 to the conquest of Carchemish by Sargon II in 717 BCE. Of the rich body of artistic material dating to this period (including monumental carved reliefs), I focus here primarily on ivories. In the first part of this paper, I review prior scholarship, which has concentrated overwhelmingly on attributing stylistic groupings of ivories mainly excavated at Nimrud in Assyria to specific centres of production in the Levant and North Syria. I argue that we need to shift from a solely attributional line of inquiry to also consider questions of human-material engagement, here posited specifically as human-style engagements. I propose an alternative approach derived from Bourdieu's theory of practice. When the ivories – especially their stylistic aspects – are approached in this manner, their central role in collective memory making strategies can be more clearly grasped. I argue that a material component of collective memory resides in, and is generated from, the ongoing practices of style. The physical and practical aspects of creating styles involve knowledge and action in a positive dialectical relationship to one another. This self-reinforcing connection between knowledge and action generates communities of what Bourdieu calls 'learned ignorance', which in turn help express and shape shared identities through tangible, though often overlooked, visual appearances.

In the second part, I take as one case study a set of distinct animal markings found across a diverse range of generally North Syrian works, most of which are of ivory. These markings belong to Kantor's 'animal style' and form the basis for Herrmann's 'Flame and Frond style-group.' While theoretically the concept of a *style-group*, as proposed by Herrmann and now adopted by many subsequent scholars of Levantine ivories, implies no direct links to geographical place or artistic workshop, in practice, these aspects (style-group–workshop–geographical location) have often been collapsed and implicitly taken as singular, unitary, and spatially bounded. I would like to suggest that we can redirect such stylistic analyses in order to consider more closely questions of continuity with Late Bronze Age ivory works, and I propose that these markings played a critical role in stylistic practices of the greater North Syrian region by enhancing a shared memory, whether consciously or unconsciously, of a Late Bronze Age heritage and a newly emerging collective identity.

First millennium Levantine ivories

The study of first millennium Levantine ivories has been inextricably bound up with attributional pursuits. Their large numbers, which permit a diverse array of similarities and differences to be enumerated across the corpus, together with the relatively early recognition that the archaeological context in which the largest number of them were excavated (the Assyrian royal city of Nimrud) was not the place of their cultural source (that is, they were not produced in an Assyrian style), have compelled scholars to focus predominately on their place and date of manufacture.

The first ivories were discovered in the 1840s at Nimrud, which is still the site that has yielded by far the largest number of them; thousands of ivories have been excavated there over the course of nearly 150 years of digging (for review of archaeological history, see Herrmann, Coffey and Laidlaw 2004, 5; Herrmann and Laidlaw 2009, 27–29).

Much smaller quantities of stylistically related ivories have been found in the greater North Syria and Levantine area,[1] as well as in far-flung locales including Hasanlu in northwest Iran, Cyprus, Greece, and Etruria (Winter 1976). It is in fact the diffuse nature of the ivories, both in terms of their stylistic delineations and their distributions patterns, that poses an ongoing challenge for attributing them to specific places and periods. While an initial survey of the material makes stylistic classifications appear straightforward, closer scrutiny has laid bare the complexity (and contentiousness) of the endeavour.

Layard, the early excavator of Nimrud, identified the ivories as non-Assyrian soon after the first discoveries were made in the 1840s (Herrmann and Laidlaw 2009, 53–55). Layard's comparative data was extremely limited at that date, and he proposed an Egyptian source, though he argued for production at Nimrud specifically for the patronage of the Assyrian kings. Later 19th-century scholars, with an expanding corpus of comparative materials, argued for Phoenician production. In 1912, Poulsen (1912, 37–59) made the enduring distinction between two groups of ivories from the Nimrud corpus, linking those with more Egyptianizing elements to Phoenicia and another group to North Syria, based on similarities to the carved reliefs of this region. Subsequently, Poulsen's work has been expanded and more systematically argued by Barnett, Winter, and Herrmann. Herrmann, in particular, has contributed to the scholarly discourse with her definition of *style-groups*, drawn from *sets* of ivories from the vast collections at Nimrud. For Herrmann (2005, 12; Herrmann and Laidlaw 2009, 56), *sets* of ivories can be 'reassembled' according to 'a similarity of size, shape, style, subject, techniques of fixing and methods of carving,' although a set need not share all these criteria. These sets then provide the basis for defining what she calls *style-groups*. According to Herrmann (Herrmann and Laidlaw 2009, 56), style-groups 'must be built employing a range of diagnostic criteria, both technical and stylistic ...'. In the wake of Herrmann's impressive cataloguing project of the Nimrud ivories, first millennium ivory studies have seen a flurry of activity by a younger generation of scholars over the last fifteen years, such as Wicke, Pappalardo, and Scigliuzzo among others (Cecchini, Mazzoni and Scigliuzzo 2009). Most significant for the purposes of this study is the predilection throughout these studies to adopt both the specific parameters of Herrmann's style-groups as well as the general concept of the *style-group* as an analytical tool.

Scholarship has reached a general consensus regarding the rough outlines of what could be called regional styles or traditions, accepting a Phoenician, North Syrian, and South Syrian/Intermediate/Syrian tradition, in addition to an Assyrian one (Herrmann and Laidlaw 2009, 56). However, little agreement has been reached in terms of more precise attributions to what are called *schools* or *workshops*, that is, to specific geographical locales of production within the broader regional designations. Because of this lack of consensus, the pursuit of attribution to workshops or schools – understood in general to mean geographical centres of production – has become the goal of most studies of first millennium ivories (*e.g.* Herrmann 2005, 15; Affanni 2009, 171). While there has been a certain amount of methodological discussion in recent years about appropriate or sufficient criteria for stylistic attribution to particular *workshops* or *schools* (Herrmann 2005; Winter 2005), only a few studies have explicitly questioned the analytical assumptions that underlie the attributional endeavour as a whole (*e.g.* di Paolo 2009).

Attributing Levantine ivories

As has already been mentioned, studies of the first millennium Levantine ivories tend to concentrate overwhelmingly on locating place(s) of production, and they do so mainly based on the internal, stylistic evidence of the ivories themselves. The goal of this endeavour is to match defined style-groups of Nimrud ivories to specific city-states in the Levant. Traditional art historical attribution proceeds by determining *a priori* a list of characteristic traits that distinguish a workshop or school. However, we have no clearly attributable corpus – no ivories can be unequivocally said to be the products of a particular place – and therefore there is no baseline from which we can determine a checklist of characteristic traits that can be clearly linked to a geographical location. Nevertheless, attempts have been made to define local stylistic characteristics; for instance, scholars have looked to the carved orthostats that adorn so many of the urban spaces in the greater North Syria region to localize workshops. Yet this, too, is not an unproblematic methodology, as relief styles are neither consistent within sites nor clearly distinct between them (Barnett 1982, 46). Moreover, the chronology of the reliefs remains contested and questions regarding regional versus chronological differences abound. This lacuna in our knowledge subjects any arguments that try to relate style-groups to past social realities (such as craft production) to an unacceptable degree of circularity (as noted by Winter 2005, 24; di Paolo 2009, 140).

Indeed, the correlation of style-groups to workshops or schools carries with it assumptions regarding social and economic modes of craft production that may not be warranted. We know practically nothing about either the mechanisms for acquiring the raw material of ivory or the organization for producing the finished objects. The question of where the ivory came from remains open. First millennium ivory is almost exclusively elephant, unlike during the preceding Late Bronze Age when hippopotamus ivory was also widespread. Because there are no specific textual references to hunting elephants in the Assyrian annals after the time of Shalmaneser III in the 9th century, Caubet and Gaborit-Chopin (2004, 29) have argued that first millennium ivories must be derived from African elephant populations. Moorey (1999 [1994], 116–117) refers to the possible population of elephants in Syria, whose presence in the second millennium is confirmed but is much more controversial for the third and first millennia. Nonetheless, he too attributes much of the first-millennium ivory to African herds due to the higher quality and larger size of African elephant tusks. Ethnographic studies of modern ivory acquisition from sub-Saharan Africa indicate that the physical and organizational skills needed to hunt vast quantities of large elephants (which are the ones that produce the largest tusks) would have restricted the activity to a small class of people who had access to resources best managed by large institutions like palaces and temples (Isaacman and Isaacman 2004, 83–122). Whether these people would have been directly dependent upon such an institution or indirectly 'commissioned' remains unknown, as does the organization for the acquisition of the raw material once extracted from the dead elephant. We have no indication of whether ivory was procured by the Levantine states through direct hunting expeditions, commercial activity, or diplomatic ties. The enormous quantities of ivory produced during a fairly short period of time (maybe two or three hundred years), the generally high-quality of its carving, and its archaeological association primarily with palatial structures when found in the Levant suggest that access to and consumption of ivory was closely linked to bodies of ruling elites and that ivory participated in a pan-Levantine culture as a prestige marker.

We also know practically nothing about the process and organization of carving ivory once procured. Wicke (2005, 71–75) calls attention to the implications of our preconceived, yet rarely acknowledged, notions of Iron Age ivory production. He notes that we have not adequately considered whether production was due to royal monopoly, commissioned as artwork, or generated within a 'free market', and that we do not fully understand the role of itinerant craftsmen. A recent article by di Paolo (2009) has brought this problem to the fore and opens the door for a critical assessment of the entire attributional endeavour. In a footnote drawing upon earlier work by Moorey (1999 [1994], 16–17), di Paolo (2009, 133 n. 1) observes that the term *workshop* is itself problematic and carries with it assumptions that may not be valid for first millennium ivory carving. What is particularly important about our lack of knowledge in this area is that, without a firm basis for understanding the organization of ivory production (which encompasses questions of acquiring/distributing the material, commissioning works, economic dependencies, apprenticeships or mechanics of training, and artisan mobility), it is practically impossible to link an unanchored 'style-group' to any specific geographical or temporal coordinates. Although Herrmann (Herrmann and Laidlaw 2009, 57) acknowledges that moving from an analytically determined style-group to any ancient social reality is fraught with problems, unexamined assumptions of 'workshop' production, organized along the lines of an Italian Renaissance master's studio, prevail and remain influential in interpretations. Winter, followed by di Paolo, has noted that there is a common tendency to slip between a *style-group*, determined solely by evidence internal to the works of art, and a *school* (which contains within it inherent social dimensions; Winter 1992, 138–139; di Paolo 2009, 139–140). Furthermore, *schools* are sometimes elided with *workshops* (that is, organized groups of artists working and training together in spatial proximity), although at other times, multiple *workshops* are taken as subgroups of a regionally understood *school*. In most ivory studies, the general working assumption, though often unstated, is that groups of stylistically similar ivories were produced in a single workshop, and that several workshops operating with similar elements belong to the same production school which coincides with an artisan center (di Paolo 2009, 14).

The nature of the stylistic variation seen among the ivories, however, problematises this straightforward equation. On the one hand, there is remarkable diversity of styles seen among the ivories, with certain traits seemingly re-occurring across enough ivories to warrant the drawing of stylistic boundaries. Yet, on the other hand, there are very few clusters of stylistic traits that *consistently* co-occur within a single style-group and *only* within that style-group. This problem can be traced through a number of Herrmann's style-groups. Here I will point out only one example, from Herrmann's so-called Flame and Frond style-group, which I will be exploring with respect to questions of social memory and communal identity in more detail at the end of this study.

Since Herrmann's initial definition of the 'Flame and Frond style-group' in the 1980s (Herrmann 1986; 1989), she has significantly expanded the number of ivories attributed to it (Herrmann and Laidlaw 2009, 91–98). Yet, in a study of sphinxes attributed to the Flame and Frond style-group, Affanni (2009) has recently pointed out the group's stylistic inconsistencies. He notes the heterogeneity of the group as currently defined, highlighting stylistic divergences among the sphinxes, some of which display traits that are usually considered part of the North Syrian tradition, while others exhibit traits typically associated with the South Syrian/Intermediate/Syrian tradition. For example, the sphinx ND 8050 (Fig. 17.1; Herrmann 1986, no. 562, pl. 131) and griffin ND 10501 (Fig. 17.2; Herrmann 1986, no. 561, pl. 130) look nothing like the animals found on the pyxides and horn from well AJ (Fig. 17.3; Herrmann and Laidlaw 2009, nos. 233–236, pls. 40–55): their bodies are more elongated and sinuous, taking S-curve shapes in their nearly upright rampant posture. Indeed, they appear more closely related, stylistically speaking, to another ivory sphinx from the Northwest Palace at Nimrud, (Fig. 17.4; ND1083; Herrmann and Laidlaw 2009, no. 19, pl. 2). This issue is further evident in Herrmann and Laidlaw's discussion of ND1083 in the catalogue: 'This panel [ND1083] shares some similarities with the human-headed, rampant sphinx, ND8050, *I.N.* IV, 144, no. 562, pl. 131, which probably forms part of the 'flame and frond' school, *I.N.* IV, 16. There is, however, no reason to place ND1083 in that style-group: note, for instance, the very different treatment of the wing and musculature.' The fact that ivories in the Flame and Frond group do not exhibit all characteristics of the group and may also include characteristics that Herrmann attributes to other style-groups demonstrates that it is not a clearly bounded homogeneous group (for similar observations regarding particular style-groups, see Winter 1992, 136–138).

The extreme heterogeneity of stylistic traits across all the Levantine ivories, despite a remarkable homogeneity in subject matter, may argue against a model of bounded, geographically anchored workshops operating in specific, politically-defined city-states (di Paolo 2009; Herrmann and Laidlaw 2009, 69–75). Herrmann (1992, 71), though still adhering to a model of singular, unified and geographically bounded workshops that produce a particular style-group, also comments tellingly on the nebulous contours of groups derived from stylistic analysis: 'Borderlines between traditions are equally hard to define… Indeed, the styles gradually meld into one another rather like the colours of the spectrum.' Recently, Suter (2008) has suggested that the ivories' stubborn refusal to divide neatly into style-groups may indicate a deliberate blurring of cultural boundaries across the Levant (including Phoenicia through North Syria). She cites a similar cultural heterogeneity in the Kilamuwa Stele from Zincirli, in which Luwian/Neo Hittite, Aramaean, Phoenician, and Assyrian elements coexist (Suter 2008; Brown 2008a). Suter concludes that the cultural mixing seen on the stele of Kilamuwa belies the complexity of the historical situation and exposes the inappropriateness of the assumed equation of style group—workshop—geo-political entity. She suggests that ivory workshops may have worked in multiple styles, regardless of their geographic location or the ethnic background of their artisans. Thus, it may not be possible to link style-groups to specific locations because stylistic practices interacted with one another across the entire Levant and North Syria to such a degree as to erase any distinct borders (see also Barnett 1982, 46; and for related argument for the Nimrud bronze bowls, see Onnis 2009). Although I consider careful stylistic analysis a central process in the study of these ivories, I suggest that attributional pursuits to singular geographic locations ultimately carry little explanatory force with respect to connecting the ivories to past social realities of workshop production.

In the studies of Levantine ivories, the relationship between human beings, geography, and culture is quite fuzzy and unarticulated, which has served to greatly confuse the attributional process. I argue here that geography and culture do play an important role in constructing identities and styles, but that they do so not through some unarticulated biological link, but instead through the social engagements and practices with a community (or communities) of other human beings. Relationships establish networks that consist of multidirectional avenues of exchange such that all participants in the network both exert a force and are acted upon by other forces. As much as a person might contribute some aspect of identity to a material product, that product in turns contributes back aspects of identity, although this process may not be symmetrical or evenly distributed across all participants in the network. Style and the practice of producing and consuming styles are central to this process of engagement. Additionally, I suggest that we can circumvent questions of artistic intentionality because, regardless of what an artist thinks s/he might be doing, her/his embeddedness in a thick web of relations means that ways of doing and reception are not monocausal but instead the result of complex and multidirectional forces. This concept of the non-atomized individual – that is, the blurring between and even interpenetration of an 'inside mind' and an 'outside world' such that 'intentionality' is intimately linked to external stimuli – is gaining ground within the field of experimental cultural psychology (Kitayama and Cohen 2007). It is from this perspective that I would like to turn to a discussion about style that addresses it from a more clearly social dimension.

The practical logic of style

I see here the potential by which a marriage of studies that stress the engagement and entanglement of human entities with the physical world and the art historical tradition of stylistic analysis provides a means for investigating a material dimension of style within social identity and memory-making processes. In particular, theories of practice derived from Bourdieu allow us to get a better handle on aspects of style by providing a theoretical construct that obviates the need to determine intentionality (authorial or otherwise) and that stresses style's social dimension. Bourdieu's concept of a practical logic (that is, the logic of his *habitus*) shows how cultural practices intersect with style and identity outside or alongside any consideration of intention or self-awareness. Such an approach can be seen to build upon and complement that of Winter (1998) who proposes artistic agency in the manipulation of visual forms, which in turn endows style with meaning. Where Bourdieu offers enrichment of these concepts is his theory's ability to transcend questions of individual intentionality.

Although Bourdieu is a common name in scholarship today and his concept of *habitus* is widely cited, the specific question at hand regarding the materiality of style within a community of practice benefits from a close review of his basic theories. This is particularly the case because of the centrality of the concept of artistic intentionality within art historical studies, a centrality that Bourdieu's work effectively destablizes. We can begin with Bourdieu's postulation (1984) that, despite an apparent ability to choose from among aesthetic options, people's aesthetic preferences strongly tie in with their social position and replicate from generation to generation. Aesthetic dispositions/tastes are therefore central to social position and power relations. They function to create a 'sense of one's place' and are internalized and embodied, becoming a naturalized entity to the individual – in other words, part of identity.

Instead of giving rational thought (and intentionality) place of importance in power relations, Bourdieu proposes that social domination and its replication were primarily enacted through bodily practices (what Bourdieu also calls 'know-how') in the social world. Social agents operate according to an implicit practical logic and bodily disposition, according to their 'feel for the game'. This sense of feeling stems from a participant's embeddedness in a *habitus*, which Bourdieu defines as the objective social structures that are inculcated into the subjective mental experiences of individuals in such a way that they become naturalized, internalized, and unquestioned. The so-called game (elsewhere in Bourdieu called the 'field') represents the moves and strategies that participants/agents make in day-to-day activities without necessarily being aware of the motivations or justifications. Bourdieu also introduces the notion of *doxa* as learned, fundamental beliefs and values that are taken as self-evident universals and that inform an individual's actions and thought within a particular field (what Bourdieu [1990, 66] calls the 'presuppositions of the game').

Central to a reconceptualisation of style as practice is Bourdieu's notion that the meaning and function of any particular practice may be solely in its doing. He speaks of such practices as being behaviour that is 'both 'sensible' and devoid of sense intention …' and of the analyst's (specifically the ethnographer's) need to produce a theory of what it is to be 'native', that is, to be in that relationship of 'learned ignorance', of immediate but unselfconscious understanding which defines the practical relationship to the world' (Bourdieu 1990, 18–19). I would like to consider how style operates at just such a level, that is, the level of 'learned ignorance' with respect to what it means to be so-and-so or such-and-such a person. This is an identity that is not rooted in any inherent, internal, essential self, but rather is taken on by individuals in their ongoing production and consumption of the style itself, or, conversely is rejected or more precisely countered in the production and consumption of different styles. Moreover, I posit that the adoption or rejection of styles is not a singular, unitary or fixed one-time act, but is always in flux. In this scenario, varying degrees of stylistic similarity and difference would be actively contributing to the construction of differing intensities of belonging or otherness.

Bourdieu (1990, 13) himself invokes artistic style in just such a manner:

> 'The coherence without apparent intention and the unity without an immediately visible unifying principle of all the cultural realities that are informed by a quasi-natural logic (is this not what makes the "eternal charm of Greek art" that Marx refers to?) are the product of the age-old application of the same schemes of action and perception which, never having been constituted as explicit principles, can only produce an unwilled necessity which is therefore necessarily imperfect but also a little miraculous, and very close in this respect to a work of art'.

What can be understood as central components of identity – what Bourdieu calls 'schemes of perception, appreciation, and action' – tend to lie outside the realm of self-reflexivity, but at the same time underlie all thought and practice. Moreover, these schemata are self-perpetuating through the actions and discourses generated by the very schemata themselves. In this way continuity can be seen to be both of critical import (not just an insignificant detail) and potentially to lie outside the realm of intended causality.

What is important here is to consider how the ongoing bodily practice of producing and consuming art in particular styles embodies a particular logic of practice (a set of dispositions that form a *habitus*). The *habitus* shapes a field of social action that we can understand today as a community of shared identity (the identity being nothing more than the putting into operation of *doxa*, that is, beliefs or the 'presuppositions of the game'; Bourdieu 1990, 66). But *doxa* are not simply immaterial ideas; rather, they are inextricably tied to bodily experiences in the world, what Bourdieu calls 'enacted belief' (Bourdieu 1990, 68). Styles, which can be understood as sets of visual traits used to associate like with like, similarly present themselves as natural and self-evident in the same manner as Bourdieu's 'practical sense' (Elsner 2003, 105–106) .

While Bourdieu orients the equation from the perspective of the person who already participates (as a 'native') within a *habitus* and thus already embodies the *doxa*/dispositions, we might reverse the vantage point to note that participation in the *habitus* (which would include style) 'nativises' the person, inculcating the *doxa* into the person in order that they appear entirely normalised, naturalised, and self-evident. This inculcation of *doxa* can be understood as identity. And style as a central, physical element that, through engagement with people, is part of *habitus* and contributes to dispositions and *doxa*, therefore, also contributes to identity. It is important here not to confuse identity with a singular concept that inheres in a physically contained biological organism (known as an individual), but rather identity here is the participation of any number of such organisms who partake of and thus share these *doxa*, *de facto* forming a community. Critically, the concept of *habitus* removes the need to be concerned with intentionality or consciousness because it produces a 'common-sense' world that is felt as self-evident and natural by the participants, while remaining regulated, thereby producing regularised action/practices without individual awareness (Bourdieu 1990, chapter 3). Likewise, unselfconsciousness or unawareness does not mean that an action is natural or biological, since it belongs to the complex social *habitus* of all action.

A critical aspect of Bourdieu's *habitus* is that it allows us to firmly distinguish between a biologically determined versus a socially conditioned notion of style (and by extension culture). In other words, it allows us to break from the idea that identity, style, culture, *etc.* exist solely inside bounded corporeal bodies and to see these aspects instead as resulting from processes of relational interactions among beings and things. *Habitus* clearly distinguishes practices from any notion of biologically programmed (and implicitly racial/nationalistic) predeterminations. Yet, at the same time, the *habitus*, as inculcated schemes of perception, appreciation, and action, generates commonalities of practical actions (and styles) that grow out of communal relations. To live in a particular community, and thus to be socialised into its *habitus*, predisposes one to act in certain ways (and to create certain styles). Thus, we can accept that styles may correspond closely to social communities (though these do not need to be bounded, contiguous, or homogeneous) and at the same time recognise shifting across, through, and in between styles to be the result of overlapping or intersecting communities of social relations and actions. In essence, this frees us from having to assume a one-to-one relationship between geographical place and artistic style, while allowing that styles do point to social communities of relatedness and belonging in their very demonstration of having been produced through connected or related practices of doing.

With Bourdieu's theory of practice, we can transition to the aspect of memory and consider memory specifically within a material dimension of style. Bourdieu (1990, 56) writes, 'The *habitus* – embodied history, internalized as a second nature and so forgotten as history – is the active presence of the whole past of which it is the product'. Style, as a materialised practice, can be understood in the same way as part of a *habitus* and thus one component (one disposition) that keeps the past alive as embodied history.

Bourdieu, however, does not account much for changes in the schemes of perception, appreciation, and action. While Bourdieu addresses aspects of change to some extent, it is the work of de Certeau (1984) that provides a fuller explanation for how (and why) *doxa*, *habituses*, and cultural fields develop, whether dramatically or incrementally. Critically, de Certeau explores the way specific (individual) strategies and tactics can affect the trajectory of the larger cultural enterprise (the *habitus*). I am not able to pursue detailed inquiries here into what these strategies and tactics might have been (or even how we might figure out a method for determining these strategies and tactics in the past); it is nonetheless essential to acknowledge that such moves enable changes over time and in fact ensure that no cultural field remains static or homogeneous.

Social memory

Connecting style with Bourdieu's notion of practical logic and the *habitus* as embodied history leads us to style's role in social memory, and I argue that in the case of the Levantine ivories style contributes to emerging Iron Age identities, not just through the production of a shared community of practical knowledge, but more precisely through one linked to the Late Bronze Age. In other words, stylistic continuity as exhibited in a number of first millennium Levantine ivories can be understood as part of a logical practice of social memory. In this, I am suggesting that social memory and shared stylistic form operate together as partners in a reciprocal relationship of dependency rather than either one existing prior to the other. The material presence of style provides visual shape to shared memories, and social recollections promote the production and consumption of similar styles.

The idea that such a thing as collective memory exists is largely credited to the early 20th-century French sociologist Halbwachs who trained with and developed the ideas of Durkheim (Halbwachs 1992; Misztal 2003). Halbwachs argues that memory is never wholly internal and individual, but rather is shaped by interactions with other people and things. His theory rests on the basic premise that *social frameworks* bind groups together. These frameworks (*cadres*), which can be fluctuating and overlapping, rely on – indeed are generated by – objects that serve as a means and repository by which networks of people find commonalities that allow them to relate to one another. In this way, objects and physical settings both reflect and construct social frameworks.

In the 1980s, the social historian Connerton expanded on Halbwachs' theories in order to consider mechanisms by which commemorative and ritual performances convey and sustain social memory. He notes that, because knowledge of the past is only possible through a knowledge of its traces, performances are most effective when they involve material objects that provide images of permanence and stability (Connerton 1989, 13, 37). Participation in ceremonial activities, which enacts and ensures membership in a group, almost always involves human-object interactions, thus according the material world a centrality in collective memory. Connerton makes the distinction between *inscribed* and *incorporated* practices. Inscribed practices entail highly self-conscious acts of identity expression; incorporated practices belong more to the realm of habit and custom. However, as we have seen in the discussion of Bourdieu's theory of practice, these two types of practices need not be mutually exclusive or even differentiated from one another. Rather, we might consider memory-making practices to span a gradual spectrum from inscribed to incorporated, with most acts embodying degrees of both.

While both Halbwachs' and Connerton's scholarship identifies a role for material objects within acts of social or collective memory making, neither scholar devotes detailed study to the objects themselves. However, archaeologists have recently taken up this question, considering the ways in which ancient peoples viewed their own pasts as part of their social memory. For example, Van Dyke and Alcock (2003) in the introduction to their edited volume *Archaeologies of Memory*, outline four intersecting venues in which archaeology can access social memory: ritual behaviours, narratives, places, and objects and representations. Ritual behaviours may be archaeologically accessible through the material dimensions of burials, feasts, or ceremonies. Narratives include stories about the past that may be codified in written form, while commemorative places are spaces inscribed with meaning, often through the erection of monuments, buildings and landscapes. Discussing objects and representations, Van Dyke and Alcock remark on their typically commemorative function, which offers a graphic, non-linguistic access to the past. Social memory for this venue is approached through either a study of images understood as laden with significant referential meaning or physical entities with life histories whose trajectories chart constructions of memory through their patterns of use and exchange.

Assmann's work on cultural memory in ancient Egypt and the Near East also has been highly influential in studies on memory in the ancient world, although his exclusive focus on textual evidence is less applicable to the material realm. Assmann (2006, 7) draws upon Halbwachs to argue for collective memory as a 'projection on the part of the collective that wishes to remember and of the individual who remembers in order to belong'. Although Assmann's discussions are less useful for my study of material culture in processes of social memory making, he nonetheless reaffirms Halbwachs' seminal contribution, namely, that collective memory has a strong connective orientation; that is, as something collective it actively connects as an entity the various constituents who participate in it (Assmann 2006, 11). This makes explicit the centrality of collective memory in community or group identities.

Style as material memory in Iron Age North Syria

Yet, I would argue that none of these lines of intellectual inquiry seriously investigate the role of style – in its visual and physical materiality and in its entanglement with human practices – as a social player in the fabric of collective memory and community identity. I would therefore like to redirect the stylistic analysis of Levantine ivories away from questions of geographical attribution and instead consider, in one particular case, how style might have functioned as material practice participating in collective memory and identity making. I take as my case study a set of markings used on animal bodies, in particular those of a leonine and bovine nature (lions, sphinxes, griffins, bulls, and also other herbivores). These markings include: a flame-like motif incised on the rear haunch, starting at the inner leg and curving back and upward; a line along the back of the animal, often highlighted with either straight denticulations, 'v's, or dots, and that ends with a series of parallel lines (often three in number) near the base of the tail; parallel lines at the rib cage, sometimes enclosed in a box; and, on leonine forms (lions, sphinxes, and griffins), a cross-hatched plaited pattern running in a strip along the belly and back of the hind leg (Figs. 17.1–17.3).

Barnett and Kantor first called attention to this set of patternings. In 1935, Barnett (1935, 195) included as one of the characteristics of his Syrian style of ivory carving 'a curious convention' of indicating the musculature on the hindquarters of lions and griffins in 'ornamental linear patterns', and he noted similar markings on the sculpture from Tell Halaf. In 1957, he refined his definition of North Syrian ivory carving, noting the 'flame-patterned haunches' as characteristic of the so-called Loftus Group of Nimrud ivories (Barnett 1975 [1957], 45–47). Reviewing the publication of the Tell Halaf reliefs by Moortgat, Kantor (1956, 173–174) more comprehensively described the series of animal markings as 'tufted manes, braided hair on belly and hindquarters, hatched dorsal border, cross-lines on the front of legs, and incised ribs' and referred to this collection of patternings as the North Syrian animal style, but did not

Fig. 17.1: Rampant sphinx, àjour ivory, ND 8050 (Herrmann 1986, no. 562, pl. 131; courtesy of The British Institute for the Study of Iraq [Gertrude Bell Memorial]).

develop the discussion further. Herrmann's 1989 article, following her 1986 publication of the ivories from SW 37 of Fort Shalmaneser at Nimrud, more systematically assembled examples of works exhibiting these markings, and she gave them the name 'Flame and Frond', which has now entered the literature of first millennium ivory studies.[2] In addition to the ivories from Nimrud – Herrmann's starting point – these markings are found on ivories, bronzes, and monumental sculpture centred on the North Syrian region with examples found at Tell Halaf (stone reliefs, gold plaques, and ivories), Tell Tayinat (bronze frontlet), Zincirli (ceramic mold), and Hama (ivories) (for references, see Herrmann and Laidlaw 2009, 96–99). Ivories with these markings have also been found at Hasanlu in north-western Iran and the Idaean Cave in Crete (for references, see Herrmann and Laidlaw 2009, 96–98). Considering these markings as quintessential traits of a single style-group or school of ivory carving, Herrmann plotted the distribution of these works and located the workshop/school at the site of Tell Halaf.

Pinpointing the geographical location of the Flame and Frond group has become one of the most contentious ongoing debates in the scholarship of Levantine ivories. Barnett (1975 [1957], 45–46), including the animal markings as a characteristic trait of the larger group of Loftus ivories, locates their 'centre of production' in Hama. Recently, Mazzoni (2009) has again made a case for Hama, although she rejects Barnett's claim (following the excavators Riis and Buhl 1990, 224) for archaeological evidence of an ivory workshop at the site. Herrmann continues to argue for a production locale at Tell Halaf (Herrmann and Laidlaw 2009, 98–99). Winter (1983; 1989) has suggested Carchemish and Zincirli as the most likely locales. Although most scholars agree that the group belongs to the North Syrian tradition, Affanni (2009) recently has argued for at least three different production locales, two in North Syria at Tell Halaf and Zincirli, and one undetermined site in South Syria (or what he calls the Intermediate School and Herrmann now calls simply Syrian). I would suggest that this group of ivories presents us with a two-fold problem along the lines discussed earlier: first, the group itself is inconsistently defined, which has confounded attempts at determining attribution to a single place and date, and second, the attributional endeavour contains flawed assumptions regarding past social and economic conditions, which lead to problematic interpretations.

How then might we understand these markings, if not as the signature of a style-group linked to a workshop located somewhere in space? Can they only be taken as characteristics of a general greater Syrian (South and North Syrian) regional tradition? On the contrary, I propose that we can say more and do more with them. Let us instead consider the markings from the perspective of practices of doing, as material *doxa* in Bourdieu's *habitus*. In other words, let us consider them as

Fig. 17.2: Rampant griffin, àjour ivory, ND 10501 (Herrmann 1986, no. 561, pl. 130; courtesy of The British Institute for the Study of Iraq [Gertrude Bell Memorial]).

part of the material practices that engender collective identity. They are the product of shared social relations that span this entire region and conversely, through their consumption, they contributed to shaping pan-regional (elite) community identities. At the same time, we should keep in mind the divergent appearance of other animal motif ivories that do not display these marks, a situation that suggests multiple (perhaps intersecting, perhaps distinct) communities of social practices across the geographical extent of the Levant and greater North Syria.

When we see these highly distinctive markings as part of the ongoing practices of producing and consuming styles that both derived from and contributed to shared identities, their visual connections with earlier artworks becomes salient in thinking about collective memory and its centrality to communal identity in early first millennium

Fig. 17.3: Detail of griffin and lion combat, carved relief ivory flask, IM 79508 (Herrmann and Laidlaw 2009, no. 236, pl. 52 middle; courtesy of The British Institute for the Study of Iraq [Gertrude Bell Memorial]).

North Syria (here taking North Syria as a broad geographical designation that encompasses the area from Hama all the way up into southeastern Turkey and Cilicia, not as the stylistic designation that divides North Syrian from South Syrian or Phoenician ivories). Since the time of Barnett's and Kantor's studies, scholars have seen earlier precedents for these animal markings in late second millennium luxury arts (*e.g.* Kantor 1956, 173–174; Barnett 1975 [1957], 43; Herrmann 1989, 104; Winter 1973, 279).

These animal markings are indeed quite distinctive of luxury arts from the Late Bronze Age, and the luxury arts that most frequently exhibit them (and variations of them) belong, as I have argued previously, to a group of diplomatically entangled prestige goods circulating in a highly structured and formal network of rhetorically equal rulers (Feldman 2006). The Late Bronze Age examples that show strong visual affinities to the first millennium pieces include a group of incised ivory inlays from Delos in the Aegean, Kition on Cyprus, and Megiddo in the southern Levant – ivories that are so similar in their execution that Kantor and I, following her, have suggested a possible shared source of production for them (Kantor 1960; Feldman 2006, 95–97).[3] Examples showing a more modelled version of the markings appear in ivory (and monumental sculpture) at Mycenae, in an ivory plaque from Byblos, an ivory pyxis from Lachish, and, from Enkomi, ivory mirror handles and an ivory gamebox (modelled and incised; for Mycenae, Byblos, and Lachish, see Feldman 2006; for Enkomi, see Murray, Smith and Walters 1900, pls. I–II: nos. 872, 883). Related markings are also found on a gold dagger sheath, gold chariot appliqués, and a gold and inlaid bow case from the tomb of Tutankhamun, a silver dish and jug from Tell Basta in lower Egypt, an ivory bas relief strip from Delos, and ivory tabletop inlays and a gold bowl from Ras Shamra-Ugarit (for images and general discussion, see Feldman 2006). For the Late Bronze Age artworks, I have proposed that the visual motifs, compositions, and idioms of execution (under which rubric I have previously classified these animal markings) all participated in and actively contributed to the formation and maintenance of an exclusive royal network based on a metaphor of brotherhood and reciprocity. In the terms of the discussion here, we might say that these idiomatic ways of doing engendered the identification of a small number of culturally and politically different kings with one another.

Style is such an effective contributor to the construction of social memory, and thereby also to communal identity, because of its dual and somewhat paradoxical nature. On the one hand, it is almost unconsidered, unthought about, secondary – simply being/existing (Elsner 2003). On the other hand, its physical presence elicits an almost visceral connection to emotive elements; without its existence, these emotive qualities would be lost. A 'logic of stylistic practice' along the model of Bourdieu allows us to see how style participates as a prime element of *habitus*, a part of a common-sense world of practical experience. Because style is so slippery a term and is used in so many ways, I have argued previously that we need to be more precise in our definition and use of the term (Feldman 2006, 90–91). Here, however, I would in fact like to remain somewhat vague in my definition – style as the manner of making or executing – in order to accommodate a range of production qualities without having to determine degrees of artistic intentionality that come into play when trying to tease out unconscious 'Morellian' stylistic traits from other 'conventional' or 'manipulated' traits (*contra* Mazzoni 2009, 110; for related multiplicity of definitions of style, see Winter 1998, 56). From this perspective, the naturalised and normalised aspect of style – it is taken as simply existing – allows it to insinuate itself unobtrusively among a host of different properties. This is exactly the kind of 'learned ignorance' that Bourdieu argues produces a common-sense world that is felt as natural and creates regularized practices without specific awareness.

To understand the logic of the stylistic practices fossilized in these animal markings – both with respect to a collective memory of the Late Bronze Age and to an emerging community identity in the Iron Age – it is useful to briefly review greater North Syria's place in the history of the early first millennium. Due to causes that still elude us, massive state collapses occurred around 1200 BCE, destroying the Hittite state and severely curtailing the ambitions of Assyria and Egypt, which retreated to their core heartlands (Ward, Joukowsky and Åström 1992). During the centuries that followed – traditionally called a Dark Age – the Near East and Mediterranean underwent radical transformations that created a very different social, economic, and political world (Liverani 2003; Sherratt 2003). The regions of North Syria, the northern Levantine coast and Cyprus seem to have emerged from the collapse and reinvented themselves the most quickly, if indeed we can consider their particular situations as collapse in the first place. In the early part of the Iron Age, certainly the 9th century and now convincingly shown even earlier in the 10th, 11th, and possibly 12th centuries, the greater North Syrian region benefited from the sudden autonomy and decentralization created by the collapse of the Hittite state, which had previously controlled this area (Dodd 2005). Sporadic finds of North Syrian luxury goods at least as early as the mid-10th century in distant places like Lefkandi and Athens in Greece indicate occasional, if not sustained, interactions with a wide, multi-cultural network (Hodos 2006, 3–5).

Yet, intense competition for territory and resources among the North Syrian states themselves also resulted (Dodd 2005; Brown 2008b). With the collapse of the great Bronze Age empires – Hatti in particular, but also the retrenchment of Egypt and Assyria – economic and political structures in areas like North Syria disappeared, creating, on the one hand, greater opportunities for growth but, on the other hand, also conflict and competition (Hawkins 1988,

Fig. 17.4: Rampant sphinx, àjour ivory, ND 1083 (Herrmann and Laidlaw 2009, no. 19, pl. 2; courtesy of The British Institute for the Study of Iraq [Gertrude Bell Memorial]).

106–108; Dodd 2005, 244). This growth finds expression in the wealth of resources used in monumental building projects at places like Carchemish and Aleppo. Conflict, however, is revealed in evidence of non-Assyrian destructions and iconoclasm at places like Tell Tayinat that have been interpreted as intra-North Syrian warfare (Harrison 2001). We might, therefore, consider that there would also have been considerable motivation for mobilising collective memory-making strategies in the construction of new community identities, both with regard to other North Syrian kingdoms and with the increasing presence of Assyria in the region beginning in the 9th century.

Indeed, several scholars have recently situated the dramatic appearance of a tradition of stone carving that included both large-scale architectural programs and smaller-scale funerary monuments within this context of autonomy and competition (*e.g.* Bonatz 2000; 2001; Brown 2008b; Dodd 2005). These scholars have implicated the carved reliefs, their architectural settings, and the urban settlements themselves in processes of tradition building in the North Syrian region in the wake of the Bronze Age collapse. The placement of carved orthostats in the urban landscape contributed to new social identities as part of a social memory of place. In contrast to Assyrian reliefs, which decorated interior spaces, North Syrian reliefs were placed mainly on exterior walls, typically in public places of gathering, performance, and celebration that relate to ritual behavior. For example, at Carchemish, complex ceremonies relating to kingship have been reconstructed as taking place in public spaces decorated by the carved reliefs (Denil 2007). Additionally, the prevalence of using carved orthostats at city gates – as liminal sites of performance related to social practices such as trade and justice – reinforces their participation in practices of social memory making. Gates were also associated with the royal ancestor cult, often expressed through the presence of a statue of a royal ancestor to whom offerings could be made, bringing together a performative dimension with a clear interest in the past (Mazzoni 1997; Cooper 2006, 234–236). On a less monumental scale, funerary stelae appear as a new type of monument at the end of the 10th and the 9th centuries, combining Bronze Age traditions of ancestor cult with new modes of expressing identity through family funerary monuments (Bonatz 2000; 2001). Their large numbers and wide distribution across North Syria point to their participation in processes of emerging landscapes of pan-regional collective memory in the Early Iron Age.

Part of this strategy relied on emphasising links with earlier Late Bronze Age cultural traditions. Several North Syrian kingdoms publically professed direct cultural and dynastic links to the former Hittite state. Here it is important to recall that the textual evidence, in the form of official seals and monumental inscriptions, not only provides us with critical historical links between the Iron Age dynasties of Carchemish and Malatya and that of the Hittite state, it also highlights the specific desire of the later rulers to promote this particular ancestry (Hawkins 1988; Dodd 2005, 250). The public expression of affiliation with the earlier Hittite state is also evident in the use of the Luwian hieroglyphic writing system for monumental display inscriptions.

This complex of intersecting landscapes and processes of social memory and community identity production can be further enriched by a careful consideration of stylistic attributes. Thus, it is within a framework of generating collective memory in a pan-regional environment of emerging socio-political identities that I propose to situate the specific body markings of Kantor's 'North Syrian animal style' and Herrmann's 'Flame and Frond style-group.' I suggest that just as the hereditary lineages and Luwian language drew upon the Late Bronze Age in order to bolster the competing claims of the various emerging North Syrian states (and, at the same time, provided a pan-regional means for resisting the encroachment of Assyria), so stylistic details were curated, passed on, and taken up as a deep-seated affiliation with the past. Style and stylistic continuity thus need to be viewed not as empty acts of making, but rather as the evocative material presence of form that delves back into a Bronze Age past. Eminently tangible yet so easily overlooked, it is the stylistic connections – offering visceral images of permanence and stability – that effectively and on an emotive level linked the present with the past.

If we can propose that the first millennium Levantine animal style ivories tapped into memories of the earlier Late Bronze Age, are we to understand their stylistic echoes to be a continuity of practice, or a rediscovery of one? Must we determine the level of awareness of the past (that is, how the past was viewed in the past) in order to propose some aspect of meaningfulness in this relationship? In reference to written texts, Assmann (2006, 117) notes that a clear distinction between old and new (that is, past and present) only comes clearly into view when a text is written in a language that is no longer used, so that it is understood as distinctly other. This raises an intriguing, but I hope to show ultimately moot, question when we consider the issue of style and collective memory: if the traits that characterise the so-called animal style belong to a collective memory drawing upon the Late Bronze Age, how are we to understand the Iron Age reception of this style – was it 'old', 'new', or simply existing? Related to this is the question of whether the animal style represents a continuity of practice from the Late Bronze Age down through the Iron Age, or was it rediscovered and in a sense reinvented? The answer to this second question, which should reside in an empirical enumeration of either continuity or break, is of course complicated by the general thinness of our evidence from the so-called Dark Age that marks the transition from the Late Bronze to Iron ages. In North Syria itself, the murkiness of this transition is beginning to come into better focus with recent archaeological discoveries, most notably the stamp seal from Lidar Höyük and the excavations at the Aleppo Citadel that establish some clearly direct links to the Late Bronze Age (although this does not negate the radically transformative character of the Late Bronze-Iron Age transition; Hawkins 1988; Kohlmeyer 2009; Gonella, Khayyata and Kohlmeyer 2005).

Regardless of whether we see continuity or rediscovery in the animal style, if we take the early Iron Age chronological horizon as an unfolding process of selecting these certain traits over and over again through a period of at least several generations, we return to the first question regarding an ancient perception of 'pastness'. This question of reception verges on similar territory as that of artistic intentionality discussed earlier in this study. Like artistic intentionality, it requires us to make impossible evaluations about ancient perceptions that must always have been multiple and in flux. However, more critical to my consideration than the irretrievability of such perceptions (for that in and of itself would not justify ignoring them) is the support provided by Bourdieu's theory of practice in which the selection choices evident in the execution of a style, regardless of how made or received in any one specific instance, simultaneously become a part of and constitute the *habitus*. It is this *habitus* that intersects with collective memory (again, regardless of whether this collective memory is openly articulated or internally normalised). The continuity of Late Bronze Age stylistic traits can therefore be understood to perpetuate a shared collective memory that may or may not (or may at some times and not at others) have been aware of these Late Bronze Age roots. These traits nonetheless tie their communities of practitioners to the Late Bronze Age, although so many other aspects of the *habitus* do not. It is this connection to a Late Bronze Age world of diplomacy and courtly luxury that I contend lies latent in the first millennium animal style ivories of North Syria, participating in a much broader and complex set of identity negotiation and competition during the centuries before (and during) Assyrian domination. Thus we can see the peculiar markings on animal bodies as part of a practical logic of style that embodied social memory and enhanced emerging communities of identity in greater North Syria at the dawn of the Iron Age.

Acknowledgments

I would like to thank the organizers of the conference, Professor Joseph Maran and Dr Philipp Stockhammer, for inviting me to participate and for preparing such a stimulating roster of speakers. Additional thanks are due for a further invitation to spend two weeks in Heidelberg as a visiting scholar, during which time I wrote a substantial part of the present paper. I would also like to thank Brian Brown, Stephanie Langin-Hooper, Claudia Suter, and Irene Winter for their close readings and perceptive feedback on several early drafts, as well as the two anonymous reviewers who commented on the manuscript draft.

Notes

1 I purposely keep vague the geographical boundaries, using various designations such as 'greater North Syria' and 'Levant', because of our increasing awareness of the fluidity of cultural connectedness across this area. My usage of the geographical area is in distinction to the stylistically determined 'North Syrian tradition'.

2 In referring to this group, Herrmann interchanges the terms workshop/school/style-group. Herrmann 1986, 16–17; 1989.

3 I do not argue for a shared biological, geographical, or cultural origin for these objects, but rather that their shared stylistic features point to shared social relations among the producers and consumers regardless of whether they were made in the Aegean, Cyprus, or the Levant or by Aegeans, Cypriots, or Levantines.

References

Affanni, G. (2009) Ivory Sphinxes of North Syrian Tradition: the Flame and Frond School. In Cecchini, Mazzoni and Scigliuzzo 2009, 171–185.

Assmann, J. (2006) *Religion and Cultural Memory*. Translated by R. Livingstone. Stanford, Stanford University Press. [Originally published as *Religion und kulturelles Gedächtnis* (2000)].

Barnett, R. D. (1935) The Nimrud Ivories and the Art of the Phoenicians. *Iraq* 2, 179–210.

Barnett, R. D. (1975 [1957]) *A Catalogue of the Nimrud Ivories*. London, The British Museum.

Barnett, R. D. (1982) *Ancient Ivories in the Middle East*. Jerusalem, The Hebrew University of Jerusalem.

Bonatz, D. (2000) Syro-Hittite Funerary Monuments: A Phenomenon of Tradition or Innovation? In G. Bunnens (ed.), *Essays on Syria in the Iron Age*. Ancient Near Eastern Studies Supplement 7, 189–210. Louvain, Peeters Press.

Bonatz, D. (2001) Mnemohistory in Syro-Hittite Iconography. In I. T. Abusch, C. Noyes, W. Hallo and I. Winter (eds), *Historiography in the Cuneiform World: Proceedings of the 45th Rencontre Assyriologique Internationale*, 65–77. Bethesda, Maryland, CDL.

Bourdieu, P. (1984) *Distinction: A Social Critique of the Judgement of Taste*. Translated by Richard Nice. Cambridge, Massachusetts, Harvard University Press.

Bourdieu, P. (1990) *The Logic of Practice*. Translated by Richard Nice. Stanford, Stanford University Press.

Brown, B. (2008a) The Kilamuwa Relief: Ethnicity, Class and Power in Iron Age North Syria. In J. M. Córdoba, M. Molist, M. C. Pérez, I. Rubio, S. Martínez (eds), *Proceedings of the 5th International Congress on the Archaeology of the Ancient Near East, Madrid, April 3–8 2006*, 339–356. Madrid, UAM Ediciones.

Brown, B. (2008b) *Monumentalizing Identities: North Syrian Urbanism, 1200–800 BCE*. Unpublished dissertation, University of California, Berkeley.

Caubet, A. and Gaborit-Chopin, D. (2004) Origines et diffusion. In *Ivoires de l'Orient ancien aux temps modernes*, 28–30. Exhibition catalogue. Paris, Editions de la Réunion des musées nationaux.

Cecchini, S. M., Mazzoni, S. and Scigliuzzo, E. (2009) *Syrian and Phoenician Ivories of the Early First Millennium BCE: Chronology, Regional Styles and Iconographic Repertories, Patterns of Inter-regional Distributions*. Acts of the International Workshop, Pisa, December 9th–11th 2004. Pisa, Edizioni ETS.

Connerton, P. (1989) *How Societies Remember*. Cambridge, Cambridge University Press.

Cooper, L. (2006) *Early Urbanism on the Syrian Euphrates*. New York and London, Routledge.

De Certeau, M. (1984) *The Practice of Everyday Life*. Translated by Steven Rendall. Berkeley, The University of California Press.

Denil, E. (2007) Ceremony and Kingship at Carchemish. In J. Cheng and M. H. Feldman (eds), *Ancient Near Eastern Art in Context: Studies in Honor of Irene J. Winter by Her Students*, 179–204. Leiden, Brill.

Di Paolo, S. (2009) What Production Model can be deduced for First-millennium BC Syro-Phoenician Ivories? In Cecchini, Mazzoni and Scigliuzzo 2009, 133–153.

Dodd, L. S. (2005) Territory, Legacy, and Wealth in Iron Age Anatolia. In B. Parker, L. Rodseth and L. Adams (eds), *Untaming the Frontier in Anthropology, Archaeology, and History*, 238–260. Tuscon, University of Arizona Press.

Elsner, J. (2003) Style. In R. S. Nelson and R. Shiff (eds), *Critical Terms for Art History*, 98–109. Second Edition. Chicago, University of Chicago Press.

Feldman, M. H. (2006) *Diplomacy by Design: Luxury Arts and an 'International Style' in the Ancient Near East, 1400–1200 BCE*. Chicago, University of Chicago Press.

Gonnella, J., Khayyata, W. and Kohlmeyer, K. (2005) *Die Zitadelle von Aleppo und der Tempel des Wettergottes*. Münster, Rhema.

Halbwachs, M. (1992) *On Collective Memory*. Edited, Translated, and with an Introduction by L. A. Coser. Chicago, University of Chicago Press. [Originally published as *Les cadres sociaux de la mémoire* (Paris 1952) and *La topographie légendaire des évangiles en terre sainte: Etude de mémoire collective* (Paris 1941)].

Harrison, T. P. (2001) Tell Ta'yinat and the Kingdom of Unqi. In P. M. Daviau, J. Wevers and M. Weigl (eds), *The World of the Aramaeans II: Studies in History and Archaeology in Honour of Paul-Eugène Dion*, 115–132. Sheffield, Sheffield Academic Press.

Hawkins, J. D. (1988) Kuzi-Tesub and the 'Great Kings' of Karkamis. *Anatolian Studies* 38, 99–108.

Herrmann, G. (1986) *Ivories from Room SW 37, Fort Shalmaneser*. Ivories from Nimrud IV. London, The British School of Archaeology in Iraq.

Herrmann, G. (1989) The Nimrud Ivories 1: The Flame and Frond School. *Iraq* 51, 85–109.

Herrmann, G. (1992) The Nimrud Ivories, 2: A Survey of the Traditions. In B. Hrouda, S. Kroll and P. Z. Spanos (eds), *Von Uruk nach Tuttul: Eine Festschrift für Eva Strommenger*, 65–79. Munich and Vienna, Profil.

Herrmann, G. (2005) Naming, Defining, Explaining: A View from Nimrud. In Suter and Uehlinger (2005), 11–21.

Herrmann, G. and Laidlaw, S. (2009) *Ivories from the North West Palace (1845–1992)*. Ivories from Nimrud VI. British Institute for the Study of Iraq.

Herrmann, G., Coffey, H. and Laidlaw, S. (2004) *The Published Ivories from Fort Shalmaneser, Nimrud: A Scanned Archive of Photographs*. London, Institute of Archaeology, University College London and the British School of Archaeology in Iraq.

Hodos, T. (2006) *Local Responses to Colonization in the Iron Age Mediterranean*. London and New York, Routledge.

Isaacman, A. F. and Isaacman, B. (2004) *Slavery and Beyond: The Making of Men and Chikunda Ethnic Identities in the Unstable World of South-central Africa, 1750–1920*. Portsmouth, New Hampshire, Heinemann.

Kantor, H. J. (1956) Syro-Palestinian Ivories. *Journal of Near Eastern Studies* 15, 153–174.

Kantor, H. J. (1960) Ivory Carving in the Mycenaean Period. *Archaeology* 13, 14–25.

Kitayama, S. and Cohen, D. (2007) *Handbook of Cultural Psychology*. New York and London, Guilford Press.

Kohlmeyer, K. (2009) The Temple of the Storm God in Aleppo during the Late Bronze and Early Iron Ages. *Near Eastern Archaeology* 72, 190–202.

Liverani, M. (2003) The Influence of Political Institutions on Trade in the Ancient Near East (Late Bronze to Early Iron Age). In C. Zaggagnini (ed.), *Mercanti e politica nel mondo antico*, 119–137. Rome, L'erma di Bretschneider.

Mazzoni, S. (1997) The Gate and the City: Change and Continuity in Syro-Hittite Urban Ideology. In G. Wilhelm (ed.), *Die orientalische Stadt: Kontinuität, Wandel, Bruch: Internationales Colloquium der Deutschen Orient-Gesellschaft, 9.–10. Mai 1996 in Halle/Saale*, 307–338. Saarbrücken, Saarbrücker Druckerei und Verlag.

Mazzoni, S. (2009) Ivories and Art Traditions in the Hama Region. In Cecchini, Mazzoni and Scigliuzzo 2009, 107–132.

Misztal, B. A. (2003) *Theories of Social Remembering*. Maidenhead and Philadelphia, Open University Press.

Moorey, P. R. S. (1999 [1994]) *Ancient Mesopotamian Materials and Industries: The Archaeological Evidence*. Winona Lake, Indiana, Eisenbrauns. [Originally published by Oxford University Press, 1994]

Murray, A. S., Smith, A. H. and Walters, H. B. (1900) *Excavations in Cyprus*. London, The British Museum.

Onnis, F. (2009) The Nimrud Bowls: New Data from an Analysis of the Objects. *Iraq* 71, 139–150.

Poulsen, F. (1912) *Der Orient und die frühgriechische Kunst*. Leipzig and Berlin, Druck und Verlag von B. G. Teubner.

Riis, P. J. and Buhl, M.-L. (1990) *Les objets de la période dite Syro-Hittite (Âge du Fer)*. Hama, fouilles et recherches de la Fondation Carlsberg 1931–1938, vol. II: 2. Copenhagen, Nationalmuseet.

Sherratt, S. (2003) 'Globalization' at the End of the Second

Millennium BCE. In W. G. Dever and S. Gitin (eds), *Symbiosis, Symbolism, and the Power of the Past: Canaan, Ancient Israel, and Their Neighbors from the Late Bronze Age through Roman Palestrina*, 37–62. Winona Lake, Indiana, Eisenbrauns.

Suter, C. E. (2008) Les ivories de Samarie, capitale de l'antique royaume d'Israël. Talk presented in the series *Actualité de la recherché archéologique*, Musée du Louvre.

Suter, C. E. and Uehlinger, C. (2005) *Crafts and Images in Contact: Studies on Eastern Mediterranean Art of the First Millennium BCE*. Orbis Biblicus et Orientalis 210. Fribourg and Göttingen, Academic Press and Vandenhoeck & Ruprecht.

Van Dyke, R. M. and Alcock, S. E. (2003) Archaeologies of Memory: An Introduction. In R. M. Van Dyke and S. E. Alcock (eds), *Archaeologies of Memory*, 1–13. Oxford, Blackwell.

Ward, W. A., Joukowsky, M. and Åström, P. (1992) *The Crisis Years: The 12th Century BC: From beyond the Danube to the Tigris*. Dubuque, Iowa, Kendall/Hunt.

Wicke, D. (2005) 'Roundcheeked and Ringletted': Gibt es einen nordwestsyrischen Regionalstil in der altorientalischen Elfenbeinschnitzerei? In Suter and Uehlinger 2005, 23–42.

Winter, I. J. (1973) *North Syria in the Early First Millennium BC, with Special Reference to Ivory Carving*. Unpublished dissertation, Columbia University.

Winter, I. J. (1976) Phoenician and North Syrian Ivory Carving in Historical Context: Questions of Style and Distribution. *Iraq* 38, 1–22.

Winter, I. J. (1983) Carchemish ša kišād puratti. *Anatolian Studies* 33, 177–197.

Winter, I. J. (1989) North Syrian Ivories and Tell Halaf Reliefs: The Impact of Luxury Goods upon 'Major' Arts. In A. Leonard, Jr and B. B. Williams (eds), *Essays in Ancient Civilization Presented to Helene J. Kantor*, 321–332. Chicago, The Oriental Institute of the University of Chicago.

Winter, I. J. (1992) Review of G. Herrmann, *Ivories from Room 37 Fort Shalmaneser*. Ivories from Nimrud 4. *Journal of Near Eastern Studies* 51, 135–141.

Winter, I. J. (1998) The Affective Properties of Styles: An Inquiry into Analytical Process and the Inscription of Meaning in Art History. In C. A. Jones and P. Galison (eds), *Picturing Science, Producing Art*, 55–77. New York and London, Routledge.

Winter, I. J. (2005) Establishing Group Boundaries: Toward Methodological Refinement in the Determination of Sets as a Prior Condition to the Analysis of Cultural Contact and/or Innovation in First Millennium BCE Ivory Carving. In Suter and Uehlinger 2005, 23–42.

18.

An introduction to the divine statues of, and the objects belonging to, the gods in Mesopotamia during the Old Babylonian Period (*c*. 2000–1595 BCE)

Michèle Maggio

Introduction

This article is an introduction to a detailed study in progress, entitled 'L´ornementation des dieux. Etude du matériel appartenant aux dieux d´après des documents de la pratique de l´époque paléo-babylonienne'. The study is a postdoctoral research project prepared for the subproject D2 of the *Cluster of Excellence: Asia and Europe in a Global Context, Shifting Asymmetries in Cultural Flows, Virtual Jaspers Centre,* University of Heidelberg, called *Materiality and Practice: Cultural Entanglements of 2nd millennium BC East Mediterranean Societies.*

From the beginning of Ancient Near Eastern studies, statues of gods have given rise to problems of identification. Many monumental statues have been found on Mesopotamian soil, but most of them are representations of kings or worshippers, rather than deities. Another problem arises in the cuneiform texts: the word 'statue' in front of the name of a deity first appears only at the beginning of the second millennium, and then only in rare or specific cases. The first part of the paper will present a number of issues relating to this problem of identification by combining archaeological evidence and cuneiform texts. The second part will present a brief overview of the objects belonging to the gods found in administrative and legal texts of the early second millennium BC. These objects consist of jewellery and garments. Finally, an attempt will be made to redefine the role of these objects in cult practices, and several methods of interpretation will be provided with respect to the materiality and the 'intentionality' of the divine statues from Mesopotamia.

Part One: the statues of the Gods and their identification

Before attempting any identification, we should first define the terms 'statue of a god' and 'cult statue'. The basic function of a cult statue is to be a material representation linking the living to the divine. In Mesopotamia, this can be expressed through three main human representations: a deity, a worshipper or a king. The statue of a deity, sometimes called 'divine statue', is only a material representation of a god on earth while the statue of the worshipper and the king can rather be the physical representation of the faithful's fervour. But for the statue of a king, we should add two possible specialised meanings: that of the good and fair leader who recalls a golden age and that of the deified king.

In time before Sargon, in the beginning of the third millennium BCE, no statues have been identified as divine. The word 'statue' (ALAN in Sumerian) never precedes a divine name in the cuneiform texts, but only that of senior dignitaries (Matthiae 1994, 40–42). At the end of the third millennium BCE, under the Dynasty of Akkad, the situation is identical. We do not find any statues of gods, or even reference to them, in the documents.

In the early second millennium BCE, mentions of divine statues appeared in the cuneiform records. Most of these occurrences can be found in the year names of kings from several dynasties or kingships. Here are few examples:

From the Dynasty of Isin (c. *2019–1794 BCE):*

- Iddin-Dagan, year 'F': mu ^{urudu}alan gu-[la] ^{d}nin-ì-si-in-

[na] mu-na-[dím] 'year, he fashioned a big copper statue for NinIsin' (Sigrist 1988, 24).

- Išme-Dagan, year 'M': mu ^{d}*iš-me-*^{d}*da-gan* lugal-e ^{urudu}alan ^{d}nin-urta [mu-na-dím] é-šu-me-ša$_{4}$ ^{urudu}éš-da-mah mu-na-gub-ba-a 'year, Išme-Dagan, the king, fashioned a copper statue for Ninurta and has placed a great vessel in the Ešumeša' (Sigrist 1988, 27).
- Enlil-bāni, year 'F': mu ^{d}en-líl-*ba-ni* lugal-e ^{urudu}alan gal-gal [3]-a-bi [^{d}]nin-urta-[ra mu-na-dím] 'year, Enlil-bāni, the king, fashioned for Ninurta three very large copper statues' (Sigrist 1988, 33).
- Enlil-bāni, year 'G': mu ^{d}en-líl-*ba-ni* lugal-e ^{urudu}alan KÙ.GI ^{d}nin-urta-ra mu-un-na-an-dím 'year, Enlil-bani, the king, fashioned for Ninurta a golden statue' (Sigrist 1988, 33).
- Enlil-bāni, year 'H': mu ^{d}en-líl-*ba-ni* lugal-e alan KÙ.GI ^{d}*na-na-a*-ra mu-na-dím 'year, Enlil-bāni, the king, fashioned for Nanāja a golden statue' (Sigrist 1988, 34).
- Zambīja, year 'A': mu ^{d}*za-am-bi-ia* lugal alan KÙ.GI 5-bi ^{d}inanna *ù* ^{d}*na-na-a*-ra mu-ne-dím OR mu ^{d}*za-am-bi-ia* lugal-e ^{giš}alan KÙ.GI 4-bi ^{d}inanna-ra mu-na-dím 'year, Zambīja, the king, fashioned 5 gold statues for Inanna and Nanāja' OR 'year, Zambīja, the king, fashioned 4 gold statues for Inanna' (Sigrist 1988, 35).

From the Dynasty of Larsa (c. *2025–1763 BC):*

- Sîn-iqīšam, year 4 : mu ^{d}EN.ZU-*i-qí-ša-am* lugal-e 14 ^{urudu}alan nibru^{ki}-šè *ù* 3 ^{giš}gu-za bára mah alan ^{d}utu ^{d}še-ri$_{5}$-da KÙ.GI šu-du$_{7}$-a é ^{d}utu-šè èš-é-babbar-šè in-ku$_{4}$-re 'year, he had 14 copper statues brought to the city of Nippur and had 3 thrones and a statue of Šamaš and Šerida brought in the chapel of the Ebabbar in the temple of Šamaš' (Sigrist 1990, 29).

From the kingships of the area of Ešnunna (c. *2010*–c. *1700 BC):*

- Ur-Ningišzida, year 'C': mu ^{urudu}alan gub-ba é ^{d}tišpak-ka ba-dím 'year, a copper standing statue for the temple Tišpak was fashioned' (Wu Yuhong 1994, 25).
- Ur-Ningišzida, year 'D': mu ^{giš}nú$^{!}$ [...] é ^{d}tišpak-ka *ù* ^{urudu}alan é [^{d}nin]-giš-zi-<da> ba-dím 'year, a wooden bed ... in the temple of Tišpak and a copper statue in the temple of Ningišzida were fashioned' (Wu Yuhong 1994, 25).
- Abī-madar, year 'C': mu ^{urudu}alan *ṣa-i-dam a-bi-ma-dar* é ^{d}EN.ZU *ú-še-ri-bu* 'year, Abī-madar brought a golden statue to the temple of Sîn' (Wu Yuhong 1994, 42).
- Sîn-abušu, year 'N': mu ^{urudu}alan-meš *a-na* é eš$_{4}$-tár *i-ru-bu* 'year, Sîn-abušu brought statues to the temple of Ištar' (Wu Yuhong 1994, 50).
- Ipiq-Adad II, year 'B1': mu 2 alan KÙ.GI *i-na-an-na in-en-ep-šu* 'year, the 2 gold statues of Inanna were made' (Wu Yuhong 1994, 75–76).
- Narām-Sîn, year 'C': mu alan KÙ.GI ^{d}*na-ra-am*-^{d}EN.ZU *a-na* é ^{d}tišpak *ú-še-ri-bu* 'year, (the divine) Narām-Sîn brought a golden statue in the temple of Tišpak' (Wu Yuhong 1994, 85).
- Narām-Sîn, year 'D': mu 2 alan KÙ.GI ù 2 alan kù-babbar ^{d}*na-ra-am*-30 *a-na* é ^{d}nin-a-zu ba-an-ku$_{4}$ 'year, (the divine) Narām-Sîn brought two golden statues and two silver statues to the temple of Ninazu' (Wu Yuhong 1994, 86).

From the kingship of Mari (reign of Zimrī-Līm, 1775–1762 BC):

- Zimrī-Līm, year 1: mu *zi-im-ri-li-im* alan *an-nu-ni-tim ša še-eh-ri-im*^{ki} *i-pu-šu* 'year, Zimrī-Līm made a statue of Annunītum of Šehrum' (Charpin and Ziegler 2003, 258).

We can also find references in administrative texts from Mari which have been selected for my study of the objects belonging to the gods in the Old Babylonian period:

- In ARMT 25 187, from the reign of Zimrī-Līm, approximately 500 g of silver was given to the statue of Annunītum of Šehrum, which can be connected to the year name 1 of Zimrī-Līm, cited above (ll. 1–4: 1 ma-na kù-babbar *i-na* [na$_{4}$-hi-a nì]-šu lugal *a-na ih-zi* [alan] *ša an-nu-ni-tim ša* [*še-eh*]-*ri-im*^{ki}).
- In ARMT 25 287 (Groneberg 1990, 168, 172), from the 10th day of the month iv in the year name 'Zimrī-Līm 4', pieces of gold were given for the statue of Dagan (ll. 3–4: [...] KÙ.GI *qé-er-re-et* alan ^{d}*da-gan*) and pieces of gold for the throne of the statue of Dagan (ll. 14– 15: 2 gín 15 še kù-babbar [*qé*]-*er-re-et* ^{giš}gu-za *ša* alan ^{d}*da-gan*).
- In the year 13 of Zimrī-Līm, ornaments has been consigned to the statue of Dagan (ARMT 25 363: [x su] 4 KÙ.GI *a-na ṣí-mi-it-ti ša* alan ^{d}*da-gan* si-lá *i-din*-eš$_{4}$-tár [it]i *a-bi-im* u$_{4}$-7-kam [mu *z*]*i-im-ri-li-im* [*áš-la*]-*ka-a*^{ki} [*ša-ni-iš*] *iṣ-ba-tu*).
- Finally, we found in an undated text, ARMT 25 626 (Durand 1990, 139), 3 kg of gold which was used to plate the statues of two deities (Dagan and Jakrub-El) and of the king (ll. 1–3: 6 ma-na KÙ.GI *ih-zu ša* 1 alan ^{d}*da-gan*1 alan lugal 1 alan ^{d}*ia-ak-ri-bi*-dingir).

The archaeological discoveries dated from the Old Babylonian period are not that representative. Only few examples of statues in terracotta or in bronze, which never exceed more than 20 cm in height, were found in the region of the Diyala. They were identified as deities because of their tiaras with horns or some inhuman characteristics (for example: four heads, *cf.* Frankfort 1943, pl. 77–79) or symbols (for example: naked women with large vulva, *cf.* Frankfort, Lloyd and Jacobsen 1940, figs. 109–112).

At the end of the second millennium BCE, during the 'Kassite' period, the symbolic representation of deities took place. Divine symbols appeared on *Kudurrus*-reliefs and we could assign them to each major god of the Mesopotamian pantheon. The crescent moon is the symbol of the god of the moon, the star represents Venus, symbol of the goddess of love, Ištar and so on.

During the first millennium BCE, it is mainly genies, and other lesser gods, that are represented (Ornan 2009, 130–134). We also find one relief from the Assyrian palaces which shows the transport of the statues (Layard 1849, pl. 65).

Apart from those discovered in the Mesopotamian plain, we must also add the discoveries of divine statues at Hazor, a Late Bronze Age site in Israel. Monumental statues were found during the first seasons of excavations in the 1950s. One of them is interesting because the sun symbol appears on his torso, which means that it should be the statue of Šamaš, the sun god (Yadin *et al.* 1961, pl. CCCXXV, 1–2).

In addition to these references, we must now look at the statues of the deified kings, which are very well documented since the beginning of Mesopotamian civilization. A very large number of statues of kings were created in the Akkadian period at the end of the third millennium BCE, of which the bronze head of Sargon (Mallowan 1936, pl. vi) or those of Gudea (Johansen 1978) are the most famous. According to later inscriptions, there was also a cult dedicated to these statues during the life of the king, and even after his death (Spycket 1968, 33 and ss.). Unlike the statues of worshipers, royal statues were fashioned in diorite. The diorite was brought from the country of Magan (the present Oman: Heimpel 1987, 48–49). It was specially used for the image of the king as representing the royal power and control over the material, and its use marked the separation of the royal sphere from the divine and human (Matthiae 1994, 44).

At the final end of the third millennium, from the Third Dynasty of Ur to the Old Babylonian period, a number of royal statues placed in temples are described in the year names (Matthiae 1994, 46–64). The king is depicted as praying or performing acts of bravery. In the year names of the Dynasty of Larsa, the kings Warad-Sîn and Rīm-Sîn, who reigned in the late 19th century BCE and in the early 18th century BCE, placed statues of their father and other kings who ruled before them in temples, especially in a chapel called Egalbarra (Matthiae 1994, 50; upon Egalbarra: George 1993, 87).

The small bronze statuettes from the Old Syrian period, between the second and first millennium BCE are also worthy of attention. Because of their tiaras with horns, they have been identified as deities. But by reference to the glyptic art, Matthiae suggested that the attitudes of these deities are identical to those of the deified Syrian kings (Matthiae 1990, 347). When he identified a shrine composed of small chapels in Ebla, he associated this discovery with them. According to Matthiae, the chapels of the shrine housed the statues of deified kings and the building as a whole was dedicated to the celebration of a new royal investiture in a ritual called *rapiu'ma* (Matthiae 1990, 353).

If every statue of a king deposited in temples played a similar role (for which, to my knowledge, no texts confirming this hypothesis), we must exclude the possibility of a genuine devotion to royal statues. Their roles could have been to perpetuate prayer and to recall a golden age by continuously serving rituals of investiture. What we do have in cuneiform literature are indications of regular offerings of food, which were brought before the royal statues in the temple. This may have perpetrated the prayer of the king before the god and was generally part of ancestor worship (Labat 1939, 371).

In conclusion, the question '*Did divine statues exist in Mesopotamia?*' can be asked. Firstly, it should be noted that there were several consecration rituals of the physical representation of the god to embody it as divine. It is the ritual of *mīs pî* 'washing the mouth' and the ritual *pīt pî* 'opening the mouth' (Walker and Dick 1999, 55–121). These rituals have generally been regarded as being performed on statues. But the same rituals were apparently also used on symbols and other objects such as weapons but this last practice seems to have been privileged during the first millennium BC (Walker and Dick 1999, 71).

In addition, we find information on transportation of treasures and statues of the gods during conquests in historical texts from the Neo-Assyrian period. In the reign of Sargon of Assyria, a text tells how he was responsible for repatriating the gods to the city of Babylon, which was then dominated by a Chaldean king (Luckenbill 1927, 33–34 no. 66). Indeed, it seems that the last king had brought them into the city of Dur-Jakin to protect them. Sargon used the pretext of repatriating idols to legitimise his warlike action against the Chaldean king (Matthiae 1994, 70). Under the reign of Sennacherib, the Babylonian gods and their possessions were in Elam. At this time, Sennacherib considered it as a great sacrilege and he immediately attacked (seventh campaign in lower Mesopotamia, Luckenbill 1927, 155 no 351; Matthiae 1994, 71). Following one victory, Assarhaddon undertook to rebuild the Babylonian temples and resettle the gods (Luckenbill 1927, 262 no 674–675; Matthiae 1994, 71–73). As for Assurbanipal, he repatriated the statue of the deity Nanāja, which had been stolen during the Third Dynasty of Ur, more than 1500 years before (Luckenbill 1927, 311 no 812–813; Matthiae 1994, 71–73).

One can also find references in the literary texts. At the time of the Kassites, a king called Agum or Agum-Kakrime described the return of the god Marduk and his consort Ṣarpanitum to Babylon in their home called Esagila, having been abducted by the Hittite king Mursili I during the conquest of Babylon in 1595 (Foster 1993, 273–277; Matthiae 1994, 74). Moreover, Agum enriched the ornamentation of the sanctuary with semi-precious stones, fashioned their tiaras with lapis lazuli and gold, fashioned crowns in semi-precious stones, symbols shaped dragon and eagle, jewellery including gold necklaces and he rearranged their room with gaskets on access doors (Foster 1993, 275). Finally, he reinstated donations (Foster 1993, 276). In a text composed around the 12th century BCE during the reign of Nebuchadnezzar I called the *Prophecy of Marduk*, Marduk described his abduction in Elam and predicted the coming of a prince (in this case Nebuchadnezzar I) to reinstate the worship of the gods in Babylon (Foster 1993, 304–307; Matthiae 1994, 74–75; see also the text named *Nabuchodonosor and Marduk*: Foster 1993, 301).

In Sumerian and Akkadian literature compositions, we find several references to the departure of the gods (statues) from their sanctuary. In the *Curse of Akkad*, we read that the goddess Inanna with her weapons, and the gods Ninurta, Utu, Enki and Anu left their sanctuary (ll. 55–80: Cooper 1983, 53–54; Matthiae 1994, 67–68). In the *Lamentation over the destruction of Ur*, Enlil decides to abandon the city of Ur with Inanna and other deities when the treasures had been stolen (ll. 149–165, 169: Michalowski 1989, 44–47; Matthiae 1994, 68). Similarly, in a poem called the *Lament of Ur*, Enlil and the goddesses Ninlil, Ninmah and Nininsiana left their residence (ll. 1–10: Jacobsen 1987, 448–449; Matthiae 1994, 69).

The literary texts demonstrate the existence of the divine statues. But why have no monumental artefacts related to these been discovered yet? It is generally acknowledged that the divine statues could be made of wood, plated with thin gold and silver plates and decorated with a multitude of semi-precious stones such as carnelian and lapis lazuli (Matshushima 1993, 215). This could explain why we have not found divine statues on Mesopotamian soil, as the wood would likely have perished and the precious materials been stolen. Besides, the word ALAN ('statue' in Sumerian) is not used in literature because the generally admitted idea is that, like the statue embodied divinity, the statue was the god him(her)self and it was not necessary to define it with the word 'statue'.

Part Two: the divine objects in the Old Babylonian everyday life texts

For this research, I selected more than 200 cuneiform texts dating from the early second millennium BCE. At that time, several dynasties were founded, the oldest of which are concentrated in southern Mesopotamia as the Dynasties of Isin, Larsa and Uruk. Further north, it was not until the late 19th century BCE when the dynasties and kingdoms such as the First Dynasty of Babylon, the Kingdoms of the region of Diyala, and the Kingdom of Mari appeared. The texts found at these sites, together with those found at surrounding sites (such as Sippar), comprise all of the documentation available to scholars for the beginning of the second millennium. The documents I used for my research consist of administrative documents, legal texts and letters. The purpose was to identify elements concerning the objects belonging to deities in the documents of everyday life. The majority of administrative texts belong to archives of administrative centres like the royal palace or temple city, but also to the archives of households.

At Ur, a series of documents called 'donation texts' were unearthed. They are small tablets that registered quantities of semi-precious stones, silver and gold given to the temple of Ningal, the goddess protector of the city of Ur (van de Mieroop 1989, 397–401). Individuals, including women, delivered the items. These documents belong to the archives of the unique religious complex of the city, which included in its centre a ziggurat. In Isin, the documentation of a tanning workshop (van de Mieroop 1987) has revealed that several divine items received particular care with a coating of varnish or glue and the addition of leather pieces. At Uruk, it is again the documentation of a workshop, which gives us information, but this time it is from a metal workshop (Sanati-Müller 1990, 131–213). The selected texts indicate that heavenly objects have undergone various repairs or coating. The same type of texts was discovered at Mari. At Sippar, legal texts indicate that one could rent divine emblems to check a harvest or use them on a trial to swear (Harris 1965, 217–224).

In addition to these different types of texts, we must look at inventories. In the region of Larsa, for example, an exceptional document identifies various jewellery and furniture that belonged to the goddess Ištar (Leemans 1952). Similar texts have also been found on other sites as Harrādum (Joannès 2007, 32, 50–51) and in the region of Diyala (al-Rawi and Black 1983, 137–143).

Finally, the year names provide important information. Some describe that the reigning king filled the temples with objects symbolizing the divine powers.

I will not discuss in detail all the objects that may have been used to adorn the statues of the gods, that is to say, jewellery and clothing but I will seek to describe the types encountered. The types of jewellery are classified according to the precious materials used in their manufacture: semi-precious stones, ivory, copper, bronze, silver and gold. The stones are always semi-precious, as precious stones, such as diamond, emerald, ruby and sapphire, were not used, having not been discovered or imported into Mesopotamia at this time. The semi-precious stones used are onyx, agate, turquoise, carnelian, garnet, lapis lazuli, amethyst, crystal rock or quartz. The identification of the terms used to designate them in Sumerian or Akkadian is known for the carnelian and lapis lazuli, the origins of which are well known. Since the third millennium BCE, carnelian is imported from the Indus Valley by sea via the Persian Gulf (Inizian 1999, 125–138) and lapis lazuli follows an overland trade route from Afghanistan (Casanova 1999, 191–210). They have moreover special characteristics of their own: carnelian, whose red colour is accentuated by heating, represents the feminine side, while the lapis lazuli, with its electric blue colour, represents the masculine side (Winter 1999, 52).

The most complete documentation of the objects made from semi-precious stones comes from Ur. The archive of the temple of the deity Ningal has more than 25 records (UET 5 278, UET 5 282, UET 5 283, UET 5 284, UET 5 285, UET 5 286, UET 5 287, UET 5 288, UET 5 289, UET 5 291, UET 5 292, UET 5 293, UET 5 295, UET 5 529, UET 5 546, UET 5 547, UET 5 548, UET 5 549, UET 5 557, UET 5 561, UET 5 564, UET 5 565, UET 5 678: van de Mieroop 1989, 397–401 and add: Nisaba 19 141, Nisaba 19 143, Nisaba 19 241, Nisaba 19 244). These semi-precious stones were offered by individuals, including women, to the temple.

In documents from one metallurgical workshop from the palace of Mari, repairs were made for necklaces in semi-precious stone that belonged to local deities in Mari (ARM 9 176, 4–5: Rouault 1977, 175; Michel 1999, 418 note 105; and ARMT 21 223, 45: Durand 1993, 236; Michel 1999, 418 note 105).

Two documents belonging to the archive of the temple of Kitītum in Nerēbtum (valley of the Diyala) indicate inventories of different semi-precious stones and jewellery items made of these materials (OBTIV 106: Greengus 1979, 46–48 and OBTIV 107: Greengus 1979, 48–50).

In the region of Larsa and further north in Harrādum, three major inventories show the richness of the jewels of the goddess Ištar: semi-precious stones and a necklace made from these materials (CM 33 1: Westenholz and Westenholz 2006, 3–81 and Haradum II 8: Joannès 2007, 32, 50–51), hand-shaped jewellery, necklaces, and a curved stick in carnelian (TLB 1 69: Leemans 1952).

Moreover, we also have information about stone objects in the year names. In Babylon, several large solar discs in lapis lazuli and agate set with silver and gold were deposited by kings in the temple Ebabbar (year names 'Abī-ešuh 10?' (for the god Nanna), 'Ammī-ditana 13', 'Samsu-ditana 7' (for the god Šamaš): Horsnell 1999). A protective deity in semi-precious stones was dedicated to Ištar of the city of Kiš (year name 'Ammī-ditana 29': Horsnell 1999) and a great emblem in lapis lazuli set with silver and gold was deposited in the temple of Marduk, the Esagila (year name 'Ammī-ṣaduqa 4': Horsnell 1999). Also in Larsa, a carnelian and lapis lazuli statue was dedicated to the moon god Nanna (year name 'Abī-sarē 8': Sigrist 1990).

As far as ivory is concerned, it was used for the manufacture of pectorals. Some were worn by deities such as Ninuruamugub (UET 5 279, 5: van de Mieroop 1989, 397 note 1) and Ningal (Nisaba 19 269, col. ii 3") in Ur and Ištar in the region of Larsa (TLB 1 69, 12: Leemans 1952).

Rings are the only copper jewellery documented (UET 5 524, 3: van de Mieroop 1989, 401 note 69), but as regards bronze objects, hand-shaped jewellery items are inventoried in the treasury of Adad in Me-turan (TH 514, col. ii 3′: al-Rawi and Black 1983, 137–143), and in Nerēbtum, the god Ilabrat received earrings in bronze (OBTIV 106, 24: Greengus 1979, 46–48).

There are several references to silver jewellery of the gods in the texts. For the goddess of love, Ištar, there are solar symbols (Haradum II 8, 8: Joannès 2007, 32, 50–51), crowns (Haradum II 8, 10: Joannès 2007, 32, 50–51) and vulvas (TLB 1 69, 8: Leemans 1952). In Nerēbtum, the goddess Kitītum received mainly rings (OBTIV 90, 1–3; OBTIV 91, 2–7; OBTIV 92, 3: Greengus 1979, 40–41; Ellis 1986, 118–120) and jewellery in the shape of a bull in silver (OBTIV 90, 4–5; OBTIV 92, 7: Greengus 1979, 40–41; Ellis 1986, 118–120). As for the goddess Ningal in Ur, it seems that a number of dignitaries offered rings (UET 5 279, 1 (for the goddess Ninuruamugub); UET 5 524, 1: van de Mieroop 1989, 397–401), crescent moons (UET 5 552, col. i 1: van de Mieroop 1989, 397 note 2) and boat-shaped jewels (UET 5 553, col. i 18, col. iii 27: van de Mieroop 1989, 397 note 1 and Nisaba 19 244, col. i 12'; Nisaba 19 245, col. ii 10′, col. iii 4"). Nanāja received several rings in Larsa (CM 33 1, col. vi 6 et ss: Westenholz and Westenholz 2006, 3–81); Adad received in Me-Turan, rings, earrings, shaped great bull jewels and even wigs breast plated in silver (TH 514, col. i 11', col. ii 1, col. ii 11', col. iii 1: al-Rawi and Black 1983, 137–143), and in Mari, two jewels in the shape of an owl belonging to Ninhursag (ARM 7 118, 1–3) and one shaped boat jewel of the god Sîn (ARMT 25 394, 2–4) are recorded to have been repaired.

The gold jewels have even more varied forms than silver ones. At Uruk, the treasure of Ištar is composed of different types of rings, shaped emblem jewels, various earrings, some of which are shaped like deer (TSKP 115: Sanati-Müller 1990, 167–170), and amulets made of different gold elements (TSKP 114: Sanati-Müller 1990, 165–166). This goddess is also decorated with various gold jewels in Lagaba: rings, vulvas, shaped fruit jewels, pectorals and earrings in gold (TLB 1 69: Leemans 1952). In Nerēbtum, the god Ilabrat and perhaps also the goddess Kitītum are not far behind. They wore bull-shaped (OBTIV 91: Greengus 1979, 40–41; Ellis 1986, 118–120), swallow-shaped (OBTIV 106: Greengus 1979, 46–47) or ant-shaped jewels (OBTIV 107: Greengus 1979, 48–50), pomegranate- (OBTIV 106: Greengus 1979, 46–47) or fruit-shaped jewels (OBTIV 107: Greengus 1979, 48–50), plant-shaped jewels (OBTIV 106: Greengus 1979, 46–47), and also rings and pectorals (OBTIV 107: Greengus 1979, 48–50). Gold jewellery offered by sovereigns of this region to the god Tišpak is also listed in the year names. We find one ring (year name 'Ipiq-Adad H?': Wu Yuhong 1994, 26), one boat-shaped jewel (year name 'Bēlakum B': Wu Yuhong

1994, 38) and one crescent moon in gold and plated with silver (year name 'Ibal-pî-El D?': Wu Yuhong 1994, 39). In Isin, the workshop of tanning affixed leather pieces on red gold rings belonging to the god Enki, the god Damu, the goddess of the city NinIsinna and the goddess Nintinuga (BIN 9 471: Richter 2004, 188). At Larsa, solar symbols and necklaces were given to Ištar and Nanāja (CM 33 1: Westenholz and Westenholz 2006, 3–81). At Ur, the goddess Bawa received earrings (UET 5 280: van de Mieroop 1989, 397 note 1), the goddess Ningal, rings (UET 5 287: van de Mieroop 1989, 397 n. 1) and the god Nanāja, a solar symbol (Nisaba 19 140). In Mari, finally, the goddess Dīrītum had earrings, solar symbols and jewels in the shape of fruit (ARMT 22 237: Durand 1990, 130); the god Adad of Aleppo, rings and earrings (ARMT 25 118; ARMT 25 154); the goddess Annunītum, a sun symbol (ARMT 25 309: Durand 1990, 129) and the god Sîn a jewel shaped like a boat (ARMT 25 394). As shown, the jewels worn by the deities are numerous, but the documentation is too brief to know exactly what jewel was preferred by a god. All we know is that all kinds of gods, whether male or female, had jewels and the forms are more varied in gold.

I also collected references on clothing worn by deities. At Larsa, a special clothing item belonged to the god Nergal and another woven garment belonged to the goddess Mammītum (TCL 10 100: Richter 2004, 394–395). In a large tablet of nine columns describing foods and objects used for rituals to various deities (CM 33 1: Westenholz and Westenholz 2006, 3–81), clothes belonged to the god Enki, the god Šamaš, the goddess Ištar, the goddess Nanāja and the god Panigarra. Heavier clothing are also attributed for Enki, Šamaš, Nanāja but also Ilabrat and Dingirmah. In addition, red clothing belonged to the god Asarluhi and was put on the gold statues of deceased kings of Larsa, Sîn-iqīšam and Warad-Sîn. In the inventory of the treasure of Ištar from Lagaba (TLB 1 69: Leemans 1952), we find several types of clothing. After their description, it is noted that these garments were placed on the goddess. In Isin, pieces of leather are added to a garment of the god Nergal (BIN 9 84: Richter 2004, 1999). At Nerēbtum, the goddess Kitītum had different clothing including headbands (OBTIV 90–92: Greengus 1979, 40–41; Ellis 1986, 118–120). Finally, in one year name of Ipiq-Adad, ruler in the region of the Diyala, a garment in gold is offered by him to the god Tišpak (year name 'Ipiq-Adad L?': Wu Yuhong 1994, 26). As was the situation with jewellery, the information about clothes of the gods are too laconic to discuss in detail the different types of garments worn by one god.

Conclusion: the objects belonging to the Gods and the adornment of the divine statues

The role of these objects becomes important when we integrate them into a specific function, that of the adornment of the divine statues. The administrative texts included in this study have not been analysed in the same way as the others yet, because they are not enough descriptive and they do not specify the function that we are attempting to highlight here. When I studied some of these documents, especially the texts of donation of the temple Ningal, for my doctoral thesis (which was about the economic activities in southern Mesopotamia in the Old Babylonian period) it was difficult for me to assign an 'economic' function to some of these administrative texts. In discussion about the inventories of the gods with Markus Hilgert, I noticed that the objects of donation had perhaps the same role as the object contained on the inventories, that of belonging to the gods. With this idea, another question must be added: What were these objects used for? Perhaps to adorn the statues. To make sure that this idea was not completely unreasonable, I looked to the worship practices of the Hellenic civilizations. I remembered the famous treasures housed in temples and I discovered that several inventories, especially those of the sanctuary of Delos and those of the Acropolis in Athens, described different types of items, including jewellery and clothes of all kinds, used to decorate shrines and adorn divine Greek statues (Hamilton 2000; Linders 1972; 1975). I also recalled processions of the Virgin Mary during my childhood in my residential area in Belgium: the statue was on this occasion richly dressed with decorated clothes and jewels kept in her chapel. However, these traditions had to be confronted with the problem of Mesopotamian divine statues discussed above that we have tried to solve. If the statues of the gods did exist and if the administrative texts tell us about some of the items adorning them, they take a physical dimension of the first order that must be now discussed.

The statues of the gods in Mesopotamia were cult statues, which required a lot of care and attention. The statues were the veritable incarnation of gods on earth; for that, they had an exceptional dimension. A statue is not just an object, but a pictorial representation. Here, as a result, the divine feeling becomes real: the statues are gods. However the human form or the anthropomorphism needs not to be discussed here, since it is men who have been made in the image of the gods according to the poem of Atra-hasīs (ll. 221–230: Lambert and Millard 1969, 59):

> 'On the first, seventh, and fifteenth day of the month,
> He (Enki) made a purifying bath,
> (The god) Wê, who had personality,
> They slaughtered in their assembly.
> With his flesh and blood
> Nintu mixed clay,
> For the rest [of time they heard the drum]
> From the flesh of the god [there was] a spirit
> It proclaimed living (man) as its sign,

And so that this was not forgotten [there was] a spirit.'

From this study, it is possible to assert that the divine statue in Mesopotamia has a unique function that is absent in other objects of this period, including ritual objects. The concept of 'object agency' of Alfred Gell can be applied confidently to the divine statue. In places besides Mesopotamia, the divine statue bore (and will still bear) a particular dimension that should be studied and better understood through the ages by the anthropologists. This dimension is the desire to make visible what is invisible; to make real, a concept, an idea. This is an 'intentionalization', a reversal of conceptualization.

Bibliographical abbreviations

ARM 7: Bottéro, J. (1957) *Textes économiques et administratifs*. Archives Royales de Mari 7. Paris, Geuthner.

ARMT 22: Kupper, J.-R. (1983) *Documents administratifs de la salle 135 du palais de Mari*. Archives Royales de Mari. Traductions 22. Paris, Éd. Recherche sur les Civilisations.

ARMT 25: Limet, H. (1986) *Textes administratifs relatifs aux métaux*. Archives Royales de Mari. Traductions 25. Paris, Geuthner.

BIN 9: Crawford, V. E. (1954) *Sumerian Economic Texts from the First Dynasty of Isin*. Babylonian Inscriptions in the Collection of James B. Nies 9. New Haven/London, Yale Univ. Press.

CM 33: Westenholz, J. G. and Westenholz, A. (2006) *Cuneiform Inscriptions in the Collection of the Bible Lands Museum Jerusalem. The Old Babylonian Inscriptions*. Cuneiform Monographs 33. Leiden/Boston, Brill.

Haradum II: Joannès, F. (with the participations of Kepinski, C. and Colbow, G.) (2007) *Haradum II. Les textes de la période paléo-babylonienne (Samsu-iluna – Ammi-ṣaduqa)*. Paris, Éd. Recherche sur les Civilisations.

Nisaba 19: Black, J. A. and Spada, G. (2008) *Texts from Ur Kept in the Iraq Museum and in the British Museum*. Nisaba 19. Messina, Dipartimento di Scienze dell'Antichità dell'Università degli Studi di Messina.

OBTIV: Greengus, S. (1979) *Old Babylonian Tablets from Ishchali and Vicinity*. Publication de l'Institut historique-archéologique néerlandais de Stamboul 44 Istanbul, Nederlands Historisch-Archaeologisch Instituut.

TLB 1: Leemans, W. F. (1962) *Old Babylonian Legal and Administrative Documents*. Tabulae cuneiformes a F.M. Th. de Liagre Böhl collectae 1. Leiden, Nederlands Inst. voor het Nabije Oosten.

TSKP: *Texte aus dem Sînkāšid Palast*.

UET 5: Figulla, H. H. and Martin, W. J. (1953) *Letters and Documents of the Old Babylonian Period*. Ur Excavations Texts 5. London.

References

al-Rawi, F. N. H. and Black, J. A. (1983) The Jewels of Adad. *Sumer* 39, 137–143.

Casanova, M. (1999) Le lapis-lazuli dans l´Orient ancient. In Caubet 1999, 189–210.

Caubet, A. (1999) *Cornaline et pierres précieuses, La Méditerranée, de l'antiquité à l'Islam; actes du colloque organisé au Musée du Louvre par le Service Culturel les 24 et 25 novembre 1995*. Paris, La documentation française.

Charpin, D. and Ziegler, N. (2003) *Florilegium Marianum V. Mari et le Proche-Orient à l'époque amorrite: essai d'histoire politique*. Mémoires de NABU 6. Paris, SEPOA.

Cooper, J. S. (1983) *The Curse of Agade*. Baltimore, John Hopkins Univ. Press.

Durand, J.-M. (1990) La culture matérielle à Mari (I): le bijou *HÚB.TIL.LÁ/'GUR$_7$.ME'. *Mari, Annales de Recherches Interdisciplinaires* 6, 125–158.

Durand, J.-M. (1993) *Textes administratifs des salles 134 et 160 du palais de Mari*. Archives Royales de Mari. Traductions 21. Paris, Geuthner.

Ellis, M. deJ. (1986) Delivery Records from the Archive of the Kititum Temple at Ishchali. In Veenhof, K. R. (ed.), *Cuneiform Archives and Libraries. Papers Read at the 30th Rencontre Assyriologique Internationale Leiden, 4–8 July 1983*. Publication de l'Institut historique-archéologique néerlandais de Stamboul 57, 112–120. Leiden, Nederlands Histor.-Archaeolog. Inst. te Istanbul.

Groneberg, B. (1990) La culture matérielle à Mari, II. Der nūbalum und seine Objekte. *Mari, Annales de Recherches Interdisciplinaires* 6, 161–180.

Foster, B. R. (1993) *Before the Muses, An Anthology of Akkadian Literature*. Bethesda, CDL Press.

Frankfort, H. (1943) *More Sculpture from the Diyala Region*. Oriental Institute Publications LX. Chicago, Univ. Press.

Frankfort, H., Lloyd, S. and Jacobsen, Th. (1940) *The Gimilsin Temple and the Palace of the Rules at Tell Asmar*. Oriental Institute Publications XLIII. Chicago, Univ. Press.

George, A. R. (1993) *House Most High, The Temples of Ancient Mesopotamia*. Winona Lake, Einsenbrauns.

Greengus, S. (1979) *Old Babylonian Tablets from Ishchali and Vicinity*. Publication de l'Institut historique-archéologique néerlandais de Stamboul 44. Leiden, Istanbul, Nederlands Historisch-Archaeologisch Instituut.

Hamilton, R. (2000) *Treasure Map. A Guide to the Delian Inventories*. Ann Arbor, Univ. Of Michigan Press.

Harris, R. (1965) The Journey of the Divine Weapon. In H. C. Güterbock and T. Jacobsen (eds), *Studies in Honor of Benno Landsberger on His Seventy-Fifth Birthday, April 21, 1965*. Assyriological Studies 16, 217–224. Chicago, Univ. of Chicago Press.

Heimpel, W. (1987) Das Untere Meer. *Zeitschrift für Assyriologie und Vorderasiatische Archäologie* 77, 22–91.

Horsnell, M. J. A. (1999) *The Year Names of the First Dynasty of Babylon. Volume 1. Chronological Matters: The Year*

Name System and the Date-Lists/Volume 2. The Year-Names reconstructed and Critically Annotated in Light of their Exemplars. Hamilton, McMaster Univ. Press.

Inizian, M.-L. (1999) La cornaline de l'Indus et la voie du Golfe au IIIe millénaire. In Caubet 1999, 125–138.

Jacobsen, T. (1987) *The Harps that once.... Sumerian poetry in translation.* New Haven, Yale Univ. Press.

Joannès, F. (with the Participations of Kepinski, C. and Colbow, G.) (2007) *Haradum II. Les textes de la période paléo-babylonienne (Samsu-iluna – Ammi-ṣaduqa).* Paris, Éd. Recherche sur les Civilisations.

Johansen, F. (1978) *Statues of Gudea Ancient and Modern.* Mesopotamia. Copenhagen Studies in Assyriology 6. Copenhagen, Akad. Forlag.

Labat, R. (1939) *Le caractère religieux de la royauté assyro-babylonienne.* Etudes d'Assyriologie 2. Paris, Adrian Maisonneuve.

Lambert, W. G. and Millard, A. R. (1969) *Atra-hasīs. The Babylonian Story of the Flood (with the Sumerian Flood Story by M. Civil).* Oxford, Clarendon Press.

Layard, A. H. (1849) *The Monuments of Niniveh: from Drawings Made on the Spot.* London.

Leemans, W. F. (1952) *Ishtar of Lagaba and her Dress.* Studia ad tabulas cuneiformes a F. M. Th. De Liagre Böhl collectas pertinentia 1/1. Leiden, Brill.

Linders, T. (1972) *Studies in the Treasure Records of Artemis Braurenia Found in Athens.* Acta Instituti Atheniensis Regni Sueciae, 4°, 19. Stockholm, Svenska Institutet i Athen.

Linders, T. (1975) *The Treasures of the Other Gods in Athens and their Functions.* Beiträge zur klassischen Philologie 62. Meisenheim am Glan, Hain.

Luckenbill, D. D. (1927) *Historical Records of Assyria from Sargon to the End.* Ancient Records of Assyria and Babylonia 2. Chicago, University of Chicago.

Mallowan, M. E. L (1936) The Bronze Head of the Akkadian Period from Niniveh. *Iraq* 3, 104–110.

Matthiae, P. (1990) A Class of Old Syrian Bronze Statuettes and the Sanctuary B2 at Ebla. In P. Matthiae, M. N. van Loon and H. Weiss (eds), *Resurrecting the Past, A Joint Tribute to Adnan Bounni.* Publication de l'Institut historique-archéologique néerlandais de Stamboul 67, 345–362. Istanbul, Nederlands Historisch-Archaeologisch Instituut.

Matthiae, P. (1994) *Il sovrano e l'opera, Arte e potere nella Mesopotmia antica.* Roma, Laterza.

Matsushima, E. (1993) Divine Statues in Mesopotamia: Their Fashioning and Clothing and Their Interaction with the Society. In E. Matsushima (ed.), *Official Cult and Popular Religion in the Ancient Near East, Papers of the First Colloquium on the Ancient Near East – The City and Its Life. Held at the Middle Eastern Culture Center in Japan (Mitaka, Tokyo) March 20–22, 1992,* 209–219. Heidelberg, Winter.

Michalowski, P. (1989) *The Lamentation over the Destruction of Sumer and Ur.* Mesopotamian Civilizations 1. Winona Lake, Eisenbrauns.

Michel, C. (1999) Les joyaux des rois de Mari. In Caubet 1999, 401–432.

van de Mieroop, M. (1987) *Crafts in the Early Isin Period: A Study of the Isin Craft Archive from the Reigns of Išbi-Erra and Šū-ilišu.* Orientalia Lovaniensia Analecta 24. Leuven, Dep. Oriëntalistiek.

van de Mieroop, M. (1989) Gifts and Tithes to the Temple in Ur. In H. Behrens, D. Loding and M. T. Roth (eds), *DUMU-E$_2$-DUB-BA, Studies in Honor of Åke W. Sjöberg.* Occasional Publications of the Samuel Noah Kramer Fund 11, 397–401. Philadelphia, Univ. Museum.

Ornan, T. (2009) In the Likeness of Man, Reflections on the Anthropocentric Perception of the Divine in Mesopotamian Art. In B. N. Porter (ed.), *What is a God? Anthropomorphic and Non-Anthropomorphic Aspects of Deity in Ancient Mesopotamia.* The Casco Bay Assyriological Institute Transactions 2, 93–151. Winona Lake, Casco Bay Assyriological Institute .

Richter, T. (2004) *Untersuchungen zu den lokalen Panthea Süd- und Mittelbabyloniens in altbabylonischer Zeit.* Alter Orient und Altes Testament 257. Münster, Ugarit Verlag.

Rouault, O. (1977) *Mukannišum. L'administration et l'économie palatiales à Mari. Transcription, traduction et étude historique.* Archives Royales de Mari 18. Paris, Geuthner.

Sanati-Müller, S. (1990) Texte aus dem Sînkašid-Palast. Dritter Teil: Metalltexte. *Baghdader Mitteilungen 21*, 131–213.

Sigrist, M. (1988) *Isin Year Names.* Institute of Archaeology Publications, Assyriologial Series 2. Berrien Springs, Andrews Univ. Press.

Sigrist, M. (1990) *Larsa Year Names.* Institute of Archaeology Publications, Assyriologial Series 3. Berrien Springs, Andrews Univ. Press.

Spycket, A. (1968) *Les statues de culte dans les textes mésopotamiens des origines à la 1re dynastie de Babylone.* Cahiers de la Revue biblique 9. Paris, Gabalda.

Walker, C. and Dick, M. B. (1999) The Induction of the Cult Image in Ancient Mesopotamia: The Mesopotamian mīs pî Ritual. In M. B. Dick (ed.), *Born in Heaven, Made on Earth: The Making of the Cult Image in the Ancient Near East,* 55–121. Winona Lake, Eisenbrauns.

Westenholz, J. G. and Westenholz, A. (2006) *Cuneiform Inscriptions in the Collection of the Bible Lands Museum Jerusalem. The Old Babylonian Inscriptions.* Cuneiform Monographs 33. Leiden/Boston, Brill.

Winter, I. J. (1999) The Aesthetic Value of Lapis Lazuli in Mesopotamia. In Caubet 1999, 43–58.

Wu Yuhong (1994) *A Political History of Eshnunna, Mari and Assyria during the Early Old Babylonian Period (from the End of Ur III to the Death of Šamaš-Adad).* Supplement to Journal of Ancient Civilizations 1. Changchun, Institute of History of Ancient Civilizations.

Yadin, Y. *et al.* (1961) *Hazor III–IV. An Account of the Third and Fourth Seasons of Excavations 1957–1958, Plates.* The James A. de Rothschild Expedition at Hazor. Jerusalem, Magnes Press.